Lecture Notes in Computer Science   13953

Founding Editors

Gerhard Goos
Juris Hartmanis

Editorial Board Members

Elisa Bertino, *Purdue University, West Lafayette, IN, USA*
Wen Gao, *Peking University, Beijing, China*
Bernhard Steffen ⓘ, *TU Dortmund University, Dortmund, Germany*
Moti Yung ⓘ, *Columbia University, New York, NY, USA*

The series Lecture Notes in Computer Science (LNCS), including its subseries Lecture Notes in Artificial Intelligence (LNAI) and Lecture Notes in Bioinformatics (LNBI), has established itself as a medium for the publication of new developments in computer science and information technology research, teaching, and education.

LNCS enjoys close cooperation with the computer science R & D community, the series counts many renowned academics among its volume editors and paper authors, and collaborates with prestigious societies. Its mission is to serve this international community by providing an invaluable service, mainly focused on the publication of conference and workshop proceedings and postproceedings. LNCS commenced publication in 1973.

Aleksander Essex · Shin'ichiro Matsuo ·
Oksana Kulyk · Lewis Gudgeon ·
Ariah Klages-Mundt · Daniel Perez ·
Sam Werner · Andrea Bracciali · Geoff Goodell
Editors

Financial Cryptography and Data Security

FC 2023 International Workshops

Voting, CoDecFin, DeFi, WTSC
Bol, Brač, Croatia, May 5, 2023
Revised Selected Papers

 Springer

Editors
Aleksander Essex (iD)
Western University
London, ON, Canada

Oksana Kulyk (iD)
IT University of Copenhagen
Copenhagen, Denmark

Ariah Klages-Mundt (iD)
Imperial College London
London, UK

Sam Werner
Imperial College London
London, UK

Geoff Goodell
University College London
London, UK

Shin'ichiro Matsuo (iD)
Georgetown University
Washington, DC, USA

Lewis Gudgeon (iD)
Imperial College London
London, UK

Daniel Perez (iD)
Imperial College London
London, UK

Andrea Bracciali (iD)
Stirling University
Stirling, UK

ISSN 0302-9743   ISSN 1611-3349 (electronic)
Lecture Notes in Computer Science
ISBN 978-3-031-48805-4   ISBN 978-3-031-48806-1 (eBook)
https://doi.org/10.1007/978-3-031-48806-1

This Springer imprint is published by the registered company Springer Nature Switzerland AG
The registered company address is: Gewerbestrasse 11, 6330 Cham, Switzerland

Paper in this product is recyclable.

VOTING 2023 Preface

These proceedings collect the papers accepted (http://fc23.ifca.ai/voting/) to the 8th Workshop on Advances in Secure Electronic Voting (Voting 2023), associated with the Financial Cryptography and Data Security 2023 conference (FC 2023). The Voting workshop was held on May 5, 2023, in Bol, on the beautiful island of Brač, Croatia. We were delighted to be back fully in-person after the prior two years of a hybrid delivery format.

This year's workshop received 18 submissions, of which 7 were accepted for publication. Thanks to the generous efforts of the PC, each paper received three reviews per submission in a double-blind review, providing constructive feedback to authors, followed by PC discussion where appropriate. We are grateful to our Program Committee for their time and effort. We thank Tamara Finogina, Rolf Haenni, and Jacob Spertus for leading a panel discussion on how the academic research community has helped shape real-world election practice.

We are grateful to Ray Hirschfeld, Carla Mascia, and IFCA for organizing the event logistics and to the FC workshop chairs and steering committee for their continued support of VOTING. The tradition of staggered chairs will continue next year, with Oksana Kulyk and Jurlind Budurushi serving as program chairs.

June 2023

Aleksander Essex
Oksana Kulyk

VOTING 2023 Organization

Program Chairs

Aleksander Essex	Western University, Canada
Oksana Kulyk	IT University of Copenhagen, Denmark

Program Committee

Roberto Araujo	Universidade Federal do Pará, Brazil
Josh Benaloh	MSR, USA
Matthew Bernhard	University of Michigan, USA
Jurlind Budurushi	Qatar University, Qatar
Jeremy Epstein	SRI International, USA
Tamara Finogina	Polytechnic University of Catalonia, Spain
Kristian Gjøsteen	Norwegian University of Science and Technology, Norway
Rajeev Gore	Technical University of Vienna, Austria and Polish Academy of Sciences, Poland
Rolf Haenni	Bern University of Applied Sciences, Switzerland
Christian Henrich	Albstadt-Sigmaringen University, Germany
Johannes Mueller	University of Luxembourg, Luxembourg
Olivier Pereira	UCLouvain, Belgium
Peter Rønne	Polish Academy of Sciences, Poland
Peter Y. A. Ryan	CNRS, LORIA, France
Steve Schneider	University of Surrey, UK
Carsten Schuermann	IT University of Copenhagen, Denmark
Philip Stark	University of California, Berkeley, USA
Vanessa Teague	Thinking Cybersecurity, Australia

CoDecFin 2023
4th Workshop on Coordination of Decentralized Finance

These proceedings collect the papers accepted at the *Fourth Workshop on Coordination of Decentralized Finance (CoDecFin* - http://fc32.ifca.ai/codecfin/*)*, associated with the Financial Cryptography and Data Security 2023 international conference (FC 2023). This year was the second opportunity to have an in-person workshop after the pandemic, and it was brilliant to have the opportunity to meet colleagues in person and exchange ideas with them during the conference and the workshop. Nonetheless, we were able to offer technical support to a number of speakers that could not yet travel to Croatia and allow them to present their contributions on-line.

The main purpose of the series of Workshop on Coordination of Decentralized Finance (CoDecFin) is to discuss multi-disciplinary issues regarding technologies and operations of decentralized finance based on permissionless blockchain.

From an academic point of view, security and privacy protection are some of the leading research streams. The Financial Cryptography conference discusses these research challenges. On the other hand, other stakeholders than cryptographers and blockchain engineers have different interests in these characteristics of blockchain technology. For example, regulators face difficulty in tracing transactions in terms of anti-money laundering (AML) against privacy-enhancing crypto-assets. Another example is consumer protection in the case of cyberattacks on crypto-asset custodians. Blockchain business entities sometimes start their business before the technology has matured, but the technology and operations are not transparent to regulators and consumers. The main problem is a lack of communication among stakeholders of the decentralized finance ecosystem. The G20 discussed the issue of insufficient communication among stakeholders in 2019. It concluded that there is an essential need to have a multi-stakeholder discussion among engineers, regulators, business entities, and operators based on the neutrality of academia.

The CoDecFin workshop was initiated in 2020 to facilitate such a multi-stakeholder discussion in a neutral academic environment. The goals of CoDecFin were to have a common understanding of technology and regulatory goals and discuss essential issues of blockchain technology with all stakeholders mentioned above. It was especially a fantastic series of academic workshops because we could involve regulators and engineers in the discussion at the Financial Cryptography Conference.

This year we had four sessions plus a Keynote: (1) Harmonization with Regulations, (2) On-Chain Governance, (3) Joint Panel with WTSC and BGIN, and (4) Lessons from the Real World.

This year's edition of CoDecFin received ten submissions by about twenty-four authors. Given the high quality of the submissions, nine papers were accepted after double-blind peer reviews. Thanks to the generous efforts of the PC, each paper received three reviews per submission in a double-blind review, providing constructive feedback to authors, followed by PC discussion where appropriate. Revised papers after the discussion at the workshop are collected in the present volume. CoDecFin also hosted, jointly with the 7th Workshop on Trusted Smart Contract (WTSC 2023), an invited talk and a joint panel discussion. This year's new and successful challenge was hosting a joint session with the Blockchain Governance Initiative Network (BGIN), a multi-stakeholder discussion body initiated from the discussion of the first CoDeFi 2020. The eighth general meeting (Block #8) of BGIN was held from May 4 to 7. The academic discussions at CoDecFin 2022 were great inputs to the discussion at BGIN.

CoDecFin 2023's chair and program committee members would like to thank everyone for their usual effort and valuable contributions: authors, reviewers, and participants, as well as the support by IFCA, the FC 2023 committees, and Ray Hirschfeld for the usual exceptional organization and coordination of the event.

June 2023   Shin'ichiro Matsuo

CoDecFin 2023 Organization

Program Committee Members

Julien Bringer	Kallistech, France
Feng Chen	University of British Columbia, Canada
Victor Garcia	Universitat Oberta de Catalunya, Spain
Joaquin Garcia-Alfaro	Télécom SudParis, France
Arthur Gervais	Imperial College London, UK
Shin'ichiro Matsuo (Chair)	Georgetown University, USA
Kanta Matsuura	University of Tokyo, Japan
Michele Benedetto Neitz	Golden Gate University, USA
Ali Nejadmalayeri	University of Wyoming, USA
Roman Danziger Pavlov	SafeStead Inc., Canada
Jeremy Rubin	Judica, USA
Robert Schwentker	DLT Education, USA
Yonatan Sompolinsky	Hebrew University of Jerusalem, DAGlabs, Israel
Ryosuke Ushida	JFSA, Japan
Robert Wardrop	University of Cambridge Judge Business School, UK
Aaron Wright	Cardozo Law School, USA
Anton Yemelyanov	Base58 Association, Canada

DeFi 2023 Organization

Program Committee

Cuneyt Akcora	University of Manitoba, Canada
Kushal Babel	Cornell University, USA
Surya Bakshi	University of Illinois, Urbana-Champaign, USA
James Hsin-yu Chiang	Technical University of Denmark, Denmark
Tarun Chitra	Gauntlet Network, USA
Jeremy Clark	Concordia University, Canada
Dominik Harz	Interlay, Japan
Ruizhe Jia	Columbia University, USA
Mahimna Kelkar	Cornell University, USA
William Knottenbelt	Imperial College London, UK
Yujin Kwon	University of California, Berkeley, USA
Jason Milionis	Columbia University, USA
Andrew Miller	University of Illinois, Urbana-Champaign, USA
Barnabé Monnot	Ethereum Foundation, Germany
Daniel Moroz	Harvard University, USA
Mahsa Moosavi	Concordia University, Canada
Alexandre Obadia	Flashbots, Monaco
Andreas Park	University of Toronto, Canada
Daejun Park	A16z Crypto, USA
David Parkes	Harvard University, USA
Julien Prat	Polytechnic Institute of Paris, France
Gengmo Qi	Dragonfly, USA
Tim Roughgarden	Columbia University, USA
Palina Tolmach	Nanyang Technological University, Singapore
Jiahua Xu	University College London, UK
Alexei Zamyatin	Interlay, UK
Ariel Zetlin-Jones	Carnegie Mellon University, USA
Fan Zhang	Yale University, USA

DeFi 2023 Preface

These proceedings collect the papers accepted at the Third Workshop on Decentralized Finance (DeFi 2023 - https://fc23.ifca.ai/defi/), held in association with the Financial Cryptography and Data Security 2023 conference (FC 2023) on May 5, 2023.

The focus of the DeFi workshop series is decentralized finance, a blockchain-powered peer-to-peer financial system. As with the first two versions of this workshop, this third version sought to solicit contributions from both academia and industry, focussed on addressing fundamental, timely, and important questions at the centre of DeFi.

The workshop received 38 submissions, of which 13 were accepted either as a short paper (5), as a talk (7) or as a demo (1). All of the short papers and a subset of the talks, as précis, appear in these proceedings. Overall, the organizers were extremely impressed by the quality of submissions received and were delighted by the strong attendance and lively discussion during the workshop.

This year's keynote was given by Dan Robinson, from Paradigm, on the subject of Decentralized Exchange (DEX). We would like to sincerely thank him for his talk.

The Organizing Committee would like to extend sincere thanks to all those who submitted their work, to the Program Committee for their careful work, and to all those who participated in the workshop.

June 2023

Lewis Gudgeon
Ariah Klages-Mundt
Daniel Perez
Sam Werner

WTSC 2023
7th International Workshop on Trusted Smart Contracts

These proceedings collect the papers accepted at the *Seventh Workshop on Trusted Smart Contracts (WTSC23* - http://fc23.ifca.ai/wtsc/), associated with the Financial Cryptography and Data Security 2023 international conference (FC 2023). This year's event was hosted in Bol, on the beautiful island of Brač, Croatia.

The WTSC series' main focus is on *smart contracts*, i.e. self-enforcing agreements in the form of executable programs and other *decentralised applications* that are deployed to and run on top of (specialised) blockchains. These technologies introduced a novel programming framework and execution environment, which, together with the supporting blockchain technologies, carry unanswered and challenging research questions, as well as new and decentralised business models and use cases. Multidisciplinary and multifactorial aspects affect correctness, safety, privacy, authentication, efficiency, sustainability, resilience and trust in smart contracts and decentralised applications.

The WTSC series aims to address the scientific foundations of Trusted Smart Contract engineering and its applications, i.e., the development of contracts that enjoy some verifiable "correctness" properties, and to discuss open problems, proposed solutions and the vision of future developments amongst a research community that is growing around these themes and brings together users, practitioners, industry, institutions and academia. Over the years, the number of theoretical problems and applications has increased and this is shown by the wide set of topics that are discussed at WTSC. The multidisciplinary Programme Committee of this seventh edition of WTSC comprises members from companies, universities and research institutions from several countries worldwide. The association with FC 2023 provided, once again, an ideal context for our workshop to be run in.

This year's edition of WTSC received fifteen submissions by about forty-five authors. Given the high quality of submissions, nine papers were accepted after double-blind peer review, with an average of four reviews per paper, some followed by discussion, providing constructive feedback to the authors of all submitted papers. We want to commend the generous efforts of the PC. Revised papers after the discussion at the workshop are collected in the present volume.

Accepted papers analyse the current state of the art of smart contracts and their development. Key recent developments addressed by papers and discussed at the workshop include Layer-2 protocols and supporting Zero-Knowledge technology, incentives and distribution of power, payment systems, privacy-preserving applications and systematisation of contract analysis. Massimo Morini, Chief Economist at Algorand, gave an invited talk on the evolution of decentralisation and governance in Proof of Stake. A round table titled "Towards decentralised governance?" was hosted, jointly with the 4th Workshop on Coordination of Decentralized Finance (CoDecFin 2023). The Block #8 meeting of the Blockchain Governance Initiative Network (BGIN - https://bgin-global.org/) was co-organised and co-hosted with WTSC at Financial Cryptography.

WTSC 2023's chairs would like to thank everyone for their usual effort and valuable contributions: authors, program committee members and reviewers, and participants, as well as the support by IFCA, the FC23 committee, and Ray Hirschfeld for the usual exceptional organisation and coordination of the event.

June 2023

Andrea Bracciali
Geoff Goodell

WTSC 2023 Organization

The WTSC 2023 Program Committee

Monika di Angelo	Vienna University of Technology, Austria
Igor Artamonov	Emerald, USA
Daniel Augot	Inria, France
Fadi Barbara	University of Turin, Italy
Massimo Bartoletti	University of Cagliari, Italy
Stefano Bistarelli	University of Perugia, Italy
Christina Boura	Versailles SQT Univ., France
Andrea Bracciali	University of Stirling, UK
Daniel Broby	Ulster University, UK
Martin Chapman	King's College London, UK
Nicola Dimitri	University of Siena, Italy
Josselin Feist	Trail of Bits, USA
Oliver Giudice	Banca d'Italia, Italy
Davide Grossi	University of Groningen, The Netherlands
Geoffrey Goodell	UCL, UK
Yoichi Hirai	BedRock Systems GmbH, Germany
Ioannis Kounelis	Joint Research Centre, European Commission, Italy
Pascal Lafourcade	University Clermont Auvergne, France
Andrew Lewis-Pye	London School of Economics, UK
Carsten Maple	Warwick University, UK
Carla Mascia	Hub Innovazione Trentino, Italy
Neil McLaren	ConsenSys, UK
Akaki Mamageishvili	Offchain Labs, Switzerland
Patrick McCorry	Pisa Research, UK
Sihem Mesnager	University of Paris VIII, France
Alex Norta	Tallin University of Technology, Estonia
Akira Otsuka	Institute of Information Security, Japan
Federico Pintore	University of Bari, Italy
Massimiliano Sala	University of Trento, Italy
Jason Teutsch	Truebit, USA
Philip Wadler	University of Edinburgh, UK

Yilei Wang   Hong Kong Polytechnic University, China
Tim Weingärtner   Lucerne University, Switzerland
Santiago Zanella-Beguelin   Microsoft, UK
Dionysis Zindros   Stanford University, USA

Contents

Voting

Belenios with Cast as Intended 3
    Véronique Cortier, Alexandre Debant, Pierrick Gaudry,
    and Stéphane Glondu

On the Auditability of the Estonian IVXV System: And an Attack
on Individual Verifiability 19
    Anggrio Sutopo, Thomas Haines, and Peter Roenne

Coercion-Resistant Cast-as-Intended Verifiability for Computationally
Limited Voters 34
    Tamara Finogina and Javier Herranz

Private Internet Voting on Untrusted Voting Devices 47
    Rolf Haenni, Reto E. Koenig, and Philipp Locher

Overstatement-Net-Equivalent Risk-Limiting Audit: ONEAudit 63
    Philip B. Stark

Risk-Limiting Audits for Condorcet Elections 79
    Michelle Blom, Peter J. Stuckey, Vanessa Teague, and Damjan Vukcevic

COBRA: Comparison-Optimal Betting for Risk-Limiting Audits 95
    Jacob V. Spertus

CoDecFin

Shaping Cryptocurrency Gatekeepers with a Regulatory "Trial and Error" 113
    Marilyne Ordekian, Ingolf Becker, and Marie Vasek

A First Dive into OFAC in DeFi Space 133
    Qin Wang, Shange Fu, Shiping Chen, and Jiangshan Yu

Proposal of Principles of DeFi Disclosure and Regulation 141
    Tomonori Yuyama, Ken Katayama, and Paul Brigner

The Hidden Shortcomings of (D)AOs – An Empirical Study of On-Chain
Governance   165
    Rainer Feichtinger, Robin Fritsch, Yann Vonlanthen,
    and Roger Wattenhofer

An Intrinsic Mechanism Deciding Hash Rates from Bitcoin Price   186
    Go Yamamoto

Stablecoins: Past, Present, and Future   197
    Ali Nejadmalayeri, Leon Molchanovsky, Bruno Woltzenlogel Paleo,
    and Rodney W. Prescott

FTX Collapse: A Ponzi Story   208
    Shange Fu, Qin Wang, Jiangshan Yu, and Shiping Chen

Policy Design of Retail Central Bank Digital Currencies: Embedding
AML/CFT Compliance   216
    Michi Kakebayashi, Gerard P. Presto, and Tomonori Yuyama

DeFi

Uniswap Liquidity Provision: An Online Learning Approach   247
    Yogev Bar-On and Yishay Mansour

Extended Abstract: The Effect of Trading Fees on Arbitrage Profits
in Automated Market Makers   262
    Jason Milionis, Ciamac C. Moallemi, and Tim Roughgarden

Concave Pro-rata Games   266
    Nicholas A. G. Johnson, Theo Diamandis, Alex Evans,
    Henry de Valence, and Guillermo Angeris

Electronic Cash with Open-Source Observers   286
    Taishi Higuchi and Akira Otsuka

Inefficiency of CFMs: Hedging Perspective and Agent-Based Simulations   303
    Samuel N. Cohen, Marc Sabaté-Vidales, David Šiška, and Łukasz Szpruch

DeFi Auditing: Mechanisms, Effectiveness, and User Perceptions   320
    Ding Feng, Rupert Hitsch, Kaihua Qin, Arthur Gervais,
    Roger Wattenhofer, Yaxing Yao, and Ye Wang

Short Squeeze in DeFi Lending Market: Decentralization in Jeopardy?   337
    Lioba Heimbach, Eric Schertenleib, and Roger Wattenhofer

WTSC

Efficient Rollup Batch Posting Strategy on Base Layer 355
  Akaki Mamageishvili and Edward W. Felten

Unlinkability and Interoperability in Account-Based Universal Payment
Channels 367
  Mohsen Minaei, Panagiotis Chatzigiannis, Shan Jin,
  Srinivasan Raghuraman, Ranjit Kumaresan, Mahdi Zamani,
  and Pedro Moreno-Sanchez

Cassiopeia: Practical On-Chain Witness Encryption 385
  Schwinn Saereesitthipitak and Dionysis Zindros

FlexiPCN: Flexible Payment Channel Network 405
  Susil Kumar Mohanty and Somanath Tripathy

Publicly Verifiable Auctions with Privacy 420
  Paul Germouty, Enrique Larraia, and Wei Zhang

Consolidation of Ground Truth Sets for Weakness Detection in Smart
Contracts 439
  Monika di Angelo and Gernot Salzer

The Principal–Agent Problem in Liquid Staking 456
  Apostolos Tzinas and Dionysis Zindros

Detecting Privileged Parties on Ethereum 470
  Michael Fröwis and Rainer Böhme

Breaking Blockchain Rationality with Out-of-Band Collusion 489
  Haoqian Zhang, Mahsa Bastankhah, Louis-Henri Merino,
  Vero Estrada-Galiñanes, and Bryan Ford

Author Index 503

Voting

Belenios with Cast as Intended

Véronique Cortier[✉], Alexandre Debant, Pierrick Gaudry,
and Stéphane Glondu

Université de Lorraine, CNRS, INRIA, LORIA, Nancy, France
veronique.cortier@loria.fr

Abstract. We propose the BeleniosCaI protocol, a variant of Belenios which brings the cast-as-inended property, in addition to other existing security properties. Our approach is based on a 2-part checksum that the voting device commits to, before being challenged to reveal one of them chosen at random by the voter. It requires only one device on the voter's side and does not rely on previously sent data like with return codes. Compared to the classical Benaloh audit-or-cast approach, we still have cast-as-intended with only some probability, but the voter's journey is more linear, and the audited ballot is really the one that is cast. We formally prove the security of BeleniosCaI w.r.t. end-to-end verifiability and privacy in a symbolic model, using the ProVerif tool.

1 Introduction

Electronic voting systems aim at guaranteeing simultaneously vote privacy (no one should know what/whom I voted for) and verifiability (my vote should be properly counted). These properties come with trust and distrust assumptions on the involved parties such as the voting server, the voting devices, the decryption authorities, or external auditors. A long-standing issue is the so-called *cast-as-intended* property: a voter should be able to control that their vote has been properly encoded and cast with their proper intention, even if their voting device tries to send a different vote.

A simple and appealing approach has been proposed by Benaloh [4] about 15 years ago. When a voter selects a vote v, their device produces a ballot b and the voter is given the choice to either cast the ballot or audit it. In the latter case, the device must produce the randomness used to form the ballot. The randomness as well as the ballot b are then sent to a second device or a third trusted party to control that b indeed encrypts v. This procedure is repeated an unpredictable number of times until the voter is convinced that their voting device behaves as expected. This approach is simple and versatile. However, user studies have shown that it is hard to use and understand in practice [26]. As a consequence, a few voters audit in real elections. Moreover, this mechanism may even threaten privacy in case voters are not properly instructed to audit ballots that contain votes that are independent of their real intention. For the Benaloh's mechanism

This work received funding from the France 2030 program managed by the French National Research Agency under grant agreement No. ANR-22-PECY-0006.

A. Essex et al. (Eds.): FC 2023 Workshops, LNCS 13953, pp. 3–18, 2024.
https://doi.org/10.1007/978-3-031-48806-1_1

to be truly secure, voters need to first roll a dice to decide whether they will vote or audit, and in the latter case, roll a dice to decide which candidate to use.

Our Contribution. We propose an audit mechanism that is part of the voter's journey (no need to choose) and in which the audited ballot is the one actually cast. Our approach works as follows. When a voter selects a vote v, an integer a is chosen at random (between 1 and μ, a positive integer larger than the number of possible values for v) and the voter is given v, a, and b such that $b = v + a \bmod \mu$. The corresponding ballot bal is formed of the respective encryption of v, a, and b, together with a zero-knowledge proof zkp that guarantees that the three ciphertexts encrypt values x, y, z such that $z = x + y \bmod \mu$.

$$\mathsf{bal} = \mathsf{enc}(v), \mathsf{enc}(a), \mathsf{enc}(b), \mathsf{zkp}$$

The voting device commits to bal on the bulletin board. Then the voter asks their device to open either the second or the third encryption (chosen at random), by revealing the randomness used to produce the ciphertext. In order to modify v, the voting device needs to modify either a or b. Hence the voter will detect a malicious device with probability $1/2$. This audit mechanism does not leak any information on v since a and b (considered separately) are perfectly random.

We integrate this mechanism into the Belenios protocol [13], yielding BeleniosCaI. Belenios is an evolution of Helios [2] that additionally provides eligibility verifiability. Belenios is used each year in about 2000 elections, that include a German political party and some EU institutions [14]. We believe that our approach could be used to add cast-as-intended to other protocols as well. Interestingly, the computation overhead remains affordable. We show that we can encode the zero-knowledge proofs of modular equality into a standard proof of set membership. Overall, the computational cost and the size of ballots are about 2–3 times bigger than their counterparts in Belenios.

We formally prove that BeleniosCaI guarantees verifiability against a compromised voting device. We also show that BeleniosCaI preserves vote secrecy (assuming an honest voting device). Specifically, we provide a formal model of BeleniosCaI using the ProVerif tool [5], a well established tool for analyzing the security of protocols. This required to reflect the theory of modular arithmetic in ProVerif, which is typically out of range of this tool. Fortunately, we could re-use the model developed in [7]. Verifiability is shown by excluding traces that do not satisfy some of the properties of modular arithmetic, using restrictions, a feature recently introduced in ProVerif [6]. Vote privacy is more involved since it is expressed as an equivalence property where the attacker tries to distinguish between different voting choices. Considering sufficient conditions is no longer appropriate. Instead, we show (in ProVerif) lemmas on traces that then allow us to conclude thanks to a theorem of [7].

Related Work. The idea of using a two-checksum a and b with $b = v + a \bmod \mu$ has been firstly developed by Neff in [28] for the specific subcase $\mu = 2$. Then, the general case has been sketched in [11] and more thoroughly introduced in [7] in the context of on-site voting. The proposed system involves printed papers with scratch-off parts, smartcards, and local observers. We adapt this idea to

Internet voting, using the Belenios protocol, with many simplifications (e.g. we no longer request a and b to be of different parity).

Many Internet voting protocols have been proposed for cast-as-intended. We refer the reader to [27] for a nice and comprehensive survey. This survey splits existing protocols into five categories: audit-or-cast, tracking data, verification devices, code sheets, delegation. Interestingly, our approach introduced a novel category that could be called audit-and-cast. We only review here the main families. In the code sheet approach, voters obtain printed code sheets during the setup, with one code assigned to each candidate. When voting for a candidate v, the voter receives a code and checks on their sheet that it indeed corresponds to v. This is the approach followed in Switzerland with CHVote [20], as well as the protocol developed by SwissPost [1] or previously by Scytl [18]. Such systems require a heavy infrastructure (e.g. a distributed voting server) and assume a honest printer that is in charge of most of the setup. Other code-sheet based systems include Demos [24] and Pretty Good Democracy [31].

Some systems assume a (second) verification device. This is for example the case in Estonia [22] where voters can use a second device and the randomness of their ballot to check it is well-formed. In Australia [8], voters simply call a server that opens their ballot and gives the vote in clear (with associated threats on vote privacy). Intuitively, BeleniosCaI allows to simplify so much the work of the second device (checking an addition) that it can be discharged on the voter.

Tracking systems include in particular sElect [25], Selene [30] and its successor Hyperion [29]. They let the voter check that their vote appears on the public bulletin board, thanks to a voting tracker. The voter may detect a misbehavior only once the election is over. In Selene and Hyperion, the validity of the tracker needs to be checked with a second device (which, in return offers some protection against vote-buying).

2   Protocol Description

We describe a voting protocol, BeleniosCaI, where voters have to select between k_1 and k_2 candidates among a list of n candidates. A vote can be represented as a vector $(v_i)_{1 \le i \le n}$, where $v_i = 1$ if candidate i has been selected and $v_i = 0$ otherwise; the condition $\sum v_i \in [k_1, k_2]$ must be satisfied. An overview of the protocol is presented in Fig. 1.

2.1   Participants and Setup

Voters are identified with their email addresses, that will be used for authentication by the **Server**. We consider two distinct roles for the Voter and their **Voting device** since our protocol is designed to protect against a malicious Voting device (w.r.t. verifiability).

During the setup phase, the **Registrar** sends a private credential cred (a signing key) to each voter. It also sends the list of corresponding public verification keys to the Server. The k **Decryption authorities** set up the public key of the election pk_E such that a threshold t of them can decrypt any message encrypted with pk_E.

We assume a **Public board** that can be accessed at any time by all the participants. How to realize a public board in practice is out of the scope of this paper and is discussed for example in [23]. We also assume that at least one honest **Auditor** checks the validity of the ballots and all the cryptographic material that appears on the public board.

2.2   Voting Phase

Ballot. Given a vote $v = (v_i)_{1 \leq i \leq n}$ and a credential cred, a ballot $\mathsf{bal} = (M, \mathsf{zkp}, \sigma)$ is formed of an encrypted matrix M, a zero-knowledge proof zkp and a signature σ defined as follows. First, a vector of audit codes $(a_i)_{1 \leq i \leq n}$ is chosen uniformly at random, where $0 \leq a_i < \mu$, that is, each a_i is a small integer (smaller than a "modulus" μ than can be thought as 2 or 10).

– The encrypted matrix $M = \begin{pmatrix} V_1 \ A_1 \ B_1 \\ \vdots \\ V_n \ A_n \ B_n \end{pmatrix}$ contains n lines. Each line is formed of V_i, A_i, B_i where $V_i = \mathsf{enc}(v_i, \mathsf{pk}_E)$ encrypts the choice v_i, $A_i = \mathsf{enc}(a_i, \mathsf{pk}_E)$ encrypts the audit code a_i, while B_i ties V_i and A_i together. Namely, $B_i = \mathsf{enc}(b_i, \mathsf{pk}_E)$ where $b_i = v_i + a_i \bmod \mu$.
– The zero-knowledge proof zkp is formed of several zero-knowledge proofs that guarantee that:
  • each V_i encrypts either 0 or 1;
  • the V_i's encrypt values v_i such that $k_1 \leq \Sigma_{i=1}^n v_i \leq k_2$.
  • for each $1 \leq i \leq n$, V_i, A_i, B_i encrypt some values v_i, a_i, b_i such that $b_i = v_i + a_i \bmod \mu$.
– Finally, σ is the signature of M and zkp with the credential cred.

Voter Experience. The voter selects their vote v on their voting device, that computes a ballot bal as described above. The voting device displays the vote v and $h = \mathsf{hash}(\mathsf{bal})$ to the voter, where h will be used as a tracking number. This step is illustrated in Fig. 2a. The voter confirms their vote, and then the device sends the ballot bal to the voting server. The voter waits for an email from the server, that contains a confirmation challenge chal (used for authentication) and their tracking number h. If the tracking number is correct, they enter chal to their voting device and starts the audit phase, as illustrated in Fig. 2b:

– the voting device displays the matrix in clear

$$m = \begin{pmatrix} v_1 + a_1 = b_1 \\ \vdots \\ v_n + a_n = b_n \end{pmatrix}$$

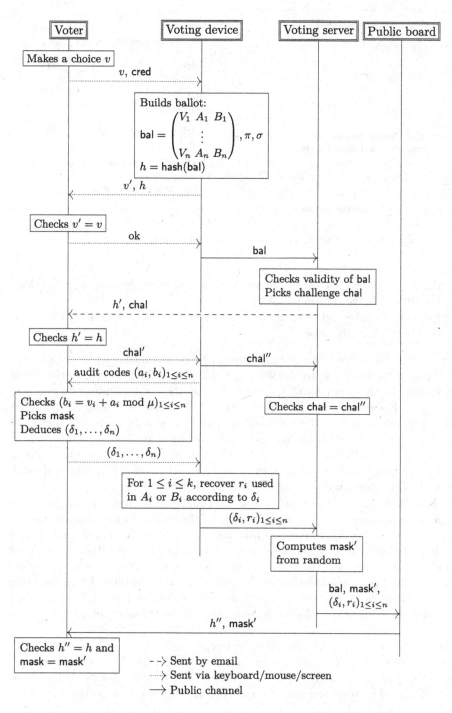

Fig. 1. Description of the voting phase of the BeleniosCaI protocol.

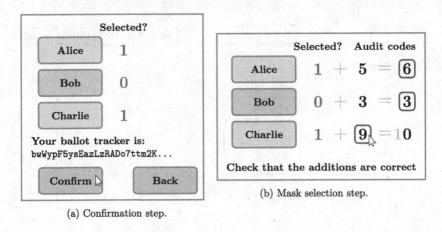

(a) Confirmation step.

(b) Mask selection step.

Fig. 2. Two steps of the voter's journey.

- the voter reviews the matrix m and checks that the sums are correct (taking $\mu = 10$ can make this step easier);
- for each line, they select either a_i or b_i, yielding a bit δ_i, where $\delta_i = 0$ if a_i is selected and 1 otherwise.

For each i, the voting device must reveal the randomness r_i used to encrypt either a_i or b_i according to the selection of the voter. The voting device sends to the server the selection $(\delta_i)_{1 \leq i \leq n}$ as well as the corresponding randomness $(r_i)_{1 \leq i \leq n}$. For each line i, the server decrypts A_i or B_i, according to δ_i, thanks to the randomness r_i and reveals on the public board the corresponding a_i or b_i. Finally, the voter checks on the public board that their tracking number h appears, as well as their selection $(\delta_i)_{1 \leq i \leq n}$ and the corresponding chosen integers. External auditors check that the decryptions of audit codes are valid, as well as the zero-knowledge proofs and signatures.

Intuitively, even if the voting device is malicious, it must commit to values v_i, a_i, b_i such that $b_i = v_i + a_i \bmod \mu$. Hence if the voting device wishes to change the vote v_i of the voter, it must also modify a_i or b_i. This will be detected with probability $1/2$ by the voter since they chose to see either a_i or b_i at random. Therefore, while a few votes may be modified without being detected, the attacker has a probability of $1/2^k$ to change k votes without being detected. This does not diminish vote privacy since only a random mask (either a_i or b_i) is revealed. We provide a formal security analysis in the next section.

Server. As in Belenios, the Server only accepts well-formed ballots, that is, ballots such that the zero-knowledge proofs are valid and the signature corresponds to a valid public verification key. Moreover, the Server ensures that a voter always uses the same credential (in case of a revote) and that no two voters use the same credential.

2.3   Tally Phase

As in Helios and Belenios, the encrypted votes $(V_i)_{1 \leq i \leq n}$ can be combined homomorphically in order to obtain an encrypted vector that corresponds to the total number of votes per candidates. The vector is decrypted by the Decryption authorities, who also provide a zero-knowledge proof of correct decryption.

2.4   Usability Considerations

In theory, the modulus μ can be as small as 2. This is enough to perfectly mask a bit. However, we do not expect typical voters to be familiar with binary arithmetic. We suggest to use $\mu = 10$, so that voters can do a classical addition, and are instructed to consider the units digit only, e.g. if the sum is 10, then we forget the 1 and get 0. Printing the 1 in gray can help as depicted in Fig. 2.

Choosing a random mask could be difficult since we expect the voters to be bad random generators in case there are many candidates. Assuming that voters can better pick numbers at random, one option is to ask voters to enter an at least 4-digit number (or maybe longer, if there are more than 13 candidates) instead of directly selecting the mask, and convert it to a mask using a predefined deterministic function. The server must then print both the mask and the number, so that the voter can check them.

3   Security Analysis

We conduct a security analysis of the BeleniosCaI protocol using the tool ProVerif.

3.1   ProVerif

ProVerif [5,6] is a state-of-the-art, automatic verification tool to prove the security of cryptographic protocols, including industrial-scale protocols such as TLS or Signal. ProVerif proves the security of protocols thanks to a (sound) transformation into first order logic. It (often) reports an attack trace when the proof fails. We recall here its main specificities and we present an overview of our model of BeleniosCaI. The full models are available at [10]. A detailed description of the syntax and semantics of ProVerif can be found in [6].

Messages. ProVerif is based on the notion of a Dolev-Yao attacker model [17] in which messages are abstracted by terms which are either an atomic data (e.g., a key, an unguessable random number, etc.) or a function symbol applied to other terms. The semantics of a message is then provided by an equational theory and/or a rewriting system. For instance, a randomized asymmetric encryption scheme is modeled by a function symbol aenc of arity 3, a symbol adec of arity 2, and a symbol pk of arity 1. The possibility to decrypt an encrypted message using the correct secret key is then modeled by the rewriting rule: $adec(y, aenc(pk(y), x, r)) \rightarrow x$ where x is the plaintext message, y the secret key corresponding to the public key $\mathsf{pk}(y)$, and r the randomness used for encryption. Most cryptographic primitives can be modeled similarly (e.g., signature, hash function, zero knowledge proof).

Roles. The different roles of the protocol are modeled through a process algebra inspired by the applied pi-calculus which includes the commands $P|Q$ to model that the processes P and Q execute in parallel, and $!P$ to model that an arbitrary number of process P can be executed in parallel. Moreover, communications on a (public or private) channel c are represented by actions $\mathsf{in}(c,x)$ and $\mathsf{out}(c,m)$ which respectively model that an agent is waiting for a message x on channel c, and an agent is sending a message m on c. In addition, the process may contain *event* actions that are used to identify specific steps in the process and to express some security properties. Finally, there are standard actions to model fresh unguessable name generations, conditionals, declarations, etc. For sake of simplicity, ProVerif supports the syntax $\mathsf{in}(c,=m); P$ as a shortcut for $\mathsf{in}(c,x); \mathsf{if}\ x = m\ \mathsf{then}\ P\ \mathsf{else}\ 0$. This notation will be used in Fig. 3.

All the processes are executed using an operational semantics presented in [6]. For instance, it formally defines that a message u can be received through an input $\mathsf{in}(c,x)$ as soon as there exists an action $\mathsf{out}(c,u)$ to execute, or if the channel c is public and the attacker is able to deduce the message u from its knowledge. Roughly speaking, the semantics formalizes the intuitive execution of the processes that the reader might think of.

Example 1. Figure 3 presents as a concrete example the process used to model the voter role. We assume that the voter securely receives their secret signing key and knows their id and the channel they will use to communicate with their device (e.g. monitor, keyboard, mouse, etc.). Finally, we assume a public channel c that will be used to communicate with the environment (i.e. the attacker).

The process then corresponds to the voter experience described in Sect. 2.2. First (l. 2–4), the voter sends their choice to their device. Second (l. 6–7), the voter reads on their device the ballot tracker and reviews their choice before confirming their vote. Third (l. 9–11), the voter receives an email from the server that contains a ballot tracker and a challenge. The ballot tracker must correspond to the one displayed on the reader. If this is the case, the voter enters their challenge in the device. Fourth (l. 13–18) the audit phase starts: the device displays the ballot and the corresponding audit codes, the voter checks the well-formedness of the ballot (i.e. $b = x + a$). The event $\mathsf{isSum}(x_B, v, x_A)$ is executed to model the check of the sum. The voter ends this phase by randomly choosing which code will be audited. Finally, (l. 20–29), the voter reads on the public bulletin board and look for an entry that matches their ballot tracker, and the expected audit codes. If everything is correct, then the voter is "happy" and can be sure that their vote will be counted, and that the ballot contains their intended choice.

The other roles of the protocol (i.e. voting device, server, tally) are modeled in a similar way.

```
1    Voter(id, c_device, ssk_id) =
2       in(c, v);    (* voter's choice chosen by attacker, to consider all cases *)
3       event HasInitiatedVote(id,v);
4       out(c_device, (v,ssk_id));
5
6       in(c_device, (=v, x_ballot_tracker));
7       out(c_device, OK);
8
9       in(c_mail(id), (=x_ballot_tracker, x_chal));
10      event Voted(id,x_ballot_tracker,x_v);
11      out(c_device, x_chal);
12
13      in(c_device, x_ballot_plaintext);
14      let (=v, x_A, x_B) = x_ballot_plaintext in
15      if x_A <> blind_code && x_B <> blind_code then
16         event isSum(x_B,v,x_A);
17         in(c, audit_choice);    (* audit choice chosen attacker, to consider all cases *)
18         out(c_device, audit_choice);
19
20         in(cell_BB, (x_vk, x_ballot, x_ballot_tracker_bb, x_rands, x_codes));
21         if audit_choice = 0 then (
22            if x_ballot_tracker_bb = x_ballot_tracker && x_codes = (x_A,blind_code) then (
23               event HappyVoter(id_voter,x_ballot_tracker,v); 0
24            ) else out(c_error, ERROR)
25         ) else if audit_choice = 1 then (
26            if x_ballot_tracker_bb = x_ballot_tracker && x_codes = (blind_code,x_B) then (
27               event HappyVoter(id_voter,x_ballot_tracker,v); 0
28            ) else out(c_error, ERROR)
29         ) else out(c, ERROR)
```

Fig. 3. ProVerif process modeling the voter actions.

Security Properties. ProVerif supports two main classes of security properties: trace properties and equivalence properties.

The trace properties express that specific *bad* states cannot be reached during the execution of the protocol. These are expressed using correspondence queries of the form

$$\bigwedge_{i\in\{1,...,n\}} E_i \Rightarrow \bigvee_{i\in\{1,...,m\}} \bigwedge_{j\in\{1,...,p\}} F_{i,j}$$

which models that whenever the events E_1, ..., E_n are executed during an execution then there must exist $i_0 \in \{1, \ldots, m\}$ such that all the facts (i.e. events, equalities, disequalities, etc.) $F_{i_0,1}$, ..., $F_{i_0,p}$ hold too. This type of queries are used to express for instance authentication, confidentiality, or integrity. In the context of our security analysis it will be used to express verifiability properties.

The equivalence properties model that two processes P and Q cannot be distinguished by an attacker interacting with them, denoted $P \approx Q$. For sake of simplicity, we intentionally decide to not recall here the formal definition of the notion of equivalence that ProVerif verifies (see [6] for details). In our context, this notion of equivalence properties will be useful to model vote secrecy.

3.2 How to Overcome ProVerif's Limitations?

The underlying symbolic model of the ProVerif tool has two main limitations to model the BeleniosCaI protocol. First, it does not allow to model associative and commutative operators which prevents an accurate modeling of the arithmetic operations in $\mathbb{Z}/\mu\mathbb{Z}$. Second, it does not model probabilistic actions that would be necessary to faithfully describe the audit mechanism of BeleniosCaI. To overcome these limitations, we leverage techniques developed in [7]. We recall here an overview of them but a detailed description and a proof of their correctness is available in the original paper.

Arithmetic Operations. To model the sum in $\mathbb{Z}/\mu\mathbb{Z}$, we assume that an event $\mathtt{isSum}(x, a, b)$ is executed each time an agent verifies that $x = a + b \mod \mu$. These events records all the equalities that must hold. Based on these events, two approaches are developed in [7] depending on the security property under study: first, for trace properties, it models the subset of properties which are relevant to make the audit mechanism secure. Specifically, it restricts the analysis to execution traces that satisfy these properties using *restrictions*. For example, we model that *"for all $a, b \in \mathbb{Z}/\mu\mathbb{Z}$ there exists a unique $x \in \mathbb{Z}/\mu\mathbb{Z}$ such that $x = a + b \mod \mu$"* using the restriction

$$\mathtt{isSum}(x, a, b) \ \wedge \ \mathtt{isSum}(x, a, b') \Rightarrow b = b'.$$

Other properties are modeled in the same way. These properties are trivially satisfied by the modular arithmetic, and actually sufficient for our verifiability properties.

Second, for equivalence properties, [7] proposes an approach based on *relation preservation* between the traces of the two processes P and Q we want to prove equivalent. Note that the previous approach, based on an over-approximation of the sum relation in $\mathbb{Z}/\mu\mathbb{Z}$ would be unsound for equivalence properties. Hence, [7] proposes to prove equivalence of processes P and Q as follows: (1) show that for any trace tr_P of P there exists an indistinguishable trace tr_Q of Q, and (2) if an event $\mathtt{isSum}(x, a, b)$ is executed in P then the same event is executed in tr_Q. The first item corresponds to the standard trace equivalence property that can be proved as usual in ProVerif, and the second item is the relation preservation property. It can be proved in ProVerif too by defining a specific lemma. An immediate consequence of item (2) is that, if the relation induced by the events $\mathtt{isSum}(x, a, b)$ models the sum in $\mathbb{Z}/\mu\mathbb{Z}$ in tr_P then it remains true in tr_Q. A detailed description of this approach and its soundness is provided in [7].

Probabilistic Actions. ProVerif does not handle probabilistic actions, and thus cannot faithfully model the random choice done by the voter to perform the audit. Like [7], to be able to conduct the security analysis, we decided to make the following reasoning on top of the modeling: because an attacker cannot know in advance which code the voter is about to audit, the attacker must be able to provide data that make the audits valid for both codes. Therefore, we model that the voter audits both codes for verifiability when it is necessary to avoid false attacks. Concretely, this means that, regarding Fig. 3, a third case is added for audit:

```
1   if audit_choice = 2 then (
2       if x_ballot_tracker_bb = x_ballot_tracker && x_codes = (x_A,x_B) then (
3         event HappyVoter(id_voter,x_ballot_tracker,v); 0
4       ) else out(c, ERROR)
```

3.3   Security Analysis and Result

We proved the security of the BeleniosCaI protocol regarding vote secrecy and verifiability. Following the approach developed in [3,12], we consider 3 sub-properties to model E2E verifiability: *cast-as-intended* to model that the voter can verify their ballot contains their intended vote, *no clash attack* to model that two voters should not agree on the same ballot, and *recorded-as-cast* to model that an attacker cannot create nor modify a ballot in the name of an honest voter. In this security analysis, we deliberately omit the eligibility property because it remains exactly the same as the current version of the Belenios protocol (eligibility is performed by both the registrar and the server).

To formalize these security properties, we define the following events:

- $\mathrm{onBoard}(vk, h, b, r, X)$ is executed each time a ballot b is added to the public bulletin board. vk is the public key associated to the signature occurring in b, h is the ballot tracker associated to b (i.e. $h = \mathsf{hash}(b)$) and (r, X) is the data published to conduct the audit.
- $\mathrm{Honest}(id, vk)$ is executed each time an honest voter id is registered with the public signing key vk.
- $\mathrm{HasInitiatedVote}(id, vk)$ is executed when the voter id with the public signing key vk has initiated a vote.
- $\mathrm{Voted}(id, vk, h)$ is executed when the voter id with the public signing key vk has confirmed their vote using the ballot tracker h.
- $\mathrm{HappyV}(X, id, h, v)$ is executed when voter id has completed the audit using the ballot tracker h and intended to vote for v. $X \in \{\mathsf{L}, \mathsf{R}, \mathsf{LR}\}$ records whether the voter audited the Left, the Right, or both (for modeling) codes.

Vote Secrecy. As usual in the symbolic analyses, we consider the vote secrecy definition proposed by Kremer *et al.* [15]: an e-voting protocol ensure vote secrecy if an attacker is not able to distinguish whether Alice voted for 0 and Bob for 1, or conversely. Formally, we note $Alice(x)$ (resp. $Bob(x)$) the process modeling the role of Alice (resp. Bob) when voting x, and P the process modeling all the other roles involved in the protocol then we want to prove that:

$$P|Alice(0)|Bob(1) \approx P|Alice(1)|Bob(0).$$

Cast-as-Intended. A protocol ensures cast-as-intended if the voter is able to verify that their ballot will be counted and contains their intended vote. We consider the following correspondence property to model cast-as-intended:

$\mathrm{HappyV}(\mathsf{LR}, id, h, v) \wedge \mathrm{Honest}(id, vk) \Rightarrow$
$\qquad\qquad \mathrm{onBoard}(vk', b, h, r, X) \wedge$ (b encrypts candidate v).

No Clash Attack. A protocol protects against clash attacks if two voters cannot agree on the same ballot. When honest devices are used, they generate ballots with different randomness, which ensure the no-clash property. This is no longer true if the voting devices are malicious and collude: they may use the same randomness and make Alice and Bob believe they own the same ballot. Interestingly, the no-clash property still holds in BeleniosCaI thanks to the fact that voters randomly choose whether they audit the left or the right code. We therefore model the no-clash property for voters that audit differently:

$$\text{HappyV}(\text{L}, id, h, v) \wedge \text{HappyV}(\text{R}, id', h, v') \Rightarrow \text{false}.$$

Note that this property is weaker than the original no-clash property, that does not need to make assumptions on voter's (audit) choices.

Recorded-as-Intended. A protocol ensures recorded-as-intended if an attacker is not able to forge a ballot in the name of an honest voter. This corresponds to the following correspondence property[1]:

$$\text{onBoard}(vk, h, b, r, X) \wedge \text{Honest}(id, vk) \Rightarrow \text{Voted}(id', vk, h). \tag{1}$$

Unfortunately, this property is not satisfied by BeleniosCaI when the voting device and the server are compromised. Indeed, as soon as the voter initiates a vote, they reveal their credential which lets the attacker completely impersonate them. We thus define a weaker property, that says that an attacker is not able to forge a ballot in the name of an honest voter, unless the voter has started a voting session:

$$\text{onBoard}(vk, h, b, r, X) \wedge \text{Honest}(id, vk) \Rightarrow \text{HasInitiatedVote}(id', vk). \tag{2}$$

Remark 1. Regarding the literature, it seems that protocols known to be verifiable assuming a compromised voting device guarantee only Property 2. This is the case, for instance, of Helios [2] or Selene [30]. Still, other protocols such as the Swiss Post [1] or BeleniosVS [12] ensure Property 1. Hence, we considered interesting to analyze the security of BeleniosCaI w.r.t. these two properties, as presented in Table 1 and 2. Recorded-as-intended corresponds to Property 2 and recorded-as-intended (strong) to Property 1.

Results. Table 1 presents the main results of the security analysis: BeleniosCaI is as secure as Belenios if we assume that the voting device is honest, i.e. it requires that either the registrar or the server is honest to ensure verifiability and that the decryption authorities are honest for vote secrecy. Moreover, it still provides verifiability when considering a malicious voting device: if the server is honest then it meets the same verifiability property as Belenios (strong E2E verifiability), while if the registrar is honest, then it ensures (only) the E2E verifiability. From the vote secrecy point of view, BeleniosCaI and Belenios are both secure as soon as enough decryption authorities are honest.

---

[1] This correspondence property identifies voters by their public signing key. This assumption is valid as long as the registrar is honest. Otherwise, when the server is honest, they can be identified by their *id* and a similar property is defined. This distinction corresponds to the approach developed in [12].

In summary, these results demonstrate that BeleniosCaI provides strictly better security guarantees than Belenios.

For interested readers, Table 2 presents the detailed results of the security analysis conducted in ProVerif. The ProVerif files are available in [10]. This table details the weakest trust assumptions in which each security property is ensured by BeleniosCaI: the less trustworthy agents there are, the more secure the protocol is. For instance, line 4 shows that the strong notion of recorded-as-cast is ensured as soon as the server is honest (i.e. even if the voting device or the registrar are compromised). Indeed, if the server is honest then the attacker will not be able to learn the challenge code sent by mail to the voter, and thus will not be able to confirm a maliciously created ballot in the name of the voter.

Table 1. Security analysis of BeleniosCaI: minimal trust assumption.

Trusted components	VD ∧ (R ∨ S) [T]	S [VD ∧ T]	R [VD ∧ T]	[VD ∧ T]
E2E verifiability (strong) (including cast-as-intended)	✓	✓	✗	✗
E2E verifiability (including cast-as-intended)	✓	✓	✓	✗
Vote secrecy	✓	✓	✓	✓

✓ = proved secure   VD = voting device, R = registrar, S = server, T = dec. auth.,
✗ = attack   [.] = extra trust assumption for vote secrecy only

Table 2. Minimal trust assumptions for each security property.

	Voter	Voting device	Server	Registrar	Dec. auth.
Cast-as-intended	☺	☹	☹	☹	☹
No clash	☺	☹	☹	☹	☹
Recorded-as-cast (strong)	☺	☺	☹	☺	☹
	☺	☹	☺	☹	☹
Recorded-as-cast	☺	☹	☹	☺	☹
	☺	☹	☺	☹	☹
Vote secrecy	☺	☺	☹	☹	☺

☺ = trustworthy   ☹ = compromised

4 Efficiency Considerations

A ballot in Belenios or Helios essentially costs one ciphertext and zero-knowledge (individual) proof per candidate, plus one zero-knowledge (overall) proof that controls the number of selected candidates. BeleniosCaI requires two extra ciphertexts and a proof of modular equality for each candidate. This essentially adds a factor between 2 and 3 to compute the ballot, as we detail now.

The zero-knowledge proofs required for forming the ballots can all be expressed as statements of the form "The cleartext of this ciphertext belongs to this finite set of possible values".

- **Individual proofs.** Each v_i belongs to $\{0,1\}$ is already in this form. This is therefore a list of 0/1 proofs. The basic approach requires 5 exponentiations. See [16,21] for ways to optimize them.
- **Overall proof.** The sum of all the v_i's is between k_1 and k_2. Due to the homomorphic property of ElGamal encryption, anyone can compute the ciphertext of this quantity, from the list of the V_i's, so that we are indeed in the claimed setting. Proving the property is then classically done as in Helios or Belenios, by rewriting it as belonging to a set of integers, with a cost that is linear in $k_2 - k_1$. Techniques exist to do this at a cost in $O(\log(k_2 - k_1))$ [9].
- **Arithmetic proofs.** The fact that V_i, A_i, B_i encrypt some values v_i, a_i, b_i such that $b_i = v_i + a_i \mod \mu$ can be rewritten as follows. First, by the homomorphic property, anyone can build the ciphertext that encrypts $v_i + a_i - b_i$ (without the modulo μ, that can not be computed homomorphically). By construction, if the ballot is correctly formed, this value must be equal to 0 or to μ. Therefore, this arithmetic proof can be rewritten as a proof of membership in a set of two elements, which is almost the same as the classical 0/1 proof. It therefore requires 5 exponentiations.

In Belenios, there is the possibility to have a special candidate representing a blank vote, and this comes with a zero-knowledge proof that either the blank vote is chosen and all the v_i's are zero, or the blank vote is not chosen, and then the sum of the v_i's is in $[k_1, k_2]$ (see [19]). Our method supports this setting: it is enough to add an arithmetic proof for this additional encrypted bit.

We also mention that in the security analysis, there is no need to have zero-knowledge proofs of the facts that the a_i's and the b_i's are in $[0, \mu-1]$. If, for some practical reasons, the server needs to detect early invalid ballots, these proofs can be added. They are of the same nature as the overall proof. However, they can be costly for the voting device of the voters, if there are many candidates.

To sum-up, compared to Belenios, for the voting device, the additional cost of forming a ballot is, for each candidate, to compute two ElGamal encryptions A_i and B_i, and to compute the arithmetic proof for them. This amounts to 9 additional exponentiations per candidate. Techniques like in [16] can be used to reduce this cost. As a rule of thumb, we can say that this will multiply the running time of forming a complete ballot by a factor between 2 and 3, the exact number depending on the number of candidates and the value of $k_2 - k_1$. For elections for which there are no more than a few dozens of candidates, this remains affordable with a Javascript/WebAssembly implementation running in a standard browser, and there is no need to have a native implementation (which would raise many issues, since this usually requires to install specific software).

References

1. Swiss post voting specification - version 1.1.1 (2022). https://gitlab.com/swisspost-evoting/e-voting/e-voting-documentation/-/tree/master/System
2. Adida, B.: Helios: web-based Open-Audit Voting. In: USENIX (2008)
3. Baloglu, S., Bursuc, S., Mauw, S., Pang, J.: Election verifiability revisited: automated security proofs and attacks on Helios and Belenios. In: CSF 2021 (2021)
4. Benaloh, J.: Simple verifiable elections. In: EVT 2006. Usenix (2006)
5. Blanchet, B.: An efficient cryptographic protocol verifier based on Prolog rules. In: CSFW 2001, pp. 82–96. IEEE (2001)
6. Blanchet, B., Cheval, V., Cortier, V.: ProVerif with lemmas, induction, fast subsumption, and much more. In: S&P 2022. IEEE (2022)
7. Bougon, M., et al.: Themis: an on-site voting system with systematic cast-as-intended verification and partial accountability. In: CCS 2022 (2022)
8. Brightwell, I., Cucurull, J., Galindo, D., Guasch, S.: An overview of the iVote 2015 voting system. New South Wales Electoral Commission, Australia (2015)
9. Canard, S., Coisel, I., Jambert, A., Traoré, J.: New results for the practical use of range proofs. In: Katsikas, S., Agudo, I. (eds.) EuroPKI 2013. LNCS, vol. 8341, pp. 47–64. Springer, Heidelberg (2014). https://doi.org/10.1007/978-3-642-53997-8_4
10. Cortier, V., Debant, A., Gaudry, P., Glondu, S.: Belenios with cast as intended. In: 8th Workshop on Advances in Secure Electronic Voting, Bol, Brač, Croatia (2023). https://hal.inria.fr/hal-04020110
11. Cortier, V., Dreier, J., Gaudry, Turuani, M.: A simple alternative to Benaloh challenge for the cast-as-intended property in Helios/Belenios (2019). https://hal.inria.fr/hal-02346420
12. Cortier, V., Filipiak, A., Lallemand, J.: BeleniosVS: secrecy and verifiability against a corrupted voting device. In: CSF 2019, pp. 367–36714. IEEE (2019)
13. Cortier, V., Galindo, D., Glondu, S., Izabachène, M.: Election verifiability for helios under weaker trust assumptions. In: Kutyłowski, M., Vaidya, J. (eds.) ESORICS 2014. LNCS, vol. 8713, pp. 327–344. Springer, Cham (2014). https://doi.org/10.1007/978-3-319-11212-1_19
14. Cortier, V., Gaudry, P., Glondu, S.: Features and usage of Belenios in 2022. In: E-Vote-ID 2022 (2022)
15. Delaune, S., Kremer, S., Ryan, M.D.: Verifying privacy-type properties of electronic voting protocols. J. Comput. Secur. **17**, 435–487 (2009)
16. Devillez, H., Pereira, O., Peters, T.: How to verifiably encrypt many bits for an election? In: Atluri, V., Di Pietro, R., Jensen, C.D., Meng, W. (eds.) ESORICS 2022. LNCS, vol. 13555, pp. 653–671. Springer, Cham (2022). https://doi.org/10.1007/978-3-031-17146-8_32
17. Dolev, D., Yao, A.: On the security of public key protocols. IEEE Trans. Inf. Theory **29**, 198–208 (1983)
18. Galindo, D., Guasch, S., Puiggalí, J.: 2015 Neuchâtel's cast-as-intended verification mechanism. In: Haenni, R., Koenig, R.E., Wikström, D. (eds.) VOTELID 2015. LNCS, vol. 9269, pp. 3–18. Springer, Cham (2015). https://doi.org/10.1007/978-3-319-22270-7_1
19. Gaudry, P.: Some ZK security proofs for Belenios (2017). https://hal.inria.fr/hal-01576379
20. Haenni, R., Koenig, R.E., Locher, P., Dubuis, E.: CHVote system specification. Cryptology ePrint Archive, Report 2017/325 (2017)

21. Haenni, R., Locher, P., Gailly, N.: Improving the performance of cryptographic voting protocols. In: Bracciali, A., Clark, J., Pintore, F., Rønne, P.B., Sala, M. (eds.) FC 2019. LNCS, vol. 11599, pp. 272–288. Springer, Cham (2020). https://doi.org/10.1007/978-3-030-43725-1_19

22. Heiberg, S., Willemson, J.: Verifiable internet voting in Estonia. In: EVOTE 2014. IEEE (2014)

23. Hirschi, L., Schmid, L., Basin, D.A.: Fixing the Achilles heel of e-voting: the bulletin board. In: CSF 2021 (2021)

24. Kiayias, A., Zacharias, T., Zhang, B.: End-to-end verifiable elections in the standard model. In: Oswald, E., Fischlin, M. (eds.) EUROCRYPT 2015. LNCS, vol. 9057, pp. 468–498. Springer, Heidelberg (2015). https://doi.org/10.1007/978-3-662-46803-6_16

25. Küsters, R., Müller, J., Scapin, E., Truderung, T.: sElect: a lightweight verifiable remote voting system. In: CSF 2016. IEEE (2016)

26. Marky, K., Kulyk, O., Renaud, K., Volkamer, M.: What did I really vote for? On the usability of verifiable e-voting schemes. In: CHI 2018 (2018)

27. Marky, K., Zollinger, M., Roenne, P.B., Ryan, P.Y.A., Grube, T., Kunze, K.: Investigating usability and user experience of individually verifiable internet voting schemes. ACM Trans. Comput. Hum. Interact. **28**, 1–36 (2021)

28. Neff, C.A.: Practical high certainty intent verification for encrypted votes (2004)

29. Ryan, P., Roenne, P., Rastikian, S.: Hyperion: an enhanced version of the Selene end-to-end verifiable voting scheme. In: E-Vote-ID 2021 (2021)

30. Ryan, P.Y.A., Rønne, P.B., Iovino, V.: Selene: voting with transparent verifiability and coercion-mitigation. In: Clark, J., Meiklejohn, S., Ryan, P.Y.A., Wallach, D., Brenner, M., Rohloff, K. (eds.) FC 2016. LNCS, vol. 9604, pp. 176–192. Springer, Heidelberg (2016). https://doi.org/10.1007/978-3-662-53357-4_12

31. Ryan, P.Y.A., Teague, V.: Pretty good democracy. In: Christianson, B., Malcolm, J.A., Matyáš, V., Roe, M. (eds.) Security Protocols 2009. LNCS, vol. 7028, pp. 111–130. Springer, Heidelberg (2013). https://doi.org/10.1007/978-3-642-36213-2_15

On the Auditability of the Estonian IVXV System
And an Attack on Individual Verifiability

Anggrio Sutopo[1], Thomas Haines[1(✉)], and Peter Roenne[2]

[1] Australian National University, Canberra, Australia
thomas.haines@anu.edu.au
[2] CNRS, LORIA & Univ Lorraine, Nancy, France

Abstract. The development and auditing processes around electronic voting implementations are much too often deficient; this is particularly true for the measures taken to prevent cryptographic errors – potentially with grave consequences for security. To mitigate this, it is common to make the code public in order to allow independent experts to help uncover such flaws.

In this paper we present our experiences looking at the IVXV system used for municipal and national elections in Estonia as well as European parliament elections. It appears that, despite the code being public for over five years, the cryptographic protocol has *not* seen much scrutiny at the code level. We describe in detail the (lack of) auditability and incentives which have contributed to this situation. We also present a previously unknown vulnerability which contradicts the claimed individual verifiability of the system; this vulnerability should be patched in the next version of IVXV system.

1 Introduction

Two fundamental requirements of any democratic election are the privacy of the voter and the integrity of the ballot. As many jurisdictions around the world move to electronic voting (e-voting), these two properties have to be guaranteed and here cryptographic techniques play a prominent role. But even the most sophisticated cryptographic techniques are useless if their software implementation contains bugs. The desire to ensure the integrity of elections, even in the presence of such bugs, no matter if accidental or malicious, has led to the notion of "software independence":

> "A voting system is software-independent if an (undetected) change or error in its software cannot cause an undetectable change or error in an election outcome" [Riv08].

Thomas Haines is the recipient of an Australian Research Council Australian Discovery Early Career Award (project number DE220100595).

This work received funding from the France 2030 program managed by the French National Research Agency under grant agreement No. ANR-22-PECY-0006.

A. Essex et al. (Eds.): FC 2023 Workshops, LNCS 13953, pp. 19–33, 2024.
https://doi.org/10.1007/978-3-031-48806-1_2

One important way to produce publicly verifiable evidence while preserving privacy is via zero-knowledge proofs (ZKP) [GMR85], which allow the demonstration of the truth of a statement without leaking additional information. Despite the name "software-independent" these systems are still dependent on the correctness of the software verifying the evidence, as we will see.

At least in part due to the complexity of the requirements and cryptography involved, electronic voting systems have a long history of insecure implementations largely as a result of insecure implementation of cryptography. For example, the Scytl-Swiss Post system contained many components which were broken despite extensive review [HLPT20]. This has been true in many systems: the iVote system [HT15], the e-voting system previously used in national elections in Estonia [SFD+14], the Moscow voting system [GG20], and the issues with Voatz [SKW20] and Democracy Live [SH20].

There is a widespread presumption that these errors are indicative of a lack of expertise within the vendors, and the companies which are paid to audit them, to develop and audit systems which securely implement cryptographic protocols. In an attempt to remedy this, it has become common to open the source code to public scrutiny to help find these errors. The IVXV system [oE] is a good example of this, having been developed and largely made public in the wake of the issues found in the previous system [SFD+14].

Haines and Roenne [HR21] argue that making the system public appears to be a necessary condition at present for developing secure systems but not a sufficient one. They make nine recommendations which are aimed at ensuring that the public code is comprehensible, and capable of being checked for the most common errors in a reasonable time frame. They further argue that unless the code meets their requirements, little progress in security can be expected.

In this work, we analyse the available information on the IVXV system with respect to these standards; despite being available for five years the system has a paltry degree of auditability. Based on this, it is to be expected that the system has errors which would have been detected already in a system with a better auditability; to this point we found a vulnerability which breaks individual verifiability which should have been caught with a quick review of the system specification (without any need to look at the code). Since the system lacks an adequate specification, this error has gone undetected until now; we conjecture the system contains more similar vulnerabilities. In our conclusion (Sect. 5) we comment on the changes that Estonia could make to the process in order to improve this situation.

1.1   E-Voting in Estonia

Estonia has been using internet voting since the early 2000s for elections. The system has had multiple changes but has maintained the same key designs, using the national ID card to verify the user's identity in the voting application.

Estonia became the first country to offer the option of voting online nationwide after implementing the first version of their online voting system in 2005. This online voting system, called Internet voting or I-voting, was first used in

2005 to vote for the municipal elections [MM06]. The system has been overhauled multiple times due to security concerns, in particular concerning the possibility that a vote might be manipulated after it has been submitted without the organiser's or voter's knowledge. A mechanism to allow a voter to verify their votes was introduced in 2013 [HW14], but within a year it was shown to have some flaws [SFD+14]. In response, a new system was implemented in 2017 in collaboration with the vendor Smartmatic - Cybernetica C.O.E for Internet Voting, called the IVXV system [HMVW16]. In the recent 2023 Estonian parliamentary election 312,181 votes were cast electronically, this means it was the first election with more than half of votes cast online [Wik]. Even further, to the best of our knowledge, this also makes it the largest online voting by participation.

1.2   The IVXV System

The IVXV system follows the basic concept of an envelope scheme [HMVW16]. In a physical election, the vote ballots are put into a sealed envelope that is only unsealed during the tally period. The IVXV system works in a similar way, where each voter sends their encrypted vote alongside their digital signature to the collector service [Sta20]. This would in theory allow the votes to remain secret while allowing the collector service to verify that the vote belongs to an eligible voter. In addition, the system also allows each voter to verify that the vote accepted by the collector service is as intended using the verification application [Sta20]. Finally, the system in theory now allows third party auditors to audit the tabulation process [HMVW16], but to our knowledge this has not occurred in the past elections using the system.

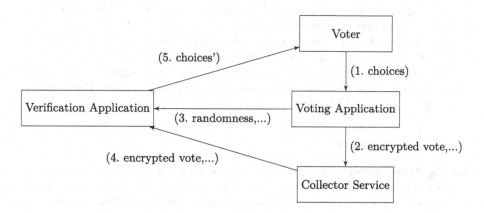

Fig. 1. Overview of vote casting and verification in the IVXV system

The IVXV system consists of a mix of services and applications that each handle a specific task, while also being connected to supporting external components [Sta19]; we highlight the main flow in Fig. 1. The internal components

include the collector service, the processing application, the key application, and
the audit application. The external components include the identification service, the signing service, and the registration service. There are also independent
but closely connected components such as the voting application, the verification
application, and the mixing application. The source code of most parts of the system can be viewed publicly in the IVXV GitHub repository, but the exact code
used in active development is kept private; nevertheless, the version of the code
used in any given election should have a corresponding commit in the GitHub
repository. In the remainder of the section, we will summarise the explanation
found in [Sta19] regarding the architecture of the IVXV system which can be
separated into the internal and external components.

Internal Components

Collector Service: The collector service is in charge of collecting the votes from
the voting application and storing them before the tallying process. It is connected to external components that are focused on supporting identification,
verification, and qualification. The service consists of several micro-services
that are all programmed in Go and are closely connected with the external
components. For brevity we omit a description of these micro-services.

Key Application: The key application is in charge of generating the vote
encryption and decryption keys for each election as well as decrypting and
counting the votes. The application is programmed in Java.

Processing Application: The processing application is in charge of verifying,
cancelling, and anonymising the votes collected over the voting period. The
application can generate a list of voters as well as the anonymised votes after
receiving the information stored in the collector service and the registration
service. The application is programmed in Java.

Audit Application: The audit application is in charge of mathematically verifying that the vote count and mixing is correct. The application generates
a detailed log containing the assessment of the audit after receiving the
anonymised votes, mixed votes, shuffle proof, and voting result. The application is programmed in Java.

External Components

Voting Application. The voting application is the program used by voters to
submit their votes to the system [HMVW16]. It is available in desktop systems
such as Windows, macOS, and Linux and can be downloaded from the election
authority's website [HW14]. *The source code of the voting application was/is
not available for scrutiny and the description below has not been checked to
match the implementation.* The system expects the process of voting to work
as follows [Sta20]:
1. The voter uses the voter application to submit their vote.
2. The collector service stores the vote.

3. The voter can use the verification application to check if their vote has been stored properly.
4. At the end of the voting period, the collector service issues the ballot box to the election organiser while the registration service issues the list of registered votes collected in the collector service.
5. The election organiser calculates the voting result.

In this section, we adopt the convention of [HMVW16] in defining the encryption used by the IVXV system. The encryption used to encrypt the votes is a homomorphic public key cryptosystem. The algorithm should follow a scheme of $\epsilon = (Gen_{enc}, Enc, Dec)$ with its key generation, encryption, and decryption functions as well as the cryptographic hash function $Hash$. The algorithm that is implemented in the current version of the system is the ElGamal cryptosystem. The election organiser generates an election key pair that is used for encrypting and decrypting the votes

$$(ek_{pub}^{elec}, ek_{priv}^{elec}) \leftarrow Gen_{enc}$$

The public key ek_{pub}^{elec} is made available to everybody and is used by both the voting and verification application to encrypt and verify the votes, respectively, while the private key ek_{priv}^{elec} is stored securely by the organiser and is used for tabulating the voting results.

The certification authority is in charge of storing the keypair $(sk_{pub}^{CA}, sk_{priv}^{CA})$ and the corresponding certificate $Cert_{CA}^{CA}$, and each eligible voter posses a unique identifier $i \in I$ as well as a certified signature keypair:

$$\forall_i \in I, (sk_{pub}^i, sk_{priv}^i) \leftarrow Gen_{sig}, Cert_{CA}^i = Sign(sk_{priv}^{CA}, (i, sk_{pub}^i))$$

The application implements the double envelope format by first encrypting the candidate choice c_v as $ballot_{c,r} = Enc(c_v, r_v, ek_{pub}^{elec})$ where $r_v \leftarrow R$ is a random number, followed by signing the encrypted vote with the voter's private key such that $vote_v = Sign(sk_{priv}^v, ballot_{c,r})$. The application then sends the voter identifier v, certificate $Cert_{CA}^v$, and signed encrypted vote $vote_v$ to the collector service, and receives a unique identifier vid and the registration service confirmation reg_{vid} which is verified using the $Hash$ of the vote. In order to verify, the identifier vid and encryption randomness r_v are presented by the voting application as a QR code that can be scanned by the verification application.

Verification Application. The verification application is used by voters to verify that their vote has been stored properly by the collector service [HMVW16]. It is available on mobile devices through either the Google App Store for Android or the Apple App Store for iOS [HW14]. The Android version is programmed in Java while the iOS version is programmed in Objective-C. The source code for the Android version is available publicly[1], as is the iOS version[2]. Even though the applications are developed on different platforms, they follow the same design for the cryptographic part, importantly

---

[1] https://github.com/vvk-ehk/ivotingverification.
[2] https://github.com/vvk-ehk/ios-ivotingverification.

they contain the same flaw, mentioned below. The description below of how the application functions is taken directly from [HMVW16].

1. The voter obtains from the voting application a QR code that encodes a unique vote identifier vid and randomness r_v after submitting their vote.
2. The voter scans the QR code using the verification application.
3. The verification application uses an authenticated TLS channel to connect with the collector service and sends the vid.
4. The collector service sends back the signed encrypted vote $vote_v$ as well as the registration service confirmation reg_{vid}. An error is returned if an unknown vid is used or if it exceeds the verification time limit.
5. The verification application verifies both the vote and the registration service confirmation then displays the identity v to the voter.
6. The verification application uses the list of candidates C and randomness r_v to find a $c' \in C$ such that $Enc(c', r_v, ek_{pub}^{elec}) = ballot_{c,r}$. The result either shows the decrypted vote or an error message. It is up to the voter to determine if their vote is correct or if they need to submit a new vote using the voting application.

Security Model. Within the repository, there are no clear claims regarding the security model desired of the system. The document available in the election information website, [Sta17], describes the system from a high level point of view, but also doesn't make any clear claims regarding which components are considered trusted. While there are several claims such as the cryptosystem used being secure and that each voter can verify their votes [Sta17], there are no information regarding which components are considered critical.

Reading between the lines, it appears that the system considers any attack that require the compromise of any part of the backend of the system to be outside the scope of the model. Whereas, an attack that can be launched by the voting device alone is in scope. Writing out the model in detail would be helpful in guiding examiners to the issues which the stakeholders care most about.

2   Scope, Methodology, and Contributions

Scope: Our work is based on version 1.7.7 of the IVXV system as it appeared at https://github.com/vvk-ehk/ivxv. In addition, we looked at selected parts of the Android verification application and the iOS verification application. Further, some information was retrieved from the election information website located on https://www.valimised.ee/en. For none of these sources was our review exhaustive; our review was limited to the documents which were available in English.

The key focus of our work is an examination of the auditability of the system with respect to the requirements listed in [HR21]. In addition, we focused on understanding the individual verifiability of the system at the code level. While we discovered an interesting vulnerability in the individual verifiability, our examination of this property was not adequate to establish the security of the system with respect to this property. In Sect. 5 we also comment on other areas of the code we are worried may negatively effect the verifiability of the system.

There is a wide range of security issues which are outside of our scope. We believe that in many of these areas, the current process in Estonia does a better job of detecting vulnerabilities in the system than it does for the cryptographic core. Overall, the vulnerabilities in the cryptography are likely to require a more sophisticated attacker to understand and exploit than other kinds; however, it is hard to evaluate this assertion since we have little idea what kinds of vulnerabilities exist within the cryptographic implementation.

Methodology: Our review methodology focused on examination of the system documents and manual code review using an IDE. Though we were unable to build the system as a whole, we did write some unit tests to test particular functionalities of the system.

Contributions: Our work highlights deficiencies in the auditability of the IVXV system. We also reveal a significant vulnerability in the individual verifiability of the system which has gone undetected for many years. Overall, our work provides a helpful resource for understanding the security of the cryptographic implementation of the IVXV system and what can be done about it.

3   Flaw in Individual Verifiability

The system has two different parts that care about the decryption of the votes. First is the key application which needs to decrypt all votes in the system that are considered valid before sending them to the tallying service. Second is the verification application which needs to extract the plaintext vote that was previously submitted by the voter using the voting application. The verification application can be separated into the Android and iOS versions. The vulnerability in the system that we found is related to the three different implementations of vote decryption, which are incomplete and cause a vulnerability that can be exploited using at least three different possible attacks. The relevant files for the key application, which can be found in the IVXV GitHub repository [ivx], are

- RecoverDecryption.java
- ElGamalPrivateKey.java
- ModPGroup.java
- Plaintext.java

The relevant files for the Android version of the verification application which can be found in https://github.com/vvk-ehk/ivotingverification are:

- DecryptionActivity.java
- DecryptionTask.java
- ElGamalPub.java

The relevant files for the iOS version of the verification application which can be found in https://github.com/vvk-ehk/ios-ivotingverification are:

- Crypto.m
- Crypto.h
- ElgamalPub.m
- ElgamalPub.h

To understand the vulnerability, we must first understand the correct implementation of the ElGamal encryption mechanism. ElGamal encryption occurs over a cyclic group G of prime order q with a generator g. The private key x is an element of $\mathbb{Z}_q$, and the public key y is g^x. Encryption of a message $m \in G$ takes a random r from $\mathbb{Z}_q^*$ and computes the tuple $(g^r, y^r m)$. The ciphertext (c_1, c_2) under a given public key g^x can be decrypted by computing c_2/c_1^x. It also possible given knowledge of r such that a given ciphertext (c_1, c_2) is equal to $(g^r, y^r m)$ to compute the message as c_2/y^r.

In the IVXV system, a voter is able to verify that their vote has been correctly submitted by the voting application by using the verification application to compute c_2/y^r such that it will display the message m which is equivalent to their recorded vote v. The interactions between a voter and the system according to the code is shown in the following process:

1. The voter submits their vote v to the voting application.
2. The voting application independently samples the random number r.
3. The voting application computes the ciphertext $(c_1, c_2) = (g^r, y^r v)$ and sends it to the collector service.
4. The voting application generates a QR code for the vote for verification.
5. The voter tries to use the verification application to verify their vote by scanning the QR code generated by the voting application.
6. The verification application receives the random number r from the voting application via the QR code.
7. The verification application receives only part of the ciphertext, $c_2 = y^r v$ from the collector service.
8. The verification application recovers v by computing c_2/y^r which the voter can check against the intended choice.
9. At the end of the election, the key application recovers v by decrypting the ciphertext $(c_1, c_2) = (g^r, y^r v)$ using the private key x.
10. The recovered vote v is sent to the tallying service.

The current design doesn't verify that c_1 is equal to g^r, and the system seems to be running under the assumption that the verification of c_1 isn't required. However, this verification is crucial in ensuring that the cryptosystem is functioning properly, and the lack of it results in a vulnerability that could be exploited in three different possible attacks of various severity. To highlight the difference in the process for each attack, the diverging step is written in italic.

3.1   Attack 1: Discarding a Vote

In the first potential attack method, an attacker is able to discard the vote of an existing voter by sending a different random number r' in place of r. The attack is executed in the following process:

- *The voting application independently samples the random numbers r and r', which will be different with overwhelming probability.*
- *The voting application computes the ciphertext $(c_1, c_2) = (g^r, y^{r'} v)$ and sends it to the collector service, note the different random numbers used.*
- *The verification application receives r' from the voting application.*
- *The verification application receives only part of the ciphertext, $c_2 = y^{r'} v$ from the collector service. Note that the application doesn't receive $c_1 = g^r$.*
- *The verification application recovers v by computing $y^{r'} v / y^{r'}$. The voter feels assured that their vote has been properly stored in the system.*
- *The key application decrypts the ciphertext $(c_1, c_2) = (g^r, y^{r'} v)$. However, since this will evaluate to $y^{r'-r} v$, which is a random element of the group, the decrypted text will not be well formed with overwhelming probability.*
- *The vote is then discarded by the key application and isn't counted by the tallying service.*

The result of this attack is that the voter is disenfranchised as their vote is discarded without their knowledge by the key application. This potential attack violates the security model as it doesn't require the attacker to be able to compromise the backend of the system; the attack only requires the adversary to control the voting application. If this attack occurred it would result in invalid votes appearing in the output. Based on the information provided by the maintainers, this attack hasn't occurred during any of the previous elections.

3.2   Attack 2: Changing a Vote with Knowledge of the Private Key

In the second attack method, an attacker is able to manipulate the vote of an existing voter into a different valid choice but requires knowledge of the private key x. The attack is executed in the following process:

- *The attacker obtains the private key x by some means. For example, accessing the part of the backend of the system where it is stored.*
- *The voting application computes the ciphertext $(c_1, c_2) = ((y^r v/v')^{1/x}, y^r v)$ and sends it to the collector service. Note that the plaintext vote in the ciphertext that is sent is now changed from v to v'.*
- *The verification application recovers v by computing $y^r v/y^r$. The voter feels assured that their vote has been properly stored in the system.*
- *At the end of the election, the key application in an offline environment recovers v' by decrypting the ciphertext $(c_1, c_2) = ((y^r v/v')^{1/x}, y^r v)$.*
- *The recovered vote v' is sent to the tallying service.*

The result of this attack is that the voter will think that their preferred choice has been stored in the system when in reality the choice that is counted is entirely different. This potential attack is considered to be outside of the security model as it requires the attacker to obtain the private key.

3.3 Attack 3: Changing a Vote Without Knowledge of the Private Key

In the third attack method an attacker is able to manipulate the vote of an existing voter into a different valid choice but requires knowledge of the discrete log relationship between the possible candidate choices in the base of the public election key. The attack is executed in the following process:

- *The attacker, by some means, gains knowledge of the discrete log relationship between two possible voting choices v and v' in the base of the public election key y, i.e. the attacker knows s in $v/v' = y^s$. For example, if the attacker is able to choose the vote encoding configuration of the system, then the relationship can easily be known.*
- *The voting application computes the ciphertext $(c_1, c_2) = (g^r, y^r v')$ and sends it to the collector service. Note that this encrypts a different vote v'.*
- The voting application generates a QR code for verification *but the QR code contains $r' = r - s$ (modulo the order of the group) instead of r.*
- The voter tries to use the verification application to verify their vote by scanning the QR code generated by the voting application.
- *The verification application receives $r' = r - s$ from the voting application.*
- *The verification application receives only part of the ciphertext, $c_2 = y^r v'$ from the collector service. The verification application doesn't receive $c_1 = g^r$.*
- *The verification application recovers v by computing $y^r v'/y^{r'} = y^r v'/y^{r-s} = v'y^s = v$. The voter feels assured that their vote has been properly stored.*
- *At the end of the election, the collector service attempts to decrypt the ciphertext $(c_1, c_2) = (g^r, y^r v')$ and will instead recover v' instead of v.*
- *The recovered vote v' is sent to the tallying service.*

The result is similar to the previous attack method, but now the attacker can execute it without prior knowledge of the private key x. We wish to thank Vanessa Teague for pointing out this variant of the attack. We believe this attack is also outside the security model because of how the encoded voting options are configured; however, we have not done a full investigation of this since the underlying vulnerability should be patched before the next election.

This attack is more interesting and concerning than the others since it is not intuitive that choosing the encodings of voting options should allow one to break individual verifiability and hence this avenue might be easier to exploit than an attack which requires knowledge of the secret key. Further, the idea of encoding votes in terms of y^v was recently used for efficiency reasons in [DPP22].

3.4 Computational Condition for Precision Attacks

We can give a precise computational necessary and sufficient condition for launching attacks changing an intended vote encoded by v into a vote encoded by v':

Theorem 1. *An adversarial algorithm can compute an ElGamal encryption of v' under the public key $y = g^x$ that will verify as a vote for v using only the second part of the ciphertext, as above, if and only if $(v'/v)^{1/x}$ can be computed.*

To see this, first assume we the adversary has created a ciphertext of v' as $(c_1, c_2) = (g^r, y^r v')$ and at the same time outputs r' such that $c_2 = y^{r'} v$. Then $v'/v = y^{r'-r} = g^{x(r'-r)}$ and hence $(v'/v)^{1/x} = g^{r'-r} = g^{r'}/c_1$ can be computed as well. On the other hand, given $(v'/v)^{1/x}$, we can choose any r' to compute $(g^{r'}(v/v')^{1/x}, y^{r'} v)$ which is a ciphertext decrypting to v' but verifying as v. If a plaintext-knowledge proof was required, such an attack would not be possible.

Given knowledge of the secret election key x, as in attack 2, or the discrete log in attack 3 immediately allows to compute $(v'/v)^{1/x}$ and launch the attack. If nothing is known about v/v' then this assumption is closely related to the 1-Diffie-Hellman Inversion Problem [PS00] of computing $g^{1/x}$ from g^x. If v'/v is directly a known power of the generator g then they are indeed equivalent. Since this is a known hard problem, also used in other voting schemes, e.g. [RRI16], we would not expect attacks from external attackers in this case.

Note that if the implementation also verified the first part of the ciphertext, it would be impossible to find an r defeating verification, and no computational assumption would be needed for the soundness of the verifiability check.

Finally, we might wonder if *auxiliary information*, such as access to decryption outcomes, would help an attacker. In general, this seems unlikely, however, there are corner cases: Consider an attacker as in Attack 3 who controls the vote encoding. If this attacker tries to launch an attack before y^x is known, it will not be possible. However, if a simple decryption of any arbitrary ciphertext (c_1, c_2) is known, then the attack can be launched since the decryption reveals c_1^x and the attacker could set $v'/v = c_1^x$ to later use it in the attack.

3.5   Solution

The solution to all three potential attacks is to redesign the verification application such that it receives c_1 which would enable it to verify that the random number r sent by the voting application satisfies the condition $c_1 = g^r$. We have informed the maintainers of the existence of the vulnerability as well as the various potential attack methods that exploit it, and they have assured us that they have started working on implementing the solution. However, at the time of writing, they haven't published their implementation of the solution, so we couldn't determine if the vulnerability is fixed or not.

The relevant stakeholders should also consider revising the security model of the system so that they and the system are prepared for more potential attacks and scenarios, especially those that involve attacks on the backend of the system.

3.6   Why wasn't This Already Noted?

The vulnerability is straightforward which makes it more concerning. The fact that is hasn't been noticed until now we put down to the fact examinations of the IVXV system, for example [Per21] focused largely on the specification level. In the next section we comment on some of the issues which make examining the code of the IVXV system so painful.

4 Analysis with Regards to Haines and Roenne 2021

This section will comment on the quality of the IXVX public information based on the standard in [HR21]. We summarise the results in Table 1 and give details in the following paragraphs.

Table 1. Summary of IVXV with respect to requirements listed in [HR21].

Property	Result
Clear claims	✗
Thorough documentation	✗
Minimality	✗
Buildable	✗
Executable	✗
Exportable	✗
Consistent documentation and source	✗
Regularly updated	✗
Minimal restriction on disclosure	✓

Clear Claims. As we noted in Sect. 1.2, the system lacks a thorough security model and claims. As such, we can consider the system to not follow this standard. We would encourage adopting standards with a similar degree of granularity as those used in Switzerland.[3]

Thorough Documentation. Within the repository, the documentation is very poor. There are no clear high level descriptions of the components contained in the repository. Inside each component's directory there is only a small description of what the directory is supposed to be inside some of the makefiles and README files. The auditor, key, processor, and voting directories seem to have a more detailed description compared to the other directories, but the additional information is about the usage of the directories and not much about the code themselves. The remaining documentation can be found in parts of the code that explain some of the functions and classes. To increase the available expertise for auditing the system it would be useful to increase the share of information that is available in English.

There are only three documents available in English: a high level overview of the system [Sta17], and the same two documents which can be generated using the source code. As such, we can consider the system to not follow this standard as the documentation is hard to find and doesn't properly describe the system as well as it could have.

Minimality. The system contains significant amounts of unused and redundant code; this unnecessary clutter hinders auditing. We are cautious about giving a specific quantitative metric for this criterion because the hindrance to

---

[3] https://www.bk.admin.ch/bk/en/home/politische-rechte/e-voting/versuchsbedingungen.html.

auditing of unused and redundant code is not independent of other issues; for example, if it was clear from the documentation what code was relevant, and what wasn't, the same level of redundant code would be less obstructive. Nevertheless, we can consider the system to not follow this standard.

Buildable. Within the repository, there are limited instructions regarding building the project. There is a main README and makefile that describes some instructions to gather the system's external dependencies, build, and test the system, but we didn't manage to pass the installation of external dependencies phase. The external packages are divided into the Java, Go, and Python dependencies. The installation instructions for these dependencies were either not working, missing key files, or unclear.

At the time of writing this paper, we have not received a response after providing the maintainers with the error messages on August 2022, so we cannot be certain if the dependencies were causing the issue. As such, we can consider the system to not follow this standard as we couldn't build the system using the provided instructions.

Executable. Since the system didn't follow the previous standard in that it couldn't be built, it is also considered to not follow this standard as the executable cannot be produced. The system does provide some documentation for running the executable files, but only for the auditor, key, and processing directories. As such, we can consider the system to not follow this standard.

Exportable. Since the system didn't manage to follow the previous standard in that it couldn't be executed, it is also considered to not follow this standard as no auditable output could be produced. The system does have some test files but we didn't manage to read through or use them as we were focused on finding the correct method of building the program. As such, we can consider the system to not follow this standard.

Consistent Documentation and Source. The system has several examples of having inconsistencies between the written documentation and the actual source files. For example, the dependencies installation instructions couldn't actually be followed because a file was missing from the repository. Another example would be the lack of clear instructions on how to run each component of the project. Most directories also lack a main overview file, and while some files that we read through had some explanation of its contents, some also lack any supporting comments on its functions. As such, we can consider the system to not follow this standard.

Regularly Updated. The system's update history can be seen through the commits page in the GitHub repository. It is very rarely updated, we can consider the system to not follow this standard.

Minimal Restrictions on Disclosure. We are not aware of any restrictions on disclosure that the system has regarding vulnerabilities. As such, we can consider the system to follow this standard.

Since the project only manages to fulfil one of the nine standards, minimal restrictions on disclosure, we foresee, inline with prior work, that the system likely has vulnerabilities. This conjecture is supported by the vulnerability discussed.

5   Conclusion

Our work highlights the significant deficiencies in the source code of the IVXV system which has been made available. These deficiencies increase the effort of examiners to audit the system and seem to have been fairly effective in preventing even simple vulnerabilities from being discovered. As an example of this, we point to the vulnerability in verifiability which should have been apparent even at the specification level. We make the following recommendations:

Revise system to allow better auditability. The system and documentation need to be reworked according to the points raised above to allow better auditability. We highlight in particular the need for clear security claims and system description. We also encourage the removal of unnecessary duplication of code from the system, particularly the numerous encoders and decoders of ballots in the different parts of the system.

Incentives examination. Further investigation is needed to determine what other unexposed issues exist in the system. We suggest encouraging such examination by introducing a bug bounty, or similar, with rewards based on the severity of vulnerabilities reported; this would be easy to define once the security requirements had been more clearly articulated. Alternatively, an approach similar to Switzerland's could be considered where auditors are asked to comment both on security of the code but also the specification.

References

[DPP22] Devillez, H., Pereira, O., Peters, T.: How to verifiably encrypt many bits for an election? In: Atluri, V., Di Pietro, R., Jensen, C.D., Meng, W. (eds.) ESORICS 2022. LNCS, vol. 13555, pp. 653–671. Springer, Cham (2022). https://doi.org/10.1007/978-3-031-17146-8_32

[GG20] Gaudry, P., Golovnev, A.: Breaking the encryption scheme of the Moscow internet voting system. In: Bonneau, J., Heninger, N. (eds.) FC 2020, Part II. LNCS, vol. 12059, pp. 32–49. Springer, Cham (2020). https://doi.org/10.1007/978-3-030-51280-4_3

[GMR85] Goldwasser, S., Micali, S., Rackoff, C.: The knowledge complexity of interactive proof-systems (extended abstract). In: STOC, pp. 291–304. ACM (1985)

[HLPT20] Haines, T., Lewis, S.J., Pereira, O., Teague, V.: How not to prove your election outcome. In: IEEE Symposium on Security and Privacy, pp. 644–660. IEEE (2020)

[HMVW16] Heiberg, S., Martens, T., Vinkel, P., Willemson, J.: Improving the verifiability of the Estonian internet voting scheme. In: Krimmer, R., et al. (eds.) E-Vote-ID 2016. LNCS, vol. 10141, pp. 92–107. Springer, Cham (2017). https://doi.org/10.1007/978-3-319-52240-1_6

[HR21] Haines, T., Roenne, P.: New standards for E-voting systems: reflections on source code examinations. In: Bernhard, M., et al. (eds.) FC 2021. LNCS, vol. 12676, pp. 279–289. Springer, Heidelberg (2021). https://doi.org/10.1007/978-3-662-63958-0_24

[HT15]   Halderman, J.A., Teague, V.: The New South Wales iVote system: security failures and verification flaws in a live online election. In: Haenni, R., Koenig, R.E., Wikström, D. (eds.) VOTELID 2015. LNCS, vol. 9269, pp. 35–53. Springer, Cham (2015). https://doi.org/10.1007/978-3-319-22270-7_3

[HW14]   Heiberg, S., Willemson, J.: Verifiable internet voting in Estonia. In: EVOTE, pp. 1–8. IEEE (2014)

[ivx]   IVXV GitHub repository. https://github.com/vvk-ehk/ivxv

[MM06]   Madise, Ü., Martens, T.: E-voting in Estonia 2005. The first practice of country-wide binding internet voting in the world. In: Electronic Voting. LNI, vol. P-86, pp. 15–26. GI (2006)

[oE]   State Electoral Office of Estonia. IVXV online voting system. https://github.com/vvk-ehk/ivxv

[Per21] Pereira, O.: Individual verifiability and revoting in the Estonian internet voting system. IACR Cryptol. ePrint Arch. 1098 (2021)

[PS00]   Pfitzmann, B.P., Sadeghi, A.-R.: Anonymous fingerprinting with direct non-repudiation. In: Okamoto, T. (ed.) ASIACRYPT 2000. LNCS, vol. 1976, pp. 401–414. Springer, Heidelberg (2000). https://doi.org/10.1007/3-540-44448-3_31

[Riv08] Rivest, R.L.: On the notion of 'software independence' in voting systems. Philos. Trans. Roy. Soc. A: Math. Phys. Eng. Sci. **366**(1881), 3759–3767 (2008)

[RRI16] Ryan, P.Y.A., Rønne, P.B., Iovino, V.: Selene: voting with transparent verifiability and coercion-mitigation. In: Clark, J., Meiklejohn, S., Ryan, P.Y.A., Wallach, D., Brenner, M., Rohloff, K. (eds.) FC 2016. LNCS, vol. 9604, pp. 176–192. Springer, Heidelberg (2016). https://doi.org/10.1007/978-3-662-53357-4_12

[SFD+14] Springall, D., et al.: Security analysis of the Estonian internet voting system. In: Proceedings of the 2014 ACM SIGSAC Conference on Computer and Communications Security, pp. 703–715. ACM (2014)

[SH20]   Specter, M., Halderman, J.: Security analysis of the democracy live online voting system (2020)

[SKW20] Specter, M.A., Koppel, J., Weitzner, D.J.: The ballot is busted before the blockchain: a security analysis of Voatz, the first internet voting application used in U.S. federal elections. In: USENIX Security Symposium, pp. 1535–1553. USENIX Association (2020)

[Sta17] State Electoral Office of Estonia. General framework of electronic voting and implementation thereof at national elections in Estonia (2017)

[Sta19] State Electoral Office of Estonia. IVXV-architecture. State Electoral Office of Estonia (2019)

[Sta20] State Electoral Office of Estonia. IVXV-protocol. State Electoral Office of Estonia (2020)

[Wik]   Wikipedia. The 2023 Estonian parliamentary election - Wikipedia. https://en.wikipedia.org/wiki/2023_Estonian_parliamentary_election. Accessed 1 Mar 2023

Coercion-Resistant Cast-as-Intended Verifiability for Computationally Limited Voters

Tamara Finogina[1,2] and Javier Herranz[1(✉)]

[1] Dept. Matemàtiques, Universitat Politècnica de Catalunya, Barcelona, Spain
javier.herranz@upc.edu
[2] Scytl Election Technologies, S.L.U., Barcelona, Spain
tamara.finogina@scytl.com

Abstract. In this work, we investigate if two essential properties in electronic voting, coercion-resistance and cast-as-intended verifiability, can be jointly achieved in settings where voters are (very) limited from a computational point of view. This may be the case in elections where voters use a voting station or webpage to cast their votes but do not have specialized software or devices to perform complicated cryptographic operations (for instance, to verify zero-knowledge proofs or to generate one-way trapdoors).

We provide a solution where the only things voters have to do are: remember and compare strings of numbers, on the one hand, and press a button at the appropriate moment, on the other hand. This button activates the participation of an online entity, which is trusted to choose a random nonce for each voter and to publish it only when that voter presses the button (and not before). The most expensive part of the verification is an OR proof of knowledge, which can be done by any (powerful enough) external verifier.

1 Introduction

Coercion resistance and cast-as-intended verifiability are two crucial but contradictory properties of electronic voting schemes. The former aims not to leak any information that can prevent voters from expressing their true intent or can facilitate vote-selling. The latter tries to ensure that a cheating voting device would not be able to modify a voter's choices undetectably. The contradiction is unavoidable: one property requires outputting as little feedback regarding the vote's content as possible, while the other demands proving that the voter's intention is encrypted correctly.

In this work, we focus on this contradiction and outline the definition of coercion-resistant cast-as-intended verification in the simplest (but maybe most realistic) case for electronic elections: a voter cannot perform any complex computations on its own, for instance, because it does not have any trusted computational device capable of doing sophisticated math.

A. Essex et al. (Eds.): FC 2023 Workshops, LNCS 13953, pp. 34–46, 2024.
https://doi.org/10.1007/978-3-031-48806-1_3

While, to our knowledge, there are no formal studies about voters' modeling or capabilities, we believe this simplest possible case is the most realistic assumption one can make about voters. It is true that, with less restrictive assumptions about voters' abilities, we perhaps can construct more elegant and secure systems. However, one may wonder - if the voter already has a trusted device or can do cryptographic operations in the head, why not use it for vote-casting directly?

As was mentioned, we consider only computationally limited voters who want to perform cast-as-intended verification while remaining safe from possible coercion threats. However, our task is not trivial: the lack of consensus regarding the coercer's abilities or voters' capabilities to withstand coercion already makes defining coercion resistance challenging. Furthermore, the matter gets more complicated by the differences in techniques for cast-as-intended verification.

1.1   On the Limitations of the Coercion and of Voters' Capabilities

Coercion is an intuitively-understandable threat. While it is clear that the goal of the coercer is to prevent free will expression, some specific details are still blurry:

- "Can a coerced prevent a voter from voting?"
- "Can an average voter extract randomness and similar secret details from the voting device (when it does not output them by default)?"
- "Are voters left without a coercer's observation during the voting?"
- "Is the coercer's goal to vote for a specific option or not?"

We can firmly agree that coercion-resistance makes sense only when the coercer has limited observational power [7], and the voter can disobey without facing high personal risks. Else, the voter has no choice but to comply [25]. Also, it was proven that resisting force-abstention attacks requires anonymous channels [13], which are incredibly hard to establish in practice. Also, we focus only on coercion that aims to change a voter's vote to a specific option or candidate. We do not deal with scenarios where the coercer wishes to delay the vote-casting process, discourage participation, or complicate voters' lives otherwise.

In this work, we assume that voters are computationally limited entities and cannot do cryptographic operations (one-way function computations, etc.). The only capability voters have is remembering and comparing strings they see - an assumption similar in spirit to [18,25]. For simplicity, we do not restrict the length of memorized data; however, we realize there is only so much information the voter can safely remember. Since we consider voters computationally limited, we exclude the possibility of force extraction of non-outputted information from an e-voting system. While it is true that, in some cases, the coercer might demand voters extract randomness used for encrypting their choice, we believe those instructions are hard to comply with for an average non-technically savvy voter.

Therefore, we consider the following scenario: a computationally limited (and potentially malicious) voter is coerced to vote for a specific option but left without supervision for (some part) of the vote-casting process. The coercer cannot:

prevent voters from voting, impersonate them, or demand data not provided by the voting protocol.

1.2 Related Work

The first proposal for cast-as-intended verification based on visual cryptography appears in Chaum's work [5], followed by an idea of simulatable zero-knowledge proofs in Neff's publication [18] the same year. In both proposals, the vote-casting happens in a polling place, and both cast-as-intended techniques require an additional trusted device (a specialized printer or randomness generator). A few years later, Benaloh [2] suggested another idea - the cast-or-challenge mechanism, which allows voters to verify multiple test ballots before finally casting the real one. It started as a pulling place testing technique based on printed commitment but quickly transformed into ballot casting assurance for remote voting [1]. Nowadays, there are many more ways to ensure a ciphertext contains the intended vote: OR proofs [10], return codes [14], tracking numbers [22], QR codes [24], etc.

The first mention of uncoercibility and receipt-freeness goes back to the election protocol designed by Benaloh and Tuinstra in 1994 [25]. A few years later, the first definition of what is now known as coercion-resistance was proposed [19]. The notion was called receipt-freeness; however, the coercer could interact with the voter during the voting phase, which implies adaptive corruption, in other words, coercion. The first widely accepted formal definition of coercion-resistance appeared only in 2010 [13]. This JCJ definition formalizes the idea of anonymous credentials and accounts for vote-selling and forced-abstention attacks. Unfortunately, achieving such a level of coercion-resistance in practice requires anonymous voting channels and effectively excludes any form of cast-as-intended verification. Interestingly, an almost unique scheme that satisfies this JCJ highly demanding notion of coercion-resistance scheme was found to leak too much information in case of re-voting, and so not to be truly coercion-resistant [6] - an attack first discovered as the "1009 attack" in [23]. Hence, the notion was enhanced by adding a cleansing-hiding procedure. The list of definitions of coercion-resistance is not limited to the JCJ derivations only. There exist many different approaches that focus on various coercion threats [4,7,9,13,16,17,25]. Unfortunately, they all struggle to capture the broadness of possible coercion strategies [11,15,21].

To our knowledge, not many articles try to combine coercion-resistance (not receipt-freeness) with any other property. We can mention: a study about relations between privacy, verifiability, accountability and coercion-resistance [20], a paper proposing to combine JCJ with Selene [12] and a discussion regarding cast-as-intended coercion resistance in settings without trusted delivery channels [8]. The solution in [12] inherits some of the (good and bad) properties of JCJ: it can resist force-abstention attacks, but the price to pay is that (i) the system must allow multiple voting, and (ii) coercers can vote on behalf of voters (which means that some part of the voting scheme is not properly authenticated).

Furthermore, all the papers mentioned in the last paragraph consider settings where the voters have the capability to run expensive/complicated (cryptographic) operations on their own. Regarding voting schemes for computationally limited (also known as human) voters, the setting we consider in this work, we can mention Neff's proposal [18], a scheme by Moran-Naor [17], Bingo voting [3] and other references therein. Authors of Bingo voting show in [3] that many of the other protocols in this setting can suffer from a specific coercion attack that they call "Babble attack". This fact leads to the idea that an external (and trusted) entity may be necessary to choose random elements on behalf of voters; this approach is taken by the Bingo voting protocol and also by the solution that we propose in this paper. We will discuss the similarities and differences between our solution and Bingo voting in Sect. 4.2.

1.3 Contributions and Organization of the Paper

In this work, we discuss voters' and coercer's limitations and propose definitions that, as we believe, capture both coercion-resistance and cast-as-intended properties without requiring voters to do complex operations (Sect. 2). The definitions are done using the standard cryptographic language for provable security (experiments, games, challengers, adversaries); furthermore, even if their goal in this paper is to analyze the security of a protocol for computationally limited voters, the definitions are written in a so general way that they could be used to analyze the cast-as-intended and coercion-resistance properties of other voting protocols.

Section 3 contains our solution of coercion-resistant cast-as-intended verification for a computationally limited voter and the proofs that it fulfills the two above-mentioned definitions. Last, we give in Sect. 4 a discussion on some practical aspects of our solution, a comparison between our solution and Bingo voting [3] and an intuitive argument on why a trusted device seems necessary in order to achieve both coercion-resistance and cast-as-intended verification in this setting of limited voters.

2 Definitions

We focus on a specific computationally limited voter $\mathcal{V}$ who wishes to cast a vote for the intent m through a voting device $\mathcal{VD}$, possibly under the coercion of an adversary $\mathcal{A}$ that prefers another option $m^\star \neq m$. Let Cpb denote the class of operations the voter $\mathcal{V}$ is supposed to be capable of doing. In the restricted setting we consider in this paper, this class contains: generating, memorizing, and comparing strings of numbers.

In such a setting, it makes perfect sense to consider the possibility that $\mathcal{V}$ gets the help of another entity or device, that we call official election device (OED for short), to execute some of the steps of the protocol. It is trusted to run the prescribed steps of the protocol correctly, and its actions are free from coercion.

We assume that the public election parameters pms include candidates, questions, election rules, mathematical descriptions of the group, a security parameter λ, hash functions, the public key pk of the encryption scheme Enc for encrypting the votes, etc. To generate pms one would run an initial protocol pms $\leftarrow$ Setup(λ).

The voting protocol itself is an interactive protocol between the voter $\mathcal{V}$ and the voting device $\mathcal{VD}$. We denote as Trc = (C, Trc$_{pub}$, Trc$_{priv}$) the result of the said interaction, where the ciphertext C encrypts (in principle) the voting option m chosen by $\mathcal{V}$ and the public trace Trc$_{pub}$ contains other messages that will be made public in the bulletin board (proofs, signatures, voter ID, etc.), along with C. The rest of voter's (private) view of the interaction with $\mathcal{VD}$ is denoted as Trc$_{priv}$.

We denote an execution of the voting protocol as:

$$\text{Trc} = (\text{C}, \text{Trc}_{pub}, \text{Trc}_{priv}) \leftarrow \text{Vote}^{\langle \mathcal{V}^{OED}, \mathcal{VD} \rangle}(\text{pms}, m, \text{Cpb}, \text{coerc})$$

Here coerc refers to a possible set of instructions forced to the voter $\mathcal{V}$ by a coercer; in case of no coercion, this variable is set to $\emptyset$. All instructions the coercer gives should be within the voter's capabilities; in other words, the actions are restricted to the class Cpb.

In our setting, where the voter has limited computational capabilities, it is clear that some part of the verification (which involves ciphertexts and thus expensive cryptographic operations) must be done by an external verifier. But of course, another part of the verification is done by the own voter $\mathcal{V}$.

The first (public) verification is done by anyone (with enough computational capabilities) by running a protocol

$$\text{ValidProof}(\text{pms}, \text{C}, \text{Trc}_{pub}) \rightarrow \{0, 1\}$$

The second (private) verification is done by $\mathcal{V}$ by running the protocol below, whose operations must belong to class Cpb:

$$\text{ValidOption}(\text{pms}, \text{C}, \text{Trc}, m, \text{Cpb}) \rightarrow \{0, 1\}$$

2.1 Cast-as-Intended Verifiability

Intuitively, this property must capture the impossibility that a dishonest voting device $\mathcal{VD}$ succeeds in cheating the voter $\mathcal{V}$ by completing an accepted execution of the protocol Vote but in which the resulting ciphertext (published in the bulletin board) encrypts something which is not the voting option chosen by $\mathcal{V}$.

The corresponding event Cheat is defined as follows:

$$\text{Cheat} = \begin{cases} \text{pms} \leftarrow \text{Setup}(\lambda) \\ \text{Vote}^{\langle \mathcal{V}^{OED}, \mathcal{VD} \rangle}(\text{pms}, m, \text{Cpb}, \emptyset) \rightarrow (\text{C}, \text{Trc}_{pub}, \text{Trc}_{priv}) \\ \text{ValidProof}(\text{pms}, \text{C}, \text{Trc}_{pub}) \rightarrow 1 // \text{ public validity} \\ \text{ValidOption}(\text{pms}, \text{C}, \text{Trc}, m, \text{Cpb}) \rightarrow 1 // \text{ private validity} \\ m \neq \text{Dec}(\text{C}, \text{sk}) // \text{ but C does not contain the intent} \end{cases}$$

Definition 1. *The protocol* Vote *enjoys Cast-as-Intended (CAI) verifiability if the probability of event* Cheat *is a negligible function of the security parameter* λ, *for any polynomial-time voting device* $\mathcal{VD}$.

2.2   Coercion-Resistance

In our setting, a coercer $\mathcal{A}$ (e.g., a vote buyer) may interact with the voter $\mathcal{V}$ before the vote-casting and force him to vote for some option m^* and to follow the instructions (belonging to the class Cpb) in coerc while executing Vote. The strategy coerc must be such that it does not affect the steps run by entity OED (which is assumed to be incoercible) and such that it leads to accepted executions of the protocol Vote. That is, we do not consider some very strong types of coercion: (1) the coercer forces a voter not to participate in the election, (2) the coercer forces a voter to misbehave during the interaction with $\mathcal{VD}$, which results in $\mathcal{VD}$ aborting the protocol and not sending any ciphertext to the ballot box.

During the execution of Vote, the adversary cannot see the interaction between $\mathcal{V}$ and $\mathcal{VD}$ (otherwise, since the voting option is sent by $\mathcal{V}$ to $\mathcal{VD}$ in clear, it would be impossible to achieve any meaningful coercion-resistance property). However, the adversary has access to the ballot box and can see the published values: the ciphertext C and the remaining public data $\mathsf{Trc}_{\mathsf{pub}}$. After the voting, $\mathcal{A}$ expects to receive from $\mathcal{V}$ the rest of the voter's view, $\mathsf{Trc}_{\mathsf{priv}}$, of the interaction.

To prevent coercion, the voter $\mathcal{V}$ must always be able to deceive the coercer. In other words, it should be able to run the protocol Vote with its voting option m and later simulate the view that would make $\mathcal{A}$ believe that Vote was run with m^* as input. All this must be done with the limited capabilities (in class Cpb) of the voter. We say the protocol Vote has coercion-resistance whenever the coercer $\mathcal{A}$ cannot distinguish between a result of voting for the coercer's preference and a simulated transcript hiding the disobedience with probability more than $1/2$. The formalization of this property is given in the following definition.

Definition 2. *The protocol* Vote *enjoys coercion-resistance (CR) if for any polynomial-time coercer* $\mathcal{A}$ *which chooses instructions* coerc $\in$ Cpb *that do not affect the steps run by* OED, *there exists a simulator* Sim $\in$ Cpb *such that, in the experiment described below,* $\left|\Pr[b' = b] - \frac{1}{2}\right|$ *is a negligible function of the security parameter* λ:

1. *pms* $\leftarrow$ Setup(λ).
2. $b \leftarrow \{0,1\}$ *is chosen uniformly at random.*
3. $\mathcal{A}(pms) \rightarrow (coerc, m^*, m)$.
4. $\mathsf{Trc}^{(0)} = \left(C^*, \mathsf{Trc}^*_{\mathsf{pub}}, \mathsf{Trc}^*_{\mathsf{priv}}\right) \leftarrow \mathsf{Vote}^{\langle\mathcal{V}^{OED},\mathcal{VD}\rangle}(pms, m^*, \mathsf{Cpb}, coerc)$
   // *obey the coercer and vote for* m^*
   If ValidProof$(pms, C^*, \mathsf{Trc}^*_{\mathsf{pub}}) \rightarrow 0$, *abort* // *happens only if instructions* coerc *invalidate the ballot*

5. $Trc = (C, Trc_{pub}, Trc_{priv}) \leftarrow Vote^{\langle \mathcal{V}^{OED}, \mathcal{VD} \rangle}(pms, m, Cpb, \emptyset)$ // disobey the coercer and vote for m

6. $Trc_{priv}^{Sim} \leftarrow Sim(Trc, m^\star, Cpb)$ // fake the voter's view

   Set $Trc^{(1)} = (C, Trc_{pub}, Trc_{priv}^{Sim})$

7. $b' \leftarrow \mathcal{A}(pms, Trc^{(b)}, Cpb)$.

3   A Construction for Limited Voters

In this section, we explore possibilities for providing coercion-resistant cast-as-intended verification to voters with (very) limited capabilities, namely those who can only generate, remember and compare strings of numbers.

We propose and analyze a simple protocol where the voter needs the help of an external device OED for string generation. The OED is expected to participate in the protocol honestly and only when the voter indicates (and not a moment before).

The idea of our solution is as follows: the voter $\mathcal{V}$ chooses one of the ℓ possible voting options $m_j \in \{m_1, m_2, \ldots, m_\ell\}$ and sends it to the voting device $\mathcal{VD}$, which encrypts the selected option into a ciphertext C. Along with C, the voting device $\mathcal{VD}$ will generate a non-interactive OR zero-knowledge proof of knowledge of the randomness r such that C is the encryption of *some* valid voting option in $\{m_1, m_2, \ldots, m_\ell\}$.

To prevent a dishonest voting device from cheating the voter by encrypting a different voting option $m^* \neq m_j$, the zero-knowledge proof must be computed in stages: first, the voting device will show the voter some values (to be memorized), then the voter will press the button generating "Nonce", and only then the voting device will be able to finish the computation of the zero-knowledge proof, by using the corresponding nonce (selected by an official election device) as an input of the hash function.

Once the final proof is published, anybody (with enough computational resources) can verify the validity of the OR proof and ensure that a ciphertext contains a valid selection. However, only the voter can ensure that the proof is consistent with the memorized values, which implies that the ciphertext encrypts the desired choice.

The simplicity of the construction allows us to analyze its coercion-resistance and cast-as-intended properties according to our definitions. The intuition says that privacy only requires that the voting device does not leak the intent to the adversary - as all client-side encryption voting schemes. Similarly, coercion-resistance holds because voters' secret is something they saw rather than any secret key or value. Cast-as-intended property is ensured due to the soundness of OR proof and randomness of the "Nonce" provided by OED.

3.1   The Protocol (for ElGamal Ciphertexts)

Let us detail the protocol that we obtain if we use the ElGamal public key encryption scheme: public election parameters of the election system must contain elements q, G, g such that $G = \langle g \rangle = \langle h \rangle$ has prime order q and two collision-resistant hash functions $H : \{0,1\}^* \to \mathbb{Z}_q$ and $\hat{H} : \{0,1\}^* \to \mathcal{X}$, where $\mathcal{X}$ is the space of strings the voter can type and memorize. The public key of the election is $y \in \langle g \rangle$. The set $\mathcal{X}$ is a set with enough entropy to avoid brute force attacks.

1. $\mathcal{V}$ chooses a voting option m_j from the set $\{m_1, m_2, \ldots, m_\ell\}$ and sends the selected index $j \in \{1, 2, \ldots, \ell\}$ to $\mathcal{VD}$.
2. $\mathcal{VD}$ encrypts m_j using ElGamal encryption protocol:
   $\mathsf{C} = (c_1, c_2) = (g^r, m_j \cdot y^r)$, for some random and uniform $r \in \mathbb{Z}_q$.
   Now $\mathcal{VD}$ starts the computation of the OR proof as follows:
   (a) choose $t_j \in \mathbb{Z}_q$ uniformly at random;
   (b) compute commitments $A_j = g^{t_j}$, $B_j = y^{t_j}$;
   (c) for each $i \in \{1, 2, \ldots, \ell\}$, $i \neq j$:
       i. choose values $z_j, e_j \in \mathbb{Z}_q$ uniformly at random;
       ii. compute $A_i = g^{z_i} \cdot (c_1)^{-e_i}$ and $B_i = y^{z_i} \cdot \left(\frac{c_2}{m_i}\right)^{-e_i}$.
   $\mathcal{VD}$ sends to $\mathcal{V}$ the value $X_j = \hat{H}(\mathsf{C}, \{(A_s, B_s)\}_{1 \leq s \leq \ell}, \{e_i\}_{1 \leq i \leq \ell, i \neq j})$, to be memorized by $\mathcal{V}$.
3. At this point, $\mathcal{V}$ presses the "Nonce" button, which makes the official election device OED choose a random nonce $\mathsf{nc}_\mathcal{V} \in \mathcal{X}$ and publish $(\mathcal{V}, \mathsf{nc}_\mathcal{V})$ in the official public board of the election. If the publication of $(\mathcal{V}, \mathsf{nc}_\mathcal{V})$ is done in any other moment (for instance, by a coerced voter, before Step 2), the voting device $\mathcal{VD}$ aborts the execution.
4. Now $\mathcal{VD}$ can finish the OR proof:
   (a) computes $e = H(\mathsf{C}, \{(A_k, B_k)\}_{1 \leq k \leq \ell}, \mathsf{nc}_\mathcal{V})$;
   (b) sets $e_j = e - \sum_{1 \leq i \leq \ell, i \neq j} e_i \mod q$;
   (c) finalizes the proof $z_j = t_j + e_j \cdot r \mod q$.
   Finally $\mathcal{VD}$ makes public the ciphertext C, the OR zero-knowledge proof $\pi = (\mathcal{V}, \mathsf{nc}_\mathcal{V}, \{(A_k, B_k, e_k, z_k)\}_{1 \leq k \leq \ell})$ and the list of couples $\{(m_k, \hat{X}_k)\}_{k \in \{1,2,\ldots,\ell\}}$, where $\hat{X}_k = \hat{H}(\mathsf{C}, \{(A_s, B_s)\}_{1 \leq s \leq \ell}, \{e_i\}_{1 \leq i \leq \ell, i \neq k})$.

Following the notation of Sect. 2, in our protocol we have:

$$\mathsf{Trc_{pub}} = (\pi, \{(m_k, \hat{X}_k)\}_{k \in \{1,2,\ldots,\ell\}})$$

$$\mathsf{Trc_{priv}} = (m_j, \{(m_i, X_i)\}_{i \in \{1,2,\ldots,\ell\}, i \neq j})$$

Private and Public Verifications. The voter $\mathcal{V}$ will accept the interaction if $\hat{X}_j = X_j$, for its chosen option m_j.

For the public verification, anybody with enough computational resources can first check that the initial couple $(\mathcal{V}, \mathsf{nc}_\mathcal{V})$ in π exists in the official public board of the election, and then ensure that all checks hold:

(i) $H(\mathsf{C}, \{(A_k, B_k)\}_{1 \leq k \leq \ell}, \mathsf{nc}_\mathcal{V}) = \sum_{1 \leq k \leq \ell} e_k \mod q$,
(ii) for each $k \in \{1, 2, \ldots, \ell\}$, $g^{z_k} = A_k \cdot (c_1)^{e_k}$,

(iii) for each $k \in \{1, 2, \ldots, \ell\}$, $y^{z_k} = B_k \cdot \left(\frac{c_2}{m_k}\right)^{e_k}$,

(iv) for each $k \in \{1, 2, \ldots, \ell\}$, $\hat{X}_k = \hat{H}(\mathsf{C}, \{(A_s, B_s)\}_{1 \leq s \leq \ell}, \{e_i\}_{1 \leq i \leq \ell, i \neq k})$

We discuss how the outputs of these verification protocols affect the election in case of a dishonest behaviour of the voting device $\mathcal{VD}$ in Sect. 4.1.

3.2   Cast-as-Intended Verifiability of the Proposed Protocol

We prove that the protocol described in the previous section achieves cast-as-intended verifiability by using the rewinds. We assume a (dishonest) voting device $\mathcal{VD}$ can break cast-as-intended verifiability. In other words, it makes the event Cheat happen with a non-negligible probability. Then, we run Vote protocol without changes until step 3, where we make a fork and send two different nonces $\mathsf{nc}_\mathcal{V} \neq \mathsf{nc}'_\mathcal{V}$ to $\mathcal{VD}$. Since we assumed that event Cheat happens with a non-negligible probability, $\mathcal{VD}$ should be able to finish the two executions successfully and produce accepted proofs π and π'.

In the two executions, since the first two steps are identical and the hash function $\hat{H}$ is collision-resistant, we have that many values in π and π' are equal: m_j, $\mathsf{C} = (c_1, c_2)$, $\{(A_s, B_s)\}_{1 \leq s \leq \ell}$, $\{e_i\}_{i \in \{1,2,\ldots,\ell\}, i \neq j}$.

But since the two nonces are different, we have with overwhelming probability $e_j \neq e'_j$ as:

$$e = H(\mathsf{C}, \{(A_k, B_k)\}_{1 \leq k \leq \ell}, \mathsf{nc}_\mathcal{V}) \neq H(\mathsf{C}, \{(A_k, B_k)\}_{1 \leq k \leq \ell}, \mathsf{nc}'_\mathcal{V}) = e'$$

Now dividing the two satisfied equations $g^{z_j} = A_j \cdot (c_1)^{e_j}$ and $g^{z'_j} = A_j \cdot (c_1)^{e'_j}$ we get $c_1 = g^{\frac{z_j - z'_j}{e_j - e'_j}}$ on the one hand.

On the other hand, dividing the two satisfied equations $y^{z_j} = B_j \cdot \left(\frac{c_2}{m_j}\right)^{e_j}$ and $y^{z'_j} = B_j \cdot \left(\frac{c_2}{m_j}\right)^{e'_j}$ we get $c_2 = m_j \cdot y^{\frac{z_j - z'_j}{e_j - e'_j}}$.

Therefore, we have $\mathsf{C} = (c_1, c_2) = (g^{r_j}, m_j \cdot y^{r_j})$ for $r_j = \frac{z_j - z'_j}{e_j - e'_j} \mod q$, which means C is an encryption of the voting option m_j. This contradicts the fact that event Cheat was happening.

3.3   Coercion-Resistance of the Proposed Protocol

Coercion resistance is easier to argue. The voter's role in the protocol is limited - only choosing the intended voting option and pressing the "Nonce" button. Hence, the coercer $\mathcal{A}$ cannot enforce an elaborate voting strategy. The only possible instruction $\mathcal{A}$ can force voters to follow would be to vote for some option $m^\star$.

Theoretically, a coercer can force the voter to press the button at the wrong moment or not press it at all, but this would lead to a non-successful execution of the protocol, which our coercion-resistance definition does not take into account.

Similarly, our notion of coercion-resistance does not cover coercion strategies that require the voter to repeat vote-casting multiple times until some arbitrary condition regarding the output is satisfied (e.g., the ciphertext starts with 42).

Assume the coercer's goal is to make the voter vote for some option $m^\star = m_w$, for some $w \in \{1, 2, \ldots, \ell\}$, likely different to the voting option $m = m_j$ that the voter wants to choose. But in this case, all that the voter (or strictly speaking, the simulator Sim) has to do to deceive the coercer $\mathcal{A}$ is to say it received value $\hat{X}_w$ (instead of $\hat{X}_j$) from $\mathcal{VD}$ in Step 2. In terminology of Definition 2, the simulated private trace $\mathsf{Trc}^{\mathsf{Sim}}_{\mathsf{priv}}$ can be obtained from $\mathsf{Trc}_{\mathsf{priv}}$ by replacing $m = m_j$ with $m^\star = m_w$ and by replacing $\hat{X}_j$ with $\hat{X}_w$. Note that all required information is available to Sim, which has the whole trace Trc and $m^\star = m_w$ as inputs. Moreover, such replacing operations performed by Sim clearly belong to the considered class Cpb, as required.

4   Discussion and Conclusions

4.1   Practical Considerations

We assume that the final output of the protocol, computed by the voting device $\mathcal{VD}$, is published immediately in the official public board of the election, which can be checked by the voter in order to run its individual verification. If this verification fails, the voter should complain and cancel the execution of the voting phase; otherwise, the voter should press a button to confirm the vote. With respect to public verification, some users/devices selected by the election will run it: only those ciphertexts corresponding to executions of the voting phase where the voter has confirmed and where public verification is valid will be moved to the ballot box for the tally phase.

In case a voter cancels the execution, the election should specify if the voter can start the voting phase again, with the same (or another) voting device.

4.2   Comparison with Bingo Voting: On the Necessity of OED

As we have commented in the introduction, our protocol is similar in spirit to Bingo voting [3]: both schemes consider computationally limited voters, and both solutions use a trusted external entity to generate a (pseudo-)random nonce. We think our solution improves Bingo voting in two aspects. First, the pre-voting phase in the Bingo scheme is quite expensive as it requires choseing and committing to many dummy values. In our protocol, there is no pre-voting phase, only the publication of the public parameters of the election. Second, in the Bingo voting, a pseudo-random nonce must be sent to the voter and the voting device $\mathcal{VD}$ through a secure channel because the privacy of the voting phase would be lost if this value was leaked during that execution. In our solution, the random nonce $\mathsf{nc}_\mathcal{V} \in \mathcal{X}$ can be (and is) made public by the official election device OED right at the moment of its generation. Therefore, our solution does not need a secure channel between the external trusted entity and the voters.

At this point, one may wonder if the help of an external trusted entity (the official election device OED in our protocol) is necessary. All in all, its only task is to generate and publish a random nonce $nc_\mathcal{V} \in \mathcal{X}$, something that even our limited voter $\mathcal{V}$ could do on its own: if we assume $\mathcal{V}$ can memorize and compare some strings of numbers, then for sure it would be able to generate a random string of numbers, as well.

But if we modify our protocol in such a way that OED disappears and Step 3 is run by the voter $\mathcal{V}$, the result is a protocol that is not coercion-resistant: a coercer who wants $\mathcal{V}$ to vote for an option $m^\star = m_w$ can ask the voter $\mathcal{V}$ to use as the nonce $\widehat{nc}_\mathcal{V}$ a value which is computed deterministically from the value $X_w = \hat{H}(\mathsf{C}, \{(A_s, B_s)\}_{1 \le s \le \ell}, \{e_i\}_{1 \le i \le \ell, i \ne w})$. For instance, to use as $\widehat{nc}_\mathcal{V}$ the first digits of X_w. The voter $\mathcal{V}$ cannot vote for another option $j \ne w$, because in such a case, $\mathcal{V}$ would get to know the value of $\hat{X}_w$ (needed to, compute $\widehat{nc}_\mathcal{V}$) only in Step 4 of the protocol, whereas the value of the nonce must be sent by $\mathcal{V}$ in Step 3.

We actually have the intuition (not formally proved) that the participation of an external entity is necessary to achieve both coercion-resistance and cast-as-intended verification in the considered setting with limited voters. The intuitive argument is as follows. At some step of the interaction, say J, between voter $\mathcal{V}$ and voting device $\mathcal{VD}$, voter has to communicate its chosen voting option m_j to $\mathcal{VD}$.

On the one hand, if the voter does not send any random values to $\mathcal{VD}$, or if all the random elements are sent to $\mathcal{VD}$ before the step J, then a malicious $\mathcal{VD}$ can break the cast-as-intended verification property, by running the fist steps $\le J$ for another voting option $m_i \ne m_j$ and then permuting the roles of indices i and j in the rest of steps of the protocol.

On the other hand, if the voter sends some random value rnd to $\mathcal{VD}$ after the voting device $\mathcal{VD}$ has computed and sent to $\mathcal{V}$ some information $info_j$ which depends on the voting option m_j, a coercer can force the voter to use as rnd a function f of $info_j$ (for instance, the first bits of it). If such coercion can be avoided by simulating execution of the voting phase for another option, but following this pattern rnd $= f(info_j)$, it seems (and this is the part that we have not been able to prove formally) that such a simulator breaks the cast-as-intended property.

This intuitive argument supports the claims made by the authors of Bingo voting: "... which strongly suggest that the voter should not be trusted to contribute her own randomness. This gives an additional motivation for the use of trusted random number generator". A formal and complete proof of the impossibility of achieving coercion-resistance and cast-as-intended verification in the limited voters setting remains an interesting open problem.

Acknowledgements. This work is partially supported by the Spanish *Ministerio de Ciencia e Innovación (MICINN)*, under Project PID2019-109379RB-I00, and by *Generalitat de Catalunya*, under Project 2018 DI 038.

References

1. Adida, B.: Helios: web-based open-audit voting. In: Proceedings of the 17th USENIX Security Symposium, pp. 335–348 (2008)
2. Benaloh, J.: Ballot casting assurance via voter-initiated poll station auditing. In: Proceedings of the USENIX Workshop on Accurate Electronic Voting Technology, EVT'07, p. 14, USA, 2007. USENIX Association (2007)
3. Bohli, J.-M., Müller-Quade, J., Röhrich, S.: Bingo voting: secure and coercion-free voting using a trusted random number generator. In: Alkassar, A., Volkamer, M. (eds.) Vote-ID 2007. LNCS, vol. 4896, pp. 111–124. Springer, Heidelberg (2007). https://doi.org/10.1007/978-3-540-77493-8_10
4. Canetti, R., Gennaro, R.: Incoercible multiparty computation. In: 37th Annual Symposium on Foundations of Computer Science, FOCS '96, Burlington, Vermont, USA, 14–16 October 1996, pp. 504–513. IEEE Computer Society, November 1996
5. Chaum, D.: Secret-ballot receipts: true voter-verifiable elections. IEEE Secur. Priv. Mag. **2**, 38–47 (2004)
6. Cortier, V., Gaudry, P., Yang, Q.: Is the JCJ voting system really coercion-resistant? Working paper or preprint, April 2022
7. Delaune, S., Kremer, S., Ryan, M.: Coercion-resistance and receipt-freeness in electronic voting. In: 19th IEEE Computer Security Foundations Workshop (CSFW'06), pp. 12–42 (2006)
8. Finogina, T., Herranz, J., Larraia, E.: How (not) to achieve both coercion resistance and cast as intended verifiability in remote evoting. In: Conti, M., Stevens, M., Krenn, S. (eds.) CANS 2021. LNCS, vol. 13099, pp. 483–491. Springer, Cham (2021). https://doi.org/10.1007/978-3-030-92548-2_25
9. Gardner, R.W., Garera, S., Rubin, A.D.: Coercion resistant end-to-end voting. In: Dingledine, R., Golle, P. (eds.) FC 2009. LNCS, vol. 5628, pp. 344–361. Springer, Heidelberg (2009). https://doi.org/10.1007/978-3-642-03549-4_21
10. Guasch, S., Morillo, P.: How to challenge *and* cast your e-Vote. In: Grossklags, J., Preneel, B. (eds.) FC 2016. LNCS, vol. 9603, pp. 130–145. Springer, Heidelberg (2017). https://doi.org/10.1007/978-3-662-54970-4_8
11. Haines, T., Smyth, B.: Surveying definitions of coercion resistance. Cryptology ePrint Archive, Report 2019/822 (2019). https://ia.cr/2019/822
12. Iovino, V., Rial, A., Rønne, P.B., Ryan, P.Y.A.: Using Selene to verify your vote in JCJ. In: Brenner, M., et al. (eds.) FC 2017. LNCS, vol. 10323, pp. 385–403. Springer, Cham (2017). https://doi.org/10.1007/978-3-319-70278-0_24
13. Juels, A., Catalano, D., Jakobsson, M.: Coercion-resistant electronic elections. In: Towards Trustworthy Elections, New Directions in Electronic Voting, pp. 37–63 (2010)
14. Khazaei, S., Wikström, D.: Return code schemes for electronic voting systems. In: Krimmer, R., Volkamer, M., Braun Binder, N., Kersting, N., Pereira, O., Schürmann, C. (eds.) E-Vote-ID 2017. LNCS, vol. 10615, pp. 198–209. Springer, Cham (2017). https://doi.org/10.1007/978-3-319-68687-5_12
15. Krips, K., Willemson, J.: On practical aspects of coercion-resistant remote voting systems. In: Krimmer, R., et al. (eds.) E-Vote-ID 2019. LNCS, vol. 11759, pp. 216–232. Springer, Cham (2019). https://doi.org/10.1007/978-3-030-30625-0_14
16. Küsters, R., Truderung, T., Vogt, A.: A game-based definition of coercion-resistance and its applications. In: 2010 23rd IEEE Computer Security Foundations Symposium, pp. 122–136 (2010)

17. Moran, T., Naor, M.: Receipt-free universally-verifiable voting with everlasting privacy. In: Dwork, C. (ed.) CRYPTO 2006. LNCS, vol. 4117, pp. 373–392. Springer, Heidelberg (2006). https://doi.org/10.1007/11818175_22

18. Neff, C.A.: Practical high certainty intent verification for encrypted votes (2004)

19. Okamoto, T.: Receipt-free electronic voting schemes for large scale elections. In: Christianson, B., Crispo, B., Lomas, M., Roe, M. (eds.) Security Protocols 1997. LNCS, vol. 1361, pp. 25–35. Springer, Heidelberg (1998). https://doi.org/10.1007/BFb0028157

20. Pankova, A., Willemson, J.: Relations between privacy, verifiability, accountability and coercion-resistance in voting protocols. Cryptology ePrint Archive, Report 2021/1501 (2021). https://ia.cr/2021/1501

21. Riou, S.; Kulyk, O.; Marcos del Blanco, D.Y.: A formal approach to coercion resistance and its application to e-voting. Mathematics **10**, 781 (2022). https://doi.org/10.3390/math10050781

22. Ryan, P.Y.A., Rønne, P.B., Iovino, V.: Selene: voting with transparent verifiability and coercion-mitigation. In: Clark, J., Meiklejohn, S., Ryan, P.Y.A., Wallach, D., Brenner, M., Rohloff, K. (eds.) FC 2016. LNCS, vol. 9604, pp. 176–192. Springer, Heidelberg (2016). https://doi.org/10.1007/978-3-662-53357-4_12

23. Smith, W.D.: New cryptographic election protocol with best-known theoretical properties. In: Workshop on Frontiers in Electronic Election (2005). https://users.encs.concordia.ca/~clark/biblio/coercion/Smith/202005-1.pdf

24. Trechsel, A.H., Vassil, K.: Internet voting in Estonia: a comparative analysis of four elections since 2005: report for the council of Europe (2010)

25. Benaloh, J., Tuinstra, D.: Receipt-free secret-ballot elections. In: STOC '94 Proceedings of the Twenty-sixth Annual ACM Symposium on Theory of Computing, pp. 544–553. Association for Computing Machinery Inc., May 1994

Private Internet Voting on Untrusted Voting Devices

Rolf Haenni[✉], Reto E. Koenig, and Philipp Locher

BFH, Bern University of Applied Sciences, Biel, Switzerland
{rolf.haenni,reto.koenig,philipp.locher}@bfh.ch

Abstract. This paper introduces a new cryptographic Internet voting protocol, which offers individual verifiability and vote privacy even on completely untrustworthy voting devices. The core idea is to minimize the voting client to a simple device capable of scanning a QR code, sending its content to the web server of the included URL, and displaying a response message to the voter. Today, QR code scanners are pre-installed into mobile devices, and users are familiar to using them for many different purposes. By reducing the voting client to an existing functionality of the voters' personal device, the implementation of the protocol is simplified significantly compared to other protocols. The protocol itself can be seen as a variant of Chaum's code voting scheme with an elegant solution to the problem of distributing the trust to multiple authorities. The approach is based on BLS signatures and verifiable mix-nets. It relies on trustworthy printing and mailing services during the election setup.

1 Introduction

A major challenge in Internet voting is the untrusted voting client. Current protocol proposals and implementations, for example the ones used in Switzerland, provide a mechanism for achieving cast-as-intended and recorded-as-cast verifiability simultaneously by returning verification codes to the voter for each submitted vote. Since the malicious voting client cannot predict these codes, manipulation attempts can be detected by the voter with high probability. However, vote privacy remains an unsolved problem on the client, because from performing the encryption of the submitted votes, the malicious voting client learns both the selected voting options and the encryption randomization. The latter serves as a receipt to prove the selected voting options to a third party. With respect to vote privacy, such systems are therefore only secure under the strong assumption of a fully trustworthy voting client.

In this paper, we introduce a fundamentally different Internet voting protocol, which offers vote privacy even in the presence of a completely untrustworthy voting client. The difference comes from minimizing the role assigned to the voting client as far as possible, in such a way that it not even learns the selected voting options. We only require the voting client of being capable of scanning a QR code, sending its content to the web server of the included URL, and displaying a response message to the voter. Since this is a pre-installed functionality

© International Financial Cryptography Association 2024
A. Essex et al. (Eds.): FC 2023 Workshops, LNCS 13953, pp. 47–62, 2024.
https://doi.org/10.1007/978-3-031-48806-1_4

of today's mobile devices, and because users are familiar to scanning QR code from different applications, we can almost entirely eliminate the complexity of designing and implementing a reliable voting web client.

Our proposal is motivated by the current situation in Switzerland, where legislation is very strict with respect to E2E-verifiability, but quite lax with respect to the privacy problem on the voting client. We interpret this unbalanced regulation as an unwanted compromise in the absence of a better solution. Our paper aims at providing a compelling solution for solving this conflict. Another motivation for our protocol is the usability study in [6], which showed that voters are able to use code voting with QR codes in an E2E-verifiable system. The paper ended with an invitation to the community for presenting corresponding cryptographic protocols. This paper is a first response to the this invitation.

1.1 Election Model and Voting Procedure

If we take the Swiss context as a reference point for designing the protocol, we cannot assume that voters possess any type of electronic credentials, which they could possibly use for authentication when submitting the ballot. On the other hand, we can assume that reliable printing and postal services are available for sending such credentials to the voters prior to an election, possibly together with other voting materials. We can also assume that with multiple simultaneous m_i-out-of-n_i elections, all possible election uses cases can be covered adequately (see discussion in [4, Section 2.2]). For reason of simplicity, we restrict ourselves in this paper to a single m-out-of-n election, but our protocol is flexible enough to support the general case with just a few additional steps.

From the voter's perspective, the election procedure starts with receiving a letter from the electoral office over postal mail. In an m-out-of-n election, this letter includes n different *voting cards*, one for each voting option, and a single *confirmation card*. Note that the optimal design of these cards is still an open question [6], but for security reasons, it is important that not all elements printed on these cards are visible at the same time. In the example shown in Fig. 1, we consider the case of a referendum (1-out-of-2 election) with two voting cards and one confirmation card. The QR codes are printed on the back of these cards to avoid making them visible together with the verification and participation codes.

Given these cards, the voting procedure is now relatively simple and efficient. It only assumes that the voter is capable of scanning QR codes and sending the scanned data to the included URL, for example using a mobile phone with a working Internet connection. Then the voting procedure consists of five steps:

1. Select m voting cards (or less to submit blank votes).
2. Scan the *voting QR codes* on the back of each selected voting card.
3. Compare the displayed codes with the *verification codes* shown on the voting cards (below the selected voting options).
4. If all codes match, scan the *confirmation QR code* on the back of the confirmation card.

Fig. 1. Example of voting and participation cards for a referendum with two voting options "YES" and "NO". The front sides of the cards are shown on top and the back sides at the bottom. The sizes of the QR codes are realistic.

5. Compare the displayed code with the *participation code* shown on the confirmation card.

For the verification codes to match in Step 3, the votes must have been cast as intended with high probability, and for the participation code to match in Step 5, the vote must have been confirmed as intended with high probability. This mechanism for achieving cast-as-intended and recorded-as-cast verifiability is exactly the same as in current approaches used in Switzerland [4,8], but in our new protocol, the voting client learns nothing about the selected voting options. Note that the general idea and the voting procedure in our approach are very similar to Chaum's *code voting* [3,7], but our new protocol requires much weaker trust assumptions for generating the codes and performing the tally.

In case the verification codes do not match in Step 3 of the above procedure, voters in Switzerland are instructed to submit the ballot on paper using the existing traditional voting channels. We adopt this convention here to handle such exceptional cases properly, i.e., without creating new security problems. In case the participation code does not match in Step 5, vote confirmation can be repeated—possibly on different devices—until the code matches. If the problem persists, voters are instructed to report the problem to the electoral office.

In the referendum example of Fig. 1, the voter simply selects one of the two voting cards with ID $i = 1823$, let's say the second one for voting option "NO", scans the QR code on the back of the card using a mobile device, checks if the verification code displayed on the device is "917B", scans the QR code on the back of the confirmation card, and finally checks if the participation code displayed on the device is "1785-9383-6912". Note that this procedure can be completed very quickly, for a single referendum possibly within a few seconds.

1.2 Contribution and Overview

This paper presents a new cryptographic voting protocol, which primarily aims at achieving vote privacy on untrustworthy voting clients. It has similarities to existing approaches [5,10], but it is quite unique in its elegant way of combining recent but well-established cryptographic primitives (BLS signatures, verifiable mix-nets, zero-knowledge proofs) with modern but wide-spread and accepted technologies (scanning of QR codes on mobile phones). Given this unique combination, we can achieve an additional important security goal simultaneously with improving the usability for the voters. Because security and usability are usually in conflict with each other, this is quite remarkable.

By limiting the responsibility of the voting client in the protocol, we also reduce the set of attack vectors and the overall complexity of the whole system. In an actual implementation, for example, since there is no need for implementing cryptography in JavaScript, developers can optimize their efforts into a single reliable back-end technology. At the same time, attacks based on injecting malicious JavaScript code become less likely and less powerful.

In Sect. 2, we start with an overview of the cryptographic primitives used in our protocol. The protocol itself is described in Sect. 3, which is the main section of this paper. The protocol description defines the involved protocol parties, the communication channels, the adversary model, and the three main protocol phases. In Sect. 4, we discuss the security properties of the proposed protocol, and Sect. 5 concludes the paper.

2 Cryptographic Background

Our protocol is based on various cryptographic primitives, which are commonly used in e-voting protocols. We briefly introduce them in the following subsections, but we refer to the literature for more details. Our protocol also relies on BLS signatures, which have not been used in e-voting very often, but which have become an established tool in other areas such as crypto-currencies. We briefly introduce BLS signatures in Sect. 2.2.

2.1 ElGamal Encryptions

The protocol as presented in this paper depends on a homomorphic asymmetric encryption scheme such as ElGamal. The choice of ElGamal is not mandatory, but we propose using it for its simplicity and maximal convenience. ElGamal is IND-CPA secure in a group, in which the DDH problem is hard. We propose the usual prime-order subgroup $\mathbb{G}_q \subset \mathbb{Z}_p^*$ of quadratic residues modulo a safe prime $p = 2q + 1$ and assume that $\mathbb{G}_q$ and a generator $g \in \mathbb{G}_q \backslash \{1\}$ are publicly known.

In this setting, we denote the generation of an ElGamal key pair consisting of a randomly selected private decryption key $dk \in \mathbb{Z}_q$ and a public encryption key $ek = g^{dk}$ by $(dk, ek) \xleftarrow{\$} \mathsf{KeyGenEnc}()$. For a given encryption key $ek \in \mathbb{G}_q$ and message $m \in \mathbb{G}_q$, we use $e \leftarrow \mathsf{Enc}_{ek}(m, r)$ to denote the encryption of m

with randomization $r \xleftarrow{\$} \mathbb{Z}_q$. The result is a ciphertext pair $e = (g^r, m \cdot ek^r) \in \mathbb{G}_q \times \mathbb{G}_q$ consisting of two group elements. For the decryption $m \leftarrow \mathsf{Dec}_{dk}(e)$ of a ciphertext $e = (a, b)$, the decryption key dk can be used to compute $m = b/a^{dk}$.

ElGamal keys can be generated in a distributed setting, in which the private decryption key of a common encryption key is shared among multiple parties. In the simplest construction of $ek = \prod_{k=1}^{s} ek_k$, all s holders of a private key share dk_k need to cooperate to perform the decryption. We use $a'_k \leftarrow \mathsf{pDec}_{dk_k}(e)$ to denote the partial decryption of a ciphertext $e = (a, b)$. The resulting values $a'_k = a^{dk_k}$ can then be used to retrieve the plaintext $m = b/\prod_{k=1}^{s} a'_k$. More involved constructions exist to enable a threshold number $t \leq s$ of key share holders to perform the decryption. This is an optional extension for our protocol.

In applications of ElGamal in e-voting, where up to m voting options can be selected from n available voting options, it is possible to encode a set of selections $S \subset [1, n], |S| \leq m$, into an ElGamal message by selecting n small prime numbers $p_1, \ldots, p_n$ from $\mathbb{G}_q \cap \mathbb{P}$ and by computing the product $\Gamma(S) = \prod_{s \in S} p_s$ over all selections. Under the condition that $\Gamma(S) < p$, such a product can be decoded into S using integer factorization. Therefore, to guarantee the uniqueness of the decoding, the maximal size of the parameters m and n is limited by p. In most practical election use cases, however, this limitation is not a real problem.

2.2 BLS Signatures

BLS signatures are defined over three groups G_1, G_2, and G_T of a bilinear map $e : G_1 \times G_2 \rightarrow G_T$. If we use the popular pairing-friendly elliptic curves from the Barreto-Lynn-Scott family, for example, we achieve approximately 128 bits of security for BLS12-381 and 256 bits of security for BLS48-581 (both curves are included in a current IETF draft [11]). In the particular case of BLS12-381, $G_1 \subset E_1[\mathbb{F}_p]$ is a prime-order subgroup of the elliptic curve $E_1 : y^2 = x^3 + 4$ over the prime-order field $\mathbb{F}_p$ for $\|p\| = 381$, $G_2 \subset E_2[\mathbb{F}_{p^2}]$ is a subgroup of the curve $E_2 : y^2 = x^3 + 4(1 + i)$ over $\mathbb{F}_{p^2}$, and $G_T \subset \mathbb{F}_{p^{12}}$ is a subgroup of the integers modulo p^{12}. The common group order $q = |G_1| = |G_2| = |G_T|$ is 256 bits long, which corresponds to 128 bits of security. Note that BLS12-381 also defines generators $g_1 \in G_1$ and $g_2 \in G_2$ for both groups.

In the BLS signature scheme, we use $(sk, vk) \xleftarrow{\$} \mathsf{KeyGenSig}()$ to denote the generation of a key pair. The private signature key $sk \in \mathbb{Z}_q$ is picked at random and the public verification key $vk = g_2^{sk}$ is computed in the group G_2.[1] For a collision-resistant hash function $\mathsf{hash} : \{0,1\}^* \rightarrow G_1$, the BLS signature of a message $m \in \{0,1\}^*$ is a single deterministic group element $\sigma = \mathsf{hash}(m)^{sk} \in G_1$. We use $\sigma \leftarrow \mathsf{Sign}_{sk}(m)$ to denote this operation. Note that such signatures are points $\sigma = (x, y) \in \mathbb{F}_p \times \mathbb{F}_p$ on the curve $E_1[\mathbb{F}_p]$, which can be represented using $\|p\| + 1$ bits ($\|p\|$ bits for x and 1 bit for the sign of $\pm y$). For BLS12-381, the signature size is therefore 382 bits (48 bytes). A BLS signature $\sigma \in G_1$ is valid if $e(\sigma, g_2) = e(\mathsf{hash}(m), vk)$, i.e., for performing the verification $\mathsf{Verify}_{vk}(\sigma, m) \in \{0, 1\}$, the pairing function needs to be computed twice.

---

[1] In our protocol, we minimize the size of the signatures by using G_1 for the signatures and G_2 for the public keys, but the roles of the groups are interchangeable.

A useful property of the BLS signature scheme is the aggregation of signatures $\sigma_k \leftarrow \mathsf{Sign}_{sk_k}(m)$ generated under multiple private keys into a single signature $\sigma = \prod_{k=1}^{s} \sigma_k$. The aggregated signature can then be verified using the combined verification key $vk = \prod_{k=1}^{s} vk_k$ of all s key holders. As in the case of ElGamal, there are more involved methods to allow the signature to be generated by a threshold number of key holders, but we will not need this in our protocol.

2.3 Non-interactive Zero-Knowledge Proofs

We use different non-interactive zero-knowledge proofs to ensure that the involved election authorities follow the protocol faithfully. First, to avoid the possibility of so-called *rogue key attacks* [9], they need to prove knowledge of the generated private ElGamal and BLS keys dk and sk, respectively. We will denote the generation of such a proof as

$$\pi^{\mathsf{key}} \xleftarrow{\$} \mathsf{NIZKP}[(dk, sk) : ek = g^{dk} \wedge vk = g_2^{sk}],$$

and the verification as $\mathsf{Verify}(\pi^{\mathsf{key}}, ek, vk) \in \{0, 1\}$. Note that π^{key} is a conjunctive composition of two non-interactive Schnorr proofs. Second, authorities need to prove the correctness of the partial decryptions $a_i' = a_i^{dk}$ for a given list $\mathbf{e} = (e_1, \ldots, e_N)$ of ElGamal ciphertexts $e_i = (a_i, b_i)$. We denote this proof as

$$\pi^{\mathsf{dec}} \xleftarrow{\$} \mathsf{NIZKP}[(dk) : ek = g^{dk} \wedge \left(\bigwedge_{i=1}^{N} a_i' = a_i^{dk} \right)],$$

which is a conjunctive composition of $N + 1$ non-interactive Schnorr proofs. For $\mathbf{a} = (a_1, \ldots, a_N)$ and $\mathbf{a}' = (a_1', \ldots, a_N')$, the proof verification is denoted by $\mathsf{Verify}(\pi^{\mathsf{dec}}, ek, \mathbf{a}, \mathbf{a}') \in \{0, 1\}$. For the details of corresponding proof generation and verification algorithms, we refer to the literature [4, Section 5.4].

2.4 Verifiable Mix-Nets

Other important cryptographic tools in our protocol are verifiable re-encryption mix-nets. The idea is to apply a series of cryptographic shuffles to an input list $\mathbf{e} = (e_1, \ldots, e_N)$ of ElGamal ciphertexts. In each shuffle, a random permutation is applied to the list, and every ciphertext of the permuted list is re-encrypted using a fresh randomization. If Ψ_N denotes the set of all permutations of size N, then $\psi \xleftarrow{\$} \Psi$ denotes picking a permutation uniformly at random, and $j = \psi(i)$ denotes the application of $\psi : [1, N] \rightarrow [1, N]$ to an input index i. The re-encryption $(\tilde{a}, \tilde{b}) \leftarrow \mathsf{ReEnc}_{ek}(e, r)$ of an ElGamal ciphertext $e = (a, b)$ is a new ciphertext $(\tilde{a}, \tilde{b}) = (a, b) \cdot \mathsf{Enc}_{ek}(1, r) = (a \cdot g^r, b \cdot ek^r)$ for a fresh randomization $r \xleftarrow{\$} \mathbb{Z}_q$.

By putting everything together, cryptographic shuffling can be defined by $\tilde{\mathbf{e}} \leftarrow \mathsf{Shuffle}_{ek}(\mathbf{e}, \psi, \mathbf{r})$, where $\tilde{\mathbf{e}} = (\tilde{e}_1, \ldots, \tilde{e}_N)$ denotes the shuffled list of re-encrypted ciphertexts $\tilde{e}_i = \mathsf{ReEnc}_{ek}(e_j, r_j)$ for $j = \psi(i)$. To prove the correctness of the shuffle, authorities need to provide a non-interactive *shuffle proof*,

$$\pi^{\mathsf{shuffle}} \xleftarrow{\$} \mathsf{NIZKP}[(\psi, \mathbf{r}) : \tilde{\mathbf{e}} = \mathsf{Shuffle}_{ek}(\mathbf{e}, \psi, \mathbf{r})],$$

which can be verified by $\text{Verify}(\pi^{\text{shuffle}}, ek, \mathbf{e}, \tilde{\mathbf{e}}) \in \{0,1\}$. We require such shuffle proofs twice in our protocol. In one of the two cases, we will need to ensure that the permutation used in the shuffle corresponds to an existing *permutation commitment* $c \leftarrow \text{Commit}(\psi, r)$. In existing constructions [2,13], such commitments are part of the proof generation and included in π^{shuffle}. Therefore, by assuming that the same algorithm generates the permutation commitment and the shuffle proof simultaneously, we can use a slightly abusive notation,

$$(\pi^{\text{shuffle}}, c, r) \xleftarrow{\$} \text{NIZKP}[(\psi, \mathbf{r}) : \tilde{\mathbf{e}} = \text{Shuffle}_{ek}(\mathbf{e}, \psi, \mathbf{r})],$$

for the proof generation and include c as an additional argument for the proof verification. For further details on theses proofs, we refer again to the literature or to the pseudocode algorithms given in [4, Sections 5.5 and 8.4].

3   Protocol Description

Our new Internet voting protocol consists of three consecutive phases called *pre-election*, *election*, and *post-election*. To specify the technical details of the protocol, we provide separate subsections for each of them. As a preparatory step at the beginning of this section, we define the set of election parameters, the protocol parties and communication channels, and the protocol's general idea.

3.1   Election Parameters

In the discussion of the election model in Sect. 1.1, we already decided to restrict our approach to single m-out-of-n elections, where n denotes the number of *candidates* (or *voting options*) and $m < n$ the maximal number of candidates to choose. For each election, we assign a *unique election identifier* U and an *election description ED*. Furthermore, we assign a unique *candidate description* CD_j to each candidate, and for an electorate of size N, we assign a unique *voter description* VD_i to each voter i. If $\mathbf{c} = (CD_1, \ldots, CD_n)$ and $\mathbf{v} = (VD_1, \ldots, VD_N)$ denote the vectors of all candidate and voter descriptions, respectively, then

$$EP = (U, ED, m, n, N, \mathbf{c}, \mathbf{v})$$

denotes the complete set of election parameters (note that $n = |\mathbf{c}|$ and $N = |\mathbf{v}|$ are redundant, but we prefer to list them explicitly). Without loss of generality, we assume that U, ED, CD_j, and VD_i are strings from a given alphabet. We also assume that these strings contain sufficient information for their specific purposes (for example, VD_i may contain the voter's name and address to enable the production of address labels by the printing service). In Fig. 1, for example, we have $U = $ "CH23-03", $ED = $ "Do you accept the tax law?", $m = 1$, $n = 2$, $CD_1 = $ "YES", $CD_2 = $ "NO", and $i = 1823$ (N and $\mathbf{v}$ are unspecified).

3.2 Protocol Parties and Communication

We distinguish five different types of protocol parties. In an implementation of the protocol, the *administrator*, the *election authorities*, and the *printing service* form the system's core infrastructure, which can be used in the same constellation for multiple elections. The *voters* are members of the electorate of a given election and the *voting clients* are the personal devices used by the voters for casting the vote. The following list describes the roles of the five party types.

Administrator. To run an election, the administrator specifies the election parameters EP, launches the three protocol phases, and finally assembles and announces the election result. The administrator does not generate or possess any cryptographic secrets other than a private signature key.

Election Authorities. In the pre-election phase, the election authorities generate a common encryption key, a common signature key, and the contents of the voting and confirmation cards in a distributed manner. During the election, they respond to submitted ballots and confirmations, and in the post-election phase, they shuffle and decrypt the list of encrypted votes. To ensure the correctness of the election and the privacy of the votes, it is assumed that at least one election authority is honest. They all possess a private signature key.

Printing Service. The printing service is responsible for printing the voting and confirmation cards and sending them to the voters. For this, it receives shares of the values to be printed from the election authorities. The printing service is trusted to assemble these shares in a deterministic manner, print them on paper, and protect the confidentiality of the received data. Otherwise, the printing service does not generate or possess any cryptographic secrets.

Voters. The voters are the main actors in the protocol. Using the voting and confirmation cards obtained from the printing service over postal mail, honest voters submit their votes according to the procedure described in Sect. 1.1. Dishonest voters may deviate from the protocol, but not if this affects the validity of the submitted vote. This implies that they keep the voting and confirmation cards secret, even in the presence of a vote buyer or coercer.

Voting Clients. The functionality of the voting clients is restricted to scanning and submitting the QR codes to the election authorities and displaying their responses to the voters. Since they are potentially dishonest, they do not generate or possess any cryptographic secrets.

To authenticate the communication channels between the infrastructure parties, we assume that the administrator and the election authorities use their private signature keys to sign all outgoing messages, and that all infrastructure parties accept incoming messages only if they contain a valid signature. Furthermore, we assume that the channels from the election authorities to the printing service and from the printing service to the voters are confidential.

Note that we do not explicitly impose the existence a public bulletin board. As we will see, every election authority in our protocol keeps a full record of all the public election data. By considering the union of their records as input for the verification, it is sufficient to have at least one honest authority for reaching a consensus about the relevant election data. This approach is consistent with the current practice and legislation in Switzerland.

3.3   General Protocol Idea

From a cryptographic point of view, the main protocol idea is to prepare for each voter a list of ciphertexts for all n possible voting options. For this, the election authorities apply a verifiable mix-net to an initial list of trivial ElGamal ciphertexts $e_j = \mathsf{Enc}_{ek}(\Gamma(j), 0) = (1, \Gamma(j))$ for all candidates $j \in [1, n]$. This leads to a matrix $\tilde{\mathbf{E}} = (\tilde{e}_{ij})_{N \times n}$ of encrypted votes, in which each row i contains encryptions of all candidates in permuted order ψ_i. The correctness of this matrix can be publicly verified by checking the shuffle proofs from the mix-net.

To submit a vote for candidate $s \in [1, n]$, the voter with voting card index i needs to know the right column index $j = \psi_i(s)$ in row i of the matrix $\tilde{\mathbf{E}}$ and submit it to the election authorities. In other words, by submitting a ballot $b = (U, i, j)$ to the authorities, the voter expresses the intention to vote in election U for candidate $s = \psi_i^{-1}(j)$. The authorities can then pick the encrypted vote $\tilde{e}_{ij}$ from $\tilde{\mathbf{E}}$ and add it to the ballot box. While this is the basic idea of the protocol, it is clear that additional security measures need to be taken.

To prevent ballot stuffing, the election authorities generate BLS signatures $\sigma_{ij} = \mathsf{Sign}_{sk}(U, i, j)$ in a distributed manner for all pairs $(i, j) \in [1, N] \times [1, n]$. To cast a valid vote, voters must then submit an extended ballot $b = (U, i, j, \sigma_{ij})$, which includes a valid signature σ_{ij} for (U, i, j). This is exactly the information that needs to be included in the QR code assigned to the voting option s. If we assume that the two voting options have been swapped in the mix-net of the example given in Fig. 1, then the QR code assigned to the second voting option NO $(s = 2)$ could be an encoding of the URL string

```
https://www.qrvote.ch?U=CH23-03&i=1823&j=1&sigma=7BM8qdOuO8gwVKpjmZ9
      hf1uO+KSotcq4DWeFgcXgn2vloWJbYLHUcl+wpUaZJgoR,
```

which directs the browser to the specified web server and submits the ballot $b =$ ("CH22-12", 1823, 1, σ) included in the query string to the election authorities. In this particular example, σ is a Base64-encoded BLS signature of length $64 * 6 = 384$ bits (48 bytes), which corresponds to an element of G_1 in BLS12-381. If σ is a valid signature, the authorities respond with a share of the corresponding verification code. The aggregation of these shares is displayed to the voter.

In an election with $m > 1$ possible selections, the authorities accept such incoming ballots until the size of the voter's ballot box reaches m. To confirm the vote, the voter submits a similar tuple $c = (U, i, \sigma_i)$, where $\sigma_i = \mathsf{Sign}_{sk}(U, i)$ is an aggregated BLS signature of (U, i), which represents the voter's intention to confirm the vote in election U. Again, if c contains a valid signature, the authorities respond with a share of the corresponding participation code, and an aggregation of these shares is displayed to the voter.

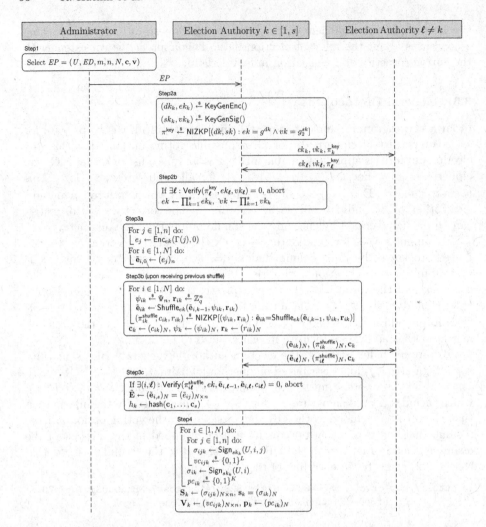

Fig. 2. First part of the pre-election phase: Election setup (Step1), key generation (Step2), ciphertext preparation (Step3), signature and code generation (Step4).

3.4 Pre-election Phase

The pre-election phase begins with an initial message EP from the administrator to the election authorities. Upon receiving this message, the election authorities generate a common ElGamal encryption key ek and a common BLS signature key vk by exchanging corresponding key shares. In Fig. 2, the key shares are generated in Step2a and the key aggregation takes place in Step2b.

In the next step of the pre-election phase, the election authorities generate the ciphertext matrix $\tilde{\mathbf{E}}$, in which each row contains ciphertexts for all candidates in permuted order. In Fig. 2, the initialization of this list is shown in Step3a, the shuffling in Step3b, and the assembling of the matrix $\tilde{\mathbf{E}}$ in Step3c. As a side-

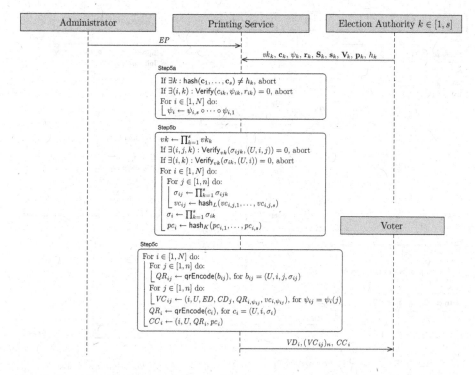

Fig. 3. Second part of the pre-election phase: Permutation composition (Step5a), signature and code aggregation (Step5b), voting card preparation (Step5c).

product of this procedure, each election authorities receives a list of permutation commitments $\mathbf{c}_\ell$ from all other authorities $\ell \neq k$. The hash $h_k = (\mathbf{c}_1, \ldots, \mathbf{c}_s)$ of these commitments is used to demonstrate to the printing service that a consensus have been reached among the election authorities about the outcome of the mixing. Another side-product are the commitment randomizations $\mathbf{r}_k$, which are given to the printing service for opening the commitments.

In Step4 of the pre-election phase, the election authorities prepare the shares σ_{ijk} of the BLS signatures for the ballots $b_{ij} = (U, i, j, \sigma_{ij})$ and the shares vc_{ijk} of corresponding verification codes vc_{ij}. Similarly, they prepare the shares σ_{ik} of the BLS signatures for the confirmations $c_i = (U, i, \sigma_i)$ and the shares pc_{ik} of corresponding participation codes pc_i. These codes are random bit strings of length L and K, respectively (in the example from Fig. 1, we have $L = 16$ and $K = 40$). Finally, the share vk_k of the verification key, the commitments $\mathbf{c}_k$, the random permutation ψ_k, the randomizations $\mathbf{r}_k$, the shares $\mathbf{S}_k$ and $\mathbf{s}_k$ of the BLS signatures, the shares $\mathbf{V}_k$ and $\mathbf{p}_k$ of the verifications and confirmation codes, and the hash value h_k of the commitments are sent to the printer.

The above messages launch the printing process. In Step5a of Fig. 3, the printing service first checks the consistency and validity of the permutation commitments and then combines the permutations into $\psi_i = \psi_{i,s} \circ \cdots \circ \psi_{i,1}$ for every $i \in [1, N]$. Similarly, in Step5b, the printing serving checks the validity of the

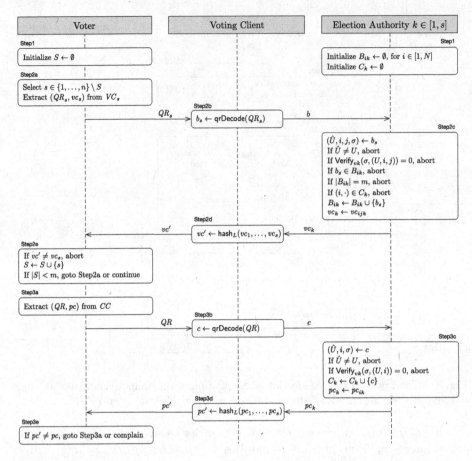

Fig. 4. Overview of the election phase: Initialization (Step1), vote casting (Step2), vote confirmation (Step3).

received signatures and then computes their aggregations σ_{ij} and σ_i. The same happens for the verification codes vc_{ij} and participation codes pc_i. From these values, the printing service assembles the voting cards VC_{ij} and confirmation cards CC_i, such that everything from Fig. 1 is included at the right place. The cards are printed and sent to the voters over a confidential channel.

3.5   Election Phase

The election phase is shown in Fig. 4. It consists of three consecutive steps. In Step1, the election authorities initialize their ballot boxes B_{ik} (one for each voter) and their confirmation box C_k. A voter, who has selected voting option $s \in [1, n]$ and is ready to vote, uses the personal device to scan QR_s on the voting card, decode QR_s into b_s, and send the ballot to the election authorities (Step2a–2b). If the ballot is valid and fresh, and if the size of the ballot box is less than m and the vote has not been confirmed yet, it is accepted into the ballot box and the

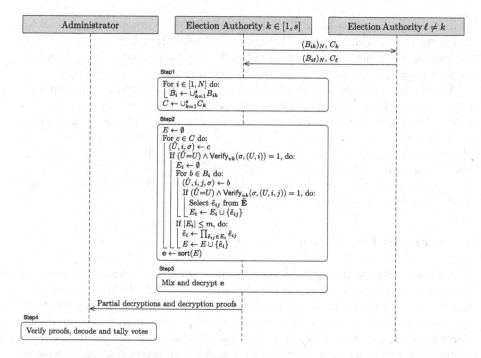

Fig. 5. Overview of the post-election phase: ballot and confirmation box synchronization (Step1), extraction of valid ciphertexts (Step2), mixing and decryption (Step3), decoding and tallying (Step4).

share of the verification code is returned (Step2c). The voting client assembles the shares and displays the code to the voter (Step2d). The voter checks the verification code and then decides to submit further ballots or confirm (Step2e).

The procedure for the vote confirmation is almost identical, i.e., the voter uses the personal device to scan QR, decode it into c, and send the confirmation to the election authorities (Step3a–3b). They check its validity and return their share of the participation code (Step3c). The voting client assembles the shares and displays the code to the voter (Step3d). Finally, the voter terminates the vote casting procedure by checking the participation code (Step3e). Note that the confirmation can be repeated multiple times, possibly on different devices.

3.6 Post-election Phase

At the end of the voting period, the election authorities first need to synchronize their ballot and confirmation boxes. This step might not be necessary in a normal protocol run, but there is no general guarantee that all submitted ballots and confirmations have reached all authorities. In Fig. 5, the synchronization takes place in Step1. To ensure that the resulting sets B_i and C only contain valid and confirmed votes, it is necessary to verify the included BLS signatures and to check that the total number of ballots does not exceed m. If this is the case for the ballots of a given voter, we use the homomorphic property of ElGamal to merge the included ciphertexts. Therefore, the resulting set E of encrypted votes contains at most one entry for each voter. To obtain an unambiguous mix-net input from Step2 of Fig. 5, we consider the list $\mathbf{e}$ obtained from sorting E.

For the two remaining steps of the post-election phase, space constraints in Fig. 5 do not allow us to give further details. In Step3, the list $\mathbf{e}$ of encrypted votes is mixed in a procedure similar to Step3 from Fig. 2, and the resulting shuffled list $\tilde{\mathbf{e}}$ is decrypted in a distributed manner as explained in Sect. 2.1. In Step4, the administrator assembles the plaintext votes from the partial decryptions and obtains the election result from applying Γ^{-1} to the plaintext votes. The correctness of the obtained election result is guaranteed by corresponding non-interactive zero-knowledge proofs π_k^{dec} and π_k^{shuffle}.

4 Security Discussion

We consider the usual active polynomial-time adversary, who might want to break vote privacy or manipulate the election result. The adversary may therefore try to corrupt as many protocol parties as needed, but we assume that the printing service and at least one election authority remain honest under all circumstances, i.e., they follow the protocol faithfully and do no disclose any of their secrets to another party. In this model, our protocol tries to achieve *covert security* [1,12], which means that corrupt parties are only cheating as long as the cheating remains undetectable and therefore has no consequences. Within this model, we also assume that voters keep their voting and confirmation cards secret from vote buyers and coercers, possibly because they fear legal consequences (see Sect. 3.2).

Below, we will briefly discuss the security properties of our protocol in the covert adversary model by giving some informal arguments relative to vote privacy and vote integrity. Verifiability arguments are the same as in other protocols based on verification codes.

Vote Privacy: Let the adversary know the assignment of the voting card indices i to the voters. A first possibility for breaking vote privacy would be to learn the combined permutation ψ_i or randomization $\mathbf{r}_i$ from the pre-election mix-net, but both ψ_i and $\mathbf{r}_i$ are only known to the trusted printing service and to the trusted group of election authorities (of which at least one is assumed trustworthy). The second possibility would be to learn the permutation ψ or randomization $\mathbf{r}$ of the post-election mix-net, and the third possibility would be to learn the aggregated private decryption key dk. In both cases, the necessary secrets are only known to the trusted group of election authorities.

Vote Integrity: For a confirmed ballot b_{ij} to appear in the final tally, both b_{ij} and c_i it must contain a valid BLS signature. Thus, a first possibility for ballot stuffing would be to generate extra signatures, but this requires the aggregated private signing key sk, which is known only to the trusted group of election authorities (of which at least one is assumed trustworthy). The second possibility would be to use the unused ballots from abstaining voters, but these ballots are only known to the trusted printing authority and to the abstaining voters themselves, who are trusted for keeping corresponding voting cards secret. For a submitted and confirmed ballot b_{ij} to drop out from the final tally, there are three possibilities: first, by preventing either b_{ij} or c_i from reaching the election authorities (but this would be detected by the voter performing the cast-as-intended and recorded-as-cast verification), second, by removing b_{ij} or c_i from the ballot boxes of all election authorities (which contradicts the assumption that at least one election authority is honest), and third, by adding additional ballots to the ballot box of at least one election authority, such that the total number of ballots exceeds m (this case can be excluded for the same reasons as ballot stuffing).

5 Conclusion

The new Internet voting protocol proposed in this paper can be seen as a modern version of Chaum's code voting scheme, in which usability concerns have been solved using the QR code scanning functionality of mobile devices and trust assumptions have been distributed to a group of election authorities, of which only one needs to be honest to prevent or detect privacy and integrity attacks. In this way, we achieve security in the covert adversary model, which is often sufficient. From the voter's perspective, the vote casting procedure in referendums or elections with a small number of candidates is intuitive, efficient, and secure. Whether this statement still holds for more complex elections is an open question. Another open issue is the current lack of a formal security proof.

References

1. Aumann, Y., Lindell, Y.: Security against covert adversaries: efficient protocols for realistic adversaries. J. Cryptol. **23**(2), 281–343 (2010)
2. Bayer, S., Groth, J.: Efficient zero-knowledge argument for correctness of a shuffle. In: Pointcheval, D., Johansson, T. (eds.) EUROCRYPT 2012. LNCS, vol. 7237, pp. 263–280. Springer, Heidelberg (2012). https://doi.org/10.1007/978-3-642-29011-4_17
3. Chaum, D.: SureVote: technical overview. In: WOTE 2001, 1st Workshop On Trustworthy Elections. Tomales Bay, USA (2001)
4. Haenni, R., Koenig, R.E., Locher, P., Dubuis, E.: CHVote protocol specification - version 3.4. IACR Cryptology ePrint Archive 2017/325 (2022)
5. Joaquim, R., Ribeiro, C., Ferreira, P.: VeryVote: a voter verifiable code voting system. In: 2nd International Conference on E-Voting and Identity, VoteID 2009, Luxembourg, pp. 106–121 (2009)
6. Kulyk, O., Ludwig, J., Volkamer, M., Koenig, R.E., Locher, P.: Usable verifiable secrecy-preserving e-voting. In: 6th International Joint Conference on Electronic Voting, E-Vote-ID 2021, Bregenz, Austria, pp. 337–353 (2021)
7. Oppliger, R.: How to address the secure platform problem for remote internet voting. In: 5th Conference on "Sicherheit in Informationssystemen", SIS 2002, Austria, Vienna, pp. 153–173 (2002)

8. Renold, H., Esseiva, O., Hofer, T.: Swiss Post Voting System - System specification - Version 1.2.0. Technical report, Swiss Post Ltd., Bern, Switzerland (2022)

9. Ristenpart, T., Yilek, S.: The power of proofs-of-possession: securing multiparty signatures against rogue-key attacks. In: Naor, M. (ed.) EUROCRYPT 2007. LNCS, vol. 4515, pp. 228–245. Springer, Heidelberg (2007). https://doi.org/10.1007/978-3-540-72540-4_13

10. Ryan, P.Y.A., Teague, V.: Pretty good democracy. In: 17th International Workshop on Security Protocols, SPW 2009, Cambridge, UK, pp. 111–130 (2009)

11. Sakemi, Y., Kobayashi, T., Saito, T., Wahby, R.S.: Pairing-friendly curves. Internet-draft, Internet Engineering Task Force (IETF) (2022)

12. Scholl, P., Simkin, M., Siniscalchi, L.: Multiparty computation with covert security and public verifiability. IACR Cryptology ePrint Archive 2021/366 (2021)

13. Terelius, B., Wikström, D.: Proofs of restricted shuffles. In: Bernstein, D.J., Lange, T. (eds.) AFRICACRYPT 2010. LNCS, vol. 6055, pp. 100–113. Springer, Heidelberg (2010). https://doi.org/10.1007/978-3-642-12678-9_7

Overstatement-Net-Equivalent Risk-Limiting Audit: ONEAudit

Philip B. Stark$^{(\boxtimes)}$ (ORCID)

University of California, Berkeley, CA, USA
stark@stat.berkeley.edu

Abstract. A procedure is a risk-limiting audit (RLA) with risk limit α if it has probability at least $1 - \alpha$ of correcting each wrong reported outcome and never alters correct outcomes. One efficient RLA method, card-level comparison (CLCA), compares human interpretation of individual ballot cards randomly selected from a trustworthy paper trail to the voting system's interpretation of the same cards (cast vote records, CVRs). CLCAs heretofore required a CVR for each cast card and a "link" identifying which CVR is for which card—which many voting systems cannot provide. This paper shows that every set of CVRs that produces the same aggregate results overstates contest margins by the same amount: they are *overstatement-net-equivalent* (ONE). CLCA can therefore use CVRs from the voting system for any number of cards and ONE CVRs created *ad lib* for the rest. In particular:

- Ballot-polling RLA is algebraically equivalent to CLCA using ONE CVRs derived from the overall contest results.
- CLCA can be based on batch-level results (e.g., precinct subtotals) by constructing ONE CVRs for each batch. In contrast to batch-level comparison auditing (BLCA), this avoids manually tabulating entire batches and works even when reporting batches do not correspond to physically identifiable batches of cards, when BLCA is impractical.
- If the voting system can export linked CVRs for only some ballot cards, auditors can still use CLCA by constructing ONE CVRs for the rest of the cards from contest results or batch subtotals.

This works for every social choice function for which there is a known RLA method, including IRV. Sample sizes for BPA and CLCA using ONE CVRs based on contest totals are comparable. With ONE CVRs from batch subtotals, sample sizes are smaller than for BPA when batches are homogeneous, approaching those of CLCA using CVRs from the voting system, and much smaller than for BLCA: A CLCA of the 2022 presidential election in California at risk limit 5% using ONE CVRs for precinct-level results would sample approximately 70 ballots statewide, if the reported results are accurate, compared to about 26,700 for BLCA. The 2022 Georgia audit tabulated more than 231,000 cards (the expected BLCA sample size was ≈103,000 cards); ONEAudit would have audited ≈1,300 cards. For data from a pilot hybrid RLA in Kalamazoo, MI, in 2018, ONEAudit gives a risk of 2%, substantially lower than the 3.7% measured risk for SUITE, the "hybrid" method the pilot used.

© International Financial Cryptography Association 2024
A. Essex et al. (Eds.): FC 2023 Workshops, LNCS 13953, pp. 63–78, 2024.
https://doi.org/10.1007/978-3-031-48806-1_5

Keywords: Risk-limiting audit · BPA · card-level comparison audit · batch-level comparison audit

A version of this paper with more numerical results is available at https://arxiv.org/abs/2303.03335.

1   Introduction: Efficient Risk-Limiting Audits

A procedure is a risk-limiting audit (RLA) with risk limit α if it guarantees that if the reported outcome is right, the procedure will not change it; but if the reported outcome is wrong, the chance the procedure will not correct it—the "risk"—is at most α. "Outcome" means who or what won, not the precise vote tallies. RLA methods have been developed for many sampling designs [10,11,16,18,20,22], and to use the audit data in different ways to measure "risk" [8,9,16–18,20–22], to accommodate legal and logistical constraints and heterogeneous equipment within and across jurisdictions.

"Card" or "ballot card" means a sheet of paper; a ballot comprises one or more cards. A "cast-vote record" (CVR) is the voting system's interpretation of the votes on a particular card. A "manual-vote record" (MVR) is the auditors' reading of the votes on a card. The main approaches to RLAs are *ballot-polling RLAs* (BPA), which examine individual randomly selected cards but do not use data from the voting system other than the totals; *batch-level comparison RLAs* (BLCA), which compare reported vote subtotals for randomly selected batches of cards (e.g., all cards cast in a precinct) to manual tabulations of the same batches; *card-level comparison RLAs* (CLCA), which compare individual CVRs to the corresponding MVRs for a random sample of cards; and *hybrid* audits, which combine two or more of the approaches above.

BLCA is closest to historical statutory audits, but requires larger sample sizes than other methods when outcomes are correct. BPA requires almost no data from the voting system. It is generally more efficient than BLCA, but its sample size grows approximately quadratically as the margin shrinks. The most efficient approach is CLCA, for which the sample size grows approximately linearly as the margin shrinks. But it requires the most information from the voting system: an exported CVR for every card and a way to link exported CVRs to the corresponding physical cards, without compromising voter privacy.

This paper shows that applying CLCA to any combination of CVRs provided by the voting system and CVRs created by the auditors to match batch subtotals or contest totals gives a valid RLA. When the CVRs are derived entirely from contest totals, the method is algebraically equivalent to BPA. When the CVRs are derived from batch subtotals, the method is far more efficient than BLCA and approaches the efficiency of 'pure' CLCA when the batches are sufficiently homogeneous.

Many modern voting systems can provide linked CVRs for some ballot cards (e.g., vote-by-mail) but not others (e.g., in-precinct voters). This has led to a variety of strategies:

- give up the efficiency of CLCA and use BPA
- *hybrid* RLAs that use different audit strategies in different strata [10,13,18, 22]
- BLCA using weighted random samples [7,10,17], with batches of size 1 for cards with linked CVRs
- CLCA that rescans some or all of the cards to create linked CVRs the voting system did not originally provide [5,12]
- CLCA using cryptographic nonces to link CVRs to cards without compromising voter privacy [19].

Section 4 develops a simpler approach that in examples is more efficient than a hybrid audit or BLCA, works even when a BCLA is impracticable, avoids the expense of re-scanning any ballots, and does not require new or additional equipment. When reporting batches are sufficiently homogeneous, the sample size for the method approaches that of CLCA.

2   Testing Net Overstatement Does Not Require CVRs Linked to Ballot Cards

2.1   Warmup: 2-Candidate Plurality Contest

Consider a two-candidate plurality contest, Alice v. Bob, with Alice the reported winner. We encode votes and reported votes as follows. There are N cards. Let $b_i = 1$ if card i has a vote for Alice, -1 if it has a vote for Bob, and 0 otherwise. Let $c_i = 1$ if card i was counted by the voting system as a vote for Alice, $c_i = -1$ if it was counted as a vote for Bob, and $c_i = 0$ otherwise. The true margin is $\sum_{i=1}^{N} b_i$ and the reported margin is $\sum_{i=1}^{N} c_i$. The *overstatement* of the margin on the ith card is $c_i - b_i \in \{-2, -1, 0, 1, 2\}$. It is the number of votes by which the voting system exaggerated the number of votes for Alice. Alice really won if the *net overstatement of the margin*, $E(\{c_i\}) := \sum_i (c_i - b_i)$, is less than the reported margin $\sum_i c_i$. Because addition is commutative and associative, if $\{c_i\}$ and $\{c_i'\}$ are any two sets of CVRs for which $\sum_i c_i = \sum_i c_i'$, then $E(\{c_i\}) = E(\{c_i'\})$: they are *overstatement net equivalent* (ONE).

$$E(\{c_i\}) := \sum_i (c_i - b_i) = \sum_i c_i - \sum_i b_i = \sum_i c_i' - \sum_i b_i = \sum_i (c_i' - b_i) = E(\{c_i'\}).$$

(1)

Hence, if we have an RLA procedure to test whether $E(\{c_i\}) < \sum_i c_i$ using the "real" CVRs produced by the voting system, the same procedure can test whether the outcome is correct if it is applied to other CVRs $\{c_i'\}$ provided $\sum_i c_i = \sum_i c_i'$, *even if the CVRs $\{c_i'\}$ did not come from the voting system.* (Audit sample sizes might be quite different.)

Thus, we can conduct a CLCA using *any* set $\{c_i'\}$ of CVRs that reproduces the contest-level results: the net overstatement of every such set of CVRs is the same. If the system reports batch-level results, we can require that the CVRs reproduce the batch-level results as well., which might reduce audit sample sizes, especially when the batches have different political preferences. If the voting system reports CVRs for some individual ballot cards, we can conduct a CLCA that uses those CVRs, augmented by ONE CVRs for the remaining ballot cards (derived from batch subtotals or from contest totals, by subtraction). Better agreement between the MVRs and VCRs will generally allow the audit to stop after inspecting fewer cards.

2.2 Numerical Example

Consider a contest in which 20,000 cards were cast in all, of which 10,000 were cast by mail and have linked CVRs, with 5,000 votes for Alice, 4,000 for Bob, and 1,000 undervotes. The other 10,000 cards were cast in 10 precincts, 1,000 cards in each. Net across those 10 precincts, Alice and Bob each got 5,000 votes. In 5 precincts, Alice showed more votes than Bob; in the other 5, Bob showed more than Alice. The reported results are thus 10,000 votes for Alice, 9,000 for Bob, and 1,000 undervotes. The margin is 1,000 votes; the *diluted margin* (margin in votes, divided by cards cast) is $1000/20000 = 5\%$. Consider two sets of precinct subtotals:

- 5 precincts show 900 votes for Alice and 100 for Bob; the other 5 show 900 votes for Bob and 100 for Alice.
- 5 precincts show 990 votes for Alice and 10 for Bob; the other 5 show 990 votes for Bob and 10 for Alice.

Construct ONE CVRs for the 10,000 cards cast in the 10 precincts as follows: if the precinct reports a votes for Alice and $1000 - a$ for Bob, the net vote for Alice is $a - (1000 - a) = 2a - 1000$. The "average" CVR for the precinct has $(2a - 1000)/1000 = 2a/1000 - 1$ votes for Alice; that is the ONEAudit CVR for every card in the precinct. For instance, a precinct that reported 900 votes for Alice and 100 for Bob has a net margin of $900 \times 1 + 100 \times -1 = 800$ for Alice, so that precinct contributes 1,000 ONE CVRs, each with $c_i = (0.9) \times 1 + (0.1) \times (-1) = 0.8$ votes for Alice (Table 1).

Table 1. Overstatement-net equivalent CVRs that match batch subtotals. If a precinct of 1000 voters reported 990 votes for Alice and 10 for Bob, the net overstatement is the same as if there had been 1,000 CVRs, one for each card, each showing 0.98 votes for Alice.

batch total	ONE CVR
990 Alice, 10 Bob	0.98 Alice
900 Alice, 100 Bob	0.8 Alice
100 Alice, 900 Bob	−0.8 Alice (0.8 Bob)
10 Alice, 990 Bob	−0.98 Alice (0.98 Bob)

To audit, draw ballot cards uniformly at random, without replacement. To find the overstatement for each audited card, subtract the MVR for the card (-1,

0, or 1) from the CVR (-1, 0, or 1) if the system provided one, or from the ONE CVR for its precinct (a number in $[-1, 1]$) if the system did not provide a CVR. Apply a "risk-measuring function" (see, e.g., [18, 22]) to the overstatements to measure the risk that the outcome is wrong based on the data collected so far; the audit can stop without a full hand count if and when the measured risk is less than or equal to the risk limit.

The random selection can be conducted in many ways, for instance, conceptually numbering the cards from 1 to 20,000, where cards 1–10,000 are the ballots with CVRs, ordered in some canonical way; cards 10,001–11,000 are the cards cast in precinct 1, starting with the top card in the stack; cards 11,001–12,000 are the cards cast in precinct 2, starting with the top card in the stack; etc. Auditors draw random numbers between 1 and 20,000, and retrieve the corresponding card. Alternatively, if the resulting number is between 1 and 10,000, retrieve the corresponding card; but if the number is larger, draw a ballot at random from the precinct that numbered card belongs to, for instance, using the k-cut method [14]. That approach avoids counting into large stacks of ballots.

Table 2 summarizes expected audit sample sizes. If there had been a CVR for every card and the results were exactly correct, the sample size for a standard CLCA with risk limit 5% would be about 125 cards. A BPA at risk limit 5% would examine about 2,300 cards. A BLCA (treating individual cards as batches for those with CVRs) using sampling with probability proportional to an error bound and the Kaplan-Markov test [21] would examine about 7250 cards on average in the 900/100 scenario and 5300 in the 990/10 scenario. For ONEAudit, the expected sample size is about 800 cards in the 900/100 scenario and 170 in the 990/10 scenario. As preferences within precincts become more homogeneous, ONEAudit approaches the efficiency of CLCA.

2.3   The General Case

We use the SHANGRLA audit framework [18] because it can be works with every social choice function for which an RLA method is known; however, ONE CVRs can be used with every extant RLA method for comparison audits. SHANRGLA reduces auditing election outcomes to multiple instances of a single problem: testing whether the mean of a finite list of bounded numbers is less than or equal to $1/2$. Each list results from applying a function A called an *assorter* to the votes on the ballots; each assorter maps votes to the interval $[0, u]$, where the upper bound u depends on the particular assorter. Different social choice functions involve different assorters and, in general, different numbers of assorters. An *assertion* is the claim that the average of the values the assorter takes on the true votes is greater than $1/2$. The contest outcome is correct if the all the SHANGRLA assertions for the contest are true.

A *reported assorter margin* is the amount by which that assorter applied to the reported votes exceeds $1/2$. For scoring rules (plurality, supermajority, multiwinner plurality, approval voting, Borda count, etc.), reported assorter margins can be computed from contest-level tallies, batch tallies, or CVRs. For auditing IRV using RAIRE [4], CVRs are generally required to construct an appropriate

Table 2. Expected RLA workloads for a two-candidate plurality contest with a 'diluted margin' of 5% at risk limit 5%. In all, 20,000 cards were cast, of which 10,000 have linked CVRs; the other 10,000 cards are divided into 10 precincts with 1,000 cards each. Among cards with CVRs, 5,000 show votes for the winner, 4,000 show votes for the loser, and 1,000 have invalid votes. In the 900/100 scenario, 5 precincts have 900 votes for the winner and 100 for the loser; the other 5 have 900 for the loser and 100 for the winner. In the 990/10 scenario, 5 precincts have 990 votes for the winner and 10 for the loser; the other 5 have 990 for the loser and 10 for the winner. BPA: ballot-polling audit. CLCA: card-level comparison audit (which would require re-scanning the 10,000 cards cast in precincts). BLCA: batch-level comparison audit. ONE CLCA: card-level comparison audit using the original 10,000 CVRs, augmented by 10,000 ONE CVRs derived from precinct subtotals. Column 4: sample size divided by BPA sample size. Column 5: sample size divided by CLCA sample size. Expected workload for BPA and CLCA is the same in both scenarios. Sample sizes for CLCA use the "super-simple" method [17], computed using https://www.stat.berkeley.edu/~stark/Vote/auditTools.htm (last visited 19 March 2023). Sample sizes for BPA use ALPHA [22].

scenario	method	expected cards	vs BPA	vs CLCA
both	BPA	2,300	1.00	18.40
	CLCA	125	0.05	1.00
900/100	BLCA	7,250	3.15	58.00
	ONE CLCA	800	0.35	6.40
990/10	BLCA	5,300	2.30	42.40
	ONE CLCA	170	0.07	1.36

set of assorters and to find their margins—but the CVRs do not have to be linked to individual ballot cards.

Let b_i denote the true votes on the ith ballot card; there are N cards in all. Let c_i denote the voting system's interpretation of the ith card. Suppose we have a CVR c_i for every ballot card whose index i is in $\mathcal{C}$. The cardinality of $\mathcal{C}$ is $|\mathcal{C}|$. Ballot cards not in $\mathcal{C}$ are partitioned into $G \geq 1$ disjoint groups $\{\mathcal{G}_g\}_{g=1}^{G}$ for which reported assorter subtotals are available. For instance $\mathcal{G}_g$ might comprise all ballots for which no CVR is available or all ballots cast in a particular precinct. Unadorned overbars denote the average of a quantity across all N ballot cards; overbars subscripted by a set (e.g., $\mathcal{G}_g$) denote the average of a quantity across cards in that set, for instance:

$$\bar{A}^c := \frac{1}{N}\sum_{i=1}^{N} A(c_i), \quad \bar{A}_{\mathcal{C}}^c := \frac{1}{|\mathcal{C}|}\sum_{i\in\mathcal{C}} A(c_i), \quad \bar{A}_{\mathcal{G}_g}^c := \frac{1}{|\mathcal{G}_g|}\sum_{i\in\mathcal{G}_g} A(c_i)$$

$$\bar{A}^b := \frac{1}{N}\sum_{i=1}^{N} A(b_i), \quad \bar{A}_{\mathcal{C}}^b := \frac{1}{|\mathcal{C}|}\sum_{i\in\mathcal{C}} A(b_i), \quad \bar{A}_{\mathcal{G}_g}^b := \frac{1}{|\mathcal{G}_g|}\sum_{i\in\mathcal{G}_g} A(b_i).$$

The *assertion* is the claim $\bar{A}^b > 1/2$. The reported assorter mean $\bar{A}^c > 1/2$: otherwise, according to the voting system's data, the reported outcome is wrong. Now $\bar{A}^b > 1/2$ iff

$$\bar{A}^c - \bar{A}^b < \bar{A}^c - 1/2. \tag{2}$$

The right hand side is known before the audit starts; it is half the "reported assorter margin" $v := 2\bar{A}^c - 1$ [18]. We assume we have a *reported assorter total* $\sum_{i \in \mathcal{G}_g} A(c_i)$ from the voting system for the cards in the group $\mathcal{G}_g$ (e.g., reported precinct subtotals) and define the *reported assorter mean* for $\mathcal{G}_g$:

$$\hat{A}^c_{\mathcal{G}_g} := \frac{1}{|\mathcal{G}_g|} \sum_{i \in \mathcal{G}_g} A(c_i). \tag{3}$$

We have

$$\bar{A}^c = \frac{\sum_{g=1}^{G} |\mathcal{G}_g| \hat{A}^c_{\mathcal{G}_g} + \sum_{i \in C} A(c_i)}{N} = \frac{\sum_{g=1}^{G} \sum_{i \in \mathcal{G}_g} \hat{A}^c_{\mathcal{G}_g} + \sum_{i \in C} A(c_i)}{N}. \tag{4}$$

Thus if we *declare* $A(c_i) := \hat{A}^c_{\mathcal{G}_g}$ for $i \in \mathcal{G}_g$, the reported assorter mean for the cards in group $\mathcal{G}_g$, the mean of the assorter applied to the CVRs—including these faux CVRs—will equal its reported value: using a "mean CVR" for the batch is overstatement-net-equivalent to any CVRs that give the same assorter batch subtotals. Condition 2 then can be written

$$\frac{1}{N} \sum_i (A(c_i) - A(b_i)) < v/2. \tag{5}$$

Following SHANGRLA [18, section 3.2]', define

$$B(b_i) := \frac{u + A(b_i) - A(c_i)}{2u - v} \in [0, 2u/(2u - v)]. \tag{6}$$

Then $\bar{A}^b > 1/2 \iff \bar{B}^b > 1/2$, which can be shown as follows, using the fact that $v := 2\bar{A}^c - 1 \le 2u - 1 < 2u$:

$$\begin{aligned} \bar{B}^b &:= \frac{1}{N} \sum_i \frac{u + A(b_i) - A(c_i)}{2u - v} \\ &= \frac{u + \bar{A}^b - \bar{A}^c}{2u - v} \\ &= \frac{u + \bar{A}^b - \bar{A}^c}{2u - 2\bar{A}^c + 1}. \end{aligned} \tag{7}$$

Thus if $\bar{B}^b > 1/2$,

$$\begin{aligned} \frac{u + \bar{A}^b - \bar{A}^c}{2u - 2\bar{A}^c + 1} &> 1/2 \\ u + \bar{A}^b - \bar{A}^c &> u - \bar{A}^c + 1/2 \\ \bar{A}^b &> 1/2. \end{aligned} \tag{8}$$

If the reported tallies are correct, i.e., if $\bar{A}^c = \bar{A}^b = (v+1)/2$, then

$$\bar{B}^b = \frac{u}{2u - v}. \qquad (9)$$

3 Auditing Using Batch Subtotals

The oldest approach to RLAs is batch-level comparison, which involves exporting batch subtotals from the voting system (e.g., for precincts or tabulators), verifying that those batch subtotals yield the reported contest results, drawing some number of batches at random (with equal probability or with probability proportional to an error bound), manually tabulating all the votes in each selected batch, comparing the manual tabulation to the reported batch subtotals, assessing whether the data give sufficiently strong evidence that the reported results are right, and expanding the sample if not [6,15,16,20,21].

BLCAs have two logistical hurdles: (i) They require manually tabulating the votes on *every* ballot card in the batches selected for audit. (ii) When the batches of cards for which the voting system reports subtotals do not correspond to identifiable physical batches (common for vote-by-mail and vote centers), the audit has to find and retrieve every card in the audited reporting batches. Those cards may be spread across any number of physical batches, which can also make recounts prohibitively expensive [1].

Both can be avoided using CLCA with ONE CVRs. The following algorithm gives a valid RLA, but selects and compares the manual interpretation of *individual* cards to the implied "average" CVR of the reporting batch each card belongs to. We assume that the canvass and a *compliance audit* [2] have determined that the ballot manifest and physical cards are complete and trustworthy.

Algorithm for a CLCA using ONE CVRs from batch subtotals.
1. Pick the risk limit for each contest under audit.
2. Export batch subtotals from the voting system.
3. Verify that every physical card is accounted for,[a] that the physical accounting is consistent with the reported votes, and that the reported batch subtotals produce the reported winners.
4. Construct SHANGRLA assorters for every contest under audit; select a risk-measuring function for each assertion (e.g., one in [22]); set the measured risk for each assertion to 1.
5. Calculate the reported mean assorter values for each reporting batch; these are the ONE CVRs.
6. While any measured risk is greater than its risk limit and not every card has been audited:
   - Select a card at random, e.g., by selecting a batch at random with probability proportional to the size of the batch, then selecting a card uniformly at random from the batch using the k-cut method [14], or by selecting at random from the entire collection of cards.

- Calculate the overstatement for the selected card using the ONE CVR for the reporting batch the card belongs to.
- Update the measured risk of any assertion whose measured risk is still greater than its risk limit.
- If the measured risk for every assertion is less than or equal to its risk limit, stop and confirm the reported outcomes.
7. Report the correct contest outcomes: every card has been manually interpreted.

---

[a] For techniques to deal with missing cards, see [3,18].

This algorithm be made more efficient statistically and logistically in a variety of ways, for instance, by making an affine translation of the data so that the minimum possible value is 0 (by subtracting the minimum of the possible overstatement assorters across batches and re-scaling so that the null mean is still 1/2) and by starting with a sample size that is expected to be large enough to confirm the contest outcome if the reported results are correct.

3.1 Numerical Case Studies

Table 3 compares expected sample sizes for BLCA to CLCA using ONE CVRs derived from the same batch subtotals, and to BPA, for two contests: the 2022 midterm Georgia Secretary of State's contest, which had a diluted margin (margin in votes divided by cards cast) of about 9.2%[1] and the 2020 presidential election in California, which had a diluted margin of about 28.7%. The Georgia contest was audited using batch-level comparisons. The Georgia SoS claims that audit was a BLCA with a risk limit of 5%, but in fact the audit was not an RLA, for a variety of reasons.[2] BPA and CLCA using ONE CVRs are generally much more efficient than BLCA when batches are large. CLCA with ONE CVRs is more efficient than BPA when batches are more homogenous than the contest votes as a whole, i.e., when precincts are polarized in different directions.

4 Auditing Heterogenous Voting Systems

When the voting system can report linked CVRs for some but not all cards, we can augment the voting system's linked CVRs with ONE CVRs for the remaining cards, then use CLCA. The ONE CVRs can be derived from overall contest results or from reported subtotals, e.g., precinct subtotals. Finer-grained subtotals generally give smaller audit sample sizes (when the reported outcome is correct) if the smaller groups are more homogeneous than the overall election.

SUITE [10], a hybrid RLA designed for this situation, was first fielded in a pilot audit of the gubernatorial primary in Kalamazoo, MI, in 2018. The stratum with linked CVRs comprised 5,294 ballots with 5,218 reported votes in the

---

[1] https://sos.ga.gov/news/georgias-2022-statewide-risk-limiting-audit-confirms-results, last visited 26 February 2023.

[2] https://www.stat/berkeley.edu/~stark/Preprints/cgg-rept-10.pdf, last visited 15 December 2022.

Table 3. Actual and estimated expected sample sizes for various RLA methods for the 2020 U.S. presidential election in California and the 2022 Georgia Secretary of State contest, at risk limit 5%. Columns 2, 3: turnout per state records. CA data from https:// statewidedatabase.org/d10/g20.html (last visited 2 March 2020); the CA Statement of Vote gives slightly smaller turnout 17,785,151 (https://elections.cdn.sos.ca.gov/sov/ 2020-general/sov/complete-sov.pdf, last visited 2 March 2023). GA data from (https:// sos.ga.gov/news/georgias-2022-statewide-risk-limiting-audit-confirms-results, last visited 26 February 2023). Column 4: approximate number of cards examined in the actual batch-level audits (which were not RLAs). Column 5: expected sample size for BLCA using the Kaplan-Markov risk function. Column 6: expected sample size for CLCA using ONE CVRs based on batch subtotals, for the ALPHA risk-measuring function with the truncated shrinkage estimator with parameters $c = 1/2$, $d = 10$, estimated from 100 Monte Carlo replications. Column 7: expected sample size for BPA using Wald's SPRT. Column 8: column 5 divided by column 6. A different risk function should reduce the GA ONE CLCA sample size to at most the BPA sample size: see Sect. 5.1. Estimates assume that reported batch subtotals are correct.

Contest	total turnout	total batches	actual sample size	K-M BLCA	ONE CLCA	Wald BP	BLCA/ CLCA
2020 CA U.S. Pres	17,785,667	21,346	≈178,000	26,700	70	72	381
2022 GA SoS	3,909,983	12,968	>231,000	103,300	1,380	700	75

contest; the "no-CVR" stratum comprised 22,372 ballots with 22,082 reported votes. The sample included 32 cards were drawn from the no-CVR stratum and 8 from the CVR stratum.[3] Table 4 summarizes the contest and audit results; auditors found no errors in the 8 CVRs, each of which yields the overstatement assorter value $u/(2u-v)$. The new method compares the 32 cards without CVRs to ONE CVRs derived from all the votes without CVRs (not from subtotals for smaller batches) by subtracting the votes on the linked CVRs from the reported contest totals. Ignoring the fact that the sample was stratified and the difference in sampling fractions in the two strata, in 100,000 random permutations of the data, the ALPHA martingale test using a fixed alternative $0.99(2u)/(2u-v)$ had a mean P-value of 0.0201 (90th percentile 0.0321), about 54% of the SUITE P-value of 0.0374 [10]. The ONEAudit P-value is larger than the P-value of the best product supermartingale test in [13], but comparable to or smaller than the P-values for the other supermartingale tests. See Table 5. If precinct subtotals were available to construct the ONE CVRs, the measured risk might have been lower, depending on precinct heterogeneity.

5   Sample Sizes for Contest-Level ONE CLCA Vs. BPA

5.1   Theory

Moving from tests about raw assorter values to tests about overstatements relative to ONE CVRs derived from overall contest totals is just an affine trans-

---

[3] See https://github.com/kellieotto/mirla18/blob/master/code/kalamazoo_SUITE.ip ynb.

Table 4. Reported votes in the stratum with CVRs and the stratum without CVRs, and the audited votes in the random sample of 32 cards from the stratum without CVRs in the 2018 RLA pilot in Kalamazoo, MI.

Candidate	CVR	no-CVR	polling sample
Butkovich	6	66	0
Gelineau	56	462	1
Kurland	23	284	0
Schleiger	19	116	0
Schuette	1,349	4,220	8
Whitmer	3,765	16,934	23
Non-vote	76	290	0
Total	5,294	22,372	32

Table 5. P-values for the 2018 RLA pilot in Kalamazoo, MI, for different risk-measuring functions. SUITE is a hybrid stratified approach [10]. Rows 2–5 are from [13, Table 3]: the ALPHA and Empirical Bernstein stratumwise supermartingales combined using either Fisher's combining function (P_F^*) or multiplication (P_M^*). The 6th row is for ONEAudit, using the ALPHA supermartingale with fixed alternative $\eta = 0.99$, a non-adaptive choice. Technically, ONEAudit should not be applied to this sample because the sample was stratified, while the risk calculation assumes the sample was a simple random sample of ballot cards: this is just a numerical illustration.

Method	P-value	SD	90th percentile
SUITE	0.037	n/a	n/a
ALPHA P_F^*	0.018	0.002	0.019
ALPHA P_M^*	0.003	0.000	0.003
Empirical Bernstein P_F^*	0.348	0.042	0.390
Empirical Bernstein P_M^*	0.420	0.134	0.561
ALPHA ONEAudit	0.020	0.010	0.032

formation: no information is gained or lost. Thus, if we audited using an affine equivariant statistical test, the sample size should be the same whether the data are the original assorter values (i.e., BPA) or overstatements from ONE CVRs.

However, the statistical tests used in RLAs are not affine equivariant because they rely on *a priori* bounds on the assorter values. The original assorter values will generally be closer to the endpoints of $[0, u]$ than the transformed values are to the endpoints of $[0, 2u/(2u - v)]$. To see why, suppose that there are no reported CVRs ($\mathcal{C} = \emptyset$) and that only contest totals are reported from the system—so every cast ballot card is in $\mathcal{G}_1$. For a BPA, the population values from which the sample is drawn are the original assorter values $\{A(b_i)\}$, which for many social choice functions can take only the values 0, 1/2, and u. For instance, consider a two-candidate plurality contest, Alice v. Bob, where Alice is the reported winner. This can be audited using a single assorter that assigns the value 0 to a card with a vote for Bob, the value $u = 1$ to a card with a vote for Alice, and the value $1/2$ to other cards. In contrast, for a comparison audit, the possible population values $\{B(b_i)\}$ are

$$\left\{\frac{1-(v+1)/2}{2-v}, 1/2, \frac{2-(v+1)/2}{2-v}\right\}.$$

Unless $v = 1$—i.e., unless every card was reported to have a vote for Alice— the minimum value of the overstatement assorter is greater than 0 and the maximum is less than u. Figure 1 plots the minimum and maximum value of the overstatement assorter as a function of v for $u = 1$.

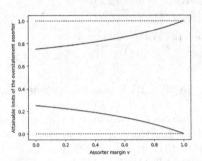

Fig. 1. Upper and lower bounds on the overstatement assorter as a function of the diluted margin v, for $u = 1$.

A test that uses the prior information $x_j \in [0, u]$ may not be as efficient for populations for which $x_j \in [a, b]$ with $a > 0$ and $b < u$ as it is for populations where the values 0 and u actually occur. An affine transformation of the over-statement assorter values can move them back to the endpoints of the support constraint by subtracting the minimum possible value then re-scaling so that the null mean is $1/2$ once again, which reproduces the original assorter, A:

$$
\begin{aligned}
C(b_i) &:= \frac{1/2}{1/2 - \frac{u-(v+1)/2}{2u-v}} \cdot \left(B(b_i) - \frac{u-(v+1)/2}{2u-v}\right) \\
&= \frac{2u-v}{2u-v-(2u-(v+1))} \cdot \left(\frac{u+A(b_i)-(v+1)/2}{2u-v} - \frac{u-(v+1)/2}{2u-v}\right) \\
&= (2u-v) \cdot \frac{A(b_i)}{2u-v} = A(b_i).
\end{aligned}
\tag{10}
$$

5.2 Numerical Comparison

While CLCA with ONE CVRs is algebraically equivalent to BPA, the performance of a given statistical test will be different for the two formulations. We now compare expected audit sample sizes for some common risk-measuring functions applied to CLCA with ONE CVRs derived from contest-level results and applied to the original assorter data. This is assessing the particular *statistical tests*, not any intrinsic difference between BPA and ONE CLCA.

Tables 7–11 in the extended version of the paper at https://arxiv.org/abs/ 2303.03335 report expected sample sizes when the reported winner received a share $\theta \in \{0.505, 0.51, 0.52, 0.55, 0.6\}$ of the reported votes, for percentages of cards that do not contain a valid vote for either candidate ranging from 10% to 75%, and various values of tuning parameters in the risk-measuring functions. Table 6 gives the geometric mean of the ratios of the mean sample size for each condition to the smallest mean sample size for that condition (across risk-measuring functions). Transforming the assorter into an overstatement assorter using the ONEAudit transformation, then testing whether the mean of the resulting population is $\leq 1/2$ using the ALPHA test martingale with the truncated shrinkage estimator of [22] with $d = 10$ and η between 0.505 and 0.55 performed comparably to—but slightly worse than—using ALPHA on the raw assorter values for the same d and η, and within 4.8% of the overall performance of the best-performing method.

Table 6. Geometric mean of the ratios of sample sizes to the smallest sample size for each condition described above. The smallest ratio is in bold font. In the simulations, for the hypothesis tests considered, the ONEAudit transformation entails a negligible loss in efficiency compared to ALPHA applied to the "raw" assorter.

Method	Parameters	Score	Method	Score
ALPHA	$\eta = 0.505\ d = 10$	1.51	ONEAudit	1.52
	$\eta = 0.505\ d = 100$	1.54		1.55
	$\eta = 0.505\ d = 1000$	1.79		1.83
	$\eta = 0.505\ d = \infty$	3.02		3.83
	$\eta = 0.51\ d = 10$	1.51		1.52
	$\eta = 0.51\ d = 100$	1.53		1.55
	$\eta = 0.51\ d = 1000$	1.72		1.80
	$\eta = 0.51\ d = \infty$	2.29		3.05
	$\eta = 0.52\ d = 10$	1.51		1.53
	$\eta = 0.52\ d = 100$	1.51		1.55
	$\eta = 0.52\ d = 1000$	1.61		1.75
	$\eta = 0.52\ d = \infty$	1.84		2.32
	$\eta = 0.55\ d = 10$	1.51		1.55
	$\eta = 0.55\ d = 100$	1.47		1.56
	$\eta = 0.55\ d = 1000$	**1.44**		1.62
	$\eta = 0.55\ d = \infty$	1.88		1.81
	$\eta = 0.6\ d = 10$	1.50		1.59
	$\eta = 0.6\ d = 100$	1.45		1.57
	$\eta = 0.6\ d = 1000$	1.51		1.52
	$\eta = 0.6\ d = \infty$	2.42		1.84
SqKelly		1.98		
a priori Kelly	$\eta = 0.505$	2.77		
	$\eta = 0.51$	1.88		
	$\eta = 0.52$	1.60		
	$\eta = 0.55$	2.14		
	$\eta = 0.6$	3.34		

6   Conclusions

Ballot-polling risk-limiting audits (BPAs) are algebraically equivalent to card-level comparison risk-limiting audits (CLCAs) using faux cast-vote records (CVRs) that match the overall reported results. Any set of CVRs that reproduces the reported contest tallies (more generally, reproduces reported assorter totals) has the same net overstatement of the margin: they are "overstatement-net-equivalent" (ONE) to the voting system's tabulation and can be used as if the voting system had exported them.

ONE CVRs let audits use batch-level data far more efficiently than traditional batch-level comparison RLAs (BLCAs) do: create ONE CVRs for each batch, then apply CLCA as if the voting system had provided those CVRs. For real and simulated data, this saves a large mount of work compared to manually tabulating the votes on *every* card in the batches selected for audit, as BLCAs require. If batches are sufficiently homogeneous, the workload approaches that of "pure" CLCA using linked CVRs from the voting system. BLCAs also require locating and retrieving every card in each batch that is selected for audit. That is straightforward when reporting batches are identifiable physical batches, but not when physical batches contain a mixture of ballot cards from different reporting batches, which is common in jurisdictions that use vote centers or do not sort vote-by-mail ballots before scanning them. In the California presidential election in 2020 and the Georgia election for Secretary of State in 2022, this approach would reduce the workload by a factor of 75 to 380, respectively, compared to the most efficient known method for BLCA.

ONE CVRs also can obviate the need to stratify, to rescan cards, or to use "hybrid" audits when the voting system cannot export a linked CVR for every card: create ONE CVRs for the cards that lack them, then apply CLCA as if the CVRs had been provided by the voting system. The same CLCA software can be used to audit voting systems that can export a linked CVR for every card and also those that cannot. For data from a 2018 pilot audit in Kalamazoo, MI, ONE CLCA gives a measured risk much smaller than that of SUITE (2% versus 3.7%), the hybrid method used in the pilot. Stratification and hybrid audits increase the complexity and opacity of audits, and rescanning substantially increases time and cost. Hence, ONEAudit may be cheaper, faster, simpler, and more transparent than previous methods. Software used to generate the tables and figures is available at https://www.github.com/pbstark/ONEAudit.

Acknowledgments. This work was supported by NSF Grant SaTC–2228884. I am grateful to Jake Spertus and Andrew Appel for helpful conversations.

References

1. Appel, A.: Sort the mail-in ballot envelopes, or don't? (2023). https://freedom-to-tinker.com/2023/05/01/sort-the-mail-in-ballot-envelopes-or-dont/. Accessed 16 June 2023

2. Appel, A., Stark, P.: Evidence-based elections: create a meaningful paper trail, then audit. Georgetown Law Technol. Rev. **4**(2), 523–541 (2020). https://georgetownlawtechreview.org/wp-content/uploads/2020/07/4.2-p523-541-Appel-Stark.pdf

3. Bañuelos, J., Stark, P.: Limiting risk by turning manifest phantoms into evil zombies. Technical report (2012). https://arxiv.org/abs/1207.3413. Accessed 17 July 2012

4. Blom, M., Stuckey, P.J., Teague, V.J.: Ballot-polling risk limiting audits for IRV elections. In: Krimmer, R., et al. (eds.) E-Vote-ID 2018. LNCS, vol. 11143, pp. 17–34. Springer, Cham (2018). https://doi.org/10.1007/978-3-030-00419-4_2

5. Harrison, A., Fuller, B., Russell, A.: Lazy risk-limiting ballot comparison audits (2022). https://doi.org/10.48550/arXiv.2202.02607

6. Higgins, M., Rivest, R., Stark, P.: Sharper p-values for stratified post-election audits. Stat. Politics Policy **2**(1) (2011). https://doi.org/10.2202/2151-7509.1031

7. Lindeman, M., McBurnett, N., Ottoboni, K., Stark, P.: Next steps for the Colorado risk-limiting audit (CORLA) program (2018). https://arxiv.org/abs/1803.00698

8. Lindeman, M., Stark, P.: A gentle introduction to risk-limiting audits. IEEE Secur. Priv. **10**, 42–49 (2012)

9. Lindeman, M., Stark, P., Yates, V.: BRAVO: ballot-polling risk-limiting audits to verify outcomes. In: Proceedings of the 2011 Electronic Voting Technology Workshop/Workshop on Trustworthy Elections (EVT/WOTE 2011). USENIX (2012)

10. Ottoboni, K., Stark, P.B., Lindeman, M., McBurnett, N.: Risk-limiting audits by stratified union-intersection tests of elections (SUITE). In: Krimmer, R., et al. (eds.) E-Vote-ID 2018. LNCS, vol. 11143, pp. 174–188. Springer, Cham (2018). https://doi.org/10.1007/978-3-030-00419-4_12

11. Ottoboni, K., Bernhard, M., Halderman, J.A., Rivest, R.L., Stark, P.B.: Bernoulli ballot polling: a manifest improvement for risk-limiting audits. In: Bracciali, A., Clark, J., Pintore, F., Rønne, P.B., Sala, M. (eds.) FC 2019. LNCS, vol. 11599, pp. 226–241. Springer, Cham (2020). https://doi.org/10.1007/978-3-030-43725-1_16

12. Rhode Island RLA Working Group: Pilot implementation study of risk-limiting audit methods in the state of Rhode Island (2019). https://www.brennancenter.org/sites/default/files/2019-09/Report-RI-Design-FINAL-WEB4.pdf

13. Spertus, J.V., Stark, P.B.: Sweeter than SUITE: supermartingale stratified union-intersection tests of elections. In: Krimmer, R., Volkamer, M., Duenas-Cid, D., Ronne, P., Germann, M. (eds.) E-Vote-ID 2022. LNCS, vol. 13553, pp. 106–121. Springer, Cham (2022). https://doi.org/10.1007/978-3-031-15911-4_7

14. Sridhar, M., Rivest, R.L.: k-cut: a simple approximately-uniform method for sampling ballots in post-election audits. In: Bracciali, A., Clark, J., Pintore, F., Rønne, P.B., Sala, M. (eds.) FC 2019. LNCS, vol. 11599, pp. 242–256. Springer, Cham (2020). https://doi.org/10.1007/978-3-030-43725-1_17

15. Stark, P.: Election audits by sampling with probability proportional to an error bound: dealing with discrepancies (2008). https://statistics.berkeley.edu/~stark/Preprints/ppebwrwd08.pdf

16. Stark, P.: A sharper discrepancy measure for post-election audits. Ann. Appl. Stat. **2**, 982–985 (2008). https://arxiv.org/abs/0811.1697

17. Stark, P.: Super-simple simultaneous single-ballot risk-limiting audits. In: Proceedings of the 2010 Electronic Voting Technology Workshop / Workshop on Trustworthy Elections (EVT/WOTE 2010). USENIX (2010). https://www.usenix.org/events/evtwote10/tech/full_papers/Stark.pdf

18. Stark, P.B.: Sets of half-average nulls generate risk-limiting audits: SHANGRLA. In: Bernhard, M., et al. (eds.) FC 2020. LNCS, vol. 12063, pp. 319–336. Springer, Cham (2020). https://doi.org/10.1007/978-3-030-54455-3_23

19. Stark, P.: Non(c)esuch ballot-level risk-limiting audits for precinct-count voting systems. In: Katsikas, S., et al. (eds.) ESORICS 2022. LNCS, vol. 13785, pp. 541–554. Springer, Cham (2023). https://doi.org/10.1007/978-3-031-25460-4_31

20. Stark, P.B.: Conservative statistical post-election audits. Ann. Appl. Stat. **2**, 550–581 (2008). https://arxiv.org/abs/0807.4005

21. Stark, P.B.: Risk-limiting post-election audits: P-values from common probability inequalities. IEEE Trans. Inf. Forensics Secur. **4**, 1005–1014 (2009)

22. Stark, P.B.: ALPHA: audit that learns from previously hand-audited ballots. Ann. Appl. Stat. **17**, 641–679 (2023). https://doi.org/10.1214/22-AOAS1646

Risk-Limiting Audits for Condorcet Elections

Michelle Blom[1]([✉]) [ID], Peter J. Stuckey[2] [ID], Vanessa Teague[3,4] [ID],
and Damjan Vukcevic[5] [ID]

[1] School of Computing and Information Systems, University of Melbourne,
Parkville, Australia
michelle.blom@unimelb.edu.au
[2] Department of Data Science and AI, Monash University, Clayton, Australia
[3] Thinking Cybersecurity Pty. Ltd., Melbourne, Australia
[4] Australian National University, Canberra, Australia
[5] Department of Econometrics and Business Statistics, Monash University,
Clayton, Australia

Abstract. Elections where electors rank the candidates (or a subset of
the candidates) in order of preference allow the collection of more information about the electors' intent. The most widely used election of this
type is Instant-Runoff Voting (IRV), where candidates are eliminated
one by one, until a single candidate holds the majority of the remaining
ballots. Condorcet elections treat the election as a set of simultaneous
decisions about each pair of candidates. The Condorcet winner is the
candidate who beats all others in these pairwise contests. There are various proposals to determine a winner if no Condorcet winner exists. In
this paper we show how we can efficiently audit Condorcet elections for
a number of variations. We also compare the audit efficiency (how many
ballots we expect to sample) of IRV and Condorcet elections.

Keywords: Condorcet Elections · Risk-Limiting Audits ·
Instant-Runoff Voting · Ranked Pairs

1 Introduction

In ranked or preferential vote elections, each ballot comprises an ordered list
of (some or all of) the candidates. The ballot is interpreted as a statement
that each candidate on the list is preferred by the voter to all the candidates
after it, and any that don't appear on the ballot. Condorcet elections treat each
election as a series of two-way contests between each pair of candidates A and
B, by saying A beats B if the number of ballots that prefer A over B is greater
than those that prefer B over A. A Condorcet winner exists if there is a single
candidate that beats all other candidates. But it is quite possible to have ranked

This work was supported by the University of Melbourne's Research Computing Services and the Petascale Campus Initiative; and by the Australian Research Council
(Discovery Project DP220101012; OPTIMA ITTC IC200100009).

A. Essex et al. (Eds.): FC 2023 Workshops, LNCS 13953, pp. 79–94, 2024.
https://doi.org/10.1007/978-3-031-48806-1_6

vote elections with no Condorcet winner. In this case there are many alternate strategies/election systems that can be used to choose a winner.

Risk-Limiting Audits (RLAs) test a reported election outcome by sampling ballot papers and will correct a wrong outcome with high probability (by requiring a full manual count of the ballots). They will not change the outcome if it is correct. The *risk limit*, often denoted α, specifies that a wrong outcome will be corrected with probability at least $1 - \alpha$. RLAs for Instant-Runoff Voting (IRV) can be conducted efficiently using RAIRE [2]. RAIRE generates 'assertions' which, if true, rule out all outcomes in which the reported winner did not win. Assertions form the basis of an RLA that can be conducted using the SHANGRLA framework [3].

In this paper we show how to use the assertion-based methodology of Blom et al. [1] to form a set of assertions sufficient to conduct an RLA for a variety of Condorcet elections. Assertions with linear dependence on transformations of the votes can easily be transformed to canonical assorter form for SHANGRLA. We contrast the estimated difficulty of these audits, in terms of sample sizes required, against auditing IRV using RAIRE.

For ranked vote elections that have a Condorcet winner, we first consider an audit that checks that the reported winner is indeed the Condorcet winner (Sect. 3). For an election with n candidates, this requires $n - 1$ assertions comparing the reported winner to each reported loser. We then consider Ranked Pairs, a Condorcet method that builds a preference relation over candidates on the basis of the strength of pairwise defeats (Sect. 4). We find, that for elections with a Condorcet winner, the expected sample sizes required to check that the reported winner is the Condorcet winner, or to audit as a Ranked Pairs or IRV election, are usually similar. In some instances, particularly those where the winner is decided by who is eliminated in the second-last round of IRV, we see more substantial differences in auditing difficulty.

To demonstrate the practicality of our auditing methods, we use IRV datasets from the Australian New South Wales (NSW) lower house elections in 2015 and 2019, in addition to a series of IRV elections held across the United States between 2007 and 2010. All of these elections have a Condorcet winner.

Finding ranked vote datasets from real elections that did not have a Condorcet winner was challenging. We were able to find some Single Transferable Vote (STV) elections, and some datasets from Preflib[1], that met this criterion. For these instances, RAIRE often struggled to terminate when finding an appropriate set of assertions to audit. Auditing these elections as if they were Ranked Pairs elections was more successful. We present these results in Sect. 9.

We finally consider three additional Condorcet methods: Minimax (Sect. 5), Smith (Sect. 6), and Kemeny-Young (Sect. 7). We found that audits for these methods were generally not practical. Minimax and Smith default to electing the Condorcet winner when one exists, and in this case we can simply use the method outlined in Sect. 3. On our instances without a Condorcet winner, we generally did not find an audit for Minimax or Smith, with our proposed methods, that was not a full manual count.

---

[1] www.preflib.org, accessed 14 Mar 2023.

Table 1. Distribution of ballot types for two example elections.

Ballot Signature	Votes
A, B	5,000
B, C	2,500
C, A, B	500
B, A	300
Total Votes	8,300

(a) Election 1

Ballot Signature	Votes
A, C, B	20,000
B, C, A	19,000
C	5,000
Total Votes	44,000

(b) Election 2

2   Preliminaries

In this paper, we consider *ranked vote elections* that require voters to cast a ballot in which they rank available candidates in order of preference, and a single winner is determined. For example, in an election with candidates A, B and C, a voter indicates which of these candidates is their most preferred, their second most preferred, and so on. Depending on the jurisdiction, voters may be required to rank all candidates (e.g., [A,B,C]) or express a partial ranking (e.g., [A, C]). The latter ballot is interpreted as expressing a preference for A over C, and that both A and C are preferred to all other candidates. The number of ballots on which a candidate is ranked first is their first-preference tally.

We define a *ranked vote election* as a pair $\mathcal{L} = (\mathcal{C}, \mathcal{B})$ where $\mathcal{C}$ is the set of candidates and $\mathcal{B}$ the multiset of ballots cast. A ballot b is a sequence of candidates π, listed in order of preference (most popular first), without any duplicates but also without necessarily including all candidates. We use list notation to define the ranking on a ballot (e.g., $\pi = [c_1, c_2, c_3, c_4]$). Given an election $\mathcal{L}$, the election system determines which candidate $c \in \mathcal{C}$ is the winner.[2]

2.1   Instant-Runoff Voting (IRV)

IRV is a type of ranked vote election. To determine the winner in an IRV election, each candidate is initially awarded all votes in which they are ranked first (known as their *first preferences*). The candidate with the smallest tally is eliminated, and the ballots in their tally pile are redistributed to the next most preferred candidate on the ballot who is still standing. For example, a ballot with the ranking [A, B, C] is first assigned to candidate A. If A were to be eliminated, the ballot would be given to candidate B, provided B has not already been eliminated. Subsequent rounds of elimination are performed in which the candidate with the smallest tally is eliminated, and the ballots in their tally pile redistributed, until we have one candidate left, or one of the remaining candidates has the majority of votes. This candidate is declared the winner.

Consider the distribution of votes present in two example elections shown in Table 1. In Election 1, candidates A, B, and C have first preference tallies of 5000, 2800, and 500, respectively. When viewed as an IRV election, candidate

[2] Ties are also possible, but very rare for elections with many ballots.

Table 2. Election 3 example: (a) distribution of ballot types; (b) calculation of comparative tallies $T(i \succ j)$ for row i and column j; (c) calculation of scores $s(i,j)$.

Ballot Signature	Votes
A, B, D, C	7,000
A, C, B, D	2,000
B, C, D, A	4,000
B, D, A, C	6,000
C, A, B, D	2,000
C, D, A, B	7,000
D, C, A, B	1,000
Total Votes	27,000

$T(i \succ j)$	A	B	C	D
A		19k	15k	11k
B	10k		17k	21k
C	14k	12k		15k
D	18k	8k	14k	

$s(i,j)$	A	B	C	D
A		9k	1k	−7k
B	−9k		5k	13k
C	−1k	−5k		1k
D	7k	−13k	−1k	

(a)   (b)   (c)

A has the majority of votes on first preferences and is declared the winner. In Election 2, A, B, and C start with 20000, 19000, and 5000 votes, respectively. Candidate C is eliminated, with all of their ballots *exhausted*. Candidate A has more votes than B and is declared the winner. For the distribution of ballots for Election 3 shown in Table 2(a), when viewed as an IRV election, candidate D is eliminated first, then A, leaving B to win with a majority of votes.

3   Risk-Limiting Audits for Condorcet Winners

In *Condorcet elections* we consider the ballots as applying to "separate" decisions about each pair of candidates $i, j \in \mathcal{C}$. A ballot b prefers i over j if i appears before j in b, or i appears on b and j does not. We define $T(i \succ j)$ to be the tally (i.e., number) of ballots $b \in \mathcal{B}$ that prefer i over j. Similarly, we define $T(j \succ i)$ to be the tally of ballots $b \in \mathcal{B}$ that prefer j over i. Note that $T(i \succ j) + T(j \succ i) \leqslant |\mathcal{B}|$ as some ballots may mention neither i nor j.

For the competition between a pair of candidates $i, j \in \mathcal{C}$, we define a *score*,

$$s(i,j) = T(i \succ j) - T(j \succ i). \tag{1}$$

In an election that satisfies the Condorcet winner criterion, the winner is the candidate $w \in \mathcal{C}$ for which $s(w,c) > 0$ for all $c \in \mathcal{C} \setminus \{w\}$. In Election 1 of Table 1, candidate A is the Condorcet winner, because $T(A \succ B)$ is 5500, $T(B \succ A)$ is 2800, $T(A \succ C)$ is 5300, and $T(C \succ A)$ is 3000; giving $s(A,B) = 2700$ and $s(A,C) = 2300$. In Election 2 candidate C is the Condorcet winner since $T(A \succ C)$ is 20000, and $T(C \succ A)$ is 24000; $T(B \succ C)$ is 19000, and $T(C \succ B)$ is 25000; giving $s(C,A) = 4000$ and $s(C,B) = 6000$. Note how a Condorcet winner need not be the IRV winner (which is A). For Election 3, shown in Table 2(a), the tallies $T(i \succ j)$ for row i and column j are shown in Table 2(b), and the scores $s(i,j)$ for row i and column j are shown in Table 2(c). There is no Condorcet winner since one of the scores in each row is negative.

We can audit the correctness of the winner in these elections by checking the assertions $s(w,c) > 0$ for all $c \in \mathcal{C} \setminus \{w\}$. This is similar to auditing first-past-the-post elections where we compare the tallies of two candidates, but rather than comparing tallies of ballots for each candidate we compare tallies of ballots that favor one candidate over the other. The tally of w, when compared with candidate c, is given by $t_w = T(w \succ c)$, and that of c is $t_c = T(c \succ w)$. Our assertion states that $t_w > t_c$ which can be transformed into an assorter as described by Blom et al. [1], and audited with SHANGRLA [3]. These assertions can be used to audit any Condorcet method where a Condorcet winner exists. We simply have to check that the reported winner is the Condorcet winner. We cannot do this for the election of Table 2, as it does not have a Condorcet winner. If the reported results indicate a Condorcet winner, but this is not actually the case, then at least one of assertions will be false, so with probability at least $1 - \alpha$ the audit will not certify. Hence this is a valid RLA.

4   Risk-Limiting Audits for Ranked Pairs Elections

Ranked Pairs [4] is a type of Condorcet election that determines a winner even if no Condorcet winner exists. Ranked Pairs elections build a preference relation among candidates. First, we compute a score for each pair of candidates, as per Eq. 1. Pairs with a positive score are called *positive majorities*. We consider each of these positive majority pairs in turn, from highest to lowest in score, and build a directed acyclic graph $\mathcal{G}$ containing a node for each candidate, and edges representing preference relationships. When we consider a pair, (i, j), we add an edge from i to j in $\mathcal{G}$, if there does not already exist a path from j to i. If such a path exists, this means that the preference $i \succ j$ is inconsistent with the stronger preference relationships already added to $\mathcal{G}$. We therefore ignore pair (i, j) and move on to the next pair. If ever there is a candidate w s.t. there is a path in $\mathcal{G}$ from w to all others, we declare w the winner.

Consider Elections 1 and 2 in Table 1. As Ranked Pairs elections, we assign the scores shown in Table 3 to each pair. For Election 1, the sorted positive majorities are (B,C), (A,B), and (A, C). We first add $B \succ C$, and then $A \succ B$, to $\mathcal{G}$. At this point, we have established that A is preferred to B, and by transitivity, that A is preferred to C. We can stop at this point, as we have established enough preference relationships to declare A as the winner, and cannot add a later preference, or generate a new transitive inference, that will be inconsistent with these relationships. In Election 2, the sorted list of positive majorities is (C,B), (C,A), and (A, B). After the first two preference relationships are added to $\mathcal{G}$, we have established that C is the winner. The Ranked Pairs winner always coincides with the Condorcet winner if one exists.

Consider Election 3 shown in Table 2. The ranked positive majorities are $(B, D), (A, B), (D, A), (B, C), (C, D)$, and (A, C). We add $B \succ D$ and then $A \succ B$ to $\mathcal{G}$. We ignore (D, A) since we have already inferred $A \succ D$ by transitivity. We then add $B \succ C$ to $\mathcal{G}$. We now have enough information to declare A the winner, as they are preferred to all other candidates through transitivity. Note that when treated as an IRV election, B is the winner.

To audit a Ranked Pairs election, we must check that all preference statements between pairs of candidates that were *ultimately used* to establish that

Table 3. Pairwise scores for pairs in Elections 1 and 2 of Table 1.

	Election 1	Election 2
$s(A, B)$	2700	1000
$s(B, A)$	−2700	−1000
$s(A, C)$	2300	−4000
$s(C, A)$	−2300	4000
$s(B, C)$	7300	−6000
$s(C, B)$	−7300	6000

the reported winner w won do in fact hold. Denote the set of preference relationships we commit to (i.e., that we add to $\mathcal{G}$) by the Ranked Pairs tabulation process up to the point at which the winning candidate is established as $\mathcal{M}$. In Election 1 of Table 1, the winner is established after the first two commits. Thus, $\mathcal{M} = \{B \succ C, A \succ B\}$. For Election 2 of Table 1, $\mathcal{M} = \{C \succ B, C \succ A\}$. For Election 3 in Table 2, $\mathcal{M} = \{B \succ D, A \succ B, B \succ C\}$.

Let $\mathcal{T}$ denote the set of *transitively inferred* preferences $i \succ j$ that were made in the tabulation process up to the point at which the winner is established. Each such inference is associated with a path in $\mathcal{G}$ from i to j. We denote the set of preferences that were used to form the transitive inference $i \succ j$ as basis($i \succ j$). This consists of all preference relationships along a path from i to j in $\mathcal{G}$. In Election 1 of Table 1, $\mathcal{T} = \{A \succ C\}$ and basis($A \succ C$) $= \{A \succ B, B \succ C\}$. For Election 3 in Table 2, $\mathcal{T} = \{A \succ D, A \succ C\}$. For these transitive inferences, basis($A \succ D$) $= \{A \succ B, B \succ D\}$, and basis($A \succ C$) $= \{A \succ B, B \succ C\}$.

We now define the assertions $\mathcal{A}$ required to audit a Ranked Pairs election. First, for each $w \succ j \in \mathcal{M}$, where w is the reported winner, we must check that $s(w, j) > 0$. This corresponds to checking that (w, j) is a positive majority, where $T(w \succ j) - T(j \succ w) > 0$. This can be achieved as outlined in Sect. 3.

Next, we must check that any transitive inference $w \succ c$, from $\mathcal{T}$, that we used to declare w the winner could not have been contradicted by a pair (c, w) that, in the true outcome, was actually stronger than one or more of the preferences used to infer $w \succ c$ in the reported outcome. In Example 1 of Table 1, this could occur if the pair (C, A) actually had a strength of 8000, for example, in place of −2300. If this were the case, $C \succ A$ should have been the first preference committed, ultimately leading to B being declared the winner in place of A.

Note that in Ranked Pairs elections where we have a Condorcet winner, we could simply verify that the reported winner was the Condorcet winner, irrespective of whether transitive inferences were used in the tabulation process. This would remove the need for an additional type of assertion, which we present in the next section. For most election instances we consider in our Results (Sect. 9), our Ranked Pairs auditing method reduces to checking the set of assertions for verifying that the reported winner is the Condorcet winner (see Sect. 3). This is because transitive inferences were not used to establish the winner in these cases.

However, checking these transitive inferences, when they are used, through the assertions developed in the next section, can sometimes be more efficient.

4.1   Assertions and Assorters for Transitive Inferences

For each transitive inference of the form $w \succ c \in \mathcal{T}$, we must check that:

$$s(i,j) > s(c,w), \quad \forall i \succ j \in \text{basis}(w \succ c).$$

We can translate this expression into the following:

$$T(i \succ j) - T(j \succ i) > T(c \succ w) - T(w \succ c)$$
$$T(i \succ j) + T(w \succ c) - T(c \succ w) - T(j \succ i) > 0 \tag{2}$$

We use the approach of Blom et al. [1] to construct an assorter for an assertion of the form shown in Eq. 2. We first form a proto-assorter

$$g(b) = b_1 + b_2 - b_3 - b_4,$$

where b is a ballot and each b_i is the number of votes the ballot b contributes to the category t_i, where $t_1 = T(i \succ j)$, $t_2 = T(w \succ c)$, $t_3 = T(c \succ w)$, and $t_4 = T(j \succ i)$. We then form an assorter, $h(b)$, for our assertion in Eq. 2 using Equation 2 of Blom et al. [1]. This equation states that $h(b) = \frac{g(b)-a}{-2a}$ where a denotes the minimum value of $g(b)$ for any b. In our case, $a = -2$, giving

$$h(b) = \frac{g(b) + 2}{4}.$$

The assorter h calculates the mean score $\bar{h}$ over the ballots b examined in an audit. By construction $\bar{h} > 1/2$ if and only if the assertion $s(i,j) > s(c,w)$ holds, to make it fit into the SHANGRLA testing framework [3].

4.2   Correctness of Audit Assertions

The assertions in the Ranked Pairs audit are then:

$$\mathcal{A} = \{s(w,c) > 0 : w \succ c \in \mathcal{M}\} \cup \tag{3}$$
$$\{s(i,j) > s(c,w) : i \succ j \in \text{basis}(w \succ c), w \succ c \in \mathcal{T}\}.$$

We now show that if these assertions are all verified to risk limit α then the declared winner is correct with risk limit α.

Theorem 1. *If the declared winner w is not the correct winner of a Ranked Pairs election, then the probability that an audit verifies all the assertions in $\mathcal{A}$ is at most α, where α is the risk limit of the audit of each individual assertion.*

Proof. Let $\mathcal{M}$ be the set of ranked pairs committed to $\mathcal{G}$ in the reported election, $\mathcal{T}$ the transitively inferred preferences from $\mathcal{M}$. Let $\mathcal{M}'$ be the set of ranked pairs committed to $\mathcal{G}$ for the actual election results, and $\mathcal{T}'$ the transitively inferred preferences from $\mathcal{M}'$. Assume that $w' \neq w$ is the actual winner.

Suppose that $w \succ w' \in \mathcal{T}$, so we audit $s(i,j) > s(w',w)$ for all $i \succ j \in basis(w \succ w')$. If all of these facts were correct then the ranked pair voting algorithm (on the true counts) would find $w \succ w'$ by transitive closure. Contradiction. So at least one of them must not hold, and the audit will accept it with probability at most α.

Otherwise $w \succ w' \in \mathcal{M}$. If $s(w',w) > 0$ then this contradicts the audited assertion, which will be accepted with probability at most α. So suppose $s(w',w) < 0$. Since w' beats w there is a w'' such that $w' \succ w'' \in \mathcal{T}'$ and $w'' \succ w' \in \mathcal{M}'$ and $s(w'',w) > s(w,w') > 0$. Now in the reported election either $w \succ w'' \in \mathcal{M}$ in which case the assertion $s(w,w'') > 0$ will be accepted with probability at most α, or $w \succ w'' \in \mathcal{T}$ and we use the argument of the previous paragraph to show that the audit will accept with probability at most α. $\square$

Consider Election 3 shown in Table 2. In the Ranked Pairs election we established A as the winner using $\mathcal{M} = \{B \succ D, A \succ B, B \succ C\}$ and $\mathcal{T} = \{A \succ D, A \succ C\}$, where $basis(A \succ D) = \{A \succ B, B \succ D\}$ and $basis(A \succ C) = \{A \succ B, B \succ C\}$. So the assertions we need to verify are $s(A,B) > 0$; $s(A,B) > s(D,A)$ and $s(B,D) > s(D,A)$; and $s(A,B) > s(C,A)$ and $s(B,C) > s(C,A)$.

Note that Tideman describes a particular approach for resolving ties between sorted majorities [4]. If the choice of which majority to process first, among those that tie, changes the ultimate winner then a full manual hand count will be required. The manner in which such ties are resolved can have an impact on the overall set of assertions formed. For example, consider a case where we have three positive majorities (A, B), (A, C), and (B, C) in a three-candidate election. The first is the strongest, while the latter two tie. Of the latter two, if we choose to process (A, C) first, then our audit will form two assertions: $s(A,B) > 0$ and $s(A,C) > 0$. If we choose to process (B, C) first then we will form the assertions: $s(A,B) > 0$, $s(A,B) > s(C,A)$ and $s(B,C) > s(C,A)$.

5 RLAs for Minimax Elections

In a Minimax election, a pairwise score is computed for each pair of candidates, c and c', denoted $ms(c,c')$. There are variations on how this score can be defined[3]. One method, denoted *margins*, is defined by:

$$ms(c,c') = T(c \succ c') - T(c' \succ c).$$

This score computation method is equivalent to that used in Ranked Pairs. We use this approach when forming assertions to audit Minimax elections. Variations

---

[3] https://en.wikipedia.org/wiki/Minimax_Condorcet_method, accessed 14 Mar 2023.

could be used instead, however their equations must be linear to be used within the assertion-assorter framework of Blom et al. [1].

If there is a Condorcet winner, then this candidate wins. Suppose it is candidate w, then we have $ms(w, c) > 0$ for all $c \in \mathcal{C} \setminus \{w\}$ when either the margins or winning votes scoring method is used. Otherwise, the winning candidate is the one with the smallest loss in pairwise contests with each other candidate.

Consider the example elections in Table 1. Table 3 records the pairwise scores for each pair of candidates. In both of our example elections, candidate A is the Condorcet winner. In Election 1, $ms(A, B) = 2700$ and $ms(A, C) = 2300$. In Election 2, $ms(C, B) = 6000$ and $ms(C, A) = 4000$.

In the case where we have a Condorcet winner w under Minimax, we simply need to audit that $ms(w, c) > 0$ for all $c \in \mathcal{C} \setminus \{w\}$, as described in Sect. 3.

In the case where we do not have a Condorcet winner, we compute each candidate c's largest margin of loss, $LL(c)$. The candidate c with the smallest $LL(c)$ is the winner. Consider a case with the pairwise scores shown below (left). In this example, we have the largest losses shown on the right. In this case, candidate B has the smallest largest loss and is the winner.

$$ms(A, B) = 2000 \qquad LL(A) = 8000$$
$$ms(B, C) = 5000 \qquad LL(B) = 2000$$
$$ms(C, A) = 8000 \qquad LL(C) = 5000$$

To audit a Minimax election, in the event that a Condorcet winner does not exist, we can first verify which pairwise defeats represent the strongest defeat for each candidate. In the example above, we could show that $A \succ B$ is the strongest defeat of B by showing that $ms(A, B) > ms(c, B)$ for all $c \in \mathcal{C} \setminus \{A\}$. We then need to show that $ms(A, B)$ is less than the score of the strongest defeat of each other candidate. In the example above, this reduces to checking that $ms(B, C) > ms(A, B)$ and $ms(C, A) > ms(A, B)$.

6 Smith

The *Smith set* in an election refers to the smallest set of candidates S such that every candidate in S defeats every candidate outside of S in a pairwise contest. For all $c \in S$ and $c' \in \mathcal{C} \setminus S$, we have $T(c \succ c') > T(c' \succ c)$. The Smith set always exists and is well defined[4]. If a Condorcet winner exists, they will be the sole member of this set. If the Smith set contains more than one candidate, IRV or Minimax can be used to select a single winner from that set. Alternatively, all candidates in the Smith set can be viewed as winners (if appropriate).

If we have a Condorcet winner, w, an audit would proceed by checking that w defeats all other candidates in a pairwise contest. Otherwise, we need to first check that the reported Smith set is correct. To do so, we first show that $T(c \succ c') > T(c' \succ c)$ for all $c \in S, c' \notin S$. Next, we must show that removing any one

---
[4] https://en.wikipedia.org/wiki/Smith_set, accessed 14 Mar 2023.

candidate from our set would violate this condition: $\forall c \in S, \exists c' \in S, T(c \succ c') > T(c' \succ c)$. In other words, that each candidate in the set is defeated by another candidate in the set. We then audit the resulting Minimax or IRV election over S. It may be that a candidate in the Smith set defeats multiple candidates in the set. For the purposes of auditing, we choose to check the defeat with the largest margin. If there are candidates in the Smith set that tie (i.e., $T(c \succ c') = T(c' \succ c)$ for some $c, c' \in S$), then a full manual count is required.

7   Kemeny-Young

Under Kemeny-Young, we start by computing pairwise scores for each pair of candidates (c, c'), $T(c \succ c')$. We then imagine all possible complete orders (rankings) among the candidates in the election. We assign a score to each ranking using the pairwise scores we have just computed. Consider the ranking $[A, B, C]$ in an election with candidates A, B and C. The ranking score is equal to $T(A \succ B) + T(A \succ C) + T(B \succ C)$. For each candidate c that appears above another c' in a ranking, we add $T(c \succ c')$ to the ranking score. The winning candidate is the candidate ranked first in the highest scoring ranking.

We can view each ranking π as an entity with a tally, $T(\pi)$. The tally for the ranking $\pi = [A, B, C]$, for example, is $T(\pi) = T(A \succ B) + T(A \succ C) + T(B \succ C)$. Let π_r denote the reported highest scoring ranking. For elections with a very small number of candidates, we can form an audit in which we check that $T(\pi_r) > T(\pi')$ for every possible ranking π' with a different first-ranked candidate to π_r. For an election with k candidates, an audit with $(k-1)!$ assertions is formed. A 13 candidate election, however, will require 4.8×10^8 assertions!

While it is technically possible to form a RLA that is not a full recount for a Kemeny-Young election, all election instances we consider in this paper have too many candidates for this method to be practical. We are not aware of any other methods for generating efficient RLAs for Kemeny-Young elections.

8   Other Condorcet Methods

Some other Condorcet methods, such as Schulze and Copeland, are not auditable by the assertion-assorter framework as it stands. To form a RLA using this framework, we need to be able to check that the reported winner won through a series of comparisons over sums of ballots. Under both the Schulze and Copeland methods, we use such comparisons to perform a meta-level reasoning step.

Under Copeland, for example, we compute each candidate c's *Copeland score* $CS(c)$, which is the number of candidates c' for which $T(c \succ c') > T(c' \succ c)$ plus a half times the number of candidates c' for which $T(c \succ c') = T(c' \succ c)$. We then elect the candidate with the highest Copeland score.

Under the Schulze method, we assign scores to each pair of candidates using the winning votes method as per Minimax (see Sect. 5). Consider a graph where for each pair of candidates, (c, c'), we have a directed edge from c to c' with a weight equal to $s(c, c')$. We define the strength of a path in this graph between candidates c and c' as the weight of the weakest link along this path. For each pair of candidates, we compute the strength of the strongest path between the pair. Where there are multiple paths between the candidates, the strongest path is the one with the largest weight on its weakest link. If there is no path, the strength of their strongest path is set to zero. Let us denote the strength of the strongest path between c and c' as $p(c, c')$. We say that $c \succ c'$ if $p(c, c') > p(c', c)$. The winner is the candidate w for which $w \succ c$ for all $c \in \mathcal{C} \setminus \{w\}$.

9   Results

We consider the set of IRV elections conducted in the 2015 and 2019 New South Wales (NSW) Legislative Assembly (lower house) elections, and a number of US-based IRV elections conducted between 2007 and 2010. For each instance, we reinterpret it as Condorcet, Ranked Pairs, Minimax and Smith elections. We report the estimated difficulty of conducting a comparison RLA for each instance when viewed as an IRV election or one of the alternative Condorcet methods. We assume a risk limit of 5%, and an error rate of 0.002. RAIRE [2] is used to generate assertions for auditing each instance as an IRV election. Note that the intention behind the reporting of these results is not to recommend one type of election over others, but to demonstrate the practicality, or lack thereof, of the auditing methods we have proposed.

We estimate the sample size (ASN) required to audit a set of assertions $\mathcal{A}$, with a chosen SHANGRLA risk function (we used Kaplan-Kolmogorov), through simulation. For each assertion $a \in \mathcal{A}$, we performed 2000 simulations in which we randomly distributed errors across the population of auditable ballots, and determined how many ballots needed to be sampled for the risk to fall below the desired threshold. We took the median of the resulting sample sizes to compute an anticipated sample size for the assertion. We took the largest of these sample sizes, across $\mathcal{A}$, as the expected sample size required for the audit. We used this process to estimate required sample sizes for all election types.

Across all the IRV instances we considered, the same winner was declared when the ballots were tabulated according to the rules of IRV, Condorcet, and Ranked Pairs. All instances have a Condorcet winner. In all but one election—a US instance, Pierce County Executive 2008—the estimated difficulty of auditing each election as either a Ranked Pairs or Condorcet election was the same. For Pierce County Executive 2008, checking each $T(w \succ c) - T(c \succ w) > 0$ assertion requires an estimated 627 ballot polls, the same ASN as the IRV audit. When audited as a Ranked Pairs election, an estimated 507 ballot polls are required. This is because in the Ranked Pairs election we are able to declare a winner before committing to all (w, c) pairs, through the use of a transitive inference. This means that in the audit, we can avoid checking one of the $w \succ c$ comparisons and instead check some easier assertions to verify the transitive inference used.

Table 4 reports the expected sample sizes required to audit selected elections that took place in the 2015–19 NSW Legislative Assembly elections as either IRV, Condorcet, or Ranked Pairs. Table 5 reports the same for selected US instances.

Table 4. Estimated sample sizes, expressed as both a number of ballots and percentage of the total ballots cast, required to audit selected IRV elections from the 2015–19 NSW Legislative Council elections (as IRV using RAIRE, Ranked Pairs [RP], and Condorcet [CDT]). Instances where the ASN for the audits across the different election types are substantially different are in bold. All instances have a Condorcet winner.

INSTANCE	RAIRE IRV		RP		CDT	
	ASN	(%)	ASN	(%)	ASN	(%)
2015						
Albury	31	0.06%	28	0.06%	28	0.06%
Auburn	74	0.15%	74	0.15%	74	0.15%
Ballina	155	0.32%	137	0.28%	137	0.28%
Balmain	99	0.20%	99	0.20%	99	0.20%
Clarence	42	0.09%	42	0.09%	42	0.09%
Coffs Harbour	32	0.07%	27	0.06%	27	0.06%
Coogee	137	0.29%	137	0.29%	137	0.29%
East Hills	1309	2.60%	1309	2.60%	1309	2.60%
Gosford	3889	7.70%	3889	7.70%	3889	7.70%
Granville	207	0.43%	207	0.43%	207	0.43%
Lismore	**1138**	**2.35%**	**4689**	**9.70%**	**4689**	**9.70%**
Manly	15	0.03%	15	0.03%	15	0.03%
Maroubra	35	0.07%	35	0.07%	35	0.07%
Monaro	152	0.32%	152	0.32%	152	0.32%
Mount Druitt	26	0.05%	26	0.05%	26	0.05%
Strathfield	227	0.46%	227	0.46%	227	0.46%
Summer Hill	45	0.09%	45	0.09%	45	0.09%
Sydney	54	0.12%	54	0.12%	54	0.12%
Tamworth	41	0.08%	38	0.08%	38	0.08%
The Entrance	1596	3.18%	1596	3.18%	1596	3.18%
2019						
Albury	25	0.05%	25	0.05%	25	0.05%
Auburn	45	0.09%	45	0.09%	45	0.09%
Ballina	98	0.19%	97	0.19%	97	0.19%
Balmain	44	0.09%	44	0.09%	44	0.09%
Coogee	248	0.52%	248	0.52%	248	0.52%
Cronulla	20	0.04%	19	0.04%	19	0.04%
Drummoyne	27	0.05%	25	0.05%	25	0.05%
Dubbo	234	0.46%	234	0.46%	234	0.46%
East Hills	1173	2.30%	1173	2.30%	1173	2.30%
Hawkesbury	25	0.05%	25	0.05%	25	0.05%
Holsworthy	130	0.25%	130	0.25%	130	0.25%
Keira	19	0.04%	19	0.04%	19	0.04%
Kogarah	236	0.49%	236	0.49%	236	0.49%
Lismore	**1363**	**2.71%**	**313**	**0.62%**	**313**	**0.62%**
Mulgoa	34	0.06%	34	0.06%	34	0.06%
Murray	129	0.26%	129	0.26%	129	0.26%
Newcastle	25	0.05%	24	0.05%	24	0.05%
Oxley	34	0.07%	28	0.06%	28	0.06%
Penrith	333	0.64%	333	0.64%	333	0.64%

Instances for which the expected sample sizes differed substantially in the different contexts are in bold. In general, there was no substantial difference in these expected sample sizes when auditing an instance as an IRV, Condorcet, or Ranked Pairs election.

Table 5. Estimated sample sizes, expressed as a number of ballots and percentage of the total ballots cast, required to audit a set of US IRV elections (as IRV using RAIRE, Ranked Pairs [RP], and Condorcet [CDT]). Instances where the ASNs are substantially different across election types are in bold. CC, CA, and CE denote City Council, County Assessor, and County Executive. All instances have a Condorcet winner.

INSTANCE	RAIRE IRV		RP		CDT	
	ASN	(%)	ASN	(%)	ASN	(%)
Aspen 2009 CC	249	10%	249	10%	249	10%
Aspen 2009 Mayor	100	3.96%	142	5.60%	142	5.60%
Berkeley 2010 D1 CC	18	0.32%	16	0.28%	16	0.28%
Berkeley 2010 D4 CC	31	0.65%	31	0.65%	31	0.65%
Berkeley 2010 D7 CC	40	0.96%	40	0.96%	40	0.96%
Berkeley 2010 D8 CC	17	0.37%	17	0.37%	17	0.37%
Oakland 2010 D4 CC	33	0.16%	31	0.15%	31	0.15%
Oakland 2010 D6 CC	18	0.14%	16	0.12%	16	0.12%
Oakland 2010 Mayor	499	0.42%	499	0.42%	499	0.42%
Pierce 2008 CC	70	0.18%	70	0.18%	70	0.18%
Pierce 2008 CA	1153	0.44%	1153	0.44%	1153	0.44%
Pierce 2008 CA	64	0.04%	64	0.04%	64	0.04%
Pierce 2008 CE	**624**	**0.21%**	**507**	**0.17%**	**624**	**0.21%**
San Francisco Mayor 2007	10	0.01%	9	0.01%	9	0.01%

9.1 IRV vs Ranked Pairs

In a small number of cases—Lismore (NSW) in 2015 and 2019; and Pierce County Executive (2008)—there was a substantial difference in the auditing difficulty in the two contexts. For Lismore (2015), we expect to audit the IRV election with a sample size of 1138 ballots, and the Ranked Pairs with 4689 ballots. For Lismore (2019), the situation is reversed, with an estimated 313 ballots required to audit the Ranked Pairs election and 1363 ballots for the IRV. In the Pierce County Executive (2008) election, we expect to sample 624 ballots for the IRV election and 507 ballots for the Ranked Pairs. All three of these instances share a common feature: when tabulated as an IRV election, the candidate who is eliminated in the last round of elimination determines the winner.

In Lismore (2015) [1138 ballots IRV vs 4689 ballots Ranked Pairs], the Nationals (NAT) candidate wins. In the last round of elimination, this candidate, alongside a Green (GRN) and a Country Labor (CLP) remain standing.

Their tallies at this stage are 20567, 12771 and 12357 votes, respectively. Given the nature of Australian politics, we would expect the majority of ballots sitting with the GRN at this stage to flow on to the CLP, if they were eliminated. Conversely, if the CLP were eliminated, we would expect ballots to flow on to both the NAT and GRN candidates. In this case, the CLP is eliminated, and we are left with the NAT on 21660 votes and the GRN on 19310. In the Ranked Pairs variation, the most difficult assertion to check is that $s(NAT, CLP) > 0$, which equates to $T(NAT \succ CLP) - T(CLP \succ NAT) > 0$. The difference in these tallies is just 186 votes. The most difficult assertion RAIRE has to check is that the GRN is not eliminated before the CLP in the context where just they and the NAT remain. Here, the tallies of the GRN and CLP differ by 414 votes.

In Lismore (2019) [1363 ballots IRV vs 313 ballots Ranked Pairs], the CLP candidate wins. In the last round of elimination, we have the CLP on 12860 votes, the GRN on 12500, and the NAT on 20094. In this case, the GRN is eliminated leaving the NAT on 20712 votes, and the CLP on 21862. In the Ranked Pairs variation, the smallest tally difference we need to check is that $T(CLP \succ NAT) - T(NAT \succ CLP) > 0$. In the reported results, the LHS equals 1150 votes. Checking that $T(NAT \succ GRN) - T(GRN \succ NAT) > 0$ is much simpler, with the LHS equal to 15494 votes. RAIRE has to show that the CLP cannot be eliminated before the GRN in that last round elimination. This is more difficult, with a difference of only 360 votes separating the two.

9.2   Elections Without a Condorcet Winner

All instances in Table 4 and Table 5 have a Condorcet winner. We have found several ranked vote datasets that, when treated as a single-winner election, do not have a Condorcet winner. Table 6 reports the estimated sample sizes required to audit these instances as IRV (using RAIRE), Ranked Pairs, Minimax, and Smith. RAIRE did not terminate in a reasonable time frame (24 h) in 6/9 of these instances. RAIRE relies on being able to prune large portions of the space of alternate election outcomes through carefully chosen assertions. In these instances, RAIRE was unable to do this. The number of votes for each ballot signature in the Preflib instances were multiplied by 1000 to form larger elections.

For the Smith method, Table 6 reports the difficulty of both checking the correctness of the Smith set, and auditing the whole election using either Minimax or IRV to find a winner from the Smith set. For the Byron instance, with 32 candidates, the estimated sample size required to verify the correctness of the Smith set is 844 ballots (4.8% of the total ballots cast). The first stage of verifying the Smith set—checking that each candidate in the set defeats all candidates outside the set—requires 112 assertions. The second stage—checking that each candidate within the Smith set defeats another candidate in the set—requires 4 assertions. Verifying the winner from the Smith set using IRV requires an estimated sample size of 327 ballots (1.84%). The ASN of the overall audit, with IRV used to select the winner, is 844 ballots. With Minimax used to select the overall winner, however, a full manual count is required.

Table 6. Estimated sample sizes, expressed as a number of ballots and percentage of the total ballots cast, required to audit a set of ranked vote election instances without a Condorcet winner (as IRV using RAIRE, Ranked Pairs, Minimax [MM], and Smith). Instances where the ASN for the audits are substantially different across election types are in bold. A '–' denotes that assertions could not be found within 24 h by the associated algorithm, and '∞' denotes that a full manual hand count is required. The overall ASN for each Smith RLA is the maximum of the cost of verifying the Smith set and verifying the winner from the Smith set using either Mimimax of IRV.

INSTANCE	RAIRE IRV	RP	MM	SMITH		
				VERIFY SS	MINIMAX	IRV
	ASN (%)	ASN (%)	ASN (%)	ASN (%)	ASN (%)	ASN (%)
2021 NSW Local Government Elections (originally STV)						
Byron	–	∞	∞	844 4.8%	∞	327 1.84%
Leeton	–	1219 2%	∞	∞	∞	∞
Parkes	–	∞	∞	∞	∞	∞
Yass Valley	–	1624 1.7%	∞	∞	∞	∞
Preflib Election Data						
ED-7-5.soi	–	2828 2.7%	2828 2.7%	∞	∞	∞
ED-7-19.soi	∞	563 0.56%	563 0.56%	∞	∞	∞
ED-10-26.soi	56 0.35%	113 0.71%	∞	∞	∞	∞
ED-10-47.soi	120 0.71%	∞	∞	120 0.71%	∞	59 0.35%
ED-34-1.soi	–	4577 1.2%	∞	∞	∞	∞

Across the ED instances, with the exception of ED-10-47, there are ties present between candidates in the Smith set, and a full manual count is required. Across the Leeton, Parkes, and Yass Valley instances, the second stage of verifying the correctness of the Smith set involves at least one comparison with a very small margin. For the ED-10-47 instance, there are tied winners under Minimax when selecting the winner from the Smith set.

10   Conclusion

We have presented methods for generating assertions sufficient for conducting RLAs for several Condorcet methods, including Ranked Pairs. We have found that auditing a ranked vote election as IRV or Ranked Pairs requires similar estimated sample sizes, in general. Most Ranked Pairs audits reduce to checking that the reported winner is the Condorcet winner. Where the election does not have a Condorcet winner, it appears that auditing the instance as a Ranked Pairs election is generally more practical than if it were an IRV election. We have considered auditing methods for other Condorcet methods, such as Minimax, Smith, and Kemeny-Young, however these were generally not practical.

References

1. Blom, M., et al.: Assertion-based approaches to auditing complex elections, with application to party-list proportional elections. In: Krimmer, R., et al. (eds.) E-Vote-ID 2021. LNCS, vol. 12900, pp. 47–62. Springer, Cham (2021). https://doi.org/10.1007/978-3-030-86942-7_4, Preprint: https://arxiv.org/abs/2107.11903arXiv:2107.11903
2. Blom, M., Stuckey, P.J., Teague, V.: RAIRE: risk-limiting audits for IRV elections (2019). https://arxiv.org/abs/1903.08804arXiv:1903.08804
3. Stark, P.B.: Sets of half-average nulls generate risk-limiting audits: SHANGRLA. In: Bernhard, M., et al. (eds.) FC 2020. LNCS, vol. 12063, pp. 319–336. Springer, Cham (2020). https://doi.org/10.1007/978-3-030-54455-3_23, Preprint: https://arxiv.org/abs/1911.10035arXiv:1911.10035
4. Tideman, T.N.: Independence of clones as a criterion for voting rules. Soc. Choice Welf. **4**(3), 185–206 (1987)

COBRA: Comparison-Optimal Betting
for Risk-Limiting Audits

Jacob V. Spertus[⊠]

Department of Statistics, University of California, Berkeley, Berkeley, USA
jakespertus@berkeley.edu

Abstract. Risk-limiting audits (RLAs) can provide routine, affirmative evidence that reported election outcomes are correct by checking a random sample of cast ballots. An *efficient* RLA requires checking relatively few ballots. Here we construct highly efficient RLAs by optimizing supermartingale tuning parameters—*bets*—for ballot-level comparison audits. The exactly optimal bets depend on the true rate of errors in cast-vote records (CVRs)—digital receipts detailing how machines tabulated each ballot. We evaluate theoretical and simulated workloads for audits of contests with a range of diluted margins and CVR error rates. Compared to bets recommended in past work, using these optimal bets can dramatically reduce expected workloads—by 93% on average over our simulated audits. Because the exactly optimal bets are unknown in practice, we offer some strategies for approximating them. As with the ballot-polling RLAs described in ALPHA and RiLACs, adapting bets to previously sampled data or diversifying them over a range of suspected error rates can lead to substantially more efficient audits than fixing bets to *a priori* values, especially when those values are far from correct. We sketch extensions to other designs and social choice functions, and conclude with some recommendations for real-world comparison audits.

Keywords: risk-limiting audit · election integrity · comparison audit · nonparametric testing · betting martingale

1 Introduction

Machines count votes in most American elections, and (reported) election winners are declared on the basis of these machine tallies. Voting machines are vulnerable to bugs and deliberate malfeasance, which may undermine public trust in the accuracy of reported election results. To counter this threat, risk-limiting audits (RLAs) can provide routine, statistically rigorous evidence that reported election outcomes are correct—that reported winners really won—by manually checking a demonstrably secure ballot trail [4]. RLAs have a user-specified maximum chance—the *risk limit*—of certifying a wrong reported outcome, and will never overturn a correct reported outcome. They can also be significantly more *efficient* than full hand counts, requiring fewer manual tabulations to verify a correct reported outcome and reducing costs to jurisdictions.

© International Financial Cryptography Association 2024
A. Essex et al. (Eds.): FC 2023 Workshops, LNCS 13953, pp. 95–109, 2024.
https://doi.org/10.1007/978-3-031-48806-1_7

There are various ways to design RLAs. Data can be sampled as batches of ballots (i.e. precincts or machines) or as individual ballot cards (hereafter, we refer to cards simply as "ballots"). Sampling individual ballots is more statistically efficient than sampling batches. In a *polling audit*, sampled ballots are checked directly without reference to machine interpretations. Ballot-polling audits sample and check individual ballots. In a *comparison audit*, manual interpretations of ballots are compared to their machine interpretations. Ballot-level comparison audits check each sampled ballot against a corresponding *cast vote record* (CVR)—a digital receipt detailing how the machine tallied the ballot. Not all voting machines can produce CVRs, but ballot-level comparison audits are the most efficient type of RLA.

Ideally, RLAs will simultaneously check multiple (potentially all) contests within a jurisdiction—a task made considerably more efficient by targeting samples with card-style data [2]. Card-style data are most feasibly derived from CVRs, in which case each contest can be audited using ballot-level comparison. Because the overall workload of the audit is aggregated across contests, optimizing the efficiency for individual contests can provide substantial workload reductions for the audit as a whole. Thus, constructing sharper ballot-level comparison audits is paramount to the implementation of real-world RLAs auditing multiple contests.

The earliest RLAs were formulated for batch-level comparison audits, which are analogous to historical, statutory audits [6]. Subsequently, the maximum across contest relative overstatement (MACRO) was used for comparison RLAs [5,7–9], but its efficiency suffered from conservatively pooling observed errors across candidates and contest. SHANGRLA [10] unified RLAs as hypotheses about means of lists of bounded numbers and provided sharper methods for batch and ballot-level comparisons. Each null hypothesis tested in a SHANGRLA-style RLA posits that the mean of a bounded list of *assorters* is less than $1/2$. If all the nulls are declared false at risk limit α, the audit can stop. Any valid test for the mean of a bounded finite population can be used to test these hypotheses, allowing RLAs to use a wide range of *risk-measuring functions*.

Betting supermartingales (BSMs)—described in Waudby-Smith et al. [14] and Stark [11]—provide a particularly useful class of risk-measuring functions. BSMs are *sequentially valid*, allowing auditors to update and check the measured risk after each sampled ballot while maintaining the risk limit. They can be seen as generalizations of risk-measuring functions used in earlier RLAs, including Kaplan-Markov, Kaplan-Kolmogorov, and related methods [7,10]. They have tuning parameters λ_i called *bets*, which play an important role in determining the efficiency of the RLA. Previous papers using BSMs for RLAs have focused on setting λ_i for efficient ballot-polling audits; betting for comparison audits has been treated as essentially analogous [11,14]. However, as we will show, comparison audits are efficient with much larger bets than are optimal for ballot-polling.

This paper details how to set BSM bets λ_i for efficient ballot-level comparison audits, focusing on audits of plurality contests. Section 2 reviews SHANGRLA notation and the use of BSMs as risk-measuring functions. Section 3 derives optimal "oracle" bets under the Kelly criterion [3], which assumes knowledge of true error rates in the CVRs. In reality, these error rates are unknown, but the oracle bets are useful in constructing practical betting strategies, which plug in estimates of the true rates. Section 4 presents three such strategies: guessing the error rates *a priori*, using past data to estimate the rates adaptively, or positing a distribution of likely rates and diversifying bets over that distribution. Section 5 presents two simulation studies: one comparing the oracle strategy derived in Waudby-Smith et al. [14] for ballot-polling against our comparison-optimal strategy, and one comparing practical strategies against one another. Section 6 sketches some extensions to betting while sampling without replacement and to social choice functions beyond plurality. Section 7 concludes with a brief discussion and recommendations for practice.

2 Notation

2.1 Population and Parameters

Following SHANGRLA [10] notation, let $\{c_i\}_{i=1}^N$ denote the CVRs, $\{b_i\}_{i=1}^N$ denote the true ballots, and $A()$ be an *assorter* mapping CVRs or ballots into $[0, u]$. We will assume we are auditing a plurality contest, in which case $u := 1$, $A(b_i) := 1$ if the ballot shows a vote for the reported winner, $A(b_i) := 1/2$ if it shows an undervote or vote for a candidate not currently under audit, and $A(b_i) := 0$ if it shows a vote for the reported loser. The *overstatement* for ballot i is $\omega_i := A(c_i) - A(b_i)$. $\bar{A}^c := N^{-1} \sum_{i=1}^N A(c_i)$ is the average of the assorters computed on the CVRs. Finally, the comparison audit population is comprised of *overstatement assorters* $x_i := (1 - \omega_i)/(2 - v)$, where $v := 2\bar{A}^c - 1$ is the *diluted margin*: the difference in votes for the reported winner and reported loser, divided by the total number of ballots cast.

Let $\bar{x} := N^{-1} \sum_{i=1}^N x_i$ be the average of the comparison audit population and $\bar{A}^b := N^{-1} \sum_{i=1}^N A(b_i)$ be the average of the assorters applied to ballots. Section 3.2 of Stark [10] establishes the relations

$$\text{reported outcome is correct} \iff \bar{A}^b > 1/2 \iff \bar{x} > 1/2.$$

As a result, rejecting the *complementary null*

$$H_0 : \bar{x} \leq 1/2 \tag{1}$$

at risk limit α provides strong evidence that the reported outcome is correct.

Throughout this paper, we ignore *understatement* errors—those in favor of the reported winner with $\omega_i < 0$. Understatements help the audit end sooner, but will generally have little effect on the optimal bets. We comment on this choice further in Sect. 7. With this simplification, overstatement assorters comprise a list of numbers $\{x_i\}_{i=1}^N \in \{0, a/2, a\}^N$ where $a := (2 - v)^{-1} > 1/2$ corresponds to the value on correct CVRs, $a/2$ corresponds to 1-vote overstatements, and 0 corresponds to 2-vote overstatements. This population is parameterized by 3 fractions:

- $p_0 := \#\{x_i = a\}/N$ is the rate of correct CVRs.
- $p_1 := \#\{x_i = a/2\}/N$ is the rate of 1-vote overstatements.
- $p_2 := \#\{x_i = 0\}/N$ is the rate of 2-vote overstatements.

The population mean can be written $\bar{x} = ap_0 + (a/2)p_1$.

2.2   Audit Data

Ballots may be drawn by sequential simple random sampling with or without replacement, but we first focus on the with replacement case for simplicity. Implications for sampling without replacement are discussed in Sect. 6. We have a sequence of samples $X_1, X_2, \ldots \overset{\text{iid}}{\sim} F$, where F is a three-point distribution with mass p_0 at a, p_1 at $a/2$, and p_2 at 0.

2.3   Risk Measurement via Betting Supermartingales

Let $T_i := 1 + \lambda_i(X_i - 1/2)$ where $\lambda_i \in [0,2]$ is a freely-chosen tuning parameter that may depend on past samples $X_1, \ldots, X_{i-1}$. Define $M_0 := 1$ and

$$M_t := \prod_{i=1}^{t} T_i = \prod_{i=1}^{t}[1 + \lambda_i(X_i - 1/2)].$$

M_t is a *betting supermartingale* (BSM) for any *bets* $\lambda_i \in [0,2]$ whenever (1) holds because

$$\bar{x} \le 1/2 \implies \mathbb{E}[X_i' \mid X_{i-1}, \ldots, X_1] \le 1/2 \implies \mathbb{E}[M_t \mid X_{t-1}, \ldots, X_1] \le M_{t-1}$$

where the first implication comes from simple random sampling with replacement.

Intuitively, M_t can be thought of as the wealth accumulated by a gambler who starts with 1 unit of capital at time $t = 0$ and at time $t = i$ stakes proportion λ_i of their current capital on observing $X_i > 1/2$. If $\lambda_i = 0$, they stake nothing and can neither gain nor lose capital on round i. If $\lambda_i = 2$, they stake everything and can lose all their capital if $X_i = 0$. For any bets that depend only on past data, the gambler cannot expect to accumulate wealth by betting that $X_i > 1/2$ when (1) is true. Ville's inequality [12] then guarantees that it is unlikely that the gambler's wealth ever becomes large:

$$\mathbb{P}(\exists\, t \in \mathbb{N} : M_t \ge 1/\alpha) \le \alpha.$$

For example, when (1) holds, the probability that the gambler ever accumulates more than 20 units of wealth is no more than 0.05.

As a matter of risk measurement, Ville's inequality implies that the truncated reciprocal $P_t := \min\{1, 1/M_t\}$ is a sequentially-valid P-value for the complementary null in the sense that $\mathbb{P}(\exists\, t \in \mathbb{N} : P_t \le \alpha) \le \alpha$ when $\bar{x} \le 1/2$ for any risk limit $\alpha \in (0,1)$. More details on BSMs are given in Waudby-Smith and Ramdas [13] Waudby-Smith et al. [14] and Stark [11]. To obtain an efficient RLA, we would like to make M_t as large as possible (P_t as small as possible) when $\bar{x} > 1/2$.

3   Oracle Betting

We begin by deriving "oracle" bets by assuming we can access the true error rates p_0, p_1, and p_2 and optimizing the expected growth of the logarithm of the martingale under these rates. We call these oracle bets because they are exactly optimal for this objective, but depend on unknown parameters and hence cannot be implemented in practice. However, oracle bets can be approximated to run efficient comparison audits with the practical betting strategies discussed in Sect. 4.

3.1   Error-Free CVRs

In the simple case where there is no error at all in the CVRs, $p_0 = 1$ and $x_i = \bar{x} = a$ for all i. When computing the BSM, it doesn't matter which ballot is drawn:

$$T_i = 1 + \lambda_i(a - 1/2) \text{ and } M_t = [1 + \lambda_i(a - 1/2)]^t.$$

Because $(a - 1/2) > 0$, the best strategy is to bet as aggressively as possible, setting $\lambda_i := 2$. Under such a bet, $M_t = (2a)^t$. Setting this equal to $1/\alpha$ yields the stopping time:

$$t_{\text{stop}} = \frac{\log(1/\alpha)}{\log(2a)} = \frac{-\log(\alpha)}{\log(2) - \log(2 - v)} \tag{2}$$

where v is the diluted margin. Ignoring understatement errors, (2) is a deterministic lower bound on the sample size of a comparison audit when risk is measured by a BSM. Figure 1 plots this as a function of the diluted margin and risk limit.

3.2   Betting with CVR Error

Usually CVRs will have at least some errors, and maximal bets are far from ideal when they do. We now show why this is true before deriving an alternative oracle strategy. In general,

$$T_i = \begin{cases} 1 + \lambda_i(a - 1/2) & \text{with probability } p_0 \\ 1 + \lambda_i(a/2 - 1/2) & \text{with probability } p_1 \\ 1 - \lambda_i/2 & \text{with probability } p_2. \end{cases}$$

If we fix $\lambda_i := \lambda$ and try to maximize M_n by maximizing the expected value of each T_i, we find $\mathbb{E}_F[T_i] = p_0[1 + \lambda(a - 1/2)] + p_1[1 - \lambda(1 - a)/2] + p_2[1 - \lambda/2] = 1 + (ap_0 + \frac{a}{2}p_1 - 1/2)\lambda$. This is linear with a positive coefficient on λ, since $ap_0 + \frac{a}{2}p_1 = \bar{x} > 1/2$ under any alternative. Therefore, the best strategy seems to be to set $\lambda := 2$ as before. However, unless $p_2 = 0$, M_t will eventually "go broke" with probability 1: $T_i = 0$ if a 0 is drawn while the bet is maximal. Then $M_t = 0$ for all future times and we cannot reject at any risk limit α. In this case, we say the audit *stalls*: it must proceed to a full hand count to confirm the reported winner really won.

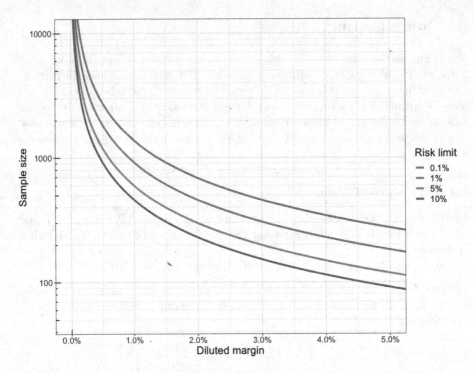

Fig. 1. Deterministic sample sizes (y-axis; $\log_{10}$ scale) for a comparison audit of a plurality contest with various diluted margins (x-axis) and risk limits (colors), with no error in CVRs and a maximal bet of $\lambda = 2$ on every draw.

To avoid stalls we follow the approach of Kelly Jr. [3], instead maximizing the expected value of $\log T_i$. The derivative is

$$\frac{d}{d\lambda}\mathbb{E}_F[\log T_i] = \frac{(a-1/2)p_0}{1+\lambda(a-1/2)} + \frac{(a-1)p_1}{2-\lambda(1-a)} + \frac{p_2}{2-\lambda}. \tag{3}$$

The oracle bet λ^* can be found by setting this equal to 0 and solving for λ using a root-finding algorithm.

Alternatively, we can find a simple analytical solution by assuming no 1-vote overstatements and setting $p_1 = 0$. In this case, solving for λ yields:

$$\lambda^* = \frac{2-4ap_0}{1-2a} \tag{4}$$

Note that $\lambda^* > 0$ since $ap_0 > 1/2$ under the alternative, and $\lambda^* < 2$ since $a > 1/2$.

3.3 Relation to ALPHA

There is a one-to-one correspondence between oracle bets for the BSM M_t and oracle bets for the ALPHA supermartingale, which reparameterizes M_t. Note that the list of overstatement assorters $\{x_i\}_{i=1}^{N}$ is upper bounded by the value of a 2-vote understatement, $u := 2/(2-v) = 2a$. Section 2.3 of Stark [11] shows that the equivalently optimal η for use with ALPHA is:

$$\eta^* := 1/2(1 + \lambda^*(u - 1/2)) = \frac{1 - 2ap_0}{2 - 4a} + 2ap_0 - 1/2.$$

Naturally, when $p_0 = 1$, $\eta^* = 2a = u$, which is the maximum value allowed for η^* while maintaining ALPHA as a non-negative supermartingale.

4   Betting in Practice

In practice, we have to estimate the unknown overstatement rates to set bets. We propose and evaluate three strategies: fixed, adaptive, and diversified betting. Throughout this section, we use $\tilde{p}_k$ to denote a generic estimate of p_k for $k \in \{1, 2\}$. When the estimate adapts in time, we use the double subscript $\tilde{p}_{ki}$. In all cases, the estimated overstatement rates are ultimately plugged into (3) to estimate the optimal bets.

4.1   Fixed Betting

The simplest approach is to make a fixed, *a priori* guess at p_k using historic data, machine specifications, or other information. For example, $\tilde{p}_1 := 0.1\%$ and $\tilde{p}_2 := 0.01\%$ will prevent stalls and may perform reasonably well when there are few overstatement error. This strategy is analagous to apKelly for ballot-polling, which fixes λ_i based on an *a priori* estimate of the population assorter mean (typically derived from reported tallies). However, Waudby-Smith et al. [14] and Stark [11] show that apKelly can become quite poor when the estimate is far from correct. This frailty motivates more sophisticated strategies.

4.2   Adaptive Betting

In a BSM, the bets need not be fixed and λ_i can be a *predictable* function of the data $X_1, \ldots, X_{i-1}$, since we condition on these data when establishing M_t as a martingale. Intuitively, the gambler can adapt their bets based on outcomes of previous rounds and, if the null is true, still cannot expect to gain capital in the next round. This fact allows us to estimate error rates based on past samples in addition to *a priori* considerations when setting λ_i. We adapt the "truncated-shrinkage" estimator introduced in Section 2.5.2 of Stark [11] to rate estimation. For $k \in \{1, 2\}$ we set a value $d_k \geq 0$, capturing the degree of shrinkage to the *a priori* estimate $\tilde{p}_k$, and a truncation factor $\epsilon_k \geq 0$, enforcing a lower bound on the estimated rate. Let $\hat{p}_{ki}$ be the sample rates at time i, e.g., $\hat{p}_{2i} = i^{-1} \sum_{j=1}^{i} 1\{X_j = 0\}$. Then the truncated-shrinkage estimate is:

$$\tilde{p}_{ki} := \frac{d_k \tilde{p}_k + i\hat{p}_{k(i-1)}}{d_k + i - 1} \vee \epsilon_k \tag{5}$$

The rates are allowed to learn from past data in the current audit through $\hat{p}_{k(i-1)}$, while being anchored to the a priori estimate $\tilde{p}_k$. The tuning parameter d_k reflects the degree of confidence in the a priori rate, with large d_k anchoring more strongly to $\tilde{p}_k$. Finally, ϵ_k should generally be set above 0 to prevent stalls.

At each time i, the truncated-shrinkage estimated rate $\tilde{p}_{ki}$ can be plugged into (3) and set equal to 0 to obtain the bet λ_i. Fixing $\tilde{p}_{1i} := 0$ allows us to use (4), in which case $\lambda_i = (2 - 4a(1 - \tilde{p}_{2i}))/(1 - 2a)$.

4.3 Diversified Betting

A weighted average of BSMs:

$$\sum_{b=1}^{B} \theta_b \prod_{i=1}^{t} [1 + \lambda_b(X_i - 1/2)],$$

where $\theta_b \geq 0$ and $\sum_{b=1}^{B} \theta_b = 1$, is itself a BSM. The intuition is that our initial capital is split up into B pots, each with θ_b units of wealth. We then bet λ_b on each pot at each time, and take the sum of the winnings across all pots as our total wealth at time t. Waudby-Smith and Ramdas [13] construct the "grid Kelly" martingale by defining λ_b along an equally spaced grid on $[0, 2]$ and giving each the weight $\theta_b = 1/B$. Waudby-Smith et al. [14] refine this approach into "square Kelly" for ballot-polling RLAs by placing more weight at close margins.

We adapt these ideas to the comparison audit context by parameterizing a discrete grid of weights for p_1 and p_2. We first note that (p_1, p_2) are jointly constrained by the hyperplane $ap_2 + (a/2)p_1 \leq a - 1/2$ under the alternative, since otherwise there is enough error to overturn the reported result. A joint grid for (p_1, p_2) can be set up by separately constructing two equally-spaced grids from 0 to v/k, computing the Cartesian product of the grids, and removing points where $ap_2 + (a/2)p_1 \geq a - 1/2$. Once a suitable grid has been constructed, the weights at each point can be flexibly defined to reflect the suspected rates of overstatements. At each point (p_1, p_2), λ_b is computed by passing the rates (p_1, p_2) into (3) and solving numerically; the weight for λ_b is θ_b. Thus a distribution of weights on the grid of overstatement rates induces a distribution on the bets.

Figure 2 illustrates two possible weighted grids for a diluted margin of $v = 10\%$, and their induced distribution on bets $\{\lambda_b\}_{b=1}^{B}$. In the top row, the weights are uniform with $\theta_b = 1/B$. In the bottom row, the weights follow a bivariate normal density with mean vector and covariance matrix respectively specified to capture a prior guess at (p_1, p_2) along with the uncertainty in that guess. The density is truncated, discretized, and rescaled so that the weights sum to unity.

5   Numerical Evaluations

We conducted two simulation studies. The first evaluated stopping times for bets using the oracle comparison bets in (4) against the oracle value of apKelly from Waudby-Smith et al. [14]. The second compared stopping times for oracle bets and the 3 practical strategies we proposed in Sect. 4. All simulations were run in R (version 4.1.2).

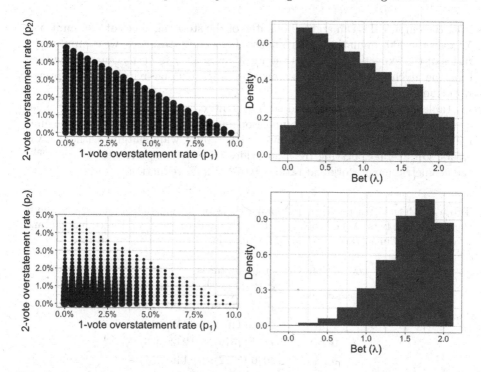

Fig. 2. Plots showing two mixture distributions over overstatement rates (left column; y-axis = 2-vote overstatement rate, x-axis = 1-vote overstatement rate; point size = mixture weight) and their corresponding induced distributions over the bets (right column; x-axis = bet, y-axis = density). The diluted margin of 10% constrains possible overstatement rates. The upper row shows a uniform grid of weights over all overstatement rates (left column) and its induced distribution on λ (right column). The bottom row plots discretized, truncated, and rescaled bivariate normal weights with parameters $(\mu_1, \mu_2) = (.01, .001)$, $(\sigma_1, \sigma_2) = (.02, .01)$, and $\rho = 0.25$ (left column) and its induced distribution on λ (right column).

5.1   Oracle Simulations

We evaluated stopping times of oracle bets at multiple diluted margins and 2-vote overstatement rates when sampling with replacement from a population of size $N = 10000$. At each combination of diluted margin $v \in \{0.05, 0.10, 0.20\}$ and 2-vote overstatement rates $p_2 \in \{1.5\%, 1\%, 0.5\%, 0.1\%, 0\%\}$ we ran 400 simulated comparison audits. We set $p_1 = 0$: no 1-vote overstatements.

The bets corresponded to oracle bets λ^* in Eq. (4) or to $\lambda^{\text{apK}} := 4\bar{x} - 2$, the "oracle" value of the apKelly strategy in Section 3.1 of Waudby Smith et al. [14] and Section 2.5 of Stark [11][1], which were originally derived for ballot-polling. λ^{apK} uses the true population mean instead of an estimate based on reported tallies. In each scenario, we estimated the expected and 90th percentile workload

---

[1] λ^{apK} implies a bet of $\eta_i := \bar{x}$ in the ALPHA parameterization.

from the empirical mean and 0.9 quantile of the stopping times at risk limit $\alpha = 5\%$ over the 400 simulations. To compare the betting strategies, we computed the ratios of the expected stopping time for λ^* over λ^{apK} in each scenario. We then took the geometric mean across scenarios as the average reduction in expected workload.

Table 1 presents the mean and 90th percentile (in parentheses) stopping times over the 400 simulations. BSM comparison audits with λ^* typically require counting fewer than 1000 ballots, and fewer than 100 for wide margins without CVR errors. On average, betting by λ^* provides an enormous advantage over λ^{apK}: the geometric mean workload ratio is 0.072, a 93% reduction.

Table 1. Mean (90th percentile) stopping times of 400 simulated comparison audits run with oracle bets (λ^*) or apKelly bets (λ^{apK}) under a range of diluted margins and 2-vote overstatement rates. DM = diluted margin; OR = overstatement rate.

DM	2-vote OR	Stopping times	
		apKelly (λ^{apK})	Oracle (λ^*)
5%	1.5%	10000 (10000)	1283 (2398)
	1.0%	10000 (10000)	482 (813)
	0.5%	7154 (7516)	242 (389)
	0.1%	4946 (5072)	146 (257)
	0.0%	4559 (4559)	119 (119)
10%	1.5%	2233 (2464)	177 (323)
	1.0%	1705 (1844)	131 (233)
	0.5%	1346 (1429)	83 (116)
	0.1%	1130 (1167)	65 (60)
	0.0%	1083 (1083)	59 (59)
20%	1.5%	339 (371)	52 (78)
	1.0%	304 (335)	42 (57)
	0.5%	272 (289)	35 (61)
	0.5%	249 (258)	30 (29)
	0.0%	245 (245)	29 (29)

5.2   Practical Simulations

We evaluated oracle betting, fixed *a priori* betting, adaptive betting, and diversified betting in simulated comparison audits with $N = 20000$ ballots, a diluted margin of 5%, 1-vote overstatement rates $p_1 \in \{0.1\%, 1\%\}$, and 2-vote overstatement rates $p_2 \in \{0.01\%, 0.1\%, 1\%\}$.

Oracle bets were set using the true values of p_1 and p_2 in each scenario. The other methods used prior guesses $\tilde{p}_1 \in \{0.1\%, 1\%\}$ and $\tilde{p}_2 \in \{0.01\%, 0.1\%\}$ as tuning parameters in different ways. The fixed method derived the optimal bet by plugging in $\tilde{p}_k$ as a fixed value. The adaptive method anchored the truncated-shrinkage estimate $\tilde{p}_{ki}$ displayed in Eq. (5) to $\tilde{p}_k$, but updated using past data in the sample. The tuning parameters were $d_1 := 100$, $d_2 := 1000$, $\epsilon_1 = \epsilon_2 := 0.001\%$. The larger value for d_2 reflects the fact that very low rates (expected for 2-vote overstatements) are harder to estimate empirically, so the prior should play a larger role. The diversified method used $\tilde{p}_k$ to set the mode of a mixing distribution, as in the lower panels of Fig. 2. Specifically, the mixing distribution was a discretized, truncated, bivariate normal with mean vector $(\tilde{p}_1, \tilde{p}_2)$, standard deviation $(\sigma_1, \sigma_2) := (0.5\%, 0.25\%)$, and correlation $\rho := 0.25$. The fact that $\sigma_2 < \sigma_1$ reflects more prior confidence that 2-vote overstatement rates will be concentrated near their prior mean, while $\rho > 0$ encodes a prior suspicion that overstatement rates are correlated: they are more likely to be both high or both low. After setting the weights at each grid point according to this normal density, they were rescaled to sum to unity.

We simulated 400 audits under sampling with replacement for each scenario. The stopping times were capped at 20000, the size of the population, even if the audit hadn't stopped by that point. We estimated the expected value and 90th percentile of the stopping times for each method by the empirical mean and 0.9 quantile over the 400 simulations. We computed the geometric mean ratio of the expected stopping times of each method over that of the oracle strategy as a summary of their performance across scenarios.

Table 2 presents results. With few 2-vote overstatements, all strategies performed relatively well and the audits concluded quickly. When the priors substantially underestimated the true overstatement rates, the performance of the audits degraded significantly compared to the oracle bets. This was especially true for the fixed strategy. For example, when $(p_1, p_2) = (0.1\%, 1\%)$ and $\tilde{p}_2 = 0.01\%$, the expected number of ballots for the fixed strategy to stop was more than 20 times that of the oracle method. On the other hand, the adaptive and diversified strategies were much more robust to a poor prior estimate. In particular, the expected stopping time of the diversified method was never more than 3 worse than that of the oracle strategy, and the adaptive method was never more than 4 times worse. The geometric mean workload ratios of each strategy over the oracle strategy were 2.4 for fixed, 1.3 for adaptive, and 1.2 for diversified. The diversified method was the best practical method on average across scenarios.

6   Extensions

6.1   Betting While Sampling Without Replacement

When sampling without replacement, the distribution of X_i depends on past data $X_1, ..., X_{i-1}$. Naively updating an *a priori* bet to reflect what we know has been sampled may actually harm the efficiency of the audit.

Specifically, recall that, for $k \in \{1, 2\}$, $\hat{p}_{ki}$ denotes the sample proportion of the overstatement rate at time i. If we fix initial rate estimates to $\tilde{p}_k$, then the updated estimate at time i given that we have removed $i\hat{p}_{k(i-1)}$ would be

$$\tilde{p}_{ki} = \frac{N\tilde{p}_k - i\hat{p}_{k(i-1)}}{N - i + 1} \quad \text{for} \quad k \in \{1, 2\}.$$

Table 2. Mean (90th percentile) stopping times over 400 simulated comparison audits with diluted margin of $v = 5\%$ and varying overstatement rates at risk limit $\alpha = 5\%$. The true overstatement rates are in the first two columns. The second two columns contain the prior guesses of the true overstatement rates, used to set bets differently in each strategy as described in Sect. 5.2. The oracle strategy uses the true rates to set the bets, so all variation over $(\tilde{p}_1, \tilde{p}_2)$ in the results for that strategy is Monte Carlo variation. Monte Carlo variation also accounts for any differences in the fixed and oracle strategies when $(\tilde{p}_1, \tilde{p}_2) = (p_1, p_2)$, since the bets are identical. Note that some stopping time distributions are highly skewed, e.g. the 90th percentile is lower than the mean for fixed bets with $(\tilde{p}_1, \tilde{p}_2) = (p_1, p_2) = (0.1\%, 0.01\%)$. OR = overstatement rate.

True ORs		Prior ORs		Stopping Times			
p_2	p_1	$\tilde{p}_2$	$\tilde{p}_1$	Oracle	Fixed	Adaptive	Diversified
0.01%	0.1%	0.01%	0.1%	124 (147)	125 (119)	124 (147)	131 (152)
			1%	124 (147)	125 (147)	125 (147)	131 (154)
		0.1%	0.1%	125 (147)	129 (151)	131 (151)	133 (155)
			1%	127 (147)	132 (153)	130 (152)	135 (157)
	1%	0.01%	0.1%	174 (229)	167 (229)	166 (229)	177 (236)
			1%	168 (229)	172 (229)	167 (229)	180 (235)
		0.1%	0.1%	176 (229)	169 (232)	175 (262)	181 (262)
			1%	159 (205)	174 (233)	180 (265)	184 (264)
0.1%	0.1%	0.01%	0.1%	146 (256)	153 (338)	159 (350)	149 (271)
			1%	151 (256)	154 (174)	150 (147)	145 (154)
		0.1%	0.1%	147 (256)	152 (256)	146 (182)	153 (259)
			1%	149 (256)	151 (244)	147 (256)	152 (265)
	1%	0.01%	0.1%	209 (351)	227 (420)	225 (460)	214 (400)
			1%	200 (324)	240 (457)	232 (500)	211 (378)
		0.1%	0.1%	204 (351)	208 (364)	210 (358)	208 (344)
			1%	208 (324)	205 (324)	205 (341)	219 (371)
1%	0.1%	0.01%	0.1%	526 (996)	13654 (20000)	1581 (3517)	888 (2090)
			1%	525 (984)	12685 (20000)	1585 (3731)	739 (1708)
		0.1%	0.1%	528 (1032)	9589 (20000)	1112 (2710)	812 (1982)
			1%	534 (985)	7247 (20000)	915 (2294)	686 (1586)
	1%	0.01%	0.1%	999 (1908)	15205 (20000)	3855 (7811)	2637 (5873)
			1%	1110 (2002)	15641 (20000)	3477 (7529)	1803 (4331)
		0.1%	0.1%	1030 (1868)	13113 (20000)	2795 (5996)	2064 (4884)
			1%	1127 (2256)	13094 (20000)	2437 (5452)	1604 (3758)

This can be plugged into (3) to estimate the optimal λ_i^* for each draw. Fixing $\tilde{p}_{1i} = 0$ and using Eq. (4) yields the closed form optimum:

$$\lambda_i^* = \frac{2 - 4a\tilde{p}_{2i}}{1 - 2a} \wedge 2,$$

where we have truncated at 2 to guarantee that λ_i^* is even a valid bet. This is necessary because the number of 2-vote overstatements in the sample can exceed the number $N\tilde{p}_2$ hypothesized to be in the entire population. If this occurs, the audit will stall if even one more 2-vote overstatement is discovered. More generally, this strategy has the counterintuitive (and counterproductive) property of betting *more* aggressively as more overstatements are discovered. To avoid this pitfall we suggest using the betting strategies we derived earlier under IID sampling, even when sampling without replacement.

6.2 Other Social Choice Functions

SHANGRLA [10] encompasses a broad range of social choice functions beyond plurality, all of which are amenable to comparison audits. Assorters for approval voting and proportional representation are identical to plurality assorters, so no modification to the optimal bets is required. Ranked-choice voting can also be reduced to auditing a collection of plurality assertions, though this reduction may not be the most efficient possible [1]. On the other hand, some social choice functions, including weighted additive and supermajority, require different assorters and will have different optimal bets.

In a supermajority contest, the diluted margin v is computed differently depending on the fraction $f \in (1/2, 1]$ required to win, as well as the proportion of votes for the reported winner in the CVRs. In the population of overstatement assorters error-free CVRs still appear as $a = (2-v)^{-1}$, but 2-vote overstatements are $(1 - 1/(2f))a > 0$ and 1-vote overstatements are $(3/2 - 1/(2f))a$. So that the population attains a lower bound of 0, we can make the shift $x_i - (1 - 1/(2f))a$ and test against the shifted mean $1/2 - (1 - 1/(2f))a$. Because there are only 3 points of support, the derivations in Sect. 3.2 can be repeated, yielding a new solution for λ^* in terms of the rates and the shifted mean.

Weighted additive schemes apply an affine transformation to ballot scores to construct assorters. Because scores may be arbitrary non-negative numbers, there can be more than 3 points of support for the overstatement assorters and the derivations in Sect. 3.2 cannot be immediately adapted. If most CVRs are correct then most values in the population will be above $1/2$, suggesting that an aggressive betting strategy with $\lambda := 2 - \epsilon$ will be relatively efficient. Alternatively, a diversified strategy weighted towards large values of $\lambda \in (0, 2]$ can retain efficiency when there are in fact high rates of error. It should also be possible to attain a more refined solution by generalizing the optimization strategy in Sect. 3.2 to populations with more than 3 points of support.

6.3 Batch-Level Comparison Audits

Batch-level comparison audits check for error in totals across batches of ballots, and are applicable in different situations than ballot-level comparisons, since they do not require CVRs. SHANGRLA-style overstatement assorters for batch-level comparison audits are derived in Stark [11]. These assorters generally take a wide range of values within $[0, u]$. Because they are not limited to a few points of support, there is not a simple optimal betting strategy. However, assuming there is relatively little error in the reported batch-level counts, will again place the majority of the assorter distribution above $1/2$. This suggests using a relatively aggressive betting strategy, placing more weight on bets near 2 (or near the assorter upper bound in the ALPHA parameterization).

Stark [11] evaluated various BSMs in simulations approximating batch-level comparison audits, though the majority of mass was either at 1 or spread uniformly on $[0,1]$, not at a value $a \in (1/2, 1]$. Nevertheless, in situations where most of the mass was at 1, aggressive betting ($\eta \geq 0.9$) was most efficient. Investigating efficient betting strategies for batch-level comparison audits remains an important area for future work.

7 Conclusions

We derived optimal bets for ballot-level comparison audits of plurality contests and sketched some extensions to broader classes of comparison RLAs. The high-level upshot is that comparison should use considerably more aggressive betting strategies than polling in practice, a point made abundantly clear in our oracle simulations. Our practical strategies approached the efficiency of oracle bets, except in cases where $p_2 = 1\%$. Such a high rate of 2-vote overstatements is unlikely in practice, and would generally imply something has gone terribly wrong: votes for the loser should not be flipped to votes for the winner.

Future work should continue to flesh out efficient strategies for batch-level comparison, and explore the effects of understatement errors. We suspect that understatements will have little effect on the optimal strategy. If anything, they imply bets should be even *more* aggressive, but already suggest placing most weight near the maximal value of $\lambda_i = 2$, diversifying or thresholding to prevent stalls if 2-vote overstatements are discovered. We hope our results will guide efficient real-world comparison RLAs, and demonstrate the practicality of their routine implementation for trustworthy, evidence-based elections.

Acknowledgements. Philip Stark and Amanda Glazer provided helpful feedback on an earlier draft of this paper. Jacob Spertus' research is supported by NSF grant 2228884.

Code. Code implementing our simulations and generating our figures and tables is available on Github at https://github.com/spertus/comparison-RLA-betting.

References

1. Blom, M., Stuckey, P., Teague, V.: RAIRE: risk-limiting audits for IRV elections (2019). https://arxiv.org/abs/1903.08804
2. Glazer, A.K., Spertus, J.V., Stark, P.B.: More style, less work: card-style data decrease risk-limiting audit sample sizes. Digit. Threats **2**(4), 1–15 (2021). ISSN: 2692-1626. https://doi.org/10.1145/3457907
3. Kelly Jr., J.L.: A new interpretation of information rate. Bell Syst. Tech. J. **35**(4), 917–926 (1956). ISSN 1538-7305. https://doi.org/10.1002/j.1538-7305.1956.tb03809.x

4. Lindeman, M., Stark, P.: A gentle introduction to risk-limiting audits. IEEE Secur. Priv. **10**, 42–49 (2012). https://ieeexplore.ieee.org/document/6175884
5. Ottoboni, K., Stark, P.B., Lindeman, M., McBurnett, N.: Risk-limiting audits by stratified union-intersection tests of elections (SUITE). In: Krimmer, R., et al. (eds.) E-Vote-ID 2018. LNCS, vol. 11143, pp. 174–188. Springer, Cham (2018). https://doi.org/10.1007/978-3-030-00419-4_12
6. Stark, P.: Conservative statistical post-election audits. Ann. Appl. Stat. **2**, 550–581 (2008). http://arxiv.org/abs/0807.4005
7. Stark, P.: Risk-limiting post-election audits: P-values from common probability inequalities. IEEE Trans. Inf. Forensics Secur. **4**, 1005–1014 (2009)
8. Stark, P.: Efficient post-election audits of multiple contests: 2009 California tests. In: 2009 Conference on Empirical Legal Studies (2009). http://ssrn.com/abstract=1443314
9. Stark, P.: Super-simple simultaneous single-ballot risk-limiting audits. In: Proceedings of the 2010 Electronic Voting Technology Workshop/Workshop on Trustworthy Elections (EVT/WOTE 2010). USENIX (2010). http://www.usenix.org/events/evtwote10/tech/full_papers/Stark.pdf
10. Stark, P.B.: Sets of half-average nulls generate risk-limiting audits: SHANGRLA. In: Bernhard, M., et al. (eds.) FC 2020. LNCS, vol. 12063, pp. 319–336. Springer, Cham (2020). https://doi.org/10.1007/978-3-030-54455-3_23. Preprint: http://arxiv.org/abs/1911.10035
11. Stark, P.: ALPHA: audit that learns from previously hand-audited ballots. Ann. Appl. Stat. **17**(1), 641–679 (2023). Preprint: https://arxiv.org/abs/2201.02707
12. Ville, J.: Étude critique de la notion de collectif (1939). http://eudml.org/doc/192893
13. Waudby-Smith, I., Ramdas, A.: Estimating means of bounded random variables by betting (2020). https://arxiv.org/abs/2010.09686. https://rss.org.uk/RSS/media/File-library/Events/Discussion%20meetings/Estimating-means-of-bounded-random-variables-by-betting.pdf
14. Waudby-Smith, I., Stark, P.B., Ramdas, A.: RiLACS: risk limiting audits via confidence sequences. In: Krimmer, R., et al. (eds.) E-Vote-ID 2021. LNCS, vol. 12900, pp. 124–139. Springer, Cham (2021). https://doi.org/10.1007/978-3-030-86942-7_9

CoDecFin

Shaping Cryptocurrency Gatekeepers
with a Regulatory "Trial and Error"

Marilyne Ordekian[(✉)], Ingolf Becker, and Marie Vasek

University College London, London, UK
{marilyne.ordekian.21,i.becker,m.vasek}@ucl.ac.uk

Abstract. In the past fifteen years, cryptocurrencies have grown from a whitepaper released on a mailing list to an ecosystem supporting millions of transactions a day using a whole host of technology never imagined before. However, governments have been slow to keep up. We present an analysis of regulatory developments from within the EU and by the Financial Action Task Force (FATF). These regulatory responses focus on intermediaries such as cryptocurrency exchanges, and wallet providers. We trace the AML/CFT policy recommendations made by the FATF, and examine the EU's Fifth Anti-Money Laundering Directive and upcoming Markets in Crypto-Assets (MiCA) regulation. Here we find a natural tension: the pace of regulation is slower than the pace of technology, so the scope is non-comprehensive, yet current trials to accelerate this pace are leading to subtle conflicting errors. These findings present a deeper understanding of the ongoing regulatory dilemma, its essence, and suggest directions for the future of cryptocurrency regulation.

1 Introduction

When Bitcoin emerged in 2008, it did not receive attention from regulators who were preoccupied with a dire financial crisis. However, the rising popularity of underground markets [18] and the collapse of Mt. Gox brought it under the radar of some spectating regulators. Yet, Bitcoin's underlying technology was too complex for many to comprehend. Consequently, policymakers globally faced colossal challenges, not knowing what or how to regulate. To this end, the cryptocurrency ecosystem entered a regulatory "trial and error" phase, where different regulators simultaneously tested diverse approaches and methods. This phase turned into a vortex swirling for more than a decade lingering its way until the present.

In 2017, an unprecedented market boom, exploding both the size and value of the ecosystem, caused this phase to start to shift. Cryptocurrency exchanges, now serving double the cryptocurrencies with more than double the value than the year before [50], caught the attention of regulators. With exchanges becoming the hidden trusted third party that Nakamoto once hoped to eliminate with the peer-to-peer system [72], regulators finally had a somewhat central body that they could reach with the existing classical regulatory methods of employing

© International Financial Cryptography Association 2024
A. Essex et al. (Eds.): FC 2023 Workshops, LNCS 13553, pp. 113–132, 2024.
https://doi.org/10.1007/978-3-031-48806-1_8

control. With this, new drawbacks started to emerge: the lack of international consensus on how to regulate these service providers, the slow procedures of taking effective actions, and the prioritization of adopting AML/CFT frameworks over creating a comprehensive regulatory environment. We will argue that the latter approach progressively causes more harm than good.

Exchanges act as *de facto* banks within an insurgent-emerging financial sector, yet, without proper governance or *de jure* regulation. They provide similar financial and custodial services but lack a long list of strict regulations and policies that banks, money services businesses, and stock exchanges employ and comply with. Thus, these proper regulation-lacking practices excite numerous predicaments beyond financial compliance. Criminals being opportunistic early adopters of new technologies [3] shifted from a highly regulated banking system to cryptocurrency intermediaries abusing the regulatory ambiguity and features such as decentralization and relative anonymity/privacy [35]. Bitcoin was soon deemed a *malum in se* for being lucrative for illegal/criminal activity [49]. Perpetrators adapted new *modi operandi* for various types of crimes, turning it into what many consider, the currency of criminals [11,20]. But, the only serious regulatory efforts concentrated on curbing the exploitation of cryptocurrencies in money laundering and terrorist financing, as the earliest and most popular policies are AML/CFT frameworks [57,59].

To this end, the international financial watchdog, FATF, has been playing a global leading role in providing recommendations, guidance, and clarification in what binds money laundering and the financing of terrorism with cryptocurrencies. Recently, the FATF recommendations have officially become inclusive of cryptocurrencies [42]. By following these, regulators are expected to impose onto exchanges the same AML/CFT frameworks that, although they were originally created and tested on the traditional financial system, seem to be tainted with weaknesses [9]. In turn, and in order to be inline and mirror these recommendations, the EU incorporated cryptocurrencies within the scope of the Fifth Anti-Money Laundering Directive (AMLD5) [29].

This route of AML/CFT rules might appeal as a right move towards bringing cryptocurrencies under the boundaries of the law. However, cryptocurrency service providers operate in an entirely different terrain than traditional banks, even when they seem to offer similar services. This application of the same regulations induces substantial hurdles. There is an emerging issue of properly adjusting and applying these frameworks in practice. The FATF itself proclaimed most exchanges and jurisdictions as non-compliant with its recommendations [45] – touching on the shortcomings, efficacy, and ill-equipment of these "strict" rules.

Additionally, cryptocurrency exchanges lack the properties, means, and other compliance standards that these heavily regulated institutions undergo, such as obligatory compliance standards relating to data protection, privacy policies, security policies, risk assessment, criminal activity detection and reporting, insurance, and consumer protection. Despite this, they are mandated to implement these AML/CFT policies that include standards such as Know Your Customer (KYC) verification, and Customer Due Diligence procedures, where a handful of customer information will be continuously collected. This is all done without the availability of any proper security or legal protection.

This article contributes in the following ways. At a high level, we stress the ramifications of adopting inapt and non-comprehensive policies within the cryptocurrency field. We outline how the regulation has evolved inconsistently over the years in Sect. 3. In response, Sect. 4 demonstrates the negative outcomes resulting from this "trial and error" phase. Policymaking should improve; Sect. 5 details concrete suggestions and overviews the latest EU regulations (MiCA/TFR).

2 Background

The anonymity over the internet drives individuals to express thoughts or do things they would not dare to do in the physical world; for some, these actions are illegal [12]. Cryptocurrencies provide certain levels of identity obfuscation and by nature, operate independently of a monitoring central body [59]. But, with the absence of a nurturing regulatory ecosystem, they were soon adopted by criminals [71], and associated with underground markets such as the Silk Road [18].

It was this link with illicit markets that had first caught the attention of regulators, and induced the need for intervention. But the technology underlying Bitcoin and its decentralized form challenged the abundant regulatory frameworks that were deemed inapplicable. To this end, three regulatory approaches emerged throughout the years. In the early days, most regulators adopted the "Wait and See" approach. They abstained from comprehensive regulation, and monitored the directions the technology was taking.

With time, others decided to take hostile directions and restricted cryptocurrencies. A report published by the Library of Congress in Nov 2021 identifies 9 jurisdictions which imposed an absolute ban on cryptocurrencies and 42 with an implicit ban [81][1]. The final approach involves interference by either integrating cryptocurrencies into certain existing regulations, or by creating new but mostly *ad hoc* frameworks. The former approach is becoming popular amongst many jurisdictions. This unfortunately prompts the lack of a fully comprehensive and enforceable standardized framework that is acceptable on a global scale.

This shift from the "Wait and See" to the intervention approach, could not have happened without the intervention of academics. As we will show, there were countless contributions throughout the years towards unravelling the mechanism of Bitcoin, its involvement with criminal activity, and the relevant scale, and characteristics such as the *mens rea, actus reus*. These eventually assisted in annihilating the Wild West that cryptocurrencies were pirouetting in.

In the early days of legislative truancy, papers discussing Bitcoin from a legal perspective had common themes and concerns, mostly directed towards its legal

---

[1] "Prohibiting banks and other financial institutions from dealing in cryptocurrencies or offering services to individuals/businesses dealing in cryptocurrencies or banning cryptocurrency exchanges are examples of implicit bans" [81].

ambiguity and the unprecedented arising risks and issues [7,10,22,61]. Issues, for instance, arising from its decentralized nature [75] and the lack of a governing-official authority [22], which incites the escape from existing controls and allows the thriving of criminal activity [18,75]. Other works helped regulators by simplifying the underlying technology [10,53], and pinpointing the ill-equipment and inflexibility of the abundant regulatory regimes in embracing cryptocurrencies [7,10]. Some explored the legal ramifications of Bitcoin's operation in a legal gray area [53], whilst many still continue the debate on legal characterization and the right choice of terminology [22,53]. Academic technologists then suggested methodologies to implement these proposals, such as clever ways of blacklisting transactions and/or coins linked to illegal activities [1,4,66,67].

With these contributions, the prospect of regulating cryptocurrencies started to gradually unfold. After all, intervention was a must, especially with the rise of haphazard and fraudulent operation of self-regulating intermediaries, which was deemed intolerable [54]. As a possible mechanism for fighting cryptocurrency crimes, governments were advised to target exchanges, as they portray the only reachable central point within an inherently decentralized ecosystem [7,75]. But this concurs with warnings about stifling innovation and punishing individuals compliant with the laws [75].

2.1   Exchanges as Gatekeepers of Illicit Financial Proceeds

Although the conventional financial and banking sectors remain the favorite methods for money laundering, criminal networks are being driven to search for alternative channels offering less surveillance and control. Cryptocurrency intermediaries seem to embody that perfect medium [36]. A major reason driving this migration is the increasing legislative noose with AML/CFT policies within the financial sector. These legislations are advanced, ad hoc, rigorous, and the result of years of tailored amendments inspired by real events, case laws, and multilateral treaties. At the moment, there exist internationally coordinated actions, consistently intending to cramp criminal organizations and their methods for laundering illicit proceeds through banks and financial services. But the cryptocurrency ecosystem lacks all this clarity and global standardization.

This prolonged regulatory void and ambiguity is causing the thriving of criminal activity associated with cryptocurrencies. Features such as pseudonymity, instant and uncontrolled transfer of unlimited funds on a global scale, and the absence of rigor regulations, appeal especially to those seeking to conceal the origins of their illicit proceeds [60].

Overall, the involvement of cryptocurrencies with money laundering takes a couple of forms and many have investigated the different ways and new *modus operandi* of money laundering [65]. Because the crime of money laundering by nature is a subsidiary class of crime, it depends on the occurrence of an initial crime. With cryptocurrencies, the originated proceeds of the initial crime can be either a non-crypto-crime or crypto-facilitated/crypto-based cybercrime [8,74]. The first method involves the conversion of illicit proceeds resulting from any crime such as drug trafficking, weaponry sale, tax evasion, bribery, theft, etc.

The process usually involves the conversion of fiat money into cryptocurrency through exchanges, peer-to-peer platforms, or cryptocurrency ATMs. The second method involves the laundering of proceeds originating from cryptocurrency-related crimes, such as ransomware ransoms, exchange theft, exit scams, and other cryptocurrency scams. In consequence, what all criminal organizations, white-collar criminals, and scammers have in common now, are the new money laundering and cashing out techniques they employ [63, 64, 82, 83].

2.2 The Current Risks of Terrorist Financing

Terrorist groups started exploiting cryptocurrencies to attain donations at an early stage [58, 77]. With work towards uncovering these activities [73], it has been unveiled that terrorists are utilizing cryptocurrencies in many ways. This includes buying weapons and explosives from the dark web [73] and running fundraising campaigns [37, 59]. Evidence even reveals the use of social media platforms to inform supporters on how to successfully donate funds [77].

The extent to which cryptocurrencies are used in relation to terrorism cannot be comparable with money laundering. At the moment, some do not consider the usage of cryptocurrencies by terrorists as a source of grave danger [37]. This is, among other things, because most terrorist groups are located in places lacking the minimum-required technological infrastructure. However, this might change.

3 Regulation Beyond the "Wait and See" Approach

In Sect. 2 we highlight the three most common regulatory approaches adopted by regulators. Following the prolonged period of the "Wait and See", the most prominent regulatory actions taken consist of AML/CFT measures targeting intermediaries as gatekeepers. The EU and FATF have been leaders in proposing and enacting strict frameworks. Yet, these rigorous polices face challenges in their enforcement due to their inflexibility, ill-suitability, locality, and vague text.

3.1 The Inconsistency in Terms and Definitions

Terminologies and definitions play a pivotal role in determining the scope of application of any legal text i.e., they define the boundaries of the text's applicability and those subjected to it. With cryptocurrencies, there is still a lack of global consensus, not only on the regulation process itself, but on terminologies and definitions, even though Bitcoin was founded more than a decade ago. This forms the first of many hurdles in building a stable-entrusting regulatory environment. As in fact, many loopholes and backdoors, which are exploited by criminals, are created based on the choice of certain terms and definitions.

In the early days when the "Wait and See" approach was dominant amongst regulators, the European Central Bank (ECB) and the FATF took the initial initiative to address cryptocurrencies. Both institutions introduced and warned of risk associations with money laundering and terrorist financing [25, 26, 39, 40].

During this time, cryptocurrencies were distinguished from E-Money, and by being ruled out of directives governing Electronic Money, they were consequently left in an unregulated terrain [27, 39].

Over the years, the ECB's and FATF's terminologies, definitions, and approaches evolved and changed. At first, the ECB referred to cryptocurrencies as Virtual Currencies [25, 26], but then settled with the term "crypto-assets", and defined them as:

> "[a] new type of asset recorded in digital form and enabled by the use of cryptography that is not and does not represent a financial claim on, or a liability of, any identifiable entity" [27].

Meanwhile the FATF exchanged the terms Virtual Currencies with "Virtual Assets" (VAs) and "Virtual Assets Service Providers" (VASPs) [40, 43], and defined a VA as:

> "a digital representation of value that can be digitally traded, or transferred, and can be used for payment or investment purposes. Virtual assets do not include digital representations of fiat currencies, securities, and other financial assets that are already covered elsewhere in the FATF Recommendations" [41, 46].

These definitions have evolved over the years and are still open to further amendments. The examples of the ECB and the FATF portraying variation, reflect a humble sample of a global inconsistency that stems critical issues.

This concern can be seen with the Fifth Anti-Money Laundering Directive.[2] In May of 2018[3], the fifth version of the directive (AMLD5) was published [29]. This expanded to encompass "Virtual Currencies" (VCs)[4], "Custodian Wallet Providers" (CWPs)[5], and "providers engaged in exchange services between virtual currencies and fiat currencies" and subjected CWPs and exchanges to regulatory requirements just as conventional financial institutions.

In order to identify what type of cryptocurrencies are incorporated within the applicability scope of the AMLD5, it is necessary to look into the presented legal definition. Article 1(2)(d)(18) defined Virtual Currencies as follows:

> "a digital representation of value that is not issued or guaranteed by a central bank or a public authority, is not necessarily attached to a legally established currency and does not possess a legal status of currency or money, but is accepted by natural or legal persons as a means of exchange and which can be transferred, stored and traded electronically".

---

[2] Within the EU, the Anti-Money Laundering Directive (AMLD), is the set of robust rules responsible for the EU's fight against money laundering/terrorist financing. The regularly amended directive aims at preventing the misuse of the financial system for economic/financial crimes, specifically ML/TF.

[3] Art. 4 of the AMLD5 mandated member states to transpose the provisions of the Directive into national AML/CFT legislation by January 2020.

[4] Art. 1(2)(d)(18), AMLD5.

[5] Art. 1(2)(d)(19), AMLD5.

In the first instance, this definition clarifies that cryptocurrencies are not a form of Electronic Money as stated in the 2009 E-Money directive, hence are not regulated by its provisions. This is expressly deduced by the condition that VCs must not be issued by any official authority. This is also expressly clarified in recital 10 as it is stated *"Virtual currencies should not be confused with electronic money as defined in point (2) of article 2 of Directive 2009/110/EC of the European Parliament and of the Council"*.

Secondly, the definition tacitly excludes what is known as utility and investment currencies or tokens. This is deduced from the phrase *"but is accepted by natural or legal persons as a means of exchange and which can be transferred, stored and traded electronically"*. Utility and investment tokens do not act as nor are used as a medium of exchange [55].

As for cryptocurrency exchanges, the AMLD5 does not provide a specific term, but rather introduces the following in article 1(1)(c)(g): *"providers engaged in exchange services between virtual currencies and fiat currencies"*. The given definition expressly obliges all fiat-to-crypto exchanges (and crypto-to-fiat) to undergo its provisions. The text does not limit the definition to a certain type of exchange. Hence, both centralized and decentralized exchanges dealing with or enabling the exchange between fiat and cryptocurrencies, are included. This clear description only including fiat/crypto exchanges, hints at the intention of the European legislator of excluding crypto-to-crypto exchanges. However, there are loopholes counter to this notion. For instance, a crypto-to-crypto exchange can still be an obliged entity under the AMLD5, if it offers "custodian wallet" services where it "safeguards private cryptographic keys" [55].

Consequently, a crypto-to-crypto exchange becomes an obliged entity, not under the definition of the aforementioned article 1(1)(c)(g) but under article 1(2)(d)(19), which reads as

> *"'custodian wallet provider' means an entity that provides services to safeguard private cryptographic keys on behalf of its customers, to hold, store and transfer virtual currencies"*.

As a result, a crypto-to-crypto exchange offering a custodian wallet service, which most exchanges do, can be subjected to the AMLD5. In contrast, the FATF's broader definition of VASPs expressly includes crypto-to-crypto exchanges within its scope of obliged entities [46].

3.2   International and European Approaches to AML/CFT

The FATF's Recommendations. The FATF incorporated VAs and VASPs in its stern recommendations by updating Recommendation 15 and publishing the Interpretative Note 15 (INR 15) [42]. This way, AML/CFT measures implemented in financial institutions became applicable to VAs and VASPs. These recommendations are not binding upon member states, but noncompliant member states often face hardship by getting listed on the grey/blacklist.

What came after the FATF's recommendations drastically changed how VASPs operated. Notable recommendations require jurisdictions to apply a risk-based approach with VAs; member states were advised to enforce registration/licensing and supervision on VASPs[6]. VASPs now have to conduct Customer Due Diligence (CDD) on transactions exceeding 1,000 USD/EUR; report, submit, and flag suspicious activities (Rec 20); and most importantly, implement the Travel Rule (Rec 16). The application of the latter rule means VASPs are enshrined to monitor transactions and collect/hold/transmit user information,[7] not only with other VASPs, but with local Financial Intelligence Units (FIUs) as well [46].

In October of 2021, the FATF expanded the scope of Recommendation 16 to VASPs and *"unhosted wallet transactions"* [46]. It also placed additional requirements on VASPs dealing with non-obliged entities[8]. Other requirements of this rule demand the freezing and prohibition of transactions designated to suspicious persons and entities. To guarantee compliance, states must deploy financial/disciplinary sanctions (withdrawal, restriction, or suspension of license), and criminal/civil/administrative sanctions on non-compliant VASPs (Rec 35).

The incorporation of the Travel Rule unleashed a major controversy within the community; it invaded one of the rather core philosophical concepts of cryptocurrencies: financial freedom, and independence from governments' surveillance. This level of proactivity with cryptocurrencies is arguably questionable. The risks associated with money laundering and cryptocurrencies are not relevantly as serious as those linked to the conventional financial system. The FATF itself stated that the trajectory of money laundering committed through the Fiat system is much more severe than in the cryptocurrency sphere. Yet evidently, we see an equivalent treatment of both high and low risk sources [38].

The EU's First Attempt with the AMLD5. Section 3.1 overviews the EU's first attempt at regulating cryptocurrencies by introducing them into the AMLD5. As discussed before, the definitions are vague, withstand interpretation, and the wording of the text is confusing [21]. But there are additional vital provisions in the directive that mandate addressing.

For instance, recital 8 details one of the means that will facilitate the fight against money laundering and terrorist financing via VCs. This includes the enabling of designated authorities to monitor the use of VCs through obliged entities incorporated within the AMLD5's scope. The purpose of this procedure is to also allow FIUs to be able to associate VC addresses to users' identities[9].

Other provisions require member states to ensure that obliged entities acquire a license with local authorities[10]. To this end, entities must follow and perform

---

[6] Para. 3 of the Interpretative Note to Recommendation 15.

[7] Information includes: Originator and beneficiary names; account numbers or wallet numbers; originator's physical address, official identification documents, place and date of birth. In Oct 2021, the FATF granted VASPs the authority to decline sharing customer information with other VASPs, on the count that the counterparty was unable to store the information securely for transactions with low risk of AML/CFT.

[8] Paras. 105–107.

[9] Recital 9, AMLD5.

[10] Art. 1(29)(1), AMLD5.

strict KYC measures, undertake CDD, monitor and report suspicious activity, carry out risk assessments, and identify and respond to threats.

When defining obliged entities under its provisions, the AMLD5 excluded certain types of tokens, ICOs, service providers, and non-custodian wallet providers. Recital 9 mentions that a large part of the cryptocurrency ecosystem will indeed remain anonymous, even with the current rules in place. This is due to the excluded parties from its scope, the abundance of purely peer-to-peer platforms, and users being able to transact directly without the need for intermediaries. The AMLD5 thus grants and proposes a self-declaration procedure to be conducted by users to the designated FIUs[11]. However, a voluntary self-declaration is unlikely to assist in fighting money laundering and terrorist financing, as parties and persons engaging in such acts will not self-declare. Therefore, some see the need to make this type of declaration a mandatory procedure [56].

4   Repercussions of the Ongoing "Trial and Error" Phase

Countries have been experimenting with regulations and policies on their own, passing laws without reaching out or initiating global collaboration. This has created an additional inconsistency amongst texts. This does not reflect well on standardizing the work and compliance of cryptocurrency service providers, on the contrary, it causes various serious repercussions.

4.1   The Lack of Consensus and Legal Uniformity

Regulatory frameworks encompassing cryptocurrencies are new and in a "trial and error" phase. The unprecedented situation drove different regulators to simultaneously test various approaches. As of January 2023, there is not a fully functional, inclusive, and globally acceptable regulatory environment accommodating cryptocurrencies that is in force.

The constant amendments and variations not only hinder users/investors from knowing their rights as consumers/customers, but also impede many service providers from the ease of complying. Furthermore, interpretable and vague texts that lack uniformity and stability can leave the doors open for gaps, loopholes, and backdoors for criminals. This can only aggravate the fight against money laundering and terrorist financing.

The essence of the issue begins with the absence of standardized-unified terms and definitions, and lingers to essential provisions and clauses where phrases are ambiguous, vague, and broad. This gives rise to different text interpretations and conclusions which can only hinder the proper application of the text.

The most basic example would be the FATF's treatment of cryptocurrencies as Virtual Assets, whilst the AMLD5 regards them as Virtual Currencies. One can argue on the distinct treatment of "assets" and "currencies" within different jurisdictions. Another example would be the characterization of cryptocurrencies as assets, commodities, or even property, as each characterization would

---

[11] Recital 9, and art. 1(41)(1)(g).

divulge distinct outcomes. For instance, the US Internal Revenue Service (IRS) considers "virtual currencies" a form of property for tax purposes. Because of this particular term (used within this specific context), general tax provisions are applicable to transactions using cryptocurrencies [80]. In contrast, the Law Commission in England and Wales is studying the recognition of a third and new category of personal properties under private property law, which would incorporate cryptocurrencies ("data objects"). This new category would entail the recognition and protection of cryptocurrencies under existing property laws [76].

Similarly, a comparison between the AMLD5 and the FATF standards would show the narrow scope of the former's provisions. For instance, the adopted definitions in the AMLD5 eliminate tokens (investment and utility) and leave out key players such as crypto-to-crypto exchanges (that do not provide custodian wallet services), non-custodial service providers, and peer-to-peer trading platforms (not acting as intermediaries) [30,55]. Thus, these services do not need to register nor deploy AML/CFT policies. This is perplexing because loopholes like these, grant criminals methods to bypass legislation, and find evasion techniques to launder illicit proceeds [23].

The lack of global harmonization and consensus worsens this problem, as regulations vary from one jurisdiction to another, are constantly amended, and are vague [51]. This is crucial as it fuels the concept of "regulatory shopping" [68], which simply allows exchanges to escape certain regulations by relocating to "friendlier" jurisdictions of their choice. A prominent example of regulatory shopping would be the case of the most popular exchange in the world, Binance which has relocated several times in, what it seems, attempts to avoid or evade certain regulations. This event has been hinted at by the FATF in 2020 as a red flag indicator for money laundering and terrorist financing [44].

4.2   Enforcement Issues with Texts and Actual Compliance

A substantial issue that also comes forth with many regulations, and is opulent in the cryptocurrency area, is the applicability of texts and their efficacious enforcement. As the mere act of adopting regulations and policies is not enough, the actual results are translated by implementations and enforcement. This predicament can be pinpointed by many factors when taking the examples of the AMLD5 and the FATF. Firstly, there have been delays by certain jurisdictions in transposing the provisions of the AMLD5 into national laws (similarly with the FATF's recommendations). The FATF states that the majority of jurisdictions are yet to fully implement its standards targeting cryptocurrencies and only 11 jurisdictions out of 98 they surveyed had started to implement and enforce the Travel Rule legislation [47].

A second factor indicating the lack of effective enforcement is the high number of laundered funds. The blockchain analytics and cryptocurrency compliance company Chainalysis found that $33bn was laundered since 2017, most onto centralized exchanges [13]. Furthermore, in 2021 alone, 47% of the funds received by centralized exchanges, being the main targets of regulators, were sent from illicit addresses. This is in a year where enforcement of robust AML/CFT policies supposedly reached its peak, as more regulators were adopting regulations, and more services were claiming to comply.

Thirdly, the shortcomings of the described regulatory situation translate into low compliance by gatekeepers [45]. This is paving the way for criminals to bypass regulations. For instance, in 2020, 56% of VASPs globally had "weak or porous KYC processes" [19]. In Europe, 60% of hosted VASPs were found to have deficient KYC procedures the highest among any other continent; meanwhile, 40% of UK VASPs had weak KYC measures [19]. Finally, only 48% of all obliged entities in Europe were registered.

These numbers, yet again, implicate the ill-translation of these policies on ground. It vastly highlights the absence of proper mechanisms that ease and ensure in-practice compliance. In essence, adopting rigour regulations alone is exasperating, and stricter does not always connote a better outcome. Actions such as sanctioning, for example, may not be very beneficial as 44% of the illicit transaction volume in the year 2022 seem to originate from activities associated with certain sanctioned entities [17]. The importance lies in enforcement and compliance too. The minacious fact is, that the exploited exchanges are not only those classified as "high risk", or those bottom-ranked or suspicious-labelled ones but are also those dominating the market with legitimate covers.

Due to these factors, criminals are thriving, and exchanges are being willingly exploited. At a time when regulators are still experimenting with laws and finding grounds for enforcement, criminals are finding alternative methods. For instance, the usage of mixers was at an all-time high in 2022 [15]. Money launderers are also resorting to the many available rogue exchanges and mixers, sponsoring the thriving gray infrastructure [35]. Unsurprisingly, criminals are also operating such services themselves (cryptocurrency laundering "As a Service" [36]). This term was pinned by the Europol following the arrest of criminal organization members, who had been operating a cryptocurrency exchange and ATMs for the sole purpose of laundering illicit proceeds [34].

4.3 The Sunrise Issue

As we have discussed in previous sections, the FATF standards were extended back in 2019 to incorporate VAs and VASPs. Starting the following year, the FATF has been publishing reports documenting the global implementation of these standards and recommendations. In the 2022 version of the report, the FATF has identified a new issue called the "Sunrise Issue" [47].

The issue emanates from the implementation challenges faced when jurisdictions regulating VAs and VASPs interact with those who do not. This comes forth, especially when implementing Travel Rule policies, where VASPs are required to share transaction and customer-related information with each other.

As a consequence, jurisdictions regulating VASPs face another challenge. This time, it is about deciding to permit regulated VASPs to interact with unregulated counterparties. According to the FATF's report, most jurisdictions have not taken a position yet, however, some plan to limit interactions with only regulated VASPs, and others plan to permit transactions with unlicensed VASPs with certain risk mitigation measures [47].

4.4 The Burden of Compliance on Small/Medium Exchanges

Cryptocurrency service providers are still in their infancy but are entrusted with running and keeping the funds of millions globally. At present, only a few exchanges can be considered major businesses; the rest are all small/medium-sized businesses with limited budgets and capabilities. Regulators are not considering this and are bombarding everyone equally with the same compliance requirements. Many exchanges are not automatically ready or trained to handle this, especially adopted policies that are tailored specifically to conventional financial institutions. Exchanges are also relatively new to KYC/AML/CFT obligations and may be "unfamiliar" with exhaustive compliance fundamentals [38].

This situation drove major services to outsource their KYC and due diligence duties to third parties, which numerous small/medium exchanges cannot afford. Inevitably, only large corporations are and will be able to implement compliance practices, while small/medium and start-up exchanges will suffer to conform. In consequence, small/medium exchanges will risk closure or relocation to friendlier jurisdictions to survive [6]. Hence this creates a market with a compliance monopoly, where only major corporations will be able to offer fully legal and compliant services to users.

It is worth mentioning that some exchanges are refusing to comply with such policies and are advertising "KYC Free" or "KYC-Less" services [69]. Exchanges are in fact able to offer such services for many reasons, one of them being regulatory shopping and the ease of relocating to other preferred jurisdictions.

5 The Future of Policymaking

Policymakers worldwide have not been triumphant in addressing the countless implications stemming from exchanges, and cryptocurrencies in general. Instead, they resorted to classical and strict AML/CFT policies, and imposed them "as is" onto exchanges, all with hopes of harvesting equivalent results to those achieved within financial institutions. However, the noticeably low percentages of compliance mentioned in Sect. 4.2, and "sporadic regulatory efforts" [68] pinpoint the grim truth. Those robust rules governing conventional institutions for years, are failing in practice within the cryptocurrency ecosystem. Even though these policies are recent, they are already considered "outdated and insufficient" [57], as well as counterproductive [68]. This is a fact acknowledged by the European Commission, European Banking Agency, and the European Securities and Markets Authority [24,28,31].

5.1 Common Regulatory Practices in Need of Change

The initial approaches that can be adopted to enhance compliance numbers can be basic and simple. Some existing regulations might in fact be sufficient, but in that case, amendments must be more accommodating and adequate. Regulators should treat innovation with innovative approaches and texts, based on scientific research and advice. It is vital to establish a continual dialogue between the legal, academic, and cryptocurrency community, to exchange knowledge and novel findings. Current conventional laws should be molded and targeted towards the specific risks and problems stemming from and relating to these exchanges, not traditional financial institutions. They must be flexible, consistent, and proactive in a manner that embraces implications and future advancements, or else they will be outdated by the time they enter into force. Most governments want to control cryptocurrencies, yet the current state of many adopted regulations is only abetting cryptocurrency exchanges to frolic. Exchanges should be more liable and accountable for their services and actions, as the early days are gone, and billions are at stake now.

The terminological ambiguity, unclear definitions and classification have been challenging issues for regulators who seek to create and enforce frameworks with boundaries [2]. We suggest that the first step in addressing these issues starts with the mere adoption of unified terms and definitions that are clear, not vague, and do not hinder enforcement due to uncertainty deriving from different text interpretations. So first and foremost, and before moving forward with comprehensive regulatory packages, it is crucial to clarify and unify definitions that assist in determining application scope [48].

5.2 The Markets in Crypto-Assets Regulation

Perhaps these aforementioned issues may partially be solved by the EU's first comprehensive piece of regulation MiCA (Markets in Crypto-Assets) [33]. MiCA is set to alleviate regulatory uncertainty and harmonize rules across the EU. The framework aims to strengthen consumer protection and establish a standardized regime for the providers of cryptocurrency services such as issuers/offerors and exchanges [33]. This will raise transparency, stability, and integrity within the cryptocurrency ecosystem and create a harmonized legal ground [84].

Whilst the territorial scope of MiCA's applicability is limited to the EU, it is anticipated to be a revolutionary piece of legislation that positively influences other jurisdictions. This is vital, especially in creating a more harmonized atmosphere, with the hopes of establishing some levels of standardization in a similar manner to what the GDPR (the EU's flagship privacy legislation) has accomplished. MiCA aims to achieve these goals without drastically stifling innovation, however, this cannot be guaranteed beforehand. Some concerns are already being raised about certain aspects of the framework even though it has not yet entered into force. Experts such as the head of the ECB, for instance, highlighted a number of shortcomings, and spoke about the need for MiCA II, especially since enforcement is delayed, whilst the field is rapidly advancing [5]. Some even consider that MiCA fails to meet one of its vital goals, which is inaugurating legal harmonization across the EU and EEA members with the application of financial concepts [84].

Overall, MiCA may diminish some of the previously raised issues, however, this will be mostly and directly bound to the EU, as the rest of globe will still continue to work independently and establish different standards and frameworks. We believe the different and distant enforcement dates with certain provisions might have negative consequences. Whilst compared to other EU legislative pieces, the provisions of MiCA do indeed have shorter enforcement dates, these are still long compared to this fast-changing ecosystem. We believe that by the time these rules become applicable, a lot of new, unpredicted, and diverse advancements would have already emerged. This could very much hinder the framework from achieving its purpose in an ultimate manner.

5.3   The Transfer of Funds Regulation

In parallel to MiCA, the EU has also adopted a legislative package called TFR (Transfer of Funds Regulation) which is intended to work in line with the framework [32]. As MiCA itself does not incorporate AML/CFT guidelines, the TFR aims to fill this gap with the purpose of strengthening the EU's existing AML/CFT and aligning them with the FATF recommendations.

One of the main additions with the TFR, is the incorporation and implementation of stricter rules like the "Travel Rule". This will assist in establishing traceability of cryptocurrency transactions, and consequently, identifying risky and suspicious activities.

Whilst the main purpose of the TFR is supposed to further align the position .of the EU with the FATF recommendations, it seems that some of its provisions will be contradictory to them. The TFR mandates the collection of information related to the originator and the beneficiary, regardless of the transferred amount of funds. This comes contrary to the FATF's recommendations that advise taking such measures only with certain amounts of funds. Contradictions like this may further complicate the aforementioned "Sunrise Situation", and overall, only hinder the creation of global harmonized standards for compliance.

5.4   The Role of Law Enforcement

It is no longer impossible to identify criminals and even return or seize illicitly acquired funds. A prominent example of this would be the Colonial Pipeline case from 2021. The company was the target of a ransomware attack that crippled its activities until it finally gave in and paid a ransom of 75 BTC. But just after a month following the attack, and with the assistance of the private sector [14], law enforcement agencies were able to identify, track, and seize 63.7 BTC the attackers intended to launder [78]. Now, results like this cannot always be achieved, especially in a short time frame; sometimes it takes years [79], or is only viable with the help of involved exchanges [70].

Overall, these abilities are only possible because academics and the private sector started using the transparency and public nature of the blockchain to develop techniques and tools, which are in turn used by governments to track and catch cryptocurrency bad actors [16,52,62]. However, to curb illegal and criminal activity, such as money laundering (Sect. 2.1) and terrorist financing (Sect. 2.2), by way of exchanges, more law enforcement agencies must be equipped with the right tools and training on blockchain forensics. At the moment, most law enforcement agencies lack these abilities, and those that have them are dependent on the private sector. This is alarming. The role of law enforcement with cryptocurrencies is increasingly privatized. Moreover, the procedures involving these investigations and forensics is not available to the public, so it is unclear whether these private companies are following relevant procedural protocols.

Utilizing the blockchain to catch more criminals, is one of the methods that will further prove that using exchanges is *ipso facto* a bad idea. At present, the tools allowing this are only accessible by a few law enforcement agencies. To play an effective role in deterring criminal activity, we see a vital need for these tools to be accessible and used by a greater number of law enforcement agencies.

6   Conclusion

Cryptocurrency exchanges accommodate the mass public with easily accessible cryptocurrency platforms. With cryptocurrencies becoming mainstream, these exchanges started to facilitate billions of legal and illegal transactions on daily basis, offering additional services such as lending, staking, stock trading, and funds safekeeping. Conventional businesses and institutions operating similar services are heavily regulated and monitored. By contrast, exchanges were long left to self-regulate, only until recently when regulators started to bombard them with AML/CFT policies.

To this end, we argue that the methods regulators resort to are inefficient, as the adopted rigorous policies are tailored to fit the conventional financial system, not mutineer technologies. This is translated into low compliance numbers, even within territories with certain regulations such as Europe. We highlight that regulators are being near-sighted, as their policies are outdated by the time they already enter into force. This causes many problems, for example, the creation of backdoors for criminals, regulatory shopping, and generally, a devious environment for consumers that lacks trust, reliability, and accountability.

Nonetheless, these findings indicate the crucial need for consensus on terms, definitions, and scope on a global scale. We worry that the continued lack of global collaboration will further weaken any compliance and control efforts. This may add additional complications onto existing issues like regulatory shopping.

In the future, the starting point is the better understanding of the specific risks and issues present within the cryptocurrency ecosystem itself, and the tailoring of policies accordingly. Policies that are not necessarily lenient but still ease and assist exchanges in being compliant with the law. Furthermore, we believe that standardizing the work of exchanges within the boundaries of the law, may not only assist in deterring future criminals from exploiting their services, but also strengthening consumer protection.

Acknowledgements. This work was supported by the Engineering and Physical Sciences Research Council [grant number EP/S022503/1].

References

1. Abramova, S., Schöttle, P., Böhme, R.: Mixing coins of different quality: a game-theoretic approach. In: Brenner, M., et al. (eds.) FC 2017. LNCS, vol. 10323, pp. 280–297. Springer, Cham (2017). https://doi.org/10.1007/978-3-319-70278-0_18
2. Allen, J.G., Lastra, R.M.: Towards a European governance framework for cryptoassets. SUERF Policy Note (2019). https://www.suerf.org/policynotes/7839/towards-a-european-governance-framework-for-crypto-assets/html
3. Anderson, R., et al.: Measuring the changing cost of cybercrime. In: Workshop on the Economics of Information Security (2019)
4. Anderson, R., Shumailov, I., Ahmed, M., Rietmann, A.: Bitcoin redux. In: Workshop on the Economics of Information Security (2018)
5. Attlee, D.: ECB head calls for separate framework to regulate crypto lending (2022). https://cointelegraph.com/news/ecb-head-calls-for-separate-framework-to-regulate-crypto-lending
6. Blandin, A., et al.: 3rd global cryptoasset benchmarking study. Available at SSRN 3700822 (2020)
7. Boehm, F., Pesch, P.: Bitcoin: a first legal analysis. In: Böhme, R., Brenner, M., Moore, T., Smith, M. (eds.) FC 2014. LNCS, vol. 8438, pp. 43–54. Springer, Heidelberg (2014). https://doi.org/10.1007/978-3-662-44774-1_4
8. Böhme, R., Christin, N., Edelman, B., Moore, T.: Bitcoin: economics, technology, and governance. J. Econ. Perspect. 29(2), 213–238 (2015)
9. Böhme, R., Grzywotz, J., Paulina, P., Ruckert, C., Safferling, C.: Bitcoin and altcoin crime prevention (2017). https://www.bitcrime.de/presse-publikationen/pdf/BITCRIME-RegulRep.pdf
10. Bollen, R.: The legal status of online currencies - are Bitcoins the future? J. Banking Financ. Law Pract. (2013)
11. Brown, S.D.: Cryptocurrency and criminality: the bitcoin opportunity. Police J. 89(4), 327–339 (2016)
12. Casey, E.: Digital Evidence and Computer Crime: Forensic Science, Computers, and the Internet. Academic Press (2011)
13. Chainalysis: The chainalysis 2022 crypto crime report (2022). https://go.chainalysis.com/2022-Crypto-Crime-Report.html
14. Chainalysis: Chainalysis in action: How FBI investigators traced DarkSide's funds following the Colonial Pipeline ransomware attack (2022). https://blog.chainalysis.com/reports/darkside-colonial-pipeline-ransomware-seizure-case-study/
15. Chainalysis: Crypto mixer usage reaches all-time highs in 2022, with nation state actors and cybercriminals contributing significant volume (2022). https://blog.chainalysis.com/reports/crypto-mixer-criminal-volume-2022/
16. Chainalysis: Introducing Chainalysis government solutions (2022). https://blog.chainalysis.com/reports/chainalysis-government-solutions-announcement/
17. Chainalysis: 2023 crypto crime trends: Illicit cryptocurrency volumes reach all-time highs amid surge in sanctions designations and hacking (2023). https://blog.chainalysis.com/reports/2023-crypto-crime-report-introduction/
18. Christin, N.: Traveling the silk road: a measurement analysis of a large anonymous online marketplace. In: Proceedings of the 22nd International Conference on World Wide Web, pp. 213–224 (2013)
19. CipherTrace: Ciphertrace geographic risk report: Vasp kyc by jurisdiction (2020). https://ciphertrace.com/wp-content/uploads/2020/10/CipherTrace-2020-Geographic-RiskReport-100120.pdf

20. Clayton, R., Moore, T., Christin, N.: Concentrating correctly on cybercrime concentration. In: Workshop on the Economics of Information Security (2015)
21. Covolo, V.: The EU response to criminal misuse of cryptocurrencies: the young, already outdated 5th anti-money laundering directive. Eur. J. Crime Criminal Law Criminal Justice **28**(3), 217–251 (2020)
22. De Filippi, P.: Bitcoin: a regulatory nightmare to a libertarian dream. Internet Policy Rev. **3**(2) (2014)
23. Dupuis, D., Gleason, K.: Money laundering with cryptocurrency: open doors and the regulatory dialectic. J. Financ. Crime (2020)
24. EBA: Report with advice for the European commission on crypto-assets (2019). https://www.eba.europa.eu/sites/default/documents/files/documents/10180/2545547/67493daa-85a8-4429-aa91-e9a5ed880684/EBA%20Report%20on%20crypto%20assets.pdf
25. ECB: Virtual currency schemes (2012). https://www.ecb.europa.eu/pub/pdf/other/virtualcurrencyschemes201210en.pdf
26. ECB: Virtual currency schemes - a further analysis (2015). https://www.ecb.europa.eu/pub/pdf/other/virtualcurrencyschemesen.pdf
27. ECB Crypto-Assets Task Force: Crypto-assets: Implications for financial stability, monetary policy, and payments and market infrastructures (2019). https://www.ecb.europa.eu/pub/pdf/scpops/ecb.op223~3ce14e986c.en.pdf
28. ESMA: Advice on initial coins offerings and crypto-assets (2019). https://www.esma.europa.eu/sites/default/files/library/esma50-157-1391_crypto_advice.pdf
29. Directive (EU) 2018/843 of the European parliament and of the council of 30 May 2018 amending directive (EU) 2015/849 on the prevention of the use of the financial system for the purposes of money laundering or terrorist financing, and amending directives 2009/138/EC and 2013/36/EU (2018)
30. Commission staff working document accompanying the document report from the commission to the European parliament and the council on the assessment of the risk of money laundering and terrorist financing affecting the internal market and relating to cross-border activities. SWD/2019/650 final (2019)
31. Commission staff working document impact assessment accompanying the anti-money laundering package: Proposal for a regulation of the European parliament and of the council on the prevention of the use of the financial system for the purposes of money laundering or terrorist financing proposal for a directive of the European parliament and of the council on the mechanisms to be put in place by the member states for the prevention of the use of the financial system for the purposes of money laundering or terrorist financing and repealing directive (EU)2015/849 proposal for a regulation of the European parliament and of the council establishing the European authority for countering money laundering and financing of terrorism, amending regulations (EU) no 1093/2010, (EU) 1094/2010 and (EU) 1095/2010 proposal for a regulation of the European parliament and of the council on information accompanying transfers of funds and certain crypto-assets SWD/2021/190 final (2021)
32. Regulation (EU) 2023/1113 of the European parliament and of the council of 31 May 2023 on information accompanying transfers of funds and certain crypto-assets and amending directive (EU) 2015/849 (2023)
33. Regulation (EU) 2023/1114 of the European parliament and of the council of 31 May 2023 on markets in crypto-assets, and amending regulations (EU) no 1093/2010 and (EU) no 1095/2010 and directives 2013/36/EU and (EU) 2019/1937 (2023)

34. Europol: Cryptocurrency laundering as a service: members of a criminal organisation arrested in Spain (2019). https://www.europol.europa.eu/media-press/newsroom/news/cryptocurrency-laundering-service-members-of-criminal-organisation-arrested-in-spain

35. Europol: Internet organised crime threat assessment (IOCTA). Publications Office of the European Union (2021). https://www.europol.europa.eu/activities-services/main-reports/internet-organised-crime-threat-assessment-iocta-2021

36. Europol: Serious and organised crime threat assessment (2021). https://www.europol.europa.eu/activities-services/main-reports/european-union-serious-and-organised-crime-threat-assessment

37. Fanusie, Y.: Terrorist networks eye bitcoin as cryptocurrency's price rises (2017). https://www.thecipherbrief.com/terrorist-networks-eye-bitcoin-cryptocurrencys-price-rises

38. FATF: 12-month review of the revised FATF standards on virtual assets and virtual asset service providers. https://www.fatf-gafi.org/publications/fatfrecommendations/documents/12-month-review-virtual-assets-vasps.html

39. FATF: Virtual currencies key definitions and potential AML/CFT risks (2014). https://www.fatf-gafi.org/media/fatf/documents/reports/Virtual-currency-key-definitions-and-potential-aml-cft-risks.pdf

40. FATF: Guidance for a risk-based approach to virtual currencies (2015). https://www.fatf-gafi.org/media/fatf/documents/reports/Guidance-RBA-Virtual-Currencies.pdf

41. FATF: The FATF recommendations (2018). https://web.archive.org/web/20181029131157/http://www.fatf-gafi.org/publications/fatfrecommendations/documents/fatf-recommendations.html

42. FATF: Guidance for a risk-based approach to virtual assets and virtual asset service providers (2019). https://www.fatf-gafi.org/publications/fatfrecommendations/documents/guidance-rba-virtual-assets.html

43. FATF: Regulation of virtual assets (2019). https://www.fatf-gafi.org/publications/fatfrecommendations/documents/regulation-virtual-assets.html

44. FATF: Money laundering and terrorist financing red flag indicators associated with virtual assets (2020). https://www.fatf-gafi.org/publications/fatfrecommendations/documents/Virtual-Assets-Red-Flag-Indicators.html

45. FATF: Second 12-month review of the revised FATF standards on virtual assets and virtual asset service providers (2021). https://www.fatf-gafi.org/publications/fatfrecommendations/documents/second-12-month-review-virtual-assets-vasps.html

46. FATF: Updated guidance for a risk-based approach for virtual assets and virtual asset service providers (2021). https://www.fatf-gafi.org/publications/fatfrecommendations/documents/guidance-rba-virtual-assets-2021.html

47. FATF: Targeted update on implementation of FATF's standards on VAs and VASPs (2022). https://www.fatf-gafi.org/en/publications/fatfrecommendations/documents/targeted-update-virtual-assets-vasps.html

48. Ferreira, A., Sandner, P.: EU search for regulatory answers to crypto assets and their place in the financial markets' infrastructure. Comput. Law Secur. Rev. **43**, 105632 (2021)

49. Foley, S., Karlsen, J.R., Putniņš, T.J.: Sex, drugs, and bitcoin: how much illegal activity is financed through cryptocurrencies? Rev. Financ. Stud. **32**(5), 1798–1853 (2019)

50. Gandal, N., Hamrick, J., Moore, T., Vasek, M.: The rise and fall of cryptocurrency coins and tokens. Decis. Econ. Finan. **44**(2), 981–1014 (2021)

51. Girasa, R.: Regulation of Cryptocurrencies and Blockchain Technologies: National and International Perspectives. Springer, Heidelberg (2018)
52. Goldfeder, S., Kalodner, H., Reisman, D., Narayanan, A.: When the cookie meets the blockchain: privacy risks of web payments via cryptocurrencies. In: Privacy Enhancing Technologies (2017)
53. Grinberg, R.: Bitcoin: an innovative alternative digital currency. Hastings Sci. Technol. Law J. **4**, 160 (2011)
54. Guadamuz, A., Marsden, C.: Blockchains and bitcoin: regulatory responses to cryptocurrencies. First Monday **20**(12–7) (2015)
55. Haffke, L., Fromberger, M., Zimmermann, P.: Cryptocurrencies and anti-money laundering: the shortcomings of the fifth AML directive (EU) and how to address them. J. Bank. Regul. **21**, 125–138 (2020)
56. Houben, R., Snyers, A.: Cryptocurrencies and blockchain: legal context and implications for financial crime, money laundering and tax evasion. Study requested by the European Parliament's TAX3 Committee (2018), no. PE 619.024
57. Houben, R., Snyers, A.: Crypto-assets. Key developments, regulatory concerns and responses. Policy Department for Economic, Scientific and Quality of Life Policies (2020)
58. Irwin, A.S., Milad, G.: The use of crypto-currencies in funding violent jihad. J. Money Laundering Control **19**(4), 407–425 (2016)
59. Keatinge, T.: Virtual currencies and terrorist financing: assessing the risks and evaluating responses: counter-terrorism. European Parliament (2018)
60. Kethineni, S., Cao, Y.: The rise in popularity of cryptocurrency and associated criminal activity. Int. Crim. Justice Rev. **30**(3), 325–344 (2020)
61. McReynolds, E., Lerner, A., Scott, W., Roesner, F., Kohno, T.: Cryptographic currencies from a tech-policy perspective: policy issues and technical directions. In: Brenner, M., Christin, N., Johnson, B., Rohloff, K. (eds.) FC 2015. LNCS, vol. 8976, pp. 94–111. Springer, Heidelberg (2015). https://doi.org/10.1007/978-3-662-48051-9_8
62. Meiklejohn, S., et al.: A fistful of bitcoins: characterizing payments among men with no names. In: Internet Measurement Conference, pp. 127–140 (2013)
63. Moore, T., Christin, N.: Beware the middleman: empirical analysis of bitcoin-exchange risk. In: Sadeghi, A.-R. (ed.) FC 2013. LNCS, vol. 7859, pp. 25–33. Springer, Heidelberg (2013). https://doi.org/10.1007/978-3-642-39884-1_3
64. Moore, T., Christin, N., Szurdi, J.: Revisiting the risks of bitcoin currency exchange closure. ACM Trans. Internet Technol. **18**(4), 50:1–50:18 (2018)
65. Möser, M., Böhme, R., Breuker, D.: An inquiry into money laundering tools in the Bitcoin ecosystem. In: 2013 APWG eCrime Researchers Summit, pp. 1–14. IEEE (2013)
66. Möser, M., Böhme, R., Breuker, D.: Towards risk scoring of bitcoin transactions. In: Böhme, R., Brenner, M., Moore, T., Smith, M. (eds.) FC 2014. LNCS, vol. 8438, pp. 16–32. Springer, Heidelberg (2014). https://doi.org/10.1007/978-3-662-44774-1_2
67. Möser, M., Narayanan, A.: Effective cryptocurrency regulation through blacklisting (2019). https://maltemoeser.de/paper/blacklisting-regulation.pdf
68. Nabilou, H.: How to regulate bitcoin? Decentralized regulation for a decentralized cryptocurrency. Int. J. Law Inf. Technol. **27**(3), 266–291 (2019)
69. Pluja: Kyc? not me (2023). https://kycnot.me/
70. Reguerra, E.: Binance recovers the majority of funds stolen from curve finance (2022). https://cointelegraph.com/news/binance-recovers-the-majority-of-funds-stolen-from-curve-finance

71. Reynolds, P., Irwin, A.S.: Tracking digital footprints: anonymity within the bitcoin system. J. Money Laundering Control **20**(2), 172–189 (2017)

72. Suga, Y., Shimaoka, M., Sato, M., Nakajima, H.: Securing cryptocurrency exchange: building up standard from huge failures. In: Bernhard, M., et al. (eds.) FC 2020. LNCS, vol. 12063, pp. 254–270. Springer, Cham (2020). https://doi.org/10.1007/978-3-030-54455-3_19

73. Teichmann, F.M.J.: Financing terrorism through cryptocurrencies-a danger for Europe? J. Money Laundering Control **21**(4), 513–519 (2018)

74. Trozze, A., et al.: Cryptocurrencies and future financial crime. Crime Sci. **11**, 1–35 (2022)

75. Turpin, J.B.: Bitcoin: the economic case for a global, virtual currency operating in an unexplored legal framework. Indiana J. Glob. Legal Stud. **21**, 335 (2014)

76. UK Law Commission: Digital assets (2022). https://www.lawcom.gov.uk/project/digital-assets/

77. US Department of Justice: Virginia teen pleads guilty to providing material support to ISIL (2015). https://www.justice.gov/opa/pr/virginia-teen-pleads-guilty-providing-material-support-isil

78. US Department of Justice: Department of justice seizes $2.3 million in cryptocurrency paid to the ransomware extortionists darkside (2022). https://www.justice.gov/opa/pr/department-justice-seizes-23-million-cryptocurrency-paid-ransomware-extortionists-darkside

79. US Department of Justice: Two arrested for alleged conspiracy to launder $4.5 billion in stolen cryptocurrency (2022). https://www.justice.gov/opa/pr/two-arrested-alleged-conspiracy-launder-45-billion-stolen-cryptocurrency

80. US Internal Revenue Service: Virtual currencies (2023). https://www.irs.gov/businesses/small-businesses-self-employed/virtual-currencies

81. US Law Library of Congress, Global Legal Research Directorate: Regulation of cryptocurrency around the world: November 2021 update (2021). https://tile.loc.gov/storage-services/service/ll/llglrd/2021687419/2021687419.pdf

82. Vasek, M., Moore, T.: There's no free lunch, even using bitcoin: tracking the popularity and profits of virtual currency scams. In: Böhme, R., Okamoto, T. (eds.) FC 2015. LNCS, vol. 8975, pp. 44–61. Springer, Heidelberg (2015). https://doi.org/10.1007/978-3-662-47854-7_4

83. Xia, P., et al.: Characterizing cryptocurrency exchange scams. Comput. Secur. **98** (2020)

84. Zetzsche, D.A., Annunziata, F., Arner, D.W., Buckley, R.P.: The markets in crypto-assets regulation (MiCA) and the EU digital finance strategy. Capital Markets Law J. **16**(2), 203–225 (2021)

A First Dive into OFAC in DeFi Space

Qin Wang[1]([✉]), Shange Fu[2]([✉]), Shiping Chen[1], and Jiangshan Yu[2]

[1] CSIRO Data61, Eveleigh, Australia
qinwangtech@gmail.com
[2] Monash University, Clayton, Australia
shange.fu@monash.edu

Abstract. *51% of Ethereum Blocks are OFAC Censored* was one of the annual headlines in the year 2022. Short for Office of Foreign Assets Control, OFAC, as a division of the U.S. Treasury Department, made itself go on the stage of decentralized finance (DeFi). OFAC was originally established to impose economic sanctions on threats to the United States national security. The jurisdiction of OFAC today, however, seems to be stretching further and further. In this work, we provide the first dive into OFAC in the DeFi space. We describe how OFAC specifically implements its sanctions, namely, on chains (in particular, Ethereum 2.0 as an example), on cryptocurrencies, and on decentralized applications. We discuss the impacts of the presence of OFAC intervention and identify future directions for DeFi products based on this fact.

Keywords: OFAC · DeFi · Ethereum 2.0

1 Introduction

Regulation on cryptocurrencies has always been under heated debate, yet is being implemented on an ongoing basis [1]. According to a varying system of legislation, different countries perform their ways of regulation in different forms. Governments such as El Salvador and Switzerland adopt a proactive method to legalize cryptocurrencies and classify them as a legitimate asset class. It usually comes with a series of regulated matters, such as implementing anti-money laundering (AML) and know-your-customer (KYC) procedures and drafting a clear legal framework for cryptocurrency transactions and investments. Some countries (e.g., US, Japan, Australia, Estonia) try to create regulations and laws that typically center around the sale, purchase, and use of cryptocurrencies, as well as requirements for crypto companies to be licensed. In some countries (e.g., China, Algeria, Iran, Nepal, Bolivia), governments take a negative view of cryptocurrencies and have banned them outright. Illegal activities involve buying, selling, or even holding cryptocurrencies within the country. Despite the complex and controversial regulatory environment surrounding cryptocurrencies, attitudes toward them, fortunately, have evolved over time. As a result, there is a recognition of the potential benefits of blockchain technology and a desire to balance innovation with consumer protection and regulatory oversight. In this work,

© International Financial Cryptography Association 2024
A. Essex et al. (Eds.): FC 2023 Workshops, LNCS 13953, pp. 133–140, 2024.
https://doi.org/10.1007/978-3-031-48806-1_9

we explore a specific regulatory approach (OFAC [2], one of the most influential agencies) that has been applied to govern cryptocurrencies (especially, DeFi protocols [3]) and provide detailed explanations of the key principles and practices involved. We aim to offer insights into the unique challenges and opportunities associated with regulating this emerging technology.

What is OFAC. OFAC, standing for the Office of Foreign Assets Control, is an agency of the United States Department of the Treasury [2]. OFAC is responsible for administering/enforcing economic sanctions against countries, organizations, or individuals with potential threats to its security, foreign policies, or economies. The sanctions include multiple types of restrictions that are not limited to national trade, financial transactions, and business dealings. The significant impact of OFAC comes from its close connection with national government agencies for accomplishing the mission. In particular, OFAC has the authority to designate individuals or entities on its Specially Designated Nationals and Blocked Persons (SDN) list [4]. This list includes individuals and organizations that are prohibited from doing business with U.S. persons or companies.

Why OFAC Has an Interest in DeFi. DeFi (Decentralized Finance) [3] refers to a new type of financial system built on blockchains with features of decentralization, permissionlessness, and automation. DeFi protocols are generally deployed on smart contract platforms (e.g., Ethereum, Avalanche), enabling developers to create a variety of decentralized applications (DApps) that operate without intermediaries. They can be used to support financial activities, including trading (DEXes like Uniswap), anchoring (stablecoins, e.g. DAI, UST), borrowing/lending (Aave, Liquity, etc.), and investing (e.g., Bancor). OFAC starts to raise interest in DeFi based on two reasons. First, most DeFi services/products can provide a high degree of anonymity and cross-border accessibility, making it attractive for those looking to conduct illicit activities as well as circumvent economic sanctions. OFAC is responsible for enforcing AML and counter-terrorism financing (CTF) laws and regulations, protecting national users from criminals. Secondly, DeFi protocols and related cryptocurrencies have become increasingly mainstream. OFAC has to start its procedure of drafting the regulatory framework and executing enforcement actions.

OFAC Sanctions in DeFi. Accordingly, OFAC has placed restrictions on certain DeFi products and the use of cryptocurrencies by individuals and entities subject to U.S. sanctions. A typical example is the sanction of the virtual currency mixer Tornado Cash (detailed in Sect. 2.2) due to its services for laundering more than $7 billion worth of cryptocurrencies since 2019. Not surprisingly, several Web3 companies, as the opponent, stood up to fight against the sanction by denying its freezing of tokens [5]. Another straightforward example is the (OFAC-) compliance of MEV-boost relay (more in Sect. 2.1). After *The Merge*, the rise of MEV-boost relays has taken over the Ethereum network. A large portion of relays is subject to regulation by OFAC, which may restrict certain transactions that violate U.S. interests. Even though regulation is inevitable, the entities operating validators outside of the U.S. should consider running non-censoring relays, as suggested by MEV Watch, for the neutrality of the network.

Our Contributions. Following similar connotation, in this paper, we delve deeper into the regulatory landscape (Sect. 1) and explore how the OFAC regulates existing DeFi protocols (Sect. 2), as well as ways to establish a better, more decentralized environment (Sect. 3). We propose three technical routes that OFAC could take to regulate DeFi, targeting the chain-, cryptocurrency-, and DApp-levels separately. In particular, we focus on the first route, which involves regulating Ethereum validators after *The Merge*. We provide a detailed analysis of the ways in which this can be done, given the high attention that this issue has received. Additionally, we discuss the necessity of OFAC's involvement in DeFi and how it may reshape the DeFi space in the future.

Related Work (US Regulations). The US government has gradually taken steps to promote innovation in the DeFi space. The Commodity Futures Trading Commission (CFTC), in 2020, filed a complaint against a cryptocurrency trading platform for fraud and misappropriation of funds. The Department of Justice has also brought criminal charges against individuals involved in cryptocurrency-related scams. Later, the Securities and Exchange Commission (SEC) has authority over initial coin offerings (ICOs) and securities offerings [6]. The Internal Revenue Service (IRS) treats cryptocurrencies as property for tax purposes. In 2021, the Office of the Comptroller of the Currency (OCC) issued guidance allowing national banks to use stablecoins and participate in blockchain networks, and SEC has proposed a regulatory framework for allowing certain cryptocurrencies to be traded on national securities exchanges. Based on the proposed rules, SEC conducted a series of sanctions against crypto-space [7], such as blaming SBF for the collapse of FTX [8] and fined Kraken with $30M for its staking-as-a-service program [9]. Also, CFTC sued a crypto trader for allegedly over $114M USD via the scams of contract swaps [10].

2   Scope of Jurisdiction

In this section, we demonstrate three distinct technical routes (targeting *chains*, *crypocurrencies*, and *DApps*) that could be applied by OFAC regulation. For each, we outline the specific approaches and provide real-world regulating cases.

2.1   Towards Chain

To enforce its regulations, the first approach of OFAC involves censoring the DeFi infrastructure, namely underlying blockchains. As a prime illustration of its reach, we select Ethereum 2.0 as our example due to its high popularity.

Ethereum 1.0 vs 2.0. Ethereum 1.0 [11] adopted the proof-of-work (PoW) consensus algorithm and required miners to solve complex mathematical problems for producing blocks and extending chains. In contrast, Ethereum 2.0 (the upgrade is called *The Merge*[1], launched on Sep. 15, 2022) utilizes the proof-of-stake (PoS)

---

[1] Ethereum: The Merge, https://ethereum.org/en/upgrades/merge/.

protocol and allows the users who have staked their cryptocurrency holdings (a.k.a. validators[2]) to participate in the consensus procedures. For advantages after the upgrade, Ethereum's energy consumption has been reduced by 99.95% and the performance is designed to increase (expected) $100X+$.

OFAC is Censoring Ethereum 2.0. According to the real-time statistics provided by MEV Watch[3], around 60% [time frame measured in ALL] of the Ethereum blocks generated after *The Merge* (including corresponding transactions) are compliant with OFAC regulations. This finding is based on an analysis of the percentage of MEV-boost proposed blocks, which are not generated by Ethereum validators but rather by MEV relays responsible for suggesting the most profitable bundle of transactions for earning MEV. It's worth noting that the extraction of MEV has become a critical aspect of Ethereum validation, with the current scale of extracted MEV amounting to an astonishing $689,906,734. It highlights the significant reliance on MEV-boost among validators.

Why Ethereum 2.0 can be OFACed. For better understanding, we now explain how to apply OFAC to Ethereum 2.0 network. Supposing the case of sending ETH from a user Bob to his friend Joe, a typical block creation cycle (compatible with both 1.0 and 2.0 versions) is stated as follows.

Creating Transaction. To initiate a transaction, Bob first signs it with his private key and then transmits it to nearby nodes. Once transmitted, the network randomly assigns the transaction to a group of mining nodes for processing.

Adding into Pools. Upon receiving the transaction, a blockchain node verifies its authenticity and adds it to the local transaction pool (equiv. mempool). The node at the same time disseminates the transaction to neighbor nodes, which must similarly verify the transaction and add it to their respective mempools.

Ordering Transaction. The validator (or miner) is responsible for arranging received transactions and appending them to the blockchain. Miners possess the autonomy to *determine the order of transactions*, e.g., based on the paid gas prices (majorly) or nonce values. Transactions with higher gas fees are usually prioritized, leading to their faster inclusion in a block.

Packing Block. Once transactions have been ordered, the validator will commence gathering all of the transactions into a "tree" structure and generate a corresponding block header by populating crucial fields such as timestamp, addresses, etc. During this process, miners must adhere to specific consensus protocols, such as PoS in Ethereum 2.0 and PoW in 1.0.

Appending to Chain. After completion, the validator shares the resulting block with the peer-to-peer network. The chain will then expand by attaching the newly received block, according to specific chain-selection rules (in particular, the GHOST&Casper in Ethereum PoS [12] and the longest-chain in PoW).

In the current stage, PoS validators are responsible for the entire cycle of block production. It is evident that PoS validators hold significant influence over the

---

[2] Since the launch of the Beacon Chain in late 2020, 16.5M ETH, worth over US$25B, has been staked via 520K+ validators, as of Feb 2023 [Data source: Binance].

[3] MEV Watch: https://www.mevwatch.info/ [Feb 2023].

arrangement of transactions in their mempool, which can enable them to profitably manipulate it. The existence of MEV, however, has created an incentive for validators to collaborate with trading firms to increase their returns. If left unaddressed, this could result in the centralization of Ethereum. Fortunately, the technique called proposer-builder separation (PBS) [13] is proposed, where validators can delegate the challenging task of building blocks to specialized entities (known as block builders). As a result, producing blocks is distributed among a wider range of proposers, resulting in the adoption of MEV-boost relays.

Root Reason Caused by MEV-Boost Relay. MEV-boost relay serves as a trusted mediator between block producers and block builders [13]. It provides the services to maximally extract the MEV profits and fairly distributed them to participants. To achieve this, the relay is typically implemented with a bot to automatically arbitrage transactions. This enables validators (node operators, staking pools) to increase their Annual Percentage Rate (APR)[4] by outsourcing their block-producing responsibilities to the highest bidder. As reported by MEV Watch, seven main relays[5] are currently in use. However, only three of these relays do not engage in censorship to comply with the requirements of OFAC. This gives the key answers to *why Ethereum 2.0 is OFACed* and leads to a negative result of breaking the credible neutrality of the entire network.

Why Other Chains Have Not Been Obviously OFACed. Though the issue of MEV may theoretically take place on any stateful blockchain, our observation is pretty straightforward: the absence of MEV-boost services creates a barrier to the application of OFAC regulations. In the case of competitive Proof-of-Stake chains like Binance Smart Chain, MEV-boosts don't have the same impact as in the Ethereum ecosystem. As for other public chains such as Avalanche and Algorand, their consensus mechanisms don't naturally facilitate the extraction of MEV. As a result, these networks may not be subject to the same regulatory scrutiny as those where MEV-boost services are more prevalent.

2.2 Towards Cryptocurrency

The second approach for implementing OFAC regulations is to directly prohibit the use of certain cryptocurrencies. In this case, we review the OFAC sanctions imposed on Tornado Cash [14]. Tornado Cash [15] is designed to be a non-custodial and privacy-focused Ethereum mixer. It enables users to anonymously exchange tokens among Ether (ETH) and ERC20 tokens. The solution leverages zero-knowledge proofs (ZKP) to obfuscate the transaction history and unlink the sender's and recipient's addresses. When a user deposits funds into its smart contract, the funds are mixed with other deposits and shuffled multiple times

---

[4] APR means validators can earn as a reward for participating in the network. It depends on a variety of factors, including the total amount of staked tokens on the network, the network's inflation rate, and the validator's performance in the network.
[5] Mainstream MEV-boost relays: Flashbots, BloXroute Max Profit, BloXroute Ethical, BloXroute Regulated, BlockNative, Manifold and Eden (cf. MEV Watch).

to make it nearly impossible to track their original source. Tornado Cash thus gained popularity in crypto communities due to its privacy-protecting nature.

However, OFAC imposed sanctions [14] on Tornado Cash and seven of its developers for their roles in facilitating the laundering of $7B USD worth of cryptocurrency and other illicit activities since its inception in 2019. It alleged that Tornado Cash was used by malicious actors to implement adequate anti-money laundering, e.g., mixing ransom payments received from victims of ransomware attacks, and facilitating transactions related to illicit activities such as drug trafficking and counter-terrorism financing U.S. citizens, As a result, are prohibited from conducting transactions with Tornado Cash, and any assets or property held by them within U.S. jurisdiction have been blocked. The aftermath also affected many DeFi protocols [16] including Aave, Uniswap, and Balancer. While it is crucial to use services like Tornado Cash responsibly and within the bounds of relevant laws and regulations, the issue of jurisdictional scope has sparked controversy among different communities. In a bid to justify its position, Tether (the issuer of USDT) has affirmed that [5] it will not impose sanctions on the smart contract addresses connected to Tornado Cash.

2.3   Towards DApp

Another dimension in the regulation scope of OFAC is DApp. DApp is an application that utilizes smart contracts to provide users with automated services such as trading, lending, and gaming in the DeFi ecosystem. Following the OFAC sanction case on Tornado Cash that we have just introduced, DApps such as Aave, Uniswap and Balancer, also ban wallets that have interacted with Tornado Cash. The power of OFAC over DApps is that it can lead DApps actively follow its actions, and it is hardly possible to deny that the existence of such a situation is a reflection of the real-world power structure. A centralized dataset maintained by TRM Labs is responsible for the accounts being banned [17]. Aave, one of the DeFi lending protocols, claimed that the TRM API on its DApp was responsible for blocking addresses that received ETH from unknown sources through Tornado Cash. However, the biggest concern is how TRM Labs decides what constitutes a sanctioned address. This may lead to an issue, and there needs to be standards and transparency as to how the community needs to be complying with this unprecedented sanction of wallets and DApps.

3   Discussion

OFAC stepping in cryptocurrency is currently a work in process. With little judicial precedent, both government and community are tentatively taking action and responding to each other, to explore the way forward. In this section, we discuss the necessity of the presence of OFAC in the DeFi space, and whether DeFi can exist on a parallel track outside of regulation.

A Symbiosis of OFAC and DeFi. Regulation imposed on cryptocurrencies, or even the entire DeFi ecosystem, is there for purposes of protecting national security and the safety of citizens' property, among others. OFAC, representing the power of the American government, is the most influential one. OFAC is claimed to defend against terrorists, narcotics dealers, targeted regimes, and other potential dangers to the homeland security of the U.S., or the economy. Cryptocurrencies that engaged in activities related to those threats have also been included in the scope of jurisdiction of OFAC in recent years. However, the spectrum of the power of OFAC is not only limited to the local United States, but worldwide, and even has a trend of forming a symbiosis with DeFi. In fact, not only OFAC, institutions such as SEC or stablecoins pegged to the USD, are all implying a deep-state-like status for the U.S. in the back of DeFi. So a question naturally arises: are we back to the point where we started? The advent of Bitcoin, as well as the following DeFi era, is a response to the 2007 United States subprime mortgage crisis, expressing disbelief in the greed of the centralized banking system. As DeFi grows and evolves, however, government departments and their regulation are coming back to the table again, going against the line of DeFi. We might expect this to continue, and a symbiosis of OFAC and DeFi is inevitable.

Ways to Re-decentralization. For the DeFi maximalists, OFAC's interference is hardly satisfying, and this also leads to a discussion on how to approach a truly decentralized financial system, as a re-decentralization exploration. We now rule out risks that individuals may or may not realize complete anonymity in reality, resulting in their restricted behavior. We instead consider ways to reinforce censorship-resistant decentralization via technical paths. The first and most straightforward method is to use alternative solutions, if available. Or to fork a protocol is also a similar idea to this; either a chain or a DApp, developers can directly replicate the same environment to bypass the regulation that has been put onward. Users will make their own choices, and they may move over time. Privacy protection technology is another alternative. This type of technology, including but not limited to ZKP, Obfuscation, and their combination with layer 2 solutions, can enable individuals to preserve their confidentiality better. Other than that, further thought is to revisit the fundamentals of PoW and PoS. PoW is rather simple to determine the content of a block by consuming more energy than others. Whereas PoS leaves much room to be interfered with (e.g., OFAC on Ethereum) as it is more complex in designs and capital-driven. A wave of reversed evolution of backing to the PoW may yield if people are getting less and less confidence in PoS.

Concluding Remarks. OFAC, abbreviated for the Office of Foreign Assets Control, is gradually taking a hand into the DeFi land. Of all the cases, more than 51% of Ethereum blocks complying with OFAC standards after The Merge is of the closest attention, and as a result, building a better-decentralized future is once again in question. This study makes a timely contribution to the entire community by providing an overall picture of OFAC as a concept. The existence of OFAC has both implicit and explicit benefits&drawbacks to the DeFi ecosystem, and most importantly, it is already in place. The symbiosis of DeFi and censorship is one path. Parallel to an environment of regulation, we have also discussed ways of achieving more desirable decentralization. A game exists between governments and communities. The evolutionary results of the game will shape where DeFi is ultimately headed.

References

1. Allen, S., et al.: Design choices for central bank digital currency: policy and technical considerations. National Bureau of Economic Research (2020)
2. Office of foreign assets control-sanctions programs and information (2023). Accessible https://home.treasury.gov/policy-issues/office-of-foreign-assets-control-sanctions-programs-and-information
3. Werner, S.M., Perez, D., Gudgeon, L., et al.: SoK: decentralized finance (DeFi). arXiv preprint arXiv:2101.08778 (2021)
4. Specially Designated Nationals and Blocked Persons List (SDN) Human Readable Lists (2023). Accessible https://home.treasury.gov/policy-issues/financial-sanctions/specially-designated-nationals-and-blocked-persons-list-sdn-human-readable-lists
5. Tether (USDT) defies treasury's sanction, says freezing Tornado Cash addresses is reckless (2022). Accessible https://www.investing.com/news/cryptocurrency-news/tether-usdt-defies-treasurys-sanction-says-freezing-tornado-cash-addresses-is-reckless-2880066
6. SEC: Spotlight on Initial Coin Offerings (ICOs) (2021). Accessible https://www.sec.gov/ICO
7. SEC Seeks to Stop the Registration of Misleading Crypto Asset Offerings (2022). Accessible https://www.sec.gov/news/press-release/2022-208
8. SEC charges Samuel Bankman-Fried with defrauding investors in crypto asset trading platform FTX (2022). Accessible https://www.sec.gov/news/press-release/2022-219
9. The SEC cracks down on crypto: Kraken and staking, Paxos and BUSD, and taxes and yachts (2023). Accessible https://www.bloomberg.com/opinion/articles/2023-02-13/the-sec-cracks-down-on-crypto
10. CFTC Sues Trader Over Alleged $114 Million Mango Markets Crypto Swaps Scam. Bloomberg (2023). Accessible https://www.bloomberg.com/news/articles/2023-01-10/cftc-sues-trader-over-alleged-114-million-mango-markets-crypto-swaps-scam
11. Wood, G., et al.: Ethereum: a secure decentralised generalised transaction ledger. Ethereum Project Yellow Pap. **151**(2014), 1–32 (2014)
12. Buterin, V., Hernandez, D., et al.: Combining GHOST and Casper. arXiv preprint arXiv:2003.03052 (2020)
13. Flashbots. MEV-related research from flashbots (2023). Accessible https://www.flashbots.net/
14. U.S. treasury sanctions notorious virtual currency mixer tornado cash (2022). Accessible https://home.treasury.gov/news/press-releases/jy0916
15. Tornado cash (2019). Accessible https://web.archive.org/web/20220808144431/https://tornado.cash/
16. LALA Tuni. Aave, uniswap, and balancer prohibit tornado cash-related wallets after OFAC sanction (2022). Accessible https://coinculture.com/au/business/aave-uniswap-and-balancer-prohibit-tornado-cash-related-wallets-after-ofac-sanction/
17. TRM Labs. Digital asset compliance & risk management (2023). Accessible https://www.trmlabs.com/

Proposal of Principles of DeFi Disclosure and Regulation

Tomonori Yuyama[1]([✉]), Ken Katayama[2], and Paul Brigner[3]

[1] Georgetown University, 3700 O St NW, Washington, DC 20057, USA
`tomonori.yuyama@toki.waseda.jp`
[2] Nomura Research Institute, Ltd., Tokyo, Japan
`k-katayama@nri.co.jp`
[3] Electric Coin, Co., Denver, USA
`paul@electriccoin.co`

Abstract. This paper proposes eight principles for DeFi disclosure and regulation based on the implications from the key challenges, risks, and questions. Such implications include Innovation Trilemma, whether a DeFi constitutes the "financial service" which participants are subject to consumer/investor protection needs to be considered, regulations from the perspective of systemic risk and anti-money laundering, establishment of a disclosure system and enforcement framework suitable for the characteristics of DeFi and crypto-assets. Creating a common disclosure platform in which national authorities and international standard-setting bodies could participate and give authority would be desirable. Such a framework would provide basic information regarding a DeFi, such as disclosure of data, governance mechanisms, token information, as well as information on audits, etc., and it would be a convenient way to check for compliance as well. Designing an appropriate common disclosure platform, that also considers participants' incentive structure, is very challenging and will be the subject of further research.

Keywords: DeFi · Regulation · Disclosure · Innovation trilemma · Token · DEX · AML/CFT

1 Introduction

After the collapse of FTX, some argued that this event was a problem with the centralized exchange (CEX), and decentralized finance (DeFi) should be

This paper owes much to the paper "Proposal of Principles of DeFi Disclosure and Regulation", which is the output paper of the IKP-WG (IAM, Key Management and Privacy Working Group) of the Blockchain Governance Initiative Network (BGIN). (BGIN Website: https://bgin-global.org/docs/). Authors (Tomonori Yuyama, Ken Katayama, and Paul Brigner) are editors of this paper. Authors would like to thank the WG co-chair Nat Sakimura (OpenID Foundation), Mitchell Travers (Soulbis Pty Ltd), the paper contributors (Tetsu Kurumizawa (Yale University), Michi Kakebayashi (UC Berkeley), Shinji Sato (Independent researcher), Stephanie Bazley (AirTree Ventures), and Yuji Suga (IIJ)), and all participants in this WG. This paper is also considered to be the paper that further updates the BGIN (2021) published by the IKPWG in the BGIN.

A. Essex et al. (Eds.): FC 2023 Workshops, LNCS 13953, pp. 141–164, 2024.
https://doi.org/10.1007/978-3-031-48806-1_10

promoted more because that there was no problem with it, and it is a source of innovation. For example, in the U.S. Senate hearings after the FTX failure[1], while some experts skeptical of crypto assets said that the FTX failure was not a problem of a CEX alone and a decentralized exchange (DEX), which is a part of DeFi, would not solve the problem, other experts said that the problem of the FTX seemed to be that failure of the CEX, not the DEX. What should we think about this issue?

DeFi itself has emerged recently and thus probably does not have a widely accepted definition (OECD [34]). Nonetheless, DeFi has been explained in various ways in papers, reports, and speeches by various public organizations and academic researchers (FSB [22], BIS [4], Ushida and Angel [41]). This paper will define DeFi as financial applications that are automatically operated by smart contracts or other code on a blockchain.

Since DeFi stands for "Decentralized Finance," the first characteristic of DeFi is that it should be "decentralized," whether it intrinsically is or not. In other words, monies (in most cases, the crypto-assets) are exchanged or lent through an automatic program without the intervention of traditional financial intermediaries such as banks and securities companies. In addition, the second characteristic of DeFi is mimicking the transactional aspects of traditional finance such as payments, exchanges, lending, lending/borrowing, investments (asset management/derivatives), and insurance. Appendix C shows the summary of existing DeFi initiatives shown in FSB [23]. Thus, the overall risk profile of a DeFi system can be dramatically lower than for alternatives in a traditional, centralized financial system. DeFi is also noted for its cost savings, traceability, and its contribution to financial inclusion.

However, while DeFi has these merits, various issues and problems have also been pointed out. In light of this situation, some regulators have argued that official regulation of DeFi may be necessary (Gensler [27]; Crenshaw [18]).

Thus, this paper discusses the issues surrounding DeFi and appropriate future regulatory considerations. Ultimately, we would like to propose principles for DeFi disclosure and regulation. Considering DeFi regulations, whether a DeFi constitutes the "financial service" which participants are subject to consumer/investor protection needs to be considered first. Additionally, regulations from the perspective of systemic risk and anti-money laundering may be important regardless of such need for protection. The most important point would be to establish a disclosure system and common platform suitable for the characteristics of DeFi and crypto-assets, as well as an enforcement framework, considering the innovation trilemma. This is because establishing a suitable disclosure system for DeFi and crypto-assets is the most essential infrastructural foundation, when considering self-regulation, enforcement by government agencies, or for investors to pursue their own responsibilities. Establishing an appropriate

---

[1] The Senate hearing can be viewed below. Also, the materials of the speakers are available for downloading. (https://www.banking.senate.gov/hearings/crypto-crash-why-the-ftx-bubble-burst-and-the-harm-to-consumers) (Last viewed on February 10, 2023).

disclosure framework is, while challenging, necessary to provide all market participants information about the potential risks and benefits for any particular DeFi applications. To create a common disclosure platform in which national authorities and international standard-setting bodies could also participate and give authority would be desirable. Such a framework would provide basic information regarding a DeFi, such as disclosure of data, governance mechanisms, token information, as well as information on audits, etc., and it is also a convenient way to check for compliance. Designing an appropriate common disclosure platform that also considers participants' incentive structure is very challenging and will be the subject of further research.

The structure of this paper is as follows. Section 2 describes benefits, advantages, and possibilities of DeFi and Sect. 3 presents the challenges, risks and questions related to DeFi. Then, Sect. 4 discusses implications for regulatory consideration, followed by the proposal of principles of DeFi disclosure and regulation. Finally, a summary and further potential topics will be presented.

2 Benefits, Advantages, and Possibilities of DeFi

The expected benefits of DeFi have been pointed out in preceding literatures (Chen [9]; FSB [22], etc.). However, some of the advantages listed below are subject to reality check.

First of all, DeFi can be identified as a potential contributor to promoting innovation and competition. Activities that used to take a lot of cost and effort in existing financial transactions can be done automatically by utilizing smart contracts (persistent scripts). As a result, it is clear that this has the potential to contribute to reducing costs and promoting innovation toward the automation of transactions. Currently, DeFi is mainly limited to crypto-asset trading. However, if the technology is extended to traditional financial institutions, it could encourage competition with existing financial institutions and thus promote innovation.

Secondly, as FSB [22] pointed out, the DeFi technology may reduce some of the financial stability risks associated with traditional financial institutions and intermediaries. In financial transactions, there is a risk called "concentration risk". "Concentration risk" refers to the risk that entire transactions will be affected if an entity that concentrates most of the transactions is in halt/insolvent. If transactions and systems were decentralized based on the blockchain (Ethereum. etc.), it would clearly contribute to reducing concentration risk. From a technical point of view, this benefit may be attributed to the feature of having no single point of failure.

Third, DeFi transactions are currently mostly traceable. As the majority of DeFi protocols currently exist on the Ethereum blockchain, rather than other blockchains, or layer two solutions (FSB [22]). As a result of this, it is relatively straightforward to trace transactions through tools such as Etherscan. This is rapidly changing, however, as centralised layer two solutions may not necessarily provide the same level of transparency. Zeroknowledge technologies, designed to obfuscate transaction history and promote privacy, are very important in preserving privacy, but may make tracking and traceability more difficult.

Fourth, transactions can take place regardless of national borders, making international transactions easier. While centralised exchanges are often bound by similar laws to banks, DeFi has proved to be a powerful asset in cross-country transactions, particularly for those in crypto-negative countries.

Fifth, their contribution to financial inclusion is often pointed out. It is estimated that about 1.7 billion adults remain unbanked—without an account at a financial institution or through a mobile money provider (The World Bank [40]). DeFi has the potential to extend the benefits of finance to many more people since financial transactions can be done with a smartphone.

Lastly, DeFi also may be the basis for a future version of the internet or Web3. Web3 is also being considered as one of the elements of the future Internet, although it has not yet been clearly defined. DeFi forms the basic structure on which a future Web3 internet may grow. By establishing financial structures that are resilient, efficient and permissionless, it could form a foundational infrastructure on which private companies may grow. Easy, trusted transactions allow payment for services, products and use of these systems, and also act as a proof of concept for emerging uses of non-financial token registration, distribution, use and transfer that we are seeing now, such as SBTs and governance. The permissionless, global nature of DeFi means that systems can be built with user bases that aren't limited by geography, political stability, or technological monopoly - as long as effective governance protects these core principles.

3   Challenges, Risks, and Questions Related to DeFi

On the other hand, a number of problems have been pointed out with DeFi, although many of them seem to come from the flip side of the advantages presented above.

3.1   Lack of AML/KYC

One of the main points of contention with DeFi is the potential for money laundering. Many DeFi platforms do not perform KYC (Know Your Customer) or identity verification for transactions. For example, a decentralized exchange or "DEX", one of the fundamental DeFi activities, allows the exchange of cryptographic assets and allows transactions across international borders without an intermediary. This may make it easy for money launderers to clean up illegal funds If the DEX's compliance system was inadequate. For example, according to Chainalysis [11], illicit DeFi transactions have risen steadily over the last three years, in terms of both raw value and also as a share of all transaction value. FATF [21] has identified this as a problem, and AML (Anti Money Laundering) is currently a significant concern in DeFi. However, since a DeFi is enabled by automated application programs, applying AML proves to be a challenge, and this point will be discussed later.

3.2   Hacking

Recently, there has been a lot of hacking related to DeFi platforms in which crypto-assets have been specifically targeted for hacking and successfully stolen. According to Chainalysis [10], in 2020, $ 162 million of crypto-assets were stolen from DeFi platforms, but in 2021, that rose significantly by about 13 times to about $ 2.2 billion.

Most instances of theft from DeFi protocols can be traced back to errors in the smart contract code governing those protocols, which hackers exploit to steal funds (Chainalysis [10]). It has also been pointed out that DeFi itself is very new, and the fact that the programs are typically open to the public makes it easier for hackers to find vulnerabilities, which may be leading to increases in hacking.

3.3   Is It Really "Decentralized"?

Many have questioned whether DeFi is truly decentralized. In fact, the definition of "decentralized" seems to be unclear. IOSCO [31] mentioned that what should be considered "decentralized" is not clear. For example, the governance functions of a DeFi, such as voting power, ownership structure, the authority to control the provision of services or products, the authority to manage customer assets, the authority to improve services or products, and so on may or may not be truly decentralized. "Decentralized" could be in some cases just a marketing word, and the actual DeFi is often centralized or near-centralized. For example, BIS [4] points out that there is a "decentralisation illusion" in DeFi due to the inescapable need for centralized governance and the tendency of blockchain consensus mechanisms to concentrate power." Chainalysis [11] also points out that, across several major DAOs, less than 1 % of all holders have 90 % of voting power.

In addition, Ushida and Angel [41] and BGIN [5] point out that some DeFi projects have a specific party with administrative authorities to modify the protocol at its discretion via private keys called "admin keys", and the existence of "admin key" can be evidence to question decentralization to a certain extent. The owner of the "admin key" may change programs and parameters related to the DeFi project without permission. As a concrete example of centralized governance in a DeFi project, Allen [1] points out that the "Badger DAO" has recently suspended smart contracts due to reports of unauthorized access. However, if they were "decentralized" they would not have been able to do this so quickly[2]. If there is no central operator, then there is no one to comply with enforcement action.

---

[2] According to Twitter, they tweeted "Badger has received reports of unauthorized withdrawals of user funds. As Badger engineers investigate this, all smart contracts have been paused to prevent further withdrawals. Our investigation is ongoing and we will release further information as soon as possible," (https://twitter.com/ BadgerDAO/status/1466263899498377218) (Last viewed on February 10, 2023).

3.4   Is It Really "Traceable"?, Is It "Accessible to All"?

Some argue that a DeFi is not traceable in practice. Crenshaw [18] points out that, as for the lack of traceability, even though all transactions are recorded on a public blockchain, in reality, DeFi investments are not fully traceable, and only a limited small group of people can read and understand the code. Even highly qualified experts miss the flaws and dangers. Thus, these facts raise concerns that (technology) insiders will reap huge profits, while ordinary investors will take more risks, be offered unfairly bad prices, and be exploited over time. It has been pointed out by Popescu [36] and others that one of the major issues to be addressed in the future is the user interface.

More concretely, many DeFi projects are funded by venture capital and professional investors, but it is not clear how much small investors understand this situation. According to Crenshaw [18], professional investors bring with them rights such as equity, options, access to project team management, involvement in governance whether formalized or informalized, nondilution rights, and control rights, which are rarely disclosed. On the other hand, they have a significant impact on investment value. It can be said that venture capital is not necessarily a good representation for public interest such as investor/consumer protection. Therefore, Crenshaw [18] pointed out that small investors are at a great disadvantage compared to professional investors, and this information gap will exacerbate the problem.

3.5   Market Manipulation and Difficulties in Investigation

It has been noted that market manipulation often occurs in the trading of crypto-assets (Gandal et al. [26]; Griffin and Shams [28]). Despite the existence of market manipulation, there are few market manipulation regulations and other significant issues exacerbating the problem. In terms of market manipulation investigations, Crenshaw [18] points out that the feature of pseudonymity can be a problem as well. In many cases, DeFi records all transaction IDs on the blockchain, they cannot be tampered with, and everyone can see them. However, the ID does not actually identify the person who controls the transaction. It merely indicates the address which is controlled by some individual. Since there is often no effective way to identify who is actually the owner of addresses, it is impossible to know, for example, whether a group of people is engaging in market manipulation, or one person is controlling multiple addresses. This makes it difficult for regulators to investigate market manipulation in DeFi market.

3.6   Does It Really Contribute to "Financial Inclusion"?

The explanation that DeFi contributes to financial inclusion is also somewhat questionable. It is true that even the unbanked people often have smartphones, so allowing financial transactions through smartphones even without a bank account certainly could promote financial inclusion. However, there are two major problems.

First of all, "Competent Knowledge and Literacy" issues can be raised. Even if a person has a smartphone, it does not mean that he or she is capable of trading through a DeFi. Rather, DeFi is likely to require a high level of skill and knowledge/literacy, which may even result in widening the disparity between those who have and haven't. Especially when DeFi is still a kind of nascent technology.

Secondly, usage is currently limited. Even if DeFi could be done through smartphones, it would only be crypto-asset trading. Although there are cases of using a DeFi to avoid high remittance costs, the scope is still limited.

3.7   Operational Risk in DeFi

Since DeFi is automatically executed by smart contract, it is generally thought that there is no operational risk, but in reality, there probably is.

First, DeFi transactions cannot be halted or undone basically. The fact that it is automatically executed by smart contract can itself be a major risk. There will be nothing that can be done even if it involves unfair trading or illicit activities where it would be desirable to order a halt or undo the trading.

Second, there is the "Oracle risk". DeFi generally refers to external information, in the form of an "oracle". However, if the reference price is incorrect or intentionally distorted, the trading price of the cryptocurrency within the service will be greatly dissociated from other services, and participants may unreasonably lose a huge amount of money. This risk is called the "oracle risk".

3.8   Characteristics of Procyclicality and the Potential for Systemic Risk Associated with It

The mechanism of procyclicality is found in a DeFi's lending as well because it is done with crypto-assets as collateral but has systemic fragility compared to traditional intermediaries who only retain collateral as insurance (Lehar et al. [32]). Since many decentralized finance (DeFi) lending protocols require loans to be over-collateralized, and loans that fall below a certain threshold are automatically liquidated by third parties. Lehar et al. [32] notes that these liquidations have a sustained cascading effect on asset prices, which often triggers further liquidations. There is another risk that when a large number of financial institutions are involved in DeFi transactions it will spill over to the financial institutions. This may lead to systemic risk.

3.9   Lack of Ability to Address Risks Associated with Information Asymmetry

From a financial theoretical point of view, financial institutions (in this case, assuming a bank) usually exist to deal with the risks associated with information asymmetry between lenders and borrowers. In other words, in the bank's example, it functions to decrease information asymmetry that exists between depositors and borrowers by analyzing the credit information of borrowers instead of depositors who lack information on borrowers, and by lending only to credit-worthy firms. Of course, there are limits to the function of banks in reducing information asymmetry, often with government support, but it is undeniable that they have a certain role to play. However, in a DeFi, there is no such financial intermediary with critical gatekeeper functions. Only financial transactions are carried out automatically according to the code. In this sense, it would seem to suggest that DeFi is not currently a viable alternative to financial institutions.

In traditional finance, credit or reputation is an important factor. The borrower has the incentive to prove their trustworthiness and the lender needs reliable information to assess the risk of the borrower. Without any reliable information, it would lead to hesitance of lending, setting a high interest rate, or requiring over-collateralization. In fact, Weyl et al. [42] has raised the problem of a DeFi not being able to replicate real world financial systems because there is currently no ground to build a reputation. They introduce an idea of Soul-bound Tokens (SBTs) which are "publicly visible, non-transferable (but possibly revocable-by-the-issuer) tokens held by the soul". A "soul" is an account or wallet which has linkage with the real world community BGIN [6].

4   Implications for Regulatory Consideration

There is no doubt that market authorities are currently in the process of seriously considering how a DeFi should be treated (the President's Working Group (PWG) [37]). IMF [30] also calls for more work needs to be done on crypto regulation. How should DeFi, where "code is law" (De Filippi [19]), be regulated? We discuss the viewpoints to be taken when considering the regulations below.

4.1   Innovation Trilemma

First of all, we consider the basic approach in applying regulations to new technologies that create innovations, such as DeFi. Brummer and Yadav [7] mentioned that applying a traditional regulatory strategy to a new technological ecosystem had proved conceptually difficult because there is a policy trilemma for introducing regulation for innovative services and products (Fig. 1). That is, when we seek to provide clear rules, maintain market integrity, and encourage financial innovation, regulators have long been able to achieve, at best, only two out of these three goals.

It is clear that the current regulations on DeFi are almost non-existent, and many problems in the market have been identified. Thus, at this point, we could sacrifice two out of the three. Therefore, the vital question will be whether to prioritize market integrity or regulatory simplicity while maintaining ongoing innovation.

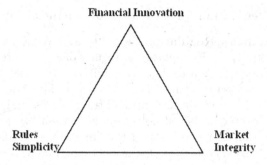

Fig. 1. Innovation trilemma (Source) Brummer and Yadav [7]

4.2 Perspectives on Whether Financial Regulations Should Be Applied

Is DeFi Really "Finance"? Since "DeFi" is an abbreviation for "Decentralized Finance", it is natural to think of it as "finance". Moreover, it is precisely whether it constitutes a "financial service". However, in reality, first of all, we need to consider whether we can really think of it as "financial service". If it is not a "financial service", then there may be less demand to regulate it as a financial product[3]. Specifically, it may not be "financial service", but part of a game. Token lending and investment-like activities in the game are, of course, not subject to financial regulations. Allen [1] stated that a DeFi is like an "incorporeal casino", and treating stablecoins like regulated deposits will provide implicit government backing to that casino, encouraging its growth. It is inappropriate and should be avoided to legitimize non-financial activities, e.g. lending and borrowing within a "game", by imposing financial regulations. It would be outside the scope of financial regulations if it is a non-financial transaction. Thus, if a particular project among a DeFi is not regarded as "financial service", then, of course, there is no need for financial regulation to apply.

Should a DeFi Participant be Subject to Investor/Consumer Protection? Even if a DeFi (or part of it) is "financial services", there is also the question of whether its participants are subject to investor/consumer protection. In other words, are DeFi market participants subject to the same protections as ordinary investors in the traditional financial markets? Even in the traditional financial market, qualified investors with a certain level of knowledge and institutional investors are professional and therefore responsible for their own investment. Nevertheless, for professional investors to make appropriate judgments, solid explanatory documents and disclosures are necessary, so it will be necessary to have a system in place to enable them to make appropriate investment decisions.

---

[3] See, for example, Armour et al. [2] for a discussion of what finance is.

4.3   Need for Regulation for Providers of Financial Functions

Safety and Soundness Regulation as a "financial Institution". When applying protection to a DeFi application, regulations to ensure the safety and soundness of regulation, similar to that of a traditional financial institution, need to be considered. Necessary regulations, such as capital adequacy regulations, entry regulations, restrictions on concentrated transactions, and transaction regulations would be on the agenda if, for example, deposit-like products were to be accepted. Risk management, such as that required of traditional financial institutions, may also be necessary. Operational risk, market risk management, and credit risk management are key examples.

How to Ensure Appropriateness as a "Financial Transaction". If transactions in a DeFi are regarded as financial transactions, then various transaction regulations would be required. The most typical regulation would be the market manipulation regulation when trading on the DEX.

How to Implement the Audit and Ensure DeFi's Reliability? Even if a disclosure mechanism for risk, governance, etc., of the code is established, the question then arises as to how to ensure its accuracy. In the normal course of business, listed companies are audited by an external auditing firm and are assured of a certain level of accuracy that investors can rely on. For corporate bonds, there are also rating agencies, such as Moody's and Standard & Poor's, that rate the credit of corporate bonds and provide information to investors.

Currently, it appears that there are indeed companies in the DeFi ecosystem that audit codes, but several issues have been raised. Conflux Network [17] indicated that audit standards were not standardized, varying from firm to firm, and it was unclear how reliable they were. When a DeFi application is recognized as a "financial service" constituting a "financial system", it will be necessary to develop an ecosystem that will ensure the reliability of such a financial system to evolve and create a system that addresses the inherent flaws, although it should be noted that these ecosystem is not infallible.

How to Establish a Regulatory Enforcement Framework? Perhaps, the most difficult question regarding DeFi is how these regulations and enforcement can be implemented, and by which authorities. Concerns have often been raised that, since some DeFi projects are further decentralized, there could be no explicit entity subject to regulation. And there may be a DeFi that claims not to belong to any country or jurisdiction. Several ideas have been suggested in this regard.

IMF [29] mentioned that, although direct bans can have a direct impact on the business of crypto exchanges (for both centralized exchanges and Decentralized exchanges), individuals are still likely to be able to trade and exchange crypto-assets by alternative means. Therefore, jurisdictions should actively coordinate with the relevant authorities and international standard-setting bodies to maximize the effectiveness of their enforcement actions and minimize regulatory arbitrage.

There is a suggestion to use soft law, such as a corporate governance code, rather than enforceable regulation by law (OECD [34]). Of course, while creating such normative standards and encouraging signatures may have a certain degree of effectiveness, bad actors may not follow these codes and may not sign them even in the first place. Therefore, it will be necessary to have certain authorities in the background of the standard. To this end, it is still essential for national authorities and international organizations to respond in a coordinated manner. It will also be necessary to deepen research on the possibility that the subject of regulation will be "code (=computer program)", by referring to the recent thinking on laws and regulations against market manipulation by AI (Bank of Japan [3]).

In addition, As Zetzsche [43] points out, DeFi could also take a completely new way of thinking about regulatory design, such as an "embedded regulation" approach. The "embedded regulation" approach is to automate the regulation itself, which may be an efficient way to regulate cyberspace in the future.

However, the question still remains. How should it be handled if it is truly decentralized, for example, the code is the operating entity. In this regard, the Tornado Cash incident was highly controversial. On August 8, 2022, the U.S. Department of the Treasury's Office of Foreign Assets Control (OFAC) sanctioned Tornado Cash, a leading crypto asset mixing platform, for engaging in money laundering of over $7 billion in crypto assets. Regarding the OFAC sanctions against Tornado Cash, some argue that OFAC sanctions against computer code exceed its legal authority and violate the Constitution (Coin Center [12]). Moreover, Coin Center, et al. v. Yellen et al. [13] pointed out that Tornado Cash did not actually provide a mixing service in that funds of users were not commingled; rather, it allowed for the deposit and withdrawal of digital assets under different, unlinkable addresses in a manner that provided the beneficial feature of privacy in an otherwise fully transparent system. The case is expected to be settled in a future court dispute.

Another controversial issue in the U.S. is the CFTC's administrative action against the Ooki DAO in September 2022[4]. The CFTC filed a lawsuit against a Decentralized Autonomous Organization (DAO) called "Ooki DAO", including those who held and voted for its governance tokens, for providing off-exchange digital asset transactions, registration violations, and non-compliance with the Bank Secrecy Act (BSA). The simple question arises as to whether the tort liability of the DAO should be considered to fall on the voters of the tokens and not on all holders of the tokens, or whether, in the case of a corporation, only the shareholders who exercise their voting rights should be held liable for the tortious acts. The main issue may be what to think about the CFTC approach of determining the

---

[4] CFTC Press release,(September 22, 2022) "CFTC Imposes $ 250,000 Penalty Against bZeroX, LLC and Its Founders and Charges Successor Ooki DAO for Offering Illegal, Off-Exchange Digital-Asset Trading, Registration Violations, and Failing to Comply with Bank Secrecy Act" (https://www.cftc.gov/PressRoom/PressReleases/859022).

liability of DAO token holders based on their participation in governance votes. In any case, the lawsuit (and the court decision based on it) is also considered to have broad implications for the crypto asset industry as a whole.

How to Establish a Disclosure System Suitable for DeFi and Crypto Assets. Blockchain is inherently traceable, so while it is already disclosed to technically sophisticated participants, it is too technical and virtually invisible to the general public and investors, which is one reason why DeFi is considered non-transparent (Brummer [8]). Ensuring a solid disclosure system will prevent the non-transparent situation that the DeFi has, and will allow investors to make appropriate decisions. Disclosure is considered necessary to a certain extent not only for investors but also for consumers, even if the product is an ordinary product. In this regard, it is essential for DeFi to provide more disclosure.

IMF [29] and OECD [34] also pointed out that establishing a disclosure framework including greater data standardization can lead to better oversight of crypto-asset markets, and in this regard, appropriate development of disclosure framework is a necessary measure. In this regard, Brummer [8] points out that the DeFi disclosure is not suitable for the SEC's EDGAR framework, as used for regular corporate disclosure and institutional investors, and requires a different framework that is preferable for investors and developers of crypto-assets. In other words, the existing disclosure systems used in finance (e.g., EDGAR) are often too detailed and too burdensome for the DeFi system to be suitable at all.

Establishing an appropriate disclosure framework, while challenging, is the most necessary thing to do in order to get the facts, and for investors to get accurate information as well. This is perhaps the issue that should be addressed most urgently. To create a common disclosure platform in which national authorities and international standard-setting bodies would also participate and give authority would be desirable to have a framework in which access to this disclosure platform would provide basic information regarding the DeFi, such as disclosure of data, governance mechanisms, token information, as well as information on audits, etc., and it is also a more convenient way to check for compliance. Designing an appropriate common disclosure platform that also considers players' incentive structure is very challenging and will be the subject of further research.

Need to Consider the Impact on the Financial System if the Scale of DeFi Becomes Large. Currently, the scale (TVL: Total Value Locked) of the DeFi markets is not significant compared to traditional financial markets. Allen [1] noted that, because DeFi still remains largely disconnected from both real-world economic applications and the established financial system, there would be limited pressure on the government to bail it out. However, as DeFi grows, the possibilities for something to go wrong, and for that something to impact the broader economy, increases.

From a simple point of view, there are two possible ways. The first is to restrict investment in DeFi by financial institutions. In other words, the exposure to DeFi itself should be reduced. This will reduce the negative linkages. Second, some kind of soundness regulation (such as capital adequacy regulation) could be introduced to maintain the soundness of the DeFi system itself. However, since such soundness regulations are entity-based, it is questionable to what extent they will be suitable for DeFi, which is the subject of the computer program.

4.4   How to Ensure AML/CFT

Whether or not DeFi is considered financial, and whether or not its participants deserve protection, at this time, the most urgent policy issue regarding DeFi would be the anti money laundering (AML). Regardless of the size of a DeFi, it should not be used to fund crime, and AML is an essential measure. To counter money laundering, KYC, such as identity verification, is necessary to be implemented into DeFi in some form. However, the issue is how to implement AML counter-measures for the DeFi, which is just an application program.

In this regard, The FATF [21] states that items with significant regulatory uncertainty, such as DeFi and stablecoins, should also comply with the "travel rule". "Travel Rule" is a set of rules for domestic and international wire transfers to prevent money laundering, and requires Virtual Asset Service Providers (VASPs) to collect and exchange information on the sender and recipient of crypto-asset transactions. And in the FATF's view (FATF 2021), almost all DeFi platforms are VASPs. The FATF has warned regulators not to accept without question the crypto-asset industry's marketing technique of broadly calling various platforms "decentralized". This is because DeFi platforms usually have a natural person (maybe not a legal entity) somewhere who "controls or influences" their activities. The point of "control or influence" is the framework for analyzing who is obligated to comply with ALT/CFT regulations.

As BGIN [5] also points out, this is a difficult matter and a number of participants expressed concerns about the AML regulations in terms of privacy, level playing fields, financial inclusion, and regulatory enforceability. However, as will be mentioned below, the key issue is how to enforce AML as the decentralized organization of DeFi further develops. Some have suggested that AML itself be embedded in the code and executed automatically, which is AML Oracle (Coinfirm [15]). AML Oracle is intended to enable AML through smart contracts, however, is in the early stage of the development and is not clear to what extent this will work practically at this moment.

5   Proposal of Principles of DeFi Disclosure and Regulation

Based on the risks and challenges seen in the previous chapters, some countries and jurisdictions are also considering regulations on DeFi[5]. However, looking at the regulatory developments on DeFi in various countries and jurisdictions, many are currently unregulated, or if they are, they are inadequate. Therefore,

---

[5] See also the IMF [30] for a detailed summary of this point.

it seems unavoidable that new regulations should be considered. In light of the points discussed so far, it would be desirable to establish the following principles for DeFi regulation and disclosure. The reason for the principle is that detailed laws and regulations are highly rigid and difficult to adapt to innovation and technological change, as well as taking a significant amount of time to enact and costing a significant amount of operational costs. Of course, this does not prevent rules and laws if they are enacted in a manner that allows them to adapt to change and operate in a manner that mitigates the disadvantages mentioned above. Several studies are also being conducted by the international organizations and regulators including IMF, FSB, FSOC, and others (see Appendix D for reference). Please note that the following principles do not apply to crypto assets in general, but only to DeFi, which is the subject of this document. The following is a proposal (as of February 17, 2023), which will be refined based on further comments and opinions to finalize the document.

(Principle 1) Need to Establish the Scope of Coverage. Regulators need to identify whether a DeFi constitutes a regulated financial activity and whether its participants fall under investor/consumer protection. The requirements for whether a DeFi constitutes a financial service should be presented in a form that is easy for participants to understand and appreciate. This coverage decision could also be considered to be made by the governing body of the globally uniform disclosure platform. once it is established, as described below.

(Principle 2) Establishment of a Disclosure Platform. Disclosure of information on DeFi could be made in a form that is easily understood and grasped by participants in transactions through the establishment of a reliable platform and their voluntary participation in it, taking into account the differences from the disclosure in securities. Disclosure information in such cases should include the following.

- Factors that have or may have a material impact on the value of the governance token, such as token governance; Founder and VC influence, conflicts of interest, economic mechanisms (additional issuance, redemption authority, splits, suspensions, etc.), token holder privileges.
- Dapp (Decentralized Applications) business model.

It is desirable to establish a globally uniform disclosure platform. The platform should be led by neutral organizations, such as multi-stakeholder organization, international standard-setting bodies, self-regulatory organizations, or international organizations. It is desirable to be approved by regulators in various countries/jurisdictions. Participating in the platform is desirable to have similar effects as registration to a regulator. This would provide an incentive to participate in a proper DeFi disclosure platform. This globally uniform disclosure platform will have the effect of providing a certain level of trust to trading participants, as only the DeFi that meet the principles will be allowed to participate. In contrast, a non-participating DeFi would also have the potential to have concerns about investor/consumer protection (Name and Shame). Disclosure platforms should aggregate, publish and provide data from participating DeFi platforms.

(Principle 3) Harmonization with Traditional Financial Regulations. If a DeFi's activity falls within the scope of financial regulatory coverage, the regulations and disclosure rules should be applied under the same risk, same activity, same regulatory outcome, and also under the principle of technology neutrality, considering the balance with normal traditional financial activities. For example, regulation in traditional finance could include: (1) Safety and soundness regulation, (2) Conflict of interest regulations (e.g., between exchanges and brokerage firms), (3) Disclosure regulation (more details below), (4) AML/CFT regulation (but this is not limited to financial activities) (5)Others.

(Principle 4) Consideration of DeFi Specialities. Even if a DeFi's activity falls within the scope of financial regulatory coverage, DeFi specific regulations and disclosures should be considered, including the fact that it is a digital activity. Specifically, for example, the most significant differences between traditional finance and DeFi, even if they are the same activity, are the following; (1) Electronic activities, (2) the ability to easily conduct cross-border activities, (3) the existence or non-existence of a central entity that can influence the activity, (4) there are cases where there is no central entity at all, even if a central entity does exist, the degree of its influence vary, (5) DeFi's specific risk called oracle risk, (6) automatic execution risk of smart contracts (a kind of operational risk), (7) Cyber security.

(Principle 5) Addressing the Potential for Systemic Risk. If the connectedness with traditional finance becomes greater, it will be necessary to consider how to deal with systemic risks, such as leverage ratios and capital adequacy ratios.

(Principle 6) Periodical Audit. DeFi participating in the disclosure platform must be subject to an audit at least once a year. A summary of the results should then be disclosed on the disclosure platform, clearly indicating that it is an appropriate DeFi. It is desirable that a uniform auditing standard be created and that they be approved by the disclosure platform.

(Principle 7) Ensuring Regulatory Effectiveness. A DeFi may not have a central entity or may have a small degree of influence on its activities, and in such cases, conduct regulations that stop the illegal activity itself may be more effective than punishment against the entity to ensure the effectiveness of the regulations. Since "decentralized" does not allow for the absence of a responsible entity in case of illegal activity, DeFi apps should include a mechanism for correcting or self-discontinuing the activity.

(Principle 8) AML/CFT and Other Measures to Legal Financial Activities. Even a DeFi that does not participate in the disclosure platform and is not regulated as financial services, it should comply with AML/CFT and other legal financial measures as prescribed by FATF standards as they are developed to apply for DeFi.

6   Conclusion

This paper summarizes the issues surrounding DeFi under these circumstances and presents some discussion points and suggestions for appropriate future regulatory considerations. We proposed principles for DeFi disclosure and regulation. In considering the principles, there were three major considerations.

Firstly, applying a traditional regulatory strategy to a new technological ecosystem has proved conceptually difficult because there is a policy trilemma called an innovation trilemma for introducing regulation for innovative services and products.

Secondly, considering DeFi regulations, whether a DeFi constitutes the "financial service" which participants are subject to consumer/investor protection need to be considered first. Additionally, regulations from the perspective of systemic risk and anti-money laundering may be important regardless of such need for protection.

Lastly, the most important point would be to establish a disclosure system and common platform suitable for the characteristics of DeFi and crypto-assets, as well as an enforcement framework, considering the innovation trilemma. This is because establishing a suitable disclosure system for DeFi and crypto-assets is the most essential infrastructural foundation, when considering self-regulation, enforcement by government agencies, or for investors to pursue their own responsibilities. Establishing an appropriate disclosure framework is, while challenging, necessary to provide all market participants information about the potential risks and benefits for any particular DeFi applications. To create a common disclosure platform in which national authorities and international standard-setting bodies could also participate and give authority would be desirable. Such a framework would provide basic information regarding a DeFi, such as disclosure of data, governance mechanisms, token information, as well as information on audits, etc., and it is also a convenient way to check for compliance. Designing an appropriate common disclosure platform that also considers participants' incentive structure is very challenging and will be the subject of further research.

These principles will be desirable to be reviewed on a continuing basis and regular basis (e.g., every two years) in the future. It is then hoped that the recognition of these principles will be shared by the participants involved in DeFi and contribute to the development of a healthy market. BGIN would also like to contribute to the healthy development of the DeFi market by communicating these views through gathering and coordinating stakeholder opinions.

Appendix

Appendix A. Terms and Definitions

This document uses the following terms as the shortcut for more complete wording provided as the definition. When the term appears within this document, it should be read as being replaced by the term.

Decentralized financial technologies	Technologies that may reduce or eliminate the need for one or more intermediaries or centralized processes in the provision of financial services [SOURCE: FSB [22]]
Decentralized financial system	A new financial system that could be the result of decentralized financial technology [SOURCE: FSB [22]]
Decentralized Finance (DeFi)	Financial applications that are automatically operated by smart contracts or other code
Smart contract	A collection of code and data (sometimes referred to as functions and state) that is deployed using crypto-graphically signed transactions on the blockchain network. The smart contract is executed by nodes within the blockchain network; all nodes must derive the same results for the execution, and the results of execution are recorded on the blockchain [Source: NIST [33]]

Appendix B. Abbreviations and Symbols

In this document, the following abbreviations and symbols are used.

AML	Anti Money Laundering
BGIN	Blockchain Governance Initiative Network
BIS	Bank of International Settlements
DeFi	Decentralized Finance
DAOs	Decentralized autonomous organizations
FATF	The Financial Action Task Force
DEX	Decentralized Exchange
FSB	Financial Stability Board
IOSCO	International Organization of Securities Commissions
KYC	Know Your Customer
SBTs	Soulbound Tokens
SEC	The U.S. Securities and Exchange Commission
NIST	National Institute of Standards and Technology

NOTE: All the abbreviations SHALL appear in this clause.

Appendix C. Summary of Existing DeFi Initiatives

	Description
Lending	By using smart contracts, users can become lenders or borrowers on DeFi platforms. Users typically post crypto-assets as collateral and then can borrow other crypto-assets. The most prominent platform typically requires $150 of collateral for every $100 of lending. Many platforms set interest rates automatically, depending on demand and supply of liquidity. Some of these platforms have characteristics analogous to commercial and/or central banks
Investment (Asset Management /Derivatives)	Many projects offer a suite of yield-generating crypto-asset products by automatically routing crypto-asset "deposits" to highest-yield opportunities within a set risk-tolerance for particular pools. Other platforms allow derivative products such as synthetic assets, options or perpetual futures as well as crypto-asset tranches
Decentralised Exchanges (DEXs)	Decentralised Exchanges claim to be peer-to-peer marketplaces based on smart contracts that allow trading in crypto-assets. They use automated liquidity pools, where investors 'lock' in their crypto-assets (in exchange for fees) to facilitate trading
Payments	Many applications focus on increasing interoperability between blockchains, with the aim to increase scaling. Others focus on increasing the safety of existing means of payment (e.g. through the use of QR codes), by using the blockchain to validate transactions in real time
Insurance	Some DeFi protocols, called discretionary mutuals, allow members to pool and share risks from smart contract failure, or mutualise premiums into smart contracts that trigger payouts when pre-defined risks or events materialise

(Source) Excerpt from FSB [23].

Appendix D. Proposals by International Organizations and Standard-Setting Bodies

(1) IMF's considerations for regulatory frameworks
IMF [30] points out the following with respect to considerations for regulatory frameworks across crypto assets.

(1) Monitoring
Authorities should first monitor developments to accurately gauge the size of the market and to identify areas of risk,

(2) Prioritization
Authorities should consider the risks of unbacked crypto assets as part of their broader regulatory and supervisory duties and determine whether the crypto asset market presents risks to their mandate that would reflect the considerable resources required to regulate and supervise crypto assets.

(3) Scope

Authorities should determine a clear scope for regulation, that is, which entities, crypto assets, and activities will fall within the regulatory scope

(4) Domestic Collaboration

Regulatory development should be a collaborative effort of financial sector regulators and relevant government departments, taking into account guidance from standard-setting bodies and regulatory approaches in peer countries

(5) Continuous Assessment of Risks

Continuous assessment of risks will be needed to identify shifting risks and business models that may require updating regulations to ensure effective protection of markets, consumers, and financial stability

(2) FSB report

FSB [24], "Regulation, Supervision and Oversight of Crypto-Asset Activities and Markets Consultative document", proposed 9 recommendations for the regulation, supervision and oversight of crypto-asset activities and markets. The summary of the proposals are below. (Excerpt from FSB [24]).

Recommendation 1: Regulatory Powers and Tools. Authorities should have the appropriate powers and tools, and adequate resources, to regulate, supervise, and oversee crypto-asset activities and markets, including crypto-asset issuers and service providers, as appropriate.

Recommendation 2: General Regulatory Framework. Authorities should apply effective regulation, supervision, and oversight to crypto-asset activities and markets – including crypto-asset issuers and service providers – proportionate to the financial stability risk they pose, or potentially pose, in line with the principle "same activity, same risk, same regulation."

Recommendation 3: Cross-Border Cooperation, Coordination and Information Sharing Authorities. Authorities should cooperate and coordinate with each other, both domestically and internationally, to foster efficient and effective communication, information sharing and consultation in order to support each other as appropriate in fulfilling their respective mandates and to encourage consistency of regulatory and supervisory outcomes.

Recommendation 4: Governance. Authorities, as appropriate, should require that crypto-asset issuers and service providers have in place and disclose a comprehensive governance framework. The governance framework should be proportionate to their risk, size, complexity and systemic importance, and to the financial stability risk that may be posed by the activity or market in which the crypto-asset issuers and service providers are participating. It should provide for clear and direct lines of responsibility and accountability for the functions and activities they are conducting.

Recommendation 5: Risk Management. Authorities, as appropriate, should require crypto-asset service providers to have an effective risk management framework that comprehensively addresses all material risks associated with their activities. The framework should be proportionate to their risk, size, complexity, and systemic importance, and to the financial stability risk that may be posed by the activity or market in which they are participating.

Authorities should, to the extent necessary to achieve regulatory outcomes comparable to those in traditional finance, require crypto-asset issuers to address the financial stability risk that may be posed by the activity or market in which they are participating.

Recommendation 6: Data Collection, Recording and Reporting. Authorities, as appropriate, should require that crypto-asset issuers and service providers have in place robust frameworks for collecting, storing, safeguarding, and the timely and accurate reporting of data, including relevant policies, procedures and infrastructures needed, in each case proportionate to their risk, size, complexity and systemic importance. Authorities should have access to the data as necessary and appropriate to fulfill their regulatory, supervisory and oversight mandates.

Recommendation 7: Disclosures. Authorities should require that crypto-asset issuers and service providers disclose to users and relevant stakeholders comprehensive, clear and transparent information regarding their operations, risk profiles and financial conditions, as well as the products they provide and activities they conduct.

Recommendation 8: Addressing Financial Stability Risks Arising from Interconnections and Inter-dependencies. Authorities should identify and monitor the relevant interconnections, both within the crypto-asset ecosystem, as well as between the crypto-asset ecosystem and the wider financial system. Authorities should address financial stability risks that arise from these interconnections and inter-dependencies.

Recommendation 9: Comprehensive Regulation of Crypto-Asset Service Providers with Multiple Functions. Authorities should ensure that crypto-asset service providers that combine multiple functions and activities, for example crypto-asset trading platforms, are subject to regulation, supervision and oversight that comprehensively address the risks associated with individual functions as well as the risks arising from the combination of functions, including requirements to separate certain functions and activities, as appropriate.

(3) IOSCO report

IOSCO [31], "Decentralized Finance Report" point out that financial innovation may lead to benefits for investors and others, but it may also present risks. Then it point out that DeFi appears to present many similar risks to investors, market integrity and financial stability as do other financial products and services, and it also poses specific and unique risks and challenges for regulators to consider. Potential regulatory concerns raised by IOSCO [31], are below.

- Asymmetry and fraud risks
- Market integrity risks
  - Front-running (or similar frauds)
  - Flash loans
- Market dependencies
- Use of leverage
- Illicit activity risks
- Operational and technology-based risks (Blockchain, Smart Contracts, Oracles)
- Cybersecurity
- Nascent stage of development (Comprehensibility, Scalability, Supportability, Reliability)
- Governance risks
- Spillover of risks to centralized/traditional markets
  - Centralized Crypto-asset Trading Platforms
  - Traditional Financial Institutions

(4) FSOC Recommendations

In the U.S., the FSOC (Financial Stability Oversight Council) suggests the following as recommendations for building regulations on crypto-graphic assets.(FSOC [25])

(Recommendation 1). Member agencies (Treasury department, SEC, OCC, FRB, FDIC, etc.) consider these general principles in their deliberations about the applicability of current authorities: Same activity, same risk, same regulatory outcome;

- Technological neutrality;
- Leveraging existing authorities where appropriate;
- Transparency in technology, including through potential future adoption and implementation of federal agency SBOM requirements by industry;
- Addressing financial stability risks before they impair the economy;
- Monitoring mechanisms through which crypto-assets could become more interconnected with the traditional financial system or increase in overall scale;
- Bringing transparency to opaque areas, including through disclosures and documentation of key issues such as inter-connectedness;
- Prioritizing timely and orderly transaction processing and legally binding settlement;
- Facilitating price discovery and fostering market integrity; and
- Obtaining, and sharing with other agencies, relevant market data from the crypto-asset market.

(Recommendation 2). Continued enforcement are needed.

(Recommendation 3). Congress pass legislation that provides for explicit rule-making authority for federal financial regulators over the spot market for crypto-assets that are not securities.

(Recommendation 4). Regulators continue to coordinate with each other in the supervision of crypto-asset entities, such as stablecoins issuers or crypto-asset platforms, particularly in cases where different entities with similar activities may be subject to different regulatory regimes or when no one regulator has visibility across all affiliates, subsidiaries, and service providers of an entity.

(Recommendation 5). Congress pass legislation that would create a comprehensive federal prudential framework for stablecoin issuers that also addresses the associated market integrity, investor and consumer protection, and payment system risks, including for entities that perform services critical to the functioning of the stablecoin arrangement.

(Recommendation 6). Congress develop legislation that would create authority for regulators to have visibility into, and otherwise supervise, the activities of all of the affiliates and subsidiaries of crypto-asset entities, in cases in which regulators do not already possess such authority.

(Recommendation 7). FDIC, FRB, OCC, and state bank regulators use their existing authorities, as appropriate, to review services provided to banks by crypto-asset service providers and other entities in the crypto-asset arena.

(Recommendation 8). Member agencies assess the impact of vertical integration (i.e., direct access to markets by retail customers) on conflicts of interest and market volatility, and whether vertically integrated market structures can or should be accommodated under existing laws and regulations.

(Recommendation 9). Coordinated government-wide approach to data and to the analysis, monitoring, supervision, and regulation of crypto-asset activities.

(Recommendation 10). Council members continue to build their capacity to analyze and monitor crypto-asset activities and allocate sufficient resources to do so.

References

1. Allen, H.: Stablecoins: How Do They Work, How Are They Used, and What Are Their Risks? Prepared Statement Before the U.S. Senate Committee on Banking, Housing, and Urban Affairs (2021)
2. Armour, J., et al.: Principles of Financial Regulation. Oxford University Press, Oxford (2016)
3. Bank of Japan (Institute for Monetary and Economic Studies): Use of Algorithms and AI in Investment Decision Making and Legal Liability (2018). (in Japanese)
4. BIS (Bank of International Settlements) (Aramonte, S., Huang, W., Schrimpf, A.): DeFi risks and the decentralisation illusion, BIS Quarterly Review (2021)
5. BGIN (Blockchain Governance Initiative Network): Present and Future of a Decentralized Financial System and the Associated Regulatory Considerations, BGIN SR 001 (2021)
6. BGIN (Blockchain Governance Initiative Network): Soulbound Tokens (SBTs) - Building and Embracing a New Social Identity Layer, BGIN SR 008 (2022)
7. Brummer, C., Yadav, Y.: Fintech and the innovation trilemma. Geo. LJ **107**, 235–307 (2018)
8. Brummer, C.: Disclosure, Dapps and DeFi, Stan. J. Blockchain Law Policy **5**(2), 137–174 (2022)
9. Chen, Y., Bellavitis, C.: Blockchain disruption and decentralized finance: the rise of decentralized business models. J. Bus. Venturing Insights **13**, e00151 (2020)
10. Chainalysis: The 2022 Crypto Crime Report (2022)
11. Chainalysis: State of Web3 Report -Your guide to how blockchains are changing the internet (2022)
12. Coin Center: Analysis: What is and what is not a sanctionable entity in the Tornado Cash case (2022). https://www.coincenter.org/analysis-what-is-and-what-is-not-a-sanctionable-entity-in-the-tornado-cash-case/
13. Coin Center, et al. v. Yellen et al.: 3:2022cv20375 (N.D. Fla., 2022)
14. Coinfirm: USA cryptocurrency Regulations (2021)
15. Coinfirm, Press release: DeFi AMLT Oracle Integrates World's Most Secure Smart Contract Network RSK (2021). https://www.coinfirm.com/blog/defi-amlt-oracle-rsk/. Accessed 17 Apr 2022
16. Coinfirm: MiCA: Markets in Crypto-Assets (2022)
17. Conflux Network: State of DeFi Audits - Taking a look at the auditing space and its importance in onboarding users by properly securing new DeFi protocols -, Medium.com (2020). https://medium.com/conflux-network/the-overlooked-element-of-defi-adoption-e3b29829e3da. Accessed 17 Apr 2022
18. Crenshaw, C.A.: (SEC Commissioner): Statement on DeFi Risks, Regulations, and Opportunities, The United States Securities and Exchange Commission (2021)
19. De Filippi, P.: Blockchain and the Law. Harvard University Press, Cambridge (2018)
20. EU (Council of the European Union): Proposal for a Regulation of the European Parliament and of the Council on Markets in Crypto-assets, and amending Directive (EU) 2019/1937 (MiCA) (2022). https://data.consilium.europa.eu/doc/document/ST-13198-2022-INIT/en/pdf
21. FATF (The Financial Action Task Force): Updated Guidance for a Risk-Based Approach to Virtual Assets and Virtual Asset Service Providers, FATF, Paris (2021)

22. FSB (Financial Stability Board): Decentralised financial technologies-Report on financial stability, regulatory and governance implications (2019)
23. FSB (Financial Stability Board): Assessment of Risks to Financial Stability from Crypto-assets (2022)
24. FSB (Financial Stability Board): Regulation, Supervision and Oversight of Crypto-Asset Activities and Markets Consultative document (2022)
25. FSOC (Financial Stability Oversight Council): Report on Digital Asset Financial Stability Risks and Regulation Table (2022)
26. Gandal, N., Hamrick, J.T., Moore, T., Oberman, T.: Price manipulation in the Bitcoin ecosystem. J. Monetary Econ. **95**, 86–96 (2018)
27. Gensler, G.: (SEC Chair): Remarks Before the Aspen Security Forum, The United States Securities and Exchange Commission (2021)
28. Griffin, J.M., Shams, A.: Is Bitcoin really untethered? J. Finance **75**(4), 1913–1964 (2020)
29. IMF (International Monetary Fund): Chapter 2: The crypto ecosystem and financial stability challenges. In: IMF, GFSR(Global Financial Stability Report) (2021)
30. IMF (Parma Bains, Arif Ismail, Fabiana Melo, and Nobuyasu Sugimoto): Regulating the Crypto Ecosystem - The Case of Unbacked Crypto Assets, FinTech Notes 2020/007 (2022)
31. IOSCO (International Organization of Securities Commissions), IOSCO Decentralized Finance Report (2022)
32. Lehar, A., Parlour, C.A., Berkeley, C.: Systemic Fragility in Decentralized Markets, Paper scheduled at American Economic Association (2022)
33. NIST (National Institute of Standards and Technology): Blockchain Technology Overview, NISTIR 8202 (2018)
34. OECD (Organization for Economic Cooperation and Development): Why Decentralized Finance (DeFi) Matters and the Policy implications (2022)
35. Pitch Book: DeFi Primer: An overview of DeFi funding activity, concepts, and select protocols (2021)
36. Popescu, A.D.: Decentralized finance (DeFi)-the Lego of finance. Soc. Sci. Educ. Res. Rev. **7**(1), 321–349 (2020)
37. PWG (President's Working Group on Financial Markets), Report on STABLE-COINS (2021)
38. Schär, F.: Decentralized finance: on blockchain-and smart contract-based financial markets. FRB of St. Louis Rev. (2021)
39. Schueffel, P.: DeFi: decentralized finance-an introduction and overview. J. Innov. Manag. **9**(3), I–XI (2021)
40. The World Bank: The Global Findex database 2017 (2017)
41. Ushida, R., Angel, J.: Regulatory considerations on centralized aspects of DeFi managed by DAOs. In: Bernhard, M., et al. (eds.) FC 2021. LNCS, vol. 12676, pp. 21–36. Springer, Heidelberg (2021). https://doi.org/10.1007/978-3-662-63958-0_2
42. Weyl, E. Glen, Ohlhaver, P., Buterin. V., : Decentralized Society: Finding Web3's Soul, Available at SSRN 4105763 (2022)
43. Zetzsche, D.A., Arner, D.W., Buckley, R.P.: Decentralized finance. J. of Fin. Reg. **6**(2), 172–203 (2020)

The Hidden Shortcomings of (D)AOs – An Empirical Study of On-Chain Governance

Rainer Feichtinger, Robin Fritsch$^{(\boxtimes)}$, Yann Vonlanthen$^{(\boxtimes)}$, and Roger Wattenhofer

ETH Zurich, Zurich, Switzerland
{rainerfe,rfritsch,yvonlanthen,wattenhofer}@ethz.ch

Abstract. Decentralized autonomous organizations (DAOs) are a recent innovation in organizational structures, which are already widely used in the blockchain ecosystem. We empirically study the on-chain governance systems of 21 DAOs and open source the live dataset. The DAOs we study are of various size and activity, and govern a wide range of protocols and services, such as decentralized exchanges, lending protocols, infrastructure projects and common goods funding. Our analysis unveils a high concentration of voting rights, a significant hidden monetary costs of on-chain governance systems, as well as a remarkably high amount of pointless governance activity.

Keywords: blockchain · decentralized autonomous organization · on-chain governance · liquid democracy · measurement study

1 Introduction

Decentralized autonomous organizations (DAOs) are already an integral part of today's blockchain ecosystem, and, as a significant innovation in organizational structures, they have the potential of impacting vast parts of business and society in the future [16]. In early 2023, DAOs are estimated to manage an equivalent of 12 billion US dollars[1]. Their goal is to enable open deliberation in a decentralized community, allow for transparent voting, and democratize resources. This has the potential of resulting in fast and well accepted decisions, something that today's centralized decision-making lacks.

With the first DAOs emerging very recently and most of them being less than a few years old, DAOs are still very much re-inventing themselves. In this work, we aim to shed light on some areas in which DAOs are facing challenges today. We take a data-first approach, and look at 21 DAOs with on-chain governance systems in depth, making the collected dataset openly accessible for each. We observe large scale phenomena, such as low decentralization of voting power, and uncover more overlooked topics, such as the high cost of DAOs performing votes on a popular blockchain such as Ethereum. Paired with a very concentrated token

---

[1] https://deepdao.io/organizations.

A. Essex et al. (Eds.): FC 2023 Workshops, LNCS 13953, pp. 165–185, 2024.
https://doi.org/10.1007/978-3-031-48806-1_11

distribution, the question of the purpose of the DAO beyond a pure marketing tool might have to be reconsidered.

In this paper, we investigate DAOs that have deployed a governance system on a blockchain to reach collective decision. These DAOs issue a governance token which represents voting rights, and distribute the token among stakeholders and the community (possibly via an airdrop or a token sale). Holders of the governance token can decide to delegate their voting rights to any representative (including themselves) to represent their interests. These so-called delegates can then use this voting power to vote on proposals which are brought forward.

The contribution of this paper is twofold: First, we make an extensive dataset on the governance systems of 21 DAOs easily accessible. The data contains a complete history of all token holders, delegations, proposals and votes. Second, we analyze the acquired dataset to get a comprehensive overview of the state of on-chain governance systems.

The first point might seem surprising, since one of the most appealing promises of blockchains is transparency: all transactions are public and can be viewed by anyone at any time. However, in practice it is not trivial to acquire all governance related information from raw blockchain data. To make the data accessible, we create a so-called *subgraph* for each of the DAOs using The Graph protocol[2]. These subgraphs allow retrieving all governance-related data though a GraphQL API. Since each governance system has its specificities, data collection had to be individually adapted to the particularities of each smart contract. All subgraph code is open source to allow for extending the dataset to include more DAOs by adding further subgraphs [12].

When analyzing the data, we focus on the distribution of voting rights and the monetary cost of the governance systems, among other aspects. While we do see a slight trend towards decentralization, voting power is still highly centralized in most DAOs. Indeed, for 17 out of the 21 analyzed governance systems, a majority of voting power, which suffices to decide any vote, is controlled by less than 10 participants. Furthermore, in most DAOs most voting power is held by delegates mainly representing a single token holder. Hence, there is little evidence of a substantial community-participation in the decision-making. Moreover, we quantify the monetary cost of the governance systems, in terms of transaction costs for delegating and voting, but also in added overhead for token transfers. This unveils significant costs, up to millions of dollars for some DAOs. Surprisingly, we also discover numerous pointless transactions, and their frequency even increasing in some cases – a sign of an immature governance systems.

2   Related Work

The history of DAOs on blockchains goes back to 2016 when a first DAO (called "The DAO") was formed on Ethereum. Unfortunately however, before becoming operational, the project suffered a severe hack which drained deposited funds from the DAO [11]. (The event was so significant that it lead to a hard fork of the Ethereum blockchain and the creation of Ethereum Classic).

---

[2] https://thegraph.com/en/.

After this failure, it took a few years before the idea of DAOs gained traction again. In 2018, the stablecoin protocol MakerDAO introduced an on-chain governance system as one of the first blockchain-based applications [21,22] (see [28] for an empirical study).

The next wave of DAOs then started entering the stage in 2020, kicked off by Compound finance [19]. Since then, more and more blockchain-based applications have followed suit and introduced an on-chain governance system, among them many decentralized finance (DeFi) protocols. (An overview and more background on DeFi can be found in [2,31,33].)

On the empirical side, there are already a number of studies of these governance systems. Some brief and early ones, such as [6,17,24,27], focus mainly the distribution of the ownership of governance tokens. In a more detailed study, Barbereau et al. consider the governance systems of nine DeFi protocols including MakerDAO, Compound and Uniswap [5]. Besides the token distribution, they also examine the voter turnout on governance decisions. More recently, a more comprehensive analysis additionally examined the voting behavior and the structure of the delegation network for three governance systems: Compound, Uniswap and ENS [14].

In contrast to this line of empirical work, Aoyogi and Ito [1] define a theoretical model of DAOs and study the competition of platforms with decentralized and centralized governance. DAOs have also been examined from a regulatory and compliance angle such as in [3], or in [10] which includes a case study of GnosisDAO. A qualitative comparison of DAO platforms can be found in [4].

The topic is also reaching mainstream attention with the World Economic Forum publishing two extensive reports on DAOs including parts on their strengths and weaknesses, the keys risks, operational processes, DAO governance processes as well as major legal and regulatory questions DAOs must face [15,16].

The voting systems used by most DAOs apply elements of *liquid democracy* (sometimes also referred to as *delegative democracy*) [7,8,13,30], in particular the possibility of delegating voting power to delegates. The main difference to liquid democracy is that most DAOs use the plutocratic "one token, one vote" approach instead of following the classic "one person, one vote" principle as outlined in liquid democracy. A second difference is that delegating is not transitive as it is in most forms of liquid democracy. (Delegations being transitive means that delegates can again delegate voting power they received by delegation to another delegate, and so on.) Instead, the systems currently implemented by DAOs only permit a single delegation step from a token holder to a delegate.

The most prominent use case of liquid democracy is an internal voting system used by the German Pirate Party which has been studied in [18,29].

There are also parallels between DAO governance's "one token, one vote" and the "one share, one vote" principle of shareholder democracy [23]. In this sense, DAO governance decisions (specially for DeFi protocols) can be seen as an equivalent to decisions at shareholder meetings of traditional companies. The voting behavior in traditional shareholder meeting has been studied in the literature, e.g. [20,32].

3   Methodology and Dataset

We analyze a total of 21 on-chain governance systems that run atop the
Ethereum blockchain, including systems that govern decentralized exchanges
(Uniswap), lending protocols (Compound, Silo, Inverse, Euler), infrastructure
(ENS, Radicle), services (GasDAO, Instadapp, Braintrust), and public goods
funding (Gitcoin). A more detailed overview of the DAOs we analyzed can be
found in Appendix A.

3.1   Data Collection

We collect data by using the open source platform called *The Graph*. The data
for each individual DAO is indexed with a so-called subgraph. As each protocol
has its specificities, we tailored each subgraph accordingly. Once indexed, these
subgraphs allow the retrieval of the pre-defined data through a GraphQL API.
All our subgraphs have been open-sourced [12][3].

For each DAO, the subgraphs store data on all token holders (their address,
their token balance, and the address they are delegating to) and all delegates
(their address, the amount of votes delegated to them, and which holders delegate to them). All this information is retrievable at an arbitrary block height.
Furthermore, the subgraphs contain details on all delegation transactions (who
delegated when to whom) and on all votes cast by delegates (how, when, on which
proposal, and with now much voting power the delegate voted). All transfers of
the governance tokens are also stored, since they are necessary to determine how
much voting power a delegate holds at any given time. Finally, metadata on the
governance systems and all proposals is included.

3.2   Dataset

Before further analyzing the data, we filter the dataset by removing smart contract accounts and accounts managed by an exchange. Usually, tokens in these
addresses are not controlled by any single user, and they cannot be used in governance. For example, a single smart contract[4] holds about 61% of the ENS tokens
at the time of writing. This contract is a time lock for ENS tokens that will only
be available over the next few years. Therefore, no one can currently participate
in governance with these tokens. Including such accounts in the analysis would
strongly distort the results, especially when analyzing the distribution of voting
power. We queried whether an account is a smart contract or not via Alchemy[5]
and we retrieved a list of accounts controlled by an exchange from Etherscan[6].

Table 1 shows an overview of the analyzed DAOs. For each, we consider the
time period between its deployment and block 16,530,000 (31 Jan 2023).

---

[3] The live subgraphs can also be found at https://thegraph.com/hosted-service/
subgraph/governancedao/NAME-governance where NAME is to be replaced by the
name of the DAO.

[4] address: *0xd7a029db2585553978190db5e85ec724aa4df23f.*

[5] https://alchemy.com.

[6] https://etherscan.io/accounts/label/exchange.

Table 1. State of the analyzed governance systems on 31 Jan 2023.

	Holders	Delegates	Proposals
Uniswap	368,193	27,805	39
Compound	208,049	4,807	147
ENS	64,290	11,834	12
Gas DAO	44,987	586	2
Gitcoin	31,595	6,341	45
Ampleforth	26,236	255	13
Fei	14,117	347	86
Hop	14,000	4,148	4
Strike	9,931	4	29
PoolTogether	8,393	466	60
Rari Capital	7,163	17	9
Radicle	6,527	75	11
Indexed	5,388	345	23
Braintrust	3,962	12	3
Idle	3,780	61	31
Instadapp	3,469	32	4
Silo	3,197	84	37
Inverse[a]	2,409	191	29
Euler	2,327	928	0
Cryptex	1,581	12	9
Babylon	1,090	47	28

[a] For Inverse, data is not included up to 31 Jan 2023, see Appendix A.

4   Distribution of Voting Power

We begin by studying the distribution of voting power in the DAOs. We do so using two measures: the Gini coefficient and the Nakamoto coefficient.

The Gini coefficient, one of the most frequently used inequality measures, was first introduced in 1912 by Corrado Gini [9]. Originally, the coefficient was used to examine income and wealth inequality within a geographical community (e.g. a nation). Nonetheless, it can be used to measure the inequality in the distribution of any fungible good, in our case voting power. Its values range from 0.0 which indicates perfect equality to 1.0 meaning the highest level of inequality (a single individual possesses everything). In most countries, the Gini coefficient of the distribution of wealth lies between 0.7 and 0.85 [25].

The Nakamoto coefficient, on the other hand, measures how decentralized a system is by counting how many parties are needed to collectively take control of the system. It was first formally described by Balaji Srinivasan in 2017 [26].

Table 2. Nakamoto and Gini coefficients of the distribution of voting power among token holders and among delegates at block 16,530,000 (31 Jan 2023).

	Nakamoto Holders	Gini Holders	Nakamoto Delegates	Gini Delegates
ENS	94	0.914	19	0.938
Gitcoin	42	0.991	10	0.993
Uniswap	30	0.992	11	0.999
Hop	30	0.902	6	0.967
Compound	25	0.996	6	0.996
PoolTogether	21	0.965	7	0.949
Indexed	16	0.935	5	0.923
Rari Capital	15	0.918	2	0.772
Babylon	13	0.937	5	0.731
Gas DAO	12	0.888	3	0.935
Braintrust	11	0.966	1	0.875
Silo	11	0.964	3	0.909
Ampleforth	9	0.984	3	0.966
Idle	7	0.960	2	0.900
Fei	7	0.975	12	0.906
Radicle	6	0.990	2	0.934
Cryptex	6	0.981	2	0.637
Instadapp	2	0.979	2	0.784
Inverse	2	0.944	2	0.937
Euler	2	0.984	3	0.980
Strike	1	1.000	1	0.667

Applied to a DAO governance system, the Nakamoto coefficient is defined as the number of addresses which together hold more than 50% of the voting power.

When analyzing the distribution of power in DAOs with delegative token governance, there are two relevant distributions to consider: the distribution of governance tokens among token holders, and the distribution of voting power among delegates (i.e. the amount of tokens delegated to them by holders). For both these distributions, Table 2 shows the Gini and Nakamoto coefficients for all analyzed DAOs on 31 Jan 2023.

With very few exceptions, the Gini coefficients are close to 1.0 indicating a highly unequal distribution of voting power. Furthermore, we observe this inequality remaining high over the whole observation period.

Regarding the values of the Nakamoto coefficient, it is notable how low they are across the board: Except for four projects, all DAOs have single digit Nakamoto coefficients for the distribution of voting power among delegates. This means that less than 10 addresses can take full control of the governance system and pass any decision they want. For half of the analyzed DAOs, the Nakamoto coefficient is even no larger than 3!

Overall, our analysis shows that there is a very high degree of centralization of voting power in current DAO governance systems. There is however a slight trend towards decentralization over time, as the increasing Nakamoto coefficients for delegates in Fig. 1 show. Nonetheless, these findings put a question mark behind the D in DAO.

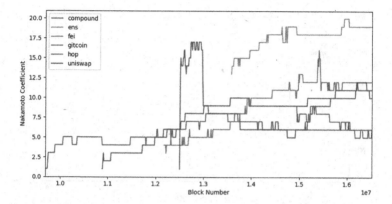

Fig. 1. Nakamoto coefficients of voting power held by delegates for six selected DAOs between block 9,690,000 (17 Mar 2020) and 16,530,000 (31 Jan 2023).

5 Structure of Voting Power Delegation

Besides the pure amount of voting power held by delegates, as analyzed in the previous section, another relevant aspect to the nature of a governance system is who the delegates are representing. Do they tend to represent large token holders (possibly themselves) or a group of community members?

In the following, we examine the structure of the delegations of voting power. To that end, we use the distinction between *single holder delegates* and *community delegates* introduced in [14]. Single holder delegates are delegates who receive more than 50% of the tokens delegated to them from a single token holder. A delegate receiving less than 50% of delegated tokens from a single holder is called a community delegate. The idea behind this definition is that single holder delegates mainly represent a single holder (and their interests). This includes the case of large token holder delegating to themselves due to the need to delegate before voting.

Furthermore, we measure the share of votes held by all community delegates. Governance systems with a large share of community delegates can be said to somewhat resemble a representative (parliamentary) system with a community electing representatives. If this share is low however, this indicates that the delegation part of the governance system is not being utilized to a large extent. Such governance systems then mainly feature direct representation of the interests of large token holders.

In Fig. 2, we see that for ENS, Gitcoin and Hop about half of all votes are in the hands of community delegates. For Compound, Fei and Uniswap on the other hand, the vote share of community delegates is low at about 10% or less. This is also the case for most other DAOs in the dataset as Table 3 shows. For many of them, almost all voting power is held by delegates who mainly represent a single holder.

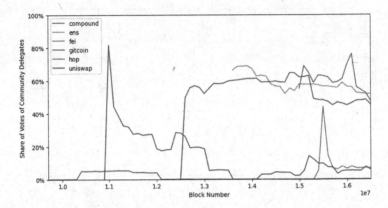

Fig. 2. Share of voting power held by community delegates (i.e. delegates who are not delegated more than 50% of their votes by a single holder) for six selected DAOs between block 9,690,000 (17 Mar 2020) and 16,530,000 (31 Jan 2023).

Again, our results show a very low degree of decentralization. Furthermore, they call into question the necessity of a delegation system, since this comes with significant cost as we will show in following sections.

6   Governance Participation

The governance participation rate can be defined in different ways, namely among tokens, delegates and voting power. The participation rate of the token holders is defined as the proportion of token holders voting out of the total number of token holders at the time of the vote. Accordingly, the participation rate among the delegates is the proportion of delegates voting among the total number of delegates. Furthermore, we consider the indirect participation rate of holder, i.e. the proportion of holders involved in a vote (voting directly or represented by a delegate) among all holders. Finally, the participation rate of voting power is the number of governance tokens voting relative to the total number of governance tokens delegated at the time of voting.

Figure 3 shows the participation rates for Compound, Uniswap, ENS and Gitcoin. The participation rate of the voting power is typically the higher than the rate for holder and delegates. This means that those voters with particularly high voting power are more active. This is not surprising since their costs relative to exercised voting power are lower. Moreover, delegates with high voting power either own many tokens themselves – and are thus strongly affected by the proposals voted on – or have many tokens delegated to them – and with that have a certain (moral) responsibility to vote. The participation rate of token holders is particularly low for all DAOs. The initially high value for Compound can be explained by the low number of token holders at the beginning of governance. The fluctuations in the participation rates also show that the interest in the proposals depends on their content.

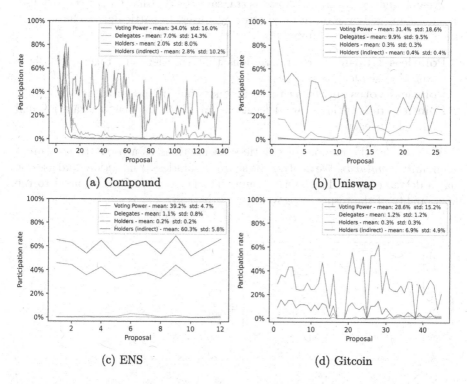

(a) Compound   (b) Uniswap

(c) ENS   (d) Gitcoin

Fig. 3. Participation rates among holders, delegates, and voting power.

The governances of ENS (Fig. 3(c)) and Gitcoin (Fig. 3(d)) show a comparatively low delegate participation rate. This phenomenon can be explained by the fact that these two protocols required delegating when claiming their airdrop. For Compound and Uniswap, only those interested in participating in proposals have to delegate. It turns out that for ENS and Gitcoin, many delegates who were created during the airdrop do not participate in governance.

On the other hand, Fig. 3(c) shows a particularly large amount of ENS token holders (on average about 60%) being represented during votes (either directly or indirectly by their delegate voting for them). This is a positive indication of a working governance system, and a pro argument for requiring delegations when for requiring delegations when claiming tokens.

7   Pointless Governance Transactions

The raw numbers of votes and delegations, as analyzed in the previous section, often do not show the whole picture of how active a DAO really is. Many transactions may simply be made by addresses hunting future airdrops, and some may be straight up mistakes.

We define *pointless transactions* as transactions that have no discernible use, and are most likely the result of an error by a user. In particular, we have found three types of pointless transactions.

- **Pointless transfers** are transactions that transfer zero tokens, or where recipient = sender.
- **Pointless votes** are votes cast by accounts holding no voting power.
- **Pointless delegations**, are delegations for which the new delegate is equal to the old delegate.

We consider the number of pointless transactions as a proxy to measure a community's *maturity*. We analyze the share of pointless transactions and assume that a decrease would hint at the community getting more accustomed to the functionality of the respective governance protocols.

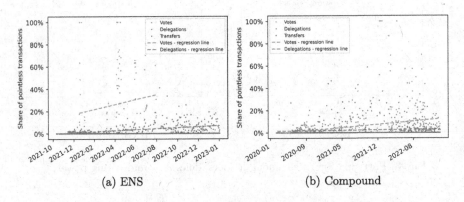

(a) ENS   (b) Compound

Fig. 4. Proportion of pointless transactions in all transactions per day.

Figure 4 shows the share of pointless transactions per day. Overall we observe that pointless transfers are rare. We assume that most users already have experience with the use of the transfers function or perform the transfer with an interface that indicates useless transfers. Astonishingly, the proportion of pointless votes, and to a lesser degree pointless delegations, is exceptionally high.

For ENS for instance, on average almost 30% of all votes per day are pointless. We suspect that many users do not realize that they must delegate their voting power to themselves before being allowed to vote. It is also remarkable that the proportion of pointless delegations and votes per day increases over time for ENS and Compound. Therefore, we conclude that DAOs are still very much in their infancy and have not reached maturity.

Table 3 shows the proportion of useless transactions when considering votes and delegations for each DAO. In general, this proportion is shockingly high with most DAOs having more than 10% useless votes and delegations, many even more than 20%. Further note that we used a very conservative definition of pointless transactions. Indeed, for Uniswap for instance, 88% of votes cast have a voting power below 10 tokens, and a staggering 47% of votes have a voting power below 1 token, while 2.5 and 40 million tokens are required to submit and pass a proposal respectively.

Note that overall ENS actually only has a few pointless transactions (¡2%). This does not contradict Fig. 4 since the majority of governance transactions occurred shortly after its airdrop, when the percentage of pointless transactions was low.

8   Monetary Price of Governance

In this section, we analyze the cost of performing governance on-chain. For each transaction carried out on blockchains such as Ethereum, a fee must be paid. The amount of the fee depends on the computational effort of the respective transactions (measured in units of gas), as well as the current price for unit of gas (which depends on the demand for block space).

To compute the monetary price of governance, we first consider transactions that handle voting, delegation voting power, and creating proposals. We define the *price of governance transactions* to be the sum of fees paid for these three types of transactions. Note that in some instances, multiple actions are combined into a single transaction. In such cases, we take special care only to include costs related to the governance actions in the transaction. A more thorough description on how this is achieved is detailed in Appendix B.

Both the gas price in ETH and the price of ETH in USD are subject to strong fluctuations. Therefore, we consider the ETH price as observed on Etherscan on the day of a transaction, and report the cost of governance in USD.

8.1   Price of Governance Transactions

Transactions that create proposals are much larger than delegation or voting transactions, and are thus much more costly. However, the number of proposals created is typically much smaller than the number of delegations and votes cast. Thus, as can be seen in Fig. 5, costs are usually dominated by delegations. One exception is Compound, the longest running DAO in the dataset, where voting costs have overtaken delegation costs.

The total governance transaction costs for all DAOs are listed in Table 3. In particular, the table shows that ENS has exceptionally high costs of the governance with about $3.5 million (costs are below $300.000 for all other DAOs). As Fig. 5(a)) shows, this is due to particularly high delegation costs following the launch of the governance system. When the previously mentioned ENS Airdrop took place in November 2021, the Ether price in USD was exceptionally high, and so was the price of a unit of gas. As virtually all delegations took place during that time (see Fig. 6(a)) due to the requirement to delegate when claiming the airdrop, this resulted in extensive amounts of fees being paid for governance transactions. On the other hand, Gitcoin, a protocol that also enforced delegations upon claiming an airdrop, started in May 2021, and thus benefitted from lower fees (see Fig. 5(b)). Of course absolutely speaking, Gitcoin also has much fewer token holders than ENS.

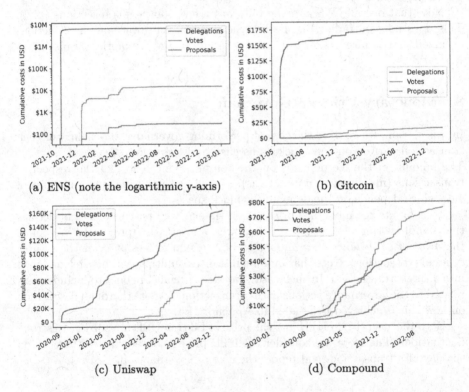

(a) ENS (note the logarithmic y-axis)   (b) Gitcoin

(c) Uniswap   (d) Compound

Fig. 5. Cost of governance: Transaction costs of delegations, votes and proposals.

In contrast to ENS and Gitcoin, Uniswap and other protocols did not implement a such delegation requirement. This lead to delegations and costs being much more spread out over time. Nonetheless, Fig. 6(b) shows a large peak between the 29 Nov 2022 and the 1 Dec 2022 for Uniswap. We trace these delegations back to newly created accounts with very low token balances and similar transaction patterns. We hypothesize that most of the observed activity in this time period comes from one or more airdrop hunters trying to set up wallets for airdrop farming.

In terms of architecture, we conclude the mandatory delegation during the airdrop can be particularly cost-intensive. However, the high costs might be justified by the hope of achieving higher participation and a more even distribution of voting power. The primary function of governance tokens is in most cases participation in governance. In this respect, it can also be argued that a token holder who does not delegate does not fulfil the actual purpose of the token.

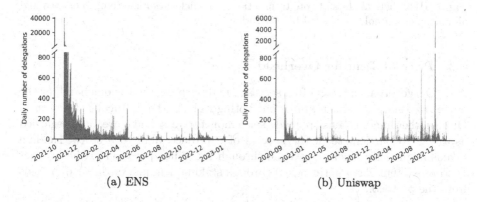

(a) ENS

(b) Uniswap

Fig. 6. Number of delegations per day.

After quantifying the costs of delegations, we quantify the cost savings they result in. Since the cost of a vote transaction is independent of the number of token holders a delegate represents, delegations lead to savings in transaction fees for voting. Figure 7 shows the cost for vote transactions that would arise if, all other things being equal, there were no delegations and all token holders represented by delegates voted individually. Comparing Figs. 5(a) and 7(a), we find that for ENS, the savings from delegations actually about make up for their costs. Finally, note that the savings from delegations are a lot smaller for Uniswap (Fig. 7(b)), in line with the observation that delegations being used less there (see Sect. 5).

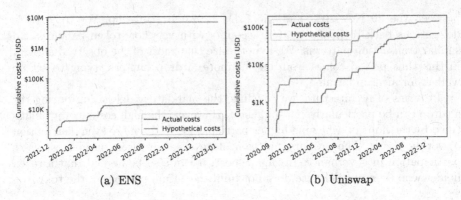

(a) ENS   (b) Uniswap

Fig. 7. Hypothetical costs of vote transactions if no delegation mechanism existed and all participation holders needed to vote individually.

8.2   Price of Transfer Overhead

A DAO's governance token often serves a dual purpose. On the one hand, as the name suggests, each token grants one voting right in the protocol's governance. On the other hand, tokens are traded as a monetary asset, and are often regarded as a way to participate in the success of a project, akin to a stock. Holding tokens might also generate revenue through their incorporation in the broader DeFi ecosystem, e.g. offering yield through staking, lending, or direct dividends from the protocol.

Generally, one would expect that the free exchange of tokens and the associated costs can be regarded separately from the price of governance. However, when a token offers the dual purpose of monetary asset and voting right, a hidden cost comes into play, that is not present for pure ERC-20 tokens.

The crucial insight is that each token transfer might change the voting power of delegates and thus requires additional smart contract logic, whose operation on the Ethereum blockchain we show to incur non-negligible additional costs. We explain how we compute these overhead costs in Appendix C.

Figure 8(a) shows that for Uniswap for instance, the costs incurred by this seemingly small variation in the smart contract has cost users just shy of 3 Million USD, and thus dwarfs the cost of direct governance transactions that amount to around 230'000 USD (see Fig. 5(c)).

The total cost of governance encompassing both the transfer overhead costs and cost of governance is shown in Table 3. Especially for projects generating low revenue, or projects that have very infrequent and inactive governance protocols, the current implementation might have to be questioned going forward.

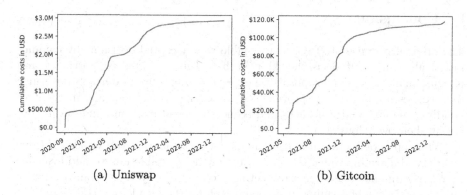

Fig. 8. Additional costs incurred by the modified transfer function.

Table 3. Characteristics of DAOs at blocks 16,530,000 (31 Jan 2023): the *share of votes held by community delegates* (cf. Sect. 5), the *participation rate of delegated voting power* (averaged over all proposals), the *cost of governance transactions* , the *total cost of governance* (additionally including added overhead costs of transfers), and the *proportion of useless transactions* (among delegation and vote transactions).

	Vote Share of Community Delegates	Participation Rate of Voting Power	Cost of Governance Transactions	Total Cost of Governance	Proportion of Pointless Transactions
Ampleforth	0.2%	77.4%	$9,303	$248,139	15.9%
Babylon	2.3%	33.8%	$13,864	$22,772	44.9%
Braintrust	0.0%	44.8%	$4,015	$30,193	28.9%
Compound	0.0%	32.2%	$147,659	$1,221,492	9.8%
Cryptex	0.0%	53.1%	$2,255	$45,282	6.8%
ENS	55.9%	39.2%	$6,501,217	$7,705,617	1.6%
Euler	2.3%	N/A	$6,832	$11,333	15.7%
Fei	0.0%	11.2%	$58,923	$312,097	23.3%
Gas DAO	38.6%	54.9%	$59,533	$351,225	15.0%
Gitcoin	43.7%	28.6%	$197,841	$316,112	9.2%
Hop	47.6%	43.8%	$217,902	$238,351	2.7%
Idle	0.0%	36.5%	$15,335	$89,350	13.2%
Indexed	0.0%	41.2%	$23,456	$99,010	18.2%
Instadapp	0.0%	39.7%	$1,843	$38,878	9.6%
Inverse	1.3%	46.7%	$41,775	$120,220	8.3%
PoolTogether	6.1%	17.6%	$38,860	$129,586	22.8%
Radicle	1.5%	58.9%	$8,446	$121,583	20.1%
Rari Capital	0.0%	24.7%	$7,673	$244,402	31.7%
Silo	29.4%	44.8%	$4,015	$30,193	28.9%
Strike	N/A	62.2%	$4,693	$29,583	1.9%
Uniswap	6.1%	20.9%	$233,559	$3,178,291	7.6%

9   Conclusion

The original promise of DAOs is to enable well accepted decisions by communities, allowing swift decision-taking both in times of great opportunity and difficult challenges. The proposals we observe and capture in our analysis range from suggesting protocol improvements, managing acquisitions and mergers, to handling the aftermath of hacks and economic downturn, sometimes even governing their own shutdown.

While open deliberation and voting is unquestionably good, we also observe a variety of alarming signs. By measuring low decentralization we find evidence that DAOs might be used as a marketing tool, or worse yet, as means to justify and veil decisions of a ruling dictatorship behind the facade of a community.

We hope that the shortcomings we lay bare can help inspire future DAO designs to also be more cost-effective and user-friendly. Finally, in the context of designing airdrop mechanisms, and in the wake of account abstraction[7] allowing for governance incentivization, our analysis sheds light on resulting costs and decentralization in various scenarios and can thus help the creation of the next generation of DAOs.

A   Short Description of Analyzed DAOs

Uniswap is the market leading decentralized exchange on Ethereum.

Compound is a decentralized on-chain money market and lending platform.

ENS stands for Ethereum Name Service, a distributed service mapping human-readable addresses to wallet addresses for example.

Gas DAO allows performing surveys among Ethereum users.

Ampleforth is a cryptocurrency with an algorithmically adjusted circulating supply.

Gitcoin is a platform designed to fund and govern open source projects.

Fei is an algorithmic stablecoin. The protocol was governed by the Tribe DAO, but after acquiring Rari Capital and repaying Hack victims, it wound down its operations, and is now discontinued. The governing Tribe DAO is said to have pioneered both the first merger and the first wind-down of a protocol in the DeFi space.

Hop is a protocol that allows transferring tokens between roll-ups.

Strike is a lending and borrowing protocol. Intriguingly, all governance proposals have been created by the same account, and apart from the first proposals this same account is the only account that has ever voted (with exactly 131'000

---

[7] https://eips.ethereum.org/EIPS/eip-4337.

tokens where the quorum of votes needed to pass a proposal consists of 130'000 votes).

PoolTogether is a protocol that awards lottery prizes to participants.

Rari Capital is a DeFi lending and borrowing platform. It has been the target of two large scale attacks, the first draining 15 million USD, the second around 80 million USD. After being acquired by Fei, its governance token was also $Tribe.

Radicle provides infrastructure for decentralized software collaboration.

Indexed was a project that provided passive portfolio management strategies for the Ethereum ecosystem. After an exploit drained a large fraction of the locked assets, the governing DAO held multiple votes regarding lawyer payment and token refunds to users.

Idle finance is a yield aggregator, offering different yield generating strategies to users. The governing DAO protocol was updated in January 2022. Both the old and the new governance contract and incorporated in the dataset.

Instadapp aims a providing infrastructure to improve the DeFi user-experience through interfaces and simplified protocols.

Braintrust is an online hiring marketplace for freelancing governed by the BTRST token.

Silo is a lending protocol, that allows the borrowing of any asset with another. Its governance token is called SILO.

Inverse is a protocol that generates yield on stablecoins and allows re-investment of the yield in a target token. We analyze the governing DAO before the smart contract was updated in October 2021.

Euler is a lending protocol controlled by a DAO. Many proposals are happening purely off-chain.

Cryptex offers exposure to market capitalization of the crypto market at large. It is governed by holders of the CTX tokens.

Babylon was a community lead asset management protocol. After being affected by the Rari Fuse Hack mentioned above, the protocol shut down in November 2022. After some back and forth between different communities and DAOs, Babylon users were eventually repaid their lost funds. The Babylon team itself bought Tribe DAO tokens, in order to vote in favor of a proposal to refund money to hack victims.

B   Computing the Cost of Governance

In order to estimate the governance costs, we extracted the gas required for the transaction and the gas price paid from the corresponding transaction receipts. Accurate measurements are complicated by the fact that the required gas for a transaction can vary widely, where delegation has taken place. More specifically, the gas requirement for a delegation varies depending on the address to which the delegation is made. In general, a delegation from delegate A to delegate B with $A \neq B$ requires more gas than a delegation from delegate A to themselves. Line 9 in Listing 1.1 is the reason for this behavior. When a participant A delegates to themselves, nothing changes regarding the delegates and therefore, the rest of the logic of the *moveDelegates* function can be skipped.

Another challenge we face is that the amount of used gas is only available for the entire transaction. However, a transaction can consist of several elements, e.g. a token claim and a subsequent delegation. In this case, if the gas consumed for the entire transaction were to be counted as governance costs, the estimate of the costs would be much higher than the effective costs. For such transactions we therefore only include the gas costs up to a fixed value, that we determine by computing the average amount of gas consumed for all isolated delegations - i.e. those transactions in which only a pure delegation was carried out.

Finally, note that the costs of executing protocol changes following a successful proposal is not included in our computed price of governance, as these costs are incurred no matter the type of governance, be it on- or off-chain.

```
1  function transferTokens(address src, address dst, uint96 amount)
       internal {
2      balances[src] = sub96(balances[src], amount);
3      balances[dst] = add96(balances[dst], amount);
4      emit Transfer(src, dst, amount);
5      moveDelegates(delegates[src], delegates[dst], amount);
6  }
7
8  function moveDelegates(address srcRep, address dstRep, uint96
       amount) internal {
9      if (srcRep != dstRep && amount > 0) {
10         if (srcRep != address(0)) {
11            #Omitted
12         }
13
14         if (dstRep != address(0)) {
15            #Omitted
16         }
17     }
18  }
```

Listing 1.1. A simplified depiction of two Solidity functions in the Uniswap smart contract.

C   Computing the Overhead Cost of Governance

In this section we outline the reason why a simple token transfer incurs higher costs if the token gives voting rights in a DAO.

In current DAOs there can be a maximum of one delegate at any given time for each address and all tokens held by that address. In other words, the voting power associated with the token of an address cannot be divided among different delegates. As a consequence, the transfer function from the ERC-20 standard[8] must be modified. Let A, B, C, D be different addresses and A delegating to C and B delegating to D. If B transfers its tokens to A, then A would have tokens whose voting power is delegated to C and tokens whose voting power is delegated to D, which contradicts the constraint that there can be at most one delegate for each address. For this reason, during each transfer it must be checked whether a delegation is necessary and if so, this delegation must be carried out. Consequently, more gas is needed for the modified transfer than for the ERC-20 standard transfer.

Thus, regardless of whether there is active participation in governance, the gas cost of a transfer increases.

We have estimated these costs with the help of remix[9]. The implementation of the *transferToken* function and the *moveDelegates* function is very similar between different projects. First, we measured the cost of calling a *transferToken* function as shown in Listing 1.1. Then we measured how the cost changes when line 5 in Listing 1.1 is removed. We estimate the additional cost of the modified transfer function to be about 4500 gas.

We multiplied the gas price at the time of a transfer by the estimated additional cost of 4500 gas. We then converted this value to USD using the same method as in the previous sections.

References

1. Aoyagi, J., Ito, Y.: Competing DAOs (2022). https://doi.org/10.2139/ssrn.4293846
2. Aramonte, S., Huang, W., Schrimp, A.:. DeFi risks and the decentralisation illusion (2021). https://www.bis.org/publ/qtrpdf/r_qt2112b.htm
3. Axelsen, H., Jensen, J.R., Ross, O.: When is a DAO decentralized? Complex Syst. Inf. Model. Q. **31**, 51–75 (2022)
4. Baninemeh, E., Farshidi, S., Jansen, S.: A decision model for decentralized autonomous organization platform selection: three industry case studies. Blockchain: Res. Appl. **2023**, 100127 (2023). ISSN: 2096-7209. https://doi.org/10.1016/j.bcra.2023.100127. https://www.sciencedirect.com/science/article/pii/S2096720923000027
5. Barbereau, T., et al.: Decentralised Finance's Unregulated Governance: Minority Rule in the Digital Wild West. SSRN (2022). https://papers.ssrn.com/sol3/papers.cfm?abstract_id=4001891
6. Barbereau, T.J., et al.: DeFi, not so decentralized: the measured distribution of voting rights. In: Proceedings of the Hawaii International Conference on System Sciences 2022, p. 10 (2022)
7. Behrens, J.: The origins of liquid democracy. In: The Liquid Democracy Journal on Electronic Participation, Collective Moderation, and Voting Systems, vol. 5 (2017). https://liquid-democracy-journal.org/issue/5/The_Liquid_Democracy_Journal-Issue005-02-The_Origins_of_Liquid_Democracy.html

---

[8] https://eips.ethereum.org/EIPS/eip-20.
[9] https://remix.ethereum.org.

8. Blum, C., Zuber, C.I.: Liquid democracy: potentials, problems, and perspectives. J. Polit. Phil. **24**(2), 162–182 (2016). https://doi.org/10.1111/jopp.12065. https://onlinelibrary.wiley.com/doi/pdf/10.1111/jopp.12065

9. Ceriani, L., Verme, P.: The origins of the Gini index: extracts from Variabilità e Mutabilità (1912) by Corrado Gini. J. Econ. Inequality **10**(3), 421–443 (2012). ISSN: 1569–1721, 1573–8701. https://link.springer.com/10.1007/s10888-011-9188-x. https://doi.org/10.1007/s10888-011-9188-x. Accessed 25 Aug 2022

10. Ding, W., et al.: A novel approach for predictable governance of decentralized autonomous organizations based on parallel intelligence. IEEE Trans. Syst. Man Cybern. Syst. **53**, 1–12 (2022). https://doi.org/10.1109/TSMC.2022.3224250

11. DuPont, Q.: Experiments in algorithmic governance: a history and ethnography of The DAO, a failed decentralized autonomous organization. In: Bitcoin and Beyond, pp. 157–177. Routledge (2017)

12. Feichtinger, R.: Subgraphs for DAOs (Git repository) (2023). https://github.com/rtfei/Subgraphs

13. Ford, B.A.: Delegative democracy. Technical report (2002). https://infoscience.epfl.ch/record/265695

14. Fritsch, R., Müller, M., Wattenhofer, R.: Analyzing voting power in decentralized governance: who controls DAOs? (2022). https://arxiv.org/abs/2204.01176. https://doi.org/10.48550/ARXIV.2204.01176

15. Gogel, D., et al.: Decentralized autonomous organization toolkit (2023). https://www3.weforum.org/docs/WEF_Decentralized_Autonomous_Organization_Toolkit_2023.pdf

16. Gogel, D., et al.: Decentralized autonomous organizations: beyond the hype (2022). https://www3.weforum.org/docs/WEF_Decentralized_Autonomous_Organizations_Beyond_the_Hype_2022.pdf

17. Jensen, J.R., von Wachter, V., Ross, O.: How decentralized is the governance of blockchain-based finance: empirical evidence from four governance token distributions (2021). arXiv: 2102.10096 [q-fin.GN]

18. Kling, C., et al.: Voting behaviour and power in online democracy: a study of liquid feedback in Germanys pirate party. In: Proceedings of the International AAAI Conference on Web and Social Media, vol. 9, no. 1, pp. 208–217 (2021). https://ojs.aaai.org/index.php/ICWSM/article/view/14618. https://doi.org/10.1609/icwsm.v9i1.14618

19. Leshner, R.: Compound Governance (2020). https://medium.com/compound-finance/compound-governance-5531f524cf68

20. Li, S.Z., Maug, E.G., Schwartz-Ziv, M.: When shareholders disagree: trading after shareholder meetings. In: Forthcoming in the Review of Financial Studies, Fifth Annual Conference on Financial Market Regulation, European Corporate Governance Institute (ECGI)- Finance Working Paper 594 (2019)

21. MakerDAO. Foundation Proposal v2 (2018). https://medium.com/@MakerDAO/foundation-proposal-v2-f10d8ee5fe8c

22. MakerDAO. What is MKR? (2015). https://medium.com/@MakerDAO/what-is-mkr-e6915d5ca1b3

23. Mitchell, D.T.: Shareholders as proxies: the contours of shareholder democracy symposium: understanding corporate law through history. Wash. Lee L. Rev. **63**(4), 1503–1578 (2006). https://heinonline.org/HOL/P?h=hein.journals/waslee63&i=1514

24. Nadler, M., Schär, F.: Decentralized finance, centralized ownership? an iterative mapping process to measure protocol token distribution (2020). https://arxiv.org/abs/2012.09306. https://doi.org/10.48550/arxiv.2012.09306

25. Shorrocks, A., Davies, J., Lluberas, R.: Credit suisse research institute global wealth databook 2022 (2022). https://www.credit-suisse.com/media/assets/corporate/docs/about-us/research/publications/global-wealth-databook-2022.pdf
26. Srinivasan, B.S., Lee, L.: Quantifying decentralization (2017). https://news.earn.com/quantifying-decentralization-e39db233c28e
27. Stroponiati, K., et al.: Decentralized governance in DeFi: examples and pitfalls (2020). https://static1.squarespace.com/static/5966eb2ff7e0ab3d29b6b55d/t/5f989987fc086a1d8482ae70/1603837124500/defi_governance_paper.pdf
28. Sun, X., Stasinakis, C., Sermpinis, G.: Decentralization illusion in DeFi: evidence from MakerDAO. arXiv preprint arXiv:2203.16612 (2022)
29. Swierczek, B.: 5 years of liquid democracy in Germany. In: The Liquid Democracy Journal on Electronic Participation, Collective Moderation, and Voting Systems, vol. 1 (2011). https://liquid-democracyjournal.org/issue/1/The_Liquid_Democracy_Journal-Issue001-02-Five_years_of_Liquid_Democracy_in_Germany.html
30. Valsangiacomo, C.: Clarifying and defining the concept of liquid democracy. Swiss Polit. Sci. Rev. **28**(1), 61–80 (2022). https://doi.org/10.1111/spsr.12486. https://onlinelibrary.wiley.com/doi/pdf/10.1111/spsr.12486
31. Werner, S.M., et al.: SoK: decentralized finance (DeFi) (2021). https://arxiv.org/abs/2101.08778. https://doi.org/10.48550/arxiv.2101.08778
32. Zachariadis, K.E., Cvijanovic, D., Groen-Xu, M.: Free-riders and underdogs: participation in corporate voting. In: European Corporate Governance Institute-Finance Working Paper 649 (2020)
33. Zetzsche, D.A., Arner, D.W., Buckley, R.P.: Decentralized finance. J. Finan. Regul. **6**(2), 172–203 (2020). ISSN: 2053–4841. https://academic.oup.com/jfr/article-pdf/6/2/172/37064506/fjaa010.pdf. https://doi.org/10.1093/jfr/fjaa010

An Intrinsic Mechanism Deciding Hash Rates from Bitcoin Price

Go Yamamoto[✉]

NTT Social Informatics Laboratories, Tokyo, Japan
go.yamamoto.public@gmail.com

Abstract. This paper presents a new theoretical approach to analyzing the relationship between Bitcoin's market price and its mining cost, aiming to substantiate the self-sustaining nature of Bitcoin's security.

Previous empirical studies reveal a long-term correlation between price and cost, while shorter-term analysis often reveals significant divergences, particularly during price bubbles. The correlation between price and cost is a critical feature for the safe confirmation of transactions and suggests that the crypto asset has a fundamental value. On the other hand, divergences, which yield profit for miners, should serve as a factor that encourages organized mining operations, raising the mining cost and thereby enhancing Bitcoin's security. Thus, Bitcoin's security seems organically maintained by an interplay of correlation and recurring divergences. Understanding the dynamics of mining costs and the mechanism driving the correlation and divergences between price and cost is essential for comprehending Bitcoin's security and how it is sustained.

By leveraging recursive methods in economics, this paper introduces a new theoretical model in which the rational decisions of miners determine mining costs. According to this model, the proof-of-work (PoW) mechanism combined with fluctuating Bitcoin price drives the long-term correlation and recurring divergences between price and cost. It demonstrates a rationale for the self-sustainability of Bitcoin's security.

1 Introduction

The fundamental value of Bitcoin is its production cost. This hypothesis is a widely held belief for the affirmative side of the argument over the value created by the energy consumed in the Bitcoin network and how the rationale behind the proof of work (PoW) is defended. This hypothesis seems to be grounded in the fact that numerous empirical studies have confirmed the correlation between the mining cost and the market price of crypto assets.

However, the relationship between market prices and mining costs is far from straightforward. Historically, significant divergences between the two have occurred many times, notably during the price bubbles. These divergences should have yielded considerable profits for the mining business, incentivizing organized mining operations and increasing mining costs, which enhances the security of Bitcoin. Thus, Bitcoin's security seems to be sustained by a complex interplay of the belief in the crypto asset's fundamental value and the mining operators' profitability.

A. Essex et al. (Eds.): FC 2023 Workshops, LNCS 13953, pp. 186–196, 2024.
https://doi.org/10.1007/978-3-031-48806-1_12

Given this complex landscape, a comprehensive understanding of Bitcoin's security requires thoroughly examining the dynamics of mining costs. Furthermore, it is critical to understand the mechanisms behind the correlation and divergences between prices and costs. This paper aims to substantiate the self-sustaining nature of Bitcoin's security by revealing the mechanism behind the interplay. For that purpose, we provide a theoretical analysis that explains the correlation and divergences between the market price and mining costs of Bitcoin caused by the intrinsic incentive mechanism.

Many empirical studies have revealed and investigated the correlation and divergence between the market price of Bitcoin and the mining cost. Hayes [7] provides a result of regression analysis that indicates the marginal mining costs explain the crypto asset prices. Hayes [6] further shows strong evidence of Granger causality from the mining cost to the market price. Kjaerland et al. [9] counterargues that hash rates do not affect the price. Some studies argue for causality from the price to the cost: Fantazzini and Kolodin [2] and Kristoufek [10] examine the Granger causality from the price to the cost or the network hash rate. Shibuya et al. [19] examines that the network hash rate tends to increase toward the break-even. These studies observed the following characteristic behaviors of the network hash rates: (A) In the short run, hash rates do not change significantly when bitcoin prices spike or fall. (B) In the long term, there is a correlation between Bitcoin prices and mining costs. Behavior (A) facilitates the formation of a price bubble, as Garcia et al. [2] discusses, while also preventing a rapid flash crash in market prices from compromising the network's security. Behavior (B) could potentially present evidence of Bitcoin's fundamental value.

So far, theoretical studies seem to have sought to explain the correlation and divergence through external mechanisms in the mining environment. Garcia et al. [3] suggests that price formation is influenced by the social information exchange based on the societal assumption that mining costs are the bottom of the price. Concerning the causality from price to cost, Marthinsen and Gordon [12] attempt to explain the causality assuming that miners may earn excess profits from price bubbles, leading to the installation of new hardware with delay. Prat and Walter [15] explain behavior (B) by the free entrance of new miners and fixed mining hardware that cannot be turned off. Behavior (A) is explained by the time to build the facilities. Garratt and Oordt [4] explain that the hash rate does not decrease significantly when the Bitcoin price falls because of the fixed asset investment in mining hardware. Pagnotta and Buraschi [14] assume that the demand for Bitcoin is backed by the value of the network, explaining that the price-cost correlation is maintained through a supply and demand analysis.

The core issue is whether it is essential to assume external influences, such as constrained hardware supply and competitive mining environment, in clarifying the relationship between Bitcoin's market price and mining costs. If such external elements are indispensable, it implies that Bitcoin's security depends on these external factors, and Bitcoin's security may not necessarily be self-sustaining.

Contrary to the conventional notions, our theoretical analysis suggests that Bitcoin's intrinsic mechanisms may play a much more significant role. We model miners' hash rate decisions by their rational risk preferences for PoW's stochastic rewards. Based on this model, we derive an estimated rational hash rate from the price of Bitcoin and the per-hash cost of mining. Interestingly, the model and the analysis predict that behaviors (A) and (B) should occur without external constraints. This finding suggests that the key dynamics of hash rates and mining costs, previously attributed to external factors, can be attributed to the combination of the intrinsic PoW mechanism and Bitcoin's price fluctuations, demonstrating a rationale for the self-sustainability of Bitcoin's security.

Our work invites further exploration of the self-sustaining nature of Bitcoin's security and value, independent of extrinsic influences, thereby contributing to the broader understanding of blockchain economics and crypto asset dynamics.

2   Rational Choice of Hash Rates

2.1   Model of Blockchain Network

We work with the following model of the PoW blockchain networks, such as Bitcoin, which simplifies and idealizes the reality concerning revenue, expense, and mining strategies of the miners, including mining pools. In reality, there are two types of policies for mining rewards for mining pools, the risk-sharing type, such as the PPLNS policy, and the risk-free type, such as the PPS policy. We explicitly model the risk-sharing type only. Miner's contribution by the risk-free type policy is interpreted as the Mining Pool's purchase of hash rates (see Remark 1).

Mining Environment. Let L be a short period of time in which we assume only at most one new block is found (for example, $L = 1$ millisecond). We employ the following parameters of the Blockchain Network processed in a period L.

B Market price of the block reward. We assume transaction fees are negligible.
H Network hash rate.
τ Expected block interval. 10 minutes for Bitcoin.
δ The difficulty parameter.
D $2^{32}\delta/\tau$.
r Risk-free rate for period L. We assume $r > 0$.

Miner and Mining Pool. We consider two types of agents. One is a Miner, and the other is a Mining Pool. We employ the following parameters for each Miner. We ignore the illiquidity of the assets for mining facilities.

w Total wealth.
Q Hash rate generated by the Miner; decision variable.
c Marginal mining cost of one hash computation, including depreciation.
M The aggregated hash rate of the Mining Pool the Miner contributes to.

Each Miner has wealth w and generates hash rate Q on its decision. It pays mining costs according to the hash rate and receives mining rewards by contributing the hash rate to a Mining Pool described below. For hash rate Q for L seconds, the cost is cLQ.

A Mining Pool is a Miner with special features. The Mining Pool accepts contributions of hash computation by a number of Miners and rewards them. The Mining Pool performs Blockchain Mining defined below with the aggregated hash rate of M and obtains a block reward by probability. When the Mining Pool has obtained the block reward, the Mining Pool distributes the block reward proportionally to the contributing Miners as the mining reward. That is, if a given Miner contributes a hash rate of Q_0, then when the Mining Pool earns a block reward B, it pays the Miner the mining reward BQ_0/M. A Mining Pool as a Miner generates a hash rate Q, contributes the hash rate Q to the self Mining Pool, and receives the mining reward from itself. A Mining Pool keeps adjusting M as well as Q. A Mining Pool can control M by promoting/restricting Miners' participation but can be subject to the limited hash supply by the Miners.

Miners, including Mining Pools, continue the computation of hash functions for an investment term. Each Miner (or Mining Pool) is interested in wealth w at the end of the term as the most preferred random variable.

Blockchain Mining and Network Hash Rate. Blockchain Mining is the process in which a Mining Pool with an aggregated hash rate M obtains reward B with probability $\frac{ML}{D\tau}$ for each short time period L.

The network hash rate H is the sum of the hash rates of all Mining Pools performing the Blockchain Mining. Difficulty δ is adjusted according to H so that $H = D$. Later in this paper, we will assume that $H = D$ always, but we will use H and D separately for convenience.

Remark 1. In reality, mining pools may incorporate contributions rewarded through risk-free type policies, such as the Pay Per Share (PPS) policy, alongside risk-sharing type policies. In our proposed model, we regard these contributions paid by the risk-free type policies as the pool's purchases of computing power from external parties to fulfill a portion of its hash rate. The mining cost should include the reward paid under the risk-free type policies. Therefore, the marginal per-hash cost c should factor in the payment for procuring such computing power.

From this perspective, our proposed model allows all mining pools to accommodate risk-sharing and risk-free type policies. A mining pool that only accepts risk-free policies is modeled as a solo miner purchasing computational power. As we will discuss later, a mining pool with considerable wealth might find it more reasonable to accept solely risk-free policies.

Expected Utility Hypothesis. We assume each agent follows the expected utility model with a utility function as the von Neumann-Morgenstern theorem (see Chapter 6 of [13]) implies.

Suppose given a family of finite random variables $\{X_s\}_{s \in S}$ valued on $\mathbb{R}$ for set S, and the agent likes to choose $s^* \in S$ such that X_{s^*} is the most preferred outcome with uncertainty. In this setting, we assume there exists a continuous function U representing the agent's preference for risk (uncertainty), and the agent chooses $s^* \in S$ that achieves $\max_{s \in S} \mathbb{E}[U(X_s)]$. The von Neuman-Morgenstern theorem shows that if the agent's preference for uncertain outcomes satisfies some axioms that look natural, we can program such a continuous function U. Two utility functions U and V represent the same risk preference in the expected utility model if and only if $U(x) = aV(x) + b$ for some $a \in \mathbb{R}^*_+$ and $b \in \mathbb{R}$. Here $\mathbb{R}^*_+ = \{x \in \mathbb{R} \mid x > 0\}$.

We assume that the agents' utility functions are increasing concave functions.

2.2   Single-Period Mining

We aim to consider Miners interested in the wealth they can accumulate over a period much longer than L, possibly spanning months or even decades. However, determining the optimal hash rates for long-term mining is generally a complex problem. Therefore, we first analyze the simplest scenario, where only one decision is made for a single short time period L.

We fix the aggregated hash rate (hereafter, the size) of the Mining Pool M and analyze the hash rate Q a Miner would like to produce to work with the Mining Pool. The revenue of the Miner with the hash rate Q who works for the Mining Pool is $R = B\frac{Q}{M}$ with probability $p = \frac{ML}{D\tau}$, and $R = 0$ with probability $1 - p$. Let R be the binary random variable for this revenue.

The Miner pays cLQ for the mining cost of one short period of L. We assume the remaining wealth produces risk-free interest. Then the amount of wealth w' after the single mining period is

$$(1) \qquad\qquad w' = R + (1 + r)(w - cLQ).$$

According to the assumption of the expected utility model, the Miner is endowed with a utility function U, and the optimal Q is obtained by solving

$$(2) \qquad\qquad \max_Q \mathbb{E}[U(w')]$$

subject to $0 \le Q \le M, \epsilon w \le -cLQ + w$ for some small constant $\epsilon > 0$. We put the latter constraint because the Miner avoids bankruptcy in the worst case. We call it the solvency constraint.

Remark 2. When the miner chooses a constant hash rate, the miner's revenue will follow a Poisson process at the limit where L approaches zero. This approximation is popular in previous studies, for example, Rosenfeldt [18]. However, we do not take the limit of L now.

We note that we do not assume that Bitcoin prices follow the geometric Brownian motion (GBM). Indeed, it is observed that Bitcoin prices exhibit significant volatility clusterings and do not follow the GBM (for example, [5] and

[8]). Removing the GBM assumption results that the classic mathematical methods developed for continuous-time portfolio theory mostly cannot be applied. Thus we dare to go back to a more fundamental approach of using backward induction in the discrete-time model.

2.3   Multi-period Mining and Dynamic Programming

We apply recursive methods to solve our problem of deciding hash rates for longer, multi-period mining. The recursive methods originally appeared in control theory and are widely applied in economics, for example, in analyzing the sequential portfolio choice problem (see [1] for example). We will apply them to our problem similarly.

Consider a discrete-time model in which a period of length L is repeated for T times. Let $t = 0, 1, \cdots, T - 1$, and denote the parameters in the t-th period with a subscript t. For example, the block reward in the t-th period is B_t.

Remark 3. Our multi-period mining model assumes that agents precisely know the future market price of the block reward at each time t. However, as we will see later, the optimal mining strategy ultimately does not depend on this future information for the settings in which we are interested. Such agents can find the optimal mining strategy without knowing the future information.

Applying Eq. (1) for $w = w_t$ and $w' = w_{t+1}$, we have

$$(3) \qquad w_{t+1} = R_t - (1 + r_t)c_t L Q_t + (1 + r_t)w_t.$$

By setting $F_i(x) = R_i - (1 + r_i)c_i L Q_i + (1 + r_i)x$ we have $w_{t+1} = F_t(w_t)$ and

$$(4) \qquad w_T = (F_{T-1} \circ \cdots \circ F_t)(w_t),$$

here $\circ$ means the composition of functions $(f \circ g)(x) = f(g(x))$.

The Miner seeks the optimal choice of hash rates for each time period that achieves the maximum expected utility at the end of the investment term, time T, so the goal is to maximize $\mathbb{E}[U(w_T)]$. Hence the miner who starts mining at time t seeks to find $Q_t, Q_{t+1}, \cdots, Q_{T-1}$ for

$$(5) \qquad V(w_t, t) := \max_{\{Q_i\}_{i \geq t}} \mathbb{E}[U((F_{T-1} \circ \cdots \circ F_t)(w_t))],$$

subject to $0 \leq Q_i \leq M, \epsilon w \leq -c_i L Q_i + w$ for each i such that $t \leq i < T$.

Finding the optimal hash rates $Q_0, Q_1, \cdots, Q_{T-1}$ may look like a problem with high complexity. However, since the random variables of incomes, R_i, are mutually independent for $i \in \mathbb{N}$, we can apply the dynamic programming method (see Sect. 2.2 of [1] for the case of the portfolio choice problems) to obtain the following equivalent form of the problem, which allows finding the sequence of $Q_{T-1}, Q_{T-2}, \cdots, Q_1, Q_0$ recursively:

$$(6) \qquad V(w_t, t) = \max_{Q_t} \mathbb{E}[\max_{\{Q_i\}_{i \geq t+1}} \mathbb{E}[U((F_{T-1} \circ \cdots \circ F_{t+1})(F_t(w_t)))]]$$

$$(7) \qquad = \max_{Q_t} \mathbb{E}[V(F_t(w_t), t + 1)]$$

subject to $0 \leq Q_t \leq M, \epsilon w \leq -c_t L Q_t + w, V(x, T) = U(x)$.

For each $i \in \{0, 1, \cdots, T-1\}$, let $U_{(i)}(w) := V(w, T-i-1)$. $U_{(i)}(w)$ defines a sequence of utility functions satisfying $U_{(0)}(w) = U(w)$ and $U_{(i+1)}(w) = \max_{Q_{T-i-1}} \mathbb{E}[U_{(i)}(F_{T-i-1}(w))]$. We call $U_{(i)}$ the i-th induced utility function.

Equation (7) is interpreted that Q_t is chosen as if the agent is doing a single period mining for time $t+1$ when the agent's risk preference is represented by the induced utility function $U_{(T-t-1)}$. It means if we know $U_{(T-t-1)}$ for some reason, we can find the optimal hash rate Q_t without knowing the distant future.

2.4 Myopic Decision of Hash Rates with Isoelastic Utility Functions

In general, $U_{(t)}(x)$ is very complex. However, when $U(x)$ is isoelastic, if we may forget constraint $Q \leq M$, we can calculate Q_0 by directly finding $U_{(T-1)}(w)$, without following the recursive steps in Eq. (7). The isoelastic utility functions are $W_\lambda(x) = \frac{x^{1-\lambda}-1}{1-\lambda}$ for $\lambda > 0$, where we set $W_1(x) = \log(x)$.

From now on, we forget constraint $Q \leq M$ and analyze the optimal hash rate $Q_{\max}$. Later we will find the condition for w for which the optimal hash rate satisfies $Q_{\max} \leq M$.

Proposition 1. *Let $U(w) = W_\lambda(w)$. For $F_t(x)$ in Eq. (4), there exists $a \in \mathbb{R}^*_+$ and $b \in \mathbb{R}$ such that $\max_{Q_t \ s.t. 0 \leq c_t L Q_t \leq (1-\epsilon)w} \mathbb{E}[U(F_t(w))] = aU(w) + b$.*

Proof. Let $\alpha = c_t L Q_t / w$ and $\rho = 1 - \lambda$. Let $X = R_t/(c_t L Q_t) - 1$. Then $F_t(w) = (\alpha(X - r_t) + (1 + r_t))w$. X is a constant of w and Q_t. Suppose $\rho \neq 0$. Since $\rho U(F_t(w)) + 1 = F_t(w)^\rho$, we have $\rho \max_{Q \ s.t. 0 \leq c_t L Q \leq (1-\epsilon)w} \mathbb{E}[U(F_t(w))] + 1 = Aw^\rho$ for $A = \max_{\alpha \ s.t. 0 \leq \alpha \leq 1-\epsilon}(\alpha(X - r_t) + (1 + r_t))^\rho$. Since $A \geq (0 + (1 + r_t))^\rho > 0$, A is a positive constant. Hence there exists $a \in \mathbb{R}^*_+$ and $b \in \mathbb{R}$ such that $\max_Q \mathbb{E}[U(F_t(w))] = aU(w) + b$. The case when $\rho = 0$ is proven in a similar way.

Corollary 1. *When $U(w) = W_\lambda(w)$, the induced utility functions $U_{(i)}(w)$ for $i \geq 0$ satisfy $U_{(i)}(w) = a_i U(w) + b_i$ for some $a_i \in \mathbb{R}^*_+$ and $b_i \in \mathbb{R}$.*

Thus miners with risk preference represented by one of the isoelastic utility functions can choose the optimal hash rate for long-term mining by finding the optimal hash rate for the immediate one-shot mining for a short period L.

2.5 Mean-Variance Approximation and Miners' Hash Rates

In a short single-period investment, the optimal portfolio for an isoelastic utility function can be well approximated by the mean-variance optimal portfolio, as economic studies have previously demonstrated [11, 16], and [17]. We apply this approximation in a specific context to estimate Miner's optimal hash rate and provide a mathematical justification for the adapted formula. Additionally, we employ the approximation technique described in Thorp [20] to formulate an estimated solution. However, unfortunately, when applied to our problem, the original technique appears to require additional assumptions for it to be justifiable. We justify its use within our particular context of estimating Miner's optimal hash rate.

Let X be a binary random variable that takes $X = u$ with probability p, and $X = d$ otherwise. Let $X_\alpha = (X - r)\alpha$ for $0 \le \alpha$. Let $\alpha_{\max}(\lambda) = \arg\max_\alpha \mathbb{E}[W_\lambda(X_\alpha + (1+r))]$ subject to $0 \le \alpha$. We find $\alpha_{\max}(\lambda)$ by solving $\partial_\alpha \mathbb{E}[W_\lambda(X_\alpha)] = 0$. Let $\mu = \mathbb{E}[X]$, $\sigma^2 = \mathbb{V}[X]$, and $\mu' = \mu - r$. The Taylor expansion of $\alpha_{\max}(\lambda)$ by μ' is $\alpha_{\max}(\lambda) = T_1 \mu' + T_2 \frac{\mu'^2}{2} + \cdots$ for $T_1 = -\frac{1}{\lambda} \frac{1+r}{(d-r)(u-r)}$, and $T_2 = \frac{(1-\lambda)(1+r)(u-2r+d)}{\lambda^2 (d-r)^2 (u-r)^2}$. In particular, we have $\alpha_{\max}(\lambda) = O(\mu')$, and $\alpha_{\max}(\lambda) = \frac{1}{\lambda} \alpha_{\max}(1) + O(\mu'^2)$.

Proposition 2. *Suppose* $\alpha = O(\mu')$. *Then* $\mathbb{E}[W_\lambda(X_\alpha + (1+r))] = W_\lambda(1+r) + \alpha \frac{\mu'}{(1+r)^\lambda} - \alpha^2 \frac{\lambda\sigma^2}{2(1+r)^{\lambda+1}} + O(\mu'^3)$ *as* $\mu' \to 0$ *for* $\sigma^2 = \mathbb{V}[X]$.

Let $g_\lambda(\alpha) = W_\lambda(1+r) + \alpha \frac{\mu-r}{(1+r)^\lambda} - \alpha^2 \frac{\lambda\sigma^2}{2(1+r)^{\lambda+1}}$. $g_\lambda(\alpha)$ is maximized when $\alpha = \alpha^*$ for $\alpha^* = (1+r)\frac{\mu-r}{\lambda\sigma^2}$. Then we have the following proposition.

Proposition 3. $\alpha_{max} = \alpha^* + O(\mu'^2)$ *and*

$$(9) \quad \mathbb{E}[W_\lambda(X_{\alpha_{max}} + (1+r))] = W_\lambda(1+r) + \frac{1}{\lambda(1+r)^{\lambda-1}} \frac{S^2}{2} + O(\mu'^3)$$

for $S = \frac{\mu-r}{\sigma}$, *the Sharpe ratio of the probabilistic return* X_{α^*}.

We approximate $Q_{\max} = \arg\max_{Q_t} \mathbb{E}[W_\lambda(F_t(w))]$ subject to $0 \le Q_t$ and $\epsilon w \le -cLQ_t + w$ using the mean-variance approximation. We assume $Y > D$ hereafter since we have $Q_{\max} = 0$ if $Y \le D$. Let Q^* be the mean-variance approximation of $Q_{\max}$. It suffices to check Q^* satisfies the solvency constraint $\epsilon w \le -cLQ^* + w$ since we assume w is small enough so that $Q_{\max} \le M$ is always satisfied. Let $\alpha = \frac{cLQ}{w}$ and $X = R/(cLQ) - 1$. $\mu = \mathbb{E}[X]$ and $\sigma^2 = \mathbb{V}[X]$ are explicitly given by $\mu = \frac{1}{cL}(\frac{BL}{D\tau} - cL)$ and $\sigma^2 = (\frac{1}{cL})^2 \frac{B^2 L(D\tau - ML)}{MD^2\tau^2}$. Substituting the above μ and σ^2 to $\alpha^* = (1+r)\frac{\mu-r}{\lambda\sigma^2}$ we obtain $\alpha^* = \frac{1}{\lambda}\frac{M}{Y}(1 - \frac{D}{Y})(L/\tau) + O((L/\tau)^2)$ for $Y = \frac{B}{(1+r)c\tau}$. Thus $\alpha^* < 1$ is satisfied when $\lambda \ge 1$, we may assume Q^* satisfies the solvency constraint when $\lambda \ge 1$. We obtain the mean-variance approximation $Q^* = \alpha^* w/(cL)$ as

$$(10) \quad Q^* = \frac{1}{\lambda} \frac{(1+r)M}{B} \left(1 - \frac{(1+r)c\tau D}{B}\right) w + O(L/\tau).$$

The Sharpe ratio $S = \frac{\mu-r}{\sigma}$ is approximated by $S_*^2 = \frac{(Y-D)^2 M}{Y^2 D}$ since

$$(11) \quad S^2 = \frac{(Y-D)^2 M}{Y^2 D}(L/\tau) + O((L/\tau)^2).$$

Equation (10) illustrates that when the market price B experiences a sudden surge, miners, who are assumed to have isoelastic utility functions, are unlikely to increase their hash rates Q in response immediately. It is because their wealth w remains largely unchanged in the short term, and their optimal choice α^* does not significantly alter in response to increases in B.

In other words, when Bitcoin's price experiences a significant increase in a short period, the hash rate does not instantly correspond with the price. The increase in hash rate only comes after the mining difficulty has risen, and miners' wealth has increased due to the higher Bitcoin prices. As such, the mining costs will begin to diverge from the Bitcoin price, and this divergence trend will continue for some time.

Equation (10) also suggests the upper bound for the amount of the total wealth w of the miners satisfying the condition $Q_{\max} \approx Q^* < M$. We note that the approximated upper bound does not depend on M. Thus, one could argue that the wealth above the level is excessive in the mining business if the agents have risk preferences represented by isoelastic utility functions.

2.6   Rational Network Hash Rate in Blockchain Network

We want to know where the network hash rate goes eventually in the long term. Hereafter we assume the difficulty is continuously adjusted, so $H = D$. We also assume that the hash supply from Miner to Mining Pool is elastic as observed in [19], so Mining Pools can choose M as desired. We assume the following for the risk preferences of Mining Pools.

Assumption 1. *Some Mining Pools have risk preferences represented by isoelastic utility functions $W_\lambda(x)$ with possibly different $\lambda \geq 1$ for each.*

For the sake of simplicity, we assume the wealth levels of Mining Pools are not high, so $Q_{\max} \leq M$ is always satisfied.

Now we stop fixing M and estimate how those Mining Pools satisfying the assumptions decide the size M.

Applying the mean-variance approximation, we assume each of the above Mining Pools decides the size M by maximizing the Sharpe ratio S_* subject to $0 \leq M$ for fixed J, where $J := H - M$. For $0 \leq M < Y - J$, the solution M^* for the condition $\partial_M S_*^2 = 0$ satisfies $M^* = \frac{(M^*+J)(Y-(M^*+J))}{Y+(M^*+J)}$. In particular M^* satisfying $0 \leq M^* < Y - J$ is unique. Hence we have the following.

Proposition 4. *Suppose a Mining Pool controls its hash rate M to maximize $S_*^2 = \frac{(Y-H)^2 M}{Y^2 H}$ with fixed $J := H-M$ subject to $0 \leq M < Y-J$. The optimal size M^* is unique and satisfies $M^* = H^* \frac{Y-H^*}{Y+H^*}$ for $H^* = M^* + J$. Here $Y = \frac{B}{(1+r)c\tau}$, the break-even hash rate.*

Suppose Assumption 1 assumes n Mining Pools $i = 1, 2, \cdots, n$ endowed with isoelastic utility functions, and each chooses the size $M_{[i]}$. Further, assume they all have the same marginal cost of hash computation c. By Proposition 4, The Nash equilibrium $M_{[i]}^*$ for Mining Pool i is unique, and $M_{[i]}^*$ satisfies

$$(12) \qquad M_{[i]}^* = H^* \frac{Y - H^*}{Y + H^*},$$

where $H^* = Z + \sum_i M^*_{[i]}$, Z is the sum of hash rates that other Mining Pools than the n isoelastic Mining Pools deploy. Other Mining Pools are not necessarily isoelastic nor may be deciding hash rates by some non-economic motivations.

Taking the sum of Eq. (12) for i, we have

$$(13) \qquad H^* - Z = nH^* \frac{Y - H^*}{Y + H^*}.$$

Let ξ be the real number satisfying $Z = \xi H^*$, where $0 \le \xi < 1$. Then by solving Eq. (13) we have $H^* = \frac{n-(1-\xi)}{n+(1-\xi)}Y$. That is, for $\hat{n} = n/(1 - \xi)$ we have

$$(14) \qquad (1 + r)c\tau H^* = \frac{\hat{n} - 1}{\hat{n} + 1}B.$$

We can interpret Eq. (14) that if we have enough numbers of Mining Pools that decide their size according to isoelastic utility functions, the rational choice of the network hash rate drives the marginal production cost to a slightly lower point than the market price of the crypto assets. It finds that the isoelastic Mining Pools adjust the network hash rate at a certain level, like a unified buffer.

3   Conclusion

We solved the problem of the rational decision of the hash rates given the stochastic reward from the mining business of PoW blockchain networks, assuming the miners are endowed with isoelastic utility functions. We observed that the hash rates do not follow the spike of crypto asset prices in the short term, but eventually, the rational choice of network hash rate matches the production cost and the crypto asset price with a slight margin. The result implies that the stochastic rewards from the PoW mechanism can explain the behavior of hash rates. It remains a subject of interest to see how closely the proposed model predicts hash rates. Quantitative evaluations through empirical studies are clear next subjects.

Acknowledgement. Part of this study was done while I was with NTT Research. I am grateful for many discussions with Tatsuaki Okamoto on using control theory to analyze hash rate dynamics. I greatly appreciate the numerous discussions with Fuhito Kojima and Aron Laszka about the behavior of miners from a microeconomic perspective in the early stages of this research. I am also thankful for many discussions with Katsumi Takahashi from NTT Social Informatics Laboratories. Any possible faults or incomplete discussions that may be present in this paper are solely my responsibility.

References

1. Brandt, M.W.: CHAPTER 5 - portfolio choice problems. In: Aït-Sahalia, Y., Hansen, L.P. (eds.) Handbook of Financial Econometrics: Tools and Techniques, pp. 269–336. North-Holland, San Diego (2010)
2. Fantazzini, D., Kolodin, N.: Does the hashrate affect the bitcoin price? MPRA Paper 103812. University Library of Munich, Germany (2020)

3. Garcia, D., Tessone, C.J., Mavrodiev, P., Perony, N.: The digital traces of bubbles: feedback cycles between socio-economic signals in the Bitcoin economy. J. R. Soc. Interface **11**(99), 20140623 (2014)
4. Garratt, R., van Oordt, M.: Why fixed costs matter for proof-of-work based cryptocurrencies. Staff Working Papers 20-27, Bank of Canada (2020)
5. Gronwald, M.: The economics of bitcoins - market characteristics and price jumps. CESifo Working Paper Series 5121, CESifo (2014)
6. Hayes, A.S.: Bitcoin price and its marginal cost of production: support for a fundamental value. Appl. Econ. Lett. **26**(7), 554–560 (2019)
7. Hayes, A.S.: Cryptocurrency value formation: an empirical analysis leading to a cost of production model for valuing bitcoin. Telemat. Inform. **34**, 1308–1321 (2016)
8. Katsiampa, P.: Volatility estimation for bitcoin: a comparison of GARCH models. Econ. Lett. **158**, 3–6 (2017)
9. Kjærland, F., Khazal, A., Krogstad, E.A., Nordstrøm, F.B.G., Oust, A.: An analysis of bitcoin's price dynamics. J. Risk Financ. Manage. **11**(4), 63 (2018)
10. Kristoufek, L.: Bitcoin and its mining on the equilibrium path. Energy Econ. **85**(C), 104588 (2020)
11. Levy, H., Markowitz, H.M.: Approximating expected utility by a function of mean and variance. Am. Econ. Rev. **69**(3), 308–317 (1979)
12. Marthinsen, J.E., Gordon, S.R.: The price and cost of bitcoin. Q. Rev. Econ. Financ. **85**, 280–288 (2022)
13. Mas-Colell, A., Whinston, M.D., Green, J.R.: Microeconomic Theory. Oxford University Press, New York (1995)
14. Pagnotta, E., Buraschi, A.: An equilibrium valuation of bitcoin and decentralized network assets. SSRN Electron. J. (2018)
15. Prat, J., Walter, B.: An equilibrium model of the market for bitcoin mining. J. Polit. Econ. **129**(8), 2415–2452 (2021)
16. Pulley, L.B.: A general mean-variance approximation to expected utility for short holding periods. J. Financ. Quant. Anal. **16**(3), 361–373 (1981)
17. Pulley, L.B.: Mean-variance approximations to expected logarithmic utility. Oper. Res. **31**(4), 685–696 (1983)
18. Rosenfeld, M.: Analysis of bitcoin pooled mining reward systems (2011)
19. Shibuya, Y., Yamamoto, G., Kojima, F., Shi, E., Matsuo, S., Laszka, A.: Selfish mining attacks exacerbated by elastic hash supply. In: Borisov, N., Diaz, C. (eds.) FC 2021. LNCS, vol. 12675, pp. 269–276. Springer, Heidelberg (2021). https://doi.org/10.1007/978-3-662-64331-0_14
20. Thorp, E.O.: The kelly criterion in blackjack sports betting, and the stock market. In: Handbook of Asset and Liability Management, pp. 385–428 (2006)

Stablecoins: Past, Present, and Future

Ali Nejadmalayeri[1]([✉]), Leon Molchanovsky[2], Bruno Woltzenlogel Paleo[3],
and Rodney W. Prescott[4]

[1] Department of Accounting and Finance, College of Business,
University of Wyoming, Laramie, USA
anejadma@uwyo.edu
[2] Galaxy Innovation Ltd., London, UK
[3] Djed Alliance, São Paulo, Brazil
[4] Technolgistkiwi, London, UK

Abstract. Since 2018, stablecoins have become the major digital currencies facilitating payment flows across various decentralized financial platforms. While in the simplest terms, stablecoins operate as low-
volatility digital cash, they are not created equal. Broadly speaking, stablecoins are dichotomized into fiat-backed or algorithmic; algorithmic
refers to a diverse set of stablecoins. By reviewing a brief history and
analyzing the current state of affairs for stablecoins, we discuss critical
facts about stablecoins and propose strategic pathways for the future.
Fiat-backed stablecoins are similar to money market funds in their function and structure. As such, the regulatory framework for money market
funds should be a guiding light. From this viewpoint, the necessary conditions for the proper functioning of fiat-backed stablecoins are: transparency, full disclosure, quality auditing, and oversight. Algorithmic stablecoins are in principle synthetic cash, or a derivative instrument. As
such, they are perfectly positioned to play pivotal roles in digital financial derivative (contingent claims) markets. Due to the heterogeneity of
their use-cases, the appropriate regulatory framework depends heavily
on the underpinning economics. Lending-related algorithmic frameworks
(i.e., credit contingent claims) can benefit from economics and regulatory
environments of collateralized repo markets and the like. Others can be
considered through the lens of derivatives instruments—futures, options,
swaps—for finding best practices and optimal strategies.

Keywords: Stablecoins · Fiat-Backed · Algorithmic

1 Introduction

In January 2017, the market value of stablecoins (almost solely represented by
Tether) stood at roughly US\$20M. By April 01, 2022, the total market cap of all

While maintaining full culpability, we would like to thank participants at Block#6 of
BGIN at UZH Blockchain Center, Block#8 of BGIN, Financial Cryptography 2023, and
University of Californinia at Santa Barbara's DeFi Seminar for their valuable comments.

A. Essex et al. (Eds.): FC 2023 Workshops, LNCS 13953, pp. 197–207, 2024.
https://doi.org/10.1007/978-3-031-48806-1_13

stablecoins (more than 100) exceeded US\$180B.[1] Tether, the largest stablecoin, had a market cap of US\$83B. Terra, the third largest stablecoin, stood at a high of US\$18B. At the time of the writing of this report in June of 2022, Tether is down to US\$69B and Terra is defunct. The month of April 2022 will go down in history with infamy as the most tumultuous month for stablecoins when the world realized stablecoins may not be as stable as we believed. But is this as unexpected as we are made to believe? Were we misguiding ourselves that stablecoins are riskless? Lastly, are all stablecoins created equal? After all, some of the largest collateralized stablecoins, Circle's USDC and Binance USD, witnessed not only a premium in their conversion rates (vis-a-vis US\$), but also have seen dramatic gains in their market shares. Since April 2022, USDC has seen a more than US\$7B increase in its market cap, nearly equal to Tether's losses. We aim to shed light on some of the existing questions, and in so doing, we hope to pave the way for a more realistic understanding of stablecoins' forms and functions.

2   Where They Came from and Why

We start with: what are stablecoins? And why do we need them? Stablecoins are digital currencies that facilitate digital financial exchanges without the extreme volatility of prototypical cryptocurrencies. Cryptocurrencies were born out of the dire need for an effective means of digital exchange. Despite the ingenuity of their design, major cryptocurrencies like Bitcoin and Ethereum lack the price stability needed for widely accepted means of exchange. In its whitepaper, Centre, the consortium that governs USDC and was created by Circle and Coinbase, notes that "... existing public blockchain implementations and crypto assets struggle to fulfill the vision in part due to three significant challenges: price stability, transaction throughput, and risks due to the lack of independent governance over standards and network participants (particularly those members offering trade capability and fiat on- and off-ramps)."

In the most intuitive sense, then, stablecoins are digital money (albeit issued in a more decentralized way). While this definition lacks details, it does strike a chord in that for an average user, money should be seamlessly acceptable for any and all transactions. Stablecoins exemplify that ethos in digital finance.

This concept is for most part a shared understanding. According to Cool-Wallet, "[a] stablecoin is a cryptocurrency that remains stable in value against a pegged external asset class. It aims to minimize price volatility, by keeping its value fixed against that of a traditional real-world assets like a single fiat currency, a combination (basket) of currencies or a valuable real-life commodity. Its primary purpose is to negate the speculative nature of most cryptocurrencies and help create a more consistent and reliable market environment in order to

---

[1] As of June 17, 2022, according to data from CoinMarketCap.com, the total market cap of the top 100 stablecoins were US\$157B with the top three (all of a collateralized variety) stablecoins-Tether, USDC and Binance USD-accounting for 90% of the total market capitalization. See: https://coinmarketcap.com/view/stablecoin/.

increase adoption of digital assets."[2,3,4] In its "Digital Currencies: The Rise of Stablecoins" blog[5], the IMF notes that the rise of stablecoins is tantamount to "[a] battle [that] is raging for your wallet. New entrants want to occupy the space once used by paper bills or your debit card."[6]

3   Current State of Stablecoins

While the IMF blog was written prior to the April 2022 crisis, some important points are worth noting. In its report, IMF notes six observations about stablecoins. First, stablecoin providers may steal away traditional deposits from banks. Second, tech giants can utilize their larger networks to create money monopolies. Third, stablecoins can replace weaker currencies as means of global exchange and payments. Fourth, stablecoins can make illicit trade easier. Fifth, stablecoins could provoke the loss of "seigniorage," because central banks can capture profits from the difference between a currency's face value and its manufacturing cost. And lastly, stablecoins can exacerbate financial consumer protection and financial inclusion concerns. For these reasons, the IMF calls for "[o]ne approach [that] would ... regulate stablecoins like money market funds that guarantee fixed nominal returns, requiring providers to maintain sufficient liquidity and capital."

Given what has transpired since early April 2022, the above observations require careful consideration. Up until recently, banks have offered near-zero interest rates. Deposit insurance has never been sufficiently large for institutional clients. As such, stablecoins do not necessarily pose a threat to prototypical bank deposits. Depending on the aggregate risk preference, stablecoins can be substitutes for money market funds or less risky alternatives to broader financial assets. According to the U.S. Fed's data, cash money increases during

---

[2] https://www.coolwallet.io/the-complete-guide-to-stablecoins-part-i-2014-2019/.

[3] There is possibility for a self-reinforcing positive feedback loop. The innate stability, theoretically, can lead to diversifying and expanding the user base, thus boosting stablecoins' utility for wider adoption. By creating more vibrant market dynamics, stablecoins in turn can strengthen stabilizing mechanisms such as cryptocurrency. Maybe, when cryptocurrencies become more stable, stablecoins will merge with more volatile cryptocurrencies, just becoming one of the varieties.

[4] One can argue that price stability depends on the economic parameters of the stablecoin tokenomics model and market forces; transaction throughput is primarily determined by its technological implementation, while independent governance is a combination of a decision-making framework and processes enabling it to ensure that all stakeholders have power to influence decisions made.

[5] https://blogs.imf.org/2019/09/19/digital-currencies-the-rise-of-stablecoins/.

[6] We clearly do not consider the case whereby different sorts of digital money (including CDBCs and corporate private money) reside in wallets. What affects the convenience and utility of the end-user is beyond the scope of this analysis. We do not deny the possibility that user experience and competition among various digital monies have profound implications for each individual provider of such money.

recessions whereas money market funds decrease. This suggests that if stable-coins (especially the fiat-backed variety) behave more like money market funds, there is no strong reason to believe they would hinder deposit taking functions of banks.

Furthermore, there is another type of cyclicality that influences the movement of money into and out of stablecoins. When the crypto market enters a downturn (a so-called crypto winter), theoretically the relative value of volatile cryptocur-rencies should decrease vis-a-vis the value locked in stablecoins. The intuition is simple: if volatile cryptocurrencies lose value against fiat, then the value of any fiat-backed asset should remain intact and, in relative terms, stronger. The rela-tive value of stablecoins has actually increased against volatile cryptocurrencies. In 2017, stablecoins accounted for nearly 0% of the total crypto market cap. After two crypto winters (in 2018 and 2022), their market cap now stands at 17% of the total crypto market. This negative comovement is independent from any competition with bank deposits and is likely to remain a major driving force for the adoption of stablecoins.

Another important consideration is that stablecoins can actually help the traditional financial intermediaries grow. The dominant type of stablecoins by market cap is the fiat-backed stablecoins (e.g., Tether, USD Coin, and Binance USD). The fiat backing of these stablecoins ought to reside somewhere in the traditional financial system: bank deposits, money market funds, etc. Therefore, fiat-backed stablecoins do not compete with such traditional stores of money but rather create an intermediation layer between them and the stablecoin users.

Tech giants such as Meta (formerly Facebook) have tried to make inroads into private currency. These attempts so far have been unsuccessful. Given the fact that the majority of cash resides in major financial institutions' balance sheets, perhaps it is not surprising that tech giants have not been able to succeed in creating private money. Since financial institutions remain the major source of systemic liquidity flow, tech giants find it difficult to replicate the legacy systems in their entirety.

In the case of cross-border payments, stablecoins may have a theoretical advantage. However, any cross-border payment faces the classic "impossible trilemma."[7] As economists John Marcus Fleming and Robert Alexander Mundell demonstrate, in international open economies, it is impossible to have all three of these facets at the same time: (1) a fixed foreign exchange rate, (2) free capital movement (absence of capital controls), and (3) an independent monetary pol-icy. Depending on what parts of the trilemma a country intends to control, the cross-country stablecoin solution may or may not prove effective. Nonetheless, there is no clear answer as to whether cross-border payment will be assisted or hindered by stablecoins.

Stablecoins pegged to stronger national currencies do indeed present a chal-lenge for central banks of weaker national currencies. For instance, stablecoins allow people in Argentina and Russia to bypass rules that limit or tax the hold-ing of USD and other foreign currencies in their bank accounts. This probably

---

[7] https://en.wikipedia.org/wiki/Impossible_trinity.

explains why USD-pegged stablecoins can be sold in peer-to-peer exchanges for a price greater than the price of USD in RUB.

The idea that stablecoins may ease illicit trades stems from the fact that transactions on a blockchain are pseudonymous. Compared to transactions via commercial banks and other financial institutions, where the identities of the parties involved in the transactions are known by the financial institutions and these financial institutions are obliged to conduct KYC/AML/CFT diligence on these transactions, it is clear that blockchains, and by extension stablecoins, can increase risks of illicit transactions. However, it I also worth noting that: a) transactions on a blockchain, despite their pseudonymity, are completely public, providing a degree of transparency that is greater than in non-blockchain-based payment infrastructures; b) this greater transparency can be and is being used to monitor transactions and fight financial crimes, as exemplified by Chainalysis; c) prototypical users will eventually have to convert stablecoins to fiat currency (i.e., the so-called "crypto off-ramp" process) to use the money within the non-crypto economy, and this process occurs through regulated financial institutions that must comply with KYC/AML/CFT; d) fiat-backed centrally-operated stablecoins typically use smart contracts that give the operating entity the power to freeze the balances of users, and this power has already been used to fulfill requests from financial authorities; e) the level of anonymity and privacy achievable with transactions on a blockchain is actually lower than that of physical cash. Transactions can be traced to the point of origin addresses, especially when corresponding hard wallets are in use.

Whether stablecoins provoke the loss of "seigniorage" is an empirical question yet to be answered, and it is likely that the answer will depend largely on predominant types of stablecoins. Fully-backed, fiat-backed stablecoins, for instance, are theoretically incapable of provoking seigniorage losses, because any amount of stablecoin issued needs to be backed by an equivalent amount of fiat currency, and seigniorage will indirectly arise from issuing the fiat currency necessary for backing. In fact, if a fiat-backed stablecoin is fully backed by the currencies issued by central banks, it may even lead to a gain of seigniorage compared to commercial bank money, which does not need to be fully backed by central-bank money within the fractional reserve banking system. On the other hand, stablecoins that are unbacked, only fractionally backed, or backed by assets that are not issued by a central bank can indeed reduce a central bank's seigniorage. Particularly in the case of crypto-backed stablecoins, it could be argued that seigniorage is being shifted away from central banks and to the entities that benefit from the increasing supply of the backing cryptocurrency. Such entities are, for instance, "miners" in the case of proof-of-work cryptocurrencies and block producers and validators in the case of proof-of-stake cryptocurrencies.

The global concerted effort to launch central bank digital currencies, at least at face value, suggests that major monetary authorities prefer to have their own digital money. The concerns about consumer access to financing services and privacy are a mixed bag. So far the largest hacks and thefts occurred on exchanges (e.g., KuCoin in 2020, Upbit in 2019, BINANCE in 2019). The flaws in security designs of the exchanges seem to be the main culprit. We really cannot blame stablecoins for that. Similarly, the consumer access question is also intimately related to decentralized applications (dApps). The diversity and design of dApps determine whether the ecosystem is consumer friendly. The variety of financial services is germane for the success of the ecosystem but stablecoins only facilitate movement of money. In short, stablecoins grease the wheels, but which direction the wheels turn is another question altogether.

Lastly, stablecoins are also a solution for an interoperability problem. Blockchains offer programmability. There are now numerous decentralized finance applications running almost autonomously on blockchains, offering a wide range of financial products and instruments such as staking, lending and borrowing, options, futures, prediction markets, crowdfunding and launchpad platforms. On these applications, end-users can use their digital assets but they cannot use their fiat currencies directly, simply because fiat currencies do not exist on blockchains. Stablecoins bridge this interoperability gap by giving people assets that are pegged to fiat currencies and that can be used within this new world of blockchain-based finance. From this point, stablecoins do not compete with fiat currencies or even CBDCs, but rather complement them by making them available within blockchain ecosystems. Indeed, this point stems from our earlier, simple, yet fundamental assertion that stablecoins are digital cash for digital economies.

4 Stablecoin Classification

In light of recent collapses and regulatory movements, it is crucial to realize that there are many different types of stablecoins and they should not all be treated in the same way. Indeed, Thomas Cowen from Paxos notes that "... Not all stablecoins are equal or even 'stable.' ... Fiat-backed stablecoins are backed by just that—fiat-denominated traditional currencies and assets. However, different fiat-collateralized stablecoins are backed by different assets depending on risk appetite."[8] One important dimension of classification is whether the stablecoin is "algorithmic." Although this word is often used to refer to stablecoins that are unbacked and uncollateralized, it actually just means that stablecoin's stabilization mechanisms follow well-defined rules, usually programmed in a smart contract. There are plenty of backed or collateralized algorithmic stablecoins, of which Djed and DAI are two examples.

Backing and collateralization are often conflated and their subtle difference is a distinguishing classification factor that is frequently overlooked. When a stablecoin is backed, it has a reserve and can be redeemed for portions of the reserve. When it is collateralized, it can be minted in the form of loans against provided collateral, but the collateral can only be retrieved by the user who generated the loan when he or she pays it back or in the event of liquidation.

---

[8] https://paxos.com/2022/07/13/its-not-either-stablecoins-or-cbdcs-its-both/.

Another important criterion for classification is governance. At one end of the spectrum, we have fiat-backed non-algorithmic stablecoins, which are governed by a single company. At the other end of the spectrum, we have fully autonomous algorithmic stablecoins, where the smart contracts run completely independently and immutably and are not governed by anyone. Somewhere in the middle of the spectrum, we may have algorithmic stablecoins that have an associated governance token that gives rights to a wide group of people to participate and influence decisions that may change aspects of the algorithm.

5   The Collapse of Luna

In April/May 2022, the Terra stablecoin collapsed. The cascading effect was an almost 50.

To answer this question, we examine whether the claim that Terra was an algorithmic stablecoin was valid. As a stablecoin, Terra's algorithmic design should have brought about economic conditions and incentives to make it secure. Terra's failure then points to flaws in the algorithm. But what were these flaws?

Terra's algorithm was originally just a variation of the seigniorage shares stablecoin algorithm[9], where the LUNA token played the role of the seigniorage share. The intuition is simple. When the value of UST is above 1 USD, LUNA holders can burn 1 USD worth of LUNA tokens in exchange for 1 UST. Then they can sell this 1 UST in the market for a value between the current market price and 1 USD, thereby profiting (in the form of indirect seigniorage revenue) and contributing to an increase in the supply of UST and, consequently, a reduction of its price in the market. Conversely, when the value of UST is below 1 USD, UST holders can burn UST in exchange for 1 USD worth of LUNA. This decreases the supply of LUNA in the open market and increases its price.

This idea seems convincing at first sight and because one can exchange UST for LUNA, UST appears to be reassuringly "backed" by LUNA. However, it is incorrect to think of this possibility of exchange as a proper form of backing; the value of LUNA is dependent on the expected future demand for the stablecoin. It is a circular dependency, which entails that UST is "backed" by itself and hence not really backed by anything else. When UST collapsed, the price of LUNA fell as well due to this circular dependency. This problem is not exclusive to Terra. It is inherent to pure seigniorage share-style algorithmic stablecoins: when the stablecoin loses the peg significantly, the seigniorage share that was allegedly "backing" it will also lose value since there won't be sufficient demand for a stablecoin that is not stable and hence the expectation of seigniorage inflow will be low.

Proper backing necessitates using assets that are independent from the stablecoin protocol itself. Thus it is more appropriate to refer to pure seigniorage share-style stablecoins as unbacked. It seems that the Terra project even realized this towards its end since a backing reserve in Bitcoin was created by the Luna

---

[9] https://blog.bitmex.com/wp-content/uploads/2018/06/A-Note-on-Cryptocurrency-Stabilisation-Seigniorage-Shares.pdf.

Foundation Guard to be non-algorithmically managed and governed. However, this reserve did not sufficiently (fully) back all UST in circulation. Furthermore, it is also possible that the purchase of Bitcoins may have been just an exit before and during the collapse by insiders.

Another problem of seigniorage share-style stablecoins is that seigniorage, which is revenue originating from increasing the supply, creates a perverse incentive to increase the supply. To increase the supply, demand for the stablecoin needs to exist. In the case of Terra, this demand was artificially generated by an annual percent rate of almost 20% for locking UST on Anchor, a lending and borrowing platform on top of Terra. At one point in time, almost 80% of the entire UST supply was deposited in Anchor. If for any reason, including but not limited to unsustainability of 20% rate, these vast amounts of UST were withdrawn from Anchor and sold in the market, there would clearly be a sudden increase in the circulating supply and a corresponding sudden crash in the UST price. A sensible course of action would have been to reduce Anchor's rate to encourage its latent supply to be withdrawn gradually. But Terra did exactly the opposite. Several weeks before the collapse, it bailed out Anchor. This decision, which goes contrary to stability, is understandable from the point of view of the perverse seigniorage incentive. The steep increase in the total supply of UST that correlated with the steep increase of deposits in Anchor had certainly been lucrative for LUNA holders so far.

Any stablecoin can be subject to a sudden supply increase and corresponding price crash, but good algorithmic stablecoins would be able to absorb the shock by buying back the excess supply. In the case of Terra, due to the joint crash of LUNA for the reasons explained above, buying back the excess supply was not possible. Good algorithmic stablecoins would also have incentives that promote stability instead of perverse incentives that encourage behaviors that cause instability.

Another issue with Terra was related to governance. When UST and LUNA crashed, Terra halted the blockchain, thereby manually preventing the algorithm from working. This is the opposite of what an "algorithmic" stablecoin should do. They were able to do this because they controlled the nodes of the blockchain. Their blockchain was not independently operated. If they had allowed the algorithm to work, UST holders would be able to exchange their UST for vast amounts of LUNA tokens, which would be dilutive and hence not beneficial to the incumbent LUNA holders. So naturally, it was not in their interest to allow the algorithm to work, even if doing so would have provided some support for the price of UST.

6   Future Directions

Challenges of stablecoins as private digital money are not trivial. Gorton, Ross, and Ross (2022) further show that "It is difficult for private agents to produce money that circulates at par with no questions asked. We study two cases of privately-produced money: pre-Civil War U.S. private banknotes and modern stablecoins. Private monies are introduced when there are no better alternatives, but they initially carry an inconvenience yield. Over time, these monies may become more money-like, but they do not always achieve a positive convenience yield. Technology advances and reputation formation pushed private banknotes toward a positive convenience yield. We show that the same forces are at work for Stablecoins." This implies that while there are no better alternatives to function as digital money, stablecoins can enjoy a collective monopolistic rent. However, the growing number of central bank digital currencies (CBDCs) is a major potential competitive threat to private money. Of course as Gorton, Ross, and Ross (2022) note, both CBDCs and stablecoins can play complementary roles. After all, money market funds and bank deposits co-exist and provide complementary services. However, building on the money market fund analogy, the emerging CBDCs may pave the way for collateralized stablecoins to function as digital private money.

More importantly, an observation of the peg and market capitalization of top stablecoins reveals stark patterns. Since April 2022, only USD Coin (USDC) has gained market share in a dramatic way. The largest, Tether, has seen a drastic decrease in its market share. According to a New York Times article, "... [a]s cryptocurrencies plummeted, a flood of investors asked to exchange their Tethers for dollars, forcing the company to pay out about an eighth of its reserves, or $10 billion, over the course of a week and a half. On cryptocurrency exchanges, Tether briefly wavered from its $1 peg." Two notable algorithmic coins, DAI and FRAX, have also lost significant market share since April 2022. By all accounts, however, backed and collateralized coins have fared well; furthermore, among these, coins with reserve or collateral assets that were perceived as less risky have fared even better (especially USDC).

In short, we can see two potential future pathways:

- Fiat-backed centrally operated stablecoins can fill a void in the digital financial services much the same way as money market funds have. But to do so, these stablecoins can take a page from money market funds' history and (1) define explicitly without ambiguity their investment strategy, (2) disclose fully the portfolio of assets that back the stablecoins, (3) adhere to highest quality auditing standards, and (4) welcome regulatory frameworks that provide clarity and protections for the well-functioning of their respective industries. Given the critical role money market funds have played in revolutionizing institutional investment, corporate treasury management, and wealth advisory services, we tend to think regulatory separation of fiat-backed stablecoins can usher in an age of near-safe, fully digital private money that can harmoniously coexist with future CBDCs. This private digital money will facilitate digital exchange needed by a fully functioning digital economy.

- Algorithmic stablecoins can continue to explore the programmability of money made possible by blockchains and smart contracts in order to automate stabilization mechanisms and ultimately offer stable digital assets with less operational overhead. To do so while having the confidence of users, these stablecoins must (1) define explicitly the stabilization mechanisms, (2) argue with more than just informal explanations why these mechanisms work, (3) be clear about the risks involved, and (4) optimize governance to limit perverse incentives of governance token holders. Given the importance of artificial intelligence, automation, and autonomy in multiple industries, it seems plausible and indeed probable that autonomy in the minting and burning of programmable digital money through smart contracts will be an inevitable part of our future. A favorable regulatory environment that enables innovation is essential for the full realization of potential algorithmic stablecoins.

The dichotomy provides a much needed pathway for algorithmic stablecoins to play a vital yet less explored role within the digital finance ecosystem. In the parlance of finance, these instruments are derivatives: they are meant to synthetically mimic the movement of their underlying assets (fiat, crypto, etc.). Since the first modern derivatives (options) started trading in the early 1970s, financial derivatives have become the largest segment of asset classes. But more importantly, they have provided innovative means for financial engineering. A case in point is the story of portfolio insurances. After the Nobel prize winning works of Black-Scholes-Merton on option pricing and proliferation of option trading in the 1970s, the decade of the 1980s brought about a new breed of derivatives: synthetics. By the early 1980s it became very clear that options have tremendous potential for risk mitigation. Put options—the bet on a price decline—were especially useful in insuring against downturns. However, outright put options are expensive insurance. American financial economists Hayne Leland and Mark Rubinstein thus invented synthetic puts. Using other cheaply available derivatives and assets, they replicated a dynamically adjusting portfolio insurance. What followed is nothing short of a miracle. The algorithmic trading accounts for the majority of the order flow and credit default swaps that dwarf the bond market are only two prominent examples of how synthetic financial products have changed the landscape of finance.

By dichotomizing stablecoins along their ultimate functions, which happens to coincide with their form, we can unleash the true potential of these products. Moreover, this change of perspective can also lead to better alignment with regulatory frameworks and disclosure rules. From a practical standpoint, this can also result in more effective risk management. Take for instance counterparty risk, which has been perhaps the singular critical reason for the recent failings in stablecoins. Fiat-backed stablecoins, which are backed by high quality, high visibility assets, should not in theory face dire credit/counterparty risk. However, as the global financial crisis of 2008 demonstrated, even the safest instruments— money markets—can face occasional bouts of extreme illiquidity shocks. The fiat-backed stablecoins thus need to have in place effective mechanisms to mitigate liquidity risk. Equally importantly, for the purpose of adhering to AML-KYC and other regulatory requirements, these stablecoins need to build strict operational risk management systems that may sacrifice flexibility expected from decentralized systems to provide soundness.

For algorithmic stablecoins, the inherent risks associated with synthetic derivatives demand sophisticated financial engineering and multi-faceted risk management mechanisms (credit, counterparty, liquidity, operational, and regulatory). But equally importantly, the success and growth of these stablecoins necessitate the lock-step development of a broad financial system. In its fully developed state, this financial system includes essential elements such as account insurance, clearinghouses, risk-based prudential capital (equity) requirements, and intersystem connectivities. Given that algorithmic stablecoins rely on multilateral financial assets' trading to maintain stability, they must implement optimal trading mechanisms that not only facilitate speedy transactions but also provide necessary backstops to prevent panic trading and suboptimal liquidations. The interconnectivity to lending platforms and leveraged instruments exacerbates the fragility of financial systems predicated on algorithmic trading. From both business longevity and community welfare standpoints, algorithmic stablecoins are well-served in implementing and maintaining a wholesome approach to risk management that expands beyond immediate peg stability and transcends to the entirety of the financial ecosystem they serve.

7   Conclusion

Stablecoins are necessary means of exchange in digital economies. Despite the failings of a few operators in this nascent industry, digital financial systems offer extraordinary opportunities: speedy transactions, access for underbanked and unbanked, and democratized exchange and trading ecosystems. However, to reach their full potential, we must first recognize that the form of stabilization mechanism fundamentally changes how stablecoins should be managed from a business perspective and be regulated from an oversight standpoint. We propose that fiat-backed stablecoins are best viewed through the lens of money market funds within traditional financial services. These stablecoins can play a similarly pivotal role in the development of digital financial services. To do so, full backing by risk-free assets, complete transparency, and audited reporting are must-haves. On the other hand, the algorithmic stablecoins are uniquely positioned to serve as synthetic cash in expanded financial ecosystems that include a wide swath of financial instruments. Prudent capital requirement, effective wholesome risk management, and liquidity shock-proof trading mechanism are critical necessary conditions for creating fragility-resistant financial systems based on algorithmic stablecoins. We hope that this document will pave the way for more constructive dialogue on the form, function, and future of stablecoins.

FTX Collapse: A Ponzi Story

Shange Fu[1](✉), Qin Wang[2](✉), Jiangshan Yu[1](✉), and Shiping Chen[2](✉)

[1] Monash University, Melbourne, Australia
{shange.fu,jiangshan.yu}@monash.edu
[2] CSIRO Data61, Sydney, Australia
qinwangtech@gmail.com, shiping.chen@data61.csiro.au

Abstract. FTX used to be the third-largest centralized exchange (CEX) in crypto space, managing over $10B in daily trading volume before its downfall. Such a giant, however, failed to avoid the fate of mania, panic, and crash. In this work, we revisit the FTX's crash by telling it as a Ponzi story. In regards to why FTX could not sustain this Ponzi game, we extract and demonstrate the three drivers of the FTX collapse, namely *FTT*, *leverage*, and *diversion*. The unfunctionality in each factor can iteratively magnify the impact of damages when the panic is triggered. Rooted in the unstable ground, FTX eventually suffered insolvency and rapidly crashed in Nov. 2022. The crisis of FTX is not an isolated event; it consequently results in the collapse of a chain of associated companies in the entire market. Recall this painful experience, we discuss possible paths for a way forward for both CeFi and DeFi implementations.

Keywords: FTX · Ponzi Model · CEX · DeFi

1 Introduction

The story of FTX started with its founder Sam Bankman-Fried (SBF in short). Though there already existed a list of cryptocurrency exchanges and strong competitors such as Coinbase and Binance, SBF still decided to launch a new crypto exchange FTX in April 2019. FTX experienced a skyrocketing development within three years and ranked as the third-largest CEX that handles over $10 active trading volume before collapsing [1]. Besides this influential trading platform, SBF also created a hedge fund called Alameda Research that manages $14.6B assets ($6B of which is FTT[1] and other assets, while $8B is debt [2]). However, FTX struck a deal for Binance and halted all non-fiat customer withdrawals. Later, FTX declared bankruptcy on Nov. 11, 2022, marking the end of the story. Negative externalities soon spread over the entire financial market. The prices of most major cryptocurrencies have plummeted more than 30% within

---

[1] FTT is the native token of the crypto derivatives created by FTX that is launched on May 8, 2019. At the time of writing, FTX token price has dropped 62X from $79.53 (9/10/2021) to $1.29 (11/29/2022) [1].

© International Financial Cryptography Association 2024
A. Essex et al. (Eds.): FC 2023 Workshops, LNCS 13953, pp. 208–215, 2024.
https://doi.org/10.1007/978-3-031-48806-1_14

hours. The collapse had a knock-on effect on a large number of crypto-projects due to their close connection with FTX (e.g., Solana [3,4]). Many traditional finance agencies such as hedge funds that have affiliated transactions with FTX also suffered serious monetary losses. U.S. Department of Justice and other federal agencies thus launched an investigation of the event [5].

Back to FTX's origin, we can observe a common pattern applied in crypto projects: issue *non-collateral tokens* (primarily in the form of ERC-20 standard [6] on Ethereum blockchain [7]) without any backed-up assets. This phenomenon is also known as ICO (short for Initial Coin Offering), which was prevalent since 2017. Not surprisingly, FTX also launched its own token FTT in 2019. Though without any collateral, the issuance of FTT raised a significant of high-liquidity crypto assets including BTC and ETH. However, such a design pattern implicitly inherits the Ponzi nature [8], where the asset manager always borrows new money to pay off the old debts until the game cannot be sustained. Typically, issuing a new token is costless most of the time.

The reasons behind the FTT price crash are not unique, though indeed it was facilitated in several innovative ways by DeFi protocols. In fact, apart from pure scams in crypto markets, many means from traditional financial markets have also been applied in today's DeFi games as an add-on, with *leverage* being the most popular one. Not limited to its classic connotation on financial derivatives such as futures or options, a more general meaning of leverage refers to the iterative magnification effect of a certain crypto asset in DeFi space. One token (FTT in this paper) can yield, perhaps, 10X or more in value after routing several centralized exchanges and DeFi protocols [9]. Another facilitator of this crash is *divert*, referring to the misappropriation of reserves. In fact, current crypto-markets are absent of formal regulation, which has spawned many types of CeFi/DeFi services without rigorous background checks or authentication. There is an undeniable fact that crypto-users, unfortunately, are keen on this kind of game due to its potential for excessive high returns. An accident similar to FTX collapse may repeat, and this motivates us to look for the root factors that may alter the ending of stories.

Contribution. We explore the reasons that cause the FTX collapse by reconstructing it in the context of the Ponzi model. We first abstract the fundamentals of Ponzi and, in particular, distinguish rational Ponzi game from other Ponzi schemes as the prerequisites to gain a deep understanding of this event (Sect. 2). Upon this theoretical basis, we decompose and analyze three major factors that lead FTX to be a broken Ponzi but not a rational Ponzi game (Sect. 3). Further, we provide discussion and advice on potential aspects, namely regulation and transparency, for future research endeavors (Sect. 4).

Related Work. Nansen [10] provides a research analysis that captures on-chain data from May 2019 – Sep 2022, focusing on both FTT and Alameda activities. Ramirez [11] sorts out the timeline and milestones of the FTX crash. Jakub [12] aims to point out the future paths for centralized exchanges. Besides, many influential companies (e.g., CoinDesk [13], Investopedia [14]) and other mainstream media (e.g., Forbes [15], Wiki [16]), also put their focus on such a historical event by recalling, analyzing, and summarizing its ins and outs. However, most of the crypto-collapse research, reports, and posts [17] [18] (topics also covering LUNA-UST's de-peg) are based on facts and explicit data without the in-depth abstraction of easy-understanding models or insights, which is the key matter that we aim to deliver in this paper.

2   What is Ponzi?

The Ponzi game, commonly referred to as the Ponzi scheme, is named after Charles Ponzi, who duped investors in the 1920s with a postage stamp speculation scheme. Ponzi is essentially a financial protocol that old liability should be financed by issuing new debt. For those who are deliberately deceptive, Ponzi scheme organizers often promise to invest your money and generate high returns with little or no risk. But in practical Ponzi schemes, fraudsters do not invest money. Instead, they use it to pay those who invested earlier and may keep some for themselves. Ponzi schemes normally share common characteristics, and U.S. Securities and Exchange Commission [19] raises "red flags" for these warning signs: (i) high returns with little or no risk; (ii) overly consistent returns; (iii) unregistered investments; (iv) unlicensed sellers; (v) secretive, complex strategies; (vi) issues with paperwork; and (vii) difficulty receiving payments.

We then demonstrate how a Ponzi scheme works (and how it may be broken) in general in Fig. 1. The green plus sign and the red minus sign represent cash inflows and cash outflows, respectively. The values in parentheses following each participant represent their corresponding utility. In a Ponzi scheme, the borrower or the issuer can always benefit from the game, and participants can reach a no-less-than-zero utility before the breaking of Ponzi; only the last wave of escapees will suffer losses. Therefore, a broken Ponzi scheme is a zero-sum game.

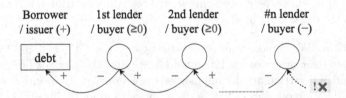

Fig. 1. How a Ponzi scheme works in general.

Rational Ponzi Game. Running a Ponzi, however, does not necessarily imply that any participant is in any sense losing out, as long as the game can be perpetually rolled over. Economists call such realization a *rational Ponzi game* [20]. A rational Ponzi game refers to a type of sustainable game that satisfies two major factors of keep running and no harm to any party. It requires monetary investment so the game should continuously operate without degrading the situation of participants. Economically, the game is measured by a utility function (a.k.a. pay-off function) based on the net cash inflows of lenders $\mathcal{I}_s$, the borrower's net indebtedness $\mathcal{D}_T$, the discount factor $\Gamma(T)$ (calculated based on the interest rate r_t), as well as the time-based counters T and s. The key principle is summarised as *current debts can always be redeemed by all future incomes in the form of present values*. It can be demonstrated in a loose mathematical model [21] which is defined as:

$$\Gamma(T)\mathcal{D}_T = \sum_{s=1}^{T} \Gamma(s)\mathcal{I}_s,$$

$$where \ \Gamma(s) \equiv \prod_{j=1}^{s} \left(1 + r_j\right)^{-1}. \tag{1}$$

The model is simulated as a sequential of debt transactions [22] that need to hold two conditions that are separately fit for different participants: firstly (♮-①), the net present indebtedness value (*left*) should always be positive for borrowers; secondly (♮-②), the game should not hurt any participating parties in the game (a.k.a. Pareto improvement [23]). These two properties guarantee a perpetually operating economical game in the context of permissionless environments. This also explains the name of *rational Ponzi* in which all the rational players will, at least, lose nothing in the game.

3   The FTX Collapse

FTX also had a potential to run itself as a rational Ponzi game by issuing its native token FTT. Founded by SBF in 2019, FTX saw a rapid growth with the help of a good market maker Alameda. Interestingly, Alameda is also founded by SBF. The tactful coordination of FTX and Alameda made FTX a leading global CEX, and made the valuation of FTX balloon in size to \$32 billion as of January 2022 [24]. With such success, FTX naturally launched its self-issued token FTT just like most centralized exchanges. However, with all the familiar stages in order - token boom and a fad for it, excessive leverage, then problem revealed and panic followed close behind, FTX finally fell into its crash. In this section, we decompose this disastrous speculation and demonstrate three facilitators that explain the FTX collapse, namely *FTT*, *leverage*, and *diversion*.

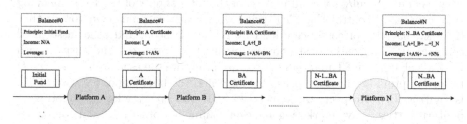

Fig. 2. The leverage mechanisms.

FTT. *FTT* is the utility token of FTX centralized exchange, mostly used for lowering trading fees on the platform. Like most other cryptocurrencies, FTT is an inherent Ponzi-type token, meaning that it is not backed by any asset. The FTT issuers raise money from the first wave of investors with a near-zero cost, just like the initiating debt in any Ponzi game. FTT may sustain, or may even achieve a rational Ponzi game if it can maintain a relatively stable or increasing market value and be actively traded in a healthy way. But unfortunately, FTT performs weaker than people previously believed. FTT does not entitle users to a part of the platform revenue or represent a share in FTX, nor give control over governance decisions or FTX's treasury. However, these are not the very causes of its own collapse; the essence of financial distress is loss of confidence. The change in the mindsets of investors from confidence to pessimism is due to the excessive *leverage* and *divert* operations conducted by FTX and Alameda.

Leverage. Though issued without any reserves, FTT was heavily used as collateral wild west [2], and thus resulted in high leverage to both FTX and Alameda, which is the second factor facilitating the crash. Leverage is the ratio of debt to capital or to equity, and we now show how leverage enlarges the available capital in general in Fig. 2. We denote money markets, including both CeFi platforms and different types of DeFi protocols, as $\{A, B, ..., N, ...\}$. Starting with the principle of an initial fund, the income of each stage is defined as $\mathcal{I}$, which could be deposit revenue, liquidity mining reward and many so on [25]. Thus, the income of A platform is identified as $\mathcal{I}_A$, with a leverage magnifier of $A\%$. At the same time, we define the life cycle of one type of asset circulating from one platform to another as one round i, where i is an integer. Therefore, we can have the combined leverage after i rounds are calculated as,

$$\sum_{i=0}^{i} \gamma = 1 + A\% + B\% + ... + N\%. \tag{2}$$

With such a financial approach, FTT was used as collateral to raise a significant amount of money in the market, covering a series of CEXes and DeFi protocols, and thus making its virtual value be magnified thousands of times (*leverage*).

Diversion. In addition to the previous two factors, the misuse of customers' funds also facilitates the FTX collapse all along. As shown in Fig. 3, FTX and Alameda only circulate a small portion of the total supply of the FTT, meaning they can easily control the FTT price with available funds. On top of this, the vast majority of coins were held by FTX, Alameda, and other associated companies. They continuously borrow money from investors and entities with FTT as collateral. FTT managers also misappropriate the users' reserves (*divert*) to further promote the asset price. In this sense, the booming of FTX and FTT is vigilant. In retrospect, we know that SBF also spent a lot in donating to political parties, heavy marketing and even bailing out other insolvent companies including Solana and BlockFi. But there are nearly no external restrictions on how he can use the funds. The game ends in a panic when all problems are revealed. At the time, FTX and Alameda were finally not solvent, and SBF paused the withdrawals, signaling the collapse of his entire empire.

The FTX crisis was not isolated but a sequel to the previous Luna/UST failure, also the beginning of a new series of collapses. The previous unexpected downfall of Three Arrows Capital and LUNA/UST meant the market participants were highly sensitive when it came to any rumors of potential insolvency. The FTX event further damaged the already shaken reputation of the crypto industry. In addition to incurring losses to customers and investors, the FTX's downfall sent shockwaves to other institutions and the entire crypto space. Solana and BlockFi are among the most severely affected entities. We refer readers interested in detailed information on this event to the reports by Coin-Desk and Nansen [10,13]. We may also likely expect to see more affected companies being revealed in the near future, and a slow recovery of belief in this market.

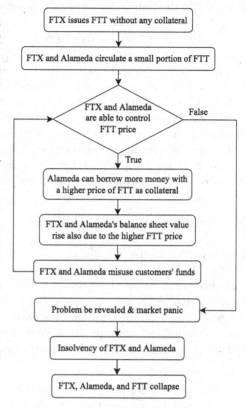

Fig. 3. The FTX collapse flow.

4   Future Directions

With lessons learned from the FTX collapse, we discuss how to better sustain CeFi and DeFi operations in this section.

Regulation. Regulation has always been a controversial topic ever since the emergence of cryptocurrencies. On the one side, users moving from traditional finance to crypto space are pursuing decentralization with strong motivations. Regulation is naturally placed in the opposite position. The FTX event raises concerns from the community about potential regulatory implications, such as the initiation of tough regulation measures, thus affecting the DeFi process. However, on the flip side, each time such a vicious incident happens, people yet paradoxically want an authority to handle it and prevent further damage. Meanwhile, the leave of some giants makes it easier for the remaining ones to form a monopoly, making regulatory intervention the only viable solution at this moment. And most importantly, regulation is already in place. With such considerations, properly introducing regulation into CEXes and even the DeFi world may seem necessary.

Transparency. Transparency is another alternative, which seems more desirable. Many CEXes have already created *proof of reserves* of assets as evidence delivered to the public. However, the proof of reserve cannot reflect the full picture of exchange solvency, such as the liabilities. CEXes and CeFi-related tools need to rely on external forces to restore market confidence. In contrast, DeFi protocols can naturally do better than CeFi in terms of transparency. Leveraging smart contracts, DeFi can realize a series of advantages such as self-custody & governance (i.e., decentralized autonomous organization, or DAO), and fair access to participants [25]. The logic and rules written in smart contracts are fully transparent that can be publicly checked by anyone. But it still is not an ideal solution due to DeFi's high-security risks. Any logic error or loop bugs will be continuously running until the system crashes, and abilities on self-calibrating & correcting are absent. Therefore, prior security audits are of particular importance to DeFi protocols when enjoying their advantage in transparency.

5   Concluding Remarks

In this paper, we dig into the root reasons for the FTX collapse. By comparing its operation of token FTT with a rational Ponzi model, we identify major violations that break the holding conditions and as a result, lead FTT to a broken Ponzi. Although there are possible ways to avoid similar disasters, none are without their flaws. Further endeavors are still required for establishing a more sustainable token operating system for both CeFi and DeFi services. At last, we deliver three pieces of home-taking messages as a summary.

> ▷ It is possible for CEX to run its native token as a rational Ponzi game if leverage is well controlled; CEX should always place sufficient security deposits while not pursuing a dangerous extension of the capital.
> ▷ Improving CeFi's transparency is an urgent task today; the proof-of-reserve standard should be widely adopted by CEXes, and the transparency of CeFi's corporate balance sheet should be enhanced.
> ▷ DeFi protocols, powered by the blockchain technology, can naturally do better than CeFi in terms of transparency. Its further development, however, still requires rigorous audit and sound governance.

References

1. CoinMarketCap. Cryptocurrency Prices, Charts And Market Capitalizations — CoinMarketCap (2022). Accessed 19 Nov 2022
2. CoinDesk. Divisions in Sam Bankman-Fried's Crypto Empire Blur on His Trading Titan Alameda's Balance Sheet (2022). https://www.coindesk.com/business/2022/11/02/divisions-in-sam-bankman-frieds-crypto-empire-blur-on-his-trading-titan-alamedas-balance-sheet/

3. Tarang, K.: Solana endures 'crucible' as ftx connection deletes 70% of tv (2022). https://thedefiant.io/solana-test-ftx-crisis
4. Aleksandar, G.: Ftx-backed bitcoin and ether tokens depeg on solana (2022). https://thedefiant.io/ftx-files-for-bankruptcy
5. Camomile, S.: Us justice department wants ftx fraud allegations to be investigated. https://www.coindesk.com/policy/2022/12/02/us-justice-department-wants-ftx-fraud-allegations-to-be-investigated/
6. Fabian, V., Vitalik, B.: Erc-20 token standard. https://ethereum.org/en/developers/docs/standards/tokens/erc-20/
7. Wood, G., et al.: Ethereum: a secure decentralised generalised transaction ledger. Ethereum Yellow Paper **151**(2014), 1–32 (2014)
8. Basu, K.: The Ponzi economy. Sci. Am. **310**(6), 70–75 (2014)
9. Werner, S.M., Perez, D., Gudgeon, L., Klages-Mundt, A., Harz, D., Knottenbelt, W.J.: Sok: decentralized finance (defi). arXiv preprint arXiv:2101.08778 (2021)
10. Li, K.Y., Sandra, L., Louisa, C., Niklas, P., Douglas, C.: Blockchain analysis: the collapse of alameda and ftx (2022). https://www.nansen.ai/research/blockchain-analysis-the-collapse-of-alameda-and-ftx
11. Ramirez, D.: Ftx crash: timeline, fallout and what investors should know (2022). https://www.nerdwallet.com/article/investing/ftx-crash
12. Jakub. Ftx collapse - what is the path forward for crypto (2021). https://finematics.com/the-ftx-collapse-explained/
13. CoinDesk. The FTX Downfall: Full Coverage - Follow the key developments of the unraveling of Sam Bankman-Fried's crypto empire and exchange, FTX (2022). https://www.coindesk.com/ftx-news-coverage/
14. Nathan, R., Vikki, V.: The Collapse of FTX: What Went Wrong with the Crypto Exchange? (2022). https://www.investopedia.com/what-went-wrong-with-ftx-6828447
15. Forbes. The Collapse Of FTX (2022). https://www.forbes.com/sites/forbesstaff/article/the-fall-of-ftx/?sh=14bbd8aa7d0c
16. Wikiwand. Bankruptcy of ftx (2022). https://www.wikiwand.com/en/Bankruptcy_of_FTX
17. Owen, F.: Crypto users jump to defi platforms in wake of ftx's cefi crash. https://thedefiant.io/defi-surge-ftx-crash
18. Owen, F.: Stablecoins show signs of stabilizing after ftx storm. https://thedefiant.io/stablecoins-show-signs-of-stabilizing-after-ftx-storm
19. Investor.gov U.S. SECURITIES AND EXCHANGE COMMISSION. Ponzi Scheme (2022). Accessed 19 Nov 2022
20. O'Connell, S.A., Zeldes, S.P.: Rational ponzi games. Int. Econ. Rev. 431–450 (1988)
21. Fu, S., Wang, Q., Yu, J., Chen, S.: Rational ponzi games in algorithmic stablecoin. arXiv preprint arXiv:2210.11928 (2022)
22. Blanchard, O.J., Weil, P.: Dynamic efficiency, the riskless rate, and debt ponzi games under uncertainty. National Bureau of Economic Research, Cambridge, Mass (1992)
23. Wiki. Pareto efficiency (2021). https://www.wikiwand.com/en/Pareto_efficiency
24. PitchBook. PitchBook Profile - FTX (2022). Accessed 19 Nov 2022
25. Qin, K., Zhou, L., Afonin, Y., Lazzaretti, L., Gervais, A.: Cefi vs. defi-comparing centralized to decentralized finance. In: Crypto Valley Conference on Blockchain Technology (CVCBT) (2021)

Policy Design of Retail Central Bank Digital Currencies: Embedding AML/CFT Compliance

Michi Kakebayashi[1]([✉]), Gerard P. Presto[2], and Tomonori Yuyama[2]

[1] University of California, Berkeley, Berkeley, USA
`michi.kakebayashi@berkeley.edu`
[2] Georgetown University, Washington, D.C., USA
`{gpp12,ty295}@georgetown.edu`

Abstract. This paper provides a foundation on how to ensure effective and efficient Anti-Money Laundering (AML) and Combating the Financing of Terrorism (CFT) compliance measures in the Central Bank Digital Currency (CBDC) system, focusing particularly on the retail CBDC in a two-tiered system. By examining the existing AML/CFT practices and those implemented in newly launched CBDC projects, we build a policy framework of AML/CFT measures that should be embedded in the CBDC system to enhance compliance. The most common enforcement of AML/CFT measures associated with CBDC balances assumes the form of transaction amount or holding amount limits based on the level of Know-Your-Customer (KYC) findings. In this paper, we examine practices beyond the initial KYC measures and explore the processes of on-boarding and on-going customer due diligence, transaction analysis and evaluation, decision making and reporting to the Financial Investigation Unit (FIU).

Keywords: CBDC - Central Bank Digital Currency · AML - Anti Money Laundering · CFT - Combating the Financing of Terrorism · DLT - Distributed Ledger Technology · FATF - Financial Action Task Force · regulatory compliance

1 Introduction

Central Bank Digital Currency (CBDC) is a digital form of sovereign currency which is the liability of the issuing central bank. A survey conducted in 2021 by the Bank for International Settlements (BIS) showed that 90% of central banks are actively exploring the development of CBDC (Kosse and Mattei, 2022).[1]

There are two types of CBDCs: wholesale and retail. Wholesale CBDC targets regulated financial institutions as users and are "intended for the settlement of interbank

---

The views expressed herein are those of the authors and do not necessarily reflect the opinions of the organizations the authors belong to. Any remaining errors are the sole responsibility of the authors.

[1] This information is based on eighty-one central banks that replied to the CBDC survey conducted by BIS (Kosse and Mattei, 2022).

© International Financial Cryptography Association 2024
A. Essex et al. (Eds.): FC 2023 Workshops, LNCS 13953, pp. 216–244, 2024.
https://doi.org/10.1007/978-3-031-48806-1_15

transfers and related wholesale transactions, for example, to settle payments between financial institutions" (BIS, 2021). Alternatively, retail CBDC is offered to the general public. The innovative aspect of the retail CBDC is that it is a direct claim on the issuing central bank (BIS, 2021).

Retail CBDC has two ways to be distributed to individuals: directly by the central bank (one-tier model) or indirectly through private intermediaries (two-tier model or intermediary model). BIS survey results showed that 70% of the central banks engaged in CBDC research were considering a two-tiered model (Kosse and Mattei, 2022). The survey also illustrated the central bank's expectation towards private intermediaries to conduct "the onboarding of clients (including know-your-customer (KYC) processes and anti-money laundering/combating the financing of terrorism (AML/CFT) procedures)" (Kosse and Mattei, 2022). In September 2022, the White House emphasized in the "Policy Objectives for a U.S. Central Bank Digital Currency System" that "[t]he CBDC system should promote compliance with AML/CFT requirements and mitigate illicit finance risks" (The White House, 2022).

Simultaneously, it is crucial to consider efficiency through the minimization of unnecessary administrative burdens, incorporation of new technologies, and elimination of obstacles.[2] In this paper, we propose a system that is purposeful, effective, and feasible for financing and allocating resources towards AML/CFT measures. Our proposed system ensures consistent, continuous, and formal enforcement of these measures.

There are several prior studies that examine AML/CFT issues as related to CBDC. Pocher and Veneris (2022) propose a regulation-by-design approach to address the trade-offs between privacy and transparency in CBDC. This approach involves embedding compliance measures into the early stages of system design or process. According to Sidorenko et al. (2021), CBDC's traceability makes it an ideal tool to combat financial crimes, and they suggest that private institutions providing interfaces for CBDC could be responsible for AML/CFT control instead of central banks. Soderberg et al. (2022) posit that CBDC could alleviate the issue of using cash for illicit activities due to its traceability and lack of anonymity. The authors also note that the reduction of illicit use of money is not a commonly stated top objective for CBDC, with the Bahamas being the only case where it has been explicitly mentioned. Mahari et al. (2022) recommend that CBDC should have strong resistance to money laundering and financing of terrorism through the implementation of robust digital identity, ongoing algorithmic transaction monitoring, and interoperable record keeping connected to customer due diligence (CDD). However, these studies have not provided a comprehensive description of the AML/CFT process, the roles and responsibilities of stakeholders, and the feasibility and effectiveness of the KYC/AML system.

---

[2] Carrington and Shams (2006) recommend that the supervisory authorities of AML/CFT "should seek, to the greatest extent possible, to minimize unnecessary regulatory burden not only in the interest of the general efficiency of the system but also to avoid the creation of incentives for the emergence of informal or parallel systems". There are cases where "regulatory burden related to AML/CFT, or uncertainties related to the implementation of these measures, and the potential reputational risk in case of noncompliance" is leading to the increasing reluctance of providing corresponding banking services in certain foreign currencies (International Finance Corporation, 2019).

The objective of this paper is to develop a framework that integrates feasible AML/CFT measures into the future design of CBDC. Specifically, the focus is on effective enforcement of CDD, transaction monitoring, reporting, and investigation of illicit activity. The paper centers on the retail two-tiered CBDC model, as this is the primary model currently under exploration by most central banks.

The remainder of the paper is organized as follows. Section 2 reviews the relevant literature on the use of CBDC in AML/CFT compliance. In Sect. 3, we discuss the design of CBDC and its associated costs. Section 4 provides an overview of the current AML/CFT system and its components. Section 5 examines several retail CBDC projects and their AML/CFT measures. Section 6 proposes a framework for embedding sustainable AML/CFT measures in CBDC. Finally, Sect. 7 concludes.

2   Proposed CBDC Model Structure and Associated AML/CFT Limitations

To initiate our review of AML/CFT measures in CBDC, we provide an overview of the model structures for CBDC that have been proposed by major central banks worldwide.

The two-tiered retail CBDC model is designed to allow for indirect access to CBDC through private intermediaries, with intermediaries serving a crucial role in processing CBDC transactions. One-tiered CBDC models, which involve direct access to the central bank, are generally considered less feasible because they limit the participation of private banking sector and the central bank cannot practically handle all aspects of CBDC transactions alone. Therefore, it is anticipated that most CBDC models will adopt a two-tiered structure to allow for efficient processing and involvement of the private sector.

Many of the suggested CBDCs are based on a distributed ledger design. In a distributed ledger, each participating user operates a node through which transactions are processed and where transaction information is stored. However, such a design also poses significant operational limitations and security concerns. A major limitation of applying a distributed ledger to a CBDC model is related to privacy issues. Transaction details are usually recorded on a public blockchain, which raises concerns about user privacy. Moreover, the implementation of privacy-enhancing technology is often costly, making it difficult to implement at scale.

To confront these privacy issues, a multi-layer blockchain-based network has been proposed wherein the participating entities of each layer are given different access permissions.[3] In a CBDC system that employs a distributed ledger design, the nodes in the regulatory layer are tasked with monitoring the entire processing of CBDC, which includes transaction verification and issuance. However, this function poses a challenge to the inherent characteristics of a blockchain, which allow the asset owner complete control over transaction details, such as when, how much, and to whom a transaction is issued, and whether the details are disclosed. As such, there exists a conflict between the auditability function and the decentralized nature of a blockchain.

---

[3] In a multilayer blockchain network, only designated nodes participate in the consensus process. Multilayer blockchain CBDC networks permit different levels of authority to different nodes.

The purpose of auditability in a CBDC is to prevent non-compliant transactions, irrespective of the owner's intent or preference. A permissioned ledger enables designated auditors to audit specific transactions. The use of a permissioned ledger and predetermined auditors in a CBDC network requires strong trust assumptions. The distribution of roles among network participants and the ledger structure are critical to achieving consensus on transaction details, which in turn determines the security of the entire ledger system. Close coordination between the central bank's infrastructure and retail connections is essential for any CBDC network. The use of privacy-enhancing technologies such as zero-knowledge proof, based on cryptography, can lead to high computational costs, which can make distributed ledger networks highly inefficient.

In a permissioned blockchain model, authorized participants who manage the transaction details are introduced to protect user privacy and achieve regulatory compliance simultaneously. However, it is essential to specify the limits of network members with higher authority who may have an incentive to act maliciously within the system. Additionally, linking a CBDC account with the identity of the real user remains necessary to maintain AML/CFT controls.

3   Total Cost Structure of CBDC

This section aims to analyze the overall cost structure of CBDC, with a specific focus on the AML/CFT measures. To provide a comprehensive understanding, we will first present the general cost structure of CBDC and then highlight the relative cost of AML/CFT measures as one of its components.

Table 1 presents the major cost components involved in building and managing a retail CBDC in a two-tiered model. The creation and operation of a new CBDC infrastructure entail significant additional costs, including expenditures on human resources and technology that are directly borne by the central bank and intermediaries. There will also be a costly alignment process as the existing financial system adapts to the features of the new CBDC system. The Financial Investigation Unit (FIU) and intermediaries will need to adopt compliance measures and adjust to the new environment created by the introduction of CBDC. Moreover, CBDC users are likely to go through an additional process to adopt and comply with the necessary measures to gain access to the CBDC. While this paper focuses specifically on the AML/CFT cost component, it is important to consider it in the broader context of the overall cost structure of CBDC.

The implementation of CBDCs has the potential to decrease service costs associated with the reduction of cash. Physical forms of currency, such as banknotes and coins, are relatively expensive to produce, handle, and distribute. For example, in 2020, the Federal Reserve spent USD 751 million on cash operations, which included the processing, paying, receiving, verification, destruction, transportation, and non-standard packaging of currency (Board of Governors of the Federal Reserve System, 2021). According to Chakravorti and Mazzotta (2013), the aggregated cost of cash on all stakeholders, including households, businesses, and governments, was estimated to be nearly USD

Table 1. Major Cost Associated with Building and Managing Retail CBDC. Notes: The stakeholders associated with the cost are in parentheses.

Increasing Cost	Decreasing Cost
a. Building cost of CBDC infrastructure *(Central Bank, Intermediary)*	a. Issuing cost of physical cash (printing banknotes and minting coins) *(Central Bank, Treasury)*
b. Maintaining cost of CBDC infrastructure *(Central Bank, Intermediary)*	b. Maintaining cost of physical cash e.g., ATM; Cash Transportation *(Every stakeholder using cash but especially Financial Institutions)*
c. Adoption cost of CBDC infrastructure (including integrating with existing system) *(Government, Business, etc.)*	c. Cash damage *(Every stakeholder using cash)*
d. Additional regulatory compliance cost (including AML/CFT) *(Financial Intelligence Unit, Intermediary, and Users)*	d. Fees e.g., Remittance and account fees; commission fees from businesses to the payment service provider *(Government, Business, and Users)*

200 billion annually in the U.S.[4] The introduction of CBDC could potentially reduce the issuing and managing costs associated with physical forms of money for both the public and private sectors.

Furthermore, Auer and Boehme (2020), "[a] trusted and widely usable retail CBDC must be secure and accessible, offer cash-like convenience and safeguard privacy". This "cash-like" feature means that it will be desirable to be able to receive and send money freely up to a certain amount. This means that CBDC could reduce various costs such as account fees, remittance fees, and commission fees.

Since all stakeholders bear some cost burden to a certain extent, it is not yet clear which stakeholder should be responsible for the additional AML/CFT compliance costs. The government has its own FIU to finance, and government expenditure cannot be easily directed to the private sector. Collecting fees for CBDC transactions to finance compliance costs, given the "cash-like" features, would only discourage the use of CBDC. Assigning responsibility to intermediaries would likely discourage private businesses from taking an active role, thus stifling innovation. CBDC systems are likely to be beneficial to many financial system participants, and there is a need for stakeholders to invest in the whole CBDC system to take off. Therefore, financial feasibility, as well as the effectiveness and efficiency of compliance, are key concepts.

---

[4] According to Chakravorti and Mazzotta (2013), the estimated cost of cash is approximately USD 200 billion, which includes various costs such as ATM fees, account fees, time costs, household thefts (worth USD 43 billion/year), armored car services, retail theft, bank robberies, new branch opening costs, ATM business operations (worth USD 55 billion/year), and new currency issuance, cash operations, and the tax gap (worth USD 101 billion/year).

4 Current AML/CFT Mechanism

In this section, we will analyze the current AML/CFT mechanism and examine the roles, responsibilities, cost and incentive structures of the stakeholders involved, as well as the capacity of human resources. The aim is to understand how the AML/CFT system could be applied in a CBDC setting.

4.1 Stakeholders

The main stakeholders involved in AML/CFT mechanisms are the Financial Intelligence Unit (FIU), businesses responsible for implementing AML/CFT procedures, and the users.[5]

The Financial Intelligence Unit (FIU) is a government agency recommended by the FATF for countries to establish. Its role is to "serves as a national centre for the receipt and analysis of: (a) suspicious transaction reports; and (b) other information relevant to money laundering, associated predicate offences and terrorist financing, and for the dissemination of the results of that analysis" (FATF, 2012).

Financial institutions play a critical role in the AML/CFT mechanism. Within the FATF's 40 Recommendations (2012), 11 are assigned to financial institutions. Additionally, in 2003, FATF extended the Customer Due Diligence (CDD) and record-keeping requirements to designated non-financial businesses and professions (DNFBPs).[6]

4.2 Process

Figure 1 shows the detailed functions and the relationship of the stakeholders based on the FATF standards. There are two layers of communication between stakeholders: the first is between the users and the financial institutions or DNFBPs, and the second is between the financial institutions/DNFBPs and the FIU.

Financial institutions and DNFBPs bear the initial responsibility for conducting the AML/CFT process. They conduct CDD and transaction monitoring based on legal requirements. The users of financial institutions or DNFBPs are required to respond to various inquiries for verification and risk assessment by the service provider.

Financial institutions need to conduct enhanced due diligence measures in cross-border correspondent banking and similar relationships. This includes gathering enough

---

[5] While we have referred to the Financial Intelligence Unit (FIU), businesses responsible for AML/CFT procedures, and the users as the main stakeholders in this paper, it is important to note that there are numerous other actors involved in AML/CFT efforts. These include regulators, tax authorities, law enforcement agencies, intelligence authorities, accrediting institutions, self-regulatory organizations, non-profit organizations (NPOs), and more.

[6] Designated non-financial businesses and professions (DNFBPs) encompass a range of industries, including casinos, real estate agents, dealers in precious metals and stones, legal professionals, and accountants, as well as trust company service providers. The CDD and record-keeping requirements mandated in Recommendations 10, 11, 12, 15, and 17 apply to all DNFBPs, as specified in Recommendation 22. In addition, other requirements outlined in Recommendations 18 to 21 apply to legal professionals and accountants, dealers in precious metals and stones, and trust company service providers, as per Recommendation 23 (FATF, 2012).

information about the respondent institution to fully understand their business, assessing their reputation and quality of supervision, and determining if they have been involved in money laundering or terrorist financing investigations or regulatory actions.

Financial institutions and DNFBPs can outsource certain elements of the CDD measures to third-party service providers, but they must ensure that specific criteria are met. However, the financial institutions and DNFBPs remain ultimately responsible for conducting the CDD measures.

Financial institutions and DNFBPs are required to submit reports on suspicious transactions to the FIU for further inspection based on their information gathering and analysis. If necessary, the FIU may make inquiries to the reporting entities for additional information.

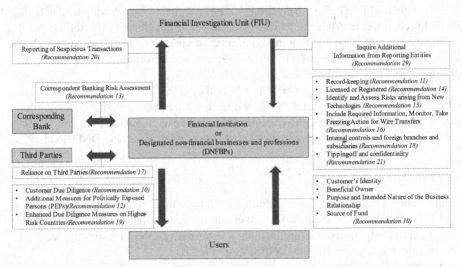

Fig. 1. Stakeholders of AML/CFT Measures. Notes: Made by the Author Based on "The FATF Recommendations" (FATF, 2012).

In the following section, we will provide a detailed explanation of the AML/CFT process carried out by financial institutions.[7] The AML/CFT process typically comprises four stages: the onboarding or account opening process, the ongoing process of periodic customer information collection and verification upon receipt of the transaction, the transaction monitoring process, and a review and feedback process. Each process involves multiple layers of operation, including the receipt of the application, verification at the time of the transaction, customer filtering, analysis and evaluation, and judgment and response (see Appendix A for details).

During the onboarding process, a financial institution initiates a relationship with its customer. At this stage, upon receiving the application, the financial institution carries out CDD by requesting customers to provide reliable identification information to verify

---

[7] DNFBPs generally follow a similar process as financial institutions for AML/CFT procedures, but there may be variations depending on the specific type of service they provide.

their identity and the purpose of the transaction.[8] While the FATF does not mandate that financial institutions conduct CDD for every transaction, they do require periodic CDD on existing customers.[9] After completing the preventive measures, the financial institution proceeds with the transaction. However, they are required to monitor the transaction for any suspicious activity and investigate any abnormal transactions that may occur. Financial institutions have a responsibility to decline suspicious applications and make a Suspicious Activity Report (SAR) to the FIU in relation to the on-boarding and transaction monitoring process. Although not required, it is important for financial institutions to conduct internal reviews and a feedback process based on suspicious activities for future compliance.[10]

4.3   Cost Structures and Incentives

In order to comply with AML/CFT measures, all stakeholders incur costs. However, cost-efficient but ineffective measures are meaningless. Therefore, it is important to estimate the true cost of AML/CFT compliance measures by looking at cases that have been evaluated as effective by the FATF. In this section, we will describe the estimated costs associated with these measures.[11]

Financial Intelligence Units (FIU)
The cost of establishing and operating an FIU can be seen in the government budget and staffing expenses. The government incurs costs in implementing preventive measures such as creating rules and guidelines, providing industry education, and promoting international cooperation. However, in this section, we will focus on the direct operating expenses of the FIU. We will examine the costs incurred by Israel, Italy, and Spain, which were evaluated as having a high or substantial level of effectiveness and compliance during the FATF Fourth Round of AML/CFT Mutual Evaluations (see Appendix B).

Within the three high-performing countries, we were able to obtain information on the operating costs and burdens of Italy and Spain. Detailed operating expenses on Spanish FIU (SEPBLAC) was disclosed, with a final budget of EUR 18.9 million (USD 18.6 million) for 2022. Personnel expenses accounted for 46.6% of these expenses, followed by expenditure on goods and services (24.2%), including IT services (11.9%),

---

[8] The purpose is "to prevent the unlawful use of legal persons and arrangements, by gaining a sufficient understanding of the customer to be able to properly assess the potential money laundering and terrorist financing risks associated with the business relationship" and "to take appropriate steps to mitigate the risks" (FATF, 2012).

[9] FATF(2012) recommends that "[f]inancial institutions should be required to ensure that documents, data or information collected under the CDD process is kept up-to-date and relevant by undertaking reviews of existing records, particularly for higher-risk categories of customers".

[10] This process may vary across different entities, but typically involves analyzing trends, evaluating and revising the transaction monitoring system and CDD process, and disseminating information to raise awareness among staff.

[11] FATF conducts peer reviews of each member on an ongoing basis to assess levels of implementation of the FATF Recommendations. The results of the mutual evaluation are disclosed on the FATF website (https://www.fatf-gafi.org/media/fatf/documents/4th-Round-Ratings.pdf).

and investments (5.3%), most of which were computer applications (La Secretaría de Estado de Presupuestos y Gastos, 2022). In 2021, the Italian FIU (UIF) received 139,524 suspicious transaction reports and analyzed 138,482 of them. The processing time for reports to the Investigative Bodies was 14 days and the percentage of reports forwarded within 30 days of receipt was 88.3%, according to the UIF's Annual Report 2021 (Banca D' Italia, 2022).

Financial Institutions and Designated Non-Financial Businesses and Professions (DNFBPs)

Financial institutions are dedicating significant resources to comply with AML/CFT measures due to the risk of severe sanctions and damage to their reputation. According to Recommendation 35 of "The FATF Recommendations" (FATF, 2012), non-compliance sanctions should be applicable not only to the financial entity but also to the directors and senior management.

The cost of the financial institutions and DNFBPs depend on the scale of the customer, volume of transactions, and the service they provide. The Government Accountability Office (GAO) reviewed 11 banks with varying characteristics and estimated that in 2018, the total direct costs for complying with the Bank Secrecy Act (BSA) ranged from about USD 14,000 to about USD 21 million. Estimated total direct costs for complying with the Bank Secrecy Act ranged from 0.4% to 4.9% of operating expenses. This includes establishing BSA/AML compliance programs, filing reports to FinCEN, and keeping records of transactions (GAO, 2020) (see Appendix C).

Users

Customers bear the burden of AML/CFT measures through fees charged by financial institutions and DNFBPs. It is the decision of private institutions whether and how to pass on these costs to end users. Although not a direct monetary cost, users may experience a time cost by having to repeatedly go through the Know Your Customer (KYC) process and submit the same information or documents each time they apply for a service from different providers (see Appendix D). For instance, in the traditional transfer agency model, if an investor subscribes to two asset managers that are both serviced by the same transfer agent, the investor would need to carry out the KYC process twice.[12]

4.4 Professional Resources in AML/CFT Measures

The current AML/CFT measures comprise both manual and automated processes for both FIUs and financial institutions/DNFBPs. However, this is a highly specialized area that requires expertise and experience. It is worth noting that professional resources are limited. The Association of Certified Anti-Money Laundering Specialists (ACAMS) provides certification for AML professionals worldwide. Although AML/CFT certification is not mandatory, the relatively low number of certified specialists worldwide,

---

[12] Deutsche Bank and Memento Blockchain's Project DAMA (Digital Assets Management Access) involved exploring the use of a digital identity token to simplify the investor KYC process. With the digital identity token, the transfer agent could perform the KYC checks for Fund Manager A and reuse the same token for Fund Manager B.

with 64,626 individuals in 190 countries/regions, highlights the scarcity of professional resources compared to the volume of transactions being conducted. Appendix F lists the top 15 countries with individuals holding any type of ACAMS certification.

5 AML/CFT Mechanisms in Retail CBDC Projects

This section explores the AML/CFT frameworks implemented in retail CBDC systems. As per the Atlantic Council CBDC tracker, there are currently four retail CBDCs that have been launched.[13] According to the publicly available information collected by the authors, the AML/CFT measures embedded in the aforementioned countries are as follows (see Appendix F).

First, the central bank authorizes the intermediaries that provide the CBDC. There is no restriction for the intermediary to be a financial institution, although currently all intermediaries participating are financial institutions. It is worth noting that in all cases, an existing financial institution is not given the license automatically.

Secondly, the roles and functions of intermediaries vary across the launched retail CBDC projects. In most cases, certified intermediaries provide digital wallets and integrate them with their existing banking services. However, the Eastern Caribbean Central Bank (ECCB) has adopted a different approach and provides a common digital wallet for all CBDC services.

Third, the KYC process is handled by intermediaries in all cases, which is reasonable given that one of the advantages of a two-tiered system is to engage intermediaries who are familiar with serving customers directly. Even though the ECCB provides digital wallets directly to the end users, it still requires intermediaries to be responsible for the KYC process. However, it is worth noting that this arrangement may change in the future as the Central Bank of Bahamas has plans to introduce a centralized KYC registry system in the mid to long term. In addition, non-distributing financial institutions have been called upon to participate in the KYC process by both the Central Bank of The Bahamas and ECCB. The Central Bank of The Bahamas has asked clearing banks and credit unions to share KYC confirmation with any Authorized Financial Institution (AFI), while ECCB has assigned non-banking financial institutions to facilitate the onboarding of users who do not have bank or credit union accounts, even if these institutions do not provide CBDC services.

Further, given that CBDC is accessed through digital wallets, providers have the more efficient way to request updated information from users for ongoing CDD purposes rather than using traditional mail or in-person methods, even after they have been onboarded.

Fourth, in order to achieve KYC, a risk-based approach is used for CBDCs. In order to promote financial inclusion through the CBDC system, the KYC process is designed to be simplified and available online. The level of KYC required may vary depending on the service, and may involve information associated with the user's existing bank account or government-issued identification (as in the cases of ECCB and Nigeria)..While one of the main goals of CBDCs is to promote financial inclusion, the CDD process still

---

[13] As of February 2023, the Central Bank of the Bahamas (Sand Dollar), Bank of Jamaica (JAMDEX), Eastern Caribbean Central Bank (DCash), and Central Bank of Nigeria (e-Naira) are among the central banks that have implemented CBDC systems.

imposes limits on holding or transaction amounts based on the level of KYC completed. Hence, an important factor to consider is how to determine the limits for CBDC services.

Sand Dollar has set a holding limit of B\$500 (USD 498), which is consistent with the "Guidelines for Supervised Financial Institutions on the Prevention of Money Laundering, Countering the Financing of Terrorism and Proliferation Financing" issued by the Central Bank of The Bahamas (2018) which allows payment institutions to "waiver customer identification procedures when the Bahamian dollar electronic payment instrument has an initial maximum stored limit of B\$500, and when it is reloadable up to a maximum value of B\$300 per month".

E-Naira has a tiered system with 4 levels that are determined by the presence of a bank account and appropriate identification. Similar to the Sand Dollar, the e-Naira's threshold is in line with the "Supervisory Framework for Payment Service Banks" issued by the Central Bank of Nigeria (2021a).

While the restrictions on CBDC holdings are closely aligned with the guidelines for non-CBDC traditional accounts, there may be slight adjustments to accommodate the unique nature of CBDCs. For example, Sand Dollar does not have restrictions on the reloadable amount. The reloadable amount up to a maximum value of B\$300 (USD 299) per month mentioned in the guideline is not applied for the Sand Dollar.

To improve financial inclusion, E-Naira has introduced Tier 0, which allows individuals without bank accounts or government IDs to participate in the CBDC system. The framework regulates on the maximum single deposit amount basis while e-Naira is based on the daily transaction limit. Tier 3 imposes stricter limit having ₦1,000,000 (USD 2,413) for daily transaction limit and the balance of ₦5,000,000 (USD 12,066) whereas the Payment Service Bank have maximum single deposit amount of ₦5,000,000 (USD 12,066) and without limit for the balance.

Finally, Financial institutions are obligated to report any suspicious activity related to CBDC transactions. To support intermediaries, ECCB provides third-party tools for anonymous transaction monitoring. In all cases except in Nigeria, the user's identity cannot be revealed to the central bank. Although the Central Bank of Nigeria can identify the users with the provided government identification records, they made it clear that they would rely on financial institutions and other payment service providers to monitor transactions.

6   Feasibility of the AML/CFT System Associated with CBDC

Looking at the current compliance process described in Sect. 5, there may be opportunities to improve the process. Table 2 outlines potential measures that could be implemented or enhanced to make the process more effective and efficient, while still remaining feasible. We will now discuss each element in detail.

Table 2. AML/CFT Process in the CBDC (○: Current Process, ■: Potential Implementation or Enhancement). Notes: Made by the author.

Operation Process	1. Account Opening	2-1. Periodic Customer Information Collection	2-2. Verification upon Receipt of Transaction	3. Transaction Monitoring	4. Review and Feedback Process
Receipt of application	○ Simplified KYC by the Digital Wallet Provider/e-KYC ■ Reliable Government ID System ■ Unification of Identification Documents for smooth KYC ■ Identity Verification through Reliance on Third Parties ■ Collaborate with other industry services (especially for 2-1 Periodic Customer Information Collection)				
Verification at the time of transaction					
Customer Filtering	○ Individual Customer Filtering by the Digital Wallet Provider ■ Automated screening of customers for adverse media/negative news. ■ Joint systems or sharing information for customer screening. ■ Registry system that could be shared between designated groups.				
Analysis and Evaluation (Alert)	○ Individual Customer Analysis by the Digital Wallet Provider automatically and manually. ■ Joint tool for transaction monitoring. ■ Sharing transaction information and trends.				
Analysis and Evaluation (Investigate)	○ AML/CFT expert conducts an investigation (information collection) on the alerted case. ○ Establish criteria and thresholds.				
Judgment and Response	○ Internal Approval Process ○ Judgement opening an account/executing a transaction or decline/suspension of transaction. ■ Automatic Process of SAR •Preparation of Reporting •Submit SAR				○ Registration of transaction monitoring systems and various databases ○ Revision of transaction monitoring system, detection routes, thresholds, and criteria ○ Revision of detection routes, detection scenarios, thresholds, and judgment criteria ○ Dissemination of information within the company ○ Consider business improvement

6.1 Tiered System Based on the Level of Assurance

In all cases, the KYC process can be simplified. The digital wallet provider requires the applicant to fill out the form. Existing customer information at financial institutions is also used in this process. At the same time, the amount of the transaction or the balance is limited based on the level of information submitted by the applicant. Even with a high amount of information, the users face a certain transaction limit. This may be partly because of the vulnerability of the KYC process. Uploading a Government ID is not a perfect solution since the issuer of the ID and the KYC verifier are unlikely to have a data-sharing process between each other.

It is therefore important to enhance the credibility of the customer's information during the KYC process. Although the Government ID system differs across countries, building a reliable digital Government ID system that is fraud-resistant is a baseline that all jurisdictions must consider. Based on this reliable Government ID system, efficiency will be enhanced by having an identification document that is easily verifiable.

At the same time, building a strong Government ID system might not necessarily be a desired or feasible option for some jurisdictions. In that case, identity verification by relying on third parties and collaboration with other industry services are other solutions to consider. As mentioned in Sect. 5, KYC is conducted in many circumstances repeatedly. The Sand Dollar project in the Bahamas asks banks and credit unions to contribute by sharing their KYC information (Sand Dollar). DCash project by the ECCB asks for non-banking financial institutions to function as DCash Agents and support the on-boarding process. This is one form of third-party reliance where there are partnerships with the institutions that are required to support the customer due diligence process. But this could be extended to other industries, especially since the user has little incentive to provide information once the account is open.

6.2 Collective Customer Due Diligence

In the aforementioned cases, the Central Bank of Bahamas and ECCB have built a framework for cooperation between non-intermediaries by sharing customer information or facilitating customer on-boarding processes for those without a bank account. This is a form of collective action for customer due diligence.

New Zealand and Australia have also implemented a scheme that asks for cooperation between entities. To make the AML/CFT process more cost-efficient, New Zealand suggested working with other institutions to reduce AML compliance costs. They recommended "form a designated business group (DBG)", "rely on another business for customer due diligence (CDD)", and "outsource CDD to a third party". DBG is "2 or more businesses or people who agree to share AML/CFT obligations such as their AML/CFT risk assessment, customer due diligence (that is, checking and verifying customers' identities and/or sources of funds), record-keeping and account monitoring, filing suspicious activity and prescribed transaction reports with the Police Financial Intelligence Unit, and annual reporting." New Zealand Government also suggested reliance on other businesses for customer due diligence (CDD) or outsourcing CDD to a third party which would be beneficial for early-stage startups or small businesses that have limited resources for building a sophisticated AML/CFT system or hiring professional staff. The Australian Government also allows DBG as in New Zealand. Allowing shared CDD operations will enhance the effectiveness and efficiency of compliance.

Having cross-entity relationships in customer due diligence could enable companies to share or pool customer information and therefore lessen the burden of collecting information. As mentioned previously, once users open an account, there is less motivation to update their information. By forming cross-industry groups, this issue could be mitigated by cross-referencing customer information. Furthermore, to the extent that the personal information is treated with caution, abiding by privacy rules, and is given consent from the customers, data collected during customer due diligence will be valuable for other industries as well. This implication shows how the cost of AML/CFT, which is initially assigned to intermediaries, could be redistributed among multiple industries in a sustainable way in the CBDC system.

6.3 Automated Analysis and Evaluation

Any investigation requires an informed decision and therefore must be done by a professional. As mentioned previously, human resources to conduct the AML/CFT process are limited compared to the huge volume of transactions. For now, CBDC is still in its early stage and the transaction amount is limited. However, with further implementation of CBDC and if the holding limits were eased, it would be necessary to improve the quality of the automated screening, especially when increasing human resources take more time to catch up with the faster-growing number of transactions. Institutions are likely to face difficulty when building these automated transaction monitoring tools. In that case, designing a joint monitoring tool between the entities and sharing transaction information would be beneficial. For example, the ECCB provides joint transaction monitoring tools. However, the provider of the tools does not necessarily have to be the central bank but private entities.

6.4 Judgment and Reporting

The automated process of suspicious activity reporting (SAR) should be enhanced. Better preparation of reporting and submission of SAR would contribute to better allocation of time and human resources. Currently, there are services that allow automated processing of AML/CFT related to transaction monitoring, investigation, and reporting. However, the system is limited to the U.S. and countries that use a system called AML Go provided by the World Bank Group. Therefore, introducing a tool that would add to the efficiency of the judgment and reporting, ideally connected to the monitoring and analysis/evaluation, would lessen the human intensity currently needed in this process.

7 Conclusion

The design of the retail CBDC is still in an early stage. The objective that a CBDC system "should promote compliance with AML/CFT requirements and mitigate illicit finance risks" is a common principle, but how to ensure the feasibility of the system remains an open question. In this paper we looked into the cost structure and incentive mechanism of KYC/AML and analyzed the associated measures in the existing retail CBDC projects. Then we have described necessary elements that must be considered for the AML/CFT system to be effective, efficient, and feasible. We suggest that tiered system based on the level of assurance, collective customer due diligence, automated analysis and evaluation, and sufficient human resource for judgement and reporting is an essential part of the CBDC design from the AML/CFT aspect. This finding provides valuable implications from the existing literature and the ongoing policy debate on the risk-management of digital currency.

Appendix A. Generalized AML/CFT Process

Table A. Generalized AML/CFT Process. Notes: Based on the Japan Financial Services Agency (2021) "Final Report of JFSA Multilateral Joint Research on Digital Identity" (for processes 1 to 3), Osawa, et al. (2022) "Theory and Practice of Anti-Money Laundering and Combating the Financing of Terrorism" (in Japanese) (for process 4).

Operation Process	1. Account Opening	2-1. Periodic Customer Information Collection	2-2. Verification upon Receipt of Transaction	3. Transaction Monitoring	4. Review and Feedback Process
Receipt of application	Receipt of application form for account opening, etc.	Regularly collect customer information (mail, phone calls, etc.) at a frequency based on customer risk and update customer information.	Receive transaction application documents from customers.	-	-
Verification at the time of transaction	• Verify the authenticity and validity of the identity evidence. • Verify objective of transaction and ultimate beneficial owner (in the case of a corporation).		• Verify the authenticity and validity of the identity evidence. • Authenticate the applicant who is conducting the transaction and verify the transaction details such as the purpose and amount of the transaction.	-	-
Customer Filtering	Prevent antisocial forces and sanctioned persons from holding accounts by checking against the list of antisocial forces and sanctioned persons, and by verifying consistency with transaction purposes, attributes, and ultimate beneficial owners.			-	-
Analysis and Evaluation	Analyze AML risk, etc., based on transaction type, customer attributes, product and service characteristics, etc., and conduct additional verification if necessary.			Detect, investigate, and determine abnormal transactions by comparing with past transaction patterns, etc., and reflecting them in the risk assessment of the relevant customers.	• Trend Analysis • Adjustment of transaction monitoring system • Examination of room for business improvement
Judgment and Response	Approve the opening of an account and notify the customer or decline the opening of an account and file a suspicious activity report, if necessary.	Approve the opening of an account and notify the customer or decline the opening of an account and file a suspicious activity report, if necessary.	Accept or reject transactions and, if necessary, file a suspicious activity report.	Continue transactions or file a suspicious activity report if necessary (including cases where transactions are processed and customers are monitored, after filing a suspicious activity report).	• Revision of detection routes, detection scenarios, thresholds, and criteria • Registration in the transaction monitoring system and various databases • Dissemination of information within the company

Appendix B. High Performing FIU (Israel, Italy, and Spain)

There are 11 effectiveness criteria to rate the effectiveness of the country's measures and 40 technical compliance criteria to reflect the implementation of the recommendations which the FATF has made. For the effectiveness criteria we used the Immediate Outcomes (IO) concerning legal and operational issues which are directly related to the FIU. These include the following; IO6 "[f]inancial intelligence and all other relevant information are appropriately used by competent authorities for money laundering and terrorist financing investigations", IO 7 "[m]oney laundering offences and activities are investigated and offenders are prosecuted and subject to effective, proportionate and dissuasive sanctions", and IO 8 "[p]roceeds and instrumentalities of crime are confiscated" (FATF, 2013). As for the technical compliance, we used the assessment of recommendations directly related to the FIU. Those are Recommendation 29 "[f]inancial intelligence units", Recommendation 30 "[r]esponsibilities of law enforcement and investigative authorities", and Recommendation 31 "[p]owers of law enforcement and investigative authorities" (See Table B1).

Table B1. High Performing FIU (Israel, Italy, and Spain). Notes: "IO" is "Immediate Outcomes", "R" is "Recommendation", "HE" is "High level of effectiveness - The Immediate Outcome is achieved to a very large extent. Minor improvements needed", "SE" is "Substantial level of effectiveness - The Immediate Outcome is achieved to a large extent. Moderate improvements needed", "C" is "Compliant".

Country	Report Date	IO6	IO7	IO8	R19	R30	R31
Israel	May, 2022	HE	SE	HE	C	C	C
Italy	Mar, 2019	SE	SE	SE	C	C	C
Spain	Dec, 2019	HE	SE	SE	C	C	C

Source: Made by the author based on FATF "Consolidated Table of Assessment Ratings" (https://www.fatf-gafi.org/media/fatf/documents/4th-Round-Ratings.pdf).

Appendix C. Compliance Cost of the Financial Institutions

According to GAO (2020), compliance costs by the financial institutions on Bank Secrecy Act in the U.S. can be broken down into five categories: Customer Due Diligence Requirements (average of 28% of the total expenses), Reporting Requirements (29%), Compliance Program Requirements (18%), Other Requirements (9%), and Software and Other Parties (17%). The amount of time the banks spend on investigating and reporting each incident was 80 h for a small community bank, whereas it was 2 h for a large bank (GAO, 2020).

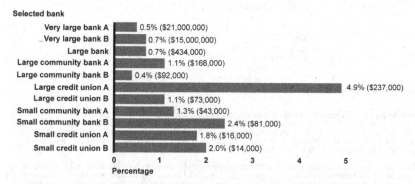

Notes: Estimated total direct compliance costs are in parentheses for each bank. Very large banks had $50 billion or more in assets. Small community banks had total of assets of $250 million or less and met the Federal Deposit Insurance Corporation's community bank definition. Small credit unions had total assets of $50 million or less.

Fig. D1. Estimated Total Direct Costs for Complying with the Bank Secrecy Act as a Percentage of Operating Expenses and Estimated Total Direct Compliance Costs for Selected Banks in 2018. Source: U.S. Government Accountability Office. 2020. "Anti-Money Laundering: Opportunities Exist to Increase Law Enforcement Use of Bank Secrecy Act Reports, and Banks' Costs to Comply with the Act Varied".

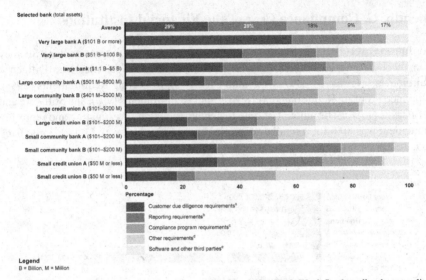

Notes: Banks are rank ordered based on total assets as of December 2018. We defined small or large credit unions using a $50 million threshold, and we defined small or large community banks using a $250 million threshold. Larger banks are those that did not meet the Federal Deposit Insurance Corporation's community bank definition (generally not specialized and with a limited geographic reach), and we defined them as large or very large using a $50 billion threshold.

a: There are four core customer due diligence requirements: (1) customer identification and verification (known as the customer identification program), (2) beneficial ownership identification and verification (for legal entities), (3) understanding the nature and purpose of customer relationships to develop a customer risk profile, and (4) ongoing monitoring for suspicious transactions and updating customer information on a risk basis. We also asked banks to include costs for additional due diligence for higher-risk customers, including for foreign correspondent accounts and private accounts for certain non-U.S. persons.

b: There are five key reporting requirements included in our review: (1) suspicious activity reporting, (2) currency transaction reporting, (3) currency transaction reporting exemptions, (4) foreign bank and financial accounts reporting, and (5) international transportation of currency or monetary instruments reporting.

c: There are four minimum compliance program requirements for a Bank Secrecy Act/Anti-Money Laundering (BSA/AML) program: (1) internal controls, (2) independent testing, (3) training, and (4) a BSA/AML officer. We do not separately report a cost for BSA/AML officers because we generally captured their direct costs in our estimates for other BSA/AML requirements.

d: Other requirements include costs for four other requirements that, on average, each comprised less than 5 percent of total direct BSA/AML costs for the 11 banks: (1) money instruments recordkeeping, (2) funds transfers recordkeeping, (3) information sharing, and (4) special measures.

e: Most of the banks used software to help comply with their customer due diligence, reporting, or other BSA/AML requirements. We report all software costs separately because the banks commonly used the same software to comply with multiple requirements and generally could not precisely allocate software costs for each requirement. Other third parties include vendors that were not associated with a specific requirement (e.g., compliance consultants).

Fig. D2. Estimated Costs for Compliance Requirements as a Percentage of Total Direct Costs for Bank Secrecy Act/Anti Money Laundering Compliance for Selected Banks in 2018. Source: U.S. Government Accountability Office. 2020. "Anti-Money Laundering: Opportunities Exist to Increase Law Enforcement Use of Bank Secrecy Act Reports, and Banks' Costs to Comply with the Act Varied".

Appendix D. Compliance Cost of the Financial Institutions

Table E shows the KYC process under different legislation in Japan. In addition to the identification requirements prescribed by laws and regulations in Table E, identification is often conducted as part of ordinances, voluntary standards of industry associations, or as an initiative of the business itself.

Some examples of identification processes not required by laws, yet still conducted in Japan include:

- Identity verification procedures when using Internet cafes in Tokyo (ordinance)
- Identity verification using official identification cards, individual financial/mobile phone numbers, etc. for shared services (industry associations)
- Identity verification procedures when accepting data communication contract applications (industry organization)
- Establishing social media usage environment according to user attributes such as age (each company's own)

Table E. Various KYC Process Users Face in Japan

	Act on Prevention of Transfer of Criminal Proceeds	Foreign Exchange Act	Act on Submission of Statement of Overseas Wire Transfers for Purpose of Securing Proper Domestic Taxation	Mobile Phone Fraud and Abuse Act for the Prevention of Unauthorized Use of Mobile Phones	Antique Dealer's Law	Act on Regulation on Soliciting Children by Using Opposite Sex Introducing Service on Internet
Target	Banking, Securities, Funds Transfer Banking, Virtual Currency, Call Reception Agent, etc.	Banking and fund transfer business, etc.	International remittances, etc.	Cell phones, voice calls etc.	Purchase of antiques, etc.	Dating sites, etc.
Aim of KYC	AML/CFT	AML/CFT	AML/CFT, Prevent tax evasion	Prevention of Crimes Using Mobile Phones	AML/CFT	Protecting youths
Identification Information	Name, Date of birth, Residence	Name, Date of birth, Address or Residence	Name, Government Issued ID Number	Name, Date of birth, Residence	Name, Date of birth, Residence, Job	Not be a child (Age)
Timing of confirmation	When opening an account. At the time of high-risk trading. Ongoing Customer Confirmation.	When remitting money overseas. When exchanging money	When remitting money overseas.	When signing up for a new line.	When transactions of 10,000 yen (USD 72) or more.	When opening an account

Sources: OpenID Foundation. 2022. "Report on KYC process for Service Providers" (in Japanese) (https://www.openid.or.jp/news/oidfj_kycwg_report_20200123.pdf).

Appendix E. Number of Certified Anti-money Laundering Specialists Graduate List (Top 15 Countries/Regions)

Notes: There were a total of 64,626 individuals on the list from 190 countries/regions. 18 individuals had no available information. If the individual had multiple certifications, they are counted by the higher certification.

Country/Region	Associate-Level Certification	Specialist-Level Certification	Advanced Specialist-Level Certification	Total
U.S.	156	20,202	184	20,542
China	16	8,391	16	8,423
Taiwan	1	4	3,602	3,607
Canada	18	3,089	15	3,122
Hong Kong	12	2,978	24	3,014
Netherlands	1,657	18	660	2,335
Singapore	17	2,190	21	2,228
Republic of Korea	1	1,871	9	1,881
India	9	12	1,532	1,553
United Kingdom	62	1,442	16	1,520
Japan	1	1,387	26	1,414
United Arab Emirates	15	16	1,262	1,293
Australia	34	15	836	885
Poland	11	8	664	683
France	4	670	1	675

Sources: ACAMS Graduate List (July 2022).

Appendix F. Current AML/CFT Measures in Two-Tiered Retail CBDC

Stakeholder and Project Name (Status)	Central Bank	Intermediary	Others	Description
Central Bank of the Bahamas Sand Dollar (Launched, October 2020)	• Monitors holdings and sponsors a centralized KYC/identity infrastructure. • On a near-to medium-term timeline, the Central Bank will also promote a government maintained centralized KYC register to maintain identification and profile data that would either mandate or allow individuals who do not maintain such information within banks or licensed intermediaries, to supply the data for the register.	• Authorized financial institution (AFI) licensed by the Central Bank is the executor of the customer due diligence process. They each provide an original digital wallet app for free and conduct KYC through it.	• Clearing banks and credit unions are expected to contribute to the customer due diligence regime. By regulations, it is proposed that a legal obligation be imposed on banks and credit unions to share customer requested KYC confirmation with any AFI provider of payments services.	• Adopt level of assurance (2 level) as follows. *Tier I Unbanked/Non-Resident/Visitors* • B\$500 eWallet holding limit, with a B\$1,500 monthly transaction limit. • Government-issued identification is not an enrollment requirement. • Cannot link to a bank account. *Tier II Others* • B\$8,000 eWallet holding limit, with a B\$10,000 monthly transaction limit. • Uploading government-issued identification is required for enrollment. • Can be linked to a bank account.

Continued on next page

Stakeholder and Project Name (Status)	Central Bank	Intermediary	Others	Description
Bank of Jamaica Jamaica Digital Exchange/ JAM-DEX (Launched, May 2022)	• When conducting transactions using CBDC user's identity is not recorded. The system only records the value of the transaction for authentication purposes.	• Wallet Providers (banks or authorized Payment Service Providers) approved by the Central Bank is the executor of the customer due diligence process. They provide an original digital wallet app for free and conduct KYC through it. • Wallet Provider is the only entity that have access to the user's information and be able see their transactions. • The Wallet Provide only shares the information only if the authorities require information for AML/CFT breaches.		• The limitations specifically for JAM-DEX are unclear. Currently, it is aligned with the existing regulation that the Bank of Jamaica has and apply the Wallet Providers' own risk-based assessment to their customers and thus determining the limit for Jam-Dex. *Simplified eKYC* • Name • Address (Must be a Jamaican resident) • Taxpayer Registration Number • Provide a valid, government issued picture ID

Continued on next page

Stakeholder and Project Name (Status)	Central Bank	Intermediary	Others	Description
Eastern Caribbean Central Bank DCash (Launched March 2021)	• The ECCB provides common application digital wallet. • Anonymized transaction monitoring data is performed by third-party tools provided by the ECCB. Data from such monitoring is stored off-ledger.	• Financial institutions licensed to conduct business, perform risk assessment on DCash as they would with any new product or service. • Shares the KYC information to the ECCB only under request as a part of its regulatory and oversight remit.	• The ECCB has designated non-banking financial institutions as DCash Agents to facilitate the on-boarding and customer service of consumers who do not have bank or credit union accounts.	• Adopt level of assurance. Wallets will have tiers with different transaction limits. The application and blockchain code will enforce these. *Registered Based Wallet* • Register with a code from the bank with the user's bank account. • The code and your bank account number. The code can be requested in person from the financial institution and is sent to the institution via email. *Value Based Wallet* • Register without a code – government-issued photo ID and a valid email address.

Continued on next page

Stakeholder and Project Name (Status)	Central Bank	Intermediary	Others	Description
Central Bank of Nigeria e-Naira (Launched, October 2021)	• Adopted an account based CBDC which the Central Bank would be able to identify users on the platform using the identify frameworks: BVN and NIN. • However, the Central Bank would rely on financial institutions and other payment service providers to deliver layered value-added services on the eNaira platform.	• Responsible for developing and/or updating reports and internal frameworks to ensure the KYC and AML/CFT checks on the users and ensuring overall compliance. • API access to connect to the Central Bank's core ledger.		• Adopt level of assurance (4 level) as follows. (No Existing Bank Account) *Tier Zero – Customers without Existing Bank Account and without Verified NIN* • Daily Transaction Limit: N20,000 • Maximum Cumulative Daily Balance: N120,000 • Minimum Account Opening Requirement: Phone Number *Tier One – Customers without Existing Bank Account,* • Daily Transaction Limit: N50,000 • Maximum Cumulative Daily Balance: N300,000 • Minimum Account Opening Requirement: National Identification Number (NIN) which is a recording of an individual's demographic data and capture of the 10 fingerprints, head-to-shoulder facial picture and digital signature

Continued on next page

Stakeholder and Project Name (Status)	Central Bank	Intermediary	Others	Description
Central Bank of Nigeria e-Naira (Launched, October 2021) (continued)				(Has Existing Bank Account) *Tier Two – Customers with Minimal Spending Abilities* •Daily Transaction Limit: N200,000 •Maximum Cumulative Balance: N500,000 •Minimum Account Opening Requirement: Bank Verification Number (BVN) is a scheme introduced by the Central Bank of Nigeria (CBN) to protect customers' transactions and enhance confidence in the Nigerian banking sector. It involves identifying an individual based on physiological or behavioral attributes, such as fingerprint, signature and others. *Tier Three – Customers with Regular Spending Abilities* •Minimum Account Opening Requirement: BVN •Daily Transaction Limit: N1,000,00, •Cumulative Balance: N5,000,000

Sources: Bahamas: Sand Dollar (2020), Jamaica: Central Bank of Jamaica, LYNC, ECCB: ECCB Digital EC Currency Pilot, DCash, Nigeria: Central Bank of Nigeria (2021 b; 2021 c)

References

Association of Certified Anti-Money Laundering Specialists. ACAMS Graduate List. https://www.acams.org/en/graduates/acams-graduate-list-cams-certified-graduates. Accessed 1 Oct 2022

Auer, R., Boehme, R.:The technology of retail central bank digital currency. BIS Q. Rev. (2020)

Australian Government. Designated Business Groups (DBG). https://www.austrac.gov.au/business/how-comply-guidance-and-resources/guidance-resources/designated-business-groups-dbg. Accessed 1 Oct 2022

Banca D' Italia. 2022. Annual Report 2021 Italy's Financial Intelligence Unit. https://uif.bancaditalia.it/pubblicazioni/rapporto-annuale/2022/annual_report_2021.pdf?language_id=1

Bank for International Settlements (BIS). Annual Economic Report 2021 (2021). https://www.bis.org/publ/arpdf/ar2021e.pdf

Board of Governors of the Federal Reserve System. Federal Reserve Board – Federal Reserve Expenses for Cash Operations. https://www.federalreserve.gov/paymentsystems/coin_expcashops.htm. Accessed 23 Sept 2022

Carrington, I., Shams, H.:Elements of an effective AML/CFT framework: Legal, regulatory and best institutional practices to prevent threats to financial stability and integrity. Presentation at Seminar on Current Development in Monetary and Financial Law, 23–27 October 2006, Washington, D.C. (2006)

Central Bank of Bahamas. Guidelines for Supervised Financial Institutions on the Prevention of Money Laundering, Countering the Financing of Terrorism Proliferation Financing (2018). https://cdn.centralbankbahamas.com/download/032474800.pdf

Central Bank of Jamaica. Jamaica's Central Bank Digital Currency (CBDC) –JAM-DEX. https://boj.org.jm/core-functions/currency/cbdc/. Accessed 1 Oct 2022

Central Bank of Nigeria. Supervisory Framework for Payment Service Banks (2021a). https://www.cbn.gov.ng/Out/2021/CCD/Supervisory%20Framework%20for%20PSBs.pdf

Central Bank of Nigeria. Design Paper for the eNAIRA (2021b). https://enaira.gov.ng/assets/download/eNaira_Design_Paper.pdf

Central Bank of Nigeria. Regulatory Guidelines on the eNAIRA (2021c). https://www.cbn.gov.ng/Out/2021/FPRD/eNairaCircularAndGuidelines%20FINAL.pdf

Chakravorti, B., Mazzotta, B.D.: The cost of cash in the United States. Institute for Business in the Global Context, The Fletcher School, Tufts University (2013)

DCash. DCash An ECCB Initiative. https://www.dcashec.com/. Accessed 1 Oct 2022

Deutsche Bank, Memento Blockchain. Project DAMA Simplifying digital fund management and investing servicing (2023). https://corporates.db.com/files/documents/publications/DB-Project-DAMA.pdf

Eastern Caribbean Central Bank. ECCB Digital EC Currency Pilot What You Should Know. https://www.eccb-centralbank.org/p/what-you-should-know-1. Accessed 1 Oct 2022

European Central Bank. The Use of DLT in Post-Trade Processes. https://www.ecb.europa.eu/pub/pdf/other/ecb.20210412_useofdltposttradeprocesses~958e3af1c8.en.pdf. Accessed 17 Dec 2022

European Commission. Distributed Ledger Technologies Basics. https://ses.jrc.ec.europa.eu/node/31971. Accessed 17 Dec 2022

Financial Action Task Force (FATF). Frequently asked questions - Money Laundering. https://www.fatf-gafi.org/faq/moneylaundering/#d.en.11223. Accessed 1 Oct 2022

Financial Action Task Force (FATF). The FATF Recommendations (2012). https://www.fatf-gafi.org/media/fatf/documents/recommendations/pdfs/FATF%20Recommendations%202012.pdf. Accessed March 2022

Financial Action Task Force (FATF). Consolidated Table of Assessment Ratings (2022). https://www.fatf-gafi.org/media/fatf/documents/4th-Round-Ratings.pdf

Govenrment of Canada. Red Tape Reduction Act. https://laws-lois.justice.gc.ca/eng/acts/R-4.5/FullText.html. Accessed 1 Oct 2022

Japan Financial Services Agency. Final Report of JFSA Multilateral Joint Research on Digital Identity (2021). https://www.fsa.go.jp/policy/bgin/ResearchPaper_NRI_en.pdf

Kosse, A., Mattei, I.: Gaining momentum - results of the 2021 BIS survey on central bank digital currencies. BIS Papers No. 125, Bank for International Settlements (2022)

La Secretaría de Estado de Presupuestos y Gastos. Proyecto del Presupuesto estimativo de los gastos de funcionamiento e inversiones del SEPBLAC para el año 2022 (2022). (In Spanish). https://www.sepg.pap.hacienda.gob.es/Presup/PGE2022Proyecto/MaestroDocumentos/PGE-ROM/doc/4/4/4/1/N_22_A_G_4_BC_P_1.PDF

Lync. JAM-DEX: Jamaica's digital currency. https://www.lynk.us/jamdex. Accessed 1 Oct 2022

Mahari, R., Hardjono, T., Pentland, A.: AML by design: designing a central bank digitalcurrency to stifle money laundering. MIT Sci. Policy Rev. 3, 57–65 (2022). https://doi.org/10.38105/spr.j0hildxtyi

New Zealand Government. Costs and benefits of AML/CFT laws. https://www.justice.govt.nz/justice-sector-policy/key-initiatives/aml-cft/costs-and-benefits/#reduce. Accessed 1 Oct 2022

OpenID Foundation. Report on KYC process for Service Providers (Service Jigyosha no tame no Honnin Kakunin (KYC) ni kansuru Chosa Report) (2022). (in Japanese). https://www.openid.or.jp/news/oidfj_kycwg_report_20200123.pdf

Osawa, T., Tsuda, K., Miyata, J.: Theory and practice of money-laundering and financing of terrorism (ManeronTerro-Shikinkyouyo Taisaku no Riron to Jitsumu). Kinyu Zaisei Jijo Kenkyu Kai (2022). (In Japanese)

Pocher, N., Veneris, A.: Privacy and transparency in CBDCs: a regulation-by-design AML/CFT scheme. IEEE Trans. Netw. Serv. Manage. 19(2), 1776–1788 (2022)

Sand Dollar. Digital Bahamian Dollar (2020). https://www.sanddollar.bs/. Accessed 1 Oct 2020

Sidorenko, E.L., Sheveleva, S.V., Lykov, A.A.: Legal and economic implications of central bank digital currencies (CBDC). In: Ashmarina, S.I., Horák, J., Vrbka, J., Šuleř, P. (eds.) IES 2020. LNNS, vol. 160, pp. 496–502. Springer, Cham (2021). https://doi.org/10.1007/978-3-030-60929-0_63

Soderberg, G., et al.: Behind the Scenes of central bank digital currency: emerging trends, insights, and policy lessons. IMF FinTech Notes No 2022/004 (2022)

The White House. September. Policy Objectives for a U.S. Central Bank Digital Currency System (2022). https://www.whitehouse.gov/wp-content/uploads/2022/09/09-2022-Policy-Objectives-US-CBDC-System.pdf

U.S. Government Accountability Office. Anti-Money Laundering: Opportunities Exist to Increase Law Enforcement Use of Bank Secrecy Act Reports, and Banks' Costs to Comply with the Act Varied (2020). https://www.gao.gov/assets/gao-20-574.pdf

DeFi

Uniswap Liquidity Provision: An Online Learning Approach

Yogev Bar-On[1](✉) and Yishay Mansour[1,2]

[1] Blavatnik School of Computer Science, Tel Aviv University, Tel Aviv, Israel
baronyogev@gmail.com
[2] Google Research, Tel Aviv, Israel

Abstract. Uniswap v3 is a decentralized exchange (DEX) that allows liquidity providers to allocate funds more efficiently by specifying an active price interval for their funds. This introduces the problem of finding an optimal strategy for choosing price intervals. We formalize this problem as an online learning problem with non-stochastic rewards. We use regret-minimization methods to show a Liquidity Provision strategy that guarantees a lower bound on the reward. This is true even for non-stochastic changes to asset pricing, and we express this bound in terms of the trading volume and the average price change.

1 Introduction

Liquidity providers (LPs) provide funds for a public pool of two assets. Traders can then send funds in the form of one asset to this pool, in exchange for funds in the form of a second asset. The pool automatically determines the price using only the data available on-chain, without outside sources, and includes a trading fee paid to the liquidity providers.

Uniswap, at the time of writing, is one of the largest DEXes, holding reserves worth more than 3 Billion US dollars on Ethereum alone [13]. Originally [3], liquidity providers on Uniswap provided two assets for a liquidity pool, and those funds could have been used by traders no matter how the price changed. This is not an efficient way of fund allocation, since a large portion of the funds would never be used, reserved for unrealistic prices.

Uniswap v3 [4] solves this problem by introducing a new type of Automated Market Maker (AMM), which allows investors to allocate liquidity in specific price ranges, instead of allowing trades in any possible price. Using this concentrated liquidity, LPs can earn more money on their investment, given a correct prediction of market prices. However, when the market price is not in their invested range, LPs lose money on potential trades. Hence, there is great interest in strategies for choosing the correct price range for each investment.

Several attempts have been made to find the optimal liquidity provision strategy given some belief on the distribution of future asset prices. Still, no work has been done on finding an LP strategy for non-stochastic prices, where we do not assume almost anything about how the future price of an asset will change.

A. Essex et al. (Eds.): FC 2023 Workshops, LNCS 13953, pp. 247–261, 2024.
https://doi.org/10.1007/978-3-031-48806-1_16

In this work, we consider the problem of liquidity provision in Uniswap v3 as an online learning problem in the non-stochastic setting. This allows us to formalize LP strategies as predictions with expert advice [5,6]. We can construct a liquidity provision algorithm using regret-minimization methods that admit a positive reward for liquidity providers. This algorithm assumes almost nothing about how future asset prices will change. Moreover - we can express a lower bound on the reward using the trading volume and the average price change during the investment time frame.

Related Work. Liquidity provision strategies on Uniswap v3 is an active research area. Neuder et al. [12] studied optimal strategies where prices evolve according to a Markov chain, and Fan et al. [9] expanded on this work with a better analysis that also takes impermanent loss into account. Heimbach et al. [11] also formalize the problem and strategy analysis in a Black-Scholes stochastic market model. Fritch [10] measures the performance of liquidity providers based on empirical data. Using online learning for market making was already considered for traditional finance. Chen and Vaughan [7] showed the connection between cost-function based prediction markets and no-regret learning. Penna and Reid [8] studied using bandit algorithms for automatic market making. Abernethy et al. [1] provided a general optimization framework for the design of securities markets, and [2] showed an adaptive market-making algorithm based on the order-book spread, using online learning techniques.

Simulations. Source code and simulations based on empirical data are publicly available on https://github.com/yogi-bo/uniswap-v3-online-framework.

2   Uniswap Overview

Any Uniswap liquidity pool holds two asset reserves, say token A reserve and token B reserve. Those assets are provided by liquidity providers, and traders can use the liquidity pool to trade between the two tokens.

When trades are made on Uniswap v2, the pool maintains an invariant on the number of tokens it holds. Let $x > 0$ and $y > 0$ be the amounts of token A and token B in the pool, respectively. The amounts must satisfy $F(x, y) \triangleq xy = L^2$, where $L > 0$, the pool's liquidity, cannot be changed by trades. This mechanism is called a Constant Product Market Maker (CPMM). Say the trader swaps Δx units of token A. They will receive Δy units of token B, such that $F(x + \Delta x, y - \Delta y) = L^2$. The motivation is supply & demand: when a token is bought, its price goes up, and when it is sold, its price goes down.

Pricing. The *spot price* is defined as the ratio of the amount of token B received to the amount of token A sent, for an infinitesimal trade. It also holds that the spot price is simply the ratio of the pool's reserves:

$$p \triangleq \lim_{\Delta x \to 0} \frac{\Delta y}{\Delta x} = \frac{y}{x}.$$

Providing Liquidity. Liquidity providers can always add liquidity to the pool, by providing a bundle of both token A and token B, such that the spot price is not changed. Since $xy = L^2$ and $p = \frac{y}{x}$, we get that to provide L units of liquidity, they need to provide the following amount of tokens:

$$x = \frac{L}{\sqrt{p}}, \qquad y = L\sqrt{p}. \tag{1}$$

Trading Fees. The incentive for LPs is that when a trade is made, e.g., from token A to token B, the trader only receives $(1 - \gamma)\Delta y$ units of token B, where $\gamma\Delta y$ is the *trading fee* that goes towards liquidity providers. γ is the *fee tier* of the pool, and is usually between 0.05% to 1%. The trading fee is distributed between all liquidity providers, proportional to their liquidity in the pool. Hence, if an LP provided L' liquidity units to a pool with L total units of liquidity, they will receive $\gamma\Delta y \frac{L'}{L}$ units of token B as a trading fee.

2.1 Uniswap v3 - Concentrated Liquidity

In Uniswap v3, the spot price domain is divided into discrete intervals: $[d^i, d^{i+1})$ for all $i \in \mathbb{Z}$, where $d > 1$ is the interval size (usually $1.0001 \leq d \leq 1.01$, varies by a *tick spacing* parameter). Each spot price interval acts as an independent CPMM liquidity pool, and liquidity providers can choose to provide liquidity only for certain intervals. This means LP's funds are allocated more efficiently, and they get more trading fees per tokens provided. However, if the spot price is outside the active interval of an LP, they will not earn any trading fees.

To achieve this, Uniswap v3 keeps track of *virtual reserves*. Say LPs invest x units of token A and y units of token B in the price range $[a, b]$. The virtual reserves x_v, y_v are defined to hold:

$$x_v = x + \frac{L}{\sqrt{b}}, \qquad y_v = y + \sqrt{a}L,$$

where $L = \sqrt{x_v y_v}$ is the amount of liquidity provided. The trade price can then be computed using the virtual reserves as if it were a Uniswap v2 pool. From Eq. 1 we get that $x_v = \frac{L}{\sqrt{p}}$ and $y_v = \sqrt{p}L$, and thus:

$$x = (\frac{1}{\sqrt{p}} - \frac{1}{\sqrt{b}})L, \qquad y = (\sqrt{p} - \sqrt{a})L \tag{2}$$

What happens when the spot price leaves the active range? In the case $p > b$, we would have no real reserve of token A, and $(\sqrt{b} - \sqrt{a})L$ units of token B. In the same way if $p < a$, we would get $(\frac{1}{\sqrt{a}} - \frac{1}{\sqrt{b}})L$ units of token A. This can be a way for LPs to make limit-order trades, trading their entire investment to a single token once the price leaves a certain range.

3   Online Learning Model

We consider a Uniswap v3 Liquidity Pool, consisting of token A and token B with an interval size $d \in [1.0001, 2)$ and a fee tier $\gamma < 1$. We now present the online learning strategy for liquidity provision, where at each time step, we re-invest our entire portfolio in a price range centered at the current spot price.

For each time step $t = 1, ..., T$, we invest a portfolio worth M_t units of token B, consisting of $Q_t^{(A)} = \frac{M_t}{2p_t}$ units of token A and $Q_t^{(B)} = \frac{M_t}{2}$ units of token B, where p_t is the spot price of token A (in terms of token B) at step t; we pick a positive *concentration controller* $n_t \in \mathbb{N} \cup \{\infty\}$ and provide liquidity in the range $[p_t d^{-n_t}, p_t d^{n_t}]$ (notice this assumes the interval size is fine enough to approximate spot prices as its exponents). Using Eq. 2, at each step t we thus have an active liquidity of

$$L_t = \frac{Q_t^{(B)}}{\sqrt{p_t} - \sqrt{p_t d^{-n_t}}} = \frac{M_t}{2\sqrt{p_t}(1 - d^{-\frac{n_t}{2}})}.$$

When the step is over, a new price $p_{t+1} = p_t d^{\rho_t}$ (where $\rho_t \triangleq \log_d \frac{p_{t+1}}{p_t}$ is the *logarithmic price change*) is revealed, along with the trading volume v_t. We then receive some reward $r_t(n_t) = \ln \frac{M_{t+1}}{M_t}$, re-balance our funds to match the new price, and invest again. Our goal is to choose optimal concentration controllers for maximizing the total reward:

$$G_T(n_1, ..., n_T) = \ln \frac{M_T}{M_1} = \sum_{t=1}^{T} r_t(n_t).$$

Note that the reward is defined in terms of token B, so it holds a hidden assumption that we care (w.l.o.g.) about maximizing our holdings in terms of token B (e.g., maximizing the number of dollars we have rather than the number of euros).

3.1   Reward Function

We will now present the formula for the reward function $r_t(n_t)$. We first make a few assumptions to simplify our model and analysis.

Total Liquidity. We assume the total active liquidity $\mathbb{L}_t$ at time step t remains constant throughout the step, and we define K_t as the equivalent virtual reserves for that amount of liquidity. Hence we get from Eq. 1:

$$K_t = 2\sqrt{p_t}\mathbb{L}_t.$$

It is useful to express the volume in terms of those virtual reserves, leading us to define the *relative trading volume* as the relation between the trading volume and the active virtual reserves:

$$u_t \triangleq \frac{v_t}{K_t} = \frac{v_t}{2\sqrt{p_t}\mathbb{L}_t}.$$

Partial Fees. We assume either the price is in our active range the entire step or not at all - meaning we get all the commission or none of it. In reality, the price can come in and out of the active range mid-step since we assume many trades can be made on the same step.

Gas Price. Gas prices are equivalent to adding a negative term, linear in T, to the total reward. To simplify our results, we ignore this term and assume re-balancing and re-investing our funds does not incur a loss.

Using those assumptions, we get the following formula:

$$r_t(n_t) = \ln \frac{M_{t+1}}{M_t} = \begin{cases} \ln \frac{1+d^{\frac{n_t}{2}}}{2} & \rho_t > n_t \\ \ln \frac{d^{\rho_t}(1+d^{\frac{n_t}{2}})}{2} & \rho_t < -n_t \\ \ln \frac{2d^{\frac{\rho_t}{2}}-d^{-\frac{n_t}{2}}(1+d^{\rho_t})+2\gamma u_t}{2(1-d^{-\frac{n_t}{2}})} & \text{else} \end{cases} \tag{3}$$

We give the full derivation in Appendix A.

4 Static Strategies

In this section, we will analyze n-static strategies in which we pick a constant concentration controller n for all steps. We will denote the total reward for static strategies as $G_T(n) = G_T(n, ..., n)$, and we will bound it in terms of the average logarithmic price change:

$$P \triangleq \frac{1}{T} \sum_{t=1}^{T} |\log_d p_{t+1} - \log_d p_t| = \frac{1}{T} \sum_{t=1}^{T} |\rho_t|,$$

which is essentially the average number of price intervals skipped each step. Proofs are given in Appendix B.

4.1 $n = \infty$

We first consider the ∞-static strategy, which will be useful as a baseline. This is equivalent to investing in a Uniswap v2 pool while re-balancing funds in each step.

Lemma 1. *For any sequence of ρ_t, u_t s.t. $u_t \leq \frac{2}{\gamma}$, the reward of the ∞-static strategy holds:*

$$G_T(\infty) \geq \frac{\gamma}{2} \sum_{t=1}^{T} u_t - \frac{T}{2} P \ln d.$$

We can already see a lower bound on the trading volume, which will ensure we get a positive reward:

Corollary 1. *For any sequence of ρ_t, u_t s.t. $u_t \leq \frac{2}{\gamma}$ and $\frac{1}{T} \sum_{t=1}^{T} u_t \geq \frac{1}{\gamma} P \ln d$, the ∞-static strategy reward is positive:*

$$G_T(\infty) \geq 0.$$

4.2 $n < \infty$

For analysis of the case where n is finite, we denote by $T_{\leq n}$ the set of time steps where the price remained in the active interval, and by $T_{>n}$ the set of steps where the price left the active interval, i.e.,

$$T_{\leq n} = \{t \mid |\rho_t| \leq n\} \qquad T_{>n} = \{t \mid |\rho_t| > n\}.$$

We show the following lower bound on the reward,

Lemma 2. *The reward of the n-static strategy holds:*

$$G_T(n) \geq \frac{n}{4}|T_{>n}| \ln d - TP \ln d + \sum_{|\rho_t| \leq n} \ln\left(1 + \frac{\gamma u_t}{1 - d^{-\frac{n}{2}}}\right).$$

From this bound, we can see that $n = 4P$ is a good choice for a concentration controller:

Theorem 1. *For any sequence of ρ_t, u_t s.t. $P \ln d \leq 1$ and $\frac{a}{\gamma}P^2 \ln^2 d \leq u_t$, the 4P-static strategy reward holds:*

$$G_T(4P) \geq |T_{\leq 4P}| \ln\left(1 + \frac{a-2}{4}P \ln d\right)$$

Thus, we can again lower bound the sufficient trading volume for a positive reward:

Corollary 2. *For any sequence of ρ_t, u_t s.t. $\frac{2}{\gamma}P^2 \ln^2 d \leq u_t$, the 4P-static strategy reward is positive:*

$$G_T(4P) \geq 0.$$

Compare this result to the ∞-static strategy. On the one hand, we assume a lower bound on the relative trading volume and not on the average trading volume. However, the required magnitude is smaller by a factor of $2P \ln d$, which is usually significantly smaller than 1.

5   Adaptive Strategy

We saw that static strategies can induce positive rewards. However, we don't know the average logarithmic price change P in advance, so we cannot choose the appropriate concentration controller. We solve this problem by using a regret-minimization adaptive algorithm called Exponential Weights Algorithm (EWA), described in Algorithm 1, to gain a reward similar to the optimal static strategy. Essentially, we are learning the optimal static concentration controller adaptively, trying to maximize our reward while doing so.

EWA analysis is given in Appendix C. We present the main result:

Algorithm 1. Exponential Weights Adaptive Strategy (EWA)

Parameters: $N \in \mathbb{N}, \eta > 0$.
Initialize: $r_0(n) \leftarrow 0$ for all $1 \leq n \leq N$.
1: **for** $1 \leq t \leq T$ **do**
2:    Set:

$$p_t(n) \leftarrow \frac{\exp\left(\eta \sum_{0 \leq \tau \leq t} r_\tau(n)\right)}{\displaystyle\sum_{1 \leq \mu \leq N} \exp\left(\eta \sum_{0 \leq \tau \leq t} r_\tau(\mu)\right)}$$

for all $1 \leq n \leq N$.
3:    For each concentration controller $1 \leq n \leq N$, provide liquidity using $p_t(n)$ of the funds, and observe the current reward $r_t(n)$.
4: **end for**

Theorem 2. *Choose $N = \lfloor \log_d 32 \rfloor$ and $\eta = \sqrt{\frac{\ln N}{128T}}$. For any sequence of ρ_t, u_t s.t. $d^{|\rho_t|} \leq 2$ and $\frac{10}{\gamma} P^2 \ln^2 d \leq u_t \leq \frac{2}{\gamma}$, the reward of the Exponential Weights Adaptive Strategy (Algorithm 1), $G_T^{(\text{EWA})}$, holds:*

$$G_T^{(\text{EWA})} \geq \frac{3}{4} T P \ln d - 23 \sqrt{T \ln \log_d 32}.$$

The intuition for the upper bound on the trading volume is that in the worst-case scenario, the best static strategy gains its entire reward in a single large-volume step, and we cannot promise our range will be active specifically in this step.

We can now see that for a large enough time period, the reward will be positive:

Corollary 3. *Choose $N = \lfloor \log_d 32 \rfloor$ and $\eta = \sqrt{\frac{\ln N}{128T}}$. For any sequence of ρ_t, u_t s.t. $d^{|\rho_t|} \leq 2$ and $\frac{10}{\gamma} P^2 \ln^2 d \leq u_t \leq \frac{2}{\gamma}$, the reward of the Exponential Weights Adaptive Strategy is positive for all sufficiently large T:*

$$G_T^{(\text{EWA})} \geq 0.$$

6   Conclusions

Uniswap v3 introduced a novel Automated Market Maker mechanism that allows for complicated investment strategies for liquidity providers. Our work demonstrates the effectiveness of using online learning methods to analyze and create such strategies. We modeled the problem of Uniswap v3 liquidity provision as an online learning problem and analyzed the reward in the context of the new formalism. In our main result (Theorem 2), we showed a dynamic strategy based on prediction with expert advice. We proved this strategy admits a positive total reward for a large enough trading volume, even in the face of non-stochastic price changes. We present the needed trading volume for a positive reward in terms of the average logarithmic price change.

Future work could improve our analysis by improving the accuracy of our formal reward function. Such improvements may include partial trading fees for steps with a significant price change or gas fees for reinvestment.

Acknowledgment. This project has received funding from the European Research Council (ERC) under the European Union's Horizon 2020 research and innovation program (grant agreement No. 882396), the Israel Science Foundation (grant number 993/17), the Yandex Initiative for Machine Learning at Tel Aviv University and a grant from the Tel Aviv University Center for AI and Data Science (TAD).

A   Reward Function Derivation

We will now derive the form of the reward function at step t, given a concentration controller n_t, trading volume v_t, and price change ρ_t. Trivially, the reward consists of the trading fees $f_{v_t}(n_t)$ we get as a commission. But it also depends on our portfolio's value at the end of the step (before re-balancing), $M_{t \to t+1}$, which is different than the beginning. Hence:

$$M_{t+1} = M_{t \to t+1} + f_{v_t}(n_t),$$

and we define the reward as the logarithmic change of value, measured in units of token B:

$$r_t(n_t) \triangleq \ln \frac{M_{t+1}}{M_t} = \ln\left(M_{t \to t+1} + f_{v_t}(n_t)\right) - \ln M_t.$$

A.1   Trading Fees

The trading fee at step t is linearly proportional to the trading volume v_t and our active liquidity, and inversely proportional to the total active liquidity in the pool, with the trading fee γ as the proportionality constant. Hence our commission is:

$$f_{v_t}(n_t) = \begin{cases} 0 & |\rho_t| > n_t \\ \gamma v_t \frac{L_t}{\mathbb{L}_t} & \text{else} \end{cases} = \begin{cases} 0 & |\rho_t| > n_t \\ \gamma u_t \frac{M_t}{(1-d^{-\frac{n_t}{2}})} & \text{else} \end{cases}.$$

A.2   Change in Value

When we invest at step t like our strategy suggests, our portfolio will consist of the following amount of tokens (see Eq. 2):

$$Q^{(A)}_{t \to t+1} = \begin{cases} 0 & \rho_t > n_t \\ L_t \frac{1}{\sqrt{p_t}}(d^{\frac{n_t}{2}} - d^{-\frac{n_t}{2}}) & \rho_t < -n_t \\ L_t \frac{1}{\sqrt{p_t}}(d^{-\frac{\rho_t}{2}} - d^{-\frac{n_t}{2}}) & \text{else} \end{cases}$$

$$Q_{t\to t+1}^{(B)} = \begin{cases} L_t\sqrt{p_t}(d^{\frac{n_t}{2}} - d^{-\frac{n_t}{2}}) & \rho_t > n_t \\ 0 & \rho_t < -n_t \\ L_t\sqrt{p_t}(d^{\frac{\rho_t}{2}} - d^{-\frac{n_t}{2}}) & \text{else} \end{cases}$$

hence, at the end of step t, our portfolio will be worth:

$$M_{t\to t+1} = p_{t+1}Q_{t\to t+1}^{(A)} + Q_{t\to t+1}^{(B)}$$

$$= \begin{cases} L_t\sqrt{p_t}(d^{\frac{n_t}{2}} - d^{-\frac{n_t}{2}}) & \rho_t > n_t \\ L_t\sqrt{p_t}d^{\rho_t}(d^{\frac{n_t}{2}} - d^{-\frac{n_t}{2}}) & \rho_t < -n_t \\ L_t\sqrt{p_t}\left(2d^{\frac{\rho_t}{2}} - d^{-\frac{n_t}{2}}(1 + d^{\rho_t})\right) & \text{else} \end{cases}$$

$$= \begin{cases} M_t\frac{1 + d^{\frac{n_t}{2}}}{2} & \rho_t > n_t \\ M_t\frac{d^{\rho_t}(1 + d^{\frac{n_t}{2}})}{2} & \rho_t < -n_t \\ M_t\frac{2d^{\frac{\rho_t}{2}} - d^{-\frac{n_t}{2}}(1 + d^{\rho_t})}{2(1 - d^{-\frac{n_t}{2}})} & \text{else} \end{cases}.$$

A.3   Total Reward

Summarizing, we get that:

$$\frac{M_{t+1}}{M_t} = \frac{M_{t\to t+1} + f_{v_t}(n_t)}{M_t} = \begin{cases} \frac{1 + d^{\frac{n_t}{2}}}{2} & \rho_t > n_t \\ \frac{d^{\rho_t}(1 + d^{\frac{n_t}{2}})}{2} & \rho_t < -n_t \\ \frac{2d^{\frac{\rho_t}{2}} - d^{-\frac{n_t}{2}}(1 + d^{\rho_t}) + 2\gamma u_t}{2(1 - d^{-\frac{n_t}{2}})} & \text{else} \end{cases},$$

and thus:

$$r_t(n_t) = \ln\frac{M_{t+1}}{M_t} = \begin{cases} \ln\frac{1 + d^{\frac{n_t}{2}}}{2} & \rho_t > n_t \\ \ln\frac{d^{\rho_t}(1 + d^{\frac{n_t}{2}})}{2} & \rho_t < -n_t \\ \ln\frac{2d^{\frac{\rho_t}{2}} - d^{-\frac{n_t}{2}}(1 + d^{\rho_t}) + 2\gamma u_t}{2(1 - d^{-\frac{n_t}{2}})} & \text{else} \end{cases}.$$

As expected, using smaller liquidity intervals leads to larger rewards, but increases the chances of losing trading fees. More specifically:

- If $\rho_t > n_t$, there are no trading fees, but the reward is larger than 0 since the value of token A is larger (in terms of token B). Once the price passed the active interval, all tokens were converted to type B - so the reward does not depend on the price, only on the concentration controller.
- If $\rho_t < -n_t$, there are no trading fees, and the portfolio's value is smaller, so the reward is less than 0. Here, the reward does depend on the price, since all tokens are converted to type A (while we measure the value in terms of token B).

- If $-n_t \leq \rho_t \leq n_t$, the reward might be either greater or less than 1. The term $2d^{\frac{\rho_t}{2}} - d^{-\frac{n_t}{2}}(1 + d^{\rho_t})$ is the effect of the price change on the reward, and γu_t is the effect of fees collected. The term $1 - d^{-\frac{n_t}{2}}$ in the denominator signifies the fact that as the liquidity is concentrated in a smaller interval, the reward is larger.

B   Proofs for Section 4

B.1   Lemma 1

For any sequence of ρ_t, u_t s.t. $u_t \leq \frac{2}{\gamma}$, the reward of the ∞-static strategy holds:

$$G_T(\infty) \geq \frac{\gamma}{2} \sum_{t=1}^{T} u_t - \frac{T}{2} P \ln d.$$

Proof. Taking the limit where $n_t \to \infty$ in Eq. 3 and getting $d^{-\frac{n_t}{2}} = 0$, we have:

$$G_T(\infty) = \sum_{t=1}^{T} r_t(\infty) = \sum_{t=1}^{T} \ln\left(d^{\frac{\rho_t}{2}} + \gamma u_t\right) \geq \sum_{t=1}^{T} \ln\left(d^{-\frac{|\rho_t|}{2}} + \gamma u_t\right)$$

$$\geq \sum_{t=1}^{T} \ln\left(d^{-\frac{|\rho_t|}{2}}(1 + \gamma u_t)\right) = \sum_{t=1}^{T} \ln(1 + \gamma u_t) - \frac{\ln d}{2} \sum_{t=1}^{T} |\rho_t|$$

$$= \sum_{t=1}^{T} \ln(1 + \gamma u_t) - \frac{T}{2} P \ln d \geq \frac{\gamma}{2} \sum_{t=1}^{T} u_t - \frac{T}{2} P \ln d$$

as desired, where the last inequality is since $\ln(1 + x) \geq \frac{x}{2}$ for $x \leq 2$.   □

B.2   Lemma 2

The reward of the n-static strategy holds:

$$G_T(n) \geq \frac{n}{4}|T_{>n}| \ln d - TP \ln d + \sum_{|\rho_t| \leq n} \ln\left(1 + \frac{\gamma u_t}{1 - d^{-\frac{n}{2}}}\right).$$

Proof. First, we will show a new representation of the total reward:

$$G_T(n) = \sum_{t=1}^{T} r_t(n) \tag{4}$$

$$= \sum_{\rho_t > n} \ln\left(\frac{1 + d^{\frac{n}{2}}}{2}\right) + \sum_{\rho_t < -n} \ln\left(d^{\rho_t}\frac{1 + d^{\frac{n}{2}}}{2}\right) + \sum_{|\rho_t| \leq n} \ln\left(\frac{2d^{\frac{\rho_t}{2}} + 2\gamma u_t - d^{-\frac{n}{2}}(1 + d^{\rho_t})}{2(1 - d^{-\frac{n}{2}})}\right) \tag{5}$$

$$= |T_{>n}| \ln\left(\frac{1 + d^{\frac{n}{2}}}{2}\right) - \ln d \sum_{\rho_t < -n} |\rho_t| + \sum_{|\rho_t| \leq n} \ln\left(\frac{2d^{\frac{\rho_t}{2}} + 2\gamma u_t - d^{-\frac{n}{2}}(1 + d^{\rho_t})}{2(1 - d^{-\frac{n}{2}})}\right) \tag{6}$$

$$= |T_{>n}| \ln\left(\frac{1 + d^{\frac{n}{2}}}{2}\right) - \ln d \sum_{\rho_t < n} |\rho_t| + \sum_{|\rho_t| \leq n} \ln\left(d^{|\rho_t|}\frac{2d^{\frac{\rho_t}{2}} + 2\gamma u_t - d^{-\frac{n}{2}}(1 + d^{\rho_t})}{2(1 - d^{-\frac{n}{2}})}\right), \tag{7}$$

where (5) follows directly from (3); in (6) we use the fact that for negative ρ_t:

$$\ln\left(d^{\rho_t}\frac{1+d^{\frac{n}{2}}}{2}\right) = \ln\left(\frac{1+d^{\frac{n}{2}}}{2}\right) - |\rho_t|\ln d,$$

and in (7) we simply add to middle summation the term $\ln d\sum_{|\rho_t|<n}|\rho_t|$, compensating it in the last summation by multiplying by $d^{|\rho_t|}$ inside the logarithm.

Since we look for a lower bound in terms of the average logarithmic price change P, we can complete the middle summation over all time steps, getting $TP\ln d$, and separate the volume term in the last summation using the fact that $d^{|\rho_t|} \geq 1$:

$$G_T(n) \geq |T_{>n}|\ln\left(\frac{1+d^{\frac{n}{2}}}{2}\right) - TP\ln d + \sum_{|\rho_t|\leq n}\ln\left(d^{|\rho_t|}\frac{2d^{\frac{\rho_t}{2}} - d^{-\frac{n}{2}}(1+d^{\rho_t})}{2(1-d^{-\frac{n}{2}})} + \frac{\gamma u_t}{1-d^{-\frac{n}{2}}}\right) \tag{8}$$

$$\geq |T_{>n}|\frac{n\ln d}{4} - TP\ln d + \sum_{|\rho_t|\leq n}\ln\left(d^{|\rho_t|}\frac{2d^{\frac{\rho_t}{2}} - d^{-\frac{n}{2}}(1+d^{\rho_t})}{2(1-d^{-\frac{n}{2}})} + \frac{\gamma u_t}{1-d^{-\frac{n}{2}}}\right) \tag{9}$$

where (9) follows from $\ln\frac{1+e^x}{2} \geq \frac{x}{2}$.

Now, consider the term $f(\rho_t) = d^{|\rho_t|}\left(2d^{\frac{\rho_t}{2}} - d^{-\frac{n}{2}}(1+d^{\rho_t})\right)$ as a function of ρ_t. We want to find a lower bound on the domain $|\rho_t| < n$; we first look for a local minimum on the differentiable domain:

$$f'(\rho_t) = d^{|\rho_t|}\ln d\left(\text{sgn}(\rho_t)\left(2d^{\frac{\rho_t}{2}} - d^{-\frac{n}{2}}(1+d^{\rho_t})\right) + d^{\frac{\rho_t}{2}} - d^{\rho_t-\frac{n}{2}}\right) = 0$$

Hence,

$$(2\,\text{sgn}(\rho_t)+1)d^{\frac{n+\rho_t}{2}} - (1+\text{sgn}(\rho_t))d^{\rho_t} - \text{sgn}(\rho_t) = 0.$$

In the case that $\rho_t < 0$, we get $d^{\frac{n+\rho_t}{2}} - 1 = 0$, which is not solvable when $|\rho_t| < n$. For $\rho_t > 0$, we get $2d^{\rho_t} - 3d^{\frac{n+\rho_t}{2}} + 1 = 0$, which is a quadratic equation on $d^{\frac{\rho_t}{2}}$ with the solution:

$$d^{\frac{\rho_t}{2}} = \frac{1}{4}(3d^{\frac{n}{2}} \pm \sqrt{9d^n - 8}).$$

Note that $\sqrt{9d^n - 8} \geq d^{\frac{n}{2}}$, so we get $d^{\frac{\rho_t}{2}} \geq d^{\frac{n}{2}}$ for the first solution, which is outside the domain. Also,

$$\sqrt{9d^n - 8} = \sqrt{(3d^{\frac{n}{2}} - 4)^2 + 24(d^{\frac{n}{2}} - 1)} \geq 3d^{\frac{n}{2}} - 4$$

so we get $d^{\frac{\rho_t}{2}} \leq 1$ for the second solution, which is impossible since we assumed $\rho_t > 0$.

In conclusion, there is no local minimum on the differentiable domain, and $f(\rho_t)$ admits a lower bound either on the domain's boundary ($\rho_t = \pm n$) or at $\rho_t = 0$ (the only non-differentiable point). Evaluating f at each of those points we get:

$$f(0) = 2(1 - d^{-\frac{n}{2}}), \qquad f(n) = d^{\frac{3n}{2}} - d^{\frac{n}{2}}, \qquad f(-n) = d^{\frac{n}{2}} - d^{-\frac{n}{2}}.$$

Note that:

$$f(-n) - f(0) = 2\left(\frac{d^{\frac{n}{2}} + d^{-\frac{n}{2}}}{2} - 1\right) \geq 0,$$

so $f(-n) \geq f(0)$. We can also see that $f(n) = f(-n)d^n \geq f(-n)$. To summarize, we have $f(n) \geq f(-n) \geq f(0)$, and thus:

$$d^{\frac{3n}{2}} - d^{\frac{n}{2}} \geq d^{|\rho_t|}\left(2d^{\frac{\rho_t}{2}} - d^{-\frac{n}{2}}(1 + d^{\rho_t})\right) \geq 2(1 - d^{-\frac{n}{2}}). \tag{10}$$

We can now plug this result in (9) to conclude our proof:

$$G_T(n) \geq \frac{n}{4}|T_{>n}|\ln d - TP\ln d + \sum_{|\rho_t| \leq n} \ln\left(1 + \frac{\gamma u_t}{1 - d^{-\frac{n}{2}}}\right).$$

$\square$

B.3   Theorem 1

For any sequence of ρ_t, u_t s.t. $P\ln d \leq 1$ and $\frac{a}{\gamma}P^2\ln^2 d \leq u_t$, the $4P$-static strategy reward holds:

$$G_T(4P) \geq |T_{\leq 4P}|\ln\left(1 + \frac{a-2}{4}P\ln d\right)$$

Proof. From our assumption on the trading volume and Lemma 2 we get:

$$G_T(4P) \geq |T_{>4P}|P\ln d - TP\ln d + \sum_{|\rho_t| \leq 4P}\ln\left(1 + \frac{\gamma u_t}{1 - d^{-2P}}\right)$$

$$= \sum_{|\rho_t| \leq 4P}\left(\ln\left(1 + \frac{\gamma u_t}{1 - d^{-2P}}\right) - P\ln d\right)$$

$$= \sum_{|\rho_t| \leq 4P}\ln\left(\frac{1 - d^{-2P} + \gamma u_t}{d^P - d^{-P}}\right)$$

$$\geq |T_{\leq 4P}|\ln\left(\frac{1 - d^{-2P} + aP^2\ln^2 d}{d^P - d^{-P}}\right).$$

Note that $e^x - 1 - e^{-x} + e^{-2x} \leq 2x^2$ for $x \leq 1$. Since we assume $P\ln d \leq 1$, we also get that $d^P - 1 - d^{-P} + d^{-2P} \leq 2P^2\ln^2 d$, and thus,

$$G_T(4P) \geq |T_{\leq 4P}|\ln\left(1 + (a-2)\frac{P^2\ln^2 d}{1 - d^{-2P} + 2P^2\ln^2 d}\right)$$

$$\geq |T_{\leq 4P}|\ln\left(1 + (a-2)\frac{P^2\ln^2 d}{1 - d^{-2P} + 2P\ln d}\right).$$

Using $d^{-2P} \geq 1 - 2P\ln d$:

$$G_T(4P) \geq |T_{\leq 4P}|\ln\left(1 + \frac{a-2}{4}P\ln d\right),$$

concluding our proof.

$\square$

C   Analysis of Algorithm 1

Since we saw $4P$ would be a good concentration controller, we want to ensure it is included in our options. Hence, we need to choose N such that $N \geq 4P$. It is reasonable to assume $d^P \leq 2$, so it is enough to choose $N \geq \log_d 16$. However we need N to be a natural number, and because $d < 2$, we can choose $N = \lfloor \log_d 32 \rfloor$.

Now we can bound the reward function:

Lemma 3. *Choose $N = \lfloor \log_d 32 \rfloor$. For any sequence of ρ_t, u_t s.t. $d^{|\rho_t|} \leq 2$ and $u_t \leq \frac{2}{\gamma}$, we have:*

$$R \triangleq \max_{t \leq T, n \leq N} r_t(n) - \min_{t \leq T, n \leq N} r_t(n) \leq 16$$

Proof. We evaluate each case in Eq. 3.

In the case that $\rho_t > n$, we have $r_t(n) = \ln \frac{1+d^{\frac{n}{2}}}{2}$. It is easy to see that $r_t(n) \geq 0$, and also:

$$r_t(n) \leq \ln \frac{1 + d^{\frac{N}{2}}}{2} \leq \ln \frac{1 + d^{\frac{\log_d 32}{2}}}{2} = \ln \frac{1 + \sqrt{32}}{2} \leq 2.$$

In the case that $\rho_t < -n$, we have $r_t(n) = \ln \frac{d^{\rho_t}(1+d^{\frac{n}{2}})}{2}$. Since $\rho_t < -n$ we get $r_t(n) \leq 0$. Using our assumption that $|\rho_t| \leq \log_d 2$, we get:

$$r_t(n) \geq \rho_t \ln d \geq -\ln 2.$$

Otherwise, if $|\rho_t| < n$, we have $r_t(n) = \ln \frac{2d^{\frac{\rho_t}{2}} - d^{-\frac{n}{2}}(1+d^{\rho_t}) + 2\gamma u_t}{2(1-d^{-\frac{n}{2}})}$. For a lower bound we can set $u_t = 0$, and get from Eq. 10 that:

$$r_t(n) \geq \ln d^{-|\rho_t|} = -|\rho_t| \ln d \geq -\ln 2.$$

For an upper bound, we use the assumption that $u_t \leq \frac{2}{\gamma}$ and again use Eq. 10:

$$r_t(n) \leq \ln \frac{d^{-|\rho_t|}(d^{\frac{3n}{2}} - d^{\frac{n}{2}}) + 4}{2(1 - d^{-\frac{n}{2}})} \leq \ln \frac{d^{\frac{3n}{2}} + 4}{2(1 - d^{-\frac{n}{2}})},$$

and since $1 \leq n \leq N \leq \log_d 32$ and $d \geq 1.0001$:

$$r_t(n) \leq \ln \frac{d^{\frac{3N}{2}} + 4}{2(1 - d^{-\frac{1}{2}})} \leq \ln \frac{32^{\frac{3}{2}} + 4}{2(1 - 1.0001^{-\frac{1}{2}})} \leq 15.$$

Overall, we get that $-\ln 2 \leq r_t(n) \leq 15$ for all t, n, and thus

$$R \leq 15 + \ln 2 \leq 16$$

as desired.   □

We will start the analysis by presenting a well-known Lemma [5,6], bounding the *regret* of our adaptive strategy:

Lemma 4. *The rewards of the Exponential Weights Adaptive Strategy hold:*

$$\sum_{t \leq T} \sum_{1 \leq \mu \leq N} p_t(\mu) r_t(\mu) \geq G_T(n) - \frac{\ln N}{\eta} - \frac{\eta}{2} T R^2$$

For all $1 \leq n \leq N$, where R is a bound on the range of the reward.

Using this lemma, we can now prove the main theorem, which we restate here:

Theorem 2. Choose $N = \lfloor \log_d 32 \rfloor$ and $\eta = \sqrt{\frac{\ln N}{128T}}$. For any sequence of ρ_t, u_t s.t. $d^{|\rho_t|} \leq 2$ and $\frac{10}{\gamma} P^2 \ln^2 d \leq u_t \leq \frac{2}{\gamma}$, the reward of the Exponential Weights Adaptive Strategy (Algorithm 1), $G_T^{(\text{EWA})}$, holds:

$$G_T^{(\text{EWA})} \geq \frac{3}{4} T P \ln d - 23 \sqrt{T \ln \log_d 32}.$$

Proof. Denote by $M_{t+1}(n)$ the value of the portfolio at $t+1$ if we were to provide liquidity at step t using only the concentration controller n, such that $r_t(n) = \ln \frac{M_{t+1}(n)}{M_t}$. Thus, due to Jensen's inequality:

$$G_T^{(\text{EWA})} = \sum_{t \leq T} \ln \left(\sum_{1 \leq n \leq N} \frac{p_t(n) M_{t+1}(n)}{M_t} \right)$$

$$\geq \sum_{t \leq T} \sum_{1 \leq n \leq N} p_t(n) \ln \frac{M_{t+1}(n)}{M_t}$$

$$= \sum_{t \leq T} \sum_{1 \leq n \leq N} p_t(n) r_t(n).$$

We can now use this result with Lemma 4. We substitute the η we chose, set $n = 4P \leq N$ and use R from Lemma 3 to get:

$$G_T^{(\text{EWA})} \geq G_T(4P) - \sqrt{512 T \ln N} \geq G_T(4P) - 23\sqrt{T \ln N}.$$

From Theorem 1, using $a = 10$, we have:

$$G_T^{(\text{EWA})} \geq |T_{\leq 4P}| \ln (1 + 2P \ln d) - 23\sqrt{T \ln N} \geq |T_{\leq 4P}| P \ln d - 23\sqrt{T \ln N}.$$

Using Markov's Inequality, we get $|T_{\leq 4P}| \geq \frac{3}{4} T$. Thus,

$$G_T^{(\text{EWA})} \geq \frac{3}{4} T P \ln d - 23\sqrt{T \ln N} \geq \frac{3}{4} T P \ln d - 23\sqrt{T \ln \log_d 32}$$

as desired.   □

References

1. Abernethy, J., Chen, Y., Vaughan, J.W.: Efficient market making via convex optimization, and a connection to online learning. ACM Trans. Econ. Comput. (TEAC) **1**(2), 1–39 (2013)
2. Abernethy, J., Kale, S.: Adaptive market making via online learning. In: Advances in Neural Information Processing Systems, vol. 26 (2013)
3. Adams, H., Zinsmeister, N., Robinson, D.: Uniswap v2 core (2020)
4. Adams, H., Zinsmeister, N., Salem, M., Keefer, R., Robinson, D.: Uniswap v3 core (2021)
5. Cesa-Bianchi, N., Freund, Y., Haussler, D., Helmbold, D.P., Schapire, R.E., Warmuth, M.K.: How to use expert advice. J. ACM (JACM) **44**(3), 427–485 (1997)
6. Cesa-Bianchi, N., Lugosi, G.: Prediction, Learning, and Games. Cambridge University Press, Cambridge (2006)
7. Chen, Y., Vaughan, J.W.: A new understanding of prediction markets via no-regret learning. In: Proceedings of the 11th ACM Conference on Electronic Commerce, pp. 189–198 (2010)
8. Della Penna, N., Reid, M.D.: Bandit market makers. arXiv preprint arXiv:1112.0076 (2011)
9. Fan, Z., Marmolejo-Cossío, F., Altschuler, B., Sun, H., Wang, X., Parkes, D.C.: Differential liquidity provision in uniswap v3 and implications for contract design. arXiv preprint arXiv:2204.00464 (2022)
10. Fritsch, R.: Concentrated liquidity in automated market makers. In: Proceedings of the 2021 ACM CCS Workshop on Decentralized Finance and Security, pp. 15–20 (2021)
11. Heimbach, L., Schertenleib, E., Wattenhofer, R.: Risks and returns of uniswap v3 liquidity providers. arXiv preprint arXiv:2205.08904 (2022)
12. Neuder, M., Rao, R., Moroz, D.J., Parkes, D.C.: Strategic liquidity provision in uniswap v3. arXiv preprint arXiv:2106.12033 (2021)
13. Uniswap info. https://info.uniswap.org. Accessed 01 Jan 2023

Extended Abstract: The Effect of Trading Fees on Arbitrage Profits in Automated Market Makers

Jason Milionis[1]($\boxtimes$) ⓘ, Ciamac C. Moallemi[2]($\boxtimes$) ⓘ,
and Tim Roughgarden[1,3]($\boxtimes$) ⓘ

[1] Department of Computer Science, Columbia University, New York, NY 10027, USA
{jm,tr}@cs.columbia.edu
[2] Graduate School of Business, Columbia University, New York, NY 10027, USA
ciamac@gsb.columbia.edu
[3] a16z Crypto, New York, NY 10010, USA

Abstract. We consider the impact of trading fees on the profits of arbitrageurs trading against an automated marker marker (AMM) or, equivalently, on the adverse selection incurred by liquidity providers due to arbitrage. We extend the model of Milionis et al. [1] for a general class of two asset AMMs to both introduce fees and discrete Poisson block generation times. In our setting, we are able to compute the expected instantaneous rate of arbitrage profit in closed form. When the fees are low, in the fast block asymptotic regime, the impact of fees takes a particularly simple form: fees simply scale down arbitrage profits by the fraction of time that an arriving arbitrageur finds a profitable trade.

Keywords: Blockchain · Decentralized Finance · Automated Market Makers

1 Introduction

For automated market makers (AMMs), the primary cost incurred by liquidity providers (LPs) is adverse selection. Adverse selection arises from the fact that agents ("arbitrageurs") with an informational advantage, in the form of knowledge of current market prices, can exploit stale prices on the AMM versus prices on other markets such as centralized exchanges. Because trades between arbitrageurs and the AMM are zero sum, any arbitrage profits will be realized as losses to the AMM LPs. Milionis et al. [1] quantify these costs through a metric called loss-versus-rebalancing (LVR). They establish that LVR can be simultaneously interpreted as: (1) arbitrage profits due to stale AMM prices; (2) the loss incurred by LPs relative to a trading strategy (the "rebalancing strategy") that holds the same risky positions as the pool, but that trades at market prices rather than AMM prices; and (3) the value of the lost optionality when an LP commits upfront to a particular liquidity demand curve. They develop formulas for LVR in closed form, and show theoretically and empirically that, once market

A. Essex et al. (Eds.): FC 2023 Workshops, LNCS 13953, pp. 262–265, 2024.
https://doi.org/10.1007/978-3-031-48806-1_17

risk is hedged, the profit-and-loss (P&L) of an LP reduces to trading fee income minus LVR. In this way, LVR isolates the costs of liquidity provision.

Despite its benefits, LVR suffers from a significant flaw: it is derived under the simplification that arbitrageurs do not pay trading fees. In practice, however, trading fees pose a significant friction and limit arbitrage profits. The main contribution of the present work is to develop a tractable model for arbitrage profits *in the presence of trading fees*. We are able to obtain general formulas for arbitrageur profits in this setting. We establish, under mild conditions, that arbitrage profits in the presence of fees are roughly equivalent to the arbitrage profits in the frictionless case (i.e., LVR), but scaled down to adjust for the fraction of time where the AMM price differs from the market price significantly enough that arbitrageurs can make profits even in the presence of fees. That is, the introduction of fees can be viewed as a rescaling of time. Finally, we prove that, under mild conditions, the total amount of arbitrage profits and fees obtained through arbitrage trades approximately equals LVR, effectively indicating that the information-theoretical role of LVR is still retained, except some of it is returned back to the AMM in the form of fees.

2   Model

Our starting point is the model of Milionis et al. [1], where arbitrageurs continuously monitor an AMM to trade a risky asset versus the numéraire, and the risky asset price follows geometric Brownian motion parameterized by volatility $\sigma > 0$. However, we assume that the AMM has a trading fee $\gamma \geq 0$, and that arbitrageurs arrive to trade on the AMM at discrete times according to the arrivals of a Poisson process with rate $\lambda > 0$. The Poisson process is a natural choice because of its memoryless nature and standard usage throughout continuous time finance. If arrival times correspond to block generation times, the parameter λ should be calibrated so that the mean interarrival time λ^{-1} corresponds to the mean interblock time.

We describe the dynamics of arrivals of arbitrageurs in terms of a mispricing process that is the difference between the AMM and market log-prices. At each arrival time, a myopic arbitrageur will trade in a way such that the pool mispricing to jumps to the nearest point in band around zero mispricing. The width of the band is determined by the fee γ. We call this band the *no-trade region*, since if the arbitrageur arrives and the mispricing is already in the band, there is no profitable trade possible.

3   Results

In our setting, the mispricing process is a Markovian jump-diffusion process. Our first result is to establish that this process is ergodic, and to identify its steady state distribution in closed form. Under this distribution, the probability that an arbitrageur arrives and can make a profitable trade, i.e., the fraction of time that the mispricing process is outside the no-trade region in steady state, is given by

$$\mathsf{P}_{\mathsf{trade}} \triangleq \frac{1}{1 + \sqrt{2\lambda}\gamma/\sigma}.$$

$\mathsf{P}_{\mathsf{trade}}$ has intuitive structure in that it is a function of the composite parameter $\eta \triangleq \gamma/(\sigma\sqrt{\lambda^{-1}/2})$, the fee measured as a multiple of the typical (one standard deviation) movement of returns over half the average interarrival time. When η is large (e.g., high fee, low volatility, or frequent blocks), the width of the no-fee region is large relative to typical interarrival price moves, so the mispricing process is less likely to exit the no-trade region in between arrivals, and $\mathsf{P}_{\mathsf{trade}} \approx \eta^{-1}$.

Given the steady state distribution of the pool mispricing, we can quantify the arbitrage profits. Denote by ARB_T the cumulative arbitrage profits over the time interval $[0, T]$. We compute the expected instantaneous rate of arbitrage profit $\overline{\mathsf{ARB}} \triangleq \lim_{T \to 0} \mathbb{E}[\mathsf{ARB}_T]/T$, where the expectation is over the steady state distribution of mispricing. We derive a semi-closed form expression (involving an expectation) for $\overline{\mathsf{ARB}}$. For specific cases, such as geometric mean or constant product market makers, this expectation can be evaluated resulting in an explicit closed form.

We further consider an asymptotic analysis in the *fast block regime* where $\lambda \to \infty$ (equivalently, the limit as the mean interarrival time $\lambda^{-1} \to 0$). In order to explain our asymptotic results, we begin with the frictionless base case of Milionis et al. [1], where there is no fee ($\gamma = 0$) and continuous monitoring ($\lambda = \infty$). Milionis et al. [1] establish that the expected instantaneous rate of arbitrage profit is

$$\overline{\mathsf{LVR}} \triangleq \lim_{T \to 0} \frac{\mathbb{E}[\mathsf{LVR}_T]}{T} = \frac{\sigma^2 P}{2} \times y^{*\prime}(P). \tag{1}$$

Here, P is the current market price, while $y^*(P)$ is the quantity of numéraire held by the pool when the market price is P, so that $y^{*\prime}(P)$ is the *marginal liquidity* of the pool at price P, denominated in the numéraire. In the presence of fees and discrete monitoring, our analysis establishes that as $\lambda \to \infty$,

$$\overline{\mathsf{ARB}} = \frac{\sigma^2 P}{2} \times \frac{y^{*\prime}(Pe^{-\gamma}) + y^{*\prime}(Pe^{+\gamma})}{2} \times \frac{1}{1 + \sqrt{2\lambda}\gamma/\sigma} + o\left(\sqrt{\lambda^{-1}}\right). \tag{2}$$

Equations (1) and (2) differ in two ways. First, (1) involves the marginal liquidity $y^{*\prime}(P)$ at the current price P, while (2) averages the marginal liquidity at the endpoints of the no-trade interval of prices $[Pe^{-\gamma}, Pe^{+\gamma}]$. This difference is minor if the fee γ is small. The second difference, which is major, is that arbitrage profits in (2) are scaled down relative to (1) by precisely the factor $\mathsf{P}_{\mathsf{trade}}$. In other words, if the fee is low, in the fast block regime we can view the impact of the fee on arbitrage profits as scaling down LVR by the fraction of time that an arriving arbitrageur can profitably trade.

Finally, conditioned on the fee γ being small in the fast block regime, we prove that the sum total of $\overline{\mathsf{ARB}}$ and the expected instantaneous rate of fees arising from arbitrage trades asymptotically equals $\overline{\text{LVR}}$. The latter fact can be interpreted as $\overline{\text{LVR}}$ being split among fees and arbitrage profits, according to P_{trade}. In particular, as blocks become more frequent (for a fixed fee γ), $\overline{\text{LVR}}$ is transferred from arbitrage profits to fees, where it is eventually consumed.

4   Conclusion

This work has broad implications around liquidity provision and the design of automated market makers. First, the model presented hereby provides a more accurate quantification of LP P&L, accounting both for arbitrageurs paying trading fees and discrete arbitrageur arrival times. As such, this model can be used for empirical analyses to evaluate LP performance both *ex post* as well as *ex ante*, when coupled with realized metrics of pool data, such as realized asset price volatility. Our results also have the potential to better inform AMM design, and in particular, provide guidance around how to set trading fees in a competitive LP market, in order to balance LP fee income and LP loss due to arbitrageurs. Finally, the asymptotic regime analysis $\lambda \to \infty$ above points to a significant potential mitigator of arbitrage profits: running a chain with lower mean interblock time (essentially, a faster chain), since we show that this effectively reduces arbitrageurs' profits without negatively impacting LP fee income derived from trading.

Disclosures. The first author was, at the time of writing, a Research Fellow with automated market making protocols, including ones mentioned in this work. The second author is an advisor to fintech companies. The third author is Head of Research at a16z crypto, which reviewed a draft of this article for compliance prior to publication and is an investor in various decentralized finance projects, including Uniswap, as well as in the crypto ecosystem more broadly (for general a16z disclosures, see https://www.a16z.com/disclosures/).

Acknowledgment. The first author is supported in part by NSF awards CNS-2212745, CCF-2212233, DMS-2134059, and CCF-1763970. The second author is supported by the Briger Family Digital Finance Lab at Columbia Business School. The third author's research at Columbia University is supported in part by NSF awards CNS-2212745, and CCF-2006737.

References

1. Milionis, J., Moallemi, C.C., Roughgarden, T., Zhang, A.L.: Quantifying loss in automated market makers. In: Proceedings of the 2022 ACM CCS Workshop on Decentralized Finance and Security, pp. 71–74. Association for Computing Machinery, New York, USA (2022). https://doi.org/10.1145/3560832.3563441

Concave Pro-rata Games

Nicholas A. G. Johnson[✉], Theo Diamandis, Alex Evans, Henry de Valence, and Guillermo Angeris

Bain Capital Crypto, Boston, USA
nicholasjohnson2015@gmail.com

Abstract. In this paper, we introduce a family of games called concave pro-rata games. In such a game, players place their assets into a pool, and the pool pays out some concave function of all assets placed into it. Each player then receives a pro-rata share of the payout; *i.e.*, each player receives an amount proportional to how much they placed in the pool. Such games appear in a number of practical scenarios, including as a simplified version of batched decentralized exchanges, such as those proposed by Penumbra. We show that this game has a number of interesting properties, including a symmetric pure equilibrium that is the unique equilibrium of this game, and we prove that its price of anarchy is $\Omega(n)$ in the number of players. We also show some numerical results in the iterated setting which suggest that players quickly converge to an equilibrium in iterated play.

Introduction

Existing blockchain systems come to consensus on transactions in batches, called blocks. Yet the economic mechanisms those transactions interact with are generally designed to process each individual transaction sequentially, making their behavior reliant on the ordering of transactions within the batch. This abstraction mismatch is the primary source of miner extractible value (MEV), defined as economic value that can be captured by the block proposer (originally the miner) who selects and sequences the transactions to be included in the batch [6].

However, rather than trying to blind the block proposer, or choose a "fair" ordering (which is difficult, if not impossible, to construct in any direct sense on current systems) within a batch, we could alternatively attempt to design economic mechanisms which do not depend on the order of transactions within a block, and instead, process each batch of transactions 'all at once'. These mechanisms would then be aligned with the actual ordering provided by the consensus mechanism, stepping from one batch of transactions to the next in the same discrete time steps in which consensus happens.

One such mechanism is a 'pro-rata mechanism'. In this mechanism, there is some known notion of value: for example, every user might want to trade some asset A for another, say B, and everyone 'pitches in' some amount of asset A into a pool. After everyone has placed their amounts, the pool, as a whole, is traded on an exchange for some amount of asset B, and the resulting amount of asset B is distributed back to each player, in proportion to how much of asset A

A. Essex et al. (Eds.): FC 2023 Workshops, LNCS 13953, pp. 266–285, 2024.
https://doi.org/10.1007/978-3-031-48806-1_18

each player placed in the pool. It is not difficult to show that such a mechanism has the desired property: the order in which players placed asset A into the collective pool does not change how much of asset B each player receives. Using some ideas from cryptography, this game can additionally be implemented in a way that does not reveal any one player's contributions or identity [9], and so may be considered a simultaneous game.

On the other hand, mechanisms of this form often lead to interesting phenomena as users must now consider the possible actions of other users when planning their own actions. A natural framework to study these kinds of problems, where players must reason about the strategies of other players, recursively, is via game theory and the study of the equilibria of games [12]. This paper serves to cleanly set up the game resulting from a pro-rata mechanism in a simple mathematical framework and derive a number of useful results for such games.

This Paper. The paper is organized as follows. We introduce the concave pro-rata game in Sect. 1 and show a few interesting properties under mild conditions. Such properties include the existence and uniqueness of a symmetric pure strategy equilibrium and an explicit way of efficiently computing this equilibrium by solving a single variable, unimodal optimization problem. We also show some simple bounds for the price of anarchy. In Sect. 2 we then describe how this type of game connects to a recent proposal for a batched decentralized exchange. We run a number of simulations in Sect. A and Sect. B, illustrating the price of anarchy and showing that in the iterated setting agents appear to converge quickly to the specified equilibrium.

1   The Concave Pro-rata Game

We will define the *pro-rata game* with n players as the game with the following payoff for player $i = 1, \ldots, n$:

$$U_i(x) = \frac{x_i}{1^T x} f(1^T x). \tag{1}$$

Here, $f : \mathbf{R}_+ \to \mathbf{R}$ is some function satisfying $f(0) = 0$, while $x \in \mathbf{R}_+^n$ is a nonnegative vector whose ith entry is the action performed by the ith player. We will say the game is a *concave* pro-rata game if the function f is a concave function. This game has a simple interpretation: every player 'pitches in' some amount x_i into a pool, totaling $1^T x$, and the pool pays out $f(1^T x)$ depending only on the total amount pitched in by all players. The amount paid out by the pool is then distributed among the players in a pro-rata way; *i.e.*, each player i receives an amount proportional to how much she put into the pool. For the remainder of this paper, we will assume that the function f is concave. We note that concave pro-rata games consist of a special case of aggregative games in which the payoff of each player is a function of their strategy and the sum of the strategies of all players (*cf.*, [11]).

Concavity. The payoff U_i is concave in the ith entry, holding the remaining entries constant. To see this, first define $y = 1^T x - x_i$ (*i.e.*, y is the sum of all entries of x except the ith entry). Overloading notation slightly for U_i, we have that

$$U_i(x_i, y) = \frac{x_i}{x_i + y} f(x_i + y).$$

We can write $U_i(\cdot, y)$ as the composition of the following two functions

$$U_i(x_i, y) = g(x_i, h(x_i)),$$

where

$$g(x_i, t) = tf\left(\frac{x_i}{t}\right) \qquad \text{and} \qquad h(x_i) = \frac{x_i}{x_i + y},$$

which are defined for nonnegative real inputs. We will use this rewriting to show that this function is concave in x_i, since, using the basic convex composition rules (*cf.*, [3, Sect. 3.2.4]) it suffices to show that (a) h is concave and (b) g is concave and nondecreasing in its second argument.

First, note that h is (strictly) concave since

$$h(x_i) = 1 - \frac{y}{x_i + y},$$

which is evidently (strictly) concave in x_i since y is a constant. We can see that g is jointly concave in its arguments as it is the perspective transform of the function f, which preserves concavity (*cf.*, [3, Sect. 3.2.6]). Finally, we need to show that g is nondecreasing in its second argument. To see this, let $0 \le t \le t'$, then we have

$$g(x_i, t') = t'f\left(\frac{x_i}{t'}\right) = t'f\left(\frac{t}{t'}\frac{x_i}{t} + \left(1 - \frac{t}{t'}\right)0\right)$$

$$\ge tf\left(\frac{x_i}{t}\right) + \left(1 - \frac{t}{t'}\right)f(0) = tf\left(\frac{x_i}{t}\right) = g(x_i, t). \tag{2}$$

The inequality follows from the definition of concavity, while the second-to-last equality follows from the fact that $f(0) = 0$.

Selfish Maximum. The fact that g is nondecreasing in its second argument also has an interesting consequence: a player never does better in the pro-rata game when compared to the 'selfish' version. In other words, for a fixed x_i, player i has the largest payoff when all other players $j \ne i$ have $x_j = 0$. This is easy to see since

$$t = \frac{x_i}{1^T x} \le 1$$

so

$$U_i(x) = g(x_i, t) \le g(x_i, 1) = f(x_i),$$

where g is as defined above. The inequality follows from the monotonicity of g in its second argument.

Strict Concavity. In the important special case where f satisfies

$$f(\alpha t) > \alpha f(t), \tag{3}$$

for every $t > 0$ and $0 < \alpha < 1$, then the function $U_i(\cdot, y)$ is strictly concave in its first argument. (We will show this soon.) Property (3) has the interpretation that any chord of the function, drawn between $(0,0)$ and any other point on the graph, lies strictly below the function itself. For example, a sufficient condition is that the function f is strictly concave, though this condition is not a necessary one as there are functions which are not strictly concave that satisfy (3). See Appendix C for a more general condition.

Since we know that h is a strictly concave function and g is a concave function, we can show that $g(x_i, h(x_i))$ is strictly concave in x_i by showing that g is strictly increasing in its second argument. Strict concavity of g follows from the usual composition rules (see [3, Sect. 3.2.4]). To show that g is strictly increasing in its second argument, let $0 < t < t'$, then:

$$g(x_i, t') = t'f\left(\frac{x_i}{t'}\right) = t'f\left(\frac{t}{t'}\frac{x_i}{t}\right) > t'\frac{t}{t'}f\left(\frac{x_i}{t}\right) = tf\left(\frac{x_i}{t}\right) = g(x_i, t),$$

where the inequality follows from an application of (3) with $\alpha = t/t'$.

Definitions. For completeness, we state several important game theoretic definitions [12]. To each player $i = 1, \ldots, n$, we associate a *strategy*, which is a probability distribution π_i over the possible actions of player i, the nonnegative real numbers. We say a strategy is *pure* if π_i is a deterministic distribution or point mass. In other words, we say a strategy is pure when the probability of choosing a specific action z is always one; *i.e.*, $\pi_i(\{z\}) = 1$ for some $z \geq 0$. Otherwise, we say the strategy is *mixed*.

A *Nash equilibrium* (simply an *equilibrium* from here on out) is a collection of strategies π_i for each player $i = 1, \ldots, n$ such that no individual player can achieve a strictly better outcome by choosing a different strategy. Concretely, let $x_i \sim \pi_i$ be a random variable chosen by player i's strategy (mixed or pure) and let $y_i \sim \pi_{-i}$ be a random variable denoting the sums of random variables from other players' strategies. The collection of strategies (π_i) consists of an equilibrium if, for each player i, we have

$$\mathbf{E}_{x_i \sim \pi_i,\ y_i \sim \pi_{-i}}\left[U_i(x_i, y_i)\right] \geq \mathbf{E}_{x_i \sim \tilde{\pi}_i,\ y_i \sim \pi_{-i}}\left[U_i(x_i, y_i)\right],$$

where $\tilde{\pi}_i$ denotes any strategy. (For the remainder of the paper, we will drop the x_i and y_i in the definition of the expectation to shorten notation.) If the above condition holds with strict inequality for all i except when $\tilde{\pi}_i = \pi_i$, the equilibrium is said to be *strict*. In words, an equilibrium is strict if each player would achieve a strictly worse outcome by choosing a different strategy. In general, we say an equilibrium is pure if all strategies of that equilibrium are pure, and mixed otherwise.

Pure Equilibria. With those definitions, we note that the strict concavity of $U_i(x_i, y)$ in x_i has an important, direct consequence: every equilibrium of this game is a pure equilibrium. Let $x_i \sim \pi_i$ be any strategy that is not pure, while $y_i \sim \pi_{-i}$ is a random variable denoting the sums of the other players' strategies, then

$$\mathbf{E}_{\pi_i, \pi_{-i}}[U_i(x_i, y_i)] = \mathbf{E}_{\pi_{-i}}[\mathbf{E}_{\pi_i}[U_i(x_i, y_i)]] < \mathbf{E}_{\pi_{-i}}[U_i(\mathbf{E}_{\pi_i}[x_i], y_i)],$$

where the strict inequality is a result of strict concavity of $U_i(\cdot, y)$ for all y and the fact that π_i is not a point mass. In other words, if $x_i \sim \pi_i$ is a mixed strategy for player i, then this player is always strictly better off playing the pure strategy $\mathbf{E}_{\pi_i}[x_i]$ instead. For the remainder of this paper, we will assume that f is concave and satisfies condition (3), unless otherwise stated. Additionally we will only discuss pure equilibria for the remainder of the paper, as all equilibria must be pure, so talking about a strategy as as a specific action $x_i \in \mathbf{R}_+$ is reasonable.

Extensions. A simple immediate extension to the concave pro-rata game is to consider payoff functions of the form:

$$U_i(x) = \frac{c_i x_i}{c^T x} f\left(c^T x\right),$$

for some strictly positive vector $c \in \mathbf{R}_{++}^n$. A more general extension is when we have a collection of n strictly increasing functions $\varphi_i : \mathbf{R}_+ \to \mathbf{R}$, where $\varphi_i(0) = 0$ and $\varphi_i(t) \to \infty$ when $t \to \infty$ for $i = 1, \ldots, n$, and

$$U_i(x) = \left(\frac{\varphi_i(x_i)}{\sum_{i=1}^n \varphi_i(x_i)}\right) f\left(\sum_{i=1}^n \varphi_i(x_i)\right).$$

In either case, all of the same properties given above apply to this slightly more general game with nearly identical proofs, but we will only consider the (often useful) special case where $\varphi_i(t) = t$.

1.1   Symmetric Pure Strict Equilibrium

There is a strict, pure equilibrium where all players have equal strategies, given by $x = (q/n)\mathbf{1}$ where q is the optimizer of the following problem:

$$\begin{aligned}
\text{maximize} \quad & q^{n-1} f(q) \\
\text{subject to} \quad & q \geq 0,
\end{aligned} \tag{4}$$

with variable $q \in \mathbf{R}$. We will show some properties of this result first and then show that the pure strategy $x = (q/n)\mathbf{1}$ is, indeed, an equilibrium.

Solution Properties. This problem has a (unique) and finite solution $q > 0$ provided $f(z) > 0$ and $f(w) = 0$ for some $0 < z < w$. The fact that $q > 0$ follows by noting that q must satisfy $q^{n-1}f(q) \geq z^{n-1}f(z) > 0$ since it is optimal. On the other hand, the fact that q is finite follows from the fact that, for any $r \geq w$, we have

$$\frac{w}{r}f(r) + \left(1 - \frac{w}{r}\right)f(0) \leq f(w) = 0,$$

where the first inequality follows from the definition of concavity. Since, by assumption, $f(0) = 0$ and $w/r > 0$, we have that $f(r) \leq 0$ so r cannot be optimal. (In fact, both statements combined prove the stronger fact that $0 < q < w$, but this is not necessary for what follows.) The uniqueness of the solution to problem (4) follows from observing that the logarithm of the objective function is strictly concave. (This is true since log is strictly increasing and $\log \circ f$ is concave if f is concave.)

Discussion. It may appear that the condition placed on f is very strong, but in fact, any f not satisfying the above condition has only trivial (or no) equilibria. In particular, since f is concave, if f does not satisfy the above condition, either (a) f is strictly positive everywhere except at $f(0) = 0$, (b) f is strictly negative everywhere except at $f(0) = 0$, or (c) $f = 0$. In the first case, there is no equilibrium as any player can improve their payoff by increasing their strategy. In the second case, any player who plays a nonzero strategy receives negative payoff (whereas playing the zero strategy would give 0 payoff). While, in the third case, any strategy is an equilibrium.

Equilibrium Properties. The collection of strategies $x = (q/n)\mathbf{1}$ is clearly pure and symmetric. To see that $x = (q/n)\mathbf{1}$ is a strict equilibrium, note that the best response for any player i, when every other player plays strategy q/n is:

$$\text{maximize} \quad \frac{x_i}{x_i + (1 - 1/n)q}f(x_i + (1 - 1/n)q) \tag{5}$$
$$\text{subject to} \quad x_i \geq 0,$$

with variable $x_i \in \mathbf{R}$. We will show that the solution to (5) is $x_i = q/n$ in two steps. First, we will show that any solution must have $x_i > 0$ and therefore that the first order optimality conditions applied to the objective suffice. We will then show that $x_i = q/n$ is a solution to the optimality conditions. This result, combined with the fact that the objective is strictly concave, implies that $x_i = q/n$ is the unique solution to the optimality conditions, which proves the final claim that this equilibrium is strict.

To see that any solution to the best response problem (5) must have $x_i > 0$, note that q/n is feasible and achieves an objective value of $f(q)/n > 0$, which is strictly greater than the objective value of zero achieved by $x_i = 0$.

Next, note that $q > 0$ must satisfy the first order optimality conditions of (4):

$$(n-1)f(q) + qf'(q) = 0. \tag{6}$$

On the other hand, the first order optimality conditions for the objective of problem (5) are that x_i must satisfy (writing $q' = (1 - 1/n)q$ for convenience)

$$\frac{q'}{x_i + q'} f(x_i + q') + x_i f'(x_i + q') = 0.$$

Choosing $x_i = q/n$ clearly satisfies this condition, since plugging this value in gives

$$\left(1 - \frac{1}{n}\right) f(q) + \frac{q f'(q)}{n} = \frac{1}{n}((n-1)f(q) + q f'(q)) = 0,$$

as required. Since the objective is strictly concave, this is the unique x_i satisfying the optimality conditions and is therefore the best response. Additionally, while we have assumed that f is differentiable, a very similar proof using subgradient calculus gives an identical result.

1.2   Uniqueness of Equilibrium

In fact, it is not hard to show that the symmetric, pure, strict equilibrium is, surprisingly, the unique equilibrium for this game, under the same conditions as (4); *i.e.*, that $f(z) > 0$ and $f(w) = 0$ for some $0 < z < w$. This proof can be broken down into a few steps. First, we will show that any equilibrium x satisfies $f(\mathbf{1}^T x) > 0$ and $x_i > 0$ for each i. This will then be used to show that there is no non-symmetric equilibrium, and, since we know that any symmetric equilibrium must satisfy Eq. (4), which has a unique solution, we then know that it is the unique equilibrium of this game.

Positivity of Equilibria. First we will show that $f(v) > 0$ for every $0 < v < w$. To see this, note that the function f is bounded from below by all of its chords, as it is a concave function. Note that the chord with endpoints $(0,0)$ and $(z, f(z))$ lies above the x-axis, except at $(0,0)$, while the chord with endpoints $(z, f(z))$ and $(w, f(w)) = (w, 0)$ lies above the x-axis, except at $(w, 0)$, which leads to the final result.

Now, suppose a collection of (pure) strategies satisfies $f(\mathbf{1}^T x) < 0$. Since $f(0) = 0$, there is some index i such that $x_i > 0$. This implies that $U_i(x_i, \mathbf{1}^T x - x_i) < 0$. But then player i can achieve a payoff equal to 0 by employing the strategy $\tilde{x}_i = 0$, which is strictly better than a negative payoff, so x cannot be an equilibrium.

On the other hand, if a collection of strategies satisfies $f(\mathbf{1}^T x) = 0$, then, from the previous discussion, we must have either $\mathbf{1}^T x = 0$ or $\mathbf{1}^T x = w$. If $\mathbf{1}^T x = 0$, any player i can obtain a strictly positive payoff by playing the strategy $\tilde{x}_i = z$. If, instead, $\mathbf{1}^T x = w > 0$, there is some index i such that $x_i > 0$. We have that the player's payoff is $U_i(x_i, \mathbf{1}^T x - x_i) = 0$ which means that

$$U_i(x_i - \varepsilon, \mathbf{1}^T x - x_i) = \frac{x_i - \varepsilon}{\mathbf{1}^T x - \varepsilon} f(\mathbf{1}^T x - \varepsilon) > 0,$$

for $\varepsilon > 0$ small enough since $f(w - \varepsilon) > 0$, so x is not an equilibrium.

Putting all of these statements together means that any equilibrium x satisfies $f(\mathbf{1}^T x) > 0$ and $\mathbf{1}^T x < w$. To see that any equilibrium must also satisfy $x > 0$, note that if there exists an index i with $x_i = 0$ for a collection of strategies with $f(\mathbf{1}^T x) > 0$, player i can always achieve a strictly positive payoff by playing $\tilde{x}_i = \varepsilon > 0$, for ε small enough.

Symmetry of Equilibria. Next, we will show that if x_i is a best response for player i, then any j for which $x_j > x_i$ is not a best response for player j, and vice versa. This will immediately show that any equilibrium must satisfy $x_i = x_j$ (*i.e.*, it is symmetric). We will show this in the case that f is differentiable, but a similar proof holds in the more general case, using subgradient calculus.

Let x be an equilibrium with $x_j > x_i$. Given that x_i is a best response, then the optimality conditions for (5) imply that:

$$\left(\frac{\mathbf{1}^T x - x_i}{(\mathbf{1}^T x)^2}\right) f(\mathbf{1}^T x) + \frac{x_i}{\mathbf{1}^T x} f'(\mathbf{1}^T x) = 0.$$

Since x is an equilibrium, from the previous discussion, we have that $f(\mathbf{1}^T x) > 0$, $x_i > 0$, and $\mathbf{1}^T x > x_i$, so $f'(\mathbf{1}^T x) < 0$. On the other hand, differentiating the objective of the best response problem (5) for player j gives

$$\left(\frac{\mathbf{1}^T x - x_j}{(\mathbf{1}^T x)^2}\right) f(\mathbf{1}^T x) + \frac{x_j}{\mathbf{1}^T x} f'(\mathbf{1}^T x) < \left(\frac{\mathbf{1}^T x - x_i}{(\mathbf{1}^T x)^2}\right) f(\mathbf{1}^T x) + \frac{x_i}{\mathbf{1}^T x} f'(\mathbf{1}^T x) = 0,$$

where the inequality follows from the fact that, since $x_i < x_j$ we have

$$\frac{\mathbf{1}^T x - x_j}{(\mathbf{1}^T x)^2} < \frac{\mathbf{1}^T x - x_i}{(\mathbf{1}^T x)^2} \quad \text{and} \quad \frac{x_j}{\mathbf{1}^T x} > \frac{x_i}{\mathbf{1}^T x},$$

so x_j cannot be a best response as it is not optimal for (5). The converse case, when $x_j < x_i$ with x_i being a best response, follows from a nearly identical proof. This immediately implies that any equilibrium must be symmetric, so, from the preceding discussion, the unique equilibrium is the one given by the solution to problem (4).

1.3 Equilibrium Payoff

Conditioned on each player receiving the same payoff (a fairness condition), the optimal allocation every player would get is

$$\frac{1}{n} \sup f,$$

which is, by definition, at least as good as the equilibrium payoff:

$$\frac{1}{n} f(q),$$

where $q > 0$ is the solution to (4). In fact, we can show that the optimal fair allocation is always strictly better than the equilibrium payoff. To see this, note that, under the assumptions on f introduced above, we know $\sup f$ is achieved by some value $0 < q^* < w$, satisfying $f'(q^*) = 0$. Rearranging the first order optimality condition for q in problem (4) gives

$$f'(q) = -(n-1)\frac{f(q)}{q} < 0,$$

for all $n > 1$ since $f(q) > 0$. This means that q does not satisfy the optimality condition for maximizing f, so $f(q) < f(q^*) = \sup f$. (In fact, this says slightly more: using the concavity of f, we have that $q > q^*$, i.e., that players 'overpay' at equilibria when $n > 1$.)

Price of Anarchy. Given the same assumptions as the beginning of Sect. 1.2 on the function f, it is not difficult to show that the price of anarchy satisfies

$$\frac{\sup f}{f(q)} \geq \Omega(n)$$

as the number of players n becomes large for some constant C. To see this, consider the first order optimality conditions for y (4):

$$(n-1)f(q) + qf'(q) = 0.$$

Note that $f'(q) < 0$ since $q > 0$ and $f(q) > 0$, so

$$f(q) = -\frac{qf'(q)}{n-1} > 0,$$

whenever $n > 1$. Since f is concave, then f' is monotonically nonincreasing, and, since $q \leq w$ for every n we have that

$$f(q) = -\frac{qf'(q)}{n-1} \leq -\frac{wf'(w)}{n-1} \leq O\left(\frac{1}{n}\right).$$

Finally, we know that $\sup f$ is constant in the number of players, so

$$\frac{\sup f}{f(q)} \geq \Omega(n).$$

2   Batched Decentralized Exchanges

In this section, we will show some basic applications of the above properties to a batched decentralized exchange, which we describe below.

Decentralized Exchanges. A *decentralized exchange* (or DEX, for short) is a type of exchange that exists on a blockchain. Such exchanges enable any agent to trade currencies without the need for a centralized intermediary. In many cases, these exchanges are organized as constant function market makers (see, e.g., [1] for a general introduction to this type of exchange), a special type of automated market maker that uses a specific function to price assets.

Batched DEXs. A *batched* decentralized exchange is a DEX where the trades are batched before they are executed. Specifically, the trades are aggregated in some way (depending on the type of batching performed) and then traded 'all together' through the DEX, before being disaggregated and passed back to the users. Though the idea of a batched exchange has been proposed many times in different contexts (see, *e.g.*, [4] and [13]), presently, almost all major decentralized exchanges are not batched. Recent work has suggested that batching is useful for privacy [5] and Penumbra [9] has proposed a design for a fully-private decentralized exchange which makes use of batching as a method for avoiding certain information leakage [2]. We describe a very simplified version of this proposal below, which will suffice for our discussion.

Batching Design. In this scenario, we have traders $i = 1, \ldots, n$ who all wish to trade some amount, say $\Delta_i \in \mathbf{R}$ of asset A for some other asset, which we will call asset B. In this case, negative values of Δ_i denote that trader i wishes to receive some amount of asset A (and will instead tender asset B to the protocol). For convenience, we will assume that $\mathbf{1}^T \Delta > 0$, *i.e.*, on net, traders want more of asset B than asset A. The batching protocol of penumbra first clears all trades to get a nonnegative vector of 'residual' trades $\Delta' \in \mathbf{R}_+^n$ with $\mathbf{1}^T \Delta = \mathbf{1}^T \Delta'$. (In other words, the protocol does not generate debts in any one side.) We can view Δ' as the 'excess demand' for asset B over A and leave the mechanism for constructing Δ' otherwise unspecified, requiring only the additional condition that, if $\Delta \geq 0$, then $\Delta' = \Delta$. (This condition can be roughly stated as: if the only trades are due to excess demand, then no clearing happens.) The protocol then pools the residual demand, $\mathbf{1}^T \Delta'$ and trades it against a constant function market maker, represented by some function g, to receive $g(\mathbf{1}^T \Delta')$ of asset B, which it then distributes to each agent i in a pro-rata way, leading to an identical form to that of the pro-rata payoff (1) with $x = \Delta'$. Constant function market makers always have concave g, known sometimes as the *forward exchange function* (*cf.*, [1, Sect. 4]), with $g(0) = 0$, and, in many practical cases, these functions are strictly concave.

2.1   Arbitrage

A common way of analyzing markets is through the lens of *arbitrage*: the ability to exploit price differences in order to make essentially risk-free profit. From before, we will write g for the forward exchange function of a constant function market maker, used by the batching design presented above.

Existence. Assuming g is differentiable at 0, we can interpret $g'(0)$ as the marginal amount of asset B that one would receive for a marginal amount of A. (The function g is often not differentiable at 0, but is one-sided differentiable at 0^+, which suffices.) If $g'(0)$ is larger than the price of an external market, say $c > 0$, then anyone who can directly trade with g can make risk-free profit by trading some (potentially small) amount, $t > 0$ of asset A for $g(t)$ of asset B, and then sell this amount of asset B to get $g(t)/c - t > 0$ of profit. (One simple way to see this is true is to use the definition of a derivative on $g(t)/c$ and send $t \downarrow 0$.)

Optimal Arbitrage. Since an agent can make risk-free profit in these cases, it is reasonable to ask: what is the maximum amount of profit an agent can make with this strategy? This is known as the *optimal arbitrage problem*, written:

$$\text{maximize} \quad g(t) - ct$$
$$\text{subject to} \quad t \geq 0,$$

with variable $t \in \mathbf{R}$. From before, if we know that $g'(0) > c$, then this problem has an optimal value that is strictly positive. If g is differentiable, the optimal solution t^* satisfies

$$g'(t^*) = c,$$

which we can see from the first-order optimality conditions for this problem. This has the interpretation that the marginal price of the CFMM after the trade t^*, given by $g'(t^*)$ should be equal to the price of the external market, which we defined to be c.

The (Aaggregated) Arbitrage Game. In the batched exchange above, arbitrageurs cannot directly trade with the constant function market maker, but must instead go through the batching process. Assuming there are n arbitrageurs competing to maximize their profit, the next question is: what are the properties of this game? Defining

$$f(t) = g(t) - ct,$$

then this game is a concave pro-rata game with function f, since the payoff (1) for player i is

$$U_i(x_i, y_i) = \frac{x_i}{x_i + y_i} f(x_i + y_i) = \frac{x_i}{x_i + y_i} g(x_i + y_i) - cx_i.$$

Note that this is exactly the amount received from the DEX with forward exchange function g, minus the cost of trading x_i with the external market, for player i. This game inherits all of the properties derived in Sect. 1. We show some numerical simulations of iterated behavior for some utility functions of this form in Appendices A and B.

3   Conclusion

We introduced concave pro-rata games and established several useful properties under relatively mild conditions. In particular, we showed the existence of a unique equilibrium that is symmetric and pure. This equilibrium can be computed efficiently by solving a single variable, unimodal optimization problem. We further established that the price of anarchy is $\Omega(n)$ in the number of players, relative to the optimal 'fair' allocation. We illustrated how concave pro-rata games connect to a recent proposal for a batched decentralized exchange and numerically studied the behavior of agents engaged in such a game in the iterated setting for a specific form of utility function. Future work includes further study of the optimal arbitrage problem for batched decentralized exchanges.

A   Numerics

The results of Sect. 1 provide insight into the equilibrium behavior of concave pro-rata games. Here we explore the transient behavior of such games through simulation.

Game Setup. Suppose that the game is played iteratively, and, at each iteration t, player i chooses some action x_i^t as the best response to the actions chosen by the other players in the previous round (denoted as x_{-i}^{t-1}), possibly subject to additional constraints. We consider the following scenarios:

1. At iteration t, player i takes action equal to the best response to x_{-i}^{t-1}.
2. At iteration t, player i takes action equal to the best response to x_{-i}^{t-1} subject to a budget constraint ($x_i^t \in [0, M_i]$).

Payoff Functions. For these simulations, we use functions f of the form $f(t) = g(t) - ct$ where $c > 0$ and $g(t) = \frac{\gamma R_2 t}{R_1 + \gamma t}$ with $0 < \gamma \leq 1$, $R_1, R_2 > 0$. The function $g(t)$ is the forward exchange function for a Uniswap V2 swap pool with reserves $R \in \mathbf{R}_+^2$ and fee parameter γ when asset 1 is being tendered and asset 2 is being received. This setting simulates n arbitrageurs competing to maximize their profit, where c denotes the external market price of asset 2. For simulations using a somewhat more simple payoff function, see Appendix B. Note that f is strictly concave and therefore satisfies condition (3), and clearly $f(0) = 0$.

Shared Equilibrium. The (unique) symmetric pure equilibrium strategy is the solution to problem (4). This is easy to compute using the first order optimality conditions for problem (4) given in (6). Plugging in this particular form of f, we obtain the following quadratic equation:

$$(cn\gamma^2)q^2 + q(\gamma^2 R_2 + 2cnR_1\gamma - \gamma^2 nR_2) + (cnR_1^2 - \gamma nR_1 R_2) = 0. \quad (7)$$

The equilibrium is then given by $x_i = q/n$, for each player $i = 1, \ldots, n$ where q denotes the positive root of (7).

Best Responses. The best response of player i, given the budget constraint $0 \leq x_i \leq M_i$ and other players' strategies $y_i = \mathbf{1}^T x - x_i$, is given by

$$\begin{aligned}
\text{maximize} \quad & U(x_i, y_i) \\
\text{subject to} \quad & x_i \in [0, M_i],
\end{aligned} \quad (8)$$

with variable $x_i \in \mathbf{R}$. This is a single-variable convex optimization problem that is easily solved in practice by any number of off-the-shelf packages [7,8]. When x_i is unconstrained, the optimal value of (8) is given by

$$x_i = \frac{1}{\gamma}\left(\sqrt{\frac{\gamma R_1 R_2 + \gamma^2 R_2 y}{c}} - R_1\right) - y$$

For more details, the code is available at (anonymized for review).

Simulation Results. In our simulations, we fix $\gamma = 0.99$, $R_1 = 200$, $R_2 = 250$, and $c = 1$. We average each reported value over 100 trials. In Fig. 1, the intial strategy of each player is drawn uniformly at random from the interval $(0, w/n)$, where w is a value such that $f(w) = 0$.

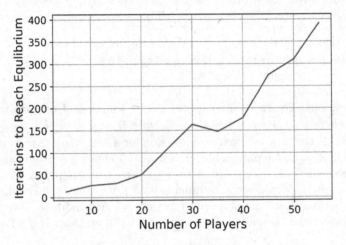

Fig. 1. Number of iterations to reach equilibrium versus the number of players in Scenario 1.

Figure 1 illustrates that the number of iterations needed to reach the unique equilibrium, in the absence of budget constraints, scales superlinearly in the number of players. We define the number of iterations to reach equilibrium as the number iterations until the strategy of every player is equal to the unique equilibrium up to the first decimal place; *i.e.*, the first round t such that

$$\max_i |x_i^t - x^*| < 0.1,$$

where x^* denotes the equilibrium strategy.

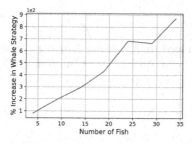
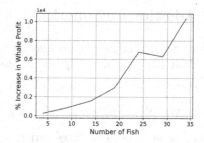

Fig. 2. Percent increase in whale strategy and whale profit versus the number of fish when compared to the unconstrained equilibrium strategy and profit.

In Fig. 2, we consider the setting where there is one player who has unlimited budget (whom we will call a *whale*) and all remaining players have some budget $M_i < q/n$ (these players are referred to as *fish*). The budgets of the fish are drawn uniformly from the interval $M_i \sim [0, q/n]$ and the initial strategy of each fish is drawn uniformly at random from the interval $[0, M_i]$. The equilibrium strategy chosen by the fish is to use their entire budget, while the whale chooses a strategy in excess of the unconstrained equilibrium strategy and is, as a result, able to extract greater profit. Figure 2 illustrates that the whale chooses an increasingly large strategy and receives an increasing profit as the number of fish increases.

Price of Anarchy. In Sect. 1 we established the order of growth of the price of anarchy. Here we illustrate the price of anarchy numerically for the specific family of payoff functions introduced previously in this section. We again fix $\gamma = 0.99, R_1 = 200, R_2 = 250$ and $c = 1$. The left plot of Fig. 3 illustrates the optimal payoff function and the equilibrium payoff function as a function of the number of players n while the right plot of Fig. 3 illustrates the price of anarchy as function of n.

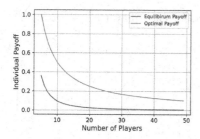
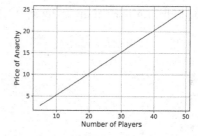

Fig. 3. (Left) Individual payoff of a player versus the number of players. (Right) Ratio of the optimal payoff divided by the equilibrium payoff versus the number of players.

B   Additional Numerics

Here we expand on the simulations introduced in Appendix A using a class of utility function that allows us to express many quantities of interest in closed form.

Game Setup. We consider the following three scenarios:

1. At iteration t, player i takes action equal to the best response to x_{-i}^{t-1}.
2. At iteration t, player i takes action equal to the best response to x_{-i}^{t-1} subject to a bounded update constraint $(|x_i^t - x_i^{t-1}| \le \delta)$.
3. At iteration t, player i takes action equal to the best response to x_{-i}^{t-1} subject to a budget constraint $(x_i^t \in [0, M_i])$.

Payoff Functions. For these simulations, we use functions f of the form $f(t) = t^\beta - \gamma t$ where $0 < \beta < 1$ and $\gamma > 0$. Note that f is concave as it is the sum of two concave functions and $f(0) = 0$. These functions also satisfy the strict concavity property (3) since

$$f(\alpha t) = \alpha^\beta t^\beta - \alpha \gamma t > \alpha t^\beta - \alpha \gamma t = \alpha f(t),$$

for $0 < \alpha < 1$.

Shared Equilibrium. The (unique) symmetric pure equilibrium strategy is the solution to problem (4). This is easy to compute using the first order optimality conditions for problem (4) given in (6). Plugging in this particular form of f, we have:

$$(n-1)(q^\beta - \gamma q) + q(\beta q^{\beta-1} - \gamma) = 0,$$

which has a solution

$$q = \left(\frac{\beta + n - 1}{n\gamma} \right)^{1/(1-\beta)}.$$

The equilibrium is then given by $x_i = q/n$, for each player $i = 1, \ldots, n$.

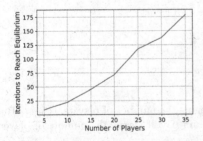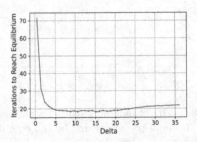

Fig. 4. (Left) Number of iterations to reach equilibrium versus the number of players in Scenario 1. (Right) Number of iterations to reach equilibrium versus δ in Scenario 2 (with $n = 10$ players).

Simulation Results. In our simulations, we fix $\beta = 0.5$ and $\gamma = 0.05$. We average each reported value over 100 trials. In Fig. 4, the intial strategy of each player is drawn uniformly at random from the interval $(0, w/n)$, where w is a value such that $f(w) = 0$.

The left plot of Fig. 4 illustrates that the number of iterations needed to reach the unique equilibrium, in the absence of budget constraints, scales superlinearly in the number of players. The right plot demonstrates that in the scenario of bounded strategy updates, for small values of δ, the number of iterations required to reach equilibrium increases significantly when compared to the unbounded strategy update scenario.

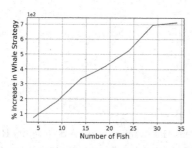 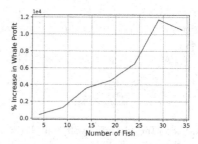

Fig. 5. Percent increase in whale strategy and whale profit versus the number of fish when compared to the unconstrained equilibrium strategy and profit.

In Fig. 5, we consider the setting where there is one player who has unlimited budget (whom we will call a *whale*) and all remaining players have some budget $M_i < q/n$ (these players are referred to as *fish*). The budgets of the fish are drawn uniformly from the interval $M_i \sim [0, q/n]$ and the initial strategy of each fish is drawn uniformly at random from the interval $[0, M_i]$. The equilibrium strategy chosen by the fish is to use their entire budget, while the whale chooses a strategy in excess of the unconstrained equilibrium strategy and is, as a result, able to extract greater profit. Figure 5 illustrates that the whale chooses an increasingly large strategy and receives an increasing profit as the number of fish increases.

Price of Anarchy. The equilibrium payoff can easibly be found to be

$$\frac{1}{n}f(q) = \left(\frac{n + \beta - 1}{\gamma n}\right)^{\beta/(1-\beta)}\left(\frac{1 - \beta}{n^2}\right).$$

Similarly, it can be show that the optimal payoff conditioned on every agent receiving the same payoff is given by

$$\frac{1}{n}\sup f = \left(\frac{\beta}{\gamma}\right)^{\beta/(1-\beta)}\left(\frac{1 - \beta}{n}\right).$$

We obtain the price of anarchy by taking the ratio of the equilibrium payoff and the optimal payoff:

$$\frac{\sup f}{f(q)} = n \left(\frac{\beta n}{n + \beta - 1} \right)^{\beta/(1-\beta)}.$$

We again fix $\beta = 0.5$ and $\gamma = 0.05$. The left plot of Fig. 6 illustrates the optimal payoff function and the equlibrium payoff function as a function of the number of players n while the right plot of Fig. 6 illustrates the price of anarchy as function of n.

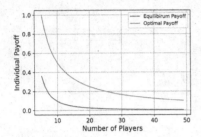 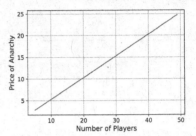

Fig. 6. (Left) Individual payoff of a player versus the number of players. (Right) Ratio of the optimal payoff divided by the equilibrium payoff versus the number of players.

C   Relaxing Strict Concavity

We do not, in fact, need strict concavity in the proofs above. Instead, we only need that f has 'some curvature' at 0. Specifically, it suffices that for all t and t' such that $0 < t < t'$, we have

$$f(t) > \frac{f(t')}{t'} t.$$

Written in English, this is the condition that the chord from 0 to t always lies strictly below the function. This condition is sometimes difficult to confirm for general functions f, so we will show that this is equivalent to the (potentially simpler-to-handle) property that all supergradients at 0 lie strictly above the function at all points. We will show that, for any concave function $f : \mathbf{R}_+ \to \mathbf{R}$ with $f(0) = 0$, the following two statements are equivalent: (a) there is some $s' > 0$ and $\alpha \in \mathbf{R}$ such that for every s with $0 \leq s \leq s'$ we have

$$f(s) = \alpha s,$$

and (b) there exists some $0 < t < t'$ such that

$$\frac{f(t)}{t} = \frac{f(t')}{t'}. \tag{9}$$

The statement above follows from the negation of both (a) and (b). This equivalence has a simple interpretation: if the point $(0,0)$ is collinear with any other two points on the graph of f, $\{(s, f(s)) \mid s > 0\}$, then the function f is a piecewise function with a linear segment starting at 0. The converse of this is that if the function f has no linear segment around 0 (*i.e.*, every linear overestimator around 0 lies strictly above f) then any chord must lie strictly below the function.

Proof. The forward implication is very easy: pick $t' = s'$ and let t be any $0 < t < s'$, then we have

$$\frac{f(t')}{t'} = \alpha = \frac{f(t)}{t}.$$

Now we'll consider the reverse implication. Given $0 < t < t'$ satisfying (9), we will show that, for any $0 \le s \le t$ we have

$$f(s) = \frac{f(t)}{t}s,$$

which satisfies the original claim with $\alpha = f(t)/t$. First, it is easy to show that

$$f(s) \ge \frac{f(t)}{t}s, \tag{10}$$

since

$$f(s) = f\left(\frac{s}{t}t + \left(1 - \frac{s}{t}\right)0\right) \ge \frac{s}{t}f(t),$$

where the inequality follows from the concavity of f and the fact that $f(0) = 0$. We will now show that any function f satisfying (10) strictly, *i.e.*,

$$f(s) > \frac{f(t)}{t}s, \tag{11}$$

for some $0 < s < t$ cannot be concave. The result follows from the contrapositive. To see this, let $0 < \gamma \le 1$ such that $t = \gamma s + (1 - \gamma)t'$, then

$$\gamma f(s) + (1 - \gamma)f(t') > \gamma\frac{f(t)}{t}s + (1 - \gamma)\frac{f(t)}{t}t' = f(t) = f(\gamma s + (1 - \gamma)t'),$$

so f cannot be concave. The inequality follows directly from conditions (9) and (11), and both the first and second equalities follow from the definition of γ.

D   Rosen Condition

Pro-rata games, even concave ones, do not satisfy the Rosen condition [10] for the uniqueness of equilibria in concave games. The Rosen condition for uniqueness is that if, there exists some $z \ge 0$ with $z \ne 0$ such that

$$\Phi(x) = \begin{bmatrix} z_1 \partial_1 U_1(x) \\ \vdots \\ z_n \partial_n U_n(x) \end{bmatrix}$$

is a strictly monotone operator; *i.e.*, for any $x \neq y$ we have

$$(y - x)^T (\Phi(y) - \Phi(x)) > 0,$$

then there is a unique equilibrium that is also pure. (Here, ∂_i denotes the ith partial derivative.) This is a common condition used to prove the uniqueness of pure equilibria in games. We will show that this condition does not hold in general for concave pro-rata games, even under most 'niceness' assumptions such as strict concavity or even strong concavity and differentiability.

Setting $2x = y = 1$ then the condition can be written as (using the definition of U)

$$(\mathbf{1}^T z/2)((1/n)(f'(n) - f'(n/2)) + (1 - 1/n)(f(n) - 2f(n/2))) > 0,$$

but this can be rewritten (since $\mathbf{1}^T z > 0$)

$$(1/n)(f'(n) - f'(n/2)) + (1 - 1/n)(f(n) - 2f(n/2)) > 0,$$

which is clearly not true for all concave functions f, since picking $f(t) = \min\{t, 3n\}$ suffices. (A mollifying argument would show that this also gives a reasonable counterexample even in the case that f is strictly concave and differentiable.) A more direct counterexample that is differentiable and strictly concave is $f(t) = (4n)^2 - (4n - t)^2$, which is slightly more difficult to verify.

References

1. Angeris, G., Agrawal, A., Evans, A., Chitra, T., Boyd, S.: Constant function market makers: multi-asset trades via convex optimization. In: Tran, D.A., Thai, M.T., Krishnamachari, B. (eds.) Handbook on Blockchain. Springer Optimization and Its Applications, vol. 194, pp. 415–444. Springer, Cham (2022). https://doi.org/10.1007/978-3-031-07535-3_13
2. Angeris, G., Evans, A., Chitra, T.: A note on privacy in constant function market makers (2021)
3. Boyd, S.P., Vandenberghe, L.: Convex Optimization. Cambridge University Press, New York (2004)
4. Budish, E., Cramton, P., Shim, J.: The high-frequency trading arms race: frequent batch auctions as a market design response. Q. J. Econ. **130**(4), 1547–1621 (2015). https://doi.org/10.1093/qje/qjv027
5. Chitra, T., Angeris, G., Evans, A.: Differential privacy in constant function market makers. In: Eyal, I., Garay, J. (eds.) FC 2022. LNCS, vol. 13411, pp. 149–178. Springer, Cham (2022). https://doi.org/10.1007/978-3-031-18283-9_8
6. Daian, P., et al.: Flash boys 2.0: frontrunning in decentralized exchanges, miner extractable value, and consensus instability. In: 2020 IEEE Symposium on Security and Privacy (SP), pp. 910–927 (2020). https://doi.org/10.1109/SP40000.2020.00040
7. Diamond, S., Boyd, S.: CVXPY: a Python-embedded modeling language for convex optimization. J. Mach. Learn. Res. **17**(83), 1–5 (2016)

8. O'Donoghue, B., Chu, E., Parikh, N., Boyd, S.: Conic optimization via operator splitting and homogeneous self-dual embedding. J. Optim. Theory Appl. **169**(3), 1042–1068 (2016). https://stanford.edu/~boyd/papers/scs.html
9. Penumbra Labs: ZSwap - The Penumbra Protocol. https://protocol.penumbra.zone/main/zswap.html
10. Rosen, J.B.: Existence and uniqueness of equilibrium points for concave N-person games. Econometrica **33**(3), 520 (1965). https://doi.org/10.2307/1911749
11. Selten, R.: Preispolitik der Mehrproduktenunternehmung in der statischen Theorie (1970)
12. Von Neumann, J., Morgenstern, O.: Theory of games and economic behavior. In: Theory of Games and Economic Behavior. Princeton University Press (2007)
13. Walther, T.: Multi-token batch auctions with uniform clearing prices (2018)

Electronic Cash with Open-Source Observers

Taishi Higuchi[1,2](✉) and Akira Otsuka[1]

[1] Institute of Information Security, Yokohama, Japan
{higuchi,otsuka}@ai.iisec.ac.jp
[2] Sakura Information Systems Co., Ltd., Minato-Ku, Japan
ta-higuchi@sakura-is.co.jp

Abstract. Electronic cash (e-cash) systems need to satisfy the property of anonymity, unforgeability, and transparency which prevent criminal activities from abuse of anonymity. Observers proposed by Chaum et al. and Brands in the '90 s are one of the cleverest solutions, where observers deployed by the authorities to the user's device only engage in legitimate anonymous payments, but never cooperate with illegal activities. In other words, observers enforce payers' legitimate behavior while the cryptographic protocols ensure the observers do not obtain private information about individual payments. However, ever-proposed observers only prevent double-spending as legitimate behavior. There had been no contributions to extend the role of observers from only double-spend prevention to general transparency enforcement required by society without sacrificing privacy. In this paper, we propose a novel concept of open-source observers which can potentially achieve both cryptographic anonymity and highly flexible transparency at the same time. In our setting, observers are published in the cloud as open-source programs and executed within a tamper-proof device with an anonymous attested execution capability, in which all outputs of the execution, with the hash value of the executed open-source program, are signed by the secure processor as formulated by Pass et al. recently. The contribution of this paper is two-fold: (1) we first defined the concept of the open-source observers and (2) we showed a construction of Brands' type provably-secure offline electronic cash scheme with observers extending the scheme by Baldimtsi and Lysyanskaya.

Keywords: Electronic Cash · Central Bank Digital Currency · Anonymity · One-more Unforgeability · Distrust dispelling · Attested Execution Secure Processors

1 Introduction

Ideal electronic cash (e-cash) systems, especially for Central Bank Digital Currency (CBDC), need to satisfy the property of anonymity, unforgeability, and transparency which prevent criminal activities from abuse of anonymity. The first anonymous electronic cash scheme was proposed by David Chaum [6,7] based on

A. Essex et al. (Eds.): FC 2023 Workshops, LNCS 13953, pp. 286–302, 2024.
https://doi.org/10.1007/978-3-031-48806-1_19

the RSA blind signature. After that, various improvements, such as introducing the notion of untraceable payments with accountability and enhancing efficiency and security, have been proposed [8,9,11,12,14]. In order to protect a user's privacy cryptographically while at the same time preventing illegal payments such as double-spending, the concept of wallets with *observers* [4,10] was invented. A wallet with observers is a combination of two device modules: One (for observers) is a tamper-proof processing unit that operates on behalf of banks and authorities. The other (for user wallets) is an arbitrary processor under the control of users. This line of research is very important to meet society's requirements for an adequate balance of anonymity and transparency.

1.1 Previous Works and Challenges

The restrictive blind signature scheme proposed by Brands [3], where the user identity is elegantly coded based on the representation problem, implements observers quite efficiently. However, the property of (one-more) unforgeability in the blind signature scheme was not proved. Baldimtsi and Lysyanskaya [1, 2] proposed a provably secure restrictive blind signature scheme, the modified Brands' one, and proved the unforgeability in the same way that Pointcheval and Stern proposed and gave the proof to the provably secure Schnorr blind signature [16]. However, their proposal does not show how to construct provably secure observers. Moreover, the ever-proposed observers only prevent double-spending as legitimate behavior and the concrete construction of observers has not been proposed.

1.2 Our Contribution

This paper contributes on the following points:

1. We first show the construction of observers over the brands' type e-cash scheme proposed by Baldimtsi and Lysyanskaya [1,2].
2. We introduce the novel concept of "open-source observers" which makes the behavior of tamper-proof devices transparent, thus it can dispel the distrust against the authorities.
3. We introduce the notion and construction of Blind Indirect Attestation as the main primitive to achieve Open-cash, an e-cash scheme with open-source observers, assuming the existence of Attested Execution Secure Processors (AESPs) [15] and the standard assumptions such as discrete logarithm problems and random oracles.
4. Our construction is efficient and almost feasible, as even modern smartphones equip with programmable secure processors.

This paper consists of the following sections: In Sect. 2, we introduce AESPs and the novel concept of Indirect Blind Attestation. We also give security notions for an e-cash scheme. In Sect. 3, we construct our Open-cash protocols concretely. In Sect. 4, the statements for the security properties of Open-cash are proposed. In Sect. 5, the conclusion of this paper is shown.

Note that the mathematical details for the protocols and the security proofs are given in Appendix A–C.

2   Preliminaries

In this section, we give several security notions and introduce AESPs. We also propose the novel concept of Blind Indirect Attestation (BIA). Note that the mathematical details for BIA are written in Appendix A.

2.1   Security Notions

We define the *secure blind signature* as digital signatures which satisfy two properties - *blindness* and *one-more unforgeability*. The secure e-cash scheme with anonymity and one-more unforgeability can be constructed based on the secure blind signature.

Blindness. The blindness ensures that a signer can sign messages without knowing them. So a malicious signer in the blind signature scheme cannot link an $(m, \sigma(m))$ pair to any particular execution of the protocol. In e-cash protocols, this blindness can separate the link between coins withdrawn and spent. The property guarantees protection for user privacy.

One-More Unforgeability. *Unforgeability* means that a correctly withdrawn coin is used only once, in other words, a coin can not be double-spent.

A user interacting with a signer S cannot output an additional, valid message/signature pair $(m, \sigma(m))$ no matter how many pairs of messages/ signatures of S he has seen (protection for the signer).

Definition 1 (Secure Blind Signature Scheme). *A blind signature scheme is secure if the two properties of Blindness and One-more unforgeability are satisfied.*

2.2   Attested Execution Secure Processors

Attested Execution Secure Processor [15] (AESP) is a formal abstraction of modern trusted hardware. As shown in Fig. 1 they defined the ideal functionality of AESP as $\mathcal{G}_{att}$ which can install any program prog inside $\mathcal{G}_{att}$, acts like a modern secure element, when receiving a message "install". It executes the installed program when receiving a message "resume". By calling resume, the program is called with the input inp, is run securely in the enclave and then outputs outp with an attestation $\sigma := \Sigma.\mathsf{Sign}_{\mathsf{sk}}(idx, eid, \mathsf{prog}, \mathsf{outp})$ with the signing key sk of $\mathcal{G}_{att}$. The attestation σ signed with a hardware key guarantees the result of calculations run there. In our Open-cash scheme, users will install an open-source observer program from the cloud in their AESPs. The observer program outputs

$\mathcal{G}_{att}[\Sigma, \text{reg}]$

// initialization:

On initialize:

   $(\text{mpk,msk}) := \Sigma.\text{KeyGen}(1^\lambda), \; T = \emptyset$

// public query interface:

On receive: getpk() from some $\mathcal{P}$

   send mpk to $\mathcal{P}$

Enclave operations

On receive: install(idx, prog) from some $\mathcal{P} \in \text{reg}$:

   if $\mathcal{P}$ is honest, assert $idx = sid$

   $eid \in \{0,1\}^\lambda$

   $T[eid, \mathcal{P}] := (idx, \text{prog}, \mathbf{0})$

   send eid to $\mathcal{P}$

On receive: resume(eid, inp) from some $\mathcal{P} \in \text{reg}$:

   let $(idx, \text{prog}, \text{mem}) := T[eid, \mathcal{P}]$

      abort if $(eid, \mathcal{P}) \notin T$

   let $(\text{outp}, \text{mem}) := \text{prog}(\text{inp}, \text{mem})$

   let $T[eid, \mathcal{P}] := (idx, \text{prog}, \text{mem})$

   $\sigma := \Sigma.\text{Sign}_{sk}(idx, eid, \text{prog}, \text{outp})$

   send (outp, σ) to $\mathcal{P}$

Fig. 1. Attested Execution Secure Processors (AESP)

the results with its attestation σ_{ATT} to prove that the Open-cash protocols, proposed in Sect. 3, were executed correctly. In our scheme, the attestation is verified indirectly using the Blind Indirect Attestation introduced in the next Subsect. 2.3, in order to keep users' private information secret.

2.3 Blind Indirect Attestation

In this subsection, we introduce a novel notion of *Blind Indirect Attestation (BIA)*, which is a variant of Direct Anonymous Attestation [5]. This can turn the direct attestation by AESP into the indirect one with blindness. In order to ensure that any open-source observer programs $Prog_{\mathcal{O}}$ (introduced in Sect. 3) correctly manage the anonymous payments, BIA enables the bank to certify indirectly that there exists an injective map to the withdrawal view from the deposit view. The bank checks that the white-listed open-source program $Prog_O$ is correctly installed in the withdrawer's AESP, thus every coin can be payable only once because $Prog_O$ maintains the payment status of each coin. On the deposit protocol, the bank confirms that the coin is acceptable by verifying the Proof of Knowledge for satisfying the witness relation, thus any valid deposit of coins at the bank is ensured to be controlled by at least one of the set of $Prog_O$.

Even if the indirect attestation is blinded its attestation ability keeps the same as the original σ_{ATT} as long as the signature is a correct (not forged) one. The blind signature enables the attestation to be executed anonymously. This feature consistently enhances the security of our Open-cash scheme we construct in the next section.

The formal definitions, theories, and proofs are written in Appendix A.

3   Construction

In this section, we propose Open-cash protocols. The detailed protocols and their sequential diagrams are shown in Appendix B.

3.1   Overview

Our Open-cash is constructed over the Brands' type blind signature scheme by Baldimtsi and Lysyanskaya [1,2]. We expand the scheme by introducing observers into it and construct Open-cash protocols to achieve a secure open-source e-cash system, where the observer is an open-source program installed in AESP. Over the Open-cash protocols proposed in Sect. 3.2, Indirect Attestation and Blind Indirect Attestation defined in Sect. 2.3 and Appendix A used to ensure our scheme to be secure.

3.2   Open-Cash Protocols

Our Open-cash consists of the following protocols - *Setup*, *Opening*, *Withdrawal*, *Spend*, and *Deposit*.

1. **Setup system:**
   Setup is executed only once. A bank picks up parameters to create a public key used in all of the Open-cash protocols.
2. **Opening protocol:**
   When a user wants to open an account in the Open-cash system he firstly executes the opening protocol (shown in Fig. 3) interacting with a bank. He should install the open-source observer program in his device distributed by the bank in advance. He and his observer pick secret parameters individually to generate a public key that serves as his account and sends it to the bank.
3. **Withdrawal protocol:**
   In the withdrawal protocol (shown in Fig. 4), a user, the user's observer and a bank are going to run a blind signature under the shared public key so

that the user can withdraw one coin signed by the bank. In this protocol, the observer picks up a random parameter as a secret key for the withdrawn coin and keeps it in its secure storage to prevent the user from double-spending the coin.

4. **Spend protocol:**
   In the spend protocol (shown in Fig. 5), a user can spend his withdrawn coin at a shop with the shop id. When a user wants to pay his coin, the shop firstly calculates a temporary id and sends it to the user. Then, the user blinds it with the parameters he only knows and sends it to his observer. The observer in the enclave of the AESP checks if the parameter corresponding to the coin to be spent is still in the secure storage, then outputs the results with its attestation. The user is going to sign the temporary id by sending it to the bank along with the coin. The shop executes the verifications and if the verifications hold, it accepts the payment and stores the payment transcript.

5. **Deposit protocol:**
   A shop should execute the deposit protocol if it wants to deposit a coin. He should send the payment transcript to the bank along with the time of the transaction. Then the bank checks the temporary id and the time in order to ensure that the shop id encoded in the temporary id corresponds to the shop's one and the shop does not try to deposit the same coin again. If something is wrong the bank doesn't accept the coin. After that, the bank verifies the signature on the coin and executes the verification equation.

4   Security

Our Open-cash scheme satisfies the security properties of anonymity and one-more unforgeability. It can also prevent double-spending attacks. The formal theories and proofs for the security notions are shown in Appendix C.

- **Anonymity**: The Open-cash scheme ensures that banks and shops can not know the private information about users from the coins on the withdrawal and spend protocol. Moreover, the views of the coins withdrawn and spent are separated.
- **One-More Unforgeability**: Malicious users can not forge a coin, i.e., $l + 1$ coins never exist for the correctly withdrawn l coins.
- **Double-Spending Protection**: Assuming AESPs are not compromised, the probability that a user can execute double-spending successfully is negligible. Moreover, even if an AESP is tampered with and double-spending is executed by an attacker, the bank can extract the double-spender's id with the observer from the two payment transcripts for the double-spent coin.

Description : Prog$_\mathcal{O}$

On input ("genKeyPair"):   On input ("Com"):

  $o_1 \leftarrow \mathbb{Z}_q, A_\mathcal{O} = G_1^{o_1}$ $o_2 \leftarrow \mathbb{Z}_q, B_\mathcal{O} = G_1^{o_2}$

  Store $(o_1, A_\mathcal{O})$ Store o_2 in $\mathcal{L}[B_\mathcal{O}]$

  return $A_\mathcal{O}$ return $B_\mathcal{O}$

                       On input ("res",$pid_0, B_\mathcal{O}$) :

                         If $B_\mathcal{O} \in \mathcal{L}[B_\mathcal{O}]$ Then

                            $o_2 \leftarrow \mathcal{L}[B_\mathcal{O}]$

                            Delete o_2 from $\mathcal{L}[B_\mathcal{O}]$

                            $p_1' = (pid_0)o_1 + o_2$

                            return p_1'

                       Else

                          ABORT

Fig. 2. The operation of the open-source Observers program in AESP

5   Conclusion

In this paper, we first defined the concept of open-source observers. And then we showed construction of Open-cash which is the Brands' type provably-secure offline electronic cash scheme with observers extending the scheme by Baldimtsi and Lysyanskaya, by newly introducing Blind Indirect Attestation with AESP attestation. We also proved that Open-cash satisfies anonymity, one-more unforgeability, and double-spending protection.

The concept of open-source observers can potentially achieve both cryptographic anonymity and highly flexible transparency at the same time while enforcing payers' legitimate behavior, which is desirable for a wide range of e-cash systems including Central Bank Digital Currency.

A   Definition of Blind Direct Attestation

We give the novel notion of *Blind Indirect Attestation* which can turn the direct attestation by AESP into the indirect one with Blindness.

A.1   Non-Blind Indirect Attestation

Firstly we consider the indirect attestation without blindness for simplicity.

Definition 2 (Proof of Knowledge *[13]*). *An interactive proof system P, V for an NP relation $\mathcal{R}$ is a proof of knowledge with knowledge error ϵ, if there*

exists a probabilistic polynomial-time extractor E such that for every w and every probabilistic polynomial-time prover P^* :

$$\Pr\left[(x, w) \in \mathcal{R} : w \leftarrow \mathcal{E}^{P^*}(x)\right] \geq \Pr\left[\langle P^*, V \rangle (x) = 1\right] - \epsilon$$

Definition 3 (Indirect Attestation). *Suppose an enclave identified by eid running a program $Prog_i$ within a session identified by sid generates (x, w) that satisfies NP-relation $\mathcal{R}$, namely, $(x, w) \in \mathcal{R}$, and outputs a*

$$(sid, eid, Prog_i, x, \sigma_{ATT})$$

as an attestation signature on an AESP as assumed and stores the witness w in securely isolated storage inside the enclave in the AESP. If malicious prover P^* succeeded in convincing a verifier that $(x, w) \in \mathcal{R}$ with the same x as in the attestation signature that P^* knows the witness w, there must exist an extractor which can output the witness w with knowledge error probability $\epsilon > 0$. More formally we have

$$\Pr\left[(x, w) \in \mathcal{R} : w \leftarrow \mathcal{E}^{P^*}(x)\right] \geq \Pr\left[\langle P^*, V \rangle (x) = 1\right] - \epsilon.$$

Theorem 1. *Suppose we have EUF-CMA signature schemes and a Schnorr [17] Proof of Knowledge protocol on a witness relation $\mathcal{R} = \{(x, w) \mid x = (g, g^w)$ where $g \in \mathbb{G}, w \in \mathbb{Z}_q^*$ and q is a prime number}. Then there exists an indirect attestation under the Random Oracle model.*

Proof (sketch) The detailed proof will be found in the full paper. □

A.2   Blind Indirect Attestation

Next, we introduce the blind version of the indirect attestation. We use a way similar to the well-known one by which several signature schemes can be turned into blind signature schemes [16].

Definition 4 (Blind Indirect Attestation). *Suppose an enclave identified by eid running a program $Prog_i$ within a session identified by sid generates $(\widetilde{x}, \widetilde{w})$ that satisfies NP-relation $\mathcal{R}$, namely, $(\widetilde{x}, \widetilde{w}) \in \mathcal{R}$, and outputs a blinded statement x such that*

$$(sid, eid, Prog_i, x, \sigma_{ATT}).$$

as an attestation signature on an AESP as assumed and stores the witness $\widetilde{w}$ in securely isolated storage inside the enclave in the AESP.

Given a blind signature of the verifier σ_V on a message $\widetilde{x}$, that is,

$$(\widetilde{x}, \sigma_V),$$

then if malicious prover P^* succeeded in convincing a verifier that $(\widetilde{x}, \widetilde{w}) \in \mathcal{R}$ with the same $\widetilde{x}$ as in the attestation signature that P^* knows the witness $\widetilde{w}$, there must exist an extractor which can output the witness $\widetilde{w}$ with knowledge error probability $\epsilon > 0$. More formally we have

$$\Pr\left[(\widetilde{x}, \widetilde{w}) \in \mathcal{R} : \widetilde{w} \leftarrow \mathcal{E}^{P^*}(\widetilde{x})\right] \geq \Pr\left[\langle P^*, V \rangle (x) = 1\right] - \epsilon.$$

If the verifier is convinced the proof of knowledge with regard to the witness $\widetilde{w}$ that satisfies the witness relation $(\widetilde{x}, \widetilde{w}) \in \mathcal{R}$, the prover must be one of the enclaves that generated the witness $(\widetilde{x}, \widetilde{w})$ that some AESP had produced the attestation signatures on the $\widetilde{x}$ in the blinded form with overwhelming probability.

Theorem 2. *Suppose we have EUF-CMA signature schemes, secure blind signature schemes and Schnorr [17] Proof of Knowledge protocol on a witness relation $\mathcal{R} = \{(\widetilde{x}, \widetilde{w}) \mid \widetilde{x} = (g, g^{\widetilde{w}})$ where $g \in \mathbb{G}, w, \widetilde{w} \in \mathbb{Z}_q^*$ and q is a prime number$\}$. Then there exists a blind indirect attestation under the Random Oracle model.*

Proof (sketch). First, we assume the signature $(\widetilde{x}, \sigma_V)$ corresponds to exactly one statement-witness pair $(x, w) \in \mathcal{R}$ and the verification algorithm outputs 1 on inputs (x, σ_V). This must be the case that the knowledge error probability of the indirect blind attestation is the same as the previous indirect attestation as stated in Theorem 1.

Therefore, we consider the probability that the verification algorithm outputs 1 but there is no corresponding statement x which appeared in one of the foregoing attestation signatures

$$(sid, eid, \text{Prog}_i, x, \sigma_{\text{ATT}}). \tag{1}$$

In the case the $\widetilde{x}$ is *forged* because the map $\varPhi$ from the set of unblinded statements $\{\widetilde{x}\}$ to the set of blinded statements $\{x\}$, namely, $\varPhi : \{\widetilde{x}\} \rightarrow \{x\}$, must be injective. The probability that $(\widetilde{x}, \sigma_V)$ is successfully forged is negligible by the One-more unforgeability property of the underlying secure blind signature. $\square$

Even if the indirect attestation is blinded its attestation ability keeps the same as the original σ_{ATT} as long as the signature is a correct (not forged) one. The blind signature enables the attestation to be executed anonymously. This feature consistently enhances the security of the Open-cash scheme.

B   Protocol Details

In this section, we give detailed cryptographical protocols and their sequential diagrams of Open-cash. The operations of the open-source observer are shown both in the diagrams of the protocols and in Fig. 2 in Sect. 3.

Note that over the following protocols, Indirect Attestation and Blind Indirect Attestation defined in Sect. 2.3 and Appendix A are used to keep our scheme secure: In the opening protocol, the execution of the generation of the statement-witness pair and the registration of the statement is over the Indirect Attestation with σ_{ATT}. In the withdrawal protocol, firstly the verification for the satisfaction of the NP-relation $(o_1; A_O)$ is executed by the PoK over the Indirect Attestation, and if the relation is satisfied, a blind signature (i.e. a coin) is issued with the Blind Indirect Attestation. In the spend protocol, the PoK for the witness of the user-id and the coin is executed over the Blind Indirect Attestation.

B.1   Setup System

Firstly we generate at random a tuple (g_2, G_1, G_2), and a number $x \leftarrow \mathbb{Z}_q$. A Bank $\mathcal{B}$ picks up two parameters $w_1, w_2 \leftarrow \mathbb{Z}_q$, and calculates $H = G_1^{w_1} G_2^{w_2}$. The pair (G_1, G_2, H) is a public key.

B.2   Opening Protocol

When a user $\mathcal{U}$ wants to open an account he installs an open-source Observers program distributed by the Bank in the AESP of his device such as a smartphone. After that, as shown in Fig. 3, $\mathcal{O}$ in the enclave of the AESP picks up at random $o_1 \leftarrow \mathbb{Z}_q$ inside, stores it in secure isolated storage, and outputs $A_\mathcal{O} = G_1^{o_1}$ with the attestation σ_{ATT}. $\mathcal{U}$ generates at random a secret number $U \leftarrow \mathbb{Z}_q$ as his identity, computes $g_1 = A_\mathcal{O}(G_1^U G_2)$ as a public key. $\mathcal{U}$ sends g_1 and the attestation σ_{ATT} along with his identification (e.g. a passport) to $\mathcal{B}$ while keeping U secret. After the verification, $\mathcal{B}$ stores the identifying information of $\mathcal{U}$ in the account database together with g_1. $\mathcal{B}$ calculates $h = g_1^{w_1} g_2^{w_3}$ from a random number $w_3 \leftarrow \mathbb{Z}_q$ and sends it to $\mathcal{U}$. $\mathcal{U}$ stores $(g_1, A_\mathcal{O}, h; U)$.

B.3   Withdrawal Protocol

In the withdrawal protocol, $\mathcal{U}$ and $\mathcal{B}$ are going to run a blind signature scheme, under the shared instance $((H, G_1, G_2), (h, g_1, g_2))$ so that the user can withdraw one coin signed by $\mathcal{B}$.

As shown in Fig. 4, the process goes on as follows: First of all, $\mathcal{O}$ in the enclave of the AESP picks up at random $o_2 \leftarrow \mathbb{Z}_q$ inside and stores it in secure isolated storage and outputs $B_\mathcal{O} = G_1^{o_2}$ with the attestation σ_{ATT}. $\mathcal{B}$ picks $(v_1, v_2, v_3) \leftarrow \mathbb{Z}_q$ uniformly at random, calculates $V_1 = G_1^{v_1} G_2^{v_2}$ and $V_2 = g_1^{v_1} g_2^{v_3}$ and then sends them to $\mathcal{U}$. After $\mathcal{U}$ receives them, he selects uniformly at random $(r', z_1', z_2', z_3') \leftarrow \mathbb{Z}_q$ and computes the simulated values $V_1' = G_1^{z_1'} G_2^{z_2'} H^{-r'}$ and $V_2' = g_1^{z_1'} g_2^{z_3'} h^{-r'}$. Then, $\mathcal{U}$ selects random parameters $(s, k) \leftarrow \mathbb{Z}_q$ uniformly and computes:

$$\tilde{h} = h^s g_2^k, \quad \tilde{g}_1 = g_1^s, \quad \tilde{V}_1 = V_1 V_1', \quad \tilde{V}_2 = (V_2 V_2')^s$$

Note that $\tilde{g}_1 = G_1^{Us} G_2^s$, where we can write $W_1 = Us$ and $W_2 = s$ and the User is actually proving that he knows a witness (W_1, W_2) such that $\tilde{g}_1 = G_1^{W_1} G_2^{W_2}$. Next U picks $e, b_1, b_2 \leftarrow \mathbb{Z}_q$ and calculates $m = G_1^{b_1} G_2^{b_2} A_\mathcal{O}^{es} B_\mathcal{O}$ and the hash

$$\tilde{r} = Hash\left(m, (H, G_1, G_2), \left(\tilde{h}, \tilde{g}_1, g_2\right), \left(\tilde{V}_1, \tilde{V}_2\right)\right)$$

and sends them to $\mathcal{B}$ the blinded value $r = \tilde{r} - r'$. At the end, $\mathcal{B}$ computes:

$$z_i = r w_i + v_1 \text{ for } i \in \{1, \ldots, 3\}$$

and sends (z_1, z_2, z_3) to $\mathcal{U}$.

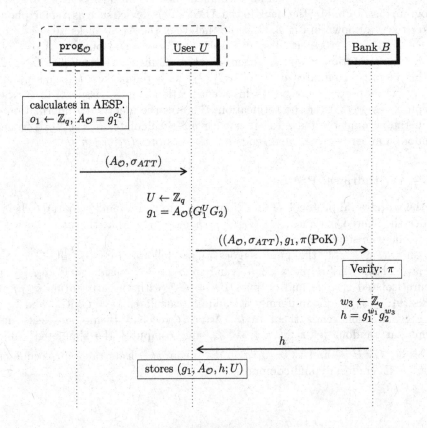

Fig. 3. Opening protocol

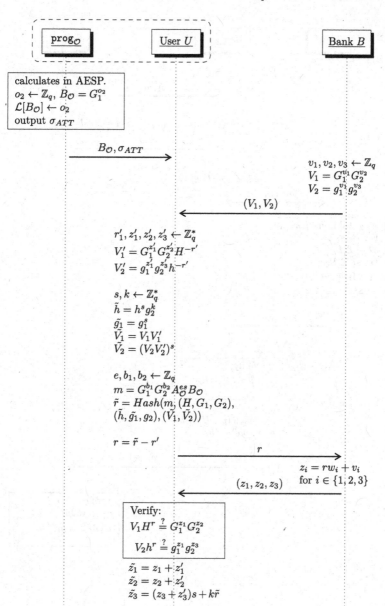

Fig. 4. withdrawal protocol

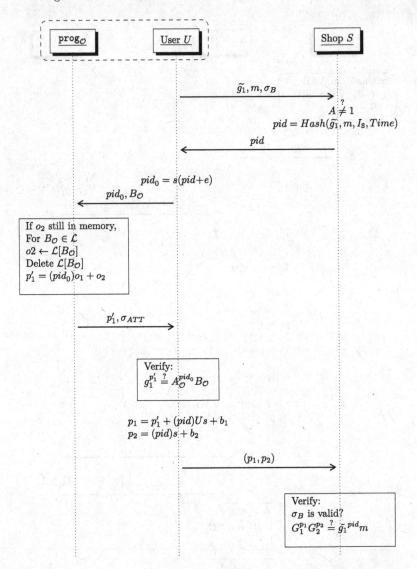

Fig. 5. spend protocol

B.4   Spend Protocol

In the spend protocol (shown in Fig. 5), $\mathcal{U}$ can spend his withdrawn coin at a shop $\mathcal{S}$ with the shop id I_s. Firstly, $\mathcal{S}$ calculates the hash

$$pid = Hash\,(\tilde{g}_1, m, I_s, \mathrm{Time})\,.$$

and sends it to $\mathcal{U}$. Then, $\mathcal{U}$ blinds it using (s, e) and sends it to $\mathcal{O}$. $\mathcal{O}$ in the enclave of the AESP checks if o_2 is still in storage, then for the $(o_2, B_\mathcal{O})$ corresponding to the coin it computes $p' = (pid_0)o_1 + o_2$ and outputs it along with the attestation σ_{ATT}. $\mathcal{U}$ is going to sign pid by sending to the bank:

$$p_1 = p_1' + (pid)Us + b_1$$
$$p_2 = (pid)s + b_2$$

along with the coin. The Shop verifies the validity of the coin and checks whether:

$$G_1^{p_1} G_2^{p_2} \overset{?}{=} m\tilde{g_1}^{pid}.$$

If the two verifications hold, $\mathcal{S}$ accepts the payment and stores $((m, \tilde{g_1}), \sigma_B, (p_1, p_2), pid)$.

B.5   Deposit Protocol

If $\mathcal{S}$ wants to deposit a coin, he should send the spending transcript, consisting of $((m, \tilde{g_1}), \sigma_B, (p_1, p_2), pid)$ to $\mathcal{B}$ along with the Time of the transaction. Then $\mathcal{B}$ checks (pid, Time) in order to ensure that the I_s encoded in the pid corresponds to $\mathcal{S}$'s one and $\mathcal{S}$ does not try to deposit the same coin again. If something is wrong the bank does not accept the coin. After that, $\mathcal{B}$ verifies the signature on the coin and that (p_1, p_2) is valid by checking whether $m\tilde{g_1}^{pid} \overset{?}{=} G_1^{p_1} G_2^{p_2}$. If so, $\mathcal{B}$ stores $((m, \tilde{g_1}), \sigma_B, (p_1, p_2), pid)$ if something does not verify, $\mathcal{B}$ rejects.

C   Security Proof

In this section, we give formal theories and prove that Open-cash satisfies anonymity, one-more unforgeability, and double-spending prevention.

C.1   Anonymity

The ideal e-cash system should be anonymous like real money, in other words, it should satisfy anonymity. In the blind signature scheme, a signer can not distinguish messages if the signature scheme satisfies blindness. Because the withdrawn coins are signatures signed by a signer (i.e. a bank), in an e-cash scheme based on a blind signature scheme, he can not know the information about the message including the identity of the user withdrawing coins. So e-cash schemes over secure blind signatures satisfy anonymity.

Lemma 1. *E-cash schemes constructed with secure blind signatures satisfy anonymity.*

The Brands' type scheme [1] satisfies anonymity, and we prove that the extension by introducing observers into the scheme does not affect the anonymity property:

Theorem 3. *Our Open-cash scheme satisfies anonymity.*

Proof. We prove that our extension does not compromise its original anonymity. In our protocol, the variables (o_1, o_2) are introduced in order to construct observers. Using them, we calculated $A_{\mathcal{O}} = G_1^{o_1}$, $B_{\mathcal{O}} = G_1^{o_2}$, $g_1 = G_1^U G_2 A_{\mathcal{O}} = G_1^{U+o_1} G_2$ and $m = G_1^{b_1} G_2^{b_2} A_{\mathcal{O}}^{es} B_{\mathcal{O}}$.

We can prove that our scheme includes the original one as a special case; by letting $o_1 = 0$ and $o_2 = 0$, then the variables in the Open-cash protocols are

$$A_{\mathcal{O}} = 1$$

$$B_{\mathcal{O}} = 1$$

$$g_1 = G_1^U G_2$$

$$m = G_1^{b_1} G_2^{b_2}.$$

This shows our protocol exactly reduces to the Brands' type scheme. So even if the bank colludes with the observer, meaning that the bank knows (o_1, o_2), the anonymity property still holds.

C.2   One-More Unforgeability

In [1,2], it was proved that blind Schnorr signatures have the property of one-more-unforgeability. The probability that legitimately withdrawn coins through the withdrawal protocol is negligible. Conversely, if a PPT adversary $\mathcal{A}$ could forge a coin, which means there exist $l+1$ coins for correctly withdrawn l coins, the adversary can forge Schnorr signatures in the random oracle and generic group model.

Theorem 4 (Theorem 3 [2]).   Consider the modified Brands' withdrawal/blind signature scheme in the random oracle model. If there exists a probabilistic polynomial time Turing machine which can perform a "one-more" forgery, with non-negligible probability, even under a parallel attack, then the discrete logarithm can be solved in polynomial time.

Theorem 5.   *Consider our e-cash scheme, based on the modified Brands' withdrawal/blind signature with Observers in the random oracle model. If there exists a probabilistic polynomial time Turing machine that can perform an "one-more" forgery, with non-negligible probability, even under a parallel attack, then the discrete logarithm can be solved in polynomial time.*

Proof. In our protocol, the cryptographic modification to the original one is the introduction of the new parameter (o_1, o_2) in order to construct observers;

$$g_1 : G_1^U G_2 \rightarrow A_{\mathcal{O}} \left(G_1^U G_2 \right) \tag{2}$$

$$m : G_1^{b_1} G_2^{b_2} \rightarrow G_1^{b_1} G_2^{b_2} A_{\mathcal{O}}^{es} B_{\mathcal{O}} \tag{3}$$

where $A_{\mathcal{O}} = G_1^{o_1}$ and $B_{\mathcal{O}} = G_1^{o_2}$.

In the proof of Theorem 4, the contents of g_1 and m do not affect both the proof logic and the conclusion, so the theorem can be proven in the same way.

C.3   Double-Spending Protection

Our Open-cash has a powerful anti-double-spending property. Under the AESP assumption, the probability that double-spending is executed successfully is negligible.

Theorem 6. *Assuming AESP is not compromised the probability that a user can execute double-spending successfully is negligible.*

Proof. In order to execute double-spending successfully in spite of the existence of BIA, the adversary must impersonate his observer, which means he must calculate o_1 for $G_1^{o_1}$ by himself.

For the probability, directly from DLA, there exists a negligible function $negl(\lambda)$ such that

$$\Pr\left[(q, G_1, G_2, G_1^{o_1}) \leftarrow S\left(1^\lambda\right); o_1' \leftarrow \mathcal{A}^{\text{Schnorr }(G_1, o_1)}\left(G_1, G_1^{o_1}\right) : o_1' = o_1\right] \leq negl(\lambda).$$

Moreover, even if the AESP assumption is broken, Open-cash enables banks to extract the id of the attacker who double-spent one coin to two different *pids*.

Theorem 7. *A bank can extract an attacker's user id with the observer if and only if the user executes a double-spending.*

Proof. When a malicious user double-spent one coin the bank will receive the same coin $((m, \tilde{g}_1), \sigma_B)$ for two different $(pid; p_1, p_2)$ and $\left(pid'; p_1', p_2'\right)$. The bank can trace the attacker who double-spent the coin by computing:

$$G_1^{\frac{p_1 - p_1'}{pid - pid'}} G_2^{\frac{p_2 - p_2'}{pid - pd'}}$$

which is equal to

$$G_1^{W_1} G_2^{W_2}$$

and by knowing $W_1 = (U + o_1)s$ and $W_2 = s$, the bank can compute the secret key (id) U of the double-spender.

References

1. Baldimtsi, F., Lysyanskaya, A.: On the security of one-witness blind signature schemes (2012)
2. Baldimtsi, F., Lysyanskaya, A.: On the security of one-witness blind signature schemes. In: Sako, K., Sarkar, P. (eds.) ASIACRYPT 2013. LNCS, vol. 8270, pp. 82–99. Springer, Heidelberg (2013). https://doi.org/10.1007/978-3-642-42045-0_5
3. Brands, S.: An efficient offline electronic cash system based on the representation problem. CWI CS-R9323, 77 (1993)
4. Brands, S.: Untraceable off-line cash in wallet with observers. In: Stinson, D.R. (ed.) CRYPTO 1993. LNCS, vol. 773, pp. 302–318. Springer, Heidelberg (1994). https://doi.org/10.1007/3-540-48329-2_26

5. Camenisch, Jan, E.B., Chen, L.: Direct anonymous attestation (2004)
6. Chaum, D.: Blind signatures for untraceable payments. In: Chaum, D., Rivest, R.L., Sherman, A.T. (eds.) Advances in Cryptology, pp. 199–203. Springer, Boston, MA (1983). https://doi.org/10.1007/978-1-4757-0602-4_18
7. Chaum, D.: Security without identification: transaction systems to make big brother obsolete. Commun. ACM **28**(10), 1030–1044 (1985)
8. Chaum, D., den Boer, B., van Heyst, E., Mjølsnes, S., Steenbeek, A.: Efficient offline electronic checks. In: Quisquater, J.-J., Vandewalle, J. (eds.) EUROCRYPT 1989. LNCS, vol. 434, pp. 294–301. Springer, Heidelberg (1990). https://doi.org/10.1007/3-540-46885-4_31
9. Chaum, D., Fiat, A., Naor, M.: Untraceable electronic cash. In: Goldwasser, S. (ed.) CRYPTO 1988. LNCS, vol. 403, pp. 319–327. Springer, New York (1990). https://doi.org/10.1007/0-387-34799-2_25
10. Chaum, D., Pedersen, T.P.: Wallet databases with observers. In: Brickell, E.F. (ed.) CRYPTO 1992. LNCS, vol. 740, pp. 89–105. Springer, Heidelberg (1993). https://doi.org/10.1007/3-540-48071-4_7
11. Ferguson, N.: Extensions of single-term coins. In: Stinson, D.R. (ed.) CRYPTO 1993. LNCS, vol. 773, pp. 292–301. Springer, Heidelberg (1994). https://doi.org/10.1007/3-540-48329-2_25
12. Ferguson, N.: Single term off-line coins. In: Helleseth, T. (ed.) EUROCRYPT 1993. LNCS, vol. 765, pp. 318–328. Springer, Heidelberg (1994). https://doi.org/10.1007/3-540-48285-7_28
13. Kogan, D.: Lecture 5: proofs of knowledge, Schnorr's protocol, NIZK p. 4
14. Okamoto, T., Ohta, K.: Universal electronic cash. In: Feigenbaum, J. (ed.) CRYPTO 1991. LNCS, vol. 576, pp. 324–337. Springer, Heidelberg (1992). https://doi.org/10.1007/3-540-46766-1_27
15. Pass, R., Shi, E., Tramèr, F.: Formal abstractions for attested execution secure processors. In: Coron, J.-S., Nielsen, J.B. (eds.) EUROCRYPT 2017. LNCS, vol. 10210, pp. 260–289. Springer, Cham (2017). https://doi.org/10.1007/978-3-319-56620-7_10
16. Pointcheval, D., Stern, J.: Provably secure blind signature schemes. In: Kim, K., Matsumoto, T. (eds.) ASIACRYPT 1996. LNCS, vol. 1163, pp. 252–265. Springer, Heidelberg (1996). https://doi.org/10.1007/BFb0034852
17. Schnorr, C.P.: Efficient identification and signatures for smart cards. In: Brassard, G. (ed.) CRYPTO 1989. LNCS, vol. 435, pp. 239–252. Springer, New York (1990). https://doi.org/10.1007/0-387-34805-0_22

Inefficiency of CFMs: Hedging Perspective and Agent-Based Simulations

Samuel N. Cohen[1,3], Marc Sabaté-Vidales[2,3], David Šiška[2,4(✉)], and Łukasz Szpruch[2,3]

[1] Mathematical Institute, University of Oxford, Oxford, UK
[2] School of Mathematics, University of Edinburgh, Edinburgh, UK
d.siska@ed.ac.uk
[3] Simtopia.ai, Edinburgh, UK
[4] Vega Protocol, Gibraltar, Spain

Abstract. We investigate whether the fee income from trades on the CFM is sufficient for the liquidity providers to hedge away the exposure to market risk. We first analyse this problem through the lens of continuous-time financial mathematics and derive an upper bound for not-arbitrage fee income that would make CFM efficient and liquidity provision fair. We then evaluate our findings by performing multi-agent simulations by varying CFM fees, market volatility, and rate of arrival of liquidity takers. We observe that, on average, with volatility set to realistic values, fee income generated from liquidity provision is insufficient to compensate for market risk. In case where the underlying pair volatility is very low the fee income exceeds market risk cost.

1 Introduction

It has been shown empirically [7] and experimentally [21] that liquidity providers (LPs) in constant function markets (CFMs) (in particular, Uniswap v3) lose money on average. Indeed, from e.g. [7, Table 2], the average LP transaction in the ETH/USDC pool (from May 2021–August 2022) resulted in a position loss of -1.64%, and fee income of 0.155% of the size of the initial trade, with an average hold time of 6.1 days.

An LP entering a position in CFM opens themselves to two risks: the impermanent loss due to price moves in the underlying asset and the risk of fee income not compensating the impermanent loss. A rational LP may choose to hedge the impermanent loss component, which is essentially a perpetual option [2]. If the fee income (from trades on the CFM) exceeds the cost of the hedge the LP is making a risk-free profit. However, if the fee income is below the cost of the hedge the LP is making a loss. We formalise this intuition using tools from continuous-time financial mathematics, to derive a theoretical, arbitrage-free upper bound on the fee income that would make the CFM efficient and LP positions fair. This is our Theorem 1. This is complementary perspective to that of loss versus rebalancing (LVR) introduced in [19].

© International Financial Cryptography Association 2024
A. Essex et al. (Eds.): FC 2023 Workshops, LNCS 13953, pp. 303–319, 2024.
https://doi.org/10.1007/978-3-031-48806-1_20

The fee income of the LP depends on the CFM fee (denoted $1-\gamma$ in Uniswap) and the trade flow. There is no canonical way to jointly model the underlying price process and the trade flow which realistically captures the interdependence of the two. For this reason we analyse the relationship between the LP fee income and the arbitrage-free upper bound using simulations involving a CFM, another liquid exchange, an arbitrageur agent and price sensitive noise traders (they choose between the exchanges based on which offers better execution price). We considered the CFM fee to be in the range 0% to 4% and in this range the simulations show that fee income due to the LP never exceeds the cost of hedging i.e. the LP is always losing money. As one would expect from Theorem 1 the loss is higher if the volatility of the underlying asset is higher. This is regardless of the rate of noise traders arriving in the market. In very low volatility regime ($< 5\%$), which is unrealistic in most CFMs used for crypto assets and defi tokens, the fee income can exceed the hedging cost, see Sect. 3. One may hope that the solution is to increase the fee the CFM charges but this reduces the trade flow thus reducing the income. Similarly, reducing the slippage by depositing more into the pool would increase trade but would not lead to lower losses for LPs as this increases the hedging cost of the LP position.

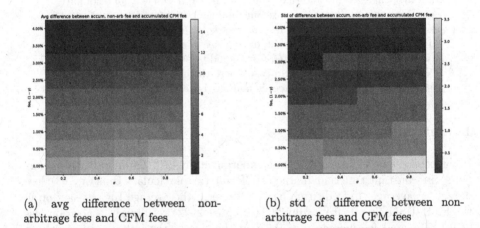

(a) avg difference between non-arbitrage fees and CFM fees

(b) std of difference between non-arbitrage fees and CFM fees

Fig. 1. Difference between premium fees and CFM fees for different values of γ, σ, positive values indicate fee income is not covering cost of hedging impermanent loss.

1.1   Literature Review

The CFM are gaining popularity in market design as they guarantee market liquidity (proportional to the amount of assets locked) and they have minimal storage and computational requirements, unlike e.g. limit-order-book-based markets. This makes them ideal for environments where computational power and storage are at a premium like Ethereum [22], or Cardano, Polkadot or Solana.

Running on blockchain gives advantages over centralised exchanges: transparency, pseudonymity, censorship resistance and security, see references in e.g. [17]. However blockchain-based CFMs suffer from a number of problems: namely questionable returns for LPs as has been already mentioned as well as traders (liquidity takers) being front-run by miners (known as miner-extractable-value) [8,10]. Attempts are being made to extend the CMF concept to reduce the loss suffered by the LPs due to toxic order flow (arbitraguer trades) by changing the underlying blockchain to make it aware of the CFM, auctioning access to blocks (which allows arbitrage trades) and re-distributing the proceeds to LPs, see [18].

Apart from the empirical study [7] mentioned in the opening paragraph there are a number of others that analysed on-chain data, see e.g. [9,13,17]. In contrast, this paper focuses on theoretical analysis and simulations. However, the conclusions are broadly similar: passive liquidity provision on various pools doesn't have returns which compensate for the risks.

Classical market clearing models suggest, see Glosten & Milgrom [11], Kyle [14,15] and Grossman & Miller [12], that the volatility of the underlying asset plays an important role in how the market makers should set bid-ask spread (which is comparable to the pool fee as it imacts execution costs). As we show in Theorem 1 the fee income due to the CFM LPs is bounded above by a product of quadratic variation of the underlying asset (which is basically volatility) and convexity of the position being hedged.

1.2   Organisation of the Paper

Section 2 includes all the theoretical findings of the paper. Some readers may wish to skim through Sect. A.1 which reviews CFMs and how liquidity provision works and fixes some notation used further in the paper. Section 2.1 recalls what a perpetual option is, Sect. 2.2 proves the main theoretical result of the paper which is Theorem 1. Section 3 describes in detail the agent-based model used and discusses the findings. Finally, in Sect. 4, we discuss the main findings, their limitations and possible further work. A full implementation of the agent-based simulation is at[1] https://github.com/simtopia/cfm-sim.

2   Liquidity Provision in Constant Function Markets

In this section, we will draw a connection between a constant function market (CFM) and a perpetual (American) options contract. We will particularly seek to derive the impermanent loss (also known as LVR) of a CFM, or equivalently the arbitrage-free streaming premium of the perpetual option.

Consider a constant function market $\Psi : \mathbb{R}_+^2 \to \mathbb{R}$, which we assume to be twice continuously differentiable and convex (see [5,6]). From Ψ one can derive $S_t \mapsto \psi(S_t)$ which provides the value of the pool in terms of price of the assets

---

[1] The link is deliberately broken to comply with the anonymous submission format.

$S_t = (S_t^1, S_t^2)$ expressed w.r.t. some numeraire asset under the assumption that arbitrageurs' ensure that the pool price and external price are in line. For details see the Appendix, Sect. A.1.

2.1   Connection with Perpetual Options

Given a payoff function ψ, there is a simple connection between liquidity provision in a CFM and investment in a perpetual American option.

We begin with a precise definition of a perpetual American contract with streaming premium. As we shall see, liquidity provision in a CFM is equivalent to entering a long perpetual derivative with the payoff dictated by the function ψ. This derivative is written on the underlying assets $S = (S_t)_{t \geq 0}$ traded in the pools. We follow the definition from [2].

Definition 1. *A perpetual contract with streaming premium, written on assets with price vector S, with payoff function $\psi : \mathbb{R}^n \to \mathbb{R}$, is a agreement between two parties, referred to as the long side and short side. The long side has the right to terminate the contract at any time $t \geq 0$, at which point it will receive a payment of $\psi(S_t)$. In return, the long-side must pay to the short side $\psi(S_0)$ at the time $t = 0$ of inception as well as a continuous cash-flow of $(g_t)_{t \geq 0}$ per unit time, referred to as the streaming premium, up until the contract is terminated.*

In order to highlight the connections between a CFM and a perpetual American option, we make the following observations. In a CFM, a liquidity provider (CFM-LP)

– initially deposits assets with value $\psi(S_0)$,
– receives fees at the rate f_t per unit time (which may vary). These fees may be withdrawn (under the Uniswap v3 protocol) at any time,
– at some future time τ (of the CFM-LPs choosing), may withdraw their assets, which will have value $\psi(S_\tau)$.

In a perpetual American option with streaming premium and payoff ψ, an investor purchasing the option

– initially purchases the option, for a cost $\psi(S_0)$,
– receives the streaming premium at a rate g_t per unit time (which may vary). This streaming premium may be positive or negative, and is received immediately,
– at some future time τ (of the investor's choosing), may exercise the option, which rewards them with value $\psi(S_\tau)$.

As we can see, assuming fees in the CFM are instantaneously predictable (i.e. the fee to be received from the CFM can be accurately estimated in advance), a no arbitrage argument suggests that we must have $f_t = g_t$, as otherwise one asset is strictly better than the other in every state of the world (over some short time horizon), which implies that an efficient market will focus all its trading in the better of these alternatives.

2.2   Model and Assumptions

We make the following assumptions about the market:

- The agent can borrow and lend any amount of cash at the riskless rate.
- The agent can buy and sell any amount of assets x^1 and x^2.
- The above transactions do not incur any transaction costs and the size of a trade does not impact the prices of the traded assets.

We denote the risk free rate (which may be stochastic) by $(r_t)_{t \geq 0}$ and model the money market as

$$dB_t = r_t B_t dt, \qquad B_0 \geq 0. \tag{1}$$

We assume $r_t \geq 0$. We further denote the drift and diffusion coefficients (again, possibly stochastic) of the risky asset shadow prices by $\mu = (\mu_t^1, \mu_t^2) \in \mathbb{R}^2$ and

$$\sigma = (\sigma_t^{(1,1)}, \sigma_t^{(1,2)}, \sigma_t^{(2,1)}, \sigma_t^{(2,2)}) \in \mathbb{R}_+^4$$

respectively, and model the shadow price of the risky asset $(S_t^i)_{t \geq 0}$ by

$$dS_t^i = \mu_t^i S_t^i dt + \sum_{j=1}^{2} \sigma_t^{(i,j)} S_t^i dW_t, \quad S_0^i \geq 0, \tag{2}$$

where $W = (W_t^1, W_t^2)$ is a 2-dimensional Brownian motion. We assume that (μ, σ) are sufficiently regular that a (unique strong) solution to (2) exists.

Remark 1. By allowing the drift and diffusion coefficients to be arbitrary processes we are just saying that the prices are non-negative and continuous: our framework incorporates a rich family of common models such as Black–Scholes, Heston, SABR or local stochastic volatility models with possibly path dependent coefficients.

We will proceed to derive an arbitrage-free fee bound in a similar way to the construction of the predictable loss in [19], and to classical arguments for no-arbitrage pricing in financial markets.

Assumption 1. The value of the pool as a function of external price process, $s \mapsto \psi(s)$ is twice continuously differentiable.

Assumption 1 holds in the case when the fee $(1 - \gamma) = 0$ and arbitrageurs continuously close the gap between S_t and the price of the CFM, as demonstrated in [19]. Hence we expect the arbitrage-free fee derived below to be a good proxy for CFMs that charge small fee (e.g Uniswap). If the CFM charges a fee $(1 - \gamma)$ which is significantly larger than 0 then the value of the pool is a function of the reserves and the price one would use for the conversion (external price S_t or pool-implied price $P_t^{2,CFM}$), see Remark 3 for more details.

Consider the wealth process Z of an agent who

- begins with zero capital[2],
- initially borrows a quantity $\psi(S_0)$ at the risk-free interest rate, which they use to establish a CFM position (which they can do by trading in the liquid market to obtain the desired risky assets for the pool),
- until time t, trades in the liquid market hold a quantity (Δ_s^i) of each asset at time s.

The dynamics of Z_t are given by

$$
Z_t = \underbrace{\psi(S_t) - \psi(S_0)}_{\text{CFM gains}} + \underbrace{\int_0^t \sum_{i=1}^2 \Delta_s^i dS_s^i}_{\text{trading gains}}
$$

$$
+ \underbrace{\int_0^t \left(Z_s - \sum_{i=1}^2 \Delta_s^i S_s^i - \psi(S_0) \right) r_s ds}_{\text{interest payments on uninvested wealth + loan}} + \underbrace{\int_0^t f_s ds}_{\text{CFM fees}}.
$$

We assumed ψ is smooth, hence we can apply Itô's lemma to obtain

$$
Z_t = \sum_{i=1}^2 \int_0^t \left[\partial_i \psi(S_s) + \Delta_s^i \right] dS_s^i + \frac{1}{2} \sum_{i,j=1}^2 \int_0^t \partial_i \partial_j \psi(S_s) d\langle S^i, S^j \rangle_s
$$

$$
+ \int_0^t \left[\left(Z_s - \sum_{i=1}^2 \Delta_s^i S_s^i - \psi(S_0) \right) r_s + f_s \right] ds.
$$

By setting $\Delta_s^i = -\partial_i \psi(S_s)$, we eliminate the first term, giving

$$
Z_t = \frac{1}{2} \sum_{i,j=1}^2 \int_0^t \partial_i \partial_j \psi(S_s) d\langle S^i, S^j \rangle_s + \int_0^t \left[\left(Z_s + \sum_{i=1}^2 (\partial_i \psi(S_s)) S_s^i - \psi(S_0) \right) r_s + f_s \right] ds.
$$

As the quadratic variation is $d\langle S^i, S^j \rangle_s = (\sigma_s \sigma_s^\top)^{(i,j)} S_s^i S_s^j ds$, this simplifies to

$$
\frac{dZ_s}{ds} = \frac{1}{2} \sum_{i,j=1}^2 \partial_i \partial_j \psi(S_s) (\sigma_s \sigma_s^\top)^{(i,j)} S_s^i S_s^j + \left(Z_s + \sum_{i=1}^2 (\partial_i \psi(S_s)) S_s^i - \psi(S_0) \right) r_s + f_s.
$$

If this quantity is positive, then we have a strategy which earns money with probability one over a short time period, that is, an arbitrage. Therefore, after rearrangement, we know that

$$
f_s + Z_s r_s \leq -\frac{1}{2} \sum_{i,j=1}^2 \partial_i \partial_j \psi(S_s) (\sigma_s \sigma_s^\top)^{(i,j)} S_s^i S_s^j - \left(\sum_{i=1}^2 (\partial_i \psi(S_s)) S_s^i - \psi(S_0) \right) r_s.
$$

As Z is increasing in f (an agent who earns more fees will be wealthier) and we assume $r \geq 0$, there is a unique value of f such that above equation is an

---

[2] This is simply to avoid having to account for the interest they should earn on their initial capital.

equality. With this CFM trading fee income per unit of time, we have $dZ_s/ds = 0$ and $Z_0 = 0$, and hence $Z_s = 0$. We denote this critical value[3]

$$\hat{f}_s = -\frac{1}{2} \sum_{i,j=1}^{2} \partial_i \partial_j \psi(S_s)(\sigma_s \sigma_s^\top)^{(i,j)} S_s^i S_s^j - \left(\sum_{i=1}^{2} (\partial_i \psi(S_s)) S_s^i - \psi(S_0) \right) r_s.$$

We have thus shown the following.

Theorem 1. *Given the model of the market given by (1) and (2) and with the assumptions stated in Sect. 2.2 we know that CFM fee income rate f_t (which depends on the trade flow and the fee $1 - \gamma$) must satisfy $f_t \leq \hat{f}_t$ where this theoretical upper bound on CFM fee income rate is*

$$\hat{f}_t = -\frac{1}{2} \sum_{i,j=1}^{2} \partial_i \partial_j \psi(S_t) \frac{d\langle S^i, S^j \rangle_t}{dt} - \left(\sum_{i=1}^{2} \partial_i \psi(S_s) S_t^i - \psi(S_0) \right) \frac{d \log B_t}{dt}.$$

Notice that the critical CFM fee income rate depends on the trading function via $\partial_i \partial_j \psi(S)$ (which is negative, as ψ is concave as long as the trading function Ψ is convex) and the quadratic variation of traded asset (which is implicitly related to the level of trading activity). On the other hand the actual CFM fee income rate depends on the trade flow in the CFM and the fee the pool sets i.e. $1 - \gamma$. It is not clear that one could bring f_t in line with $\hat{f}_t$ as increasing $1 - \gamma$, the fee charged by the CFM will likely lead to decreased trade flow.

Note that this argument only uses a long-position in the CFM, and only establishes[4] the inequality $f_t \leq \hat{f}_t$. If it were possible to perfectly short-sell the CFM (or the corresponding perpetual option), then a similar argument would yield the converse inequality. This may explain why the fee rate in Uniswap v3, is systematically below the critical fee rate, which is related to liquidity provision in CFMs yielding persistently poor returns.

Example 1. For clarity of presentation we set the risk free interest rate $r = 0$, and assume that asset S^2 is a numeraire (hence the agent only invests in asset $S = S^1$). This means that $\psi(S_t) = \psi(S_0) \left(\frac{S_t}{S_0} \right)^\theta$. The second derivative of ψ is given by $\partial_S^2 \psi(S_t) = \theta(\theta - 1) \frac{\psi(S_0)}{S_0^2} \left(\frac{S_t}{S_0} \right)^{\theta-2}$, which is negative since $\theta \in (0, 1)$. The critical fee rate is then given by

---

[3] [7] give a similar calculation, to obtain a closely related quantity, which they call the permanent loss of the CFM.

[4] The presentation above assumes the agent starts at time 0, and derives the critical fee rate on this basis. To obtain the inequality bound $f_t \leq \hat{f}_t$ for all times, we formally have to consider starting with zero capital at a time where the inequality is not satisfied, and showing that this gives a short-term arbitrage opportunity.

$$\hat{f}_t = \frac{-1}{2}\theta(\theta-1)\frac{\psi(S_0)}{S_0^2}\left(\frac{S_t}{S_0}\right)^{\theta-2}\sigma_t^2 S_t^2$$

$$= \frac{\theta(1-\theta)}{2}\sigma_t^2\psi(S_0)\left(\frac{S_t}{S_0}\right)^\theta = \frac{\theta(1-\theta)}{2}\sigma_t^2\psi(S_t) \geq 0\,.$$

As mentioned above, by analyzing the data in the Uniswap v3 pool (e.g. [7]) one can see that, in general, the fee rate is below critical fee rate. Nevertheless, since one cannot simply short position at the Uniswap (unless using an over-the-counter bespoke arrangement) it is not clear how one could realise a potential arbitrage opportunity when $f < \hat{f}$.

3   An Agent-Based Model

We design an Agent-Based-Model with the aim to compare the accumulated fees by a CFM defined as in Example 2 with $\theta = 1/2$ in a period of time $[0, T]$ against the accumulated non-arbitrage fee derived in Sect. 2.2.

3.1   Model Description

We consider the CFM with x^1 being the numeraire. Price discovery occurs in a second reference market, where S_t denotes the price of asset x^2 in terms of the numeraire x^1 at time t. We model the price S_t by a Geometric Brownian Motion

$$dS_t = \sigma S_t dW_t, \quad S_0 > 0.$$

Whenever the price of asset x^2 in terms of the numeraire x^1 in the CFM is different than S_t, there might be an arbitrage opportunity. An arbitrageur will automatically make the necessary trades to maximise their profit. Furthermore we model the arrival of liquidity takers by Poisson process $(N_t)_t$ with intensity λ. We run the simulation of discrete times $\Pi := \{0, t_1, t_2, ..., T\}$ and initialise the simulation with reserves (x_0^1, x_0^2) and fee $(1-\gamma)$; initial price S_0 and volatility σ; liquidity takers arrival intensity λ. We run the following simulation. For every $t \in \Pi$:

- The arbitrageur makes the necessary trades resulting from optimisations (7) (8) in the CFM and in the reference market to make a risk-free profit.
- If $N_t - N_{t_-} = 1$ then a price-sensitive liquidity trader arrives and trades $\Delta_t \in \mathbb{R}$ sampled from $\mathcal{N}(0,1)$ of asset x^1. The noise trader chooses the market with better execution price with some high probability p, i.e. we allow for the noise trader to be irrational with probability $(1-p)$.[5]

We take $\sigma \in \{0.025, 0.05, 0.1, 0.2, 0.4, 0.6, 0.8\}, \lambda \in \{50, 75, 100\}, p \in \{0.5, 0.9\}$ and fix $S_0 = 10, x_0^1 = 100, x_0^2 = 10$ and run the above simulation 100 times for different values of $\gamma \in [0.96, 1]$.

---

[5] Perfectly rational liquidity trader would consider splitting the order to optimise the execution cost. We omit this extension in our simulations.

3.2   High Fee and Low Fee $1 - \gamma$

Figures 5, 2, 6 and 3 consider two simulated scenarios: high fee value $\gamma = 0.96$ (i.e. fee 4%); low fee value $\gamma = 0.997$ of (i.e. fee 0.3%), $\lambda = 50$ and $\sigma = 0.4$. Figures 5 and 6 provide the evolution of the price process for the two simulated scenarios in the CFM for the same price process S_t in the reference market. The smaller the fee (the higher the value of γ) the closer the CFM price process depicted in blue follows the reference market price S_t. For these two scenarios, the CFM and arbitrage-free fee rates are shown in Figs. 2 and 3, and the area under the fee rates corresponds to accumulated fees in that particular simulation. High values of fees (low values of γ) indicate less arbitrage opportunities, and therefore the number of trades will be lower than in the low fees scenarios. Hence increasing the fee rate does not necessarily lead to higher fee income. However, in higher fees regimes, the trade sizes will necessarily be higher (there will only be an arbitrage opportunity when the gap between the CFM price and the reference price is big enough to compensate for the fee).

Fixing $\lambda = 50$, Fig. 1 aggregates the generated results for all the considered $\gamma \in [0.96, 1], \sigma \in \{0.2, 0.4, 0.6, 08\}$. Figure 1a indicates that higher trades will bring higher fees on average, yet they will not be able to cover the cost of hedging the impermanent loss, which increases with the volatility σ.

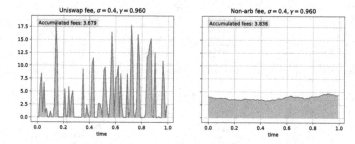

Fig. 2. CFM fees (left) and non-arbitrage fees (right) for a simulation with $\gamma = 0.96, \sigma = 0.4$

3.3   Impact of Noise Trader Arrival Rate λ

Figure 4 aggregates all the simulations for the three considered intensity regimes for the noise trader and the two considered rationality regimes also for the noise trader. We see that for low values of $\sigma \in \{0.025, 0.05\}$, the non-arbitrage fee is low, and the CFM fee can cover the cost of hedging impermanent loss if it is high enough (above 1%). For higher values of σ, the CFM fee does not cover the cost of hedging impermanent loss. We see that if the liquidity takers only trade on the better priced venue with probability $p = 0.5$ then increasing λ increases the LP profits, as one would expect. With $p = 0.9$ increasing λ does not increase the LP

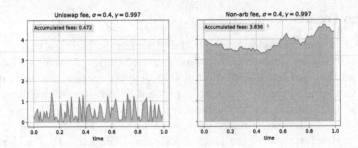

Fig. 3. CFM fees (left) and non-arbitrage fees (right) for a simulation with $\gamma = 0.997, \sigma = 0.4$

profit much. Why? In the simulation the arbitrageur executes their trade first. This leaves the pool in the "no-arbitrage" bounds with respect to the external venue. This means that the external venue gives better price to the liquidity taker and they utilise it with $p = 0.9$. Hence the LP sees very little benefit from increase in λ.

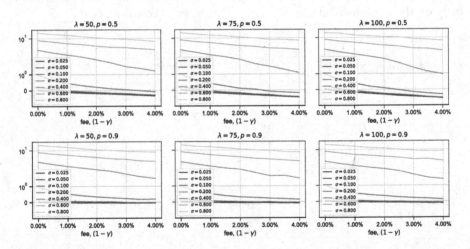

Fig. 4. Average difference between non-arbitrage fees and CFM fees for different values of γ, σ, λ

4   Conclusion and Future Work

In Theorem 1 we have derived an upper bound on the fee income for an LP placing liquidity in a CFM which does not lead to arbitrage when compared to the cost of hedging the risk of the underlying price moves (referred to as impermanent loss). These findings are augmented by agent based simulations which indicate that at least in some market regimes LP providers in CFMs are not being adequately compensated for the impermanent loss risk they take on.

The theoretical model used to derive Theorem 1 makes a number of simplifying assumptions that are common in financial mathematics but on top of that it only applies in the low fee regime of CFMs, as discussed in Remark 3. To better study the higher fee regimes one would need to jointly model the trade flow and its impact on the underlying price or to model the joint evolution of the reserves and the underlying asset price. This, mathematically more challenging problem, is left for future work. More realistic agent order flow could be based directly on empirical data e.g. from [20]. This would, in particular, allow more informed choice of λ. Getting accurate estimates for the p (probability of trading on the pool vs. another venue) is harder to establish as this would require access to client/trade data from centralised venues. The liquidity takers could not only choose the venue which provides better execution price but could split their orders for lowest overall execution cost. Furthermore, most arbitrageurs do not to realise the arbitrage in one "step"; instead they should consider multistep optimisation with penalty for inventory leading to dynamic-programming problems (or, if we assume that the model of underlying price is unknown, to a reinforcement learning problem). Again, this more involved investigation is left for future work.

Acknowledgements. SC and LS acknowledge the support of the UKRI Prosperity Partnership Scheme (FAIR) under EPSRC Grant EP/V056883/1 and the Alan Turing Institute. SC also acknowledges the support of the Oxford–Man Institute for Quantitative Finance.

A   Appendix

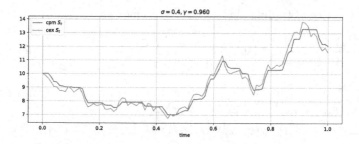

Fig. 5. Price processes for a simulation with $\gamma = 0.96, \sigma = 0.4$

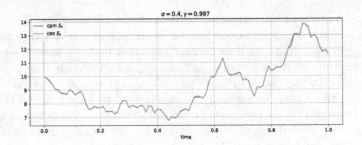

Fig. 6. Price processes for a simulation with $\gamma = 0.997, \sigma = 0.4$

A.1   An Overview of CFMs

A constant function market (CFM) is characterised by

i) The reserves $(x^1, x^2) \in \mathbb{R}_+^2$ describing amounts of assets in the pool.
ii) A constant function market $\Psi : \mathbb{R}_+^2 \to \mathbb{R}$ which determines the state of the pool after each trade according to the acceptable fund positions:

$$\left\{ (x^1, x^2) \in \mathbb{R}_+^2 \ : \ \Psi(x^1, x^2) = \text{constant} \right\}.$$

iii) A trading fee $(1 - \gamma)$, for $\gamma \in (0, 1]$.

To acquire Δx_t^1 of asset x^1 at time t a trader needs to deposit a quantity $\Delta x^2 = \Delta x^2(\Delta x^1)$ of asset x^2 into the pool, and pay a fee $(1 - \gamma)\Delta x^2$.[6] Δx^2 and Δx needs to satisfy the equation

$$\Psi(x_t^1 - \Delta x^1, x_t^2 + \Delta x^2) = \Psi(x_t^1, x_t^2).$$

Once the trade is accepted the reserves are updated according to

$$x_{t+1}^1 = x_t^1 - \Delta x^1 \quad \text{and} \quad x_{t+1}^2 = x_t^2 + \Delta x^2. \tag{3}$$

The relative price of trading Δx^1 for Δx^2 is defined as

$$\frac{P_t^{1,CFM}(\Delta x^1)}{P_t^{2,CFM}(\Delta x^2)} := \frac{\Delta x^2}{\Delta x^1} \quad \text{subject to} \quad \Psi(x_t^1 - \Delta x^1, x_t^2 + \Delta x^2) = \Psi(x_t^1, x_t^2).$$

Observe that

$$\begin{aligned} 0 =& \Psi(x_t^1 - \Delta x^1, x_t^2 + \Delta x^2) - \Psi(x_t^1, x_t^2) \\ =& -\partial_{x^1}\Psi(x_t^1, x_t^2)\Delta x^1 + \partial_{x^2}\Psi(x_t^1, x_t^2)\Delta x^2 + \mathcal{O}((\Delta x)^2). \end{aligned}$$

Hence the relative price of trading an infinitesimal amount of Δx^1 for Δx^2 is given by

$$\frac{P_t^{1,CFM}}{P_t^{2,CFM}} := \lim_{\Delta x^1 \to 0} \frac{P_t^{1,CFM}(\Delta x^1)}{P_t^{2,CFM}(\Delta x^2)} = \frac{\partial_{x^1}\Psi(x_t^1, x_t^2)}{\partial_{x^2}\Psi(x_t^1, x_t^2)}.$$

---

[6] The fee in Uniswap-V3 is not added to the pool reserves [1]. This is in contrast to Uniswap-V2.

Assume that there is an external market where assets x^1 and x^2 can be traded (without frictions) at the prices $S_t = (S_t^1, S_t^2)$. The no-arbitrage condition in the case of no fees ($\gamma = 1$) implies that

$$\frac{P_t^{1,CFM}}{P_t^{2,CFM}} = \frac{S_t^1}{S_t^2} \tag{4}$$

Conversely, if 4 would not hold, then (in a market with no fees) there would be an arbitrage opportunity between CFM and the external market (assuming frictionless trading is possible), as it would be possible to purchase a combination of assets cheaply in one market, and then sell it in the other.

Example 2 (GMM). Consider the trading function

$$\Psi(x^1, x^2) = (x^1)^\theta (x^2)^{1-\theta}$$

for $\theta \in (0,1)$. The no arbitrage relationship (4), in GMM is given by

$$\frac{P_t^{1,CFM}}{P_t^{2,CFM}} = \frac{S_t^1}{S_t^2} \,.$$

The value of the liquidity pool at any time $t \in [0, \infty)$, is given by

$$\psi(S_t; x_t) := x_t^1 \cdot S_t^1 + x_t^2 \cdot S_t^2 \,,$$

and using (5) we can show that

$$\psi(S_t; x_t) = \frac{1}{\theta} S_t^1 x_t^1 \quad \text{or} \quad \psi(S_t) = \frac{1}{1-\theta} S_t^2 x_t^2 \,.$$

In the Appendix, see Example 3, we derive an alternative representation for ψ_t, that does not depend on (x_t^1, x_t^2),

$$\psi(S_t) = \psi(S_0) \cdot \left(\frac{S_t^1}{S_0^1}\right)^\theta \cdot \left(\frac{S_t^2}{S_0^2}\right)^{1-\theta} \,.$$

The above example, also studied in [9], demonstrates two key properties of CFMs:

- A GMM automatically re-balances liquidity pools so that the value of the pools with asset x^1 and x^2 is $\theta \cdot \psi(S_t)$ and $(1 - \theta)\psi(S_t)$, respectively
- Providing liquidity to a CFM Ψ is equivalent to entering a long position on a perpetual derivative on the underlying asset with the payoff dictated by the value (in terms of price) ψ.

As observed in [3,4], for any CFM ψ for any non-negative, non-decreasing, concave, 1-homogenous[7] payoff function ψ, there exists a trading function Ψ, such

---

[7] That is, $\lambda\psi(S) = \psi(\lambda S)$ for all $\lambda > 0$ and S. Equivalently, we can assume that one of the assets in S_t is the numeraire asset, in which case the 1-homogeneity assumption is not needed.

that the value of the liquidity provision in CFM with with function Ψ matches this payoff function. In other words, a CFM with appropriately designed trading function Ψ dynamically adjusts portfolio held by liquidity providers so that the value of this portfolio, at any time, is described by the payoff function ψ. This gives us two ways to understand a CFM:

- Through the defining trading function Ψ, indicating valid combinations of the two assets.
- Through the valuation function ψ, indicating the value of the CFM pool in terms of the prices of the two assets.

Concentrated liquidity, introduced in Uniswap V3, gives individual LPs control over what price ranges their capital is allocated to. This gives a practical way of creating liquidity provision that replicates a given function ψ, and has been observed and described in [16].

Example 3 (Derivation of ψ for the Geometric Mean Market). Consider the trading function

$$\Psi(x^1, x^2) = (x^1)^\theta (x^2)^{1-\theta}$$

for $\theta \in (0,1)$. In the setting with no fees, $\gamma = 1$, we have $(x_t^1)^\theta (x_t^2)^{1-\theta} = (x_0^1)^\theta (x_0^2)^{1-\theta}$. The no arbitrage relationship (4), in GMM is given by

$$\frac{P_t^{1,CFM}}{P_t^{2,CFM}} = \frac{\theta x_t^2}{(1-\theta)x_t^1} = \frac{S_t^1}{S_t^2}. \tag{5}$$

The value of the liquidity pool at any time $t \in [0,\infty)$, is given by

$$\psi(S_t) := x_t^1 \cdot S_t^1 + x_t^2 \cdot S_t^2 .$$

Note that, under no arbitrage and no fee assumptions, it makes no difference whether the accounting is being done in S or P.

Using (5) we can show that

$$\psi(S_t) = \left(\frac{1-\theta}{\theta} + 1 \right) S_t^1 x_t^1 = \frac{1}{\theta} S_t^1 x_t^1$$

or equivalently

$$\psi(S_t) = \left(\frac{\theta}{1-\theta} + 1 \right) S_t^2 x_t^2 = \frac{1}{1-\theta} S_t^2 x_t^2 .$$

From here we see that the value of the sub-pools with assets x^1 and x^2 are $\theta \cdot \psi(S_t)$ and $(1-\theta)\psi(S_t)$, respectively.

Next, we derive an alternative representation for V_t that does not depend on (x_t^1, x_t^2). To do that, note that

$$1 = \frac{\psi(S_t)}{\psi(S_t)} = \frac{S_t^2 x_t^2}{1-\theta} \frac{\theta}{S_t^1 x_t^1} .$$

Hence

$$\psi(S_t) = \left(\frac{S_t^1 x_t^1}{\theta}\right)^{\theta} \cdot \left(\frac{S_t^1 x_t^1}{\theta}\right)^{1-\theta}$$

$$= \left(\frac{S_t^1 x_t^1}{\theta}\right)^{\theta} \cdot \left(\frac{S_t^1 x_t^1}{\theta}\right)^{1-\theta} \cdot \left(\frac{S_t^2 x_t^2}{1-\theta} \frac{\theta}{S_t^1 x_t^1}\right)^{1-\theta}$$

$$= (x_t^1)^{\theta} (x_t^2)^{1-\theta} \left(\frac{S_t^1}{\theta}\right)^{\theta} \cdot \left(\frac{S_t^2}{1-\theta}\right)^{1-\theta} .$$

Since

$$(x_t^1)^{\theta} (x_t^2)^{1-\theta} = (x_0^1)^{\theta} (x_0^2)^{1-\theta} , \quad \text{and} \quad \psi(S_0) = (x_0^1)^{\theta} (x_0^2)^{1-\theta} \left(\frac{S_0^1}{\theta}\right)^{\theta} \cdot \left(\frac{S_0^2}{1-\theta}\right)^{1-\theta} ,$$

we have

$$\psi(S_t) = \psi(S_0) \cdot \left(\frac{S_t^1}{S_0^1}\right)^{\theta} \cdot \left(\frac{S_t^2}{S_0^2}\right)^{1-\theta} .$$

Remark 2 (Convex duality approach). We begin by observing that if Ψ defines a constant function market, then it is possible to apply the implicit function theorem to construct a convex function $\phi : \mathbb{R} \to \mathbb{R}$, called the *trading function,* such that

$$\Psi(x^1, x^2) = \kappa^2 \qquad \Leftrightarrow \qquad \phi(x^1) = x^2.$$

That is, ϕ determines the amount of asset x we hold, when we have a given quantity y. We assume for simplicity that ϕ is continuously differentiable. Given the reserves (x_t^1, x_t^2), an agent willing to sell Δx^1 to the pool will receive Δx^2 such that

$$x_t^2 - \Delta x^2 = \phi(x_t^1 + \Delta x^1) \implies \frac{\Delta x^2}{\Delta x^1} = -\frac{\phi(x_t^1 + \Delta x^1) - \psi(x_t^1)}{\Delta x^1} .$$

As in (4) the no-arbitrage condition (in the case of no fees ($\gamma = 1$)) implies that

$$- \partial_x \phi(x_t^1) = S_t . \qquad (6)$$

As ψ is convex, we can take its Legendre transform, to define

$$\phi^*(s) = \sup_x \left\{ s \cdot x - \phi(x) \right\}.$$

Note that right hand side achieves its (unique) supremum when $\partial_x \phi(x) = s$. From (6) we see that for $s = -S_t$, we have $x = x_t^1$. Hence

$$-\phi^*(-S_t) = S_t \cdot x_t^1 + \phi(x_t^1) = S_t \cdot x_t^1 + x_t^2 = \psi(S_t) .$$

Hence the value of the LP position in the pool is $-\phi^*(-S_t)$ and can be readily computed using any off-the-shelf convex optimisation algorithm. As ϕ^* is a convex function, we see that ψ is concave, and as ϕ is decreasing, we see that ψ is increasing.

Example 4 (Uniswap V2 via convex duality). For a constant product market (as in Uniswap V2), $\Psi(x^1, x^2) = x^1 \cdot x^2 = \kappa^2$, so $\phi(x^1) = \kappa^2/x^1$. We compute $\phi^*(s) = -2\kappa\sqrt{-s}$, and hence $\psi(s) = 2\kappa\sqrt{s}$.

Remark 3 (Comments about the derivation of the arbitrage-free fee rate bound). The derivation of the arbitrage-free fee rate bound is done under the Assumption 1 which, as we explained, holds in the case when $(1 - \gamma) = 0$. If for each trade the CFM charges a fee it can be easily shown that this optimal arbitrage trades will not lead to condition (4). We demonstrate this on Fig. 5. Indeed the arbitrageur who trades $(\Delta x^1, \Delta x^2)$ when reserves are (x^1, x^2) will incur cost $f(\gamma, x^1, x^2, \Delta x^1, \Delta x^2)$ and solves the optimisation problem $\Delta x^{2,*} := \max(\Delta x^2_{\text{CFM, CEX}}, \Delta x^2_{\text{CEX, CFM}})$, where

$$\Delta x^2_{\text{CFM, CEX}} := \underset{\Delta x^2}{\operatorname{argmax}} \, \Delta x^1 \cdot S^1 - \Delta x^2 - f(\gamma, , x^1, x^2, \Delta x^1, \Delta x^2)$$

$$\text{such that } \Psi(x_1 - \Delta x^1, x_2 + \Delta x^2) = \Psi(x_1, x_2), \quad \Delta x^2 \geq 0, \qquad (7)$$

$$\Delta x^1 \cdot S^1 - \Delta x^2 - f(\gamma, x^1, x^2, \Delta x^1, \Delta x^2) \geq 0$$

and

$$\Delta x^2_{\text{CEX, CFM}} := \arg\max_{\Delta x^2} \Delta x^2 - \Delta x^1 S^1 - f(\gamma, x^1, x^2, \Delta x^1, \Delta x^2)$$

$$\text{such that } \Psi(x_1 + \Delta x^1, x_2 - \Delta x^2) = \Psi(x_1, x_2), \quad \Delta x^2 \geq 0, \qquad (8)$$

$$\Delta x^2 - \Delta x^1 S^1 - f(\gamma, x^1, x^2, \Delta x^1, \Delta x^2) \geq 0$$

where the subindexes of $\Delta x^2_{.,.}$ denote the order of the markets where the arbitrageur goes short and long in asset x^2. If $\Delta x^{2,*} = 0$, then there is no possible trade for which an arbitrageur makes a profit. When condition (4) does not hold, the model to calculate the arbitrage fee rate bound $\hat{f}_t$ needs to be generalized. A first step in this direction is to re-rewrite the value function as a function of (x^1, x^2, S_t). Furthermore, using Implicit Function Theorem for trading function $\Psi(x^1, x^2)$, there is function g such that $x^2 = g(x^1)$. Hence, assuming x^1 is the numeraire so that $S^1_t = 1$,

$$\psi(x^1_t, S_t) = x^1_t + g(x^1_t) \cdot S^2_t.$$

Applying Itô formula to ψ we get

$$d\psi(x^1_t, S^2_t) = \partial_x \psi(x^1_t, S^2_t) dx^1_t + \partial_S \psi(x^1_t, S^2_t) dS^2_t + \partial_x \partial_S \psi(x^1_t, S^2_t) d\langle x^1, S^2 \rangle_t$$

$$+ \frac{1}{2} \partial^2_x \psi(x^1_t, S^2_t) d\langle x^1, x^1 \rangle_t + \frac{1}{2} \partial^2_S \psi(x^1_t, S^2_t) d\langle S^2, S^2 \rangle_t.$$

One can see that to analyse the evolution of the value of the pool one needs to model the evolution of reserves and its dependence on S. Instead of performing analysis under various sets of assumptions we turn to simulations.

References

1. Adams, H., Zinsmeister, N., Salem, M., Keefer, R., Robinson, D.: Uniswap v3 core. Technical report, Uniswap (2021)

2. Angeris, G., Chitra, T., Evans, A., Lorig, M.: A primer on perpetuals. arXiv preprint arXiv:2209.03307 (2022)
3. Angeris, G., Evans, A., Chitra, T.: Replicating market makers. arXiv preprint arXiv:2103.14769 (2021)
4. Angeris, G., Evans, A., Chitra, T.: Replicating monotonic payoffs without oracles. arXiv preprint arXiv:2111.13740 (2021)
5. Angeris, G., Kao, H.T., Chiang, R., Noyes, C., Chitra, T.: An analysis of uniswap markets. arXiv preprint arXiv:1911.03380 (2019)
6. Capponi, A., Jia, R.: The adoption of blockchain-based decentralized exchanges. arXiv preprint arXiv:2103.08842 (2021)
7. Cartea, A., Drissi, F., Monga, M.: Decentralised finance and automated market making: permanent loss and optimal liquidity provision (2022). https://papers.ssrn.com/sol3/papers.cfm?abstract_id=4273989
8. Daian, P., et al.: Flash boys 2.0: frontrunning, transaction reordering, and consensus instability in decentralized exchanges. arXiv:1904.05234 (2019)
9. Evans, A.: Liquidity provider returns in geometric mean markets (2021)
10. Flashbots. Mev-explore v0. https://explore.flashbots.net
11. Glosten, L.R., Milgrom, P.R.: Bid, ask and transaction prices in a specialist market with heterogeneously informed traders. J. Financ. Econ. 14, 71–100 (1985)
12. Grossman, S.J., Miller, M.H.: Liquidity and market structure. J. Financ. 43, 617–633 (1988)
13. Heimbach, L., Schertenleib, E., Wattenhofer, R.: Risks and returns of uniswap v3 liquidity providers. arXiv preprint arXiv:2205.08904 (2022)
14. Kyle, A.S.: Continuous auctions and insider trading. Econometrica 53, 1315–1335 (1985)
15. Kyle, A.S.: Informed speculation with imperfect competition. Rev. Econ. Stud. 56, 317–455 (1989)
16. Lambert, G., Kristensen, J.: Panoptic: a perpetual, oracle-free options protocol. arXiv preprint arXiv:2204.14232 (2022)
17. Loesch, S., Hindman, N., Richardson, M.B., Welch, N.: Impermanent loss in uniswap v3. arXiv:2111.09192 (2021)
18. McMenamin, C., Daza, V., Mazorra, B.: Diamonds are forever, loss-versus-rebalancing is not. arXiv preprint arXiv:2210.10601 (2022)
19. Milionis, J., Moallemi, C.C., Roughgarden, T., Zhang, A.L.: Automated market making and loss-versus-rebalancing. arXiv preprint arXiv:2208.06046 (2022)
20. Miori, D., Cucuringu, M.: DeFi: data-driven characterisation of Uniswap v3 ecosystem & an ideal crypto law for liquidity pools. arXiv:2301.13009 (2022)
21. Sabate-Vidales, M., Šiška, D.: The case for variable fees in constant product markets: an agent based simulation. In: Matsuo, S., et al. (eds.) FC 2022. LNCS, vol. 13412, pp. 225–237. Springer, Cham (2022). https://doi.org/10.1007/978-3-031-32415-4_15
22. Wood, G.: Ethereum: a secure, decentralised generalised transaction ledger. Ethereum Proj. Yellow Pap. 151, 1–32 (2014)

DeFi Auditing: Mechanisms, Effectiveness, and User Perceptions

Ding Feng[1], Rupert Hitsch[2], Kaihua Qin[3], Arthur Gervais[4],
Roger Wattenhofer[2], Yaxing Yao[5], and Ye Wang[1(✉)]

[1] University of Macau, Macau, China
{mc25944,wangye}@um.edu.mo
[2] ETH Zurich, Zurich, Switzerland
wattenhofer@ethz.ch
[3] Imperial College London, London, UK
kaihua.qin@imperial.ac.uk
[4] University College London, London, UK
a.gervais@ucl.ac.uk
[5] University of Maryland, Baltimore County, Baltimore, USA
yaxingyao@umbc.edu

Abstract. Decentralized Finance (DeFi), a blockchain-based financial ecosystem, suffers from smart contract vulnerabilities that led to a loss exceeding 3.24 billion USD by April 2022 [67]. To address this, blockchain firms audit DeFi applications, a process known as DeFi auditing. Our research aims to comprehend the mechanism and efficacy of DeFi auditing. We discovered its ability to detect vulnerabilities in smart contract logic and interactivity with other DeFi entities, but also noted its limitations in communication, transparency, remedial action implementation, and in preventing certain DeFi attacks. Moreover, our interview study delved into user perceptions of DeFi auditing, unmasking gaps in awareness, usage, and trust, and offering insights to address these issues.

Keywords: Decentralized finance · auditing · blockchain

1 Introduction

Decentralized Finance (DeFi), an ecosystem built on blockchain's smart contracts, has experienced significant growth, with a Total Value Locked (TVL) surpassing 110 billion USD in 2022. Despite its expansion, DeFi is frequently targeted by cyber-attacks due to the lack of legal and industry standards and its inherent decentralization. The immutable nature of deployed DeFi project code, coupled with potential user vulnerabilities, worsens the scenario. An escalating number of auditing firms are striving to meet the demand for dependable safety assessments.

Nonetheless, DeFi projects continue to be compromised despite these audits, questioning these firms' reliability and credibility. Additionally, a universal standard for DeFi auditing is currently lacking. Consequently, our study explores the following crucial questions:

© International Financial Cryptography Association 2024
A. Essex et al. (Eds.): FC 2023 Workshops, LNCS 13953, pp. 320–336, 2024.
https://doi.org/10.1007/978-3-031-48806-1_21

RQ1 How does DeFi auditing identify DeFi application security vulnerabilities?
RQ2 Which vulnerabilities persist despite DeFi auditing?
RQ3 How do DeFi users perceive the role of DeFi auditing in DeFi?

We analyze the mechanisms and effectiveness of DeFi auditing in our study by conducting mixed-method research across nine top DeFi auditing firms, 45 DeFi projects, and real-world DeFi incidents. Furthermore, we explore user perception through interviews, revealing that DeFi auditing steps are largely unknown to users, suggesting an understanding deficit in this field.

2   Data Collection

We curated a dataset of DeFi auditing through three main avenues: DeFi attacks, DeFi auditing firms and DeFi applications, and DeFi vulnerabilities.

2.1   DeFi Attacks

We examined real-world DeFi attacks between April 2018 and April 2022, using a dataset encompassing 181 attacks reported on platforms such as Rekt News [4], SlowMist [5], PeckShield [3], and Medium [2]. Each attack can be instigated by multiple vulnerabilities across several system layers, adding complexity to their logistics.

2.2   DeFi Auditing Firms and DeFi Applications

We selected nine prominent auditing firms, based on criteria like number of completed audits, reputation of audited DeFi projects, and development of popular security tools. Security information was collected from the firms' websites and social media.

Furthermore, 45 recent projects audited by these firms were selected to explore current DeFi auditing practices. Our dataset included the audit reports, official websites, and social media of these projects. Refer to Table 4 for detailed information.

2.3   DeFi Vulnerabilities and Taxonomy

We adopted Zhou et al.'s [67] taxonomy to categorize DeFi vulnerabilities, focusing on smart contract layer, protocol layer, and third-party layer vulnerabilities. We derived our vulnerability dataset from academic papers and 45 audit reports, resulting in 49 identified vulnerabilities. See Appendix A for a detailed list and explanation of these vulnerabilities.

3   DeFi Auditing Mechanisms

In this section, we elucidate how DeFi auditing discovers DeFi application security vulnerabilities (**RQ1**).

3.1 DeFi Auditing Workflow

Method. To understand DeFi auditing mechanisms, we reviewed 45 audit reports from nine different firms (Table 4), as well as their official websites. We identified various auditing steps each firm took during their audit process. This was done by direct mentions or inferences made from reading audit reports in depth. Inclusion was also made for steps cited on the firms' websites and GitHub pages detailing their audit process. We assumed all tools developed by the firms were employed for auditing when their websites mentioned them.

Findings. We find that DeFi audits can be divided into two distinct methodologies: tool-assisted analysis and manual analysis. Additionally, auditors recommend solutions for any problems identified through the utilization of these techniques. The statistics and further explanation of these audit steps are presented in Appendix C.

4 Effectiveness of DeFi Auditing

We scrutinize the efficiency of DeFi auditing via a detailed analysis, focusing on its merits and flaws in real-life situations to answer **RQ2**.

4.1 Audited vs Non-audited Projects - Vulnerabilities and Attacks

Method. We studied harmful DeFi attacks and classified them as audited or non-audited projects based on the occurrence of audits prior to the attack. The nature of exploited vulnerabilities and the handling of identified vulnerabilities in audits were analysed. We also investigated the rectification status of these vulnerabilities to discern if the exploits were due to negligence or inadequate rectification.

Findings. The dataset included 189 exploited vulnerabilities, out of which 140 were from non-audited projects and 43 from audited ones. Most vulnerabilities were located at the smart contract and protocol layers. While audited projects had a slightly higher proportion of vulnerabilities at the smart contract layer, non-audited projects had a significantly higher proportion at the third-party layer. The efficacy of auditing in curbing third-party layer issues was statistically confirmed using a U test method. Refer to Fig. 1 for detailed information.

DeFi Auditing Detection Capability. We found that in 43 audited projects that were attacked, the audit reports mentioned the exploited vulnerabilities in 7 instances, searched for but did not detect the vulnerabilities in 11 instances, and did not mention the exploited vulnerabilities in 25 instances. The statistics of these three groups are presented in Table 6, 7 and 8.

Mentioned: Out of the 7 projects, two fixed the mentioned vulnerabilities, one partially resolved them, three did not address the vulnerabilities, and in one project the resolution status was unclear. This indicates the project owners' lack of urgency in addressing security risks.

Searched For, Not Detected: In 11 instances, auditors failed to detect the vulnerabilities they searched for, implying limitations in the detection mechanisms.

Not Mentioned: 25 attack causes weren't mentioned in audit reports, highlighting potential limitations in audit scope or transparency in communication.

5   DeFi Auditing: User Perceptions

This study explores users' perceptions of DeFi auditing, a security practice in the DeFi ecosystem. It examines how DeFi users understand the role of DeFi auditing in affecting their transactions and investments. We conducted interviews with DeFi users to explore their perceptions of DeFi auditing.

Necessity of DeFi Auditing. Users viewed DeFi auditing as necessary for three reasons: it helps non-technical users understand potential security issues, enhances DeFi project security, and showcases a project's commitment to improving security.

Information Delivery of Auditing. Some users found the technical nature of auditing findings challenging to comprehend, indicating a need for more accessible explanations. Others mentioned difficulties finding specific information within audit reports due to either overly abstract reporting or the absence of certain audit aspects.

Auditing Effectiveness. Despite acknowledging the importance of DeFi auditing, most interviewees felt the auditing effectiveness was inadequate. Reasons include irregular quality among audit firms, difficulty covering all vulnerabilities technically, and a flawed auditing workflow focusing too much on technical issues without considering underlying business logic.

Acknowledgement. This work was supported by grants from the Science and Technology Development Fund (FDCT) Macau SAR (File no. 0129/2022/A) and the University of Macau (File no. MYRG-CRG2022-00013-IOTSC-ICI, no. APAEM/SG/0005/2023 and no. SRG2022-00032-FST).

A   DeFi Vulnerability

A.1   Smart Contract Layer Vulnerabilities

1. Under-priced Opcodes: An imbalance between the gas price of executing an operation in the EVM and the resource consumption (CPU time, memory

etc.) can be exploited, e.g. by flooding the network, leading to "denial of service" [59].

2. Outdated Compiler Version: The smart contract is compiled using an outdated compiler version, which might contain unresolved bugs and vulnerabilities [35, p.6].

3. Compiler version not fixed/Different Solidity versions used: The source code specified the compiler version with the caret operator "^", allowing it to be compiled with a future compiler version, which might not ensure backward compatibility, be buggy, or introduce syntax changes [20].

4. Call to the unknown: The smart contract calls other smart contracts that execute untrusted code, such as some of the primitives used in Solidity to invoke functions and to transfer ether, e.g. *call*, may have the side effect of invoking the fallback function of the callee or recipient. [8, p.169]

5. Reentrancy: The external callee's contact calls back a function in the caller's contract (that is, a circular call) before the caller's contract expires, allowing an attacker to bypass validation until the calling contract runs out of ether or the transaction runs out of gas [19, p.9].

6. Delegatecall/call injection: To facilitate code-reuse, the Ethereum Virtual Machine (EVM) provides an opcode, *delegatecall*, for inserting a callee contract's bytecode into the bytecode of the caller contract, [19, p.9] hence the malicious callee contract is called in the context of caller contract and can directly modify or manipulate its state variables.

7. Unchecked call return value/Unhandled or mishandled exception: Return values of functions may return important information about the program state, or success or failure of execution. A discrepancy exists in Solidity's handling of exceptions occurring in the execution of callee contracts: If the exception occurs directly referencing a callee contract's instance, the transaction is reverted and the exception is propagated to the caller, if the exception occurs by invoking *send*, *call*, or *delegatecall*, false is returned to the caller [8, p.170 f.].

8. Call stack depth limit: The EVM implementation limits the call stack's depth to 1024 frames and deliberately exceeding the call stack's depth limit causes instructions to fail. [19, p.13].

9. Locked or frozen assets: Allowing users to deposit their money to their contract accounts, but preventing them from spending their money from those accounts, effectively freezing their money. This can be accomplished by e.g. contracts not providing any function for spending money, relying on the money-spending function of another contract, e.g. a library, and the library being killed [19, p.9].

10. Integer overflow or underflow: The result of an arithmetic operation can fall outside of the range of a Solidity data type, causing e.g. unauthorized manipulation of balance or state variables [19, p.10].

11. Absence of coding logic or sanity check: Method arguments and return values that could cause malicious actions during the execution of the method are not checked or validated.

12. Short address: Manipulation of the data padding scheme to change function parameters (e.g. ether value) by providing an address, which is too short, as a function parameter.

13. Casting: The Solidity compiler does not check if types match in all cases and does not throw exceptions, hence the caller is not aware that code is executed in an unexpected manner [8, p.172].

14. Unbounded or gas costly operation: Each block has a "gas limit" field that specifies the maximum total amount of gas that can be consumed by the transactions in a block. When the amount of gas required for executing a contract exceeds the block gas limit, e.g. by looping over a large data structure, the transaction will not be executed [19, p.11].

15. Other arithmetic mistakes: Programming oversight when performing computer arithmetic, not unique to smart contracts.

16. Other non-arithmetic mistakes: Programming oversight not relating to computer arithmetic, from erroneous constructor names to faults in translating business logic into smart contract code.

17. Inconsistent or improper access control: The smart contract does not adequately authenticate access to restricted fields, allowing e.g. permissions to be overwritten or funds to be siphoned to external accounts.

18. Visibility error: Solidity provides four types of visibility to restrict access to a contract's functions, namely, public, external, internal, and private, which respectively says that a function can be called arbitrarily, only externally, only within the contract and derived contracts, or only within the contract. When visibility is incorrectly specified, it can permit unauthorized access [19, p.10].

19. Lackluster test coverage: The percentage of smart contract code, for which functionality tests are written, is too low, or the tests do not sufficiently test corner cases.

20. Other smart contract layer vulnerabilities: Other security vulnerabilities located in the smart contract layer according to the taxonomy laid out in Sect. 2.3.

A.2 Protocol Layer Vulnerabilities

1. Front-running: The result of certain transactions depends on the order in which they are executed. Since transactions are publicly broadcast to the network, a malevolent Externally Owned Account (EOA) can offer a higher gas price to have its transactions included in blocks sooner than others'. Moreover, a malicious miner can always pick up its own transactions irrespective of the gas price [19, p.13].

2. Back-running: The result of certain transactions depends on the order in which they are executed. Since transactions are publicly broadcast to the network, a malevolent EOA can offer a lower gas price to have its transactions included in blocks later than others'. Further, a malicious miner can always pick up its own transactions irrespective of the gas price [19, p.13].

3. Sandwiching: An attacker observes a non-executed transaction purchasing an asset and quickly front-runs it by purchasing that asset for a low price. As the supply of the twice-bought asset is low, its value increases by the design of the bonding curve. The attacker then back-runs by selling the asset shortly after the victim transaction to make a profit [66, p.1].

4. Other transaction order dependency: The result of certain transactions depends on the order in which they are executed, which can be manipulated by means other than front-/back-running or a combination thereof.

5. Transaction/strategy replay: Transactions are often validated with digital signatures. If a digital signature does not depend on due information, e.g. a nonce, a malicious entity could use a digital signature multiple times, e.g. to withdraw extra payments.

6. Randomness: Relying on the pseudo-random or predictable data, such as the block number or timestamp, as a source of randomness, e.g. for encryption, is not safe, since it can allow a prediction of the next "random" number [19, p.13f.].

7. Other block state dependency: Other means by which manipulable elements of the block state are depended upon, e.g. a contract may use the block timestamp, which can be manipulated as a triggering condition to execute some critical operations [36, p.4].

8. On-chain oracle manipulation: To circumvent relying on third parties for pricing assets, some DeFi applications solely retrieve prices from on-chain oracles, which can be manipulated, e.g. with flash loans [31].

9. Governance flash borrow or purchase: Protocols that implement decentralized governance may employ governance tokens, holders of which can propose and vote to change the protocol. Through flash loans [31], entities may temporarily amass a large enough share of tokens to unilaterally change the protocol.

10. Fake token: Real tokens have certain token standards to abide by and fraudulent token creators build in mechanisms to steal token owners' money, not adhering to these standards. Fake tokens may pose as legitimate tokens, though they are not of equal value, for instance, in attempts to extract information about unsuspecting users [37].

11. Token standard incompatibility: Token standards like ERC20 are Ethereum's technical standards for the implementation of cryptocurrency tokens. They define a standard list of rules that tokens should follow within the larger Ethereum ecosystem, allowing developers to predict exactly how the tokens will interact. Smart contracts are missing return values or missing functionality specified in the standard, potentially leading to undefined behavior. Alternatively, smart contract code is not compatible with special types of tokens, e.g. deflationary tokens [58].

12. Other unsafe DeFi protocol dependency: Other DeFi protocol risks that may occur due to external dependencies.

13. Unfair slippage protection: When performing trades on a blockchain, where asset prices adapt according to the order in which trades are executed, users may wish to only execute a trade if the price variation does not exceed a

previously specified tolerance ("slippage"). Applications may not execute trades according to the user-defined slippage.

14. Unfair liquidity providing: Liquidity providers may manipulate the supply of liquidity to control the price of currencies in a liquidity pool [6], e.g. through variants of sandwich attacks.

15. Other unsafe DeFi protocol interaction: Other ways in which interacting with a DeFi protocol could be unsafe.

16. Other protocol layer vulnerabilities: Other security vulnerabilities located in the protocol layer according to the taxonomy laid out in Sect. 2.3.

A.3   Third-Party Layer Vulnerabilities

1. Compromised private key/wallet: The attacker can gain control of the private key or wallet and is able to extract all money, ransoms the account, or the attacker disables wallet usage.

2. Weak password: A third party can hack into an ether account and steal funds by simply correctly guessing a weak password.

3. Deployment mistake: Deployment of smart contracts suffers from risks of regular software deployment, e.g. deploying code manually (inconsistently), not tracking code changes properly between different versions [34], but also suffer deployment challenges related to interoperability between different blockchains [7].

4. Malicious oracle updater: Entities responsible for updating real-time data feeds may benefit from providing manipulated information, often to the detriment of users, e.g. in prediction markets, where people can trade contracts that pay based on the outcomes of unknown future events [32, p.22].

5. Malicious data source: Centralized data feeds provide arbitrary data from a single centralized source, and they build on existing blockchain platforms. Centralized data feeds rely on a trusted party that may misbehave or accidentally produce wrong data, harming users in the process [32, p.22].

6. External market manipulation: Adversaries can manipulate the market price of assets off-chain by disseminating false or misleading information about a company, engaging in a series of transactions to make it appear that the security is being traded more actively, or rigging prices, quotes, or trades to manipulate the perception of demand [1].

7. Backdoor/Honeypot: Honeypots are smart contracts that have an obvious flaw in their design, where users a priori commit a certain amount of ether to a contract, thus allowing ether to be extracted from the contract. However, if a user were to attempt to exploit this apparent vulnerability, it would open a second, as-yet-unknown trapdoor for him, preventing him from successfully ejecting ether. [60, p.3]. The attacker takes the money that the victim lost in the exploitation attempt.

8. Insider activities: Since DeFi is less regulated than CeFi, acting on confidential or non-public information for one's benefit or collusion is more common.
9. Phishing attack: Phishing is a form of social engineering in which an attacker sends deceptive messages or deploys malicious software designed to cajole people into disclosing sensitive information to the perpetrator. As a result, unwanted funds are transferred to the attacker [33, p.1].
10. Authority control or breach of promise: Creators or administrators of DeFi projects, such as coins or platforms, may act maliciously by breaking implicit or explicit commitments of trustworthiness to users.
11. Faulty wallet provider: Third-party wallet providers, which DeFi projects rely on, may include, deliberately or negligently faulty, exploitable code in the provided wallets.
12. Faulty API/RPC: The JSON-RPC of an Ethereum client exposes various APIs for EOAs to communicate with the Ethereum network. For security reasons, an attacker could access his client remotely via a JSON request, so the interface should not be reachable from the internet [19, p.17].
13. Other third-party layer vulnerabilities: Other security vulnerabilities located in the third-party layer according to the taxonomy laid out in Sect. 2.3 (Table 1, 2 and 3).

Table 1. Smart contract layer vulnerabilities grouped by their respective causes. Explanations of each vulnerability can be found in Appendix A.1.

Vulnerability Cause	Vulnerability Type
State transition design/implementation error	Under-priced opcodes
	Oudated compiler version
	Compiler version not fixed/Different Solidity versions used
Untrusted callee	Call to the unknown
	Reentrancy
	Delegatecall/call injection
Coding mistake	Unchecked call return value/Unhandled or mishandled exception
	Call-stack depth limit
	Locked or frozen assets
	Integer overflow or underflow
	Absence of coding logic or sanity check
	Short address
	Casting
	Unbounded or gas costly operation
	Other arithmetic mistakes
	Other non-arithmetic mistakes
Access control error	Inconsistent or improper access control
	Visibility error
Sub-par code maintenance	Lackluster test coverage
Other	Other smart contract layer vulnerabilities

Table 2. Protocol layer vulnerabilities grouped by their respective causes. Explanations of each vulnerability can be found in Appendix A.2.

Vulnerability Cause	Vulnerability Type
Transaction order dependency error	Front-running
	Back-running
	Sandwiching
	Other transaction order dependency
Replayable design error	Transaction/strategy replay
Block state dependency error	Randomness
	Other block state dependency
Unsafe DeFi protocol dependency	On-chain oracle manipulation
	Governance flash borrow or purchase
	Fake token
	Token standard incompatibility
	Other unsafe DeFi protocol dependency
Unsafe DeFi protocol interaction	Unfair slippage protection
	Unfair liquidity providing
	Other unsafe DeFi protocol interaction
Other	Other protocol layer vulnerabilities

Table 3. Third-party layer vulnerabilities grouped by their respective causes. Explanations of each vulnerability can be found in Appendix A.3.

Vulnerability Cause	Vulnerability Type
Faulty operation	Compromised private key/wallet
	Weak password
	Deployment mistake
Off-chain oracle manipulation	Malicious oracle updater
	Malicious data source
	External market manipulation
Greedy project owners or other internet entities	Backdoor/Honeypot
	Insider activities
	Phishing attack
	Authority control or breach of promise
Faulty blockchain service provider	Faulty wallet provider
	Faulty API/RPC
Other	Other third-party layer vulnerabilities

B   Data Collection

Table 4. The sampled DeFi applications of each audit company.

Company	Sampled DeFi Projects
CertiK	Vicstep [18], The Space [17], Argo [14] Hunny Swap [16], Decaswap Finance [15]
ConsenSys	Fei Labs [25], pSTAKE Finance [22], Gluwacoin [21] Gamma [23], Notional Protocol [24]
Trail of Bits	Advanced Blockchain [61], DeGate [62], Looks Rare [63] Maple Labs [64], Perpetual Protocol V2 [65]
Beosin	Alpha Quark [12] Clip [9], SeasonSwap [13] MasterChefV2 [11], Crafting [10]
SlowMist	ROTL [53], LaqiraToken [56], CheersUp [55] Arowana [54], Starcrazy [57]
PeckShield	DeFiAI [40], KaoyaSwap [42], ArthSwap [38] eamswap [39], Duet Bond [41]
Quantstamp	PlaySwoops [46], CapsuleNFT [43], Pine [45] Rara [47], Nomad [44]
Hacken	Paribus [27], TheNextWar [29], VYNKSAFE [30] Onechain [26], Bolide [28]
Runtime Verification	Algofi [50], EXA Finance [52], Blockswap Stakehouse [49] Atlendis Protocol [51], Alchemix v2 [48]

C   Auditing Mechanism Findings

Table 5. Core steps of DeFi auditing. We include companies if they consider the specific step during their audits. A: CertiK, B: ConsenSys, C: Trail of Bits, D: Beosin, E: SlowMist, F: PeckShield, G: Quantstamp, H: Hacken, I: Runtime Verification.

Category	Auditing Step	Companies
Tool-Assisted Analysis	Static Analysis	A, B, C, D, E, F, G, H, I
	Symbolic Execution	B, C, G, H, I
	Fuzzing	B, C, D, E, H
	Formal Verification	A, B, C, D, I
Manual Analysis	Vulnerability Verification and Testing	A, B, C, D, E, F, G, H, I
	Advanced DeFi Scrutiny	A, B, C, D, E, F, G, H, I
	Semantic Consistency Analysis	A, B, D, F, G, H, I
Suggest Remediations	Vulnerability Remediation	A, B, C, D, E, F, G, H, I
	Coding Practice Recommendation	A, B, C, D, E, F, G, H, I

Tool-assisted analysis aims to identify potential vulnerabilities in smart contract codes through automated scrutiny, negating the need for an in-depth analysis of the protocol's business logic. Various tools are used to achieve this, with firms like Quantstamp and Trail of Bits explicitly mentioning their usage of specific tools such as Slither and Echidna respectively in their reports (Table 5).

Manual Analysis is often employed to expand the scope and increase the accuracy of vulnerabilities identified. This step is crucial as automated tools may generate false positives. After collecting potential vulnerabilities identified by tools, auditors manually verify them, perform code testing, and conduct advanced DeFi scrutiny and semantic consistency analysis.

Remediation Suggestion provides solutions for each identified vulnerability. Audit reports contain detailed descriptions of all vulnerabilities found, including their severity, type, example exploit, and remediation recommendations. They also provide suggestions for coding practices improvement and compliance with industry standards. The reports also state whether the vulnerabilities have been resolved after auditing, with statuses categorized as Resolved, Partially resolved, Acknowledged, or No Information provided.

D   Auditing Effectiveness Findings

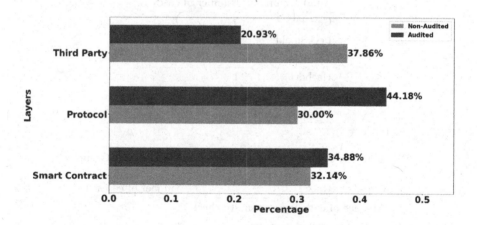

Fig. 1. Percentage distribution of 43 exploited vulnerabilities across different layers.

Table 6. The frequency of appearance of auditing firms in Not Mentioned Group

Audit Company	Number of cases
CertiK	8
Haechi	2
Solidity	2
OpenZepplin	2
ZOKYO	2
Harborn	1
Onmniscia	1
Arcadia	1
Cleanunicorn	1
InterFi Network	1
Consensys	1
Hacken	1
Solidified	1
Nick Johnson(Personal)	1

Table 7. The frequency of appearance of auditing firms in Searched For Group

Audit Company	Number of cases
CertiK	5
PeckShield	2
TechRate	1
Harborn	1
Quantstamp	1
Personal Audit	1

Table 8. The category of vulnerabilities in Searched For Group

Cause of attack	Number of cases
Absence of code logic or sanity check	5
Call to untrusted contract	3
Reentrancy	1
Oracle manipulation	1
Fake Token	1

References

1. Market manipulation. https://www.investor.gov/introduction-investing/investing-basics/glossary/market-manipulation. Accessed 1 Aug 2022
2. Medium. https://medium.com/. Accessed 5 Sept 2022
3. Peckshield. https://peckshield.medium.com/. Accessed 5 Sept 2022
4. rekt. https://rekt.news/. Accessed 5 Sept 2022
5. Slowmist hacked. https://hacked.slowmist.io/en/. Accessed 5 Sept 5 2022
6. What are liquidity pools in DeFi and how do they work? https://academy.binance.com/en/articles/what-are-liquidity-pools-in-defi. Accessed 5 Sept 2022
7. What are cross-chain smart contracts? (2022). https://blog.chain.link/cross-chain-smart-contracts/. Accessed 5 Sept 2022
8. Atzei, N., Bartoletti, M., Cimoli, T.: A survey of attacks on Ethereum smart contracts (SoK). In: Maffei, M., Ryan, M. (eds.) POST 2017. LNCS, vol. 10204, pp. 164–186. Springer, Heidelberg (2017). https://doi.org/10.1007/978-3-662-54455-6_8
9. Beosin: clip smart contract security audit (2022). https://beosin.com/audits/CLIP_202205101825.pdf. Accessed 13 June 2022
10. Beosin: crafting smart contract security audit (2022). https://beosin.com/audits/Crafting_202204141429.pdf. Accessed 13 June 2022
11. Beosin: MasterChefV2 smart contract security audit (2022). https://beosin.com/audits/MasterChefV2_202204211554.pdf. Accessed 13 June 2022
12. Beosin: NFTAQ721 smart contract security audit (2022). https://beosin.com/audits/NFTAQ721_202204181629.pdf. Accessed 13 June 2022
13. Beosin: season swap smart contract security audit (2022). https://beosin.com/audits/SeasonSwap_202204221127.pdf. Accessed 13 June 2022
14. CertiK: Security assessment argo - audit - addendum (2022). https://www.certik.com/projects/argo. Accessed 13 June 2022
15. CertiK: security assessment DecaSwap finance (2022). https://www.certik.com/projects/decaswap-finance. Accessed 13 June 2022
16. CertiK: Security assessment hunny swap (2022). https://www.certik.com/projects/hunny-swap. Accessed 13 June 2022
17. CertiK: security assessment the space (2022). https://www.certik.com/projects/the-space. Accessed 13 June 2022
18. CertiK: security assessment vicstep (2022). https://www.certik.com/projects/vicstep. Accessed 13 June 2022
19. Chen, H., Pendleton, M., Njilla, L., Xu, S.: A survey on Ethereum systems security: vulnerabilities, attacks, and defenses (2020). https://par.nsf.gov/servlets/purl/10197180. Accessed 7 Sept 2022
20. ConsenSys: locking pragmas. https://consensys.github.io/smart-contract-best-practices/development-recommendations/solidity-specific/locking-pragmas/. Accessed 3 Sept 2022
21. ConsenSys: Gluwacoin erc-20 wrapper (2021). https://consensys.net/diligence/audits/2021/10/gluwacoin-erc-20-wrapper/. Accessed 13 June 2022
22. ConsenSys: pstake finance (2021). https://consensys.net/diligence/audits/2021/08/pstake-finance/. Accessed 13 June 2022
23. ConsenSys: Gamma (2022). https://consensys.net/diligence/audits/2022/02/gamma/. Accessed 13 June 2022
24. ConsenSys: Notional protocol (2022). https://consensys.net/diligence/audits/2022/03/notional-protocol-v2.1/. Accessed 13 June 2022

25. ConsenSys: Tribe dao - flywheel v2, xtribe, xerc4626 (2022). https://consensys.net/diligence/audits/2022/04/tribe-dao-flywheel-v2-xtribe-xerc4626/. Accessed 13 June 2022

26. Hacken: smart contract code review and security analysis report for oneChain (2022). https://hacken.io/wp-content/uploads/2022/06/Summonersarena_010620 22_SCAudit_Report.pdf. Accessed 13 June 2022

27. Hacken: smart contract code review and security analysis report for paribus (2022). https://hacken.io/wp-content/uploads/2022/06/Paribus_25052022_SCAudit_Report_2.pdf. Accessed 13 June 2022

28. Hacken: smart contract code review and security analysis report for tencoins (2022). https://hacken.io/wp-content/uploads/2022/06/Bolide-Strategy_08062022_SCAudit_Report_3.pdf. Accessed 13 June 2022

29. Hacken: smart contract code review and security analysis report for thenextwar (2022). https://hacken.io/wp-content/uploads/2022/05/The_Next_War_02042022_SCAudit_Report_1.pdf. Accessed 13 June 2022

30. Hacken: smart contract code review and security analysis report for VYNKSAFE (2022). https://hacken.io/wp-content/uploads/2022/05/VYNKSAFE_03052022 SCAudit_Report1.pdf. Accessed 13 June 2022

31. Hertig, A.: What is a flash loan? https://www.coindesk.com/learn/2021/02/17/what-is-a-flash-loan/. Accessed 31 July 2022

32. Homoliak, I., Venugopalan, S., Reijsbergen, D., Hum, Q., Schumi, R., Szalachowski, P.: The security reference architecture for blockchains: toward a standardized model for studying vulnerabilities, threats, and defenses (2020). https://ieeexplore.ieee.org/stamp/stamp.jsp?arnumber=9239372. Accessed 7 Sept 2022

33. Jakobsson, M., Myers, S.: Phishing and Countermeasures: Understanding the Increasing Problem of Electronic Identity Theft. Wiley, Hoboken (2006)

34. Jurzik, H.: 5 most common deployment mistakes (2021). https://deploybot.com/blog/5-most-common-deployment-mistakes. Accessed 5 Sept 2022

35. Kaleem, M., Mavridou, A., Laszka, A.: Vyper: a security comparison with solidity based on common vulnerabilities (2020). https://arxiv.org/pdf/2003.07435.pdf. Accessed 7 Sept 2022

36. Luu, L., Chu, D.H., Olickel, H., Saxena, P., Hobor, A.: Making smart contracts smarter. In: Proceedings of the 2016 ACM SIGSAC Conference on Computer and Communications Security, pp. 254–269 (2016). https://eprint.iacr.org/2016/633.pdf, https://github.com/enzymefinance/oyente. Accessed 1 June 2022

37. Ng, F.: More than \$4.7m stolen in Uniswap fake token phishing attack (2022). https://cointelegraph.com/news/more-than-4-7m-stolen-in-uniswap-fake-token-phishing-attack. Accessed 5 Sept 2022

38. PeckShield: smart contract audit report for ArthSwap MasterChef (2022). https://github.com/peckshield/publications/blob/master/audit_reports/PeckShield-Audit-Report-ArthSwap-MasterChef-v1.0.pdf. Accessed 13 June 2022

39. PeckShield: smart contract audit report for beamswap (2022). https://github.com/peckshield/publications/blob/master/audit_reports/PeckShield-Audit-Report-Beamswap-v1.0.pdf. Accessed 13 June 2022

40. PeckShield: smart contract audit report for defiai (2022). https://github.com/peckshield/publications/blob/master/audit_reports/PeckShield-Audit-Report-DeFiAI-v1.0.pdf. Accessed 13 June 2022

41. PeckShield: smart contract audit report for duet bond (2022). https://github.com/peckshield/publications/blob/master/audit_reports/PeckShield-Audit-Report-Duet-Bond-v1.0.pdf. Accessed 13 June 2022

42. PeckShield: smart contract audit report for kaoyaswap (2022). https://github.com/peckshield/publications/blob/master/audit_reports/PeckShield-Audit-Report-KaoyaSwap-v1.0.pdf. Accessed 13 June 2022
43. Quantstamp: Quantstamp security assessment certificate capsulenft (2022). https://certificate.quantstamp.com/full/capsule-nft. Accessed 13 June 2022
44. Quantstamp: Quantstamp security assessment certificate nomad (2022). https://certificate.quantstamp.com/full/nomad. Accessed 13 June 2022
45. Quantstamp: Quantstamp security assessment certificate pine (2022). https://certificate.quantstamp.com/full/pine. Accessed 13 June 2022
46. Quantstamp: Quantstamp security assessment certificate playswoops (2022). https://certificate.quantstamp.com/full/play-swoops. Accessed 13 June 2022
47. Quantstamp: Quantstamp security assessment certificate rara (2022). https://certificate.quantstamp.com/full/rara. Accessed 13 June 2022
48. RuntimeVerification: Audit report alchemix v2 (2022). https://github.com/runtimeverification/publications/blob/main/reports/smart-contracts/Alchemix_v2.pdf. Accessed 13 June 2022
49. RuntimeVerification: audit report blockswap stakehouse (2022). https://github.com/runtimeverification/publications/blob/main/reports/smart-contracts/Blockswap_Stakehouse.pdf. Accessed 13 June 2022
50. RuntimeVerification: security audit report algofi amm and nanoswap (2022). https://github.com/runtimeverification/publications/blob/main/reports/smart-contracts/Algofi-dex-nanoswap.pdf. Accessed 13 June 2022
51. RuntimeVerification: security audit report atlendis protocol (2022). https://github.com/runtimeverification/publications/blob/main/reports/smart-contracts/atlendis-audit-report.pdf. Accessed 13 June 2022
52. RuntimeVerification: security audit report exa finance smart contracts (2022). https://github.com/runtimeverification/publications/blob/main/reports/smart-contracts/EXA_Finance.pdf. Accessed 13 June 2022
53. SlowMist: smart contract security audit report rotl (2021). https://github.com/slowmist/Knowledge-Base/blob/master/open-report-V2/smart-contract/SlowMist%20Audit%20Report%20-%20ROTL_en-us.pdf. Accessed 13 June 2022
54. SlowMist: smart contract security audit report arowana (2022). https://github.com/slowmist/Knowledge-Base/blob/master/open-report-V2/smart-contract/SlowMist%20Audit%20Report%20-%20Arowana_en-us.pdf. Accessed 13 June 2022
55. SlowMist: smart contract security audit report cheersup (2022). https://github.com/slowmist/Knowledge-Base/blob/master/open-report-V2/smart-contract/SlowMist%20Audit%20Report%20-%20CheersUp_alpha8_en-us.pdf. Accessed 13 June 2022
56. SlowMist: smart contract security audit report laqiratoken (2022). https://github.com/slowmist/Knowledge-Base/blob/master/open-report-V2/smart-contract/SlowMist%20Audit%20Report%20-%20LaqiraToken_en-us.pdf. Accessed 13 June 2022
57. SlowMist: smart contract security audit report starcrazy (2022). https://github.com/slowmist/Knowledge-Base/blob/master/open-report-V2/smart-contract/SlowMist%20Audit%20Report%20-%20Starcrazy_en-us.pdf. Accessed 13 June 2022
58. Stevens, R.: Inflationary and deflationary cryptocurrencies: what's the difference? https://www.coindesk.com/learn/inflationary-and-deflationary-cryptocurrencies-whats-the-difference/. Accessed 5 Sept 2022

59. Swende, M.H.: Eip-1884: repricing for trie-size-dependent opcodes. https://eips.ethereum.org/EIPS/eip-1884#motivation. Accessed 31 July 2022

60. Torres, C.F., Steichen, M., et al.: The art of the scam: demystifying honeypots in ethereum smart contracts (2019). https://www.usenix.org/system/files/sec19-torres.pdf. Accessed 7 Sept 2022)

61. TrailofBits: advanced blockchain security assessment (2022). https://github.com/trailofbits/publications/blob/master/reviews/AdvancedBlockchainQ12022.pdf. Accessed 13 June 2022

62. TrailofBits: Degate security assessment (2022). https://github.com/trailofbits/publications/blob/master/reviews/DeGate.pdf. Accessed 13 June 2022

63. TrailofBits: Looksrare security assessment (2022). https://github.com/trailofbits/publications/blob/master/reviews/LooksRare.pdf. Accessed 13 June 2022

64. TrailofBits: maple labs security assessment (2022). https://github.com/trailofbits/publications/blob/master/reviews/MapleFinance.pdf. Accessed 13 June 2022

65. TrailofBits: perpetual protocol v2 security assessment (2022). https://github.com/trailofbits/publications/blob/master/reviews/PerpetualProtocolV2.pdf. Accessed 13 June 2022

66. Wang, Y., Zuest, P., Yao, Y., Lu, Z., Wattenhofer, R.: Impact and user perception of sandwich attacks in the DeFi ecosystem. In: CHI Conference on Human Factors in Computing Systems, pp. 1–15 (2022)

67. Zhou, L., et al.: Sok: decentralized finance (DeFi) attacks. Cryptology ePrint Archive (2022)

Short Squeeze in DeFi Lending Market: Decentralization in Jeopardy?

Lioba Heimbach$^{(\boxtimes)}$, Eric Schertenleib, and Roger Wattenhofer

ETH Zürich, Zürich, Switzerland
{hlioba,ericsch,wattenhofer}@ethz.ch

Abstract. Anxiety levels in the Aave community spiked in November 2022 as Avi Eisenberg performed an attack on Aave. Eisenberg attempted to short the CRV token by using funds borrowed on the protocol to artificially deflate the value of CRV. While the attack was ultimately unsuccessful, it left the Aave community scared and even raised question marks regarding the feasibility of large lending platforms under decentralized governance.

In this work, we analyze Avi Eisenberg's actions and show how he was able to artificially lower the price of CRV by selling large quantities of borrowed CRV for stablecoins on both decentralized and centralized exchanges. Despite the failure of his attack, it still led to irretrievable debt worth more than 1.5 Mio USD at the time and, thereby, quadrupled the protocol's irretrievable debt. Furthermore, we highlight that his attack was enabled by the vast proportion of CRV available to borrow as well as Aave's lending protocol design hindering rapid intervention. We stress Eisenberg's attack exposes a predicament of large DeFi lending protocols: limit the scope or compromise on 'decentralization'.

Keywords: blockchain · DeFi · lending protocols · price manipulation

1 Introduction

While borrowing assets serves a whole host of purposes, perhaps none have gained such an infamous reputation as short-selling. Thereby, a market participant borrows funds but immediately upon entering the borrowing contract, sells the asset ('selling it short') in the hope of re-acquiring it ('covering the short') before the lending contract expires at a lower price. A short-seller thus profits if the asset loses value. However, short-selling naturally involves risks for the speculator – mainly that the asset appreciates in value. In this case, the borrower must buy back the asset at a higher price than they sold it for. In dramatic cases, the borrower becomes at risk of defaulting on the loan, and the lender may demand the repayment, thus, forcing the borrower to cover the short ('short squeeze').

In traditional finance, banks or brokers provide loans that enable short-selling. The conditions of the loan are typically set by the lender or are agreed upon by the involved parties. Thus, the loan must be approved by the lender, and the lender naturally closely monitors the financial situation of the borrower and employs complex active risk management to safeguard their funds.

© International Financial Cryptography Association 2024
A. Essex et al. (Eds.): FC 2023 Workshops, LNCS 13953, pp. 337–351, 2024.
https://doi.org/10.1007/978-3-031-48806-1_22

In contrast, *Decentralized Finance (DeFi)* aims to build a financial ecosystem that provides the financial services of the traditional financial sector without relying on a central authority or placing any trust in a counterparty. Given its role as a cornerstone of finance, it is not surprising that DeFi protocols were launched that enable borrowing and lending. One of the most well-known lending protocols is *Aave* [1]. On Aave's V2-version users could borrow a host of different ERC20 tokens, including the *Curve DAO token (CRV)*, the utility token of the decentralized exchange Curve [11]. The key to offering loans in a trustless setting is requiring users to deposit collateral of greater value than the debt taken out (*over-collateralization*). Loans at risk of becoming under-collateralization are offered for liquidation at a discount to protect lenders and avoid irretrievable debt on the protocol.

In October 2022, Avi Eisenberg began publicly discussing ideas on how to attack Aave, i.e., burdening the protocol with irretrievable debt for his profit. He had previously gained a reputation by extracting more than 100 Mio USD from the DeFi protocol Mango Markets [12] using price manipulation – fooling the protocol about the value of the pledged collateral [13]. The ideas discussed for Aave were of similar nature. Then, in November 2022, Avi Eisenberg began his attack on Aave by shorting CRV. In particular, he deposited USDC, a stablecoin[1], as collateral on Aave and sold CRV short. His actions led to a rapid price decrease and thereby devalued the collateral of users who had deposited CRV. These developments lead to significant anxiety in the Aave community. They feared being left with irretrievable debt, which ultimately did materialize, despite the failure of the attack.

Our Contribution. In this work, we dissect Avi Eisenberg's actions and use this as a case study to highlight threats to the viability of DeFi lending protocols. In particular, we observe Eisenberg selling his borrowed CRV on both decentralized and centralized exchanges for stablecoins. We further analyze Eisenberg's effect on the CRV borrowing market and show that Eisenberg selected CRV for a good reason. Aave offered significant liquidity relative to CRV's market capitalization enabling him to greatly affect the price of CRV using the borrowed assets. Finally, we discuss the aftermath of the attack. We show that a single (failed) attack quadrupled the amount of bad debt on Aave, underscoring the threat posed to the whole DeFi lending market. Further, we review the actions taken by Aave to rectify the situation and discuss the viability of 'decentralized' lending platforms.

2   Background

Lenders require that the borrower puts up collateral to secure the loan. While in traditional finance, this 'collateral' is at times only limited to the borrower's creditworthiness and their promise to repay (unsecured debt), this approach

---

[1] Stablecoins are cryptocurrencies that are pegged to a 'stable' asset – typically the USD. For our purposes, we can use USDT, USDC, and BUSD (Binance USD) as synonymous with USD.

does not adhere to the trustless principle of decentralized finance. Furthermore, both borrowers and lenders often rely on third-party intermediaries like banks to facilitate the transaction.

DeFi lending protocols, on the other hand, seek to offer these services without a trusted third-party or prior clearance of either borrower or lender. Instead, users deposit assets that the protocol supports, such as CRV for Aave V2, thereby becoming *liquidity providers*. Liquidity providers earn interest on their funds locked in the protocol. Users seeking to borrow can use the deposited funds as collateral to take out debt. The required collateral significantly exceeds their maximal debt in value. Thus, the borrower is required to *over-collateralize*. This over-collateralization allows users to borrow without prior clearance.

The parameters of Aave's smart contract determine the terms of borrowing and lending. The formula for the rates is included in Appendix A. Qualitatively, it is important to note that the rates are determined by the *utilization*, i.e., the fraction of deposited funds that have been borrowed, and the risk parameters set by the protocol in accordance to the perceived risk of the asset. Furthermore, note that there is a maximal borrowing rate that can be reached. In the case of CRV, the rate is limited to 307%.

In the event that the collateralization of the borrower becomes insufficient, the position can be liquidated. The threshold for this is given by the *health factor* H reaching 1, where

$$H = \frac{\sum_{i \in A}(C_i \cdot l_i)}{\sum_{i \in A} D_i}.$$

Here, the sum running over the set assets available on the protocol A, C_i is the collateral deposited in currency i, l_i is the liquidation threshold for asset i, and D_i is the debt in token i. Once the health factor drops below 1, its collateral is auctioned off at a discount to a liquidator who must repay the debt. In the case of CRV, Aave V2 uses a liquidation threshold of 89%.

To calculate the health factor and other asset price dependent quantities, lending protocols rely on *price oracles*. For example, Aave V2 uses Chainlink's price oracle [9]. Chainlink thus provides Aave with information on the price the asset is currently trading at on centralized markets. Finally, we note that like many DeFi protocols, Aave is governed by a *decentralized autonomous organization (DAO)*. Holders of the Aave token (native token of Aave) comprise the DAO of Aave. They can vote on proposals such as changing the protocol's risk parameters. The procedure for such changes must abide to rules that are enforced by the protocol's smart contract. Therefore, such changes do take several days to get implemented.

3 Related Work

Early research by Bartoletti et al. [17] on DeFi lending protocols, which became widely adopted amidst the excitement of the 2020 DeFi summer, provides a systematization of knowledge regarding lending protocols as well as a formal framework to model them. Gudgeon et al. [21] further present an empirical study of interest rate rules utilized by lending protocols.

Lending protocols are a DeFi corner stone, as Aramonte et al. [16] point out they allow users to easily take on leverage and are mainly used to facilitate cryptocurrency price speculation. The central position of lending protocols in DeFi, thus, makes cryptocurrency prices increasingly sensitive as Chiu et al. [18] note. Our work studies exactly how leveraged trading on lending protocols affects cryptocurrency prices by examining a case study in detail.

Heimbach et al. [22] investigate the effects of the Merge on Ether rates on Aave and Compound. They discuss how the DAOs of the respective protocols took actions to prevent exorbitant rates leading to mass liquidations. In contrast to the Merge, the short-selling we investigate was not announced well in advanced, giving less time for the protocols to adapt and thus posing a different kind of challenge to the lending protocols.

Attacks, arbitrage opportunities and trading strategies on DeFi protocols are frequent and well-studied studied in previous work [20, 24–29]. As opposed to these works, our work studies a novel attack on lending protocols by examining the CRV short-selling attempt that was facilitated by through lending activity on Aave.

4 Data Collection

We collect both Ethereum blockchain data, as well as data from centralized exchanges. To gather the on-chain data we run an erigon [23] archive node. In particular, we filter the transaction logs for those that relate to the Aave lending market and query the historical state of the Aave contracts to obtain the relevant data. Additionally, we inspect the logs to identify the value and target of all CRV transfers originating from Avi Eisenberg's wallet [14]. For centralized exchanges, we collect data from Binance and OKX. The former, as it is the largest crypto exchange and its price is therefore very reliable. The latter, as the short-seller transferred the vast majority of the borrowed funds to his OKX account. For Binance data, we connect to their API to get aggregated price, and volume data of CRV-BUSD [8]. OKX provides aggregated trade data on a daily basis. We downloaded all aggregated trade data for the month of November and analyze the four pools they offer containing CRV: Ether (ETH), Bitcoin (BTC), and the two stablecoins USDT and USDC.

5 Avi Eisenberg's Attack

In this section, we focus on Eisenberg's attack. We first discuss an attack he had previously suggested and transition to his actual attack. We trace his money flows to decentralized and centralized exchanges. Then, we investigate why Eisenberg likely selected CRV and what his intentions may have been.

Naturally, lending protocols are required to closely monitor the price of the assets supported on the protocol to determine quantities such as the value of the collateral, line of credit, or the liquidation threshold. An attacker or an external event causing a rapid price change can catch other users of the protocol off guard. For example, a rapid increase in price of a borrowed token or pledged collateral can lead to a short-squeeze, and, in dramatic cases, lead to a situation where not all debt can be retrieved (bad debt). This bad debt is from the perspective of the liquidity providers lost money. Thus, rapid price movements pose a threat to lending protocols.

This was highlighted in October 2022 when Avi Eisenberg, at the time already well-known for his attack on Mango Markets, began floating the idea of attacking Aave in a series of tweets [10]. Essentially his idea boils down to using borrowed assets to artificially inflate the value of the pledged collateral, and, in the end, taking out more loans than the original value of the collateral. We discuss his proposed attack in more detail in Appendix D. It is important to note that what Eisenberg proposes is in fact an attack on the lending protocol. He has no intention of repaying the debt but solely attempts to borrow more than he posted as collateral. Shortly after his comments and possibly in response, Aave froze the lending pool for REN – the asset Eisenberg suggested for the attack – and a few other assets [4].

In November 2022, Avi Eisenberg himself began targeting Aave by borrowing CRV and dumping it on the market. In Fig. 1, we show the CRV price on Binance. We observe a significant and rapid price drop on November 22, which, as discussed below, is also the date Eisenberg dumps most his borrowed CRV on to the market.

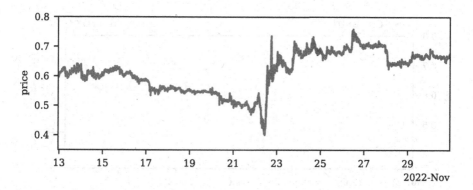

Fig. 1. Price of CRV on Binance during the in November (CRV-BUSD pool). We observe large price movements around November 22, the main date during Eisenberg's attack.

Eisenberg started his move on November 13 by depositing approximately 39 Mio USDC on Aave V2. The next day he took out his first CRV loan. Initially, the short-seller's activity was a relatively small scale. Until the end of November 15, Eisenberg had borrowed 6 Mio CRV (approx 3.6 Mio USDC) of which he sold about 2.2 Mio through the decentralized exchange aggregator 1inch [6].

From November 17 to 22 he stepped up his strategy by further borrowing more than 68 Mio CRV. Eisenberg borrowed nearly all available CRV which in turn also led to a spike in borrowing rates. We show the available liquidity and borrowing rates in Appendix A. We note that even though the high borrowing rates is an expense the attacker must shoulder, the short duration of the attack hardly makes an annualized borrowing rate of around 300% prohibitive.

From November 16 on, Avi Eisenberg no longer sold his tokens on 1inch. Rather, he transferred large amounts of borrowed CRV to the centralized exchange OKX – 71.6 Mio CRV of the total 77 Mio he borrowed over the course of November. While centralized exchanges do not offer the same transparency and it is therefore not possible to exactly track his transactions, we can gather several clues. OKX provides aggregated trade data, i.e., for every trade we know the price at which the trade occurred, the timestamp as well as the transaction size.

When analyzing the four pools that OKX offers, CRV-USDT, CRV-UST, CRV-ETH, and CRV-BTC, we notice a conspicuous jump in trading volume in the CRV-USDT pool. In Fig. 2, we show the CRV-USDT price and the hourly volume. We observe that the trading volume dramatically jumps after Eisenberg deposited significant funds to OKX – indicated by dashed vertical lines. In fact, trading volume is orders of magnitudes larger than usual for this pool. Note that while he had already deposited some of the borrowed CRV on OKX before November 22, those amounted to significantly less than the deposits on the 22nd (11.6 Mio CRV before November 22 vs. 60 Mio CRV on November 22).

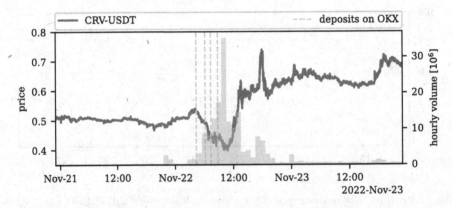

Fig. 2. Plot of the CRV-USDT price on OKX (blue) and the hourly trading volume measured in CRV (yellow). The dashed vertical lines indicate the times at which the short-seller deposited significant amounts of CRV on OKX. We observe significant volume shortly after the these deposits. (Color figure online)

Thus, it is highly likely that Avi Eisenberg sold his borrowed CRV on OKX primarily for the stablecoin USDT in the hope of causing a large enough price drop. We note that he likely chose a centralized exchange like OKX rather than a decentralized exchange as both Aave's price oracle, Chainlink, as well as arbitrage bots often assume the centralized exchange price to be the 'true' price. Further, the liquidity depth is on centralized markets is typically larger and, thus, could likely expect a better price.

Naturally, the question arises why the short-seller ultimately targeted CRV. A lot of the public discourse around Eisenberg's attack focuses on the debt position of the Curve founder, Michael Egorov, who had deposited significant amounts of CRV on Aave and borrowed against it. The theory is that Eisenberg attempted to cause such a price drop, leading to the liquidation of Egorov's debt [19]. This liquidation would then lead to a further decrease in price, benefiting the short-seller. We plot the health factor of the Curve founder's debt position in Appendix C in Fig. 7. We see that his health factor is around 1.5 around the attack but does fluctuate significantly.

While it is possible that Eisenberg attempted to get the debt position liquidated, and he did allude to this [2], this represents quite a fanciful plan. Egorov's debt was quite far from liquidation, making a large price drop necessary. Additionally, the Curve founder has significant funds at his disposal to post additional collateral – something he ultimately did. Thus, it appears that this plan would only had slim chances of success to begin with.

Rather than solely focusing on the Curve founder's debt, we stress that there were further reasons for Eisenberg targeting CRV. For an attack relying on borrowed funds to move the price, the amount of liquidity available to borrow must be significant relative to the total market capitalization of the token. Further, if the total market capitalization is too large, the short-seller may simply lack the funds for the attack, even if a large proportion of the assets were available on Aave.

In Fig. 3a, we plot the liquidity deposited as a function of the tokens total market capitalization for each asset available on Aave V2. The data is as of November 1 and the market capitalization data is taken from CoinMarketCap. Similarly, Fig. 3b shows the liquidity *available* to a borrower as a function of the market capitalization. The color of the data points has the following meaning: we plot tokens for which Aave disabled borrowing before Eisenberg's attack but after his October tweets in yellow. Purple points represent tokens for which Aave froze borrowing after the attack (such as CRV) and assets that can still be borrowed are displayed in blue.

As we can see, CRV must have seemed a very attractive option for Eisenberg given that the available liquidity relative to the market capitalization was very high at more than 15% (top left corner of the plot). We conclude from Fig. 3 that CRV was Eisenberg's best option for the attack.

This highlights that CRV was an attractive option for Eisenberg irrespective of the debt of Egorov. We further point out that Eisenberg could have also been attempting a modification of his originally proposed attack discussed in Appendix D.

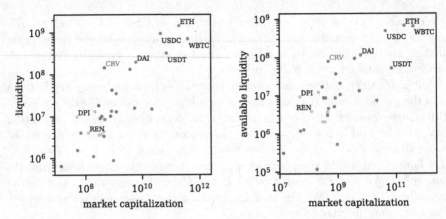

(a) Liquidity deposited on Aave V2 relative to the token's market cap.

(b) Liquidity available to borrow on Aave V2 relative to the token's market cap.

Fig. 3. Plot showing the liquidity (left) and available liquidity (right) of different tokens offered on Aave V2 on November 1 2022 as a function of market capitalization. For the short seller CRV is an attractive choice as it has a large proportion of its market cap on Aave (top left corner in the respective plots). Tokens for which Aave froze lending before Eisenberg's attack are represented as yellow points. Purple points represent tokens for which lending was de-activetad after the attack and for tokens plotted in blue borrowing remains possible. (Color figure online)

1. The attacker deposits USDC to borrow significant amounts of CRV
2. The attacker sells all CRV on a centralized exchange lowering the price. The funds received cover some of the debt taken out but also lead to a devaluation of the debt and a reduction in debt to collateral ratio.
3. The attacker uses the lower debt level to take out a loan in USDT.

The proceeds in step 2) as well as the loan in step 3) would fund his attack. A liquidation of Egorov's debt or panic-selling of CRV holders during the price devaluation would boost the attacker's profit. Note that strategy should be considered an attack rather than short-selling, as unlike a short-seller the attacker has no intentions of repaying the borrowed tokens. This underscores that the ramifications of such strategies for lending protocols are far greater than mere short-selling.

6 Aftermath

After initially managing to reduce the price of CRV by around 20%, the CRV price surged later on November 22, jumping by about 75% (cf. Fig. 2). This rapid price jump led to the liquidation of Eisenberg's debt. However, the sheer size of his debt had negative implications for the protocol. In Fig. 4, we plot the total value of all bad debt as well as all debt on Aave V2 measured in ETH. Note that we obtain the total (bad) debt by identifying all users that ever borrowed assets on Aave V2. We then, on a daily basis, query the value of their collateral and debt. The debt of positions with a debt value larger than the collateral value is bad debt. We observe that the total amount of bad debt more than quadruples due to the activities of Eisenberg. This highlights the severe impact that the short-seller's activity had. Furthermore, we note that this is the damage incurred due to the failed attack. Had the attack succeeded the implications would have likely been far graver. Furthermore, we note that in this instance the bad debt was, in the end, covered by the protocol.

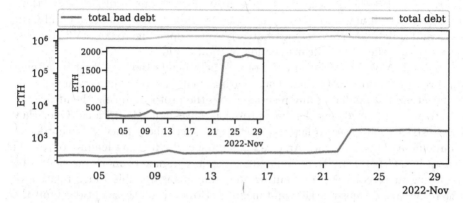

Fig. 4. Plot of the total debt (green) and bad debt, i.e., the debt of liquidated positions that has become irretrievable, on Aave V2. Note that the short-squeeze of Avi Eisenberg quadrupled the amount of bad debt, highlighting the strain the actions of the short-seller exerted on the protocol. (Color figure online)

It has been suggested that the delay of the price oracle has aggravated the bad debt. In Appendix B, we plot the health factor of Avi Eisenberg both using the Binance price as well as the oracle price. While differences are visible, the ultimate effect of this price delay is rather limited.

What, however, could cause potentially fatal delays is Aave's reliance on comparatively slow moving DAO votes. While the protocol has a proven track-record of successfully updating its risk parameters to face changing market environment such as during the Merge [22], these changes do require a few days. In this instance, Aave was not oblivious to the threats of Eisenberg's proposed attack and froze borrowing of assets like REN (yellow points in Fig. 3) only weeks after Eisenberg mused about this potential attack [4]. While we cannot be certain that Aave disabled borrowing for these tokens as a consequence of Eisenberg's comments, the timing of their actions and the discussions in the governance forum lead us to believe that the two are not unrelated. However, reacting to CRV developments proved difficult as the majority of the short-selling occurred on a single day. In the aftermath of the attack Aave V2 disabled several further tokens including CRV (purple points in Fig. 3) [5].

346 L. Heimbach et al.

7 Discussion

Given their size lending protocols like Aave are rightly considered one of the most successful applications of DeFi. However, the attack of Avi Eisenberg demonstrated that despite – or in some cases due to – this success vulnerabilities remain. An attack like the one proposed by Eisenberg is facilitated by two key features.

First, Eisenberg relied on Aave holding a significant portion of all available CRV tokens (>30% of market cap). The large amount of funds available to borrow enabled the attacker to significantly move the price of the asset, thus, effectively manipulating the price and thereby altering the valuation of all CRV debt and collateral. This avenue of attack is only open due to Aave V2's success in attracting such a significant portion of total liquidity.

Second, Aave V2 relies on a set of risk parameters that can only be altered by a relatively slow DAO vote. Thus, during such an attack the parameters are, in effect, static, hindering any response from the protocol during the attack.

To face this challenge lending protocols have multiple options. One, they can restrict themselves to large market cap tokens whose price is far harder to manipulate. This is a route Aave V2 has pursued by freezing lending of several assets like CRV. Two, they could make their parameters more restrictive by requiring more collateral or limiting the amount of available funds relative to the respective token's market capitalization. However, all these options limit the scope of the protocol and may make the protocol less attractive to certain users.

Alternatively, they can rely more heavily on active risk management, allowing the risk parameters to change rapidly in response to altering market conditions. As has been suggested, this could be accomplished by employing a feedback loop that automatically updates the risk parameters [3]. This would, however, inadvertently add additional layers of complexity and potentially open new avenues of attack as the feedback loops would likely rely on further market parameters fed by oracles.

Instead, lending protocols could rely on an active risk manager who has the flexibility to intervene. This is the route Aave has chosen for its newest version, V3. On Aave V3, the DAO can elect a 'risk admin' who has the power to change the risk parameters without a governance vote [7]. However, this naturally compromises the protocol's decentralization.

Finally, we note that a future attack could use multiple protocols to borrow a total amount sufficient for price manipulation. Thus, with the growing popularity of DeFi lending protocols, the inter-dependencies and complexities will also increase, necessitating cross-protocol risk management.

8 Conclusion

In this work, we use Avi Eisenberg's actions as a case study. We investigate his money flows across both DeFi and centralized exchanges. Furthermore, we show that Eisenberg selected CRV as, among other reasons, Aave at the time had more than 30% of the market capitalization locked on its protocol, making large-scale price manipulations feasible. Despite the failure of the attack, it still led to irretrievable debt worth more than 1.5 Mio USD at the time, quadrupling the protocol's irretrievable debt.

In summary, Eisenberg's attack highlighted that DeFi lending protocols that contain a large portion of a token's market capitalization enable price manipulations. The slow-moving governance votes are ill-suited to react to such an attack. This has left large lending protocols in predicament: either limit their offering or place their trust in active risk management.

A   Borrowing Rates

The parameters of Aave's smart contract determine the terms of borrowing and lending. The rates are ultimately determined by the *utilization*, i.e., the fraction of deposited funds that have been borrowed. In the case of CRV the borrowing rate at time t as a function of the utilization U_t is given as

$$r_t = \begin{cases} r_0 + \frac{U_t}{U_{\text{optimal}}} r_{\text{slope}_1} & \text{if } U_t \leq U_{\text{optimal}}, \\ r_0 + r_{\text{slope}_1} + \frac{U_t - U_{\text{optimal}}}{1 - U_{\text{optimal}}} r_{\text{slope}_2} & \text{if } U_t > U_{\text{optimal}}, \end{cases}$$

with $r_0 = 0$, $U_{\text{optimal}} = 45\%$, $r_{\text{slope}_1} = 7\%$, and $r_{\text{slope}_2} = 300\%$. Note that the rate r_t is given as an annualized rate and has a kink at the 'optimal utilization' U_{optimal}. Furthermore, the rates are capped at a maximum of $r_{\text{slope}_1} + r_{\text{slope}_2} = 307\%$. The aforementioned risk parameters differ across cryptocurrencies and are set by the protocol in accordance to the perceived risk of the asset.

Eisenberg started his move on Nov-13 by depositing approximately 39 Mio USDC on Aave V2. The next day he took out his first CRV-loan. Initially, the short-seller's activity was on quite a small scale. Until the end of November 15, Eisenberg had borrowed 6 Mio CRV (approx 3.6 Mio USDC) of which he sold about 2.2 Mio through the decentralized exchange 1inch [6]. From November 17 to 22 he stepped up his strategy by borrowing more than 68 Mio CRV. As shown in Fig. 5a the available liquidity (in yellow) in Aave's CRV-pool dropped to zero, signaling that the short-seller borrowed the maximal possible amount. Consequently, the borrowing rates also spiked (cf. Fig. 5b).

B   Latency of Price Oracle

Apart from the danger's posed by rapid price changes, inaccuracies of the protocol's oracle price can also pose significant threats. In Fig. 6, we plot the health factor of Eisenberg using both Aave's oracle price as well as the Binance price. While small differences are visible the oracle price reflected the Binance quite accurately. Observe that between 5 and 6 p.m. the price increase rapidly bringing down the health factor from just above 1 to under 0.89 in a matter of minutes, the later threshold indicates the value at which irretrievable debt begins to accumulate. This highlights that the time window for liquidations can be very short

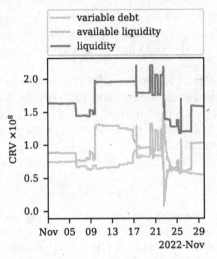
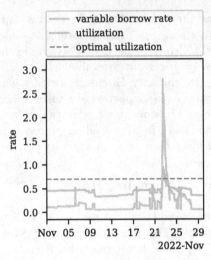

(a) Debt (green), available liquidity (yellow), and total liquidity (violet) in Aave's CRV pool.

(b) Borrowing rate (green) and utilization (yellow) of CRV on Aave V2 during November.

Fig. 5. Total volume of debt taken out (left) and borrowing rates (right) are both ploted in green. Note the total debt taken out peaked at about 150 Mio CRV (approx. 90 Mio USD at the time) which corresponds to basically all liquidity that was available on Aave V2 at the time. (Color figure online)

and was very short for this case study. The liquidations, nevertheless, succeeded in retrieving the majority of the debt. However, the combination of the sheer volume of the position's debt and the limited time the protocol had to liquidate the position, in the end, left the protocol with the significant amount of irretrievable debt which in the end the protocol covered.

C   Curve Founder's Position on Aave

In Fig. 7 we plot the health factor of the position of the Curve founder's wallet on Aave [15]. Even though, it was suggested by Avi Eisenberg himself and repeated in multiple articles discussing the attack, we do not believe that Avi Eisenberg attack was solely focused around causing a liquidation of this position. While liquidations of a position with such a significant volume of CRV collateral would have lead to a further decrease in price, we believe that this strategy would have been fanciful. The position's health factor never dropped significantly below a health factor of 1.5 during the attack and it is further hard to believe that the Curve founder would not have the funds available to prevent his liquidation.

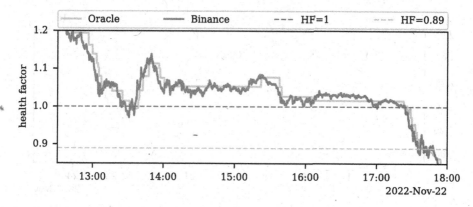

Fig. 6. Health factor of Eisenberg using the oracle price (green) and the Binance price (blue). A health factor below 1 makes liquidations possible, whereas, the yellow line indicates the price at which bed debt would remain. (Color figure online)

D Attack Proposed by Avi Eisenberg

Avi Eisenberg suggested the following attack on Aave's REN-pool [10]. An attacker has two wallets, A and B, where initially 100% of his assets are in wallet A. We here sketch the idea of the attack:

1. From wallet A deposit 100% of the assets as USDC as collateral to borrow all REN possible on Aave. Using USDC as collateral, a user can borrow 85% of the USDC value (loan to value).
2. The attacker's borrowed REN (85% of initial assets) is transferred to wallet B. The attacker uses the REN as collateral to borrow USDC on Aave. At the time the loan to value for REN was 60%, so from wallet B the attacker could borrow approximately $85\% \cdot 60\% \approx 50\%$ of the initially deposited USDC.
3. The attacker uses the borrowed USDC to buy REN on centralized exchanges to drive up the price of REN[2].
4. This increases the value of the collateral of wallet B, allowing the attacker to take out more USDC loans.

The collateral in wallet A will be liquidated by the price increase caused in step 3. Additionally, given the price increase was created by artificial buying pressure, it is likely that the price of REN reverts close to it's original value, thus, also liquidating the collateral in step 2. However, if this price increase is sufficiently large, the additional USDC that can be extracted in step 4 as well as to proceeds of selling the REN acquired in step 3, pays for the attack.

---

[2] The thereby acquired REN could be used to go back to step 2 to borrow more USDC to repeat the cycle. Given the loan to value of 60%, the hypothetical limit the 50% of assets borrowed in step 2 can be increased to using this loop is given by the geometric series, i.e. $50\%/(1 - 60\%) = 125\%$.

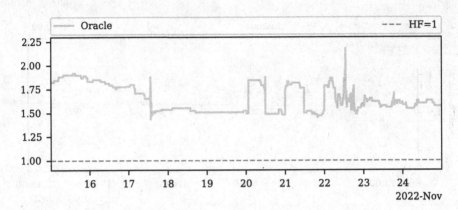

Fig. 7. Health factor of Curve founder using the oracle price (green). A health factor below 1 makes liquidations possible, the position did not come close to the liquidation threshold. (Color figure online)

Note that an attacker may deliberately target a lending protocol for more reasons than pure profits. An attacker looking to damage a protocol, thus, might execute this attack for a small profit or even at a small cost just to make a point.

Finally, we note that for this attack to work, the amount of REN available on Aave must be significant to allow the attacker to use the borrowed REN to create a significant uptick in price. Thus, the proportion of the market cap available on Aave for borrowing must be significant.

References

1. Aave (2022). https://aave.com/
2. Eisenberg Tweet from Nov-20 (2022). https://twitter.com/avi_eisen/status/1594293743380615168?cxt=HHwWgMCinc7tiKAsAAAA
3. Report on code at risk: an in-depth analysis of how AAVE's $1.6 million bad debt was created (2022). https://drive.google.com/file/d/1u3vtcsQ1qfclt6Od8aZx5DkvuQRE4GMH/view
4. Risk parameter updates for Aave V2 ETH market (2022–11-12) (2022). https://app.aave.com/governance/proposal/?proposalId=117
5. Risk parameter updates for Aave V2 Ethereum liquidity Pool (2022–11-25) (2022). https://governance.aave.com/t/risk-parameter-updates-for-aave-v2-ethereum-liquidity-pool-2022-11-25/10824
6. 1inch (2023). https://app.1inch.io
7. Aave V3 Risk (2023). https://docs.aave.com/risk/
8. Binance API (2023). https://github.com/binance/binance-public-data
9. Chainlink (2023). https://chain.link/
10. Chainlink (2023). https://twitter.com/avi_eisen/status/1582763707742183424
11. Curve (2023). https://curve.fi/
12. Mango Markets (2023). https://mango.markets/
13. Mango Markets Mangled by Oracle Manipulation for 112M (2023). https://blockworks.co/news/mango-markets-mangled-by-oracle-manipulation-for-112m

14. Wallet of Avi Eisenberg: 0x57e04786e231af3343562c062e0d058f25dace9e (2023)
15. Wallet of Curve Founder: 0x7a16ff8270133f063aab6c9977183d9e72835428 (2023)
16. Aramonte, S., Doerr, S., Huang, W., Schrimpf, A., et al.: DeTi lending: intermediation without information? Technical report, Bank for International Settlements (2022)
17. Bartoletti, M., Chiang, J.H., Lafuente, A.L.: SoK: lending pools in decentralized finance. In: International Conference on Financial Cryptography and Data Security (2021)
18. Chiu, J., Ozdenoren, E., Yuan, K., Zhang, S.: On the inherent fragility of DeFi lending (2022)
19. EigenPhi: cleaning Up of the Battlefield of Avi and Curve (2022). https://eigenphi.substack.com/p/cleaning-up-of-the-battlefield-of
20. Eskandari, S., Salehi, M., Gu, W.C., Clark, J.: SoK: oracles from the ground truth to market manipulation. arXiv preprint arXiv:2106.00667 (2021)
21. Gudgeon, L., Werner, S., Perez, D., Knottenbelt, W.J.: DeFi protocols for loanable funds: interest rates, liquidity and market efficiency. In: Proceedings of the 2nd ACM Conference on Advances in Financial Technologies, pp. 92–112 (2020)
22. Heimbach, L., Schertenleib, E., Wattenhofer, R.: DeFi lending during the merge. arXiv preprint arXiv:2303.08748 (2023)
23. ledgerwatch: Erigon (2023). https://github.com/ledgerwatch/erigon
24. Perez, D., Werner, S.M., Xu, J., Livshits, B.: Liquidations: DeFi on a knife-edge. In: Borisov, N., Diaz, C. (eds.) FC 2021. LNCS, vol. 12675, pp. 457–476. Springer, Heidelberg (2021). https://doi.org/10.1007/978-3-662-64331-0_24
25. Qin, K., Zhou, L., Gamito, P., Jovanovic, P., Gervais, A.: An empirical study of DeFi liquidations: incentives, risks, and instabilities, pp. 336–350. IMC 2021 (2021)
26. Qin, K., Zhou, L., Gervais, A.: Quantifying blockchain extractable value: how dark is the forest? In: 2022 IEEE Symposium on Security and Privacy (SP), pp. 198–214. IEEE (2022)
27. Torres, C.F., Camino, R., State, R.: Frontrunner jones and the raiders of the dark forest: an empirical study of frontrunning on the Ethereum blockchain. arXiv preprint arXiv:2102.03347 (2021)
28. Yaish, A., Tochner, S., Zohar, A.: Blockchain stretching & squeezing: manipulating time for your best interest. In: Proceedings of the 23rd ACM Conference on Economics and Computation, pp. 65–88 (2022)
29. Zhou, L., Qin, K., Torres, C.F., Le, D.V., Gervais, A.: High-frequency trading on decentralized on-chain exchanges. In: 2021 IEEE Symposium on Security and Privacy (SP), pp. 428–445. IEEE (2021)

WTSC

Efficient Rollup Batch Posting Strategy on Base Layer

Akaki Mamageishvili[✉] and Edward W. Felten

Offchain Labs, Zürich, Switzerland
akaki@inf.ethz.ch

Abstract. We design efficient and robust algorithms for the batch posting of rollup chain calldata on the base layer chain, using tools from
operations research. We relate the costs of posting and delaying, by con-
verting them to the same units and adding them up. The algorithm that
keeps the average and maximum queued number of batches tolerable
enough improves the posting costs of the trivial algorithm, which posts
batches immediately when they are created, by 8%. On the other hand,
the algorithm that only cares moderately about the batch queue length
can improve the trivial algorithm posting costs by 29%. Our findings can
be used by layer two projects that post data to the base layer at some
regular rate.

1 Introduction

Ethereum blockchain satisfies high security and decentralization requirements,
but it is not scalable. Namely, transaction fees are too high for running computationally heavy smart contracts. Also, it can only record a low number of
transactions on each block. To improve scalability, several different solutions
were proposed. Among them, one of the most successful solutions are layer two
(shortly L2) networks, called rollup protocols. Several rollup protocols that build
on top of Ethereum were proposed [7,9]. While the designs of these protocols of
how heavy computation is delegated to them are different, they share one thing
in common: from time to time they post (compressed) batches of transactions
on the Ethereum main chain, referred to as a base layer or a layer one (L1).
These recorded transactions on the base layer can be later used as a reference
for rollup protocols and smart contracts governing them if there is a dispute
about the state of execution of transactions. Rollup protocols create new economic design questions to solve. In this paper, we address one of them. Namely,
we study the question of posting data batches of layer two rollup chains on a base
layer, which constitutes most of the costs the rollup chains incur. User transactions sent to the rollup protocol are grouped together with fixed frequency and
compressed, which creates a batch. We study the question of how to decrease

We thank Lee Bousfield, Chris Buckland, Aysajan Eziz, Tim Roughgarden, and
Thomas Thiery for valuable feedback.

© International Financial Cryptography Association 2024
A. Essex et al. (Eds.): FC 2023 Workshops, LNCS 13953, pp. 355–366, 2024.
https://doi.org/10.1007/978-3-031-48806-1_23

these costs in this paper. We try to find an efficient strategy for when to post transaction batches as the L1 price of posting data fluctuates. The trade-off is clear: avoid posting batches when the price is high, but at the same time, avoid delaying the posting. Such an algorithm adds to the robustness of the system, and overall, to its security.

The question is motivated by historical experience with the Ethereum *base fee*, which fluctuates in a partially predictable way, and occasionally, when some major product is deployed on it, has intervals of very high base fee[1]. Such intervals are not too long and not too frequent, which gives a hope that after some delay posting costs will be lower and posting can be resumed.

We decompose the cost in two parts: a posting cost that can be directly observed when posting batches, and a delay cost that is not directly measurable. More concretely, we interpret the total cost as the sum of posting and delay costs. Delay cost has several components. The first is psychological: users do not like when the batches are not posted for long period, as it may suggest to them that components of the system are down or unavailable. The second part is related to delayed finality: L2 transactions are not fully final until they are posted as part of a batch and that batch posting has finality on L1. Until that time, users must either wait for finality or trust the L2 system's sequencer to be honest and non-faulty. Delayed finality imposes costs on some applications. The third part is related to the specific technical nature of transaction fee computation on L2 rollups. Namely, a transaction fee is calculated when transactions are created, not when they are posted on L1. Therefore, more delay causes less precise estimates of the L1 cost to attribute to L2 transactions, increasing the risk of unfair or inefficient pricing of rollup transactions.

We model the problem as a Markov decision process. In each round, we calculate total costs independently from the past rounds. Each round is characterized by the current queue size and price, which constitutes a state. The price in the next round is modeled as a random variable, which depends on the current price. Depending on the strategy in the current round, the random variable indicating the price in the next round moves the state to the next state. For practical implementation, we discretize the price space and use a discrete approximation of a continuous random variable. To solve the optimization problem of finding the optimal strategy in each round, we use tools from dynamic programming, in particular, q-learning. The structure of the solution allows us to design a practical batch posting algorithm, which turns out to be intuitive and simple. The algorithm is characterized by only two parameters. We test the algorithm against a few natural benchmark algorithms, on the previous year's Ethereum base fee data[2]. Back-testing allows us to find optimal parameter sets for all algorithms and compare their performances. A comprehensive theoretical analysis of the EIP-1559 gas fee scheme is given in [8].

---

[1] A memorable instance involved a base fee of more than 100 times the norm for a period of several hours. At least one rollup protocol (Arbitrum) decided to take manual control of the batch posting policy during that instance.

[2] The data covers the full period from the introduction of EIP-1559 in August 2021 until November 2022.

Related Literature

The optimization problem at hand is very similar to the inventory policy (IP) problem, long studied in economics and operations research literature, see [1] and [6]. In IP problems, the newly produced items need to be sold for some price, and the demand price distribution is given. Therefore, the IP optimization problem is to maximize revenue, by maximizing revenue from trade and minimizing maintenance costs, while our problem is to minimize both costs. These two are dual. The only difference between our optimization problem and IP problems is that the delay cost in IP problems is linear in the inventory size, as the cost is interpreted as the maintenance cost of stored items, whereas we model the cost as superlinear in the number of delayed items. The optimality of pure stationary strategies in a wide range of Markov decision processes is shown in [2]. The main tool for solving our optimization problem is Q-Learning, which was introduced in [10]. Linear delay cost of transaction inclusion is discussed in [4]. The convergence of the dynamic programming algorithm that covers our case as well is discussed in [5].

2   Model

There is a discrete time with an infinite horizon. In round $i \in \mathbb{N}$, one new batch is created. The number of batches currently queued is denoted by Q_i. P_i is the price of posting a batch in the round i.

At each round, the batch poster chooses a number of batches to publish, denoted by N_i. It is proved in the operations research literature that the optimal way of doing so is to apply a stationary strategy. Namely, by applying a strategy function S which must satisfy $0 \leq S(P_i, Q_i) \leq Q_i$. That is, it is optimal to assume that $N_i = S(P_i, Q_i)$ is only a function of the posting price in the current round and the queue size. By default, the algorithm posts batches that were created earliest (i.e., in FIFO order). Intuitively, S should be weakly increasing in Q_i (if more batches to post, we should not post less) and weakly decreasing in P_i (if more expensive to post, we should not post more). This intuition can be used to test any (heuristic) solution we obtain.

In round i, the system incurs a cost

$$C_i = C_{i,\text{posting}} + C_{i,\text{delay}} = P_i N_i + c(Q_i - N_i)^2. \tag{1}$$

In this paper, we assume that $C_{i,\text{posting}} := P_i N_i$ and $C_{i,\text{delay}} := c(Q_i - N_i)^2$, where the $c > 0$ coefficient represents the relative weight of the second component.

The first term represents the cost of posting batches. Here we assume that the posting price is not affected by how many batches we post in each round. This assumption could be violated in practice if N_i is very large. The second term represents the cost of delaying the posting of batches that remain in the queue after this round, essentially assuming that the cost of delaying a batch until

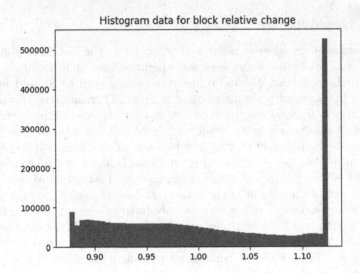

Fig. 1. Relative change of the Ethereum base fee per block, over the past year. Each data point represents the ratio of the base fee in block $i+1$ to the base fee in block i. The large bar at 1.125 is the case where block $i+1$ is completely full so the base fee is increased by the maximum amount.

the next round is linear in how long that batch has already been waiting[3]. The non-linear cost of delay is natural and is well-studied in the economics literature.

To move to the next round, we update:

$$Q_{i+1} := Q_i - N_i + 1,$$

representing posting of N_i batches in round i and the arrival of one more batch in the queue in round $i+1$, and

$$P_{i+1} := R(P_i),$$

where R is some random function that models the fluctuation of the batch posting price. Here we are making another implicit assumption that the L2 batch posting strategy does not affect the future base fee. This is a reasonable approach especially if the number of batches posted is not very large. Also, batches are created at a regular rate and their sizes are equal. The latter is relevant as the price of posting is measured in gas units, that is, the real cost is multiplied by how large the batches are in gas units.

To begin, we consider the price of the next block to be uniformly distributed at the interval $[P_i \cdot t_1, P_i \cdot t_2]$, where $t_1 = \left(\frac{7}{8}\right)$ and $t_2 = \left(\frac{9}{8}\right)$, as the base fee may change by $\frac{1}{8}$ either direction in every 12 seconds. Note that $t_1 \cdot t_2 \approx 0.984$

---

[3] Strictly speaking, the exact functional form of such delay would be $\sum_{i=1}^{Q_i-1} i = \frac{Q_i(Q_i-1)}{2}$, however, we approximate by ignoring the linear term in Q_i and we absorb the factor of two into the coefficient c.

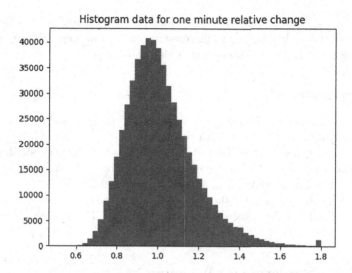

Fig. 2. Relative change of the Ethereum base fee per minute, over the past year. Each data point represents the ratio of the base fee at $i + 1$ minutes to the base fee at i minutes. The distribution is similar to the result of composing five steps drawn independently from the distribution in Fig. 1.

is smaller than 1, that is, the distribution is slightly skewed to the left. For a more realistic distribution, we need to look at the data. We assume that each batch is generated every minute (60 s), and the distribution of $R(P_i)$ is a result of uniform distribution convoluted 5 times: $R(R(R(R(R(P_i)))))$. Theoretically, this approaches the normal distribution for a large enough number of convolutions. For data on the Ethereum one-minute base fee changes, see Fig. 2. Note that there is a skew to the left direction, and there is an outlier at point 1.8, which is caused by a large outlier in the block base fee change data, see Fig. 1. A large outlier corresponds to full blocks and a small outlier corresponds to empty blocks. Both outliers are observed in a theoretical setup with rational miners (block proposers), that maximize their own tips, see [3].

Although we do see a large peak at the max increase in the per-block data, we do not see a similarly large peak at the max increase in the per-minute data. This suggests that the per-minute data is likely more consistent with the hypothesis that per-block changes are independent of each other, and not that there are extended periods of the maximum price increase. Perhaps a large number of completely full blocks is due to different block producers having different lower bounds on the tip they require so that when a block producer with a low tip bound makes a block, that block includes a lot more transactions. That would be consistent with an assumption of independence between the base fee change in consecutive blocks.

An especially interesting factor is a potential support size of $R(P_i)$. The right endpoint of the support turns out to be $1.8P_i$. The reason is that $1.8 \approx (\frac{9}{8})^5$, and it seems to happen often that price increases $\overline{\text{e}}$xponentially[4]. In fact, if we look at block data, the maximum increase appears to happen 15% of the time. The left endpoint is $0.6P_i$. The reason is that $0.6 \approx (\frac{7}{8})^5$.

Objective functions

Our goal is to minimize the expected value of the total cost. We assume there is an infinite horizon of rounds with discounted costs: we minimize $\sum_{i=0}^{\infty} C_i \delta^i$, where $\delta < 1$ is a discount of future costs. This variant is very similar to the inventory policy problem, with the only difference being that the delay cost in inventory policy problems is linear in the delayed number.

As a side note, we optimize the cost with a finite number of rounds n: In this variant, we minimize the total sum of costs $\sum_{i=1}^{n} C_i$. The solution is described in Sect. 5.

3   Bellman Equation/Q-Learning

We now turn to solve the main variant with an infinite number of rounds and future cost discounting. To this end, we apply Q-Learning. Using standard notation[5], we calculate the following two matrices: $Q[s_t, a_t]$ and $O[s_t]$. s_t is the current state and a_t is an action. In our case, s_t is a pair of (Q_i, P_i), while a_t is any natural number between 0 and Q_i. The action a_t corresponds to how many batches to post at round t. $Q[s_t, a_t]$ denotes the total cost, discounting the future cost. $O[s_t]$ denotes the optimal action given the state s_t, that is, the action that minimizes the total cost from this point on. We initialize $O[s_t]$ with Q_i, that is, the initial assumption that the optimal move is to publish all batches at each point. The value update iteration step is the following:

$$Q^{new}[s_t, a_t] := (1 - \alpha)Q[s_t, a_t] + \alpha(c_t + \delta \cdot \mathbb{E}_R[\min_a Q[s_{t+1}, a]]).$$

c_t is the cost incurred by taking action a_t, in this (stationary) round. That is, in our setting, this is $c_t := a_t \cdot P_i + c(Q_i - a_t)^2$. α is a learning rate, as in the computation of the new matrix Q, we take the previously computed matrix Q with weight $1 - \alpha$ and new improved values with weight α. After updating all states of the Q matrix, we update all values of the O matrix. Note that O matrix values appear in the calculation of $\min_a Q[s_{t+1}, a]$ which is replaced with $Q[s_{t+1}, O[s_{t+1}]]$.

We arbitrarily[6] initialize $Q[s_t, a_t]$ as $a_t \cdot P_i + c(Q_i - a_t)^2$ and $O[s_t]$ as Q_i, consistent with an initial hypothesis, to be refined by Q-Learning, that the optimal move at each point in time is to publish all batches.

---

[4] Somewhat against the assumption of uniform distribution.

[5] See Bellman equation: https://en.wikipedia.org/wiki/Q-learning.

[6] Any other initialization works, for example, we can assign 0 to all entries of Q matrix. The only difference is in the convergence. While the rate stays the same, good initialization gives fewer iteration steps.

3.1 Implementation

We discretize the continuum price space by taking a bounded interval. That is, we assume that the price of batch posting will not go above some high bound. This is a reasonable assumption in our context. The space complexity of the implementation is $\Theta(PQ^2)$, where P is the number of price points and Q is the maximum number of batches we allow in the queue. To enforce this upper bound on queue length, we impose an infinite cost for exceeding the bound.

The run-time complexity of the system is $\Theta(IPQ^2 f(P))$, where I is the number of iterations before convergence, which depends on the convergence rate, which itself depends on the learning rate α and future discount δ. $f(P)$ is an average of support sizes of $R(P_i)$ random variables. In the case of a normal random variable, $f(P) \in \Theta(P)$. When generating a random variable for the close-to-boundary prices, we put weights only up until the upper bound price, as we do not have Q matrix values. This irregularity of implementation creates misleading O values for high prices, as the expectation by the implementation is that the price goes down in the next rounds, while theoretically, we would like to study a general case where there is no upper bound on the price.

Higher δ means that we care about the future costs more. For the implementation, we take $\delta = 0.999$, which is close enough to 1, but not too close, as it slows down the computation considerably[7].

We take $P = 400$ and $Q = 300$. The ratio of the highest to lowest Ethereum base fee in our data is around 6000. Therefore, to approximate the real price data with our discrete points, we multiply all prices by $\frac{6000}{400} = 15$. We take the learning rate $\alpha = 0.1$. At this threshold, we observe that the values of the Q matrix for large values of P and Q are stabilized. Generally speaking, lower α improves the precision of the Q matrix calculation, but it increases computation time. Namely, the number of iterations is higher. In our case, we did not observe major qualitative or quantitative differences by choosing different values of α. We assume that the algorithm has converged when the change in every entry in Q is less than $\epsilon = 0.01$, that is when:

$$\max_{s_t, a_t} Q^{new}[s_t, a_t] - Q[s_t, a_t] < \epsilon.$$

The program takes 72 hours to finish, for approximately 14000 iterations, on the input described above on Intel Core i7-8565U CPU @ 1.80 GHz × 8. The current implementation is without parallelism. Note that Q^{new} matrix calculation depends only on Q, therefore, full parallelization is feasible.

3.2 Observations

Running the Q-learning algorithm and analyzing its output yields a few observations:

---

[7] It also increases the magnitude of values in the matrix Q, as we weight future costs more.

1. There is a threshold price, below which all batches are posted. That is, there exists T_P, so that when $P_i < T_P$, $S_i(P_i, Q_i) = Q_i$.
2. Above this threshold price, there exists a threshold on the number of batches that depends on the posting price, so that, below this threshold, no batches are posted. That is, there exists $T_Q(P_i)$, so that, when $Q_i < T_Q(P_i)$, $S_i(P_i, Q_i) = 0$.
3. On the other hand, if $Q_i > T_Q(P_i)$, then $S_i(P_i, Q_i) = Q_i - T_Q(P_i) - 1$. That is, the minimum number of batches is posted, to guarantee that in the next round if the price does not change, the threshold condition on the number of batches will still hold.

We conjecture that for any plausible functional form of the delay term of the cost, and for most smooth and convex/concave random distributions R on price changes, these observations should hold. Verifying the hypothesis that this is the case for a given delay cost with a (smooth) version of random variable future batch posting price, by solving a dynamic programming problem for a given R, is left for the future. The functional form of the function $T_Q(P)$ depends on the delay cost. For the quadratic delay cost, we conjecture that for $P > T_P$, the optimal threshold on the queue size, $T_Q(P)$, is of order $\Theta(\sqrt{P})$.

4   Back-Testing Results

In this section, we compare the performance of the algorithm based on our Q-Learning analysis to three other algorithms' performances. We calculate how much each algorithm would spend and how much delay cost each would incur, on the last year's time-series data of Ethereum base fees, taken after every minute, that is, after every fifth block[8]. It is assumed that each batch has the same unit size, which is a good approximation in practice. If batches are created with less frequency, we can easily modify the test set and optimize parameters accordingly.

For each algorithm, we measure a few properties: publishing cost; delay cost; the average and worst-case delays experienced by batches; and the maximum number of batches posted in any one round. The last measure is an important robustness measure, as posting too many batches at the same time may affect the future price or even be impossible to perform given the L1 block space constraints. All performances given in the following subsections are on the Pareto-efficient curve of the pair of publishing and delay costs. Back-testing algorithms were optimized for approximately 100 different instances. All algorithms described below are linear in the data size, as the decision in each round depends only on the current round price and queue size.

4.1   Current Arbitrum Algorithm

The first algorithm is currently deployed by Arbitrum. We denote it by $\mathcal{O}$. $\mathcal{O}$ is characterized by 3 parameters, over which we minimize its total cost:

---

[8] Before the Ethereum Merge on 6 September 2022, the time between blocks was about 12 s on average. Since the Merge, the interval between blocks is fixed at 12 s.

- ap, intuitively an *acceptable price* measured in GWEIs,
- e, an exponent,
- and ut, an *update time* in minutes.

Every batch has these three features. If the base fee is lower or equal to ap, the batch is posted. After ut time passes and the batch is still not posted on L1, the new acceptable price becomes e times bigger. That is, $ap^{new} := e \cdot ap$.

The performance of the algorithm $\mathcal{O}$ for a few parameter sets is documented in the following table.

Parameters (e, ap, ut)	Publishing cost	Delay cost	Maximum delay	Avg. delay
$(1.2, 144, 60)$	$2.598e + 07$	$5.99e + 09$	773	39.7986
$(2, 96, 120)$	$3.170e + 07$	$6.456e + 07$	193	2.23403
$(2.8, 72, 140)$	$3.271e + 07$	$1.866e + 07$	165	0.949142

Note that publishing cost increases and maximum delay and average delay decrease by increasing e. Both behaviors are natural as the algorithm posts more aggressively for higher e. There is no clear upper bound on the delay in round i as a function of posting price P_i, as it depends on when the exponential function catches up with the price, i.e., it depends on the history as well.

The following table shows the performance of the Arbitrum algorithm where the acceptable price does not do a step-function doubling every update time but instead increases in a smooth exponential curve with the same doubling time. That is, the exponent in each round is equal to $e^{\frac{1}{ut}}$.

Parameters (e, ap, ut)	Publishing cost	Delay cost	Maximum delay	Avg. delay
$(1.2, 144, 60)$	$2.60294e + 07$	$4.73071e + 09$	771	33.5433
$(2, 96, 120)$	$3.19334e + 07$	$1.72324e + 07$	183	1.08583
$(2.8, 72, 140)$	$3.31778e + 07$	$4.86956e + 06$	164	0.429163

Compared to the step algorithm described above, publishing costs are slightly increasing and delay costs are slightly decreasing. But qualitatively, the results are very similar.

4.2   Q-Learning Algorithm

The second algorithm, $\mathcal{Q}$, is based on Q-Learning. We optimize over two parameters: d and T_p, when minimizing the cost of the $\mathcal{Q}$ algorithm. In particular, we test $T_Q(P) = \frac{\sqrt{P - T_P}}{d}$ and $T_P := T_p$.

The performance of the algorithm $\mathcal{Q}$ for a few parameter sets is documented in the following table.

Parameters (T_p, d)	Publishing cost	Delay cost	Max. delay	Avg. delay	Max. posted
$(60, 2)$	$3.420e + 07$	$1.283e + 06$	42	1.699	5
$(60, 1.6)$	$3.383e + 07$	$2.339e + 06$	52	2.127	7
$(80, 1.2)$	$3.324e + 07$	$4.111e + 06$	69	2.00	10

Note that both delay cost and maximum delay are increasing in decreasing d, while publishing cost is decreasing. The publishing cost is decreasing and the delay cost is increasing with increasing T_P. As a robust measure for T_P, we can take the value that is 80% percentile of the base fee data distribution. This allows the algorithm to be fully automatic, by updating T_P every month or two weeks, to adjust to the current trend of prices. We do not include a maximum posted number in the performance of the other algorithms as this number is equal to the maximum delay by definition. Unlike the previous algorithm, the algorithm in this section gives an upper bound on the delay in each round i as a function of the price of posting P_i, which is equal to $\frac{\sqrt{P_i - T_P}}{d}$ and adds to the robustness of the system. This gives a global upper bound $\frac{\sqrt{P_{\max} - T_P}}{d}$ on the maximum delay, where $P_{\max}$ is the maximum posting price. Note that the maximum base fee was about 8200 GWEIs and the maximum delays in the table approximately correspond to this upper bound. For example, $\frac{\sqrt{8200}}{1.2} \approx 74 > 69$. In general, the upper bound does not have to be achieved, as the price may increase very quickly and the delay queue size may not catch up.

4.3   Price Minimizing Algorithm

The third algorithm, $\mathcal{D}$, delays posting until the price drops below a certain threshold T and then posts all batches.

The performance of the algorithm $\mathcal{D}$ for a few parameters is documented in the following table.

Parameters T	Publishing cost	Delay cost	Maximum delay	Avg. delay
60	$2.237e + 07$	$2.658e + 12$	14975	584.191
80	$2.632e + 07$	$2.683e + 11$	8448	124.4
100	$2.896e + 07$	$3.835e + 09$	1394	15.66

Notice that a huge value of the maximum delay would violate our assumption that the price of posting in each round is not affected by how many batches we post. We do not include a maximum posted number in the performance of the other algorithms as this number is equal to the maximum delay by definition.

4.4   Trivial Algorithm

A trivial algorithm, denoted by $\mathcal{T}$, posts every batch immediately. $\mathcal{T}$ has its own merits. First, it keeps the delay costs to 0, which imposes a minimal load on the system. Second, it is simple to interpret and easy to implement.

Testing on the same data as the above algorithms, we find that a trivial algorithm has publishing costs equal to $3.6e+07$. Note that it does not have any parameters and the delay cost is equal to 0. We use this result as a benchmark to measure the performance of other algorithms with respect to the cost of publishing.

4.5   Tips

In the paper so far, we ignored tips that are given to L1 block builders for inclusion in the block in the design and analysis of efficient batch posting strategy. These tips should in principle be counted towards the price of publishing. For example, Arbitrum has a fixed tip, 1 GWEI per gas, which is enough to get included in 95% of the cases. If we count the minimum tips to be included in each block towards the total price of being posted and run the same algorithms as before, we get very similar results as before, namely, in 1% proximity of both, publishing and delay costs. One potential explanation is that when tips to be included are high, base fees are also high, therefore, none of the algorithms post their batches. These observations can be seen as indicators to simplify the decision problem by including the tips directly towards the cost of publishing, instead of choosing them strategically.

5   Dynamic Programming with Fixed Prices

In this section, we discuss the case where there is a fixed number of rounds n, and posting prices in each round are fixed and given in advance. At the end of the last round, we publish all batches that are left unpublished. The use-case of this algorithm, for example, is if there are futures contracts on base fees.

The optimum solution can be found by dynamic programming with run-time $\Theta(n^3)$ as described in the following. In $dp[i][j]$, we store the minimum cost incurred if in the first i rounds we publish exactly j batches. We iterate i through all rounds in the outermost loop, contributing the first multiplicative factor n. In the second loop, we iterate j between 0 and i, contributing another multiplicative factor n. In the third and innermost loop, we iterate $take$ over newly published batches, between 0 and $i+1-j$, therefore, contributing the last multiplicative factor n. We update $dp[i+1][take+j]$ with the maximum between the following two values:

$$dp[i+1][take+j] := \max(dp[i+1][take+j], dp[i][j] + cost), \qquad (2)$$

where $cost$ is calculated as $c(i-j-take+1)^2$. We also record $take$ that gives the minimum answer for each i and j, which will allow us to recover the answer, and the number of batches published at each round to minimize global cost. The global cost is located at $dp[n][n]$ and we can reconstruct the answer of how many to publish at each round using a backtracking algorithm.

We generated prices according to different distribution functions and observed that it is almost always optimal to publish zero or all batches.

6   Conclusions

We initiate the study of an efficient batch posting strategy by L2 rollup chains on the L1 chain as a calldata. As an outcome, we obtain efficient algorithms with robustness guarantees. Namely, in each round, the new algorithm does not post too many batches and the number of batches kept in the queue is bounded by a function of posting price in each round. Future avenues of research include the optimization problem where current and future prices depend on the number of batches posted in each round. This may be the case if rollup protocols become dominant in the scalability of the base fee. Finding out the optimal constant tip is also left for future research.

References

1. Arrow, K.J., Harris, T., Marschak, J.: Optimal inventory policy. Econometrica **19**(3), 250–272 (1951)
2. Gimbert, H.: Pure stationary optimal strategies in Markov decision processes. In: Thomas, W., Weil, P. (eds.) STACS 2007. LNCS, vol. 4393, pp. 200–211. Springer, Heidelberg (2007). https://doi.org/10.1007/978-3-540-70918-3_18
3. Hougaard, J.L., Pourpouneh, M.: Farsighted miners under transaction fee mechanism EIP1559. In: Working Paper (2022)
4. Huberman, G., Leshno, J.D., Moallemi, C.: Monopoly without a monopolist: an economic analysis of the bitcoin payment system. Rev. Econ. Stud. **88**(6), 3011–3040 (2021)
5. Jaakkola, T.S., Jordan, M.I., Singh, S.P.: On the convergence of stochastic iterative dynamic programming algorithms. Neural Comput. **6**(6), 1185–1201 (1994)
6. Veinott Jr, A.F.: The optimal inventory policy for batch ordering. Oper. Res. **13**,424–432 (1965)
7. Kalodner, H., Goldfeder, S., Chen, X., Weinberg, S.M., Felten, E.W.: Arbitrum: scalable, private smart contracts. In: Enck, W., Felt, A.P. (eds.) 27th USENIX Security Symposium, USENIX Security 2018, Baltimore, MD, USA, 15–17 August 2018, pp. 1353–1370. USENIX Association (2018)
8. Leonardos, S., Monnot, B., Reijsbergen, D., Skoulakis, E., Piliouras, G.: Dynamical analysis of the EIP-1559 Ethereum fee market. In: Baldimtsi, F., Roughgarden, T. (eds.) AFT 2021: 3rd ACM Conference on Advances in Financial Technologies, Arlington, Virginia, USA, 26–28 September 2021, pp. 114–126. ACM (2021)
9. Nehab, D., Teixeira, A.: The core of cartesi. White Paper (2018)
10. Watkins, C.J.C.H.: Learning from delayed rewards (1989)

Unlinkability and Interoperability in Account-Based Universal Payment Channels

Mohsen Minaei[1]([✉]), Panagiotis Chatzigiannis[1], Shan Jin[1],
Srinivasan Raghuraman[1], Ranjit Kumaresan[1], Mahdi Zamani[1],
and Pedro Moreno-Sanchez[2]

[1] Visa Research, Foster City, USA
{mominaei,pchatzig,shajin,srraghur,rakumare,mzamani}@visa.com
[2] IMDEA Software Institute, Pozuelo de Alarcón, Spain
pedro.moreno@imdea.org

Abstract. Payment channels allow a sender to do multiple transactions with a receiver without recording each single transaction on-chain. While most of the current constructions for payment channels focus on UTXO-based cryptocurrencies with reduced scripting capabilities (e.g., Bitcoin or Monero), little attention has been given to the possible benefits of adapting such constructions to cryptocurrencies based on the account model and offering a Turing complete language (e.g., Ethereum).

The focus of this work is to implement efficient payment channels tailored to the capabilities of account-based cryptocurrencies with Turing-complete language support in order to provide scalable payments that are interoperable across different cryptocurrencies and unlinkable for third-parties (e.g., payment intermediaries). More concretely, we continue the line of research on cryptocurrency universal payment channels (UPC) which facilitate interoperable payment channel transactions across different ledgers in a hub-and-spoke model, by offering greater scalability than point-to-point architectures. Our design proposes two different versions, UPC and AUPC. For UPC we formally describe the protocol ideas sketched in previous work and evaluate our proof-of-concept implementation. Then, AUPC further extends the concept of universal payment channels by payment unlinkability against the intermediary server.

1 Introduction

Payment channels [2,11] aim at scaling blockchain payments throughput and latency, by "off-loading" payment transactions to an off-chain communication channel between the sender and the receiver of the payment. The channel is "opened" through an on-chain funding transaction followed by any number off-chain transactions. Eventually, when one or both parties agree, the channel is

---

We also point the reader to the full version of our paper [28].

© International Financial Cryptography Association 2024
A. Essex et al. (Eds.): FC 2023 Workshops, LNCS 13953, pp. 367–384, 2024.
https://doi.org/10.1007/978-3-031-48806-1_24

"closed" through another on-chain transaction. This design mitigates both the costs and the latency associated with on-chain operations, effectively amortizing the overhead of on-chain transactions over many off-chain ones. However, basic payment channels lack *universality* since they only enable transactions within the same ledger; and *connectivity* since only payments between the two parties that share the channel are possible.

Payment Channel Networks/Hubs. To tackle the connectivity challenge, a payment channel network (PCN) can be treated as a graph in which nodes are senders and receivers, and edges are the payment channels between them. Several proposals improve upon the initial design of payment channels to support multi-hop payments [32] (e.g., for improving scalability [12], security [22,23], programmability [3], privacy [16] and collateral efficiency [27]). PCNs however come with additional challenges: (a) minimizing the overhead of finding paths between the users and maintaining the network topology and (b) privacy concerns when payments are performed through sequential channel updates between senders and receivers, especially though a single intermediary. Tumblers or payment channel hubs (PCHs) were introduced to address the above challenges, which act as gateways to receive the payments from the senders and route them to the corresponding receivers. Recent proposals such as Tumblebit [18], A^2L [35] and A^2L+ [15] are examples of such PCHs. While these proposals reduce the storage overhead on the underlying blockchain, they are designed for the UTXO model. It would be interesting to borrow these designs to the account-based model.

More recently, Universal Payment Channels (UPC) were proposed [10] as a protocol relying on hashed time-lock contracts (HTLCs) (which are common throughout the cryptocurrency ecosystem) and on generic accumulator data structures, tied to a hub-and-spoke model, where end users need to register with a UPC hub in order to send and receive payments. This protocol enabled *universality*, i.e. enabling transactions across different ledgers, and *concurrency*, i.e. parallelizing the internal flow of transactions to maximize throughput.

Confidentiality and Anonymity. Many blockchain-based payment systems such as Bitcoin [31] provide a (false) sense of privacy by using "pseudo-anonymous" addresses. However, academic efforts [26,34] and the surveillance industry [19] have demonstrated that it is possible to associate those addresses with real identities, for instance using clustering techniques [26]). To protect user privacy, systems were specifically designed with privacy in mind such as Zcash [7] or Monero [36]. Note that "privacy" in financial transactions typically implies both the aspect of *confidentiality* and *anonymity* (or unlinkability), which imply preventing the leakage of information about the transaction value and the transacting parties from external observers respectively [9]. Therefore, it is expected that the payment channel hub used in UPC will also provide such privacy guarantees, without being able to learn information about transactions routed through it. A^2L [35] and A^2L+ [15] focus on this issue and provide a solution for a secure PCH which preserves anonymity. In addition, they only rely on digital signatures and timelock functionalities, making it interoperable across different ledgers.

In summary, we are currently missing an approach for universal, efficient, privacy-preserving scalable payments with small blockchain storage overhead for cryptocurrencies based on the account model. Such a proposal would be of interest to the blockchain community since it would be possible to be deployed in many blockchains, e.g., those based on the Ethereum Virtual Machine (EVM).

Our Contributions. In our work, we start from the basic idea of Universal Payment Channels [10,29] (UPC). We first formalize the UPC ecosystem by providing a complete set of protocols that describe the system as a whole. Then, being inspired from A²L [35] and A²L+ [15], we augment it with anonymity properties (resulting in AUPC), while preserving the core UPC properties, namely universality and concurrency. Finally, we evaluate UPC through a proof-of-concept implementation, which showcases its feasibility in a practical deployment, while providing insights towards a fully private and auditable payment hub.

2 Preliminaries and Building Blocks

In this section, we provide an overview of the cryptographic primitives, the background and the related works necessary for building our protocols.

Standard Cryptographic Building Blocks. We consider a digital signature scheme consisting of algorithms KeyGen(), Sign() and SigVerify() and a commitment scheme P_{COM}. We also consider non-interactive zero-knowledge proof scheme NIZK := (P_{NIZK}, V_{NIZK}) where $\pi \leftarrow P_{NIZK}(x, w)$ and $V_{NIZK}(x, \pi) := \{0, 1\}$ are the prover's algorithm and verifier's algorithm respectively for statement x and witness w and NP relation $R(x, w)$. We refer to Appendix A in [28] for formal definitions of the above primitives.

Blinded Randomizable Signature (BRS) Scheme. A BRS scheme consists of algorithms: (i) $\widetilde{\sigma} \leftarrow$ BlindSign(com, sk), that generates a blinded signature given a commitment com to a message m; (ii) $\sigma :=$ UnBlindSign($\widetilde{\sigma}$, decom), that unblinds $\widetilde{\sigma}$ to produce a valid signature σ based on the decommitment information decom; (iii) and $\sigma' \leftarrow$ RandSign(σ), that generates a randomized signature σ' based on a valid signature σ.

Adaptor Signatures. Let statement/witness pair $(x, w) \in R$ where R is a hard relation, and secret/public key pair (sk, vk). At a high level, an adaptor signature scheme [5] allows a party to pre-sign a message m w.r.t. some statement x of a hard relation R, while that pre-signature $\hat{\sigma}$ can be adapted into a full valid signature σ by any party knowing the witness w. Also, the adaptor signature scheme makes possible to extract the witness w by any party which knows both the pre-signature and the adapted full signature. We refer to Appendix A in [28] for a formal definition of adaptor signatures.

Randomizable Puzzles. A randomizable puzzle scheme RnP with a solution space $\mathcal{S}$ and a function ϕ which acts on $\mathcal{S}$, consists of the following algorithms: (a) $(pp, td) \leftarrow$ PSetup(1^λ) where pp are the public parameters and td is the trapdoor. (b) $Z \leftarrow \mathrm{PGen}(\mathrm{pp}, \zeta)$ where ζ is a puzzle solution, and Z is the generated puzzle (c) $\zeta := \mathrm{PSolve}(\mathrm{td}, Z)$ (d) $(Z', r) \leftarrow \mathrm{PRand}(\mathrm{pp}, Z)$ where r is a randomization factor and Z' is a randomized puzzle with the solution as $\phi(\zeta, r)$.

Note that it is assumed that there exists a deterministic function ϕ such that for a puzzle Z with the corresponding solution ζ, given its randomized version Z' with the randomization factor r, it has $\phi(\zeta, r) \in \mathcal{S}$ is a solution to Z'.

Hash-Time Lock Contract (HTLC). A HTLC is a smart contract built upon *timelocks* and *hashlocks*. A timelock implements the "locking" of funds on a transaction until a predetermined time is reached, when the funds will return to the sender. A hashlock implements the "locking" of funds on a transaction until the hash preimage is revealed, where the funds are released to the receiver.

Accumulators. An accumulator acc enables a succinct and binding representation of a set of elements S and supports constant-size proofs of (non) membership on S. We consider *trapdoorless* accumulators to prevent the need for a trusted party that holds a trapdoor and could potentially create fake (non)membership proofs. An accumulator acc typically consists of the following algorithms [6]: $(\mathrm{pp}, D_0) \leftarrow \mathrm{AccSetup}(n_{acc})$ generates the public parameters pp and instantiates the accumulator initial state D_0; $\mathrm{Add}(D_t, x) := (D_{t+1}, \mathrm{upmsg})$ adds element x to accumulator D_t, outputting D_{t+1} and upmsg such that witness holders can update their witnesses; $\mathrm{MemWitCreate}(D_t, x, S_t) := w_x^t$ Creates a membership proof w_x^t for element x where S_t is the set of elements accumulated in D_t; $\mathrm{MemWitUp}(D_t, w_x^t, x, \mathrm{upmsg}) := w_x^{t+1}$ Updates membership proof w_x^t for element x after it is added to the accumulator; $\mathrm{VerMem}(D_t, x, w_x^t) := \{0, 1\}$ Verifies membership proof w_x^t of x in D_t.

Notation. We present the notations that are used through the rest of the paper using Table 1. In Sect. 3 we begin introducing the UPC protocol and later modify the protocol to achieve AUPC, we denote with blue color the added variables and functions and with red color the removals to modify UPC to AUPC.

3   Universal Payment Channels (UPC)

The goal of Universal Payment Channels (UPC) is to facilitate digital token transfers of funds across different ledgers between two parties A and B, thus achieving interoperability between those ledgers. UPC follows a hub-and-spoke design for scalability purposes, where a trustless UPC hub H plays a central role in the system. In this section, we provide an overview of the basic UPC system as well as its core protocols which serve as foundations towards constructing its privacy-preserving version AUPC. Next, we provide a high level description of the UPC system, and provide a detailed description for all of its functionalities and formal descriptions of the respective protocols in Appendix A in [28].

Registration and UPC Contract. After both parties have registered their public keys with H (Appendix B.1 in [28]), an instance of the UPC contract (described in Appendix B.2 in [28] and Fig. 3) is deployed between each party

Table 1. Details of the variables used in the UPC smart contract, Receipt (R), Promise (P), and Channel(C) objects.

Contract Variables	
chanId	channel identifier
vk_H&vk_C	public key of the server and client respectively
claimDuration	duration to submit claims before channel termination
status	channel's status ("Active", "Closing", "Closed")
$deposit_H$&$deposit_C$	server's and client's deposit amounts on-chain
$lock_C$	client's locked amounts on-chain
$credit_H$&$credit_C$	server's and client's aggregated amounts received off-chain
chanExpiry	channel's expiry time, to be set at the time of channel closing
acc_H&acc_C	accumulators storing pending transactions for server and client
Secrets	mapping of claimed promises and corresponding secrets
Solutions	mapping of solved puzzle and corresponding solution
closeRequester	first party finalizing the closure of the channel
Channel (C)	
cid	channel identifier
contract	contract object from the contract deployment
params	parameters initialized at contract deployment
$credit_{in}$&$credit_{out}$	(in)outgoing credits respectively
$Promises_{in}$&$Promises_{out}$	(in)outgoing promises respectively
acc_{in}&acc_{out}	accumulator for (in)outgoing pending promises
$accAux_{in}$&$accAux_{out}$	auxiliary info used by (in)outgoing accumulators
$netProm_{in}$& $netProm_{out}$	aggregate of (in)outgoing pending promise amounts
receipt	latest receipt received from the counter party
ledger	ledger that the channel resides on.
Receipt (R)	
credit	total promises' amounts for which a secret has been received
acc	accumulator for tracking pending promises
σ	valid signature on the values cid, credit and acc
Promise (P)	
credit	total promises' amounts for which a secret has been received
amount	amount of coins to be transferred in this transaction
hash&secret	hash value of a preimage secret for this transaction
$Z := (A_\alpha, c_\alpha)$	puzzle with statement A_α and encrypted solution c_α for this transaction
α	puzzle solution for this transaction
expiry	timestamp that this promise expires
proof	membership proof of this promise in an accumulator
$\hat{\sigma}$	pre-signature on the values cid, credit, amount, A_α, expiry
σ	signature on the values cid, credit, amount, hash (or A_α), expiry

and the hub on the party's respective ledger (using protocols described in Appendix B.3 and Fig. 6 in [28])[1].

Payment Channel Funding and Monitoring. After the contract deployment by each party and the hub, the next step is to open a payment channel

---

[1] For ease of notation we have considered that the each instance of the UPC contract is between the Hub and a single party, however, it can easily be extended to consider all the parties within a single blockchain to use the same contract.

between them. This is achieved through the deposit on-chain protocol described in Appendix B.3 and Fig. 6 in [28] which in turn invokes the UPC contract's deposit function. UPC contract also includes on-chain protocols for closing a payment channel, as well as a continuous process being run by the UPC parties to monitor the state of the contract and take any on-chain action as needed.

UPC Payments. After each party A and B has established a payment channel through the payment hub H and have agreed on the transaction parameters, (i.e., transaction amounts and expiry), the receiving party B samples a secret value and creates its hash $= h(x)$. Then it requests payment from A by sending the payment details, which includes amount$_B$, a time expiry and the hash value. Then, A creates a *promise*, which is a signed message containing amount$_A$, hash and expiry, and sends it to H (using `CreatePromise` in Fig. 4). After H verifies the promise (using `VerifyPromise` in Fig. 4), it sends a similar promise to B that consists of amount$_B$, hash and expiry (using `CreatePromise` in Fig. 4). Finally, B sends secret to H, which is also forwarded to A. The transfer of amount$_A$ from A to H and amount$_B$ from H to B is completed by updating the channel parameters and finalizing through a signed Receipt message (using `UpdateChannel` and `CreateReceipt` in Fig. 4). The payment flow described above is depicted in Fig. 1 and described in details in Appendix B.4 in [28].

Fig. 1. Overview of off-chain steps taken by the parties to send payments from a sender to a receiver via the intermediary server

Concurrent Payments. To provide maximum parallelization for a receiver that can process multiple promises simultaneously, UPC allows the sender to submit multiple promises without waiting for each promise to be processed (we refer to this property as *non-blocking/concurrent* payments). The UPC provides this feature by asking the parties to commit to the set of pending promises along with every receipt to prevent double-spending (promises are added to the pending list in `CreatePromise` and committed to when `CreateReceipt` is called in Fig. 4).

As the list of pending promises grows linearly, it is inefficient to send the entire list in every receipt exchange. To address this issue, UPC uses cryptographic accumulators (e.g., Merkle tree and RSA accumulator). This allows to reduce the asymptotic bandwidth/fee overhead of inclusion proofs to a logarithm (e.g., for a Merkle tree) or a constant (e.g., for an RSA accumulator) in the number of pending promises.

Channel Closing. When a party decides to close the channel, they can initiate the closure by invoking the UPC contract (Fig. 3). We can consider two main scenarios. In the optimistic case, after a promise is sent from the sender, the receiver releases the secret and consequently, the sender sends a corresponding receipt to the receiver (the receipt has the aggregated amount of all previously completed promises). In such a scenario, the receiving party invokes the `ReceiptClaim` function of the UPC contract using the latest *receipt* object (Fig. 3). However, in the pessimistic case, where the receiving party releases the secret but does not receive a receipt, it first invokes the `ReceiptClaim` function to present its latest receipt and then submits the corresponding *promise* object using the `PromiseClaim` function.

4   Privacy-Preserving AUPC

In UPC, the payment hub learns all payment details routed through it: sender, receiver and transaction amounts. As discussed in the introduction, such a significant exposure of the transacting parties' privacy towards the hub can be problematic in many cases. Therefore, being inspired from A^2L and A^2L+, we describe how to modify UPC discussed in the previous section which enables transacting parties to maintain their anonymity against the hub, by making them unlinkable by the hub when a large number of parties transact through it. We first provide below a short high-level description of A^2L, then we discuss the modifications in the smart contract and both the on-chain and off-chain protocols at a high level, and we provide the detailed protocols in Appendix C in [28]. We use color coding for the changes in the respective figures imported from UPC.

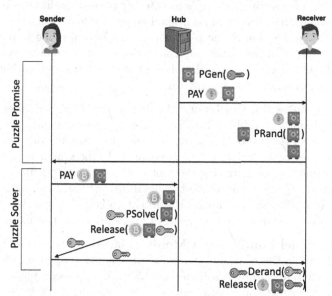

Fig. 2. Off-chain steps in A^2L to send payments via an intermediary server.

A²L Overview. The goal of A²L [35] is to improve on existing solution (Tumblebit [18]) which implemented a protocol to facilitate privacy-preserving payments between parties through an untrusted payment channel hub (PCH). A²L improves over Tumblebit by enabling the protocol to be *interoperable* across different cryptocurrencies. In addition, it improves on communication costs and addresses potential denial of service (DoS) attacks, where an attacker could potentially ask the PCH to initiate a large number of transactions without intending to complete them.

A²L follows the paradigm of Tumblebit: it consists of two phases, a "Puzzle Promise" and a "Puzzle Solver" phase, as shown in Fig. 2. The Puzzle Promise phase takes place between PCH H and B, where H computes an adaptor signature $\hat{\sigma}_G$ and a *re-randomizeable* puzzle holding a secret value k that can be solved using some ephemeral secret. Then B re-randomizes the puzzle (denoted by PRand()) using randomness r_B and forwards the new puzzle to A.

Next in the "Puzzle Solver" phase, A re-randomizes the puzzle again using randomness r_A, and computes an adaptor signature $\hat{\sigma}_A$ which is sent to H. Now H can solve A's puzzle using its ephemeral secret (denoted by PSolve()) and extract the product of $r_A \cdot r_B \cdot k$ and use it to complete the adaptor signature $\hat{\sigma}_A$ and get paid by A. Now A due to the properties of adaptor signatures, can extract the randomized solution and send after removing r_A from the solution, can obtain $r_B \cdot k$ and send it to B. Lastly, B removes r_B from the solution and recovers k which can be used to complete $\hat{\sigma}_G$ and get paid by H. Note that the re-randomizations described throughout this process are crucial to prevent H from being able to link payments between parties.

A²L+. Follow-up work [15] addresses potential attack vectors to A²L which would result into recovering the hub's private key or into stealing coins from the hub. These are addressed by two additional steps, the first being a NIZK proof during the first interaction of the parties with the hub, proving that its public key is in the support of the public-key encryption scheme, and the second being a check by the hub during the puzzle solver phase, that A's verification key is in the support of the adaptor signature scheme.

Registration and AUPC Contract. The first major change in order to follow the A²L paradigm is to replace hash values by "puzzle promises". In addition, because the flow of the protocol first requires the establishment of a "promise" to the intended received on behalf of the payment hub, the sender is first required to lock some funds before initiating the protocol to prevent "griefing" attacks by malicious actors, which would make the payment hub establish such promises without the initiating sender having the intent to complete the protocol. The registration process is described in detail in Fig. 9 in the Appendix of [28].

Payment Channel Funding and Monitoring. After the sender has locked the needed funds in the contract, the payment channel is opened between each party and the hub in a similar fashion as in UPC. Also, a second modification is required in the contract state monitoring process, which now tracks the existence of puzzle solutions and puzzle expiries instead of hash preimages (or "secrets").

The changes are discussed in Appendix B.2 in [28] and shown in Fig. 3 using our color-coding (i.e., by removing the steps in blue color and adding those in red).

AUPC Payments. The off-chain payment protocols for AUPC are similar to UPC payments described in Sect. 3 with the following differences: (a) There is no need to agree on the transaction amount, as this is fixed and pre-determined for any transaction facilitated through that particular hub. (b) HTLCs are replaced by rerandomizeable puzzles. (c) In CreatePromise(), the signed message is replace by an adaptor signature as in A^2L. (d) A PreVerifyPromise() function used by B to pre-verify the validity of the pre-signature and the proof of knowledge of puzzle solution received from H. (e) VerifySecret() is replaced by VerifySolution() function to verify the rerandomizeable puzzle solution. Those differences are highlighted with color code in Fig. 4.

Summary. We observe that no extensive changes are required to modify the UPC protocol to construct the privacy-preserving AUPC, and those changes are mostly related to the corresponding primitives utilized by A^2L, i.e., rerandomizeable puzzles and adaptor signatures instead of hashes and standard signatures. Therefore, we can consider the two versions of UPC to be modular, where only a few functions (e.g., PreVerifyPromise, VerifySolution) and variables need to be modified. We thereby present the details of two systems that provide a tradeoff in terms of efficiency and privacy guarantees. We expand on this and other discussion points in Sect. 6.

5 Implementation and Evaluation

We have created a simple proof of concept implementation of our UPC protocol detailed in Sect. 3. The platform we used for our evaluation is 2.6 GHz 6-Core Intel Core i7 laptop. In addition, we have developed a mobile client for the users to interact with the UPC protocol and show the feasibility of our solution.

5.1 Accumulators

In this work, we considered two types of accumulators namely the Merkle Tree and RSA accumulators. We compared the efficiency of the two by different operations in the Ethereum network using Solidity contracts, shown in Fig. 5. We observe that the Merkle tree is the better choice as it has less run-time for a practical number of in-flight transactions per channel (less than 60K at a time), and less gas cost for membership proof verification (450K gas compared to 20K when $100,000$ promises are stored in the accumulator).

5.2 UPC Smart Contract Implementation

The ledger contract presented in Fig. 3 has been implemented using the programming language Solidity for the Ethereum blockchain. Users within the Ethereum network communicate with the network through the means of transactions. The

---

UPC Contract

Init(cid, vk$_1$, vk$_2$, T):
1. Set (chanId, vk$_H$, vk$_C$, claimDuration) ← (cid, vk$_1$, vk$_2$, T);
2. Set status ← "Active";
3. Set (deposit$_H$, deposit$_C$, lock$_C$, credit$_H$, credit$_C$, chanExpiry) ← $(0,0,0,0,0,0)$;
4. Set (acc$_H$, acc$_C$, Secrets, Solutions, closeRequester) ← $(\bot, \bot, \bot, \bot, \bot)$;

GetParams():
Output [chanId, vk$_H$, vk$_C$, claimDuration].

Deposit(amount):
1. Abort if status ≠ "Active" or caller.vk ∉ {vk$_H$, vk$_C$};
2. If caller.vk = vk$_H$, then set deposit$_H$ ← deposit$_H$ + amount;
3. If caller.vk = vk$_C$, then set deposit$_C$ ← deposit$_C$ + amount.

Lock(amount):
1. Abort if status ≠ "Active" or caller.vk ∉ {vk$_C$};
2. If caller.vk = vk$_C$, then set lock$_C$ ← lock$_C$ + amount.

PromiseClaim(P):
1. Abort if status ≠ {"Active", "Closing"} or caller.vk ∉ {vk$_H$, vk$_C$};
2. Abort if now ≥ P.expiry or Hash(P.secret) ≠ P.hash or Secrets[P.hash] ≠ $\bot$ or Solutions[P.Z] ≠ $\bot$ or $P.\sigma \neq$ Adapt($P.\hat\sigma, P.\alpha$);
3. If caller.vk = vk$_H$, then set vk ← vk$_C$, credit ← credit$_H$, and acc ← acc$_H$; Otherwise, set vk ← vk$_H$, credit ← credit$_C$, and acc ← acc$_C$;
4. Abort if SigVerify($P.\sigma$, [chanId, P.credit, P.amount, P.expiry], vk);
5. Abort if P.credit < credit and ACC.VerifyProof(acc, P.hash, P.Z, P.proof) = 0;
6. If caller.vk = vk$_H$, then set credit$_H$ ← credit$_H$ + P.amount; Otherwise, credit$_C$ ← credit$_C$ + P.amount;
7. Set Secrets[P.hash] ← P.secret Solutions[P.Z] ← $P.\alpha$.
8. If status = "Active", then set chanExpiry ← now + claimDuration, and status ← "Closing".

ReceiptClaim(R):
1. Abort if status ≠ {"Active", "Closing"} or caller.vk ∉ {vk$_H$, vk$_C$};
2. If caller.vk = vk$_H$, then:
   (a) Abort if SigVerify($R.\sigma$, [chanId, R.credit, R.acc], vk$_C$) = 0;
   (b) Set credit$_H$ ← R.credit, and acc$_H$ ← R.acc;
   Otherwise:
   (a) Abort if SigVerify($R.\sigma$, [chanId, R.credit, R.acc], vk$_H$) = 0;
   (b) Set credit$_C$ ← R.credit, and acc$_C$ ← R.acc;
3. If status = "Active", then set chanExpiry ← now + claimDuration, and status ← "Closing".

Close():
1. Abort if status ≠ {"Active", "Closing"} or caller.vk ∉ {vk$_H$, vk$_C$};
2. If closeRequester = $\bot$, then set closeRequester ← caller.vk;
3. If closeRequester ≠ caller.vk, then set status ← "Closed";
4. If status = "Active", then set chanExpiry ← now + claimDuration, and status ← "Closing".

Withdraw():
1. Abort if status ≠ {"Closing", "Closed"};
2. Abort if status = "Closing" and now < chanExpiry;
3. Invoke ledger.transfer(vk$_H$, deposit$_H$ + credit$_H$ − credit$_C$) and ledger.transfer(vk$_C$, deposit$_C$ + credit$_C$ − credit$_H$);

Unlock():
1. Abort if status ≠ {"Closing", "Closed"};
2. Abort if status = "Closing" and now < chanExpiry;
3. Invoke ledger.transfer(vk$_C$, lock$_C$);

Fig. 3. UPC smart contract.

Off-Chain Functions

CreatePromise(C, amount, hash, Z, expiry, sk):
cid $\leftarrow$ C.cid;   credit $\leftarrow$ C.credit$_{out}$;
1. $P \leftarrow$ [credit, amount, hash, expiry, σ], where
   $\sigma \leftarrow$ Sign([cid, credit, amount, hash, expiry], sk)
   $P \leftarrow [m, Z := (A_\alpha, c_\alpha), \hat{\sigma}, \sigma]$,
   where $\hat{\sigma} \leftarrow$ PreSign(m, A_α, sk), $\sigma = \perp$ and $m = $ [cid, credit, amount, expiry];
2. Add P to C.Promises$_{out}$;
3. ACC.Insert(C.acc$_{out}$, hash, Z, C.accAux$_{out}$);
4. Output P.

PreVerifyPromise(P, promiseSender, C, amount, Z, expiry, vk):
cid $\leftarrow$ C.cid;   credit $\leftarrow$ C.credit$_{in}$;
1. If promiseSender = "Server" then deposit $\leftarrow$ C.contract.deposit$_H$;
   else deposit $\leftarrow$ C.contract.deposit$_C$
2. If [PreVerify($P.\hat{\sigma}$, [cid, credit, amount, expiry], A_α, vk) = 0] $\vee$ [C.credit$_{in}$+C.netProm$_{in}$+amount $>$
   deposit + C.credit$_{out}$] then output 0; else output 1.

VerifyPromise(P, promiseSender, C, amount, hash, Z, expiry, vk):
cid $\leftarrow$ C.cid;   credit $\leftarrow$ C.credit$_{in}$;
If promiseSender = "Server" then deposit $\leftarrow$ C.contract.deposit$_H$;
Otherwise, deposit $\leftarrow$ C.contract.deposit$_C$
1. Output 0 if any of the following conditions is true:
   - SigVerify($P.\sigma$, [cid, credit, amount, hash, expiry], vk) = 0
   - C.credit$_{in}$ + C.netProm$_{in}$ + amount $>$ deposit + C.credit$_{out}$;
   - P.expiry $-$ now $\leq$ C.params.claimDuration
2. Add P to C.Promises$_{in}$ and set C.netProm$_{in}$ $\leftarrow$ C.netProm$_{in}$ + amount;
3. ACC.Insert(C.acc$_{in}$, hash, Z, C.accAux$_{in}$);
4. Output 1.

VerifySecret(C, P, secret):
Output 0 if any of the following conditions is true; otherwise output 1:
   - $P \neq C$.Promises$_{out}$;
   - Abort if Hash(secret) $\neq$ P.hash;
VerifySolution(C, P, σ, A_α):
Output 0 if any of the following conditions is true; otherwise output 1:
   - $P \neq C$.Promises$_{out}$;
   - Abort if $\alpha = \perp$ where $\alpha := $ Ext(σ, $P.\hat{\sigma}$, A_α);
UpdateChannel(C, P, updateDirection):
If updateDirection = "outgoing", then
1. Set C.credit$_{out}$ $\leftarrow$ C.credit$_{out}$ + P.amount;
2. Remove P from C.Promises$_{out}$;
3. ACC.Delete(C.acc$_{out}$, P.hash, $P.Z$, C.accAux$_{out}$);
Otherwise,
1. Set C.credit$_{in}$ $\leftarrow$ C.credit$_{in}$ + P.amount;
2. Remove P from C.Promises$_{in}$;
3. ACC.Delete(C.acc$_{in}$, P.hash, $P.Z$, C.accAux$_{in}$)
CreateReceipt(C, sk):
cid $\leftarrow$ C.cid;   credit $\leftarrow$ C.credit$_{out}$;   acc $\leftarrow$ C.acc$_{out}$;
Output $\sigma \leftarrow$ Sign([cid, credit, acc], sk);
VerifyReceipt(R, P, C, vk): cid $\leftarrow$ C.cid;   credit $\leftarrow$ C.credit$_{in}$;   acc $\leftarrow$ C.acc$_{in}$;   accAux $\leftarrow$ C.accAux$_{in}$;
1. ACC.Delete(acc, P.hash, $P.Z$, accAux);
2. Return SigVerify($R.\sigma$, [cid, credit + P.amount, acc], vk).

Fig. 4. Off-Chain Functions

finality of a transaction is dependent on the block creation rate (i.e., about 13 s in Ethereum) and the fee associated to the transaction. In this section, we will be focusing on the fees associated to the transaction calls made to the smart

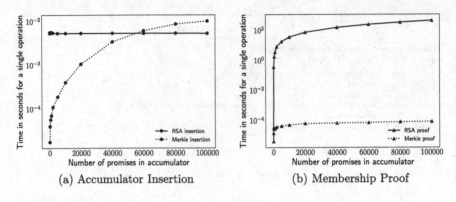

(a) Accumulator Insertion   (b) Membership Proof

Fig. 5. Performance comparisons between Merkle Tree and RSA accumulators

contract, which is captured with the *gas* value. The gas refers to the unit that measures the amount of computational effort required to execute specific set of operations in the Ethereum network. Moreover, the final price of a transaction fee depends on the exchange rate between gas and Ether known as the *gas price*. The gas price is chosen by the sender of the transaction, however acceptable gas prices by the miners of the blocks would be dependent on the demand and network congestion. At the time of writing (Jan 25th 2023) the average gas price for Ethereum is 24 Gwei and 51 Gwei for the Polygon network. Furthermore, ETH is priced at 1544 USD and MATIC[2] at 0.95 USD.

We begin by evaluating the gas needed for the deployment of the contract. The UPC contract requires $1,532,271$ gas (56.55 USD for Ethereum and 0.1 USD for Polygon) to be deployed on the respective blockchain. We emphasize that in our implementation we did not aim to optimize gas costs and further optimizations can reduce the gas. respectively. The gas usages for different functions of UPC contract are reported in Table 2.

In the case of HTLC payments, we can consider two main scenarios. In the optimistic case, after a promise is sent from the sender, the receiver releases the secret for the HTLC and consequently, the sender sends a corresponding receipt to the receiver. In such a scenario, the receiving party will submit the receipt to the contract and close accordingly. However, in the pessimistic case, where the receiving party releases the secret but does not receive a receipt, it goes on-chain and first submits its latest receipt. Next, it submits the promise for the HTLC where the party can reveal the secret of HTLC. Comparing the two scenarios and referencing the Table 2, we see that in the pessimistic case, about 70K more gas (2.50 USD) will be needed to resolve the promise.

Off-chain Evaluation. To evaluate the protocol's runtime, we conducted a test with ten clients simultaneously sending transactions to a single server. Each client transmitted 1,000 transactions, resulting in a total of 10,000 promises, secret reveals, and receipts. We achieved an end-to-end throughput of 110

---

[2] MATIC is the native token used in the Polygon blockchain.

Table 2. UPC contract's functions Gas Prices. USD amounts reflect the date Jan 25th, 2023.

Functions	Gas Units	USD-ETH	USD-Polygon
Deposit	45,079	1.67	0.002
ReceiptClaim	75,336	2.80	0.004
Promise Claim	65,954 (w/o. proof)	2.45	0.003
	66,196 (Merkle-1 tx)	2.46	0.003
	74,755 (Merkle-1K txs)	2.78	0.004
	80,750 (Merkle-100K txs)	3.00	0.004
	524,378 (RSA)	19.48	0.026
Close	48,089 (initial)	1.79	0.002
	32,250 (final)	1.20	0.002
Withdraw	29,089	1.08	0.001

TPS, encompassing random secret generation, secret hashing, promise creation, promise verification, secret revealing, secret verification, receipt creation, and receipt verification. We note that optimizing the off-chain code and using a more capable server machine could further enhance the performance.

AUPC Overhead. As described in Sect. 4, inspired from the A^2L work we can modify UPC to achieve transactional unlinkability. We refer readers to Sect. 6 of [15] for the overhead of A^2L and A^2L + for providing privacy.

6 Discussion

6.1 Security

The two intuitive security properties we require for both UPC and AUPC to satisfy are:

1. *Theft prevention*, meaning the funds of all honest participants in the system are protected despite adversarial actions.
2. *Balance*, meaning the total funds in the system do not increase with time (or in other words, an adversary cannot double-spend).

In addition, AUPC needs to satisfy *anonymity*, meaning a malicious payment hub which does not collude with other parties cannot infer any information between the sender and receiver of a transaction.

Informally, the properties of theft prevention and balance are satisfied through the sequence of hashed secrets and signed promises in UPC and the rerandomizeable puzzles and adaptor signatures in AUPC, which guarantee *atomicity*, i.e., either the payment is successful with the funds transferred simultaneously, or the funds are returned back to the sender, as discussed in the optimistic and pessimistic scenarios in Sect. 5.2. Also anonymity is achieved through the series of rerandomizeable puzzles, as for the case of A^2L and A^2L+ discussed in Sect. 4.

6.2 Tradeoffs Between UPC and AUPC

We now discuss the advantages and disadvantages of AUPC over UPC (other than privacy, which was the intended goal for AUPC):

HTLCs vs Timelocks. Since UPC relies on HTLCs (hashed time-lock contracts), it is only interoperable across chains that use the same hash function. In contrast, the conditions in AUPC only rely on time-locks, which allows it to be interoperable between ledgers that do not support the same hash function.

Fixed vs. Variable Amounts: While UPC supports arbitrary amounts, AUPC inherits a limitation from A^2L, where the amount for each transaction should be fixed (since arbitrary amounts could be used to link the sender and receiver, thus defeating privacy). Therefore, to send an arbitrary amount, multiple transactions may be required. For example, consider the case that the fixed amount for each payment is set to 0.1 ETH. To send a transaction of amount 0.7 ETH, seven transactions are required. As we can see, there is a tradeoff between transaction efficiency (e.g., tx fees, tx finality) and privacy. As a result, given this tradeoff, in some cases users may opt to use the UPC protocol instead of AUPC.

6.3 Related Work

In addition to A^2L and A^2L+ which inspired AUPC, a work closely related to ours is Raiden [3], which like UPC, focuses on Ethereum and ERC-20 tokens, and additionally relies on HTLCs to route payments through the Raiden network.[3] Furthermore, Raiden supports concurrent transactions and makes use of a Merkle tree to commit to the set of pending payments. However, it faces a major limitation in the low number of in-flight payments (limited to 160 at a time[456]) Also, as pointed out earlier, Raiden off-chain payments are *simple* payments as opposed to *conditional* payments *a la* HTLCs. For this reason, Merkle paths

---

[3] Notably they employ a separate SecretRegistry contract [27] to ensure that worst case delays are independent of the length of the payment route.

[4] As noted in [4], this is to avoid the risk of not being able to unlock the transfers, as the gas cost for this operation grows linearly with the number of the pending locks and thus the number of pending transfers.

[5] The limit, currently set to 160, is a rounded value that ensures the gas cost of unlocking will be less than 40% of Ethereum's traditional pi-million (3141592) block gas limit.

[6] Lightning has a similar limitation in that it supports 483 (unidirectional) concurrent payments owing to block size limits in Bitcoin [1,30].

corresponding to *all* pending payments are opened (and in particular, checked for expiry) before allowing the parties to withdraw from their Raiden channel at settlement time. In contrast, in UPC, pending payments that have expired do not need to be opened on-chain. While this may seem a minor improvement in the context of off-chain payments, this turns out to have a significant impact in larger applications (such as atomic swaps or secure computation with penalties [8,33]) that rely on HTLCs. If UPC is used to implement HTLCs in these applications, then a counterparty that aborts without claiming the HTLC payment (i.e., the HTLC payment refunds the money back to the sender), does not incur any additional (gas) cost to the honest sender. Finally, we note that to the best of our knowledge, Raiden has not been formally described.

Next, we discuss a work on virtual payment channels [12], which constructs the so called *ledger channels* between participants, such that parties that have a ledger channel with an intermediary party, can send payments to each other via a *virtual channel* that does not require interaction with the intermediary for every payment. Note that interaction with the intermediary is required for sending the first payment (and for closing the virtual channel), and thus the benefits are obtained only if parties send at least two or more payments over the virtual channel. Additionally, participants have to pre-allocate (i.e., lock) funds on the ledger channel for every virtual channel. This may cause a large payment on a given virtual channel to fail unless funds are re-allocated by closing multiple existing virtual channels (each of which would require interaction with server). On the one hand, UPC requires interaction with the UPC Hub for authorization of every off-chain payment. On the other hand, UPC clients do not have to perform any additional pooling of funds as long as they have sufficient balance on the UPC channel.

Other works focus on efficient cross-chain atomic swaps [37] or off-chain trading platforms [14], and require clients to hold accounts on both chains (required per definition of the atomic swap problem [13]). UPC, on the other hand, can allow payments between two clients who do not share a common blockchain. Also, several works in addition to A^2L focus on providing privacy and/or anonymity in payment channels [16,16,18,21,24,25] for blockchains based on the UTXO model. However, we are currently missing an approach for universal, efficient, privacy-preserving scalable payments account based blockchains.

Finally, there have been other scalability approaches like rollups or sharding [17,20] which are orthogonal to our work.

7 Conclusion and Future Work

We presented two implementations of UPC, or Universal Payment Channels: A first implementation is UPC which uses HTLC contracts to enable payment channels between a sender and a receiver through a payment hub, and AUPC which only uses time-locks and digital signatures compatible with adaptor signatures, in the respective contracts (making it interoperable across a broader family of ledgers) and offers unlinkability against the payment hub. However, the tradeoff in AUPC is that it does not support arbitrary amounts, which implies that in practice, payments utilizing AUPC would require more transactions to complete. Moreover, we could foresee that in practice, different denominations might be supported by different hubs and this would require users to interact with multiple hubs, each serving a different fixed amount.

One exciting research direction for future work is to consider auditability guarantees and how to add support to UPC and AUPC in order to be able to enforce policies such as anti money-laundering (AML).

Acknowledgements. This work has been partially supported by Madrid regional government as part of the program S2018/TCS-4339 (BLOQUES-CM) co-funded by EIE Funds of the European Union; by grant IJC2020-043391-I/MCIN/AEI/10.13039/501100011033; by PRODIGY Project (TED2021-132464B-I00) funded by MCIN/AEI/10.13039/ 501100011033/ and the European Union NextGenerationEU/PRTR.

References

1. Bolt #2: peer protocol for channel management. https://github.com/lightningnetwork/lightning-rfc/blob/master/02-peer-protocol.md#rationale-7. Accessed 22 Sept 2020
2. Payment channels - bitcoin wiki. https://en.bitcoin.it/wiki/Payment_channels. Accessed 05 May 2021
3. Raiden. https://raiden.network/. Accessed 04 May 2021
4. Raiden. https://raiden-network-specification.readthedocs.io/en/latest/mediated_transfer.html#limit-to-number-of-simultaneously-pending-transfers. Accessed 04 May 2021
5. Aumayr, L., et al.: Generalized bitcoin-compatible channels. Cryptology ePrint Archive, Report 2020/476 (2020)

6. Baldimtsi, F., et al.: Accumulators with applications to anonymity-preserving revocation. In: IEEE EuroS&P (2017)
7. Ben-Sasson, E., et al.: Zerocash: decentralized anonymous payments from bitcoin. In: 2014 IEEE Symposium on Security and Privacy, pp. 459–474. IEEE Computer Society Press (2014). https://doi.org/10.1109/SP.2014.36
8. Bentov, I., Kumaresan, R.: How to use bitcoin to design fair protocols. In: Garay, J.A., Gennaro, R. (eds.) CRYPTO 2014. LNCS, vol. 8617, pp. 421–439. Springer, Heidelberg (2014). https://doi.org/10.1007/978-3-662-44381-1_24
9. Chatzigiannis, P., Baldimtsi, F., Chalkias, K.: SoK: auditability and accountability in distributed payment systems. In: Sako, K., Tippenhauer, N.O. (eds.) ACNS 2021. LNCS, vol. 12727, pp. 311–337. Springer, Cham (2021). https://doi.org/10.1007/978-3-030-78375-4_13
10. Christodorescu, M., et al.: Universal payment channels: an interoperability platform for digital currencies. CoRR abs/2109.12194 (2021). https://arxiv.org/abs/2109.12194
11. Decker, C., Wattenhofer, R.: A fast and scalable payment network with bitcoin duplex micropayment channels. In: Pelc, A., Schwarzmann, A.A. (eds.) SSS 2015. LNCS, vol. 9212, pp. 3–18. Springer, Cham (2015). https://doi.org/10.1007/978-3-319-21741-3_1
12. Dziembowski, S., Eckey, L., Faust, S., Malinowski, D.: Perun: virtual payment hubs over cryptocurrencies. In: 2019 IEEE Symposium on Security and Privacy (SP), pp. 106–123. IEEE (2019)
13. Heilman, E., Lipmann, S., Goldberg, S.: Atomic swaps. https://en.bitcoin.it/wiki/Atomic_swap. Accessed 04 May 2021
14. Heilman, E., Lipmann, S., Goldberg, S.: The Arwen trading protocols. In: Bonneau, J., Heninger, N. (eds.) FC 2020. LNCS, vol. 12059, pp. 156–173. Springer, Cham (2020). https://doi.org/10.1007/978-3-030-51280-4_10
15. Glaeser, N., Maffei, M., Malavolta, G., Moreno-Sanchez, P., Tairi, E., Thyagarajan, S.A.: Foundations of coin mixing services. Cryptology ePrint Archive, Report 2022/942 (2022). https://eprint.iacr.org/2022/942
16. Green, M., Miers, I.: Bolt: anonymous payment channels for decentralized currencies. In: Proceedings of the 2017 ACM SIGSAC Conference on Computer and Communications Security, pp. 473–489. ACM (2017)
17. Gudgeon, L., Moreno-Sanchez, P., Roos, S., McCorry, P., Gervais, A.: SoK: layer-two blockchain protocols. In: Bonneau, J., Heninger, N. (eds.) FC 2020. LNCS, vol. 12059, pp. 201–226. Springer, Cham (2020). https://doi.org/10.1007/978-3-030-51280-4_12
18. Heilman, E., Alshenibr, L., Baldimtsi, F., Scafuro, A., Goldberg, S.: TumbleBit: an untrusted bitcoin-compatible anonymous payment hub. In: NDSS 2017. The Internet Society (2017)
19. Chainalysis Inc.: Chainalysis: blockchain analysis. https://www.chainalysis.com/
20. Khalil, R., Zamyatin, A., Felley, G., Moreno-Sanchez, P., Gervais, A.: Commit-chains: Secure, scalable off-chain payments. Cryptology ePrint Archive, Report 2018/642 (2018). https://eprint.iacr.org/2018/642
21. Le, D.V., Hurtado, L.T., Ahmad, A., Minaei, M., Lee, B., Kate, A.: A tale of two trees: one writes, and other reads: optimized oblivious accesses to bitcoin and other UTXO-based blockchains. Proc. Priv. Enhancing Technol. **2020**(2), 519–536 (2020). https://doi.org/10.2478/popets-2020-0039. https://par.nsf.gov/biblio/10200542
22. Lind, J., Eyal, I., Pietzuch, P.R., Sirer, E.G.: Teechan: payment channels using trusted execution environments (2016). http://arxiv.org/abs/1612.07766

23. Lind, J., Naor, O., Eyal, I., Kelbert, F., Sirer, E.G., Pietzuch, P.: Teechain: a secure payment network with asynchronous blockchain access. In: Proceedings of the 27th ACM Symposium on Operating Systems Principles, pp. 63–79. SOSP 2019, Association for Computing Machinery, New York, NY, USA (2019). https://doi.org/10.1145/3341301.3359627

24. Malavolta, G., Moreno-Sanchez, P., Kate, A., Maffei, M., Ravi, S.: Concurrency and privacy with payment-channel networks. In: Thuraisingham, B.M., Evans, D., Malkin, T., Xu, D. (eds.) ACM CCS 2017. pp. 455–471. ACM Press (2017). https://doi.org/10.1145/3133956.3134096

25. Malavolta, G., Moreno-Sanchez, P., Schneidewind, C., Kate, A., Maffei, M.: Anonymous multi-hop locks for blockchain scalability and interoperability. In: NDSS 2019. The Internet Society (2019)

26. Meiklejohn, S., et al.: A fistful of bitcoins: characterizing payments among men with no names. Commun. ACM (2016)

27. Miller, A., Bentov, I., Bakshi, S., Kumaresan, R., McCorry, P.: Sprites and state channels: payment networks that go faster than lightning. In: Goldberg, I., Moore, T. (eds.) FC 2019. LNCS, vol. 11598, pp. 508–526. Springer, Cham (2019). https://doi.org/10.1007/978-3-030-32101-7_30

28. Minaei, M., et al.: Unlinkability and interoperability in account-based universal payment channels. Cryptology ePrint Archive, Paper 2023/916 (2023). https://eprint.iacr.org/2023/916

29. Minaei Bidgoli, M., Kumaresan, R., Zamani, M., Gaddam, S.: System and method for managing data in a database (2023). https://patents.google.com/patent/US11556909B2/

30. Mizrahi, A., Zohar, A.: Congestion attacks in payment channel networks. https://arxiv.org/pdf/2002.06564.pdf. Accessed 04 May 2021

31. Nakamoto, S.: Bitcoin: a peer-to-peer electronic cash system (2009). http://bitcoin.org/bitcoin.pdf

32. Poon, J., Dryja, T.: The bitcoin lightning network: scalable off-chain instant payments. http://lightning.network/lightning-network-paper.pdf. Accessed 22 Sept 2020

33. Kumaresan, R., Vaikuntanathan, V., Vasudevan, P. N.: Improvements to secure computation with penalties. In: CCS, pp. 406–417 (2016)

34. Ron, D., Shamir, A.: Quantitative analysis of the full bitcoin transaction graph. In: Sadeghi, A.-R. (ed.) FC 2013. LNCS, vol. 7859, pp. 6–24. Springer, Heidelberg (2013). https://doi.org/10.1007/978-3-642-39884-1_2

35. Tairi, E., Moreno-Sanchez, P., Maffei, M.: A^2l: anonymous atomic locks for scalability in payment channel hubs. In: 42nd IEEE Symposium on Security and Privacy, SP 2021, San Francisco, CA, USA, 24–27 May 2021, pp. 1834–1851. IEEE (2021). https://doi.org/10.1109/SP40001.2021.00111

36. Van Saberhagen, N.: Cryptonote v 2.0 (2013). https://cryptonote.org/whitepaper.pdf

37. Zamyatin, A., Harz, D., Lind, J., Panayiotou, P., Gervais, A., Knottenbelt, W.: XCLAIM: trustless, interoperable, cryptocurrency-backed assets. In: IEEE Security and Privacy. IEEE (2019)

Cassiopeia: Practical On-Chain Witness Encryption

Schwinn Saereesitthipitak[(✉)] and Dionysis Zindros

Stanford University, Stanford, USA
schwinn@stanford.edu

Abstract. Witness Encryption is a holy grail of cryptography that remains elusive. It asks that a secret is only revealed when a particular computational problem is solved. Modern smart contracts and blockchains make assumptions of "honest majority", which allow for a *social* implementation of Witness Encryption. The core idea is to make use of a partially trusted committee to carry out the responsibilities mandated by these functionalities - such as keeping the secret private, and then releasing it publicly after a solution to the computational puzzle is presented. We propose Cassiopeia, a smart contract Witness Encryption scheme (with public witness security) and provide an open source composable implementation that can be utilized as an oracle by others within the broader DeFi ecosystem. We devise a cryptoeconomic scheme to incentivize honest participation, and analyze its security under the honest majority and rational majority settings. We conclude by measuring and optimizing gas costs and illustrating the practicality of our scheme.

Keywords: Witness Encryption · Publicly Verifiable Secret Sharing · Smart Contract

1 Introduction

Witness Encryption [16] is a cryptographic scheme where a message is encrypted such that it can only be decrypted when a solution (also called the "witness") to a computational puzzle is presented. For example, a message may be witness-encrypted such that it can only be decrypted if for some connected graph, a Hamiltonian cycle is found. A particularly useful instantiation of Witness Encryption in the blockchain setting is Timelock Encryption [25,27,29], where a message is encrypted such that it can only be decrypted after a set unlock time. This enables important use cases in DeFi such as sealed bid auctions and front-running prevention [1].

Though Witness Encryption is still impractical under standard assumptions, the "honest majority" assumption in modern blockchains can be leveraged to make Witness Encryption practical. We do so by asking a committee to keep

© International Financial Cryptography Association 2024
A. Essex et al. (Eds.): FC 2023 Workshops, LNCS 13953, pp. 385–404, 2024.
https://doi.org/10.1007/978-3-031-48806-1_25

the secret and release it for us when the witness is presented. As long as a majority of the committee is honest, the secret is revealed at the right time. Our goal is to make Witness Encryption practical and composable for use in DeFi. Furthermore, we hold committee members accountable for releasing correct decryption keys in a timely manner.

Our Contributions. We summarize our contributions as follows:

1. We put forth a smart contract-based construction for Witness Encryption.
2. We explore whether our scheme is correct and secure under the honest majority and rational majority settings.
3. We implement the construction as an open-source Solidity smart contract, benchmark gas usage on Ethereum, and provide our parameterization of the scheme.

Construction Overview. Suppose Alice wants to encrypt a secret with an instance of a puzzle. Alice will entrust a fixed committee to keep her secret and release it if someone presents a solution to the puzzle to the smart contract. She trusts that the majority of the committee are honest. Alice splits her secret into shares, one for each committee member, such that a majority of them are required to reconstruct the original secret and each committee member is only able to decrypt its own share. Alice then calls a smart contract function to publish the encrypted shares for them to access. She also attaches a zero-knowledge proof of knowledge of the secret (in the form of a zkSNARK) to ensure she is honest and actually knows the secret. The contract verifies that Alice split her secret into shares correctly. When the contract receives a solution to the puzzle, it enables committee members to submit their decrypted shares to the contract. When a committee member submits a share, the contract verifies that it is consistent with the corresponding encrypted share Alice posted before accepting the share. As long as at least a majority of the committee members revealed their shares, Alice's secret can be reconstructed by anyone.

We also propose an incentivized version of the above scheme which includes fees and slashing. Each committee member deposits collateral into the contract. If a committee member correctly reveals its decrypted shares, it is awarded a fee. Otherwise, its collateral is slashed. We ensure the fee is sufficient to incentivize honest committee member participation, using the risk-free rate as a benchmark for the opportunity cost. Note that the incentivized version of the scheme requires Alice to provide a maximum secret lifespan upfront after which the secret can be decrypted even without a witness.

Related Work. General-purpose Witness Encryption was introduced by Garg et al. [16]. The standard security definition of Witness Encryption is *extractable security* [18]. Most current Witness Encryption schemes are based on multilinear maps [16,17] or on indistinguishability obfuscation (iO) [15]. Both construction paths require strong assumptions and are computationally impractical. One alternative is to use weaker variants of Witness Encryption that encompass only a specific subset of NP [4].

Another alternative to build practical Witness Encryption, which we explore in this work, is to do *social witness encryption* where a committee is entrusted up to an adversarial threshold. Goyal et al. [19] were the first to propose an extractable social Witness Encryption scheme constructed from Proactive Secret Sharing (PSS) that leverages a blockchain and its Proof-of-Stake validators as the committee. Though there have been multiple previous works proposing social WE equivalents [8,12,19], we are the first to provide an incentivized smart contract instantiation. One particularly useful application of Witness Encryption and blockchains is Timelock Encryption [25,27,29]. Social Timelock Encryption leveraging Identity-Based Encryption (IBE) [6] has been put forth in i-TiRE [1] and tlock [24]. Dottling et al. [12] proposed a social Timelock Encryption scheme using a weaker Signature-based Witness Encryption (SWE) scheme.

The critical building block for social Timelock Encryption and Witness Encryption is a Secret Sharing Scheme [32]. In the blockchain setting, threshold encryption was previously explored in works by Benhamouda et al. [3] and Goyal et al. [19]. For accountability, we use Publicly Verifiable Secret Sharing (PVSS) [10,33]. For our implementation, we use SCRAPE [9] as the underlying PVSS scheme.

Applications. Witness Encryption can be used to build powerful cryptographic primitives such as succinct Functional Encryption [7,28] for Turing machines [18]. When combined with a blockchain, Witness Encryption can also be leveraged to achieve fairness against dishonest majority in a secure multiparty computation protocol [11]. More practically, it can also be used to instantiate Timelock Encryption, which can be applied towards building new forms of wallets [34] among other applications.

2 Preliminaries

2.1 Symmetric Encryption

Let s be the secret key and m be the message to encrypt. A symmetric encryption scheme contains an encryption algorithm $Enc_s(m)$ that produces a ciphertext c and a decryption algorithm $Dec_s(c)$ that produces the original message m.

2.2 Secret Sharing

A threshold secret sharing scheme [32] consists of a dealer D, a secret s, a committee of n participants $p_1, p_2, \ldots, p_n$, and a threshold t. To share the secret, D calls a function share(s) which splits s into shares $s_1, s_2, \ldots, s_n$ and distributes these to participants such that each participant p_i only has access to s_i. A set of at least t participants can work together to combine their shares $s_{i_1}, s_{i_2}, \ldots,$ using the function recover($s_{i_1}, s_{i_2}, \ldots$) to obtain the original secret. On the other hand, if less than t participants work together to combine their shares, no information can be learned about the secret.

2.3   Publicly Verifiable Secret Sharing (PVSS)

Publicly verifiable secret sharing schemes [9,10,23,30,31,33] are augmentations of secret sharing schemes such that any verifier V (who does not need to be the dealer or part of the committee) can verify that the secret shares are valid. PVSS schemes generally follow the steps below [9]:

- **Setup:** Given a security parameter λ, each participant p_i calls $\mathsf{Gen}(1^\lambda)$ to generate a public-private key pair (pk_i, sk_i) and shares pk_i publicly.
- **Distribution:** Let s be the secret to be shared by the dealer. The dealer calls $\mathsf{genDist}(s, [pk_i])$ to generate shares $s_1, \ldots, s_n$ and encrypts each share s_i with pk_i to produce $\hat{s}_i$. The dealer also generates a proof π_D that all $\hat{s}_i$ are valid and consistent with one another.
- **Verification:** Any external verifier V calls $\mathsf{verifyDist}([\hat{s}_i], [pk_i], \pi_D)$ to non-interactively verify, using all publicly available information, that the encrypted shares are consistent with one another.
- **Reconstruction:**
  - Each p_i publishes $s'_i = \mathsf{decrypt}(\hat{s}_i, sk_i)$, along with a proof π_i that $s'_i = s_i$.
  - V calls $\mathsf{verifyShare}(i, \hat{s}_i, s'_i, \pi_i)$ for every participant's contribution to verify that all $s'_i = s_i$.
  - With all shares known, anybody can call $\mathsf{reconstruct}(s'_{i_1}, \ldots, s'_{i_t})$ on the revealed shares to obtain the secret s.

PVSS schemes generally have the following properties [23]:

- **Correctness:** If the dealer is honest and a set of at least t parties are honest, then $\mathsf{verifyDist}$ passes during distribution, $\mathsf{verifyShare}$ passes during reconstruction for all honest parties, and $\mathsf{reconstruct}$ yields the original secret.
- **Verifiability:** If $\mathsf{verifyDist}$ passes, then $\hat{s}_i$ are consistent secret shares with overwhelming probability, and if $\mathsf{verifyShare}$ passes, then $\hat{s}'_i = s_i$ with overwhelming probability.
- **Secrecy:** Prior to reconstruction, any set of less than t participants cannot learn any information about the secret.

2.4   Zero-Knowledge Succinct Non-Interactive Argument of Knowledge (zkSNARK)

Let C be an efficiently computable boolean circuit. We define the relation $\mathcal{R}_C = \{(x_C, w_C) \mid C(x_C, w_C) = 1\}$, where (x_C, w_C) is an instance-witness pair. A zkSNARK consists of a triple of probabilistic polynomial time algorithms (G, P, V) as follows [5,21]:

- G is a generator that, upon receiving a security parameter input λ, generates a *reference string* σ and a *verification state* τ.
- A prover $P(\sigma, x_C, w_C)$ that outputs a proof π for the instance x_C and the witness w_C.
- A verifier $V(\tau, x_C, \pi)$ that outputs 1 if the proof is valid and 0 otherwise.

zkSNARKs have the following properties:

- **Correctness**: An honestly-generated proof π is always accepted by an honest verifier V.
- **Soundness**: A proof π generated with an invalid witness will not be accepted by an honest verifier V with overwhelming probability.
- **Zero Knowledge**: The interaction between prover and verifier reveals negligible information about the witness.

2.5 Witness Encryption

In a Witness Encryption scheme, a message is encrypted such that the cipher-text can only be decrypted if a witness is presented as a solution to an NP problem [16]. For example, a message can be encrypted such that it can only be decrypted with a solution to an instance of the 3-SAT problem. Concretely, let $\mathcal{R}$ be a relation of an NP language $\mathcal{L}$ such that for each $x \in \mathcal{L}$, there exists some w such that $(x, w) \in \mathcal{R}$ and for all $x \notin \mathcal{L}$ such a witness does not exist. The scheme has public witness security if the witness is public during decryption, and the message is revealed publicly. A Witness Encryption scheme, parameterized by a security parameter λ, consists of PPT encryption and decryption functions $\mathsf{WE.Enc}_{\mathcal{R}}(1^\lambda, x, m)$ and $\mathsf{WE.Dec}_{\mathcal{R}}(c, x, w)$ such that the following properties hold [25]:

- *Correctness*: For any plaintext message m, instance $x \in \mathcal{L}$, and witness w such that $(x, w) \in \mathcal{R}$, $\mathsf{WE.Dec}_{\mathcal{R}}(\mathsf{WE.Enc}_{\mathcal{R}}(1^\lambda, x, m), x, w) = m$.
- *Extractable Security*: A PPT adversary given $c = \mathsf{WE.Enc}_{\mathcal{R}}(1^\lambda, x, m)$ is only able to extract information about m if she can also produce a witness w such that $(x, w) \in \mathcal{R}$, except with negligible probability.

2.6 Risk-Free Rate

The fees awarded to committee members should be at least the return on an exogenous risk-free source of yield, otherwise rational committee members will stop participating in the protocol. Therefore, we assume there exists a per-block risk-free rate r agreed upon by all parties participating in the protocol. At any block, anyone can deposit M and earn $M(1+r)$ after one block via an exogenous risk-free source of yield. The opportunity cost for not earning risk-free yield on M for k blocks is $M(1 + r)^k - M$.

3   Construction

The Cassiopeia smart contract is instantiated for a fixed committee with known public keys of size n and a threshold t. The threshold t is a public parameter indicating the minimum number of honest committee members required for the construction to be correct and secure. Correctness means that the secret can be decrypted if the witness becomes available. Security means no information about the secret can be obtained unless a witness becomes available.

Suppose the dealer wants to perform *social* Witness Encryption with public witness security on a message m (Algorithm 1). First, the dealer chooses a relation $\mathcal{R}$ and a corresponding instance x. Then, the dealer generates a random bit string s that can be simultaneously used as the secret in a PVSS scheme and the key of a symmetric encryption scheme. The dealer runs PVSS.genDist($s, [pk_i]$) to generate the encrypted secret shares $[\hat{s}_i]$ along with a proof π_D that the generated encrypted secret shares are consistent with one another. Note that a valid proof π_D guarantees that Cassiopeia.encrypt prevents committee members from maintaining shares of invalid secrets. It becomes vital to correctness in the incentivized construction in Sect. 4.

Denote $c = ([\hat{s}_i], \pi_D)$ as the *PVSS ciphertext*. Using a symmetric encryption scheme, the dealer encrypts m with the key s to produce $\hat{c} = Enc_s(m)$. The dealer calls the smart contract function encrypt to register the PVSS ciphertext and instance on chain. The contract checks whether the proof π_D is valid, and if so, makes the encrypted secret shares available to the committee members. A unique identifier for the secret id is returned. Subsequently, $\hat{c}$ is dispersed to *public storage* (using the function disperse), either off-chain to optimize gas costs (e.g. IPFS) or on-chain for data availability.

Algorithm 1. Off-chain procedure run by dealer to witness-encrypt a secret

1: **function** WE.Enc$_{\mathcal{R}}(1^\lambda, x, m)$
2:     $s \xleftarrow{\$} \{0,1\}^\lambda$
3:     $\hat{c} \leftarrow Enc_s(m)$
4:     $c \leftarrow$ PVSS.genDist($s, [pk_i]$)
5:     $y \leftarrow H(s \,\|\, c \,\|\, \mathcal{R} \,\|\, x)$
6:     $\pi \leftarrow P(\sigma, (c, \mathcal{R}, x, y, [pk_i]), s)$
7:     $id \leftarrow$ Cassiopeia.encrypt($c, \mathcal{R}, x, y, \pi$)
8:     disperse($id, \hat{c}$)
9: **end function**

Anybody who obtains a valid witness w can call the smart contract function claim to start decryption (Algorithm 2). The smart contract checks that w is indeed a valid witness such that $(x, w) \in \mathcal{R}$. If so, a flag M_{id} is set indicating the secret has been claimed. Note that to support private decryption, one could provide a zkSNARK proof as the witness w for a boolean circuit corresponding to x and $\mathcal{R}$ [19]. This way, w reveals nothing about the actual secret witness while still retaining the same correctness and security properties.

Now, committee members will decrypt their encrypted shares $\hat{s}_i$ and submit the result on chain (Algorithm 3). A committee member does so by first using PVSS.decrypt to obtain a decryption s'_i and a proof π_i that s'_i is a valid decryption, i.e. $s'_i = s_i$. The committee member then submits the share on-chain by calling the smart contract function submitShare, which verifies the proof and stores s_i' in the set of decrypted shares S_{id} inside the contract. Once $|S_{id}| \geq t$, anyone can reconstruct the secret s using PVSS.reconstruct. To obtain the original message, $\hat{c}$ is fetched from *public storage* (using the function fetch) and decrypted using s as the key to produce $m = Dec_s(\hat{c})$. Note that for our correctness proof to follow, we assume committee members submit their shares within Δ blocks of the secret being claimed, where Δ is a fixed parameter. The full decryption procedure is written in pseudocode below.

Algorithm 2. Off-chain decryption procedure run by anyone in possession of the witness w

---
1: $id \leftarrow$ identifier of secret to decrypt
2: **function** WE.Dec$_{\mathcal{R}}(1^\lambda, c, x, w)$
3:     Cassiopeia.claim(id, w)
4:     ▷ *Wait for committee members to submit shares*
5:     **upon** $|$Cassiopeia.$S_{id}| \geq t$ **do**   ▷ Monitor smart contract for state change
6:         $s \leftarrow$ reconstruct(Cassiopeia.S_{id})
7:         fetch$(\hat{c})$
8:         $m \leftarrow Dec_s(\hat{c})$
9:     **end upon**
10: **end function**

Algorithm 3. Off-chain procedure run by any committee member submitting shares

---
1: $i \leftarrow$ index of own public key in $[pk_i]$
2: **upon** Cassiopeia.$M_{id} =$ CLAIMED **do**   ▷ Monitor smart contract for state change
3:     $([\hat{s}_i], \pi_D) \leftarrow$ Cassiopeia.$C_{id}.c$
4:     $(s_i', \pi_i) \leftarrow$ PVSS.decrypt$(\hat{s}_i, sk_i)$
5:     Cassiopeia.submitShare(s_i', π_i, id, i)
6: **end upon**

However, this protocol still vulnerable to malleability attacks. Concretely, let x' be an instance of relation $\mathcal{R}'$ for which the adversary already knows a valid witness w'. The adversary can act as a malicious dealer, calling encrypt with c and x' instead of x, then call claim with w' to notify committee members to start submitting their shares (and thereby start decryption). Therefore, the adversary can bypass the requirement of finding a valid witness w for x to decrypt the secret encoded by c.

To mitigate this issue, we ask the dealer to provide a proof in zero knowledge that he knows s and he intends to encrypt s with the instance x. In particular, the dealer generates a commitment to the secret and ciphertext, tying it to $\mathcal{R}$ and x by computing $y = H(s \,\|\, c \,\|\, \mathcal{R} \,\|\, x)$, where H is a hash function modeled as a random oracle. The dealer then generates a zkSNARK proof of knowledge of

s such that if the encrypted shares were decrypted and recombined, the result would be s, and that $y = H(s \,\|\, c \,\|\, \mathcal{R} \,\|\, x)$. More formally, the dealer generates the proof $\pi = P(\sigma, (c, \mathcal{R}, x, y, [pk_i]), s)$ in Line 6 of Algorithm 1 using the boolean circuit in Algorithm 4. Without knowledge of s, an adversarial dealer cannot use the same ciphertext c with another instance x'.

Algorithm 4. zkSNARK circuit defined by $\mathcal{R}_C$

Require: $x_C = (c, \mathcal{R}, x, y, [pk_i])$, $w_C = s$
1: $y' \leftarrow H(s \,\|\, c \,\|\, \mathcal{R}, x)$
2: $c' \leftarrow \mathsf{PVSS.genDist}(s, [pk_i])$
3: **return** $y' = y \wedge c' = c$

When the dealer calls encrypt, he must include y and π. The contract verifies that the zero knowledge proof π is valid with respect to c, $\mathcal{R}$ and y, on top of already verifying the PVSS ciphertext as outlined above. Concretely, the π must be valid according to $V(\tau, (c, \mathcal{R}, x, y, [pk_i]), \pi) = 1$. Without a valid π, an adversary would not be able to carry out a malleability attack. The Cassiopeia smart contract is written in pseudocode in Algorithm 5.

Algorithm 5. Cassiopeia Smart Contract

```
 1: contract Cassiopeia
 2:     C, S, M ← ∅
 3:     function encrypt(c, R, x, y, π)
 4:         ([ŝᵢ], π_D) ← c
 5:         require(V(τ, (c, R, x, y, [pkᵢ]), π) = 1 ∧ PVSS.verifyDist([ŝᵢ], [pkᵢ], π_D))
 6:         id ← H(c, R, x)
 7:         C_id ← (c, R, x)
 8:         return id
 9:     end function
10:     function claim(id, w)
11:         {R, x, ...} ← C_id
12:         require((x, w) ∈ R)
13:         M_id ← CLAIMED
14:     end function
15:     function submitShare(s'ᵢ, πᵢ, id, i)
16:         require(M_id = CLAIMED)
17:         ([ŝᵢ], ⊥) ← C_id.c
18:         PVSS.verifyShare(i, ŝᵢ, s'ᵢ, πᵢ)
19:         S_id,i ← s
20:     end function
21: end contract
```

4   Incentives

Here, we augment the scheme in Sect. 3 to incentivize committee members to act honestly. We will create incentives for the committee to reveal on time so that the secret is recoverable. This will be done by paying out a reward to the committee members who reveal at the right time, while slashing committee members who do not. If every committee member is honest, everyone will be rewarded. This way, we will ensure correctness. Unfortunately, we cannot use slashing to ensure security, as malicious committee members can always reveal confidential information off-chain and the smart contract has no way of knowing this, so our goal will only be correctness.

Initially, the dealer chooses a *reparation price*, which they are guaranteed to be paid in case the secret is irrecoverable. Next, the dealer calculates a *holding fee* which is a function of the reparation price. The larger the reparation price, the larger the holding fee must be. He begins the Witness Encryption procedure by paying the holding fee into the contract. The holding fee is the incentive for committee members to participate honestly in the protocol. At the same time, each committee member puts in a certain *collateral*, which is held by the contract in escrow until the completion of protocol. If the majority of committee members are dishonest and the secret is irrecoverable, the slashing amounts are sufficient to add up to the reparation price which is used to appease the dealer in the case of failure.

Consider the happy path, where the dealer and all committee members are honest. After a call to claim with a valid witness, committee members submit their shares. As soon as a committee member submits a valid share, they receive their reward. Let f be the holding fee of the secret. The holding fee is split equally amongst all committee members to cover their reward payments, so each committee member's reward is $\frac{f}{n}$.

Now consider the scenario where the committee has at least t honest members, but not all of them are honest. Dishonest committee members may choose to not submit their shares. If any committee member does not submit their share, they do not receive their reward of $\frac{f}{n}$. Instead, it is transferred back to the dealer.

Now consider the case where the secret is irrecoverable. In particular, there are less than t honest committee members who submit their shares. Every dishonest committee member has their collateral slashed equally, on top of already not receiving their reward. Note that we mentioned in Sect. 3 that the proof π_D is needed to ensure correctness incentives in this scheme. This is because if we did not check that the PVSS output was consistent, the adversary could generate invalid secret shares, yet the committee members would be slashed.

Suppose only t' committee members reveal valid shares and the reparation price is a. The sum of every dishonest committee member's slashed collateral and forfeited reward must add up to a. Therefore, the amount of collateral slashed per committee member $b = \frac{a}{n-t'} - \frac{f}{n}$. The contract keeps track of the collateral balance cl_i for each committee member i that is deducted when slashed and added to when rewards are earned from submitting valid shares. We introduce a function slash (Algorithm 6) that slashes committee members and transfers the reparation price to the dealer as outlined above.

Algorithm 6. Cassiopeia slash function

1: **function** slash(i)
2:     require($M_{id} = $ CLAIMED $\land$ block.number $\geq D_{id}$)
3:     $\{$dealer$, a, f, \dots\} \leftarrow C_{id}$
4:     $t' \leftarrow |S_{id}|$
5:     $G \leftarrow 0$
6:     $b \leftarrow \frac{a}{n-t'} + \frac{f}{n}$
7:     $\hat{b} \leftarrow \frac{a}{n-t+1} + \frac{f}{n}$ ▷ Equation 1
8:     **for** $i \in [n]$ **do**
9:         **if** $S_{id,i} = \bot$ **then**
10:            **if** $t' < t$ **then**
11:                $cl_i \leftarrow cl_i - b$
12:                $G \leftarrow G + b$
13:            **end if**
14:            $G \leftarrow G + \frac{f}{n}$
15:        **end if**
16:    **end for**
17:    dealer.send(G)
18:    $l \leftarrow l - \hat{b}$
19:    $M_{id} \leftarrow$ SLASHED
20: **end function**

To ensure the contract can use a committee member's collateral to pay the reparation price, the committee member must have deposited at least b inside the contract before encrypt can be called. However, the number of honest committee members who will submit valid shares t' is unknown at the time of an encrypt request. Therefore, the contract must ensure that each committee member has deposited at least the maximum slashable amount given the reparation price. Let $\hat{b}$ be the amount of funds a committee member is required to deposit.

$$\hat{b} = \max_{0 \leq t' \leq t-1} b = \frac{a}{n-t+1} - \frac{f}{n} \tag{1}$$

Notice that each committee member's collateral is locked inside the contract for the lifetime of the secret. However, the locked funds do not earn interest, which introduces an opportunity cost for committee members. To incentivize committee members to participate in the protocol honestly, the reward must be higher than the opportunity cost. Concretely, let d be the *maximum lifespan* of the secret in blocks. The opportunity cost for locking $\hat{b}$ as collateral inside the contract for d blocks is

$$o = \hat{b}((1+r)^d - 1) \tag{2}$$

where r is the per-block risk-free rate agreed upon by all committee members.

In fact, we will see that the reparation price a is limited by the fee and the risk free rate. Intuitively, the higher the risk free rate is and the lower the fee is, the lower the maximum reparation price will be. Suppose committee members agree upon a target time-valued net profit β for honest committee members, where $\beta = \frac{f}{n} - o$. Combining this with Eq. 1 and Eq. 2, we have that the maximum value of a is:

$$a = \frac{(\frac{f}{n}(1+r)^d - \beta)(n - t + 1)}{(1+r)^d - 1} \tag{3}$$

Instead of letting the user specify the reparation price, we would like the contract to compute the reparation price a directly from the holding fee. To do so, the maximum lifespan of the secret d must be known. However, for an arbitrary relation $\mathcal{R}$ the witness may take an arbitrary amount of time to be found. Therefore, we require the dealer to also provide the maximum number of blocks T that committee members will keep the secret for. Let st be the block where the encryption request was first made. We modify the original claim function to start decryption at block $st + T$ even if no valid witness has been revealed. Alternatively, the protocol could also be defined such that all secret shares are destroyed after time $st + T$.

The lifespan of the secret d also includes the number of blocks between when the secret is claimed and when committee members are slashed, after which the secret can be decrypted. For the maximum lifespan of the secret to be known, everyone must agree upon a share submission deadline D_{id} after which committee members are slashed. The deadline D_{id} is set to Δ blocks (corresponding to the liveness parameter of the blockchain [14]) after the secret is claimed. Honest committee members must submit their shares by block D_{id}. Therefore, the secret's maximum lifespan is $d = T + \Delta$, and is known at encryption time. We modify the claim function as in Algorithm 7.

Algorithm 7. Modified Cassiopeia claim function

1: **function** claim(id, w)
2:     require($M_{id} = \bot$)
3:     $\{st, x, T\} \leftarrow C_i$
4:     require(block.number $\geq st + T \vee (x, w) \in \mathcal{R}$)
5:     $D_{id} \leftarrow$ block.number $+ \Delta$
6:     $M_{id} \leftarrow$ CLAIMED
7: **end function**

We call a secret *active* if slash has not been called for the secret. Because many secrets may be active, the contract must ensure it has sufficient funds in escrow to cover all potential reparations. Let l be the sum of $\hat{b}$ for all secrets. In encrypt, the contract ensures the remaining collateral $cl_i - l$ is at least the new secret's $\hat{b}$. The fully modified encrypt function is shown below in Algorithm 8.

Algorithm 8. Modified Cassiopeia encrypt function

1: **function** encrypt$(c, \mathcal{R}, x, T, y, \pi)$ **payable**
2:     ▷ *Incentives*
3:     $d \leftarrow T + \Delta$
4:     $f \leftarrow$ msg.value
5:     $a \leftarrow \frac{(\frac{f}{n}(1+r)^d - \beta)(n-t+1)}{(1+r)^d - 1}$ ▷ Equation 3
6:     $\hat{b} \leftarrow \frac{a}{n-t+1} - \frac{f}{n}$ ▷ Equation 1
7:     **for** $i \in [n]$ **do**
8:        require$(cl_i \geq l + \hat{b})$
9:     **end for**
10:    $l \leftarrow l + \hat{b}$
11:    $st \leftarrow$ block.number
12:    ▷ *Verify PVSS and zkSNARK*
13:    $([\hat{s}_i], \pi_D) \leftarrow c$
14:    require$(V(\tau, (c, \mathcal{R}, x, T, y, [pk_i]), \pi) = 1 \wedge \mathsf{PVSS.verifyDist}([\hat{s}_i], [pk_i], \pi_D))$
15:    $id \leftarrow H(c, \mathcal{R}, x, T)$
16:    $C_{id} \leftarrow \{c, \mathcal{R}, x, T, [\hat{s}_i], f, a, st\}$
17:    **return** id
18: **end function**

Lastly, we must allow committee members to deposit and withdraw their collateral to collect fees or stop participating in the protocol. The only requirement is that the remaining collateral is sufficient to cover the worst case reparation price for all active secrets. Concretely, committee member i can withdraw δ_{cl} only if $cl_i - \delta_{cl} \geq l$.

5 Analysis

We assume a synchronous network model where there exists a probabilistic polynomial time adversary. The adversary controls some committee members, which can do whatever they like. Let $\mathsf{PVSS} = (\mathsf{genDist}, \mathsf{verifyDist}, \mathsf{decrypt}, \mathsf{verifyShare}, \mathsf{reconstruct})$ be a correct and verifiable PVSS scheme that has secrecy, (G, P, V) be a correct and extractably secure zkSNARK scheme, (Enc, Dec) be a correct and secure symmetric encryption scheme, $\mathbb{L}$ be a safe and live ledger, and H be a random oracle. We will analyze the security properties of both the non-incentivized and incentivized constructions.

5.1 Security Analysis of Non-incentivized Construction

Theorem 1. *Correctness (Informal). Consider an honest dealer and a committee of size n such that at least t members are honest. The social Witness Encryption construction in Sect. 3 is correct. See Appendix A for proof.*

Theorem 2. *Security (Informal). Consider an honest dealer, and a committee of size n such that less than t members are adversarial. The social Witness Encryption construction in Sect. 3 is extractably secure. See Appendix B for proof.*

At the heart of the proof of security lies the following Lemma. Intuitively, the attack that Lemma 1 ensures protection from is a malleability attack. In particular, an adversary may use the arguments $(c, \mathcal{R}, x, y, \pi)$ of a previous encrypt call to generate arguments $(c', \mathcal{R}', x', y', \pi')$ such that the decryption of c' can be used to infer the decryption of c (i.e. the original secret).

Lemma 1. *Suppose an adversary is given the values $c, \mathcal{R}, x, y, \pi$ for secret s generated by an honest dealer, and the adversary interacts with the contract. The adversary cannot obtain s without a witness w such that $(x, w) \in \mathcal{R}$. See Appendix B for proof.*

Now, we analyze the security properties of the non-incentivized scheme under honest majority. Let h be the number of honest committee members. Assume that a majority of committee members are honest (i.e. $h \geq \frac{n}{2} + 1$). If $t = \frac{n}{2}$, then the construction is correct, since $h \geq t$. Furthermore, the construction is also extractably secure, because the number of adversaries $n - h \leq \frac{n}{2} - 1 < t$.

Note that the construction may be instantiated with different values of t. Since the minimum number of honest committee members needed to ensure correctness and security is t and $n - t + 1$ respectively, higher t ensures a higher degree of correctness for lower security and vice versa. When both correctness and security are desired with the lowest possible minimum required number of honest committee members, we optimize for $\arg\min_t \min(t, n - t + 1)$, which occurs when $t = \frac{n}{2}$, corresponding with the honest majority case.

5.2   Security Analysis of Incentivized Construction

We assume there exists a fixed per-block risk-free rate r, as outlined in Sect. 2.6.

Lemma 2. *If a committee member submits a valid share within the grace period, its time-valued net compensation is at least β.*

Proof (Sketch). Since the PVSS scheme is verifiable, the contract will only accept the dealer's PVSS ciphertext c if it is valid. Furthermore, the contract will only accept a committee member's encrypted share if it is correct. Therefore, a committee member will only be paid its reward of $\frac{f}{n}$ if it submits a valid share. Let d be the maximum lifetime of the secret. Since the committee member also deposits its collateral for d blocks, the committee member's time-valued net compensation is

$$\frac{f}{n} - o = \frac{f}{n} - \left(\frac{a}{n - t + 1} - \frac{f}{n}\right)((1 + r)^d - 1) = \beta$$

Theorem 3. *Correctness (Informal). Consider an honest dealer, and a committee of size n such that all maintain sufficient collateral for the holding f and at least t members are rational. The social Witness Encryption construction in Sect. 4 is correct.*

Proof (Sketch). We follow the same proof as that of Theorem 1 but with added steps. If a committee member does not submit a valid share by the deadline, they forfeit both their reward and are slashed. By Lemma 2, a committee member who submits their shares will receive a net gain of β. Since we assume that β is a sufficient reward, rational committee members will choose to submit valid shares of the secret on time. Because we assume all committee members hold sufficient collateral in the contract, WE.Enc$_\mathcal{R}$ completes in polynomial time. Since there are at least t rational committee members, S_{id} contains at least t valid shares. As in the proof of Theorem 1 above, the correctness of PVSS ensures that reconstruct$(S_{id}) = s$, and by the correctness of the symmetric encryption scheme, $Dec_s(\hat{c}) = m$. Therefore, WE.Dec$_\mathcal{R}$ correctly recovers m in polynomial time.

Theorem 4. *Payout (Informal). Consider an honest dealer, and a committee of size n such that all maintain sufficient collateral for the holding f. If less than t committee members submit valid shares, the dealer receives a.*

Proof (Sketch). Let t' be the number of committee members who did not submit valid shares. Committee members who do not submit valid shares do not receive their reward, which is given to the dealer in Line 14 of Algorithm 6, along with their share of the reparation fee $\frac{a}{|t'|} - \frac{f}{n}$. The reparation fee can always be deducted from each committee member's collateral because $\hat{b} \geq \frac{a}{|t'|} - \frac{f}{n}$. Therefore, the dealer receives a in total.

6   Implementation

We implement all on-chain components of the non-incentivized scheme in Solidity and off-chain components in Typescript and Rust. We use SCRAPE [9] as the underlying PVSS scheme by adapting the implementation given by Gurkan et al. [22]. Since SCRAPE relies on Type 3 pairings, our PVSS ciphertext is instantiated using the curve BN254 [2], as at the time of writing only it is the only curve with Type 3 pairings available as precompiles on Ethereum. Similar to the scheme presented by Schoenmakers [31], SCRAPE's dealer shares the secret s but the committee recovers h^s, where h is the generator of $\mathbb{G}_2$ in BN254. Therefore, our implementation of the scheme requires the dealer to produce $\hat{c}$ by encrypting m with the truncated SHA256 hash of a h^s rather than use s directly.

Though BN254 is not a SNARK friendly curve, we have optimized the proving time of the zkSNARK circuit from Algorithm 4 by leveraging the fact that SCRAPE's instantiation of PVSS.verifyDist allows us to be convinced that PVSS.genDist$(s, [pk_i]) = c$ just by checking $F_0 = g^s$ (where g is the generator of $\mathbb{G}_1$). Since PVSS.verifyDist already checks consistency of F_0 with the rest of the ciphertext, we only need to check whether $\log F_0 = s$. This involves only one BN254 exponentiation inside of Algorithm 4 and makes the circuit size constant, allowing proving time to be constant. To optimize the proving time of the zkSNARK further, we compress the problem instance by first hashing $(c, \mathcal{R}, x)$ before passing it into H, and instantiate H using Poseidon [20], a SNARK friendly hash function. The primary bottleneck of performance is PVSS.verifyDist, which occurs on chain and has optimal $O(n)$ complexity using SCRAPE.

We use a Hardhat node to measure the on-chain gas cost paid for by the dealer in WE.Encrypt$_\mathcal{R}$, relative to n and t. As can be seen in Fig. 1, the maximum committee size that does not consume more gas than the block gas limit is 56. The code for the implementation can be found at https://github.com/galletas1712/cassiopeia.

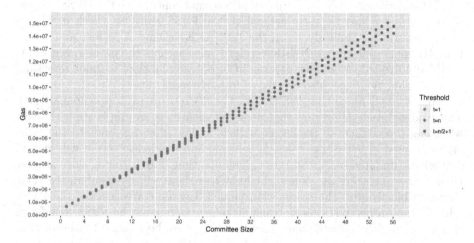

Fig. 1. Gas cost of encrypt vs committee size

7 Conclusion

In this work, we propose Cassiopeia, a social Witness Encryption scheme instantiated as an on-chain smart contract, along with an incentivized version of the scheme. Our construction combines a publicly verifiable secret sharing scheme and zkSNARKs to provide security against malleability attacks. In doing so, the scheme is also resistant to front-running attacks which are widespread when interacting with smart contracts. We also provide a Solidity smart contract implementation of the non-incentivized scheme. The non-incentivized construction is correct and secure under honest majority, and the incentivized construction is correct under rational majority.

Future work will focus on ensuring security for the incentivized scheme under rational majority. Threshold Information Escrows have been proposed with incentivized security [26], and could potentially be integrated with our work. Furthermore, we could also allow for a dynamic committee by using proactive secret sharing, which would make our protocol more robust to security attacks.

8 Appendix A: Proof of Correctness for Non-incentivized Construction

Theorem 5. *Correctness (Informal). Consider an honest dealer and a committee of size n such that at least t are honest. The social Witness Encryption construction in Sect. 3 is correct.*

Proof (Sketch). First, we will prove that $WE.Enc_{\mathcal{R}}(1^{\lambda}, x, m)$ successfully returns the secret identifier id in polynomial time. Since $Enc, PVSS.genDist, H, P$ are all PPT algorithms, they all return in polynomial time. Since the PVSS scheme is correct and c was honestly generated, the PVSS.verifyDist check in Line 5 of encrypt passes. Similarly, since the zkSNARK scheme is correct and π was honestly generated, the zkSNARK verifier V also accepts the proof π. Since $\mathbb{L}$ is a safe and live ledger, encrypt returns id in polynomial time without reverting. By extension, $WE.Enc_{\mathcal{R}}$ also returns id in polynomial time.

Now, we will prove that $WE.Dec_{\mathcal{R}}(1^{\lambda}, x, id)$ returns m in polynomial time. The random oracle H ensures that no secret identifiers are duplicate with overwhelming probability, so the secret with identifier id corresponds to the same one encrypted in $WE.Enc_{\mathcal{R}}$. Since $\mathbb{L}$ is a safe and live ledger, claim will update M_{id} will be updated to CLAIMED in polynomial time. Furthermore, since at least t committee members are honest, at least t of them will have submitted their shares Δ blocks after the secret was claimed. By the correctness of the PVSS scheme, the shares of all honest committee members pass the PVSS.verifyShare check in Line 18 of submitShare. Therefore, $|S_{id}|$ will be at least t after all honest committee members submit their shares. Furthermore, reconstruction of the secret is also polynomial time. Since the symmetric encryption scheme is correct and $\hat{c}$ was produced honestly, $Dec_s(\hat{c})$ returns m in polynomial time. By extension, $WE.Dec_{\mathcal{R}}$ also returns m in polynomial time.

9 Appendix B: Proof of Security for Non-incentivized Construction

Lemma 3. *Suppose an adversary is given the values $c, \mathcal{R}, x, y, \pi$ for secret s generated by an honest dealer, and the adversary interacts with the contract. The adversary cannot obtain s without a witness w such that $(x, w) \in \mathcal{R}$.*

Proof (Sketch). The only way the adversary can obtain any information about s interacting with the contract is to first call encrypt with $(c', \mathcal{R}', x', y', \pi')$, then performing $WE.Dec_{\mathcal{R}'}(1^{\lambda}, c', x', w')$ to retrieve the secret s', where w' is a witness for $\mathcal{R}'$ and x' already known to the adversary. The adversary aims to deduce non-negligible information about s from s' and $(c, \mathcal{R}, x, y, \pi)$.

Suppose the adversary can extract non-negligible information about s. Because the PVSS scheme has secrecy, s cannot be extracted from c, since c is an encryption of s. Since y is the output of a random oracle, all preimages are equally probable, so y contains no information about s. By the zero knowledge property of the zkSNARK scheme, π does not reveal any information about the private input s. Therefore, the adversary deduces information about s using s'.

Consider when $s' = s$ and $c' = c$. When the adversary calls encrypt, the ledger's safety and liveness ensures she must specify $y' = H(s \parallel c \parallel \mathcal{R}' \parallel x')$ and produce a valid zkSNARK proof π for the circuit in Algorithm 4. By the extractable soundness property of the zkSNARK, the adversary must know the entire preimage of y' prior to encrypt. The adversary must also provide s such that $c = \mathsf{PVSS.genDist}(s, [pk_i])$. Furthermore, since the preimage of y and y' are not equal, y cannot be used in place of y', nor is it related to y' is any way. Therefore, the adversary must know s prior to encryption. However, since the dealer is honest, the adversary cannot have access to s prior to encryption, which is a contradiction.

Now consider when $s' \neq s$ and $c' \neq c$. Since s' is the decryption of c', c' must have encrypted some information about s. But y contains no information about s, c' must have been derived from c. When the adversary calls encrypt, the ledger's safety and liveness ensures she must specify $y' = H(s' \parallel c' \parallel \mathcal{R}' \parallel x')$ and produce a valid zkSNARK proof π for the circuit in Algorithm 4. Because the zkSNARK is extractably sound, y' is the output of a random oracle function, and $c' = \mathsf{PVSS.genDist}(s', [pk_i])$ is enforced in the zkSNARK circuit, the adversary must know s' prior to the computation of y' (i.e. before the call to encrypt). But this means the adversary can know s with knowledge of only $c, \mathcal{R}, x, y, \pi$, which is a contradiction.

In either case, the adversary cannot obtain s even by interacting with the contract.

Theorem 6. *Extractable Security (Informal). Consider an honest dealer, and a committee of size n such that less than t are adversarial. The social Witness Encryption construction in Sect. 3 is extractably secure.*

Proof (Sketch). First, consider the case where the contract will accept only one secret to encrypt in its lifetime. The dealer is honest, so no other party (including the adversary) has access to s. Since s is a bit string of length λ and the symmetric encryption scheme is secure, $\hat{c}$ reveals nothing about s. Similarly, since the PVSS scheme has secrecy, the PVSS ciphertext c reveals nothing about s. Furthermore, because less than t committee members are adversarial, no coalition of adversarial committee members can learn any information about the secret. The random oracle H ensures that y is uniformly distributed and $Pr[y = H(s \parallel c \parallel \mathcal{R} \parallel x) \mid c, \mathcal{R}, x]$ is negligible, so a PPT adversary cannot learn anything about s from y. By the zero knowledge property of the zkSNARK, the proof π also reveals nothing about s. Therefore, all public values reveal nothing about s.

Now, suppose the contract may accept multiple secrets in its lifetime. By Lemma 3, no matter what other encryption requests the adversary makes, she cannot learn any information about s, even if she has access to the public arguments of all encrypt calls that will ever occur.

Without having submitted a valid witness w, the adversary does not learn any information about s, whether from public data or from interacting with the contract. Therefore, if the adversary learns any information about s, they must know a valid witness w, and the construction is extractably secure.

References

1. Baird, L., Mukherjee, P., Sinha, R.: i-TiRE: incremental timed-release encryption or how to use timed-release encryption on blockchains? Cryptology ePrint Archive, Paper 2021/800 (2021). https://eprint.iacr.org/2021/800
2. Barreto, P.S.L.M., Naehrig, M.: Pairing-friendly elliptic curves of prime order. In: Preneel, B., Tavares, S. (eds.) SAC 2005. LNCS, vol. 3897, pp. 319–331. Springer, Heidelberg (2006). https://doi.org/10.1007/11693383_22
3. Benhamouda, F., et al.: Can a public blockchain keep a secret? Cryptology ePrint Archive, Paper 2020/464 (2020). https://eprint.iacr.org/2020/464
4. Benhamouda , F., Lin, H.: Multiparty reusable non-interactive secure computation. Cryptology ePrint Archive, Paper 2020/221 (2020). https://eprint.iacr.org/2020/221
5. Bitansky, N., Chiesa, A., Ishai, Y., Paneth, O., Ostrovsky, R.: Succinct non-interactive arguments via linear interactive proofs. In: Sahai, A. (ed.) TCC 2013. LNCS, vol. 7785, pp. 315–333. Springer, Heidelberg (2013). https://doi.org/10.1007/978-3-642-36594-2_18
6. Boneh, D., Franklin, M.: Identity-based encryption from the weil pairing. In: Kilian, J. (ed.) CRYPTO 2001. LNCS, vol. 2139, pp. 213–229. Springer, Heidelberg (2001). https://doi.org/10.1007/3-540-44647-8_13
7. Boneh, D., Sahai, A., Waters, B.: Functional encryption: definitions and challenges. Cryptology ePrint Archive, Paper 2010/543 (2010). https://eprint.iacr.org/2010/543
8. Campanelli, M., David, B., Khoshakhlagh, H., Konring, A., Nielsen, J.: Encryption to the future. In: Agrawal, S., Lin, D. (eds.) ASIACRYPT 2022. LNCS, vol. 13793, pp. 151–180. Springer, Cham (2023). https://doi.org/10.1007/978-3-031-22969-5_6
9. Cascudo, I., David, B.: Scrape: scalable randomness attested by public entities. Cryptology ePrint Archive, Paper 2017/216 (2017). https://eprint.iacr.org/2017/216
10. Chor, B., Goldwasser, S. Micali, S., Awerbuch, B.: Verifiable secret sharing and achieving simultaneity in the presence of faults. In: 26th Annual Symposium on Foundations of Computer Science (sfcs 1985), pp. 383–395 (1985)
11. Choudhuri, A.R., Green, M., Jain, A., Kaptchuk, G., Miers, I.: Fairness in an unfair world: fair multiparty computation from public bulletin boards. In: Proceedings of the 2017 ACM SIGSAC Conference on Computer and Communications Security, CCS 2017, pp. 719–728. Association for Computing Machinery New York, NY, USA (2017)
12. Döttling, N., Hanzlik, L., Magri, B., Wohnig, S.: McFly: verifiable encryption to the future made practical. Cryptology ePrint Archive, Paper 2022/433 (2022). https://eprint.iacr.org/2022/433
13. Ende, M.: Momo. Puffin, München (2009)
14. Garay, J., Kiayias, A., Leonardos, N.: The bitcoin backbone protocol: analysis and applications. In: Oswald, E., Fischlin, M. (eds.) EUROCRYPT 2015. LNCS, vol. 9057, pp. 281–310. Springer, Heidelberg (2015). https://doi.org/10.1007/978-3-662-46803-6_10

15. Garg, S., Gentry, C., Halevi, S., Raykova, M., Sahai, A., Waters, B.: Candidate indistinguishability obfuscation and functional encryption for all circuits. In: 2013 IEEE 54th Annual Symposium on Foundations of Computer Science, pp. 40–49 (2013)
16. Garg, S., Gentry, C., Sahai, A., Waters, B.: Witness encryption and its applications. In: Proceedings of the Forty-Fifth Annual ACM Symposium on Theory of Computing, STOC 2013, pp. 467–476. Association for Computing Machinery New York, NY, USA (2013)
17. Gentry, C., Lewko, A.B., Waters, B.: Witness encryption from instance independent assumptions. Cryptology ePrint Archive, Paper 2014/273 (2014). https://eprint.iacr.org/2014/273
18. Goldwasser, S., Kalai, Y., Popa, R.A., Vaikuntanathan, V., Zeldovich, N.: How to run turing machines on encrypted data. Cryptology ePrint Archive, Paper 2013/229 (2013). https://eprint.iacr.org/2013/229
19. Goyal, V., Kothapalli, A., Masserova, E., Parno, B., Song, Y.: Storing and retrieving secrets on a blockchain. In: Hanaoka, G., Shikata, J., Watanabe, Y. (eds.) PKC 2022 Part I. LNCS, vol. 13177, pp. 252–282. Springer, Cham (2022). https://doi.org/10.1007/978-3-030-97121-2_10
20. Grassi, L., Khovratovich, D., Rechberger, C., Roy, A., Schofnegger, M.: Poseidon: a new hash function for zero-knowledge proof systems. In: Proceedings of the 30th USENIX Security Symposium, pp. 519–535. USENIX Association. United States Conference date: 11-08-2021 Through 13-08-2021 (2021)
21. Groth, J.: Simulation-sound NIZK proofs for a practical language and constant size group signatures. In: Lai, X., Chen, K. (eds.) ASIACRYPT 2006. LNCS, vol. 4284, pp. 444–459. Springer, Heidelberg (2006). https://doi.org/10.1007/11935230_29
22. Gurkan, K., Jovanovic, P., Maller, M., Meiklejohn, Stern, G., Tomescu, A.: Aggregatable distributed key generation. Cryptology ePrint Archive, Paper 2021/005 (2021). https://eprint.iacr.org/2021/005
23. Heidarvand, S., Villar, J.L.: Public verifiability from pairings in secret sharing schemes. In: Avanzi, R.M., Keliher, L., Sica, F. (eds.) SAC 2008. LNCS, vol. 5381, pp. 294–308. Springer, Heidelberg (2009). https://doi.org/10.1007/978-3-642-04159-4_19
24. Labs, P.: tlock: Timelock encryption/decryption made practical. https://github.com/drand/tlock
25. Liu, J., Jager, T., Kakvi, S.A., Warinschi, B.: How to build time-lock encryption. Des. Codes Crypt. 86(11), 2549–2586 (2018)
26. Mangipudi, E.V., Lu, D., Psomas, A., Kate, A.: Collusion-deterrent threshold information escrow. Cryptology ePrint Archive, Paper 2021/095 (2021). https://eprint.iacr.org/2021/095
27. Mao, W.: Timed-release cryptography. Cryptology ePrint Archive, Paper 2001/014 (2001). https://eprint.iacr.org/2001/014
28. Mascia, C., Sala, M., Villa, I.: A survey on functional encryption (2021)
29. Rivest, R.L., Shamir, A., Wagner, D.A.: Time-lock puzzles and timed-release crypto. Technical report, USA (1996)
30. Ruiz, A., Villar, J.L.: Publicly verifiable secret sharing from paillier's cryptosystem. In: Wulf, C., Lucks, S., Yau, P.-W. (eds.) WEWoRC 2005 - Western European Workshop on Research in Cryptology, pp. 98–108. Gesellschaft für Informatik e.V, Bonn (2005)

31. Schoenmakers, B.: A simple publicly verifiable secret sharing scheme and its application to electronic voting. In: Wiener, M. (ed.) CRYPTO 1999. LNCS, vol. 1666, pp. 148–164. Springer, Heidelberg (1999). https://doi.org/10.1007/3-540-48405-1_10

32. Shamir, A.: How to share a secret. Commun. ACM **22**(11), 612–613 (1979)

33. Stadler, M.: Publicly verifiable secret sharing. In: Maurer, U. (ed.) EUROCRYPT 1996. LNCS, vol. 1070, pp. 190–199. Springer, Heidelberg (1996). https://doi.org/10.1007/3-540-68339-9_17

34. Zindros, D.: Hours of horus: keyless cryptocurrency wallets. Cryptology ePrint Archive, Paper 2021/715 (2021). https://eprint.iacr.org/2021/715

FlexiPCN: Flexible Payment Channel Network

Susil Kumar Mohanty and Somanath Tripathy[✉]

Department of Computer Science and Engineering, Indian Institute of Technology
Patna, Bihta, Patna 801106, India
{susil_1921cs05,som}@iitp.ac.in

Abstract. Payment Channel Network (PCN) is a widely recognized and
effective off-chain solution used to reduce on-chain operational costs.
PCN is designed to address the scalability challenge and throughput
issues in permissionless blockchains. Though transaction throughput is
improved, many issues remain, like no flexibility, channel exhaustion,
poor sustainability, etc. A separate deposit is required for each payment
channel between two users, which locks a substantial amount of coins for
a long period of time. Therefore, the flexibility to move these locked coins
across channels is impossible through off-chain. Moreover, the channels
get exhausted due to unbalanced (unidirectional) transfer. This causes
the channel to become unsustainable (dead) until the PCN is rebalanced.
This work presents a novel payment protocol called Flexible Payment
Channel Networks (FlexiPCN), which allows users to deposit coins per
user rather than per channel. So, users can move coins flexibly from one
channel to another without the help of the blockchain or setting the cycle
off-chain. FlexiPCN has been proven to be secure under the Universal
Composability framework.

Keywords: Blockchain · Payment channel network · Security ·
Privacy

1 Introduction

In the past decade, blockchain technology has rapidly developed, making it possible to conduct secure transactions in a distributed and trustless environment
[18,25]. It supports complex transaction logic using smart contracts [23], which
are a few lines of code that run on the blockchain [25]. It is a robust technology
because of its consensus mechanism (like PoW[1]), which allows all peers to have
a consistent view of transactions [18]. However, its wide adoption is limited due
to scalability issues (low transaction throughput, high transaction fees, and high
latency) [3,20]. For example, Bitcoin [18] executes 5–7 transactions per second
(TPS) and takes approximately 60 minutes to finalize a transaction. Similarly,

---

[1] Adam Back. "HashCash: A popular PoW system". First announced in March 1997.

© International Financial Cryptography Association 2024
A. Essex et al. (Eds.): FC 2023 Workshops, LNCS 13953, pp. 405–419, 2024.
https://doi.org/10.1007/978-3-031-48806-1_26

Ethereum [25] executes 15-20 TPS and takes approximately 6 minutes to finalize a transaction. However, traditional payment systems like Visa process about 47,000 TPS[2] To solve the scalability issue, a novel off-chain (layer 2) mechanism known as payment channels has been introduced [20]. Payment channel enables two users to deposit and lock funds in the blockchain, as well as make payments without broadcasting or recording transactions on the blockchain. Off-chain payments are processed and confirmed instantly since they only need the consent of channel users instead of all peers on the blockchain. If any dispute arises between the channel users, it is resolved through the blockchain. Payment channels are extended to the payment channel network (PCN), allowing users without a direct payment channel to perform multi-hop payments without creating a new payment channel. For example, the Lightning Network (LN) [20] and Raiden Network (RN) [1] are payment channel networks deployed on top of Bitcoin and Ethereum, respectively. For more information about PCN, see [4,6], related security and privacy issues [7,8,15,19,22], and application in social internet of vehicles (SIoV) [17].

Even though PCN has better scalability, it still has many problems. In PCNs, users must deposit separately for each channel [14], and significant amounts of coins are locked up in advance. Payment flows over a channel are not equal in both directions, so funds accumulate gradually in one direction. Consequently, over time, the balance in one direction of channels gradually becomes exhausted because of imbalanced channel transfers [21]. In such a case, the following issues may arise:

1. Any further payments are not processed because there are insufficient funds in the required channel.
2. It must either be revoked from the blockchain or refunded by closing the payment channel and then reopening it. These are on-chain operations, which are time-consuming and costly.
3. Whenever a channel is exhausted, owners lose the opportunity to receive off-chain payments as relay fees.
4. PCN payment routing becomes more difficult because the user must find a payment path with enough capacity. Also, the success rate of probing may decrease.

Therefore, channel exhaustion is an important issue in PCN.

There are several existing works that address this issue. The trivial approach is to refund the channel by closing and reopening the channel, which requires two on-chain transactions that are costly and time-consuming. LOOP[3] reduces the refund costs to one on-chain transaction. Refunding still needs to interact with the blockchain. Another approach is Revive [10], where channels are refunded by reallocating deposits from adjacent channels, known as "rebalancing". The entire process is off-chain, so rebalancing is cost-free for multiple times, and the underlying blockchain is relieved of the transaction load. The rebalancing operation works well in PCN; provided i) when both channel users who wish to rebalance and the direction of desired coin flows can form directed cycles; ii) a fair leader is required to collect users' rebalancing demands, identify the directed cycles, and generate transactions for cycles; and iii) the cycle users should cooperate. Finally, a minimum rebalancing amount can be achieved among the cycle users. Because of this, it suffers from low feasibility for large-scale applications, such as LN [20]. PnP [11] is another solution that relies on carefully planning the initial balance on each channel to reduce the chance of channel exhaustion. It delays the occurrence of channel exhaustion by guaranteeing a good probability of success for off-chain transactions. It is very difficult to estimate node-to-node payment requirement correctly, a prior. Since PCN is trustless by nature, malicious nodes may compromise the balance planning service. PnP [11] cannot recover nearly exhausted channels. CYCLE [9] is an asynchronous rebalancing approach for sustainable PCN that allows the channels to rebalance during off-chain payment execution. It consistently balances PCN channels and prevents channel freezing while ensuring privacy and security of users. Shaduf [5], is a payment channel rebalancing scheme that doesn't require any cycles. It allows users to shift coins off-chain, several times after an on-chain binding operation is performed. The binding process is an on-chain operation, so it becomes time-consuming and expensive. Thus, channel exhaustion issue in PCN has not yet been fully resolved by the off-chain method. It is also not flexible because funds are locked into the blockchain for a specific channel.

This work introduces a flexible payment channel network called FlexiPCN, a purely off-chain based rebalancing technique, which allows users to freely allocate and share funds across all of their payment channels. It keeps funds per user rather than per channel, facilitate users to use funds more flexibly and improves payment success rates. Therefore, channel exhaustion only occurs when the user has exhausted all its funds or if the payment amount exceeds their current balance.

The rest of this paper is structured as follows. Section 2 explains the background concept. System model and formal model is described in Sect. 3, and the proposed FlexiPCN method is described in Sect. 4. Security analysis is presented in Sect. 5. Section 6 discusses the conclusion and future scope of the paper.

2   Background

Payment Channel Network (PCN): A payment channel enables several payments to be made between two parties without recording each transaction to the blockchain. A PCN is made up of peer-to-peer multi-hop payment channels. It is still possible to conduct payments via PCN even if there is no direct channel between two peers. It is created when two peers deposit coins into a shared account and add double-signed transactions to a blockchain. When the channel does not require or one party's coins run out, coins are distributed based on its final state, and closes the channel is recorded on the blockchain. The deposit will be refunded to each user according to their mutually agreed channel state. A PCN is made up of peer-to-peer multi-hop payment channels. It is still possible to conduct payments via PCN even if there is no direct channel between two peers. For more information about PCN, see [12,13,16].

Off-chain Contracts: Off-chain contracts [20] are smart contracts in which the contract logic is not executed by miners. It is carried out by all participants involved in making the contract. It is possible to execute computationally intensive operations without involving the blockchain, so long as all participants are honest. An honest participant can prove the correct state of the contract. It is impossible to cheat because all the participants must sign a contract. Whenever a malicious participant broadcasts an incorrect state in the blockchain, the counterparty can dispute it and broadcast the correct state. An example of such contact is HTLC[4], which is used in PCN.

Hashed Time-Lock Contracts (HTLC): An off-chain payment transferred from sender to receiver must be atomic. Either the payment channel balances are entirely updated or terminated. PCN [20] accomplishes atomicity by incorporating Hashed Time-Lock Contracts (HTLC)[4]. For more information about HTLC, see [12,13,16,24]. To build an HTLC contract, the receiver first chooses a random string and then transmits the hash of the string to the sender. The sender computes the total amount (including forwarding fees), time-lock for all the channels on the path. Next, it locks funds and sends payment to the subsequent user. During the locking phase, each intermediary user forwards the payment to the next neighbor along the path by deducting time-lock and forwarding fees from its preceding user's payment request. During the releasing phase, upon receiving the preimage from its right neighbor within the time-lock, it releases the coin to the next neighbor and reveals the preimage to its previous neighbor. Any disagreement would be handled through blockchain. For more information about HTLC, see [13,16].

Table 1. Notations

Notation	Description	Notation	Description
$\mathbb{G} := (\mathbb{V}, \mathbb{E}, \Omega)$	Payment channel network	ω_i	User u_i's collaterals or sum of neighboring channel's collateral
$c_{\langle u_i, u_j \rangle}$	Channel identifier	v	Actual amount sender u_0 wants to transfer to receiver u_n
$\mathcal{B}$	Blockchain	Υ_{ij}	Collateral or available balance in channel $c_{\langle u_i, u_j \rangle}$ ($u_i \to u_j$)
$\mathcal{G}$	Elliptic curve base point	$c_{\langle u_i, u_j \rangle}$	Payment channel identifier (between user u_i and u_j)
$\mathcal{P}$	Payment path	t_{ij}	Expiration time of the transaction corresponding to user u_i
u_0 & u_n	Sender & Receiver	f_{ij}	Payment relay fee of channel $c_{\langle u_i, u_j \rangle}$
$\{u_i\}_{i \in [1, n-1]}$	Intermediate users	sk_i & pk_i	Secret key of user u_i & Public key of user u_i
$\mathcal{A}$	Attacker	$\mathcal{AL}$ & $\mathcal{CL}$	Active channel list & Closing channel list
$\mathcal{F}$	Ideal functionality	$PK, R, \& S$	Aggregated public key, partial nonce, & signature
$\mathcal{C}_{ij}$	Channel capacity	$\mathcal{B}[u_i]$	On-chain balance of the user u_i
$\mathcal{T}$	Coin Allocation Table	ν_{ij}	The amount required to shift for fulfilling the payment request
$\mathcal{T}_i$	Transaction log of user u_i	σ_{ij}	Signature signed by the user u_i and send its neighbor u_j

---

[4] https://en.bitcoin.it/wiki/Hash_Time_Locked_Contracts.

3   System and Adversary Model

3.1   System Model

We model FlexiPCN as a bi-directed and weighted graph $\mathbb{G} := (\mathbb{V}, \mathbb{E}, \Omega)$, where $\mathbb{V}$ denotes the set of blockchain users (nodes) with a weight function w, $w :$ $\mathbb{V} \times \mathbb{V} \rightarrow \mathbb{R}^+$ denotes the collateral between users, $\mathbb{E} \subseteq \mathbb{V} \times \mathbb{V}$ denotes the set of active payment channels between two user's wallets, and $\omega_u \in \Omega$ is the collateral of user u. Each user $u_i in \mathbb{V}$ has a collateral of $\omega_i = \sum_{j=1}^{k} \Upsilon_{ij}$, where Υ_{ij} represents the collateral balance of u_i with u_j. An off-chain payment is denoted as $\mathtt{Payment}(u_0, u_n, v_{01}, t_{01}, \mathcal{P})$, where u_0 is the sender, u_n is the receiver, $v_{01} = v + \sum_{i=1}^{n-1} f_{\langle i,i+1 \rangle}$ is the total payment amount including relaying fees, and t_{01} is the time period within which the payment must be completed. $f_{\langle i,i+1 \rangle}$ represents the relay fee that an intermediate user $u_i \in \mathbb{V}$ charges for relaying a payment from u_i to u_{i+1}. A payment path $\mathcal{P}$ between u_0 and u_n is denoted as $\{u_0 \rightarrow u_1 \rightarrow \cdots \rightarrow u_n\}$. For readability, we present the most frequently used notations in Table 1.

3.2   Adversary Model

We assume that each pair of users uses a secure and authenticated channel to exchange payment information. Neither the sender nor the receiver have a secure channel with the intermediate users, but both have a secure channel with each other. Intermediary nodes are only aware of their previous and next neighbors. The sender, however, has detailed information about the network topology, including the identity of the user, lock-time, relay fees of the intermediate nodes, channel identifier, and node capacity but not the channel capacity, etc. There must be at least one payment path between the sender and receiver, and the associated payment channels must meet the collateral requirements (either from one channel or by moving coins from other channels) to process off-chain transactions. Each neighboring user has a pre-established payment channel with zero collateral.

Security threats occur either from internal or from external sources. So, our adversary model considers both inside and outside PCN adversaries. We consider both honest-but-curious and malicious models. Assume that $\mathcal{A}$ is a computationally efficient adversary who corrupts one or more PCN users. Once $\mathcal{A}$ has corrupted some users, it gains access to their internal states and information flows, as well as complete control over them. Compromised users can work together to challenge PCN security, and steals off-chain payment relay fees from honest intermediaries. $\mathcal{A}$ can impersonate any corrupted user and sends arbitrary messages. Assume that intermediate users are honest-but-curious and that they are interested in analyzing the sender's privacy and communication patterns or behaviors. The target of the adversary is to exhaust a payment channel, so that it can no longer participate in the payment execution.

3.3 Ideal World Model

The security model of FlexiPCN follows [5,12,16,24] which is based on the universal composable (UC) framework [2]. The simulator S is a probabilistic polynomial-time algorithm that simulates the off-chain FlexiPCN protocol in a hybrid world model. The output in S must be indistinguishable in communication with the ideal functionality $\mathcal{F}$, even if some users are corrupt. The environment $\mathcal{Z}$ represents all events that occur outside the protocol execution, which would influence the protocol execution. It gives the input to the user and obtains the output from the user. $\mathcal{Z}$ could compromise certain users for obtaining access to their internal states and to manage their execution. But, $\mathcal{Z}$ does not interact with S, while getting executed by corrupted users. Since honest users interact through secure and authorized channels, the adversary $\mathcal{A}$ cannot retrieve any confidential information. The ideal functionality $\mathcal{F}_{\texttt{FlexiPCN}}$ uses $\mathcal{F}_{\texttt{ECDSA}}$ (used for digital signatures), $\mathcal{F}_{\mathcal{B}}$ (used to maintain blockchain and its operations), $\mathcal{F}_{\mathcal{C}}$ (used for maintaining contract instances), and $\mathcal{F}_{anon}$ (used for anonymous communication) as subroutines, i.e., our protocol is specified in the $(\mathcal{F}_{\texttt{ECDSA}}, \mathcal{F}_{\mathcal{B}}, \mathcal{F}_{\mathcal{C}}, \mathcal{F}_{anon})$-hybrid model. Internally, $\mathcal{F}_{\texttt{FlexiPCN}}$ maintains two lists, namely an active channel list $\mathcal{AL}$ and a closed channel list $\mathcal{CL}$. It also maintains a table called transaction log or state $\mathcal{T}$.

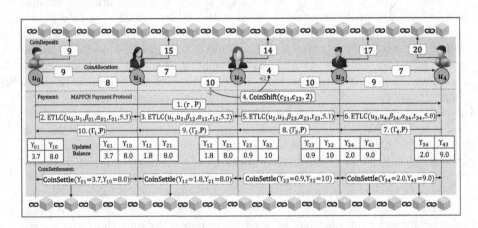

Fig. 1. FlexiPCN: Flexible Payment Channel Network Overview

4 The Proposed Protocol: FlexiPCN

4.1 Overview

We provide an overview of payment execution in FlexiPCN. Consider the simple PCN structure shown in Fig. 1, in which payment channels are established between users with no collateral. In order to participate in off-chain payment execution, each user deposits a certain amount of coins to the blockchain $\mathcal{B}$, such as 9, 15, 14, 17, and 20 coins deposited by u_0, u_1, u_2, u_3, and u_4, respectively. Then, each user distributes the deposited coins to their corresponding payment channels, such as u_0 allocates 9 coins to channel $c_{\langle u_0, u_1 \rangle}$; u_1 allocates 8 and 7 coins to channel $c_{\langle u_1, u_0 \rangle}$ and $c_{\langle u_1, u_2 \rangle}$, respectively; u_2 allocates 10 and 4 coins to channel $c_{\langle u_2, u_1 \rangle}$ and $c_{\langle u_2, u_3 \rangle}$, respectively; u_3 allocates 10 and 7 coins to channel $c_{\langle u_3, u_2 \rangle}$ and $c_{\langle u_3, u_4 \rangle}$, respectively; u_4 allocates 9 coins to channel $c_{\langle u_4, u_3 \rangle}$. Note that users are aware of all other users' node balances, but are only aware of the channel balances of their previous and next users. Suppose u_0 is the sender who wishes to send 5 coins to the receiver u_4. For that, u_0 chooses a payment path $\mathcal{P} : \{u_0 \rightarrow u_1 \rightarrow u_2 \rightarrow u_3 \rightarrow u_4\}$. For the payment operation, we use the existing protocol MAPPCN [24] to ensure user privacy and anonymity. u_0 initiates the payment operation by sending $\langle r, P \rangle$ to u_4 over a secure channel, where r is a random number and P is the base point of the Elliptic curve $\mathbb{E}_p$. Then, u_0 establishes an $\mathbf{ETLC}(\mathbf{u_0}, \mathbf{u_1}, \beta_{01}, \alpha_{01}, \mathbf{t_{01}}, \mathbf{v_{01}})^5$ contract with u_1, where β_{01} and α_{01} are the secret parameters, t_{01} is the expiration time period to lock v_{01} amount of coins ($v_{01} = 5.3$ is the sum of payment amount $v = 5$ and relay fees of intermediate users $f = \sum_{i=1}^{3} f_{\langle i, i+1 \rangle} = 0.3$). Later, each intermediate user u_i generates ℓ_i randomly, computes secret parameters $\beta_{\langle i, i+1 \rangle} = \ell_i \cdot \beta_{\langle i-1, i \rangle}$ and $\alpha_{\langle i, i+1 \rangle} = \ell_i \cdot \alpha_{\langle i-1, i \rangle}$ to establish an $\mathbf{ETLC}(\mathbf{u_i}, \mathbf{u_{i+1}}, \beta_{\langle i, i+1 \rangle}, \alpha_{\langle i, i+1 \rangle}, \mathbf{t_{\langle i, i+1 \rangle}}, \mathbf{v_{\langle i, i+1 \rangle}})$ contract. When u_2 receives the ETLC request from u_1, it is unable to forward it to u_3 due to insufficient balance at channel $c_{23} = 4$, which requires at least 5.1 coins after deducting the relay fee. Therefore, u_2 performs a coin shifting operation to shift 2 coins from channel c_{21} to channel c_{23} in order to complete the payment execution. Then, u_2 establishes an $\mathbf{ETLC}(\mathbf{u_2}, \mathbf{u_3}, \beta_{23}, \alpha_{23}, \mathbf{t_{23}}, \mathbf{v_{23}})$ contract with u_3, which continues until u_4 is reached. Therefore, upon receiving $\mathbf{ETLC}(\mathbf{u_3}, \mathbf{u_4}, \beta_{34}, \alpha_{34}, \mathbf{t_{34}}, \mathbf{v_{34}})$ request from u_3, u_4 validates $r \cdot \beta_{34} \cdot P \overset{?}{=} \alpha_{34}$, computes $\Gamma_{34} = r \cdot \beta_{34}$, and returns $\langle \Gamma_4, P \rangle$ to u_3 in order to satisfy the ETLC contract condition. After receiving $\langle \Gamma_{i+1}, P \rangle$ from u_{i+1}, each intermediate user u_i validate $\Gamma_{i+1} \cdot P \overset{?}{=} \alpha_{\langle i, i+1 \rangle}$. Upon satisfying the contract condition, u_i releases the locked coins to u_{i+1} and returns $\Gamma_i = \ell_i^{-1} \cdot \Gamma_{i+1}$ to u_{i-1} in order to satisfy the ETLC contract condition. As a result, each user on the payment path receives their committed coins. When a user wants to settle coins, it must first finish all pending payments and share the latest state with its neighbors. Then it invokes coin settlement on the blockchain $\mathcal{B}$ by submitting the latest state with its signature. The user account is then updated by $\mathcal{B}$. If a neighbor raises a dispute, the neighbor user sends the most recent state to $\mathcal{B}$, and $\mathcal{B}$ is solved as a dispute resolution.

4.2   FlexiPCN Operations

FlexiPCN consists of seven primary operations: 1) OpenChannel, 2) Coin Deposit, 3) CoinAllocation , 4) Payment, 5) CoinShift, 6) CoinSettlement, and 7) CloseChannel.

---

5 ETLC: Elliptic Curve based Time-Lock Contract [24].

1. OpenChannel : This is an on-chain (blockchain) operation that is triggered by the user u_i in order to establish a payment channel with the user u_j, and it returns the channel identifier $c_{\langle u_i, u_j \rangle}$.

2. CoinDeposit : This is an on-chain operation initiated by user u_i, which deposits the amount of coins ω_i with signature σ_i in order to participate in the payment execution and returns $\top$ as confirmation.

3. CoinAllocation : This is an off-chain operation initiated by the user u_i that distributes coins equally to each active adjacent channel user u_j so that it can participate in payment execution. Each adjacent user returns σ'_{ji} as their agreement confirmation.

4. Payment : This is an off-chain operation initiated by the sender u_0 who wants to transfer some coins (v) to u_n via some intermediate users. This is accomplished by using the ETLC[5] contract, which updates the channel balances atomically.

5. CoinShift : This is an off-chain operation triggered by an intermediate user u_i between two channels that do not have enough channel balance to send the ETLC payment request to the next user u_j. In order to fulfill the payment request, u_i moves the required amount of coins ν from its adjacent channel(s) to another.

6. CoinSettlement : This is an on-chain operation initiated by any user u_i, by sending the recently updated state Ψ with its agreement σ_i for coin settlement after all pending payment requests are completed.

7. CloseChannel : This is an on-chain operation that can be initiated by any channel user to close the payment channel and return the off-chain balance to the blockchain.

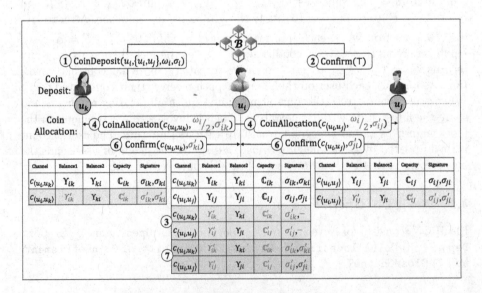

Fig. 2. Coin Deposit and Allocation Operation

Algorithm 1: FlexiPCN Protocol Operations

OpenChannel($u_i, u_j, T_{ij}, T_{ji}, f_{ij}, t_{ij}$) :
1: **if** $(\{u_i, u_j\} \in \mathcal{B}$ and $c_{\langle u_i, u_j \rangle} \notin \mathcal{AL})$ **then**
2:     **create**: channel identifier $c_{\langle u_i, u_j \rangle}$
3:     $T_{ij} = 0, T_{ji} = 0, C_{ij} = 0$
4:     **write**: open($c_{\langle u_i, u_j \rangle}, C_{ij}, f_{ij}, t_{ij}$) to $\mathcal{B}$
5:     **store**: $(c_{\langle u_i, u_j \rangle}, T_{ij}, T_{ji}, C_{ij}, f_{ij}, t_{ij})$ in $\mathcal{AL}$
6:     **send**: $c_{\langle u_i, u_j \rangle}$ to both u_i and u_j
7: **else**
8:     Abort
9: **end if**

CoinDeposits($u_i, \{u_j\}, \omega_i, \sigma_i$) :
1: **if** $(u_i \in \mathcal{B}$ and $\omega_i \leq \mathcal{B}[u_i])$ **then**
2:     **for** all neighbor u_j **do**
3:         **if** $(c_{\langle u_i, u_j \rangle} \in \mathcal{AL})$ **then**
4:             **add**: $c_{\langle u_i, u_j \rangle}$ in $\mathcal{T}$
5:         **else**
6:             Abort
7:         **end if**
8:         **write**: CoinDeposit($u_i, \{u_j\}, \omega_i, \sigma_i$) to $\mathcal{B}$
9:         **send**: $\top$ to u_i
10:    **end for**
11: **else**
12:     Abort
13: **end if**

CoinAllocation($u_i, \{u_j\}, \omega_i$) :
1: **for** all neighbor u_j **do**
2:     **if** $(c_{\langle u_i, u_j \rangle} \in \mathcal{AL}$ and $c_{\langle u_i, u_j \rangle} \in \mathcal{T})$ **then**
3:         **update**: $(c_{\langle u_i, u_j \rangle}, T'_{ij} = \frac{\omega_i}{|\{u_j\}|}, T_{ji}, C'_{ij} = T'_{ij} + T_{ji}, \langle \sigma'_{ij}, - \rangle)$ in $\mathcal{T}$
4:         **send**: $(c_{\langle u_i, u_j \rangle}, \frac{\omega_i}{|\{u_j\}|}, \sigma'_{ij})$ to u_j
5:         **receive**: σ'_{ji} from u_j
6:         **update**: $(c_{\langle u_i, u_j \rangle}, \cdot, \cdot, \cdot, \langle \cdot, \sigma'_{ji} \rangle)$ in $\mathcal{T}$
7:     **else**
8:         Abort
9:     **end if**
10:    **send**: $\top$ to u_i

11: **end for**
Payment: Refer MAPPCN [24].

CoinShift($\{c_{\langle u_i, u_k \rangle}\}, c_{\langle u_i, u_j \rangle}, \nu_{ik}$) :
1: **for** each channel $c_{\langle u_i, u_k \rangle}$ **do**
2:     **if** $(c_{\langle u_i, u_k \rangle} \in \mathcal{AL})$ **then**
3:         **send**: $(c_{\langle u_i, u_k \rangle}, c_{\langle u_i, u_j \rangle}, \nu_{ik})$ to u_k
4:         **receive**: $(T''_{ik}, C''_{ik}, \sigma''_{ki})$ from u_k
5:         **update**: $(c_{\langle u_i, u_k \rangle}, T''_{ik}, \cdot, C''_{ik}, \langle \sigma''_{ik}, \sigma''_{ki} \rangle)$ in $\mathcal{T}$
6:         **update**: $(c_{\langle u_i, u_j \rangle}, T''_{ij}, \cdot, C''_{ij}, \langle \sigma''_{ij}, - \rangle)$ in $\mathcal{T}$
7:         **send**: $(c_{\langle u_i, u_k \rangle}, c_{\langle u_i, u_j \rangle}, T''_{ij}, \cdot, C''_{ij}, \langle \sigma''_{ij}, \sigma''_{ik}, \sigma''_{ki} \rangle)$ to u_j
8:         **receive**: σ''_{ji} from u_j
9:         **update**: $(c_{\langle u_i, u_j \rangle}, \cdot, \cdot, \cdot, \langle \cdot, \sigma''_{ji} \rangle)$ in $\mathcal{T}$
10:        **send**: $\langle \sigma''_{ik}, \sigma''_{ij}, \sigma''_{ji} \rangle$ to u_j
11:    **end if**
12: **end for**

CoinSettlement($u_i, \{u_j\}, \Psi, \sigma_i$) :
1: **send**: $(c_{\langle u_i, u_j \rangle}, \Psi)$ to u_j
2: **write**: CoinSettle(u_i, Ψ, σ_i) to $\mathcal{B}$
3: **send**: $\top$ to u_i

CloseChannel($c_{\langle u_i, u_j \rangle}$,) :
1: **if** $(c_{\langle u_i, u_j \rangle}, C_{ij}, f_{ij}, t_{ij}) \in \mathcal{B}$ and $(c_{\langle u_i, u_j \rangle}, T_{ij}, T_{ji}, C_{ij}, f_{ij}, t'_{ij}) \in \mathcal{AL}$ **then**
2:     **if** $(c_{\langle u_i, u_j \rangle} \in \mathcal{CL}$ or $t'_{ij} > |\mathcal{B}|)$ **then**
3:         Abort
4:     **else**
5:         **remove**: $(c_{\langle u_i, u_j \rangle}, T_{ij}, T_{ji}, C_{ij}, f_{ij}, t'_{ij})$ from $\mathcal{AL}$
6:         **write**: close($c_{\langle u_i, u_j \rangle}, C_{ij}, f_{ij}, t'_{ij}$) to $\mathcal{B}$
7:         **store**: $c_{\langle u_i, u_j \rangle}$ in $\mathcal{CL}$
8:         **send**: $(c_{\langle u_i, u_j \rangle}, \top)$ to both u_i and u_j
9:     **end if**
10: **else**
11:     Abort
12: **end if**

4.3 FlexiPCN Operational Details

The open channel and close channel operations are the same as the existing payment protocols like MAPPCN [24], but there is no initial channel balance. However, for the payment operation, we use the existing mechanism of MAPPCN [24] to ensure the anonymity and privacy of the user. Algorithm 1 depicts all the operations of the FlexiPCN protocol. The remaining operations are described in detail as follows:

$\texttt{CoinDeposit}(u_i, \{u_j\}, \omega_i, \sigma_i)$: As illustrated in Fig. 2, user u_i wishes to deposit some coins onto blockchain $\mathcal{B}$, it first invokes $\texttt{CoinDeposit}(u_i, \{u_j\}, \omega_i, \sigma_i)$ and passes the parameters: active neighboring set $\{u_j\}$, amount to be deposited ω_i, and signature σ_i. After receiving $\texttt{CoinDeposit}$ request, the blockchain $\mathcal{B}$ checks $u_i \in \mathcal{B}$, $c_{\langle u_i, u_j \rangle} \in \mathcal{AL}$, and $\omega_i \leq \mathcal{B}[u_i]$. If all of these conditions are met, $\mathcal{B}$ updates the account balance of u_i $\mathcal{B}[u_i] = \mathcal{B}[u_i] - \omega_i$ and sends $\top$ to u_i as confirmation. Then, u_i adds the channel $c_{\langle u_i, u_j \rangle}$ into the transaction state table $\mathcal{T}$.

$\texttt{CoinAllocation}(u_i, \{u_j\}, \omega_i, \sigma'_{ij})$: As illustrated in Fig. 2, the user u_i allocates collateral to each adjacent channel $c_{\langle u_i, u_j \rangle}$ by using the coin allocation policy is $\frac{\omega_i}{|\{u_j\}|}$ along with signature σ'_{ij} for each u_j. After that, each neighbor u_j confirms their agreement by sending their signature σ'_{ji} to u_i. Each user maintains a transaction log (state) $\mathcal{T}$ table.

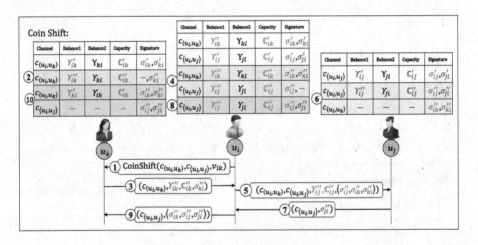

Fig. 3. Coin Shift Operation

$\texttt{CoinShift}(c_{\langle u_i, u_k \rangle}, c_{\langle u_i, u_j \rangle}, \nu_{ik})$: As illustrated in Fig. 3, the user u_i moves ν_{ik} amount of coins from one (or more) neighboring channel(s) to $c_{\langle u_i, u_j \rangle}$ in order to fulfill the off-chain payment request routed through it. To do this, u_i sends a $\texttt{CoinShift}(c_{\langle u_i, u_k \rangle}, c_{\langle u_i, u_j \rangle}, \nu_{ik})$ request to its neighbor u_k (assuming channel $c_{\langle u_i, u_k \rangle}$ has more collateral than ν_{ik} according to $\mathcal{T}$ maintained by u_i). After

u_k updates the channel balance $\Upsilon_{ik} = \Upsilon_{ik} - \nu_{ik}$ and channel capacity $C_{ik} = \Upsilon_{ki} + (\Upsilon_{ik} - \nu_{ik})$, u_k sends signature σ_{ki}'' to u_i. Then, u_i updates the channel balances $\Upsilon_{ik} = \Upsilon_{ik} - \nu_{ik}$ and $\Upsilon_{ij} = \Upsilon_{ij} + \nu_{ik}$, as well as channel capacity $C_{ik} = \Upsilon_{ki} + (\Upsilon_{ik} - \nu_{ik})$ and $C_{ij} = \Upsilon_{ji} + (\Upsilon_{ij} + \nu_{ik})$, and stores σ_{ki}'' in T. After that, u_i sends signatures $\langle \sigma_{ij}'', \sigma_{ik}'', \sigma_{ki}'' \rangle$ to u_j. Then, u_j updates the channel balance $\Upsilon_{ij} = \Upsilon_{ij} + \nu_{ik}$ and channel capacity $C_{ij} = \Upsilon_{ji} + (\Upsilon_{ij} + \nu_{ik})$, stores signatures, and sends σ_{ji}'' to u_i. Next, u_i stores σ_{ji}'' and sends $\langle \sigma_{ik}'', \sigma_{ij}'', \sigma_{ji}'' \rangle$ to u_k. Finally, all users u_i, u_j, and u_k have the same state.

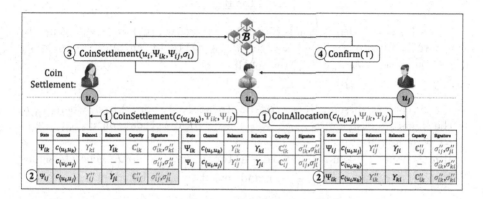

Fig. 4. Coin Settlement Operation

CoinSettlement$(\mathtt{u_i}, \{\mathtt{u_j}\}, \Psi, \sigma_i)$: As illustrated in Fig. 4, the user u_i informs each neighbor u_j of their most recent updated state $\langle c_{\langle u_i, u_j \rangle}, \Psi_{ij} \rangle$ before initiating the coin settlement operation. Then, u_i writes CoinSettle$(\mathtt{u_i}, \{\mathtt{u_j}\}, \Psi, \sigma_i)$ on the blockchain $\mathcal{B}$. $\mathcal{B}$ validates the Ψ and updates the on-chain balances. If this operation is successful, $\mathcal{B}$ returns success with $\top$ to u_i; otherwise, it returns fail with $\bot$. If any of the neighbors u_j, does not agree with the updated balances, the blockchain can be used to resolve the conflict by providing the transaction state Ψ_{ij}.

5   Security Analysis

Theorem 1. *FlexiPCN protocol UC-realizes the ideal functionality $\mathcal{F}_{\mathtt{FlexiPCN}}$: $(\mathcal{F}_{\mathtt{ECDSA}}, \mathcal{F}_{\mathcal{B}}, \mathcal{F}_C, \mathcal{F}_{\mathtt{anon}})$-hybrid model, provided that the digital signature scheme is existentially unforgeable.*

Proof. The OpenChannel and CloseChannel operations are discussed in [5], and Payment operation is also discussed in [24]; so here we are focusing on the remaining operations: CoinDeposit, CoinAllocation, CoinShift, and CoinSettlement. This simulator $\mathcal{S}$ uses a secure cryptographic primitive called Elliptic Curve Digital Signature Algorithm (ECDSA), which is assumed to be secure.

CoinDeposit

$\underline{u_i}$ **is honest:** When u_i sends $(\underline{\texttt{CoinDeposit}}, \texttt{u}_\texttt{i}, \{\texttt{u}_\texttt{j}\}, \omega_\texttt{i}) \hookrightarrow \mathcal{F}$, generate signature σ_i of user u_i on message $(\{u_j\}, \omega_i)$ where $\{u_j\}$ is the set of active adjacent channel user, ω_i is the amount to be deposited or locked in the contract functionality $\mathcal{C}$, and sends $(\underline{\texttt{CoinDeposit}}, \texttt{u}_\texttt{i}, \{\texttt{u}_\texttt{j}\}, \omega_\texttt{i}, \sigma_\texttt{i})$ to $\mathcal{C}$ on behalf of user u_i. $\mathcal{C}$ returns $(\texttt{deposit} - \texttt{confirm})$ to $\mathcal{F}$, and $\mathcal{F}$ returns $\top$ to u_i.

$\underline{u_i}$ **is corrupt:** When u_i sends $(\underline{\texttt{CoinDeposit}}, \texttt{u}_\texttt{i}, \{\texttt{u}_\texttt{j}\}, \omega_\texttt{i}, \sigma_\texttt{i}) \hookrightarrow \mathcal{C}$, $\mathcal{C}$ sends $(\underline{\texttt{CoinDeposit}}, \texttt{u}_\texttt{i}, \{\texttt{u}_\texttt{j}\}, \omega_\texttt{i}, \sigma_\texttt{i}) \hookrightarrow \mathcal{F}$ on behalf of u_i. $\mathcal{F}$ returns $\bot$ to u_i.

CoinAllocation :

$\underline{u_i}$ **is honest:** When u_i sends $(\underline{\texttt{CoinAllocation}}, \texttt{u}_\texttt{i}, \{\texttt{u}_\texttt{j}\}, \omega_\texttt{i}) \hookrightarrow \mathcal{F}$, generate signature σ_i' of u_i on $(u_i, \{u_j\}, \omega_i)$, sends $(\underline{\texttt{CoinAllocation}}, \texttt{c}_{\langle\texttt{u}_\texttt{i},\texttt{u}_\texttt{j}\rangle}, \frac{\omega_i}{|\{u_j\}|}, \sigma_{ij}')$ to each adjacent user $u_j \in \{u_j\}$ on behalf of u_i.

For each $u_j \in \{u_j\}$:

- If u_j is corrupt: It sends $(\texttt{confirm} - \texttt{allocate}, \texttt{c}_{\langle\texttt{u}_\texttt{i},\texttt{u}_\texttt{j}\rangle}, \sigma_{ji}')$ to u_i where σ_{ji}' is the signature of u_j on $(c_{\langle u_i,u_j\rangle}, \frac{\omega_i}{|\{u_j\}|})$, send $(\underline{\texttt{CoinAllocation}}, \texttt{c}_{\langle\texttt{u}_\texttt{i},\texttt{u}_\texttt{j}\rangle}, \frac{\omega_i}{|\{u_j\}|}) \hookrightarrow \mathcal{F}$ on behalf of u_j.
- If u_j is honest: It sends $(\texttt{confirm} - \texttt{allocate}, \texttt{c}_{\langle\texttt{u}_\texttt{i},\texttt{u}_\texttt{j}\rangle}) \hookrightarrow \mathcal{F}$, generate signature σ_{ji}' of u_j on $(c_{\langle u_i,u_j\rangle}, \frac{\omega_i}{|\{u_j\}|})$, and sent it to u_i on behalf of u_j.

$\underline{u_i}$ **is corrupt:** When u_i sends $(\underline{\texttt{CoinAllocation}}, \texttt{c}_{\langle\texttt{u}_\texttt{i},\texttt{u}_\texttt{j}\rangle}, \frac{\omega_i}{|\{u_j\}|}, \sigma_{ij}')$ to u_j, where $u_j \in \{u_j\}$ and u_j is honest, send $(\underline{\texttt{CoinAllocation}}, \texttt{c}_{\langle\texttt{u}_\texttt{i},\texttt{u}_\texttt{j}\rangle}, \frac{\omega_i}{|\{u_j\}|}) \hookrightarrow \mathcal{F}$ on behalf of u_i and send $(\texttt{allocate} - \texttt{request}, \texttt{u}_\texttt{j})$ to $\mathcal{F}$.

For each $u_j \in \{u_j\}$:

- If u_j is corrupt: It sends $(\texttt{confirm} - \texttt{allocate}, \texttt{c}_{\langle\texttt{u}_\texttt{i},\texttt{u}_\texttt{j}\rangle})$ to $\mathcal{F}$ on behalf of u_j.
- If u_j is honest: It sends $(\texttt{confirm} - \texttt{allocate}, \texttt{c}_{\langle\texttt{u}_\texttt{i},\texttt{u}_\texttt{j}\rangle}) \hookrightarrow \mathcal{F}$, generate signature of u_j on $(c_{\langle u_i,u_j\rangle}, \frac{\omega_i}{|\{u_j\}|})$ and send $(\underline{\texttt{CoinAllocation}}, \texttt{c}_{\langle\texttt{u}_\texttt{i},\texttt{u}_\texttt{j}\rangle}, \frac{\omega_i}{|\{u_j\}|}, \sigma_{ij}')$ to u_i on behalf of u_i.

CoinShift :

$\underline{u_i}$ **is honest:** When u_i sends $(\underline{\texttt{CoinShift}}, \texttt{c}_{\langle\texttt{u}_\texttt{i},\texttt{u}_\texttt{k}\rangle}, \texttt{c}_{\langle\texttt{u}_\texttt{i},\texttt{u}_\texttt{j}\rangle}, \nu_\texttt{ik}) \hookrightarrow \mathcal{F}$, send $(\underline{\texttt{CoinShift}}, \texttt{c}_{\langle\texttt{u}_\texttt{i},\texttt{u}_\texttt{k}\rangle}, \texttt{c}_{\langle\texttt{u}_\texttt{i},\texttt{u}_\texttt{j}\rangle}, \nu_\texttt{ik})$ to u_k on behalf of u_i.

- If u_k is honest: It generates signature σ_{ki}'' on $(c_{\langle u_i,u_k\rangle}, \Upsilon_{ik}'', \mathsf{C}_{ik}'')$ and send $(c_{\langle u_i,u_k\rangle}, \Upsilon_{ik}'', \mathsf{C}_{ik}'', \sigma_{ki}'') \hookrightarrow \mathcal{F}$. $\mathcal{F}$ sends $(c_{\langle u_i,u_k\rangle}, \Upsilon_{ik}'', \mathsf{C}_{ik}'', \sigma_{ki}'')$ to u_i on behalf of u_k. u_i sends $(c_{\langle u_i,u_k\rangle}, \texttt{c}_{\langle\texttt{u}_\texttt{i},\texttt{u}_\texttt{j}\rangle}, \Upsilon_{ij}'', \mathsf{C}_{ij}'') \hookrightarrow \mathcal{F}$. $\mathcal{F}$ generates signatures σ_{ik}'' on $(c_{\langle u_i,u_k\rangle}, \Upsilon_{ik}'', \mathsf{C}_{ik}'')$ and σ_{ij}'' on $(c_{\langle u_i,u_j\rangle}, \Upsilon_{ij}'', \mathsf{C}_{ij}'')$, send $(\texttt{c}_{\langle\texttt{u}_\texttt{i},\texttt{u}_\texttt{k}\rangle}, \texttt{c}_{\langle\texttt{u}_\texttt{i},\texttt{u}_\texttt{j}\rangle}, \Upsilon_{ij}'', \mathsf{C}_{ij}'', \langle\sigma_{ij}'', \sigma_{ik}'', \sigma_{ki}''\rangle)$ to u_j on behalf of u_i.
  - If u_j is honest: It sends $(\texttt{coin} - \texttt{shift} - \texttt{ok}) \hookrightarrow \mathcal{F}$, generate signature σ_{ji}'' on $(c_{\langle u_i,u_j\rangle}, \Upsilon_{ij}'', \mathsf{C}_{ij}'')$, send $(\texttt{c}_{\langle\texttt{u}_\texttt{i},\texttt{u}_\texttt{j}\rangle}, \langle\sigma_{ik}'', \sigma_{ij}'', \sigma_{ji}''\rangle)$ to u_k on behalf of u_i.

- If u_j is corrupt: It sends signature $\sigma_{ji}^{''}$ on $(c_{\langle u_i,u_j \rangle}, \Upsilon_{ij}^{''}, C_{ij}^{''})$ to u_i, sends $(c_{\langle u_i,u_j \rangle}, \langle \sigma_{ik}^{''}, \sigma_{ij}^{''}, \sigma_{ji}^{''} \rangle)$ to u_k on behalf of u_i.

- If u_k is corrupt: It generates signature $\sigma_{ki}^{''}$ on $(c_{\langle u_i,u_k \rangle}, \Upsilon_{ik}^{''}, C_{ik}^{''})$ and sends $(c_{\langle u_i,u_k \rangle}, \Upsilon_{ik}^{''}, \sigma_{ki}^{''})$ to u_i. u_i sends $(c_{\langle u_i,u_k \rangle}, c_{\langle u_i,u_j \rangle}, \Upsilon_{ik}^{''}, C_{ik}^{''}, \sigma_{ki}^{''}) \hookrightarrow \mathcal{F}$, generates signatures $\sigma_{ik}^{''}$ on $(c_{\langle u_i,u_k \rangle}, \Upsilon_{ik}^{''}, C_{ik}^{''})$ and $\sigma_{ij}^{''}$ on $(c_{\langle u_i,u_j \rangle}, \Upsilon_{ij}^{''}, C_{ij}^{''})$, send $(c_{\langle u_i,u_k \rangle}, c_{\langle u_i,u_j \rangle}, \Upsilon_{ij}^{''}, C_{ij}^{''}, \langle \sigma_{ij}^{''}, \sigma_{ik}^{''}, \sigma_{ki}^{''} \rangle)$ to u_j on behalf of u_i.

  - If u_j is honest: It sends $(\texttt{coin} - \texttt{shift} - \texttt{ok}) \hookrightarrow \mathcal{F}$, generate signature $\sigma_{ji}^{''}$ on $(c_{\langle u_i,u_j \rangle}, \Upsilon_{ij}^{''}, C_{ij}^{''})$, send $(c_{\langle u_i,u_j \rangle}, \langle \sigma_{ik}^{''}, \sigma_{ij}^{''}, \sigma_{ji}^{''} \rangle)$ to u_k on behalf of u_i.
  - If u_j is corrupt: It sends signature $\sigma_{ji}^{''}$ on $(c_{\langle u_i,u_j \rangle}, \Upsilon_{ij}^{''}, C_{ij}^{''})$ to u_i, sends $(c_{\langle u_i,u_j \rangle}, \langle \sigma_{ik}^{''}, \sigma_{ij}^{''}, \sigma_{ji}^{''} \rangle)$ to u_k on behalf of u_i.

$\underline{u_i \textbf{ is corrupt:}}$ When u_i sends $(\underline{\texttt{CoinShift}}, c_{\langle u_i,u_k \rangle}, c_{\langle u_i,u_j \rangle}, \nu_{ik}) \hookrightarrow \mathsf{u}_k$.

- If u_k is honest: It generates signature $\sigma_{ki}^{''}$ on $(c_{\langle u_i,u_k \rangle}, \Upsilon_{ik}^{''}, C_{ik}^{''})$ and send $(c_{\langle u_i,u_k \rangle}, \Upsilon_{ik}^{''}, C_{ik}^{''}, \sigma_{ki}^{''}) \hookrightarrow \mathcal{F}$. $\mathcal{F}$ sends $(c_{\langle u_i,u_k \rangle}, \Upsilon_{ik}^{''}, C_{ik}^{''}, \sigma_{ki}^{''})$ to u_i on behalf of u_k. u_i generates signatures $\sigma_{ik}^{''}$ on $(c_{\langle u_i,u_k \rangle}, \Upsilon_{ik}^{''}, C_{ik}^{''})$ and $\sigma_{ij}^{''}$ on $(c_{\langle u_i,u_j \rangle}, \Upsilon_{ij}^{''}, C_{ij}^{''})$, and send $(c_{\langle u_i,u_k \rangle}, c_{\langle u_i,u_j \rangle}, \Upsilon_{ij}^{''}, C_{ij}^{''}, \langle \sigma_{ij}^{''}, \sigma_{ik}^{''}, \sigma_{ki}^{''} \rangle)$ to u_j.

  - If u_j is honest: It sends $(\texttt{coin} - \texttt{shift} - \texttt{ok}) \hookrightarrow \mathcal{F}$. u_i generate signature $\sigma_{ji}^{''}$ on $(c_{\langle u_i,u_j \rangle}, \Upsilon_{ij}^{''}, C_{ij}^{''})$, send $(c_{\langle u_i,u_j \rangle}, \langle \sigma_{ik}^{''}, \sigma_{ij}^{''}, \sigma_{ji}^{''} \rangle)$ to u_k.
  - If u_j is corrupt: It generates signature $\sigma_{ji}^{''}$ on $(c_{\langle u_i,u_k \rangle}, c_{\langle u_i,u_j \rangle}, \Upsilon_{ij}^{''}, C_{ij}^{''})$ and sends $(c_{\langle u_i,u_j \rangle}, \sigma_{ij}^{''})$ to u_i, it sends $(c_{\langle u_i,u_j \rangle}, \langle \sigma_{ik}^{''}, \sigma_{ij}^{''}, \sigma_{ji}^{''} \rangle)$ to u_k.

- If u_k is corrupt: It generates signature $\sigma_{ki}^{''}$ on $(c_{\langle u_i,u_k \rangle}, \Upsilon_{ik}^{''}, C_{ik}^{''})$ and sends $(c_{\langle u_i,u_k \rangle}, \Upsilon_{ik}^{''}, C_{ik}^{''}, \sigma_{ki}^{''})$ to u_i. It generates signatures $\sigma_{ik}^{''}$ on $(c_{\langle u_i,u_k \rangle}, \Upsilon_{ik}^{''}, C_{ik}^{''})$ and $\sigma_{ij}^{''}$ on $(c_{\langle u_i,u_j \rangle}, \Upsilon_{ij}^{''}, C_{ij}^{''})$, and sends $(c_{\langle u_i,u_k \rangle}, c_{\langle u_i,u_j \rangle}, \Upsilon_{ij}^{''}, C_{ij}^{''}, \langle \sigma_{ij}^{''}, \sigma_{ik}^{''}, \sigma_{ki}^{''} \rangle)$ to u_j.

  - If u_j is honest: It sends $(\texttt{coin} - \texttt{shift} - \texttt{ok}) \hookrightarrow \mathcal{F}$, generate signature $\sigma_{ji}^{''}$ on $(c_{\langle u_i,u_j \rangle}, \Upsilon_{ij}^{''}, C_{ij}^{''})$, send $(c_{\langle u_i,u_j \rangle}, \langle \sigma_{ik}^{''}, \sigma_{ij}^{''}, \sigma_{ji}^{''} \rangle)$ to u_k.
  - If u_j is corrupt: It generates signature $\sigma_{ji}^{''}$ on $(c_{\langle u_i,u_k \rangle}, c_{\langle u_i,u_j \rangle}, \Upsilon_{ij}^{''}, C_{ij}^{''})$ and sends $(c_{\langle u_i,u_j \rangle}, \sigma_{ij}^{''})$ to u_i, it sends $(c_{\langle u_i,u_j \rangle}, \langle \sigma_{ik}^{''}, \sigma_{ij}^{''}, \sigma_{ji}^{''} \rangle)$ to u_k.

CoinSettlement :

$\underline{u_i \textbf{ is honest:}}$ When u_i sends $(\underline{\texttt{CoinSettlement}}, \mathsf{u}_i, \Psi) \hookrightarrow \mathcal{F}$ where Ψ is the most recent updated state of the payment channels, generate signature σ_i of user u_i on Ψ, and sends $(\underline{\texttt{CoinSettlement}}, \mathsf{u}_i, \{\mathsf{u}_j\}, \omega_i, \sigma_i)$ to $\mathcal{C}$ on behalf of user u_i. If the pending payment requests are completed and updated channel balances, $\mathcal{C}$ sends confirmation $(\texttt{settlement} - \texttt{confirm})$ to $\mathcal{F}$, and $\mathcal{F}$ returns $\top$ to u_i.

$\underline{u_i \textbf{ is corrupt:}}$ When u_i sends $(\underline{\texttt{CoinSettlement}}, \mathsf{u}_i, \Psi, \sigma_i) \hookrightarrow \mathcal{C}$, $\mathcal{C}$ sends $(\underline{\texttt{CoinSettlement}}, \mathsf{u}_i, \{\mathsf{u}_j\}, \Psi, \sigma_i) \hookrightarrow \mathcal{F}$ on behalf of u_i. $\mathcal{F}$ returns $\bot$ to u_i.

6   Conclusion

In this paper, we have proposed a novel flexible payment channel network called FlexiPCN, which rebalances the channel completely off-chain. In FlexiPCN, coins can be deposited per user instead of per channel, allowing users to move coins between channels without going on-chain or setting up a cycle. We have formalized and studied the security of the FlexiPCN protocol using the Universal Composability (UC) framework. The implementation of FlexiPCN is in progress, and we are looking at various applications like SIoVChain [17].

Acknowledgement. We acknowledge the Ministry of Education (MoE), Government of India for providing fellowship under Ph.D. program to complete this work.

References

1. Raiden Network: Fast, cheap, scalable token transfers for Ethereum (2018). https://raiden.network/
2. Canetti, R.: Universally composable security: a new paradigm for cryptographic protocols. In: Proceedings 42nd IEEE Symposium on Foundations of Computer Science, pp. 136–145. IEEE (2001)
3. Croman, K., et al.: On scaling decentralized blockchains. In: Clark, J., Meiklejohn, S., Ryan, P.Y.A., Wallach, D., Brenner, M., Rohloff, K. (eds.) FC 2016. LNCS, vol. 9604, pp. 106–125. Springer, Heidelberg (2016). https://doi.org/10.1007/978-3-662-53357-4_8
4. Dotan, M., Pignolet, Y.A., Schmid, S., Tochner, S., Zohar, A.: SOK: cryptocurrency networking context, state-of-the-art, challenges. In: Proceedings of the 15th International Conference on Availability, Reliability and Security, pp. 1–13 (2020)
5. Ge, Z., Zhang, Y., Long, Y., Gu, D.: Shaduf: non-cycle payment channel rebalancing. In: 29th Annual Network and Distributed System Security Symposium, NDSS 2022, San Diego, California, USA (2022)
6. Gudgeon, L., Moreno-Sanchez, P., Roos, S., McCorry, P., Gervais, A.: SoK: layer-two blockchain protocols. In: Bonneau, J., Heninger, N. (eds.) FC 2020. LNCS, vol. 12059, pp. 201–226. Springer, Cham (2020). https://doi.org/10.1007/978-3-030-51280-4_12
7. Harris, J., Zohar, A.: Flood & loot: a systemic attack on the lightning network. In: Proceedings of the 2nd ACM Conference on Advances in Financial Technologies, pp. 202–213 (2020)
8. Herrera-Joancomartí, J., Navarro-Arribas, G., Ranchal-Pedrosa, A., Pérez-Solà, C., Garcia-Alfaro, J.: On the difficulty of hiding the balance of lightning network channels. In: Proceedings of the 2019 ACM Asia Conference on Computer and Communications Security, pp. 602–612 (2019)
9. Hong, Z., Guo, S., Zhang, R., Li, P., Zhan, Y., Chen, W.: Cycle: sustainable off-chain payment channel network with asynchronous rebalancing. In: 2022 52nd Annual IEEE/IFIP International Conference on Dependable Systems and Networks (DSN), pp. 41–53. IEEE (2022)
10. Khalil, R., Gervais, A.: Revive: rebalancing off-blockchain payment networks. In: Proceedings of the 2017 ACM SIGSAC Conference on Computer and Communications Security, CCS, Dallas, TX, USA, pp. 439–453 (2017)

11. Li, P., Miyazaki, T., Zhou, W.: Secure balance planning of off-blockchain payment channel networks. In: IEEE INFOCOM 2020-IEEE Conference on Computer Communications, pp. 1728–1737. IEEE (2020)
12. Malavolta, G., Moreno-Sanchez, P., Kate, A., Maffei, M., Ravi, S.: Concurrency and privacy with payment-channel networks. In: Proceedings of the 2017 ACM SIGSAC Conference on Computer and Communications Security, pp. 455–471 (2017)
13. Malavolta, G., Moreno-Sanchez, P., Schneidewind, C., Kate, A., Maffei, M.: Anonymous multi-hop locks for blockchain scalability and interoperability. In: 26th Annual Network and Distributed System Security Symposium, NDSS 2019, San Diego, California, USA (2019)
14. Mavroudis, V., Wüst, K., Dhar, A., Kostiainen, K., Capkun, S.: Snappy: Fast on-chain payments with practical collaterals. arXiv preprint arXiv:2001.01278 (2020)
15. Mizrahi, A., Zohar, A.: Congestion attacks in payment channel networks. In: Borisov, N., Diaz, C. (eds.) FC 2021. LNCS, vol. 12675, pp. 170–188. Springer, Heidelberg (2021). https://doi.org/10.1007/978-3-662-64331-0_9
16. Mohanty, S.K., Tripathy, S.: n-htlc: Neo hashed time-lock commitment to defend against wormhole attack in payment channel networks. Comput. Secur. **106**, 102291 (2021)
17. Mohanty, S.K., Tripathy, S.: Siovchain: time-lock contract based privacy-preserving data sharing in siov. IEEE Trans. Intell. Transp. Syst. **23**(12), 24071–24082 (2022)
18. Nakamoto, S.: Bitcoin: a peer-to-peer electronic cash system (2008). http://bitcoin.org/bitcoin.pdf
19. Pérez-Solà, C., Ranchal-Pedrosa, A., Herrera-Joancomartí, J., Navarro-Arribas, G., Garcia-Alfaro, J.: LockDown: balance availability attack against lightning network channels. In: Bonneau, J., Heninger, N. (eds.) FC 2020. LNCS, vol. 12059, pp. 245–263. Springer, Cham (2020). https://doi.org/10.1007/978-3-030-51280-4_14
20. Poon, J., Dryja, T.: The Bitcoin Lightning Network: Scalable Off-Chain Instant Payments (2016). https://lightning.network/lightning-network-paper.pdf
21. Rohrer, E., Malliaris, J., Tschorsch, F.: Discharged payment channels: quantifying the lightning network's resilience to topology-based attacks. In: 2019 IEEE European Symposium on Security and Privacy Workshops (EuroS&PW), pp. 347–356. IEEE (2019)
22. Rohrer, E., Tschorsch, F.: Counting down thunder: timing attacks on privacy in payment channel networks. In: Proceedings of the 2nd ACM Conference on Advances in Financial Technologies, pp. 214–227 (2020)
23. Szabo, N.: The idea of smart contracts. Nick Szabo's papers and concise tutorials **6**(1), 199 (1997)
24. Tripathy, S., Mohanty, S.K.: MAPPCN: multi-hop anonymous and privacy-preserving payment channel network. In: Bernhard, M., et al. (eds.) FC 2020. LNCS, vol. 12063, pp. 481–495. Springer, Cham (2020). https://doi.org/10.1007/978-3-030-54455-3_34
25. Wood, G., et al.: Ethereum: a secure decentralised generalised transaction ledger (2014). https://ethereum.github.io/yellowpaper/paper.pdf

Publicly Verifiable Auctions with Privacy

Paul Germouty, Enrique Larraia$^{(\boxtimes)}$, and Wei Zhang

nChain, London, UK
{p.germouty,e.larraia,w.zhang}@nchain.com

Abstract. Online auctions have a steadily growing market size, creating billions of US dollars in sales value every year. To ensure fairness and auditability while preserving the bidder's privacy is the main challenge of an auction scheme. At the same time, utility driven blockchain technology is picking up the pace, offering transparency and data integrity to many applications. In this paper, we present a blockchain-based first price sealed-bid auction scheme. Our scheme offers privacy and public verifiability. It can be built on any public blockchain, which is leveraged to provide transparency, data integrity, and hence auditability. The inability to double spend on a blockchain is used to prevent bid replay attacks. Moreover, our scheme can achieve non-repudiation for both bidders and the auctioneer without revealing the bids and we encapsulate this concept inside the public verification of the auction. We propose to use ElGamal encryption and Bulletproofs to construct an efficient instantiation of our scheme. We also propose to use recursive zkSNARKs to reduce the number of comparison proofs from $N-1$ to 1, where N is the number of bidders.

Keywords: Auction · Blockchain · Privacy · Public Verifiability

1 Introduction

In the last few decades, online auctions are becoming an important vehicle to advertise and trade assets. They connect buyers and sellers dispersed geographically and allows them to perform the exchange without being in the same location physically. In traditional online auctions platforms (such as eBay), the auctioneer is entrusted to conduct the entire auction correctly. This design demands a high degree of trustworthiness on auctioneer's side. Fortunately, we can leverage a blockchain's built-in consensus and data-integrity to add transparency to the process. This can be done in two ways. The blockchain can be used as a bulletin board where data is posted publicly by bidders and the auctioneer. Afterwards, an independent party can verify the auction using the (immutable) information on the blockchain. The other possibility is to delegate the verification to the blockchain itself, yielding a self-enforcing transparent auction. In both cases, blockchains can be effectively used to verify the correctness of the auction result.

The challenge is to design a blockchain-based auction that does not compromise privacy. In a sealed-bid auction, only the winning bid is revealed by

A. Essex et al. (Eds.): FC 2023 Workshops, LNCS 13953, pp. 420–438, 2024.
https://doi.org/10.1007/978-3-031-48806-1_27

the auctioneer, and the other bids are kept private (as opposed to open-outcry auctions, where all the bids are known to everyone). The most common types of sealed-bid auctions are first and second price winning auctions.

- First-price sealed-bid auction (FPSBA). The bidder with the highest bid wins and pays the value of the bid to the seller.
- Second-price sealed-bid auction (Vickrey auctions [29]). The bidder with the highest bid wins, but pays an amount equal to the value of the second highest bid.

In this work we focus on FPSBA for simplicity, but we emphasize that with slight modifications our system can be applied to Vickrey auctions as well. We refer to [28] for more information about the different types of auctions.

1.1   Auction Model

Security: Building on [19] we define security of a blockchain-based FPSBA with the following properties:

- **Bid privacy**. No information about non-winning bids can be inferred from the result (beyond that the winning bid is the highest bid).
- **Bid independence**. Bids are independent from each other. A (possibly malicious) bidder cannot construct their bid based on a bid from an honest bidder.
- **Bid binding**. After the bid phase is closed, bidders cannot change their mind and bid differently.
- **Public verifiability**. The correctness of the result (namely, the winner is the one claimed by the auctioneer) and the correct behaviour of the auctioneer, can be verified by anyone using public information only.

Public verifiability is sometimes referred as *universal verifiability*, and bid binding as *non-repudiation* or *non-cancellation* [16]. As noted in [15], these security definitions borrow from the e-voting literature, wherein individual/universal verifiability, eligibility and accountability are well-established notions.

Adversary Model. To achieve bid privacy we assume the auctioneer is *semi-honest*. Specifically, they do not share private information. For the remaining security properties, the auctioneer and the bidders can be *malicious* (they may deviate from the protocol instructions and share information). We observe that an auction with bid independence implies that there cannot be replay attacks.

Trustless Verification. Public verification should be conducted based only on public information. This means that neither the auctioneer nor the bidders need to disclose private information. In most cases, all public information can be fetched from the blockchain. Public verifiability, as defined above, also captures the case of verifying that a bid has been discarded by the auctioneer because it is indeed malformed (e.g. out of range). If the chosen blockchain supports contract automation and enforcement, the verification can be embedded in blockchain transactions and conducted by the blockchain network.

Complexity: We identify metrics relating to the complexity of the auction scheme.

Communication Overhead (CO). The amount of data published on the blockchain by the bidders and the auctioneer. For scalability, it should be linear in the number of bidders $\mathcal{O}(\lambda N)$. Ideally, any party publishes $\mathcal{O}(\lambda)$ bits to the blockchain, where λ is the security parameter.

Rounds of Interaction (Blockchain Latency). This can be defined as the minimum number of blocks elapsed while executing an auction. Ideally, bidders only interact with the blockchain in the bid phase, and do not participate in the result phase nor in the public verification.

Verification Overhead (VO). The complexity of the public verification algorithm. This affects the feasibility and cost of self-enforced verification in the blockchain. Public verification uses on-chain information, thus a lower bound is the communication overhead.

Financial Fairness: Some schemes require that dishonest behaviour should be financially penalised. In this work we do not detail how to achieve financial fairness. However, since we obtain public verifiability we can ask bidders to deposit funds in the blockchain and only return the funds if they behave as they should. There are a number of ways this can be implemented in practice. For example, using smart contracts in an Ethereum-like blockchain as in [19,22] or using multi-signatures escrow payments in a Bitcoin-like blockchain. However, care must be taken as publicly disclosing the deposit (which is greater but not necessarily equal than the bid) may influence the strategic interaction and equilibrium bidding behaviour [27]. Even worst, it might conflict with bid privacy or bid independence.

1.2 Related Work

Since the early works of Nurmi and Salomaa [26] and Franklin and Reiter [18] many auction schemes secured by cryptography have followed [4,7,9,12,19,24, 25]. Some works rely on Yao's millionaire's problem [12], others are based on garbled circuits [25], or homomorphic encryption [1,4,24]. These protocols require a third party (the auctioneer) that should remain honest and does not collude with bidders. Other schemes aim to eliminate the auctioneer [9] and achieve fairness with low complexity [3,14]. For example, in [9] Brandt exploits the homomorphic property of ElGamal encryption with a combination of discrete-log based zero-knowledge proofs (ZKP) to construct a multiparty protocol for fully-private auctions (whereby the winning bid is not public). However, all these works require some degree of interaction of bidders in the result phase. A recent survey of auction schemes [2] offers detailed descriptions of the security properties and technologies used in those works.

Blass and Kerschbaum present Strain in [7], which is an auction protocol for blockchains secure against a malicious bidder. The scheme uses Goldwasser-Micali's homomorphic encryption [20] scheme which has large ciphertexts and ZKPs of order N. While the scheme preserves bid privacy, the comparison of two bids requires interaction between the bidders. Lafourcade et al. in [22] propose Auctionity, a scheme for open-outcry auctions (where all bids are public) using Ethereum to secure deposits, and analyse its security in a symbolic model.

In a different fashion, Galal and Youssef in [19] describe a blockchain-based FPSBA deployed in Ethereum. Bidders commit to their bids using Pedersen commitments and send the commitments to the auction contract. Bids are integers in $\mathbb{Z}_p$ where p is the size of the Pedersen group $\mathbb{G}_p$. Only after the auction contract has been updated with all commitments, the bidders encrypt their bids and the Pedersen openings with an asymmetric public-key encryption scheme using the public key of the auctioneer and send the ciphertexts to the auctioneer. The auctioneer (which is semi-honest only for bid privacy) uses ZKPs to prove the statement "$x_w > x_i$" where x_w is the winning (highest) bid, and x_i is any other bid. To create the comparison ZK proofs they use the following implication, which holds for any positive integer $B \leq p/2$:

$$x_w, x_i, (x_w - x_i) \mod p, \in [0, B) \Rightarrow x_w > x_i \tag{1}$$

Since x_w is publicly announced, the comparison proof can be reduced to two range proofs for the statements "$x_i \in [0, B)$" and "$\Delta_i \mod p \in [0, B)$", where $\Delta_i := x_w - x_i$. For the range proof they use a non-interactive Σ-protocol by Brickwell et al. [10]. However, the soundness of one such ZKP proof is for 1 bit, so they need to repeat the protocol λ times (per non-winning bid x_i). This introduces significant complexity and high gas fees on the chosen blockchain. As a result, they report an implementation with the security parameter heavily restricted to $\lambda = 10$. Also, their scheme uses a dispute-resolution technique that forces bidders to disclose their bids on-chain to prove their honesty when a malicious auctioneer falsely claim that their bids are invalid. Last, in [23] Bulletproofs for bid comparison is used, however all bidders need to participate in the verification phase.

1.3   Our Contributions and Techniques

We describe how to conduct FPSBA over *any* public blockchain. We focus on making an auction publicly verifiable, using the blockchain for an audit trail without breaching the privacy of the non-winning and honest bidders. In our scheme, the auctioneer generates *short* ZKPs (specifically, we use SNARKs) which greatly improves the complexity of the solution compared to previous work.

Summary of Our Main Contributions. We develop a generic methodology to ensure bid privacy and bid independence using any encryption scheme and non-malleable commitments. We describe a concrete and practical instantiation using ElGamal encryption [17], Bulletproofs [11] to generate the comparison proofs, and salted hashes to commit ciphertexts. In this instantiation, the auctioneer needs to generate one comparison proof per non-winning bidder, and hence the communication overhead is linear in the number of bidders. We explain how to achieve *constant* communication overhead and sub-linear verification using recursive SNARKs for the comparison proofs. Last, both instantiations have only four rounds of interactions with the chosen blockchain: two rounds for the bid phase and one round for each of the result phase and verification phase.

It is also worth noting that in our scheme the auctioneer can prove a bid is out of range without interacting with the disputed bidder. This eliminates the need of dispute-resolution mechanisms. Further, we identify a flaw in the comparison proof used by Galal and Youssef in [19]. This flaw is described in Appendix A.

Our Techniques. We implement the bid phase in two rounds. In the first round, bidders encrypt their bids and commit to their ciphertexts with a non-malleable commitment. In the second round, the bidders open the commitments to the ciphertexts by publishing the opening and the ciphertext. The bids are kept private 'inside' the ciphertexts, and the ciphertexts (hence the bids) are independently generated. We call this two-round protocol *sealed encryption*. As in [19], we reduce the i-th comparison proof "$x_w > x_i$" to two range proofs. Bids are encrypted with ElGamal over a cyclic group $\mathbb{G}_p$ of order p. One can derive Pedersen commitments for x_i and $\hat{\Delta}_i := (x_w - x_i) \mod p$ using the ElGamal ciphertexts ct_i and ct_w. Our main observation is that the secret key (of the auctioneer) can be seen as the *opening* information. Thus, the auctioneer can use these two Pedersen commitments as the public inputs, and his secret key as the private input to prove with Bulletproof range proof system that $\forall x_i, \hat{\Delta}_i \in [0, B)$, for upper bound $B := 2^n$.

In Sect. 4, we describe a generic method using recursive SNARKs to generate a single proof attesting to the validity of all statements "$x_w > x_i$", for $i \leq N, i \neq w$. The auctioneer organizes the $N - 1$ ciphertexts of the non-winning bids into a Merkle tree, and recurse proof generation over the tree. We explain how to do sequential recursion and somewhat-parallel recursion during the proof generation.

Comparison with Other Blockchain-Based Auctions. We compare the reviewed auction protocols with ours in Table 1. We chose to use only one security parameter λ for both security of the encryption and soundness of the argument of knowledge. N is the number of bidders, and bids are in the range $[0, 2^n - 1]$ for some integer n. In our schemes we have $3 + 1$ rounds, where the last round is for public-verifiability. The communication overhead during the bid and result phases directly affect the cost of implementing the auction on a blockchain, as most blockchains charge fees based on the size of transactions or data. In the case of an automated verification, the verification runtime is also important as it affects the cost of executing an automated contract on-chain.

Table 1. Asymptotic comparison of our work

Scheme	Rounds	Communication		Verification runtime	Public verifiability	
		Bid phase	Result phase	($\#\mathbb{G}_p$ operations)	Bid correctness	Result correctness
[7]	4	$\mathcal{O}(n\lambda^2)$	$\mathcal{O}(N^2\lambda)$	$\mathcal{O}(n\lambda)$	✗	✓
[19]	$2(\lambda+1)$	$\mathcal{O}(\lambda)$	$\mathcal{O}(N\lambda^2)$	$\mathcal{O}(N\lambda^2)$	✗	✓
Ours (Sect. 3)	3+1	$\mathcal{O}(\lambda)$	$\mathcal{O}(\lambda N \log(n))$	$\mathcal{O}(\lambda N \frac{n}{\log(n)})$	✓	✓
Ours (Sect. 4)	3+1	$\mathcal{O}(\lambda)$	$\mathcal{O}(\lambda \log(n))$	$\mathcal{O}(\lambda \log(n))$	✓	✓

2 Preliminaries

In this section we describe the building blocks that we use in our auction scheme, namely: commitments, public-key encryption and zero-knowledge proofs.

Notation. We denote a finite cyclic group of prime order p with $\mathbb{G}_p$, and vectors of group elements in bold $\mathbf{v}$. We write $x \xleftarrow{\$} D$ to mean x is picked uniformly at random from domain D. We will use λ for the security parameter, N for the number of bidders that participate in an auction, and $n \ll \log(p)$ for an upper bound of the bids $x \in [0, 2^n)$.

2.1 Public Key Encryption

A public-key encryption scheme PKE has four probabilistic polynomial time (PPT) algorithms:

- Setup(1^λ) takes as input the security parameter λ, and outputs the public parameters param of the scheme.
- KeyGen(param) outputs a pair of keys, a (public) encryption key pk and a (private) decryption key sk;
- Encrypt(pk, m; r) takes as input the public key pk a plaintext m, and randomness r. It outputs a ciphertext ct.
- Decrypt(sk, ct) takes as input the secret key sk and a ciphertext ct. It outputs a plaintext m or a decryption error $\perp$.

ElGamal Encryption. It is a public-key encryption scheme [17] instantiated over a cyclic group $\mathbb{G}_p$ with generator g. A ciphertext consist of a pair of group elements ct $= (d, e)$, and we set the plaintext space to $[0, 2^n) \subset \mathbb{Z}_p$. The decryption requires a precomputed lookup table storing pairs of the form $(x, g^x) \in [0, 2^n) \times \mathbb{G}_p$ where x is from the plaintext space. See Fig. 1 for a description.

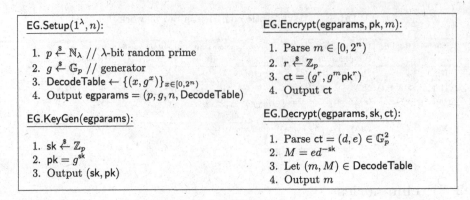

Fig. 1. ElGamal Encryption scheme

2.2 Commitments

A commitment scheme Com enables the generation of a commitment to a message, which can be used to verify the message when it is revealed with an opening. It consists of four PPT algorithms:

- Setup(1^λ) outputs the public parameters param of the scheme.
- KeyGen(param) generates a public commitment key ck.
- Commit(ck, m; r) takes as input ck and a message m. It outputs the commitment c and the randomness r used to commit (the opening value).
- VerCom(ck, c, m, r) outputs true if message m was committed in c using r. Otherwise, it outputs false.

Intuitively, a commitment scheme is *binding* if it is infeasible to find messages $m' \neq m$ and openings r, r' such that Commit(ck, m; r) = Commit(ck, m'; r'). It is *hiding* if it is infeasible to infer any information about m from c without the knowledge of the opening r (the probabilities of both events are negligible in the security parameter λ).

In our auction scheme we will commit to values using a cryptographic hash function Hash as described in Fig. 2. This commitment scheme does not have a commitment key, and it is well-known to be binding and hiding in the random oracle model. The range of the hash should be set to 2λ for the binding property (preimage resistance), and use a λ-bit random salt for the hiding property. This commitment scheme is also non-malleable.

Setup(1^λ): Output Hash : $\{0,1\}^* \rightarrow \{0,1\}^{2\lambda}$

Commit(m):

1. $r \xleftarrow{\$} \{0,1\}^\lambda$
2. $c = \mathsf{Hash}(m||r)$
3. Output (c, r)

VerCom(m, c, r):

1. If $c = \mathsf{Hash}(m||r)$ output true
2. Else output false

Fig. 2. Salted hash commitment.

2.3 Zero-Knowledge Proofs

Given a fixed finite field $\mathbb{F}_p$ and an $\mathbb{F}_p$-arithmetic circuit $C : \mathbb{F}_p^n \times \mathbb{F}_p^h \to \{0,1\}$, a preprocessing, zero-knowledge, succinct, non-interactive, argument of knowledge (zkSNARK —see e.g. [6]) for the NP relation

$$\mathcal{R}_C := \{(x; w) \in \mathbb{F}_p^n \times \mathbb{F}_p^h \mid C(x, w) = 1\},$$

is a triplet of algorithms SNARK = (Setup, Prove, Verify) such that:

- Setup($1^\lambda, \mathcal{R}_C$) takes as input a security parameter λ and the description of a circuit C it outputs a pair of keys pk, vk.
- Prove(pk, x, w) takes the proving key pk, the public instance x and the private witness w as input and outputs a proof π.
- Verify(vk, x, π) takes the verification key vk, the public instance x, and the proof π as input and outputs either accept or reject.

The zkSNARK is *complete* if Verify always accepts proofs π generated by Prove on inputs $(x; y) \in \mathcal{R}_C$. It is *succinct* if $|\pi| = \mathcal{O}_\lambda(1)$, and it has a succinct verifier (sometimes also referred as fully succinct) if Setup runs in time $\mathcal{O}_\lambda(|x|)$. It is zero-knowledge if no information about the witness w is leaked from the proof.

Knowledge Soundness. It must be possible to efficiently extract a witness from any (possibly cheating) prover Prove* that outputs an accepting pair (x, π). More formally, for every polynomial-time adversary Prove*, there exists a polynomial-time extractor Extract$_{\text{Prove*}}$, such that for every large-enough security parameter λ,

$$P\left[\begin{array}{l} \text{Verify(vk}, x, \pi) = 1 \\ (x; y) \notin \mathcal{R}_C \end{array} \middle| \begin{array}{l} (\text{pk}, \text{vk}) \leftarrow \text{Prove}(1^\lambda, C) \\ (x, \pi) \leftarrow \text{Prove*}(\text{pk}, \text{vk}) \\ y \leftarrow \text{Extract}_{\text{Prove*}}(\text{pk}, \text{vk}) \end{array}\right] \leq \text{negl}(\lambda).$$

Bulletproofs. Bulletproofs [11] is a SNARK used to prove interval membership $x \in [0, 2^n)$. The public input is a Pedersen commitment $C = \text{Commit}(\text{ck}, x; r) := g^x h^r$ of the integer x under commitment key ck $:= (g, h) \in \mathbb{G}_p^2$. A prover convinces the verifier that a given $x \in \mathbb{Z}_p$ lies in range $[0, 2^n)$ by showing it knows the bit decomposition $\mathbf{b}$ of x. Specifically, the NP relation is:

$$\mathcal{R}_{\text{BP}} = \{(g, h, C \in \mathbb{G}_p, n \in \mathbb{N}); (x, r \in \mathbb{Z}_p) \mid C = g^x h^r, x \in [0, 2^n)\} \qquad (2)$$

The high-level idea is to prove in zero-knowledge that the following constraints are satisfied:

$$\langle \mathbf{b}, \mathbf{2}^n \rangle = x; \text{ and } \mathbf{b} \circ \mathbf{b}' = \mathbf{0}; \text{ and } \mathbf{b}' = \mathbf{b} - 1$$

Above, $\mathbf{2}^n$ is a vector of all the powers of 2 up to 2^{n-1}, and $\circ$ denotes component-wise product. The second and third constraints proves that elements in $\mathbf{b}$ are indeed bits, and the first constraint shows that $\mathbf{b}$ is the bit decomposition of x. To achieve logarithmic communication in n, satisfiability of the above constraints is reduced to a inner product argument (sound but not zero-knowledge) in which the prover commits to messages $\mathbf{m} \in \mathbb{Z}_p^{2n}$ of $2n$ elements using a (binding-only) length-reducing Pedersen vector commitment with key $\mathsf{ck} := \mathbf{g} \in \mathbb{G}_p^{2n}$, setting $\mathsf{Commit}(\mathsf{ck}, \mathbf{m}) := \prod_{i=1}^{2n} g_i^{m_i}$. The triplet of algorithms $\mathsf{BP} = (\mathsf{BP.Setup}, \mathsf{BP.Prove}, \mathsf{BP.Verify})$ is as follows:

- $\mathsf{BP.Setup}(1^\lambda, n)$ takes as input a security parameter λ and the description of the range $[0, 2^n)$. It outputs a pair of keys $\mathsf{pk}_{\mathsf{bp}} = \mathsf{vk}_{\mathsf{bp}} = \mathbf{g} \in \mathbb{G}_{p(\lambda)}^{2n}$.
- $\mathsf{BP.Prove}(\mathsf{pk}_{\mathsf{bp}}, (g, h, C), (x, r))$ takes the proving key $\mathsf{pk}_{\mathsf{bp}}$, the public instance (g, h, C) and the private witness (x, r) and outputs a proof π_{bp}.
- $\mathsf{BP.Verify}(\mathsf{vk}_{\mathsf{bp}}, (g, h, C), \pi_{\mathsf{bp}})$ takes the verification key $\mathsf{vk}_{\mathsf{bp}}$, the public instance (g, h, C), and the proof π_{bp}, and it outputs accepts or rejects.

The soundness of Bulletproofs relies on the assumption that there is no known relationship between the group elements $\mathbf{g}, g, h$. Recall $\mathbf{g}$ is the Vector Pedersen key used to commit to internal messages in the proving and verification algorithms of BP, and g, h is the Pedersen key (part of the public instance) used to commit to x in relation $\mathcal{R}_{\mathsf{BP}}$—see Eq. (2). The publicly-verifiable correctness of the result of our auction scheme will rely on the following theorem proved in [11].

Theorem 1 (Corollary 2 of [11], informal). *If there is no known relationship between the group elements $g, h, \mathbf{g}$, then* BP *with* $\mathsf{pk}_{\mathsf{bp}} = \mathsf{vk}_{\mathsf{bp}} = \mathbf{g}$ *is knowledge sound.*

Recursive Proof Composition. This is useful to prove that a function is applied iteratively $x_1 = f(x_0), \ldots, x_n = f(x_{n-1})$. Proving the correct iteration of f can be done with proof composition. A proof π_n for the statement "$x_n = f(x_{n-1})$" also attests to the existence of valid proofs π_i for the statements "$x_i = f(x_{i-1})$" for each $i = 1 \ldots, n-1$. In a recursive SNARK_r, the verification logic of the base SNARK_b is implemented as part of the prover. Thus, if the base circuit is "$\mathcal{C}_b(x_i, x_{i-1}) = 1$ iff $x_i = f(x_{i-1})$", the recursive algorithm Prove_r proves satisfiability of the augmented circuit:

$$\text{``}\mathcal{C}_r((x_i, \mathsf{vk}_b), (x_{i-1}, \pi_{i-1})) = 1 \text{ iff } x_i = f(x_{i-1}) \wedge \mathsf{Verify}_b(\mathsf{vk}_b, x_{i-1}, \pi_{i-1}) = \mathsf{true}\text{''}.$$

The main benefit of recursive proofs is that the prover can be parallelised. Of course, it also reduces the number of proofs that need to be transmitted from $N - 1$ (using a non-recursive SNARK) to just one. Proof composition was first constructed using cycles of pairing-friendly curves [5] and can be recursed assuming the base verifier is succinct (it runs in logarithmic time). Further works [8, 21], reduce the recursion overhead without requiring a succinct base verifier.

3   Description of Our Scheme

In this section we describe the details of our auction scheme. The interactions after setup, between the blockchain and the participants of the auction are

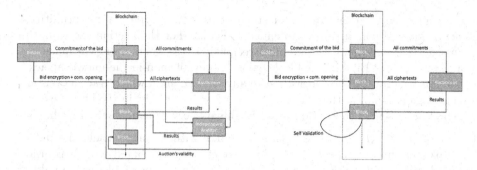

Fig. 3. Auction schemes interaction with independent public verification

Fig. 4. Auction schemes interaction with automated verification

described in Fig. 3 and Fig. 4. The verification of the auction can be conducted by an independent party or automated on the blockchain. Our auction scheme has four phases: setup, bid, result, and public verification. It can be implemented with appropriate choices of commitments, public-key encryption and ZKPs. We give a concrete instantiation by setting the commitment to salted hashes, encryption to ElGamal [17] and the ZKP to Bulletproof [11]. The details of these building blocks can be found in Sect. 2. In Fig. 8 we describe the implementation of our auction scheme.

3.1 Setup Phase

In this phase, the auctioneer sets time bounds T_b, T_r, T_v for each subsequent phase (e.g. given by block heights). It then generates the following scheme parameters:

- Select a cyclic group $\mathbb{G}_p$ of prime order $p = p(\lambda)$.
- Set the upper bound of the bids to $n < \log(p) - 1$. Thus the bid range is $[0, 2^n)$ for $2^n < p/2$.
- Generate $2n + 1$ group elements $g, \mathbf{g} \in \mathbb{G}_p^{2n+1}$. These group elements are generated in a publicly-verified way to ensure no discrete-log relation is known. The proving key (and verification key) of Bulletproofs is set to $\mathbf{g}$. The group generator of ElGamal is set to g.
- Compute the ElGamal decoding table $\mathsf{DecodeTable} = \{(x, g^x)\}_{x \in [0, 2^n)}$ and his secret/public key pair $(\mathsf{pk}_A, \mathsf{sk}_A)$.

Then, the auctioneer publishes $(n, p, g, \mathbf{g}, \mathsf{pk}_A, T_b, T_r, T_v)$ and the description of the goods to the blockchain. It keeps the decryption key sk_A private.

3.2 Bidding Phase

We design a new protocol for the bid phase called *sealed encryption* and described in Fig. 5. This new protocol allows for a message to be committed and revealed to an intended recipient at a later stage. It uses two cryptographic primitives: encryption and commitment as defined in Sect. 2. For the auction use case, the message is the bid and the intended recipient is the auctioneer. We make use of the security of Bitcoin-like blockchains to prevent man-in-the-middle attacks. Our construction can be generalized to any blockchain of which transactions are secure against man-in-the-middle attacks. More concretely, in the bid phase, we instantiate a sealed encryption using ElGamal encryption and salted hash:

Commit phase: the bidder encrypts his bid x with ElGamal using the public key pk_A of the auctioneer. The ciphertext ct is concatenated with a transaction identifier $txid_0$, corresponding to a transaction tx_0 spendable by the bidder. Then $ct\|txid_0$ is committed in c using randomness r. Finally, c is pushed on the blockchain by embedding it in a transaction tx_1 that spends tx_0.

Reveal phase: the bidder publishes his ciphertext ct and the opening randomness r on the blockchain by embedding them in a transaction tx_2 that spends tx_1.

3.3 Result Phase

In this phase, the auctioneer identifies the winning bid x_w and announces it publicly in the blockchain. The auctioneer does the following:

- Obtain and decrypt all ElGamal ciphertexts $\{ct_i\}_{i\leq N}$ from the bid phase using his secret key sk_A.
- Discard incorrect bids: If an opening to a ciphertext ct_i is incorrect add i to a list of incorrect openings $L_{BadComm}$. If it decrypts to group element X_i that cannot be decoded (bid out of range) add i to a list of bad encryptions L_{BadEnc}. The auctioneer disqualify all bidders in $L_{BadComm} \cup L_{BadEnc}$. Else, he adds i to a list of honest bidders L_{HB}.
- Identify the highest bid x_w from the set of honest bids L_{HB}.
- Prove correctness of his computations. He creates a correct decryption proof $\pi_{dec,w}$ to prove ct_w decrypts to x_w, and (at most) $N-1$ comparison proofs $\pi_{cmp,i}$ to prove that $x_w > x_i$ for each $i \neq w, i \in L_{HB}$. He also creates proofs $\pi_{dec,i}$ of correct decryption to out of range bid X_i for each $i \in L_{BadEnc}$. (See next paragraphs for more information.)

SE.Commit(param, $\mathcal{M}$, pk):

1. Pick an unspent transaction $txid_0$
2. Compute $ct = Encrypt(param, pk, m)$
3. Pick $r \xleftarrow{\$} \mathbb{Z}_p$
4. Compute $c = Commit(ck, ct\|txid_0; r)$
5. Embed c in the transaction $txid_1$ spending the transaction $txid_0$

SE.Reveal(ct, r, $txid_1$):

1. Embed ct, $txid_0$ and r in the transaction $txid_2$ spending $txid_1$.

SE.Verify(ct, r, c, $txid_2$) :

1. Verify c lies inside the parent transaction of $txid_2$ and child transaction of $txid_0$.
2. Output $VerCom(ck, c, ct\|txid_0; r)$

SE.Open(ct, r, c, $txid_2$, sk):

1. Run SE.Verify(param, ct, r, c, $txid_2$) if it ouputs 0 then output $\bot$
2. $m \leftarrow Decrypt(param, sk, ct)$
3. Output m

Fig. 5. Sealed Encryption Protocol

- Publish to the blockchain the winner bid x_w, the list of ZKP proofs $L_{zkp} = \{\pi_{dec,w}, \{\pi_{cmp,h}\}_{h\neq w, h\in L_{HB}}, \{\pi_{dec,c}\}_{c\in L_{BadEnc}}\}$, and the list of honest bidders L_{HB} and disqualified bidders $L_{BadComm} \cup L_{BadEnc}$.

Correct Decryption Proof. This is essentially a proof of equal discrete logarithms. Let the auctioneer ElGamal public key $pk_A = h = g^{sk_A}$, and let the ElGamal ciphertext $ct_w = (d_w, e_w) = (g^r, g^{x_w}h^r)$. If the ciphertext decrypts to x_w under secret key sk_A, then it holds $e_w x_w^{-1} = h^r = d_w^{sk_A}$. Thus, the auctioneer proves in zero-knowledge that the group elements $e_w x_w^{-1}$ and h have the same discrete logarithm sk_A in basis d_w, g respectively. We use the Σ-protocol of Chaum and Pedersen [13] to prove equality of discrete logs on public basis. For completeness, we describe the non-interactive version $CDEC = (CDEC.Prove, CDEC.Verify)$ in Fig. 6.

CDEC.Prove$((g, pk_A, ct, x), sk_A)$:	CDEC.Verify$((g, pk_A, ct, x), \pi_{dec})$:
1. Parse $ct = (d, e) \in \mathbb{G}_p^2$	1. Parse $ct = (d, e) \in \mathbb{G}_p^2$
2. $s \xleftarrow{\$} \mathbb{Z}_p$	2. Parse $\pi_{dec} = (c, z) \in \mathbb{Z}_p^2$
3. $(a, b) = (g^s, d^s)$	3. $a = g^z pk_A^{-c}$,
4. $c = Hash(g, pk_A, x, ct, a, b) \in \mathbb{Z}_p$	4. $b = d^z (eg^{-x})^{-c}$
5. $z = s + c sk_A$	5. If $c = Hash(g, pk_A, ct, x, a, b)$ output true
6. Output $\pi_{dec} = (c, z)$	6. Else, output false

Fig. 6. Non-interactive sigma protocol to prove correct decryption of ct to x using decryption key sk_A. Based on equality of discrete logs [13].

Comparison Proof. The auctioneer needs to prove that for each $i \neq w$ the bid x_w encrypted in the ElGamal ciphertext $ct_w = (d_w, e_w)$ is greater than the bid x_i encrypted in $ct_i = (d_i, e_i)$. As in [19], we reduce bid comparison to checking interval membership, namely that $x_w, x_i, \hat{\Delta}_i := (x_w - x_i) \mod p \in [0, B)$ for some fixed bound $B := 2^n \leq p/2$ —see implication (1). The NP relation $\mathcal{R}_{CMP}$ for bid comparison is then as follows:

$$\mathcal{R}_{CMP} = \left\{ \begin{array}{l} g, d_w, e_w, d_i, e_i \in \mathbb{G}_p, n \in \mathbb{N}; \\ x_w, x_i, sk_A \in \mathbb{Z}_p \end{array} \middle| \begin{array}{l} e_w = g^{x_w} d_w^{sk_A} \\ e_i = g^{x_i} d_i^{sk_A} \\ \hat{\Delta}_i = x_w - x_i \mod p \\ x_i, \hat{\Delta}_i \in [0, 2^n - 1] \end{array} \right\} \quad (3)$$

We use Bulletproofs [11] as a building block. Recall from Sect. 2.3 that Bulletproofs take as public input a Pedersen commitment $C = g^x h^r \in \mathbb{G}_p$, and as private input the integer $x \in [0, 2^n)$ and the opening $r \in \mathbb{Z}_p$. Our observation is that an ElGamal ciphertext $ct = (d, e) \in \mathbb{G}_p^2$, encrypted with public key $pk = g^{sk}$ can be seen as a Pedersen commitment under commitment key $ck = (g, d)$. More precisely, the second ciphertext component e can be seen as a Pedersen commitment with opening the secret key sk:

$$ct = (d, e) = (g^r, g^x h^r) = (g^r, g^x g^{skr}) = (d, g^x d^{sk}) \quad (4)$$

The above equation means that the auctioneer can use the ciphertext $ct_i = (d_i, e_i)$ and his private key sk_A to prove with Bulletproofs that what the ciphertext decrypts to (the bid x_i) is in the valid range $[0, 2^n)$. Since ElGamal is additively homomorphic, the auctioneer can also derive a ciphertext for the difference $\hat{\Delta}_i = (x_w - x_i) \mod p$ setting

$$ct_{\hat{\Delta}_i} = (d_{\hat{\Delta}_i}, e_{\hat{\Delta}_i}) := (d_w d_i^{-1}, e_w e_i^{-1}) = (g^{r_w - r_i}, g^{\hat{\Delta}_i} pk_A^{r_w - r_i}) = (d_{\hat{\Delta}_i}, g^{\hat{\Delta}_i} d_{\hat{\Delta}_i}^{sk_A}) \tag{5}$$

and prove $\hat{\Delta}_i \in [0, 2^n)$. In Fig. 7 we detail the snark CMP = (CMP.Setup, CMP.Prove, CMP.Verify) to prove correct bid comparison. Thus, it proves that $((g, ct_w, ct_i, n); (x_w, x_i, sk_A)) \in \mathcal{R}_{CMP}$.

Soundness of the Comparison Proof. Due to lack of space we just give the intuitions of why the comparison proofs $\pi_{cmp,i}$ are sound. We just have to argue for honest bidders. If the i-th non-winning bidder is honest, he will not reveal the encryption randomness r_i used to encrypt $ct_i = (d_i, e_i) = (g^{r_i}, g^{x_i} pk_A^{r_i})$ to the auctioneer. Thus, the auctioneer does not known the discrete-log relationship between g, and $d_i = g^{r_i}$, where g is the ElGamal generator. Now, because no one knows a discrete-log relationship between the group elements $g, \mathbf{g}$ that form the verification key vk_{cmp} (they are generated in a publicly verifiable way), it is not difficult to see that $g, d_i, \mathbf{g}$ are also independent elements from the point of view of the auctioneer. Using Theorem 1, the soundness of the bulleproof π_i generated in step 5 of algorithm CMP.Prove of Fig. 7 is guaranteed.

The same applies when arguing the soundness of the bulleptroof $\pi_{\hat{\Delta}_i}$ generated in step 7 of CMP.Prove. The elements $g, d_{\hat{\Delta}_i}, \mathbf{g}$ are independent for the auctioneer, where $d_{\hat{\Delta}_i}$ is the first component of the (homomorphically derived) ciphertext $ct_{\hat{\Delta}_i}$ encrypting $\hat{\Delta}_i := (x_w - x_i) \mod p$. Indeed if r_i is unknown, then g and $d_{\hat{\Delta}_i} = g^{r_w + r_i}$ are independent elements for the point of view of the auctioneer (see Eq. (5)). Therefore, the i-th comparison proof $\pi_{cmp,i} = (\pi_i, \pi_{\hat{\Delta}_i})$ is sound.

CMP.Setup($1^\lambda, n$):

1. $g, \mathbf{g} \xleftarrow{\$} \mathbb{G}_{p(\lambda)}^{2n+1}$ // Independent generators.
2. Output $pk_{cmp} = vk_{cmp} = (g, \mathbf{g})$ // $\mathbf{g}$ for Bulletproofs, and g for ElGamal.

CMP.Prove($pk_{cmp}, (ct_w, ct_i), (x_w, x_i, sk_A)$):

1. Parse $pk_{cmp} = (g, \mathbf{g})$
2. Parse $ct_w = (d_w, e_w), ct_i = (d_i, e_i)$
3. Set $\hat{\Delta} = x_w - x_i \mod p$
4. Set $d_{\hat{\Delta}} = d_w d_i^{-1}, e_{\hat{\Delta}} = e_w e_i^{-1}$
5. $\pi_i \leftarrow$ BP.Prove($\mathbf{g}, (g, d_i, e_i, n), (x_i, sk_A)$)
6. $\pi_{\hat{\Delta}} \leftarrow$ BP.Prove($\mathbf{g}, (g, d_{\hat{\Delta}}, e_{\hat{\Delta}}, n), (\hat{\Delta}, sk_A)$)
7. Output $\pi_{cmp,i} = (\pi_i, \pi_{\hat{\Delta}})$

CMP.Verify($vk_{cmp}, (ct_w, ct_i), \pi_{cmp,i}$):

1. Parse $vk_{cmp} = (g, \mathbf{g})$
2. Parse $ct_w = (d_w, e_w), ct_i = (d_i, e_i)$
3. Parse $\pi_{cmp,i} = (\pi_i, \pi_{\hat{\Delta}})$
4. Set $d_{\hat{\Delta}} = d_w d_i^{-1}, e_{\hat{\Delta}} = e_w e_i^{-1}$
5. $b_i =$ BP.Verify($\mathbf{g}, (g, d_i, e_i, n), \pi_i$)
6. $b_{\hat{\Delta}} =$ BP.Verify($\mathbf{g}, (g, d_{\hat{\Delta}}, e_{\hat{\Delta}}, n), \pi_{\hat{\Delta}}$)
7. If $b_i = 0, b_{\hat{\Delta}} = 0$ output 0 (accept)
8. Else output 1 (reject).

Fig. 7. SNARK to compare two bids x_w, x_i encrypted in ElGamal ciphertexts ct_w, ct_i. Internally, it uses Bulletproofs [11].

3.4   Public Verification

In this phase, the auditor verifies the correct behaviour of all bidders and the auctioneer. Namely, they obtain and verify correct openings of all commitments c_i to ciphertexts ct_i for $i \leq N$, and that the ZKP proofs of the auctioneer are valid. Note that the verifier can be automated on the blockchain in some cases.

The verifier maintains a running list $\mathsf{L_{HB}}$ of honest bids, initially set to all bidders. It does the following:

- *Verify correct openings of commitments to ciphertexts.* Use the algorithm VerCom which in our instantiation takes as input the commitment c_i, the randomness r_i and the ciphertext concatenated with transaction id $ct_i\|txid_i$ and output true if $c_i = \mathsf{Hash}(ct_i\|txid_i\|r_i)$. If the check fails, remove i from the list of honest bidders $\mathsf{L_{HB}}$.
- *Verify incorrect encrypted bids* For each bidder $c \in \mathsf{L_{HB}}$ for which the auctioneer claims ct_c decrypts to incorrect X_c, verify the correct decryption proof $\pi_{\mathsf{dec},c}$ on public input $(g, \mathsf{pk}_A, ct_w, X_c)$. Here g is the ElGamal generator from setup and pk_A is the public key of the auctioneer (can be found on the blockchain). Then, verify X_c is not in the decoding table DecodeTable. Last, remove c from the list of honest bidders $\mathsf{L_{HB}}$.
- *Verify correct decryption of ct_w to winning bid x_w.* First check $w \in \mathsf{L_{HB}}$. Then, run the verification algorithm CDEC.Verify on public input $(g, \mathsf{pk}_A, ct_w, g^{x_w})$ and proof $\pi_{\mathsf{dec},w}$.
- *Verify x_w is the highest bid.* For each non-winning bidder $i \neq w, i \in \mathsf{L_{HB}}$, run the verification algorithm CMP.Verify on public input (ct_w, ct_i) and proof $\pi_{\mathsf{cmp},i}$ using the verification key $\mathsf{vk_{cmp}}$. Here $\mathsf{vk_{cmp}}$ was made publicly available by the auctioneer during setup, ct_w is the ciphertext of the winning bid (for which correct decryption is checked), and for each $i \neq w$ in the honest list, the ciphertext ct_i was published in the bid phase.

An invalid commitment opening to a ciphertext ct_i or an out of range ciphertext ct_i means the i-th bidder is dishonest, so his bid has been discarded correctly. An invalid or missing ZKP proof means the auctioneer is dishonest. If all the ZKP proofs are valid, the auction is valid and the winner wins the auction item and pays the amount x_w.

4   Reducing the Number of Comparison Proofs

The approach described in Sect. 3 requires the auctioneer to generate $N-1$ comparison proofs, one per non-winning bidder. In this section we explain a generic approach that leverages recursive SNARKs to produce a single comparison proof attesting for the $N-1$ comparisons. Note that reducing the number of comparison proofs minimizes the overall proof size, and simplifies the process of verifying the correctness of the auction result. Another interesting effect of the proof size reduction is the cost of publishing the proof on the blockchain. Since it is of size $\mathcal{O}(\log(n))$ the modified scheme is very scalable.

Auction.Setup(1^λ): // Auctioneer

1. Set time bounds T_b, T_r, T_v
2. Set $n \in \mathbb{N}$ // Upper bound for bids $x \in [0, 2^n)$
3. $\mathsf{pk_{cmp}} = \mathsf{vk_{cmp}} = (g, \mathbf{g}) \leftarrow \mathsf{CMP.Setup}(1^\lambda, n)$ // Transparent setup (see Figure 7)
4. ElGamal setup: // Equivalent to EG.Setup (see Figure 1)
   (a) DecodeTable $\leftarrow \{(x, g^x)\}_{x \in [0, 2^n)} \subset \mathbb{Z}_p \times \mathbb{G}_p$
   (b) Set egparams $= (p, g, n)$ and DecodeTable
5. $(\mathsf{pk}_A, \mathsf{sk}_A) \leftarrow \mathsf{EG.KeyGen}(g)$
6. Publish param $:= (n, \mathsf{egparams}, \mathsf{vk_{cmp}}, \mathsf{pk}_A, T_b, T_r, T_v)$ on the blockchain

Auction.Bid(egparams, pk_A, x): // Bidders. On input bid $x \in [0, 2^n)$:

1. $(c, ct, r, tx_1) \leftarrow \mathsf{SE.Commit}(x, \mathsf{pk}_A)$ // tx_1 hs commitment c
2. Publish tx_1 on the blockchain
3. $tx_2 \leftarrow \mathsf{SE.Reveal}(ct, r, txid_1)$ // tx_2 spends tx_1 and contains encrypted bid ct and commitment opening r.
4. Publish tx_2 on the blockchain

Auction.Result(egparams, $\mathsf{pk_{cmp}}, \mathsf{L_{ct}}, \mathsf{L_{com}}, \mathsf{L_{op}}, \mathsf{sk}_A$): // Auctioneer. Let lists of commitments, openings and ciphertexts $\mathsf{L_{com}} = \{c_i\}_{1 \le i \le N}$, $\mathsf{L_{op}} = \{r_i\}_{1 \le i \le N}$, $\mathsf{L_{ct}} = \{ct_i, tx_{2,i}\}_{1 \le i \le N}$ from the bid phase (before time T_b)

1. $\mathsf{L_{HB}}, \mathsf{L_{BadComm}}, \mathsf{L_{BadEnc}} \leftarrow \emptyset$ // List of honest bidders, bad commitments, and bad encryptions
2. Open sealed bids from bidders. For $i \in [0, N]$:
   (a) $(b_i, x_i) \leftarrow \mathsf{SE.Open}(ct_i, r_i, c_i, tx_{2,i}, \mathsf{sk}_A)$ // Verify opening and decrypt
   (b) If $b_i = \mathsf{true}$ add i to $\mathsf{L_{HB}}$.
   (c) Else, if c_i cannot be decommitted, add i to $\mathsf{L_{BadComm}}$. Else ct_i decrypts to out of range bid X_i, add i to $\mathsf{L_{BadEnc}}$
3. Let $x_w = \max_{i \in \mathsf{L_{HB}}}\{x_i\}$ // The winning bid
4. Create ZKP proofs:
   (a) $\pi_{\mathsf{dec}} = \mathsf{CDEC.Prove}((\mathsf{egparams}, \mathsf{pk}_A, ct_w, x_w), \mathsf{sk}_A)$ // Correct decryption to winning bid x_w
   (b) $\pi_{\mathsf{cmp},i} = \mathsf{CMP.Prove}(\mathsf{pk_{cmp}}, (ct_w, ct_i), (x_w, x_i, \mathsf{sk}_A))$ // Correct comparison for $i \in \mathsf{L_{HB}} \setminus \{w\}$
   (c) $\pi_{\mathsf{dec},i} = \mathsf{CDEC.Prove}((\mathsf{egparams}, \mathsf{pk}_A, ct_i, X_i), \mathsf{sk}_A)$ // Correct decryption to bid X_i out of range for $i \in \mathsf{L_{BadEnc}}$
   (d) Set list $\mathsf{L_{zkp}} := (\pi_{\mathsf{dec}}, \{\pi_{\mathsf{cmp},i}\}_{i \in \mathsf{L_{HB}} \setminus \{w\}}, \{X_i, \pi_{\mathsf{dec},i}\}_{i \in \mathsf{CBList}})$
5. Publish winning bid x_w and lists $\mathsf{L_{HB}}, \mathsf{L_{BadComm}}, \mathsf{L_{BadEnc}}, \mathsf{L_{zkp}}$ to the Blockchain

Auction.Verify(egparams, $\mathsf{vk_{cmp}}, \mathsf{L_{ct}}, \mathsf{L_{op}}, x_w, \mathsf{L_{HB}}, \mathsf{L_{BadComm}}, \mathsf{L_{BadEnc}}, \mathsf{L_{zkp}}$) // Independent party or Blockchain. On input $\mathsf{L_{com}}, \mathsf{L_{op}}, \mathsf{L_{ct}}$ from the bid phase, winning bid x_w, and lists $\mathsf{L_{HB}}, \mathsf{L_{BadComm}}, \mathsf{L_{BadEnc}}, \mathsf{L_{zkp}}$, from the result phase. If any check fails the auctioneer is dishonest, else the result is valid:

1. Check $[1, N] = \mathsf{L_{HB}} \cup \mathsf{L_{BadComm}} \cup \mathsf{L_{BadEnc}}$
2. Verify openings:
   (a) Check True $= \mathsf{SE.Verify}(ct_i, r, c, tx_{2,i})$ // for $i \in \mathsf{L_{HB}} \cup \mathsf{L_{BadEnc}}$
   (b) Check False $= \mathsf{SE.Verify}(ct_i, r, c, tx_{2,i})$ // for $i \in \mathsf{L_{BadComm}}$
3. Check $w \in \mathsf{L_{HB}}$ for winning bid x_w
4. Verify ZKPs:
   (a) Check True $= \mathsf{CDEC.Verify}((\mathsf{egparams}, \mathsf{pk}_A, ct_w, x_w), \pi_{\mathsf{dec}})$ // Correct decryption for x_w
   (b) Check True $= \mathsf{CMP.Verify}(\mathsf{vk_{cmp}}, (x_w, ct_i), \pi_{\mathsf{cmp},i})$ // for $i \in \mathsf{L_{HB}}, i \ne w$
   (c) Check True $= \mathsf{CDEC.Verify}((\mathsf{egparams}, \mathsf{pk}_A, ct_i, X_i), \pi_{\mathsf{dec},i})$ // ct_i decrypts to X_i for $i \in \mathsf{L_{BadEnc}}$
   (d) Check $X_i \notin$ DecodeTable // X_i out of range for $i \in \mathsf{L_{BadEnc}}$

Fig. 8. Auction Scheme with ElGamal encryption and Bulletproofs

Our proposal allows to use any encryption scheme $\mathsf{PKE} = (\mathsf{Setup}, \mathsf{KeyGen},$ $\mathsf{Encrypt}, \mathsf{Decrypt})$ for which it is possible to prove in zero-knowledge correct key-pair generation and correct decryption (namely, without revealing the decryption key). We define the comparison predicate $\mathcal{C}_{\mathsf{CMP}}$ in Fig. 9. In a nutshell, the circuit enforces $x_w > x_i$ and that x_i can be decrypted from an input ciphertext ct_i using the secret key sk_A corresponding to the auctioneer public key pk_A.

Public input Winning bid x_w, auctioneer public key pk_A, i-th ciphertext ct_i.
Private input i-th bid x_i, auctioneer secret key sk_A, randomness r for key generation.
Steps Enforce the following.
   1. $x_w > x_i$
   2. $x_i = \mathsf{Decrypt}(\mathsf{sk}, \mathsf{ct}_i)$
   3. $(\mathsf{pk}_A, \mathsf{sk}_A) = \mathsf{KeyGen}(\mathsf{param}; r)$

Fig. 9. Comparison predicate $\mathcal{C}_{\mathsf{CMP}}$ for a generic encryption scheme.

We also need to ensure recursive comparison is done exactly on the bids encrypted in the ciphertexts $\{\mathsf{ct}_i\}_{i \neq w}$ posted in the blockchain in the bid phase. We propose two ways of enforcing this.

Sequential Recursion. For simplicity, below we assume $N - 1 = 2^d$. We see the 2^d ciphertexts as the leaves of a Merkle tree, whose root is given as public input. An extra gadget is added to the comparison predicate $\mathcal{C}_{\mathsf{CMP}}$: it receives the root of the tree as public input, and the Merkle proof for the i-th leaf as private input. It enforces ct_i is in the tree using the Merkle proof. This approach has the disadvantage that proof generation is sequential. Thus, the auctioneer cannot generate $\pi_{\mathsf{cmp},i}$ at the same time than $\pi_{\mathsf{cmp},i-1}$.

Parallel Recursion. Now we assume $N - 1 = 2^d - 1$. To be able to batch proof generation we see the ciphertexts as the $2^d - 1$ root nodes of a Merkle tree of depth $d - 1$. We define the hash at node i as $h_i = \mathsf{Hash}(\mathsf{ct}_i, h_{i,0}, h_{i,1})$, where $h_{i,b}$ denotes the hashes of the two children of node i. The extra gadget of $\hat{\mathcal{C}}_{\mathsf{CMP}}$ this time receives as public input the hash h_i, and as private inputs, the two child ciphertexts and the two child hashes. It enforces correct hash generation. The downside with respect the previous approach is that the complexity is increased because now two child proofs must be verified in the recursive circuit $\hat{\mathcal{C}}_{\mathsf{CMP}}$ (instead of one proof verification as in the sequential recursion). However, note that to generate proofs at layer k of the tree, the recursive prover only needs two proofs from the previous layer $k - 1$, and all the proofs in the same layer can be parallelised. Thus, we can parallelise proof generation in batches of $2^{d-1}, 2^{d-2}, \ldots, 2$ sizes.

A Bypassing the Comparison Proof of [19]

Let x_w the winning bid, and let x_i any other bid. The authors of [19] observe that if $x_w, x_i, \Delta_i \mod q \in [0, q/2]$, where $\Delta_i := x_w - x_i$, then $x_w > x_i$. Thus, since the winning bid x_w is known to everyone, the comparison proof for "$x_w > x_i$" can be accomplished with two range proofs: one to prove "$x_i \in [0, q/2)$", and another to prove "$\Delta_i \bmod q \in [0, q/2)$".

The range proof used in [19] is the Σ-protocol due to Brickell et al. [10]. See Fig. 10 for a description of the protocol. An (honest) prover, that knows an integer $x \in [0, B)$, convinces the verifier that $x \in [-B, 2B)$. Note the gap in the ranges, which is also observed in [19]. Since bids cannot be negative (at least if aim to be the highest bid), the authors assumed that the interval membership was reduced to $[0, 2B)$ and set the upper bound to $B = q/4$ accordingly. Our observation is that the difference $\Delta_i = x_w - x_i$ (without modulus reduction) can be negative. Below we show how a malicious prover (auctioneer) can generate a valid proof for $\Delta_i \in [-B, 0)$ that convinces the verifier that $\Delta_i \in [-B, 2B)$. In other words, how the malicious auctioneer can generate a valid comparison proof that does not attest for the veracity of "$x_w > x_i$".

The Attack. Suppose the difference between the highest bid x_1, and the second-highest bid x_2, is less than $B < q/4$ and that a malicious auctioneer announces the winning bid to be $x_w := x_2$. Thus $\Delta_1 = x_w - x_1 \in [-B, 0]$. The malicious prover (auctioneer), instead of following the steps of Fig. 10 proceeds slighlty different:

- In step 1 (commit), the only difference is that the auctioneer chooses $w_1 \in [-\Delta, B]$ (instead of $w_1 \in [0, B]$).
- In step 3 (response), if challenge bit is $e = 1$ the auctioneer always sends $m = \Delta + w_1$, (and the other response n).

To see why verification passes, it is enough to observe that $w_1 \in [0, B]$ (because $-\Delta$ is positive), so the verifier checks will pass in case the challenge bit is $e = 0$. Also, $m \in [0, B]$ which follows from assuming $\Delta \in [-B, 0]$ and $w_1 \in [-\Delta, B]$, so if $e = 1$ the verifier checks will also pass.

Public input Pedersen commitment $C = G^x H^o$, and upper bound B.
Private input Integer $x \in [0, B)$, and opening o.

1. **Commit.** The prover (auctioneer) picks $w_1 \in [0, B]$, sets $w_2 = w_1 - B$ and commits to w_1, w_2 with Pedersen using openings r_1, r_2. It sends commitments $W_1 = G^{w_1} H^{r_1}, W_2 = G^{w_2} H^{r_2}$ to the verifier.
2. **Challenge.** The verifier picks a random challenge bit e and sends it to the prover.
3. **Response.** The prover sends one of the following responses to the verifier, based on the challenge bit e:
   - If $e = 0$ the prover sends w_1, w_2, r_1, r_2 to the verifier. The verifier checks $w_1 \in [0, B]$, $w_2 = B - w_1$, and $W_i = G^{w_i} H^{r_i}$ for $i \in \{1, 2\}$.
   - Else $e = 1$, and the prover sends $m = x + w_j$, opening $n = o + r_j$, and index j such that $m \in [0, B]$. The verifier checks $C W_j = G^m H^n$, and $m \in [0, B]$.

Fig. 10. Range proof from [10] used in the comparison proof of [19]. It convinces the verifier that $x \in [-B, 2B]$

References

1. Abe, M., Suzuki, K.: M + 1-st price auction using homomorphic encryption. In: Naccache, D., Paillier, P. (eds.) PKC 2002. LNCS, vol. 2274, pp. 115–124. Springer, Heidelberg (2002). https://doi.org/10.1007/3-540-45664-3_8
2. Alvarez, R., Nojoumian, M.: Comprehensive survey on privacy-preserving protocols for sealed-bid auctions. Comput. Secur. **88** (2020). https://doi.org/10.1016/j.cose.2019.03.023
3. Bag, S., Hao, F., Shahandashti, S.F., Ray, I.G.: SEAL: sealed-bid auction without auctioneers. IEEE Trans. Inf. Forensics Secur. **15**, 2042–2052 (2020)
4. Baudron, O., Stern, J.: Non-interactive private auctions. In: Syverson, P. (ed.) FC 2001. LNCS, vol. 2339, pp. 364–377. Springer, Heidelberg (2002). https://doi.org/10.1007/3-540-46088-8_28
5. Ben-Sasson, E., Chiesa, A., Tromer, E., Virza, M.: Scalable zero knowledge via cycles of elliptic curves. In: Garay, J.A., Gennaro, R. (eds.) CRYPTO 2014. LNCS, vol. 8617, pp. 276–294. Springer, Heidelberg (2014). https://doi.org/10.1007/978-3-662-44381-1_16
6. Bitansky, N., et al.: The hunting of the SNARK. J. Cryptol. **30**(4), 989–1066 (2017). https://doi.org/10.1007/s00145-016-9241-9
7. Blass, E.-O., Kerschbaum, F.: Strain: a secure auction for blockchains. In: Lopez, J., Zhou, J., Soriano, M. (eds.) ESORICS 2018. LNCS, vol. 11098, pp. 87–110. Springer, Cham (2018). https://doi.org/10.1007/978-3-319-99073-6_5
8. Bowe, S., Grigg, J., Hopwood, D.: Halo: recursive proof composition without a trusted setup. Cryptology ePrint Archive, Report 2019/1021 (2019). https://eprint.iacr.org/2019/1021
9. Brandt, F.: How to obtain full privacy in auctions. Int. J. Inf. Secur. **5**(4), 201–216 (2006)
10. Brickell, E.F., Chaum, D., Damgård, I.B., van de Graaf, J.: Gradual and verifiable release of a secret (extended abstract). In: Pomerance, C. (ed.) CRYPTO 1987. LNCS, vol. 293, pp. 156–166. Springer, Heidelberg (1988). https://doi.org/10.1007/3-540-48184-2_11
11. Bünz, B., Bootle, J., Boneh, D., Poelstra, A., Wuille, P., Maxwell, G.: Bulletproofs: short proofs for confidential transactions and more. In: 2018 IEEE Symposium on Security and Privacy, pp. 315–334. IEEE Computer Society Press, San Francisco, CA, USA, 21–23 May 2018. https://doi.org/10.1109/SP.2018.00020
12. Cachin, C.: Efficient private bidding and auctions with an oblivious third party. In: Motiwalla, J., Tsudik, G. (eds.) ACM CCS 99, pp. 120–127. ACM Press, Singapore, 1–4 November 1999. https://doi.org/10.1145/319709.319726
13. Chaum, D., Pedersen, T.P.: Wallet databases with observers. In: Brickell, E.F. (ed.) CRYPTO 1992. LNCS, vol. 740, pp. 89–105. Springer, Heidelberg (1993). https://doi.org/10.1007/3-540-48071-4_7
14. David, B., Gentile, L., Pourpouneh, M.: FAST: fair auctions via secret transactions. In: Ateniese, G., Venturi, D. (eds.) Applied Cryptography and Network Security. ACNS 2022. LNCS, vol. 13269, pp. 727–747. Springer, Cham (2022). https://doi.org/10.1007/978-3-031-09234-3_36
15. Dreier, J., Jonker, H., Lafourcade, P.: Defining verifiability in e-auction protocols. In: Chen, K., Xie, Q., Qiu, W., Li, N., Tzeng, W. (eds.) 8th ACM Symposium on Information, Computer and Communications Security, ASIA CCS '13, Hangzhou, China, 08–10 May 2013, pp. 547–552. ACM (2013)

16. Dreier, J., Lafourcade, P., Lakhnech, Y.: Formal verification of e-auction protocols. In: Basin, D., Mitchell, J.C. (eds.) POST 2013. LNCS, vol. 7796, pp. 247–266. Springer, Heidelberg (2013). https://doi.org/10.1007/978-3-642-36830-1_13

17. ElGamal, T.: A public key cryptosystem and a signature scheme based on discrete logarithms. In: Blakley, G.R., Chaum, D. (eds.) CRYPTO 1984. LNCS, vol. 196, pp. 10–18. Springer, Heidelberg (1985). https://doi.org/10.1007/3-540-39568-7_2

18. Franklin, M.K., Reiter, M.K.: The design and implementation of a secure auction service. IEEE Trans. Softw. Eng. **22**(5), 302–312 (1996)

19. Galal, H.S., Youssef, A.M.: Verifiable sealed-bid auction on the Ethereum blockchain. In: Zohar, A., et al. (eds.) FC 2018. LNCS, vol. 10958, pp. 265–278. Springer, Heidelberg (2019). https://doi.org/10.1007/978-3-662-58820-8_18

20. Goldwasser, S., Micali, S.: Probabilistic encryption. J. Comput. Syst. Sci. **28**(2), 270–299 (1984)

21. Kothapalli, A., Setty, S., Tzialla, I.: Nova: Recursive zero-knowledge arguments from folding schemes. In: Dodis, Y., Shrimpton, T. (eds.) Advances in Cryptology – CRYPTO 2022, Part IV. CRYPTO 2022. LNCS, vol. 13510, pp. 359–388. Springer, Cham (2022). https://doi.org/10.1007/978-3-031-15985-5_13

22. Lafourcade, P., Nopere, M., Picot, J., Pizzuti, D., Roudeix, E.: Security analysis of auctionity: a blockchain based e-auction. In: Benzekri, A., Barbeau, M., Gong, G., Laborde, R., Garcia-Alfaro, J. (eds.) FPS 2019. LNCS, vol. 12056, pp. 290–307. Springer, Cham (2020). https://doi.org/10.1007/978-3-030-45371-8_18

23. Li, H., Xue, W.: A blockchain-based sealed-bid e-auction scheme with smart contract and zero-knowledge proof. Secur. Commun. Netw. **2021**, 5523394:1–5523394:10 (2021)

24. Lipmaa, H., Asokan, N., Niemi, V.: Secure vickrey auctions without threshold trust. In: Blaze, M. (ed.) FC 2002. LNCS, vol. 2357, pp. 87–101. Springer, Heidelberg (2003). https://doi.org/10.1007/3-540-36504-4_7

25. Naor, M., Pinkas, B., Sumner, R.: Privacy preserving auctions and mechanism design. In: Feldman, S.I., Wellman, M.P. (eds.) Proceedings of the First ACM Conference on Electronic Commerce (EC-99), Denver, CO, USA, 3–5 November 1999, pp. 129–139. ACM (1999). https://doi.org/10.1145/336992.337028

26. Nurmi, H., Salomaa, A.: Cryptographic protocols for Vickrey auctions. Group Decis. Negot. **2**(4), 363–373 (1993)

27. Schlegel, J.C., Mamageishvili, A.: On-chain auctions with deposits. CoRR abs/2103.16681 (2021). https://arxiv.org/abs/2103.16681

28. Shi, Z., de Laat, C., Grosso, P., Zhao, Z.: Integration of blockchain and auction models: a survey, some applications, and challenges. IEEE Commun. Surv. Tutor. **25**(1), 497–537 (2023). https://doi.org/10.1109/COMST.2022.3222403

29. Vickrey, W.: Counterspeculation, auctions, and competitive sealed tenders. J. Financ. **16**, 8–37 (1961)

Consolidation of Ground Truth Sets for Weakness Detection in Smart Contracts

Monika di Angelo$^{(\boxtimes)}$ and Gernot Salzer

TU Wien, Vienna, Austria
{monika.di.angelo,gernot.salzer}@tuwien.ac.at

Abstract. Smart contracts are small programs on the blockchain that often handle valuable assets. Vulnerabilities in smart contracts can be costly, as time has shown over and over again. Countermeasures are high in demand and include best practice recommendations as well as tools supporting development, program verification, and post-deployment analysis. Many tools focus on detecting the absence or presence of a subset of the known vulnerabilities, delivering results of varying quality. Most comparative tool evaluations resort to selecting a handful of tools and testing them against each other. In the best case, the evaluation is based on a smallish ground truth. For Ethereum, there are commendable efforts by several author groups to manually classify contracts. However, a comprehensive ground truth is still lacking.

In this work, we construct a ground truth based on publicly available benchmark sets for Ethereum smart contracts with manually checked ground truth data. We develop a method to unify these sets. Additionally, we devise strategies for matching entries that pertain to the same contract, such that we can determine overlaps and disagreements between the sets and consolidate the disagreements. Finally, we assess the quality of the included ground truth sets. Our work reduces inconsistencies, redundancies, and incompleteness while increasing the number of data points and their heterogeneity.

Keywords: analysis · benchmark · Ethereum · security · vulnerability

1 Introduction

To support the development of Ethereum smart contracts (SCs) and to analyze SCs that have been deployed, over 140 tools were released until mid-2021 [11], and new tools keep appearing. The sheer number of tools makes it difficult to choose an appropriate one for a particular use case. Moreover, it is difficult to assess the effectiveness of the many methods proposed, and to judge the relevance of various extensions. Tool comparisons can facilitate the selection process. However, many tool surveys are based on academic publications that focus on the methods employed by the tools, or on whitepapers of the tools themselves. For a thorough quality assessment of the tools, it is necessary to also install and systematically test the tools – preferably with an appropriate ground truth set of SCs.

© International Financial Cryptography Association 2024
A. Essex et al. (Eds.): FC 2023 Workshops, LNCS 13953, pp. 439–455, 2024.
https://doi.org/10.1007/978-3-031-48806-1_28

Given the scarce availability of an appropriate ground truth, tool developers adopted the practice of comparing their tool to previous ones, often with the somewhat biased intention of demonstrating the superiority of their tool in a particular respect. This approach is justified by the need for an evaluation despite the lack of an established ground truth. However, there are major concerns about the validity of such evaluations.

Undetermined Quality of Tools: Since the point of reference is unclear, a comparison to something of unknown quality only provides relative information.

Dependence Between Tools: When a new tool builds on tools published earlier, there is a tendency to compare it to exactly those tools in order to show the improvements. With the quality of the base tool(s) not clearly determined, the relative quality assessment remains vague.

Ground Truth (GT). In our context, a *ground truth* for a particular program property is a set of smart contracts (given as source or bytecode) together with assessments that state for each contract whether it satisfies the property or not. As the term truth suggests, these assessments are supposed to be definitive and reliable. To foster trust into the ground truth, it may be accompanied by a specification of the process how the assessments were obtained (e.g. by expert evaluation) or by objective arguments for the assessments (e.g. by specifying program inputs that solicit behavior satisfying the property, or by showing that such inputs do not exist).

Goals and Approach. The primary goal of this work is to compile a unified and consolidated ground truth of SCs with manually labeled properties, starting from GT sets that are publicly available and documented. Ultimately, we aim at a uniformly structured collection of contracts with verified properties that harnesses the individual efforts that have been invested into the original datasets.

Unification. From related work, we collect benchmarks containing GT data. We extract information on the corresponding contracts (like address, source code, bytecode, location of the issue) as well as classifications (properties tested, assessments) and introduce a unique reference for every entry in the original dataset. We clean the data by repairing obvious mishaps and complete it using our database of source codes and chain data.

Consolidation. To consolidate the datasets, we introduce four attributes per contract: the address (with chain and creation block) if the contract has been deployed, as well as unique fingerprints of the source code, the deployment and the deployed bytecode. Based on these attributes, we determine and eliminate discrepancies within the individual datasets. Then, we map the classifications to a common frame of reference, the SWC[1] classes and the DASP[2] scheme. Relying again on the attributes, we determine overlaps between datasets, detect disagreements, and examine their cause.

Quality Assessment. Based on the taxonomy by Bosu et al. [2] for assessing data quality in software engineering, we assess the included GT sets set with regard

---

[1] https://swcregistry.io.
[2] https://dasp.co/.

to the three aspects accuracy, relevance, and provenance. For accuracy, we consider incompleteness, redundancy, and inconsistency; for relevance, we consider heterogeneity, amount of data, and timeliness; for provenance, we consider accessibility and trustworthiness.

2   Definition of Terms

To discuss the data, we use the following terms.

Property, Weakness, Vulnerability: Most contract properties addressed in datasets constitute program weaknesses, with a few exceptions like honeypots. In software engineering at large, vulnerabilities are weaknesses that can be actually exploited, while blockchain literature tends to use the two terms synonymously. Throughout the paper, we prefer the term *weakness*, and use *property* for general statements.

Judgment: If a property holds, the corresponding judgment is "positive". If a property does not hold, the judgment is "negative". If the assessment is inconclusive or does not make sense, the judgment is "not available" (n/a).

Assessment: a triple consisting of a contract, a single property, and a judgment of the latter in the context of the former.

Entry: smallest unit of a dataset according to its authors. Depending on the structure of the dataset, an entry consists of a single assessment or of multiple assessments pertaining to the same contract. We use the term mainly to relate to the original publication accompanying the dataset.

Contradiction: a group of two or more assessments for the same contract and property, but with conflicting judgments.

Duplicates: multiple assessments for the same contract and property with identical judgments.

3   Benchmark Sets with Ground Truth Data

In this section, we specify the selection of the benchmarks sets and give an overview of the contents in the included sets.

3.1   Selection of GT Sets

From the systematic literature review [11], where Rameder et al. identified benchmark sets of smart contracts for the quality assessment of approaches to weakness or vulnerability detection, we extracted all references that contain a ground truth. Moreover, for the years 2021 and 2022, we searched for further GT sets.

Inclusion Criteria. We include all sets that provide a ground truth by either manually checking the contracts or by generating them via deliberate and systematic bug injection.

Exclusion Criteria. We omit sets that reuse the samples of other sets without contributing assessments of their own. Moreover, we exclude sets having been assessed automatically, e.g. by combining the results of selected vulnerability detection tools by majority voting. While they may constitute interesting test data, they do not qualify as a ground truth.

3.2   Structure of the Included Sets

Table 1 lists the datasets that we selected as the basis of our work. They differ regarding the number of assessments per entry, the identification of contracts, the way assessments are specified, and the information provided per contract.

Identification: Usually, contracts are given either by a file with the Solidity source or by a chain address. Only one dataset specifies just an internal identifier, which in most cases contains an address.

Assessments: The majority of datasets provides the assessments in a structured form as `csv`, `json`, `xlsx` or `ods` files. Five datasets encode the weakness and partly also the judgment in the filepath or use prose.

Contract Information: The datasets may provide chain addresses, Solidity sources from Etherscan or elsewhere, deployment and/or runtime bytecodes.

Crafted and Wild Sets. Depending on the provenance of the contracts, we divide the datasets into two groups. The *wild* group comprises eight collections of contracts that have been deployed either on the main or a test chain, hence they all provide chain addresses or source code from Etherscan. The *crafted* sets contain at least some contracts that have not been deployed to a public chain[3]. One set has been obtained from the SWC registry, where it illustrates the SWC taxonomy. Two sets, JiuZhou and SBcurated, are related to tool evaluations. The set NotSoSmartContracts is intended for educational purposes, and the set SolidiFI was generated from Solidity sources by injecting seven types of bugs.

3.3   Summary of Assessments in the Included Sets

Table 1 gives an overview of the assessments in the sets. The first column contains a reference to the publication presenting the set, while the second one gives the number of entries. The subsequent columns quantify the assessments, specifying the total number as well as a breakdown by judgment type. The column for ignored assessments indicates the number of duplicate or contradicting assessments, as discussed in Sect. 5.2.

To compare the weaknesses covered by the sets, we map the individual assessments to the taxonomy provided by the SWC registry (Table 2). Section 5.3 discusses the mapping in detail. Properties not represented in the SWC registry

---

[3] The distinction between *crafted* and *wild* sets is not strict. Crafted sets may contain some contracts from public chains in modified or unmodified form.

Table 1. Included GT Sets.

	Set	reference	entries	total	positive	negative	n/a	ignored	unmapped	weaknesses	SWC classes
				assessments							
wild datasets	CodeSmells	[3]	587	11740	2293	9073	374	1330	5870	20	10
	ContractFuzzer	[8]	379	379	379	0	0	4	0	7	7
	Doublade	[16]	319	319	152	167	0	40	0	5	5
	eThor	[13]	720	720	196	512	12	18	0	1	1
	EthRacer	[10]	127	127	69	47	11	16	0	2	1
	EverEvolvingG.	[19]	344	344	344	0	0	52	271	5	3
	NPChecker	[15]	50	250	28	222	0	31	0	5	5
	Zeus	[9]	1524	10533	2726	7807	0	3210	0	7	7
crafted	JiuZhou	[18]	168	168	68	100	0	3	39	53	33
	NotSoSmartC.		31	34	24	10	0	0	2	18	12
	SBcurated	[5]	143	145	145	0	0	16	0	10	16
	SolidiFI	[6]	350	350	350	0	0	7	0	7	7
	SWCregistry		117	117	76	41	0	1	0	33	33

remain unmapped, leading to unmapped assessments. The last two columns of Table 1 give the number of weaknesses as defined by the set and the number of covered SWC classes. When the number of weaknesses is larger than the number of SWC classes covered, it either means that there are unmapped assessments or that several weaknesses are mapped to the same SWC class.

4   Unified Ground Truth

In this section, we describe the process of merging the selected sets into a unified ground truth. We extract relevant data items, assign unique identifiers to the entries, repair mishaps, normalize the data to obtain a common format, add missing information from other data sources and investigate data variability.

4.1   Extracting Data from the Original Sets

For each repository selected (Sect. 3), we identify the parts pertaining to a ground truth, and use a Python script to extract relevant items. At a minimum, we need information to identify a contract, a property, and a corresponding judgment.

Most sets have not been designed for automated processing. They contain inconsistencies, errors, and information only intelligible to humans. We encountered numerous invalid Ethereum addresses, inconsistent spellings, invalid data formats, and wrong information (like bytecode not corresponding to the given source code). For the sake of transparency, we left the original sets unchanged and integrated the fixes into the Python scripts.

4.2   Completing the Data

To identify duplicate or contradicting assessments, and to arrive at a consolidated ground truth usable in different scenarios, each contract should be given by its source, deployment and runtime code as well as by its chain address (if deployed). Most repositories contain only some of this information. With the help of data from Ethereum's main chain and Etherscan's repository of source code, we were able to complete most missing data.

Contracts with Addresses: [4] We query the respective chain for the bytecodes, and Etherscan for the source code (if available).

Contracts with Source Code: We use the fingerprint of the source code to look it up in an internal database. If there is a match, we retrieve the deployment address and proceed as above. Otherwise, the source code can be compiled to obtain the corresponding bytecode. Given the variability of compilation, this step most likely will not result in code matching code obtained elsewhere, and is thus inferior when searching for duplicates.

Contracts with Bytecode: The contracts considered here all come with an address or some source code. However, to cross-check and to confirm guesses about the chain, we use fingerprints of any provided bytecode to look up public deployments. Moreover, we extract the runtime code from given deployment code.

Fingerprints. To detect identical contracts, we use fingerprints of the code. For source code, we eliminate comments and white space before computing the MD5 hash. A second type of fingerprint additionally eliminates `pragma solidity` statements prior to hashing. For bytecodes, we replace metadata sections inserted by the Solidity compiler with zeros before computing the MD5 hash.

4.3   Variability in the Unified GT Set

We portrait the variability with regard to the contract language (Solidity or EVM bytecode) as well as the range and distribution of Solidity versions and time of deployment.

Contract Identification. We need some reference to a contract, be it an address or a source file. Figure 1 depicts the number of entries in the unified GT set, for which we have an address, a source, both, or neither.

---

[4] Addresses by themselves are not sufficient to identify a contract. Apart from information about the chain, we also need the deployment time if the contract or an ancestor is the result of a CREATE2 operation. However, as the data in the repositories mostly predates the introduction of this operation, we encountered no contract of this type. Hence, for our purposes knowing the address and chain is sufficient. We use the block numbers of deployments only for analyzing changes over time.

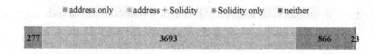

Fig. 1. Addresses (orange and yellow) and Solidity source files (yellow and green) in the entries in the unified GT set. (Color figure online)

In the unified set, there are 4 859 entries in total, of which 4 559 (93.8 %) come with a Solidity source and 3970 (81.7 %) with a deployment address. While 3693 (76.0 %) entries are associated with both, address and source, there are 866 (17.8 %) entries with a Solidity source only, and 277 (4.6 %), for which a source file is neither provided not can be retrieved. This concerns 28 entries in the set EverEvolvingGame, 131 in Zeus, and 118 in eThor. Moreover, 23 entries indicate neither an address nor a source file, but refer to a Solidity file without providing it (all in Zeus).

Chains. Entries with address refer to 2731 unique addresses, with the majority (2461) from the main chain, 268 from Ropsten, and one from Rinkeby. For one address in Zeus, we were not able to locate it on any public chain.

Solidity Versions. Solidity, the main programming language for smart contracts on Ethereum and beyond, has been evolving with several breaking changes so far. In the included sets, we see predominantly versions 0.4.x as depicted in the left part of Fig. 2. While the versions 0.4.x were current throughout 2017 up to early 2018, versions 0.8.x started December 2020 and are still current in mid 2023. The highest Solidity version in the GT sets is v0.6.4.

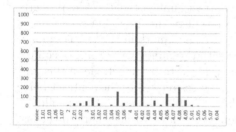

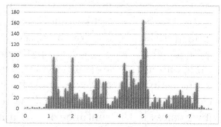

Fig. 2. Distribution of Solidity versions in the included GT sets.

Fig. 3. Distribution of contract deployments/addresses in the included GT sets on a time line (in million blocks).

Deployment Blocks and Forks. To put the addresses into a temporal context, we depict the deployment block in Fig. 3. We count the deployments in bins of 100 000 blocks and depict them on a timeline of blocks (ticks per million blocks).

The latest block in the GT sets is 8 M, while by the end of 2022, the main chain was beyond block 16.3 M. The deployment block also indicates, which EVM opcodes (introduced by a regular fork) were available.[5] This information

---

[5] An important opcode change occurred at block 7.28 M with the introduction of the shift operations, which now appear in most contracts, and CREATE2. At block 9.069 M, SELFBALANCE and CHAINID got introduced, and at block 12.9 M BASEFEE.

may be critical if a detection tool was developed before a particualar opcode was introduced.

5   Consolidated Ground Truth

In this section, we describe the consolidation of the unified GT set. It consists of (i) identifying entries pertaining to the same contract, (ii) marking conflicts within sets, (iii) mapping all assessments to a common taxonomy, (iv) determining the overlaps between the included sets, and (v) analyzing disagreements between the sets.

5.1   Matching Contracts

To detect assessments referring to the same contract, we match the address and the fingerprints of the codes (cf. Sect. 4.2) according to the following considerations:

- Same address and chain means same contract, since none of the contracts in the sets was deployed via CREATE2.
- Most assessments are based on the Solidity source code. As the source usually specifies the admissible compiler versions (except when the missing directive is actually the weakness), the semantics of the program is fixed. So, if two source codes have identical fingerprints and the names of the contracts under consideration are the same, the assessments refer to the same contract.
- Assessments referring to deployment bytecodes with the same fingerprint can be considered as assessing the same contract, unless the checked property is tied to Solidity (like inheritance issues). For the SWC classes, Table 2 indicates the visibility of the weakness by a checkmark in the last column.
- Assessments referring to runtime codes with the same fingerprint are comparable only if the checked property is guaranteed to be detectable in this part of the code. Typically, this holds for weaknesses related to the contract being called by an adversary. For the SWC classes, Table 2 indicates the visibility of a weakness in the runtime code by a non-parenthesized checkmark in the last column. A checkmark in parentheses indicates that the weakness may occur in the constructor and thus is not necessarily detectable in the runtime code.

5.2   Assessments Excluded from the Consolidated Set

For obvious reasons, we ignore assessments where either the judgment is n/a, or where the object of the assessment is ill defined. The first condition affects 397 assessments, mostly from the set CodeSmells. The second one eliminates 153 assessments from the Zeus set, as some contract identifiers do not allow us to extract a valid chain address, and the set does not provide further information.

It is well known that contracts like wallets or tokens have been deployed identically numerous times. Often, this fact is not taken into account when collecting contract samples, such that the same contract may end up in a set multiple

Table 2. Coverage of SWC Classes in the Consolidated GT Set.

SWC-id	#Sets	pos.	neg.	Weakness	Bytecode
100	1	1	1	Function Default Visibility	
101	7	807	322	Integer Overflow and Underflow	(✓)
102	1	1	0	Outdated Compiler Version	
103	3	513	46	Floating Pragma	
104	10	426	1402	Unchecked Call Return Value	(✓)
105	4	62	5	Unprotected Ether Withdrawal	✓
106	3	7	3	Unprotected SELFDESTRUCT	✓
107	12	354	2087	Reentrancy	✓
108	2	3	1	State Variable Default Visibility	
109	3	6	3	Uninitialized Storage Pointer	
110	2	15	8	Assert Violation	(✓)
111	2	2	2	Use of Deprecated Solidity Functions	
112	4	33	6	Delegatecall to Untrusted Callee	(✓)
113	8	331	1359	DoS with Failed Call	(✓)
114	8	535	726	Transaction Order Dependence	✓
115	7	79	1619	Authorization through tx.origin	(✓)
116	5	174	1	Block values as a proxy for time	(✓)
117	2	3	2	Signature Malleability	(✓)
118	4	9	3	Incorrect Constructor Name	
119	3	4	3	Shadowing State Variables	
120	8	315	1423	Weak Sources of Randomness	(✓)
123	1	1	1	Requirement Violation	(✓)
124	4	10	4	Write to Arbitrary Storage Location	✓
125	2	2	2	Incorrect Inheritance Order	
127	2	2	1	Arbitrary Jump	✓
128	5	25	529	DoS With Block Gas Limit	(✓)
129	2	4	1	Typographical Error	
130	2	2	1	Right-To-Left-Override control character	
131	1	2	2	Presence of unused variables	(✓)
132	5	16	566	Unexpected Ether balance	(✓)
133	2	2	3	Hash Collisions	(✓)
134	2	18	0	Message call with hardcoded gas amount	(✓)
135	2	12	525	Code With No Effects	(✓)
136	2	3	3	Unencrypted Private Data On-Chain	
995	2	2	1	Short Address Attack	✓
996	3	51	1	Honey Pot	✓
997	3	86	530	Locked Ether	(✓)
999	1	3	7	Other Arithmetic Issue	(✓)

(✓) provided the weakness does not occur exclusively in the constructor

448   M. di Angelo and G. Salzer

times, albeit under different addresses. Therefore, we check the sets for multiple assessments of the same code, to find contradictions and duplicates.

Surprisingly, the Zeus set contains 18 contradictions already on the level of its own identifiers (meaning that the same identifier is listed multiple times, with diverging assessments) and 30 more when applying the criteria laid out in the last section. Moreover, we find 103 conflicts in the set CodeSmells, 6 in Doublade, and 3 in JiuZhou. These assessments are excluded from the consolidated set.

For duplicates, all but one assessment are redundant and can be ignored. We find duplicates in almost every set (the number in parentheses gives the ignored assessments): CodeSmells (853), ContactFuzzer (4), Doublade (34), eThor (6), EthRacer (5), EverEvolvingGame (52), NPChecker (31), SBcurated (16), SolidiFI (7), SWCregistry (1), and Zeus (3009).

For a summary of the exclusions, see the column 'ignored' in Table 1.

5.3 Mapping of Individual Assessments to a Common Taxonomy

To compare assessments in different sets, we map the properties of each set to classes of a suitable taxonomy. The SWC registry[6] provides such a widely used taxonomy with 37 weakness classes. Each has a numeric identifier, a title, a CWE parent and some code samples.

Coverage of SWC Classes. Table 2 shows how well the SWC classes are covered by positive and negative assessments, and how many sets contribute assessments to the class. Popular weaknesses with seven or more contributing GT sets are marked in gray. At the bottom, we add the classes 995–999 to account for weaknesses missing from the SWC registry.

Even after combining all GT sets into a unified ground truth, the coverage of the SWC classes remains highly uneven. This can be attributed to the intention behind most benchmark sets: to support the test of tools for automated vulnerability detection. And tools aim for "interesting" weaknesses.

Comparison of Weaknesses. It is intrinsically difficult to compare weaknesses across GT sets due to (i) vague or missing *definitions* of weaknesses, (ii) the unclear *relationship* between definitions, (iii) the ambiguous *mapping* of a weakness to a corresponding class, and (iv) heterogeneous *criteria for structuring* weaknesses, mixing cause and effect or different levels of the protocol/software stack. The definitions provided by GT authors are rarely a perfect match for a taxonomy. Therefore, when comparing weaknesses via a taxonomy, we have to check disagreements manually to distinguish mismatches of definitions from contradicting assessments.

5.4 Overlaps

To find disagreements between the cleaned GT sets, we first determine their overlap. For each pair of sets, Table 3 gives the number of non-ignored assessments that map to the same SWC class. The diagonal shows the total number

---
[6] https://swcregistry.io.

Table 3. Overlap of Mapped Assessments in the Consolidated GT Set.

Set	CodeSmells	ContractFuzzer	Doublade	eThor	EthRacer	EverEvolvingG	NPChecker	Zeus	JiuZhou	NotSoSmartC	SBcurated	SolidiFI	SWCregistry
CodeSmells	5300	6	4	26	0	0	14	145	0	1	0	0	0
ContractFuzzer	6	375	6	0	0	0	3	15	0	0	10	0	0
Doublade	4	6	279	2	0	0	2	10	0	0	7	0	0
eThor	26	0	2	702	0	0	25	691	0	0	0	0	0
EthRacer	0	0	0	0	111	0	0	5	0	0	0	0	0
EverEvolvingG.	0	0	0	0	0	65	0	0	0	0	0	0	0
NPChecker	14	3	2	25	0	0	219	128	0	0	0	0	0
Zeus	145	15	10	691	5	0	128	7323	0	0	1	0	0
JiuZhou	0	0	0	0	0	0	0	0	129	0	0	0	2
NotSoSmartC	1	0	0	0	0	0	0	0	0	32	7	0	0
SBcurated	0	10	7	0	0	0	0	1	0	7	129	0	31
SolidiFI	0	0	0	0	0	0	0	0	0	0	0	343	0
SWCregistry	0	0	0	0	0	0	0	0	2	0	31	0	116

of mapped assessments per GT set. The upper-left block relates *wild* sets, while the lower-right block concerns the *crafted* ones. As to be expected, there is more overlap within the *wild* group than within the *crafted* one or between the groups. SBcurated mixes crafted and wild contracts, with some crafted ones taken from the SWCregistry. Of 20 498 cleaned assessments, 18 409 appear in only one set, while 2 089 occur in two or more.

5.5 Disagreements and Errors

In Table 3, overlaps with disagreements are marked gray. Of the 2 098 overlapping assessments, 458 disagree with at least one other, involving eight GT sets and six SWC classes (Table 4).

The disagreements constitute an interesting area of investigation. While some disagreements are due to diverging definitions of weaknesses that were mapped to the same SWC class, quite a few turn out to be inconsistencies under the authors' original definitions. Table 4 summarizes the results of our manual evaluation. For each affected set, it gives the total number of assessments that disagree with an assessment of another set as well as a breakdown by SWC class. A table entry is marked red if our evaluation revealed assessment errors, giving also the number of such errors.

Table 4. Number of Disagreements in the Unified GT Set, with the Errors.

Dataset	total	104	107	113	114	120	997
CodeSmells	34	8	6 of 9	8	:	7 of 7	2 of 2
ContractFuzzer	13	7	:	:	:	4 of 4	2
Doublade	6	3	3 of 3	:	:	:	:
eThor	166	:	166	:	:	:	:
EthRacer	2	:	:	:	2 of 2	:	:
NotSoSmartC	1	:	1	:	:	:	:
NPChecker	25	3 of 6	1 of 7	7	1 of 2	2 of 3	:
Zeus	211	18	3 of 163	15	1 of 4	11	:

Table 5. Number of Manually Checked Assessments, with the Errors.

Set \ SWC	101	104	107	112	113	114	115	120	997
CodeSmells	:	1	3	:	3	:	:	:	2 of 7
ContractFuzzer	:	10	3	4 of 11	:	:	:	4	9
Doublade	:	1	2	:	:	:	1	:	:
NPChecker	:	1 of 4	:	:	:	:	:	:	:
SBcurated	:	1	2	:	:	:	:	:	:
Zeus	4 of 6	7	:	:	1	4	:	:	:

Since reentrancy is the most popular weakness, it appears in 12 GT sets and gives rise to most overlaps: of the 2 098 overlapping assessments, 1 480 pertain to reentrancy (SWC 107). Thus, it is not surprising that we observe the highest number of disagreements (182) and errors (13) for reentrancy.

With 42 disagreements, SWC 104 is second. However, we identified only three errors, with the other disagreements resulting from diverging definitions. While SWC 113 shows no errors, half of the disagreements for SWC 114, 120 and 997 are errors.

To gain further insights into the quality of the assessments, we randomly select 80 assessments from the consolidated ground truth, in order to manually check them. Table 5 shows, for each GT set and SWC class, the number of checked assessments as well as the number of errors.

6   Discussion

6.1   Data Quality

To assess the data quality of the GT sets along the dimensions proposed by Bosu et al. [2], we define scores for each criterion as specified in Table 6. The resulting overview of the data quality is shown in Table 7.

Table 6. Criteria for Data Quality Assessment.

	Aspect	Score	Criterion
Accuracy	completeness	+	source and bytecode are provided (and addresses if any)
		o	some source and bytecodes provided
		−	no code files are provided
	irredundancy	+	duplicates [%] ≤ 1
		o	$1 >$ duplicates [%] < 10
		−	duplicates [%] ≥ 10 (without bytecode)
	consistency	−	the dataset shows contradictions and conflicts
		o	Tables 4 or 5 show inconsistent or incorrect assessments
		+	otherwise
Relevance	heterogeneity		Sections 4.3 and 6.1 detail the heterogeneity of the GT sets
		−	All sets show low heterogeneity.
	data quantity		Table 1 lists the number of assessments A and weaknesses W
		+	$A > 1000 \wedge W > 5$
		−	$A < 500 \wedge W < 5$
		o	otherwise
	timeliness	−	All sets lack recent contracts (Sect. 4.3).

Table 7. Data Quality of Ground Truth Sets.

Quality Aspect		Set	CodeSmells	ContractFuzzer	Doublade	eThor	EthRacer	EverEvolvingG	NPChecker	Zeus	JiuZhou	NotSoSmartC	SBcurated	SolidiFI	SWCregistry	Consolidated GT
						wild							crafted			
Accuracy	completeness		−	+	o	+	−	−	−	−	o	o	o	o	+	+
	irreduncancy		o	+	o	+	o	−	−	−	+	+	+	o	+	+
	consistency		−	o	−	+	o	+	o	−	−	+	+	+	+	o
Relevance	heterogeneity		−	−	−	−	−	−	−	−	o	−	o	−	o	o
	data quantity		+	o	o	o	−	o	o	+	o	o	o	o	o	+
	timeliness		−	−	−	−	−	−	−	−	−	−	−	−	−	−

Accuracy. All sets provide a minimum of data, but we had to complete the data of about two thirds of the sets. Redundancy exists in many *wild* GT sets, to varying degrees. The main concern regards inconsistencies – the key aspect of a GT – which we encountered in six *wild* GT sets. We improved the data quality (i) by data completion, (ii) by eliminating redundant and contradictory assessments within sets, and (iii) by resolving disagreements between sets. Thus, we could increase the accuracy in the consolidated GT set in all aspects. However, random inspections revealed further inconsistencies; the overall accuracy would benefit from further checks.

Relevance. The GT sets mostly lack heterogeneity, often provide a smallish amount of data, and above all lack recent data. By merging 13 GT sets, we could improve the amount of data (number of positive and especially negative samples) and some aspects of heterogeneity, like the number of weaknesses covered. However, there is still a bias towards a small range of Solidity versions, deployments between 2016 and 2018, source code that has been published for some reason on Etherscan, and popular vulnerabilities.

6.2   Related Work

Each of the thirteen original datasets can be regarded as distantly related work; see Sect. 3 for a description. Concerning the construction of a unified GT set, we only find AutoMESC [14]. In this work, Soud et al. choose five source code datasets [4,7,12,17,18] that address 10 vulnerabilities, which are detected by one or more of the tools HoneyBadger, Mythril, Maian, Osiris, Slither, SmartCheck, Solhint. They apply as inclusion criteria: recent (up to three years old), public, Ethereum, corresponding publication or GitHub repo; and exclude commercial and competition datasets, and sets that just provide one sample per vulnerability. For unification, they use a file-ID per contract (without checking for non-obvious duplicates). For consolidation (identifying duplicates, mapping the assessments to a common taxonomy, and resolving contradictory assessments), they discard the original classification, and replace it with a simple majority vote of the seven selected tools if those claim to detect the weakness (after mapping the tool findings to a common taxonomy). They claim that there is neither redundancy nor inconsistency in the five datasets included.

6.3   Challenges in Identifying Weaknesses

Ambiguous Definitions of Weaknesses. Hardly any weakness possesses a commonly accepted, precise definition. As a consequence, seemingly contradictory assessments of a contract by different datasets may actually result from applying subtly different definitions.

Weakness vs. Vulnerability. There is no agreement among dataset authors whether to aim for exploitable or potential issues.

Intended Purpose. The verdict on whether a weakness is considered a vulnerability also depends on the purpose of a contract. An apparent weakness may be actually the intended behavior of the contract (e.g. a faucet that "leaks" Ether).

Contracts in Isolation. The included datasets consider single-contract weaknesses only (discounting the attack contract). However, vulnerabilities may be the result of several interacting contracts. A single contract may not provide sufficient context to be classified as vulnerable on its own.

6.4   Reservations About Majority Voting

Due to the scarcity of GT data, some authors resort to pseudo-GT data. They run several vulnerability detection tools on selected contracts and obtain the judgment by comparing the number of positive results to a threshold. This approach is debatable for the following reasons.

Weakness vs. Vulnerability. Most tools detect code patterns that indicate a weakness, regardless of whether it can be actually exploited. Hence, false positives (and, to a lesser extent, false negatives) are rather the norm than the exception. Thus, majority vote may turn false positives into a positive assessment.

Tool Genealogy. Tools form families by being derived from common ancestors (like Oyente), by implementing the same approach (like symbolic execution, taint analysis, or fuzzing), or by relying on the same basic components (like GigaHorse, Rattle, Z3, or Soufflé). Related tools may misjudge a contract in a similar way and outnumber tools with the correct result.

Diverging Definitions of Weaknesses. Even if labeled the same, the weaknesses detected by any two tools are not quite the same. Rather, we are faced with tools voting on a weakness that is more or less similar to what they can detect.

7   Conclusion

Publicly available ground truth data for smart contract weaknesses is scarce, but much needed. Our consolidated ground truth is an appreciation of the commendable efforts by others and hopefully renders the included GT sets more usable to the community. The consolidated ground truth described in this paper is available from http://github.com/gsalzer/cgt For an extended version of this paper, see [1].

Future Work. *Granularity.* This unified and consolidated GT set is constructed on contract level. Information on the location of weaknesses within the contracts, like the line number in the source or the offset in the byte code, is available only for two small datasets, and was omitted here. *Severity Level.* Assigning a severity level to a weakness would further improve the GT set, but is a difficult topic on its own. *Updates* are important. We invite everyone to contribute by adding GT collections, taxonomies, levels of granularity or severity, proofs and exploits.

References

1. di Angelo, M., Salzer, G.: Consolidation of ground truth sets for weakness detection in smart contracts. arXiv preprint 2304.11624 (2023). https://doi.org/10.48550/arXiv.2304.11624
2. Bosu, M.F., MacDonell, S.G.: A taxonomy of data quality challenges in empirical software engineering. In: 2013 22nd Australian Software Engineering Conference, pp. 97–106. IEEE (2013). https://doi.org/10.1109/ASWEC.2013.21
3. Chen, J., Xia, X., Lo, D., Grundy, J., Luo, X., Chen, T.: Defining smart contract defects on ethereum. IEEE Trans. Softw. Eng. (2020). https://doi.org/10.1109/TSE.2020.2989002
4. Durieux, T., Ferreira, J.F., Abreu, R., Cruz, P.: Empirical review of automated analysis tools on 47,587 Ethereum smart contracts. In: Proceedings of the ACM/IEEE 42nd International Conference on Software Engineering, pp. 530–541. ACM, New York, NY, USA (2020). https://doi.org/10.1145/3377811.3380364
5. Ferreira, J.F., Cruz, P., Durieux, T., Abreu, R.: SmartBugs: a framework to analyze solidity smart contracts. In: 35th IEEE/ACM International Conference on Automated Software Engineering (ASE 2020), pp. 1349–1352. ACM (2020). https://doi.org/10.1145/3324884.3415298
6. Ghaleb, A., Pattabiraman, K.: How effective are smart contract analysis tools? evaluating smart contract static analysis tools using bug injection. In: Proceedings of the 29th ACM SIGSOFT International Symposium on Software Testing and Analysis, pp. 415–427. ISSTA 2020, Association for Computing Machinery (2020). https://doi.org/10.1145/3395363.3397385
7. Grech, N., Brent, L., Scholz, B., Smaragdakis, Y.: Gigahorse: thorough, declarative decompilation of smart contracts. In: 2019 IEEE/ACM 41st International Conference on Software Engineering (ICSE), pp. 1176–1186. IEEE (2019). https://doi.org/10.1109/ICSE.2019.00120
8. Jiang, B., Liu, Y., Chan, W.K.: Contractfuzzer: fuzzing smart contracts for vulnerability detection. In: Proceedings of the 33rd ACM/IEEE International Conference on Automated Software Engineering, pp. 259–269. ASE 2018, Association for Computing Machinery (2018). https://doi.org/10.1145/3238147.3238177
9. Kalra, S., Goel, S., Dhawan, M., Sharma, S.: ZEUS: analyzing safety of smart contracts. In: NDSS Symposion. NDSS, Internet Society (2018). https://doi.org/10.14722/ndss.2018.23082
10. Kolluri, A., Nikolic, I., Sergey, I., Hobor, A., Saxena, P.: Exploiting the laws of order in smart contracts. In: Proceedings of the 28th ACM SIGSOFT International Symposium on Software Testing and Analysis, pp. 363–373. ISSTA 2019, Association for Computing Machinery, New York, NY, USA (2019). https://doi.org/10.1145/3293882.3330560
11. Rameder, H., Angelo, M.D., Salzer, G.: Review of automated vulnerability analysis of smart contracts on ethereum. Front. Blockchain - Smart Contracts (2022). https://doi.org/10.3389/fbloc.2022.814977
12. Ren, M., et al.: Empirical evaluation of smart contract testing: what is the best choice? In: Proceedings of the 30th ACM SIGSOFT International Symposium on Software Testing and Analysis, pp. 566–579 (2021). https://doi.org/10.1145/3460319.3464837
13. Schneidewind, C., Grishchenko, I., Scherer, M., Maffei, M.: EThor: practical and provably sound static analysis of ethereum smart contracts. In: Proceedings of the ACM Conference on Computer and Communications Security, pp. 621–640 (2020). https://doi.org/10.1145/3372297.3417250

14. Soud, M., Qasse, I., Liebel, G., Hamdaqa, M.: Automesc: automatic framework for mining and classifying ethereum smart contract vulnerabilities and their fixes. arXiv preprint arXiv:2212.10660 (2022). https://doi.org/10.48550/arXiv.2212.10660

15. Wang, S., Zhang, C., Su, Z.: Detecting nondeterministic payment bugs in ethereum smart contracts. Proc. ACM Program. Lang. (PACMPL) 3(189), 1–29 (2019). https://doi.org/10.1145/3360615

16. Xue, Y., et al.: Doublade: unknown vulnerability detection in smart contracts via abstract signature matching and refined detection rules. arXiv preprint arXiv:1912.04466 (2019). https://doi.org/10.48550/arXiv.1912.04466

17. Yashavant, C.S., Kumar, S., Karkare, A.: Scrawld: a dataset of real world ethereum smart contracts labelled with vulnerabilities. arXiv preprint arXiv:2202.11409 (2022). https://doi.org/10.48550/arXiv.2202.11409

18. Zhang, P., Xiao, F., Luo, X.: A framework and dataset for bugs in ethereum smart contracts. In: IEEE International Conference on Software Maintenance and Evolution (ICSME), pp. 139–150. ICSME 2020, IEEE (2020). https://doi.org/10.1109/icsme46990.2020.00023

19. Zhou, S., Yang, Z., Xiang, J., Cao, Y., Yang, Z., Zhang, Y.: An ever-evolving game: evaluation of real-world attacks and defenses in ethereum ecosystem. In: 29th USENIX Security Symposium (USENIX Security 20), pp. 2793–2810. USENIX Security 2020, USENIX Association (2020). https://www.usenix.org/conference/usenixsecurity20/presentation/zhou-shunfan

The Principal–Agent Problem in Liquid Staking

Apostolos Tzinas[1,3(✉)] and Dionysis Zindros[2,3]

[1] National Technical University of Athens, Athens, Greece
tzinas@tzinas.com
[2] Stanford University, Stanford, USA
[3] Common Prefix, Athens, Greece

Abstract. Proof-of-stake systems require stakers to lock up their funds in order to participate in consensus validation. This leads to capital inefficiency, as locked capital cannot be invested in Decentralized Finance (DeFi). *Liquid staking* rewards stakers with fungible tokens in return for staking their assets. These fungible tokens can in turn be reused in the DeFi economy. However, liquid staking introduces unexpected risks, as all delegated stake is now fungible. This exacerbates the already existing Principal–Agent problem faced during any delegation, in which the interests of the delegator (the Principal) are not aligned with the interests of the validator (the Agent). In this paper, we study the Principal–Agent problem in the context of liquid staking. We highlight the dilemma between the choice of *proportional representation* (having one's stake delegated to one's validator of choice) and *fair punishment* (being economically affected only when one's choice is misinformed). We put forth an attack illustrating that these two notions are fundamentally incompatible in an adversarial setting. We then describe the mechanism of *exempt delegations*, used by some staking systems today, and devise a precise formula for quantifying the correct choice of exempt delegation which allows balancing the two conflicting virtues in the rational model.

1 Introduction

When a validator participates in a proof-of-stake protocol, they *bond* their stake, locking it up for a period of time in exchange for rewards. This locked-up stake is *slashed* in case of validator misbehavior such as equivocation. Stakeholders *delegate* their stake to *validators* to also earn rewards. If the validator misbehaves, the funds of the delegator are also slashed. This introduces a *Principal–Agent* problem [20,29] in which the actions of the validator (the *Agent*) affect the capital of the delegator (the *Principal*).

However, staked assets are *illiquid* and cannot be used for other purposes such as in DeFi applications [32] because they are locked up. *Liquid staking* [24] is

A. Tzinas—Supported in part by the Algorand Centres of Excellence MEGA-ACE programme.

A. Essex et al. (Eds.): FC 2023 Workshops, LNCS 13953, pp. 456–469, 2024.
https://doi.org/10.1007/978-3-031-48806-1_29

an attempt to solve this problem by issuing *token representations* of the staked assets that can be freely traded and utilized by stakeholders elsewhere in the blockchain ecosystem.

Liquid staking token representations are most valuable when they are *fungible*. However, this fungibility exacerbates the Principal–Agent problem of delegated stake. A liquid staking system *pools together* stakes from different participants, prompting the question of whom to delegate these pooled funds to. If the system has *proportional representation*, every pool participant decides whom to delegate to *in proportion* to their contributed shares. The crux of the issue arises from the fact that a malicious pool participant can choose to delegate to a colluding validator who then equivocates. This causes a portion of the pooled money to be slashed, affecting every pool participant in proportion to their contributed stake, even if they made no *unwise* delegation decisions, in a situation of *unfair punishment*. This causes a drop in the price of the liquid staking tokens. A rational attacker profits from this price drop by shorting the token.

Our Contributions. Our contributions in this paper are as follows:

1. We introduce two desirable properties in the context of Liquid Staking: *Proportional Representation* and *Fair Punishment*.
2. We showcase the Principal–Agent problem in the Liquid Staking setting by describing a concrete attack leveraging it.
3. We give a precise description of the market conditions that enable this attack, and a formula for a liquid staking system configuration which can avoid it.

Related Work. Proof-of-stake (PoS), introduced by PeerCoin [22], was formalized in later works [5,6,16,18,21]. Slashing [11] is a technique used to achieve economic safety [12] in many PoS systems, among others PoS Ethereum [13,14] and Cosmos [8–10]. Outside of centralized exchanges, liquid staking was introduced independently by the team of Joe Bowman, Brian Crain, Felix Lutsch, Dev Ojha, Meher Roy (from Chorus One and Sikka), and Hyung Yeon Lee (from B-Harvest) in June 2019. First reported as *Delegation Vouchers* [23] they were later analyzed in a comprehensive report [24] with the help of the Liquid Staking Working Group. Lido [1] and Rocket Pool [28] popularized liquid staking in Ethereum, and Quicksilver [7], Stride [30] and pStake [27] in Cosmos. Quicksilver is the first protocol to propose proportional representation, but this is not yet implemented. Besides liquid staking, stake rehypothecation takes the form of restaking (EigenLayer [17]) and cross staking [3]. Exempt delegations, with one name or another, are used in Rocket Pool, and have been proposed for Cosmos [25].

2 Preliminaries

Loans. For the attack we will describe in this paper, some upfront capital is required. Sometimes a portion of this capital is needed only throughout *one* transaction. Towards this purpose, a *flash loan* [19] is obtained, which has zero duration and no funds at risk. We assume that a loan of duration Δt for capital u has an *upfront* cost factor β, an *interest rate* r and the amount to be repaid, including both the principal and interest, is $((1+r)^{\Delta t}+\beta)u$. The term β models the cost factor of a flash loan, which has duration 0. In order to take a non-flash loan, collateral in a different currency must be deposited for the duration of the loan. DeFi protocols typically require overcollateralization. We denote by $\gamma \geq 1$ the collateral ratio required by the loan provider. To take a loan of z in one currency, one must deposit the equivalent value of γz in another currency.

Proof-of-Stake. Proof-of-stake systems are secured by *validators* who propose and vote on blocks. To become a validator in a slashably safe [12] system, a stakeholder must *bond* their stake which locks it up for a particular period of time in return for rewards. Validators promise they will not *equivocate* by signing conflicting blocks. In case of equivocation, a percentage $0 < p \leq 1$ of the locked stake is *slashed* and the validator is permanently deactivated. In the cryptographic model, validators can be *honest* or *adversarial*. The honest validators run the prescribed protocol, and hence never equivocate, whereas the adversarial validators can deviate from the protocol arbitrarily.

Delegation. Since not everyone has the capacity to become a validator, a stakeholder can *delegate* their stake to a validator to participate in the validation process in their stead. The voting power of the validator accounts for the delegated stake, and delegated stake is also slashed in case of validator misbehavior. The stake bonded by a validator themselves and not delegated from others is known as *self-delegation*. Self-delegations as well as stake delegated from others is known as *delegated stake*, and the capital holder of delegated stake is known as the *delegator*, but will also be referred to as the *principal*. A principal can *undelegate* or *redelegate* at any time, but must wait[1] for an *unbonding period* δ.

Liquid Staking. Delegated stake earns rewards, but remains locked and is illiquid. Principals often wish to rehypothecate their delegated stake, for example to take loans [19] or to, more broadly, participate in the DeFi [32] economy. Protocols that enable this ability are known as *liquid staking protocols* [24]. Some such protocols [1,30] operate in the form of smart contracts (*e.g.*, Lido and Rocket Pool in Ethereum) or separate appchains[2] (*e.g.*, Stride, pStake, and Quicksilver in Cosmos). Stakeholders *deposit* their funds into the liquid staking protocol. Upon deposit, these contracts act as delegators and delegate

---

[1] The waiting period may sometimes be *waived* and redelegations allowed instantly if no other redelegations have happened within δ, such as in Cosmos [15]. The important point for us is that, after redelegation has commenced, the redelegated stake is still prone to slashing due to the *old* validator's misbehavior for a period of δ.

[2] An appchain is a separate Cosmos zone, connected with other Cosmos zones using IBC/ICA [33] and functions similarly to a smart contract.

the incoming funds to their choice of validators. They collect this delegated stake into a *pool* and receive staking rewards from these holdings. During the deposit, a new derivative asset is minted, which is given to the depositor as a claim to the delegated stake held by the liquid staking contract. Such derivative tokens, when issued from the same liquid staking contract, are fungible with one another[3]. We are only concerned with liquid staking protocols that are fully fungible. At any time, the derivative asset holder can *redeem* their derivative asset. During redemption, the contract burns the holder's derivative assets and returns the respective assets to the holder. For completeness, we illustrate the basic deposit and withdrawal functionalities of any liquid staking protocol in the full version of this paper [31]. In our treatment, we consider a generic asset that we denominate in ASSET and the respective derivative token, that we denominate in stASSET, issued by an arbitrary liquid staking protocol. We assume a perfectly efficient market for ASSET and stASSET, as well as a sufficiently deep loan market with rates r_A, β_A, and r_{st}, β_{st} respectively.

Exchange Rates. Initially, ASSET and stASSET are priced at a 1:1 exchange rate, as one can be exchanged for the other by redeeming or withdrawing. However, the balance of the liquid staking protocol in ASSET holdings can change with time due to two reasons. Firstly, it continuously receives rewards for staking the ASSET (these rewards are auto-compounded). Secondly, if a validator it delegates to misbehaves, a portion of its ASSET can get slashed. These events do not change the supply of stASSET in the market. The deposit and redemption operations must adjust their price. Let b_0 ASSET denote the amount of ASSET holdings of the liquid staking protocol, and s_0 stASSET denote the total market supply of stASSET that the protocol has issued. When the user deposits b ASSET, the protocol mints $s = b\frac{s_0}{b_0}$ stASSET. On the other hand, when the user burns s ASSET, the protocol returns $b = s\frac{b_0}{s_0}$ delegated ASSET to the user. These delegated ASSET can be unbonded to convert them to ASSET. Because the user can always go back to the protocol and exchange b for s or vice versa, we assume that the price of stASSET denominated in ASSET in the market is the same as the quoted protocol price. We refine this assumption in the full version of this paper [31]. Users can buy and sell stASSET*s* by *swapping* them on-chain [4].

Governance. The choice of which validator the liquid staking protocol's assets are delegated to depends on the particularities of the protocol. In centralized protocols, the decision is taken by a central party or central committee of parties, who may not be the liquid stake holders themselves. Some protocols allow the principals to vote. During the voting process, anyone can propose for a proportion of the protocols's assets to be delegated to a validator of their choosing.

---

[3] The exact fungibility constraints depend on the protocol. For example, stATOM in Stride [30] and stETH in Lido [1] are fully fungible. However, in the proposed Liquidity Staking Module [2] of Cosmos, derivative tokens are only fungible when they have been delegated to the same validator in the same batch.

Each principal can then vote *yes* or *no* to the proposal. Decisions are often taken by weighted majority.

3 Representation

In a staking protocol, whether liquid or not, each principal has an opinion about which validator they wish to delegate to.

Definition 1 (Delegation Wish). *For each principal, we define their delegation wish to be a particular validator of their choice.*

It will generally be desired that these delegation wishes point to honest validators. We formalize this in the notion of *wisdom*.

Definition 2 (Wisdom). *A principal is* wise *if their delegation wish points to an honest validator. Otherwise, the principal is* unwise.

In the liquid staking protocols described in Sect. 2, the decision of which validators to delegate to is up to the majority of the stakeholders. This creates a problem. A stakeholder holding a minority of the stake may wish to delegate this stake to a particular validator, but the rest of the stakeholders can overturn him by a majority vote. Hence, in these protocols we have a situation of *only the majority* being represented, instead of *everyone being equally represented* [26].

On the contrary, in a *proportional representation* system, the majority of the stakeholders decide where to delegate the majority of the stake, but the minority of the stakeholders also decide where to delegate the minority of the stake.

Definition 3 (Proportional Representation). *In a* proportionally represented *liquid staking protocol, each validator is delegated a proportion of the liquid staking pool's* ASSET *equal to the sum of the proportions of* stASSET *held by the principals who wish to delegate to that validator.*

To achieve this, the process of liquid staking becomes different: Each principal must *signal* their *intent* indicating which validator they wish the pool to delegate to. This election mechanism was introduced by Quicksilver [7] even though it has not yet been implemented, at the time of writing.

First, the principal deposits ASSET into the protocol and signals delegation intent to the validator of their choice. Then, the protocol delegates the deposited ASSET to that validator. The principal is now a holder of tradable stASSET representations of the delegated ASSET. This stASSET can now be transferred to a different owner.

At some later time, the stASSET holder may wish to redelegate their underlying ASSET to a new validator. The stASSET holder can *resignal* their delegation intent and the protocol will redelegate the underlying ASSET to the new validator. The goal is for all stASSET holders to be represented proportionally to their stake.

Note that proportional representation may not be instant. Redelegation speeds are limited by the underlying blockchain's unbonding period. Hence, a stASSET holder may have to wait δ before their corresponding ASSETs are redelegated to the validator of their choice.

4   The Principal–Agent Problem

In the proof-of-stake systems described in the previous sections, principals grant permission of their funds to validators so they can participate in consensus on their behalf. Principals have ownership of the stake, but validators have control over it. The stakeholders rely on validators to act according to their best interest: Stay online and follow the protocol. However, validators (the agents) may have extrinsic motivation to misbehave and plot against principals. This creates a conflict of interest that is known as the Principal–Agent problem.

For example, a malicious validator can equivocate, which causes the principal's funds to be slashed. If the malicious validator has limited self-delegation and no reputation to lose, the validator may be able to profit from the principal's loss. However, a validator with a larger self-delegation will themselves be affected by the slashing. This is why self-delegation offers a layer of protection against the Principal–Agent problem.

In traditional staking protocols, principals have the responsibility to delegate their funds *wisely*. When a malicious validator misbehaves, only the stake of unwise principals is slashed. No wise principal gets *unfairly punished.*

Definition 4 (Fair Punishment). *A staking protocol has Fair Punishment if no wise principal's stake gets slashed as a result of a malicious validator's actions.*

With the introduction of liquid staking protocols, the principal is no longer directly delegating to the validator of their choice. Instead, the protocol is now responsible for the delegation process and stake allocation to validators. Although the principal can express their delegation wish, ultimately it is the protocol that decides where funds are delegated based on its *delegation strategy*. All liquid staking tokens are fungible, hence all validators delegated to by the protocol become agents for all principals. The Principal–Agent problem is exacerbated. The principal's funds are now effectively delegated to validators he has not necessarily chosen, some with mischievous intentions.

5   Attack

We now describe an attack an adversary can conduct which leverages the Principal–Agent problem of liquid staking. First, we observe that fair punishment in the class of protocols we are concerned about is impossible.

Claim. Any *fungible* liquid staking protocol with *Proportional Representation* deployed over any proof-of-stake consensus protocol which slashes equivocating validators by a rate of $p > 0$ cannot have *fair punishment.*

Demonstration. To see why the above claim holds, consider the following simplistic attack illustrated in Fig. 1. Let b_0 be the amount of delegated ASSET in the protocol's delegation pool, and s_0 be the total amount of stASSET tokens outstanding before the attack commences. The initial quoted price of stASSET is $\frac{b_0}{s_0}$.

Initially, the adversary $\mathcal{A}$ creates a new validator $\mathcal{V}$ under her control[4]. We do not require any of the existing protocol participants to delegate to this validator for the attack to work, i.e., we assume, without loss of generality, that all participants are wise and all other validators are honest. At time t_2, the adversary deposits b ASSET to the protocol, signalling delegation intent to $\mathcal{V}$. Due to proportional representation, the protocol respects this intent and delegates b ASSET to $\mathcal{V}$. The protocol now holds b delegated ASSET to $\mathcal{V}$. Through this deposit, the adversary obtains $s = \frac{s_0}{b_0}b$ stASSET, and the quoted price remains $\frac{b_0+b}{s_0+s} = \frac{b_0}{s_0}$. Lastly, at time $t_4 > t_2$, validator $\mathcal{V}$ equivocates. This causes a proportion p of the capital b to be slashed. The rest $(1-p)b$ ASSET is returned back to the protocol. However the amount of stASSET circulating in the market remains $s_0 + s = s_0 + b\frac{s_0}{b_0}$. The new quoted price is now $\frac{b_0+(1-p)b}{s_0+s} = \frac{b_0}{s_0}(1 - p\frac{b}{b_0+b}) < \frac{b_0}{s_0}$.

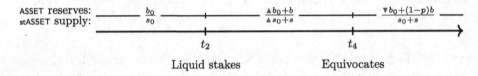

Fig. 1. Timeline of the simplistic attack.

Because stASSET is fungible, *every* stakeholder is negatively affected, proportionally to their holdings. The losses are socialized. As everyone else was wise, this constitutes unfair punishment.   ◇

The above attack requires the adversary to expend capital b to cause harm to others, and is irrational. In the remainder of this section, we explore how to make this attack profitable. The profitable attack works for protocols with an *unbonding period* $\delta > 0$. First, we show how to attack without adversarial losses; later, how to profit.

Attack with No Initial Capital. With a subtle change to the above construction, the attack can be performed without the adversary expending any capital (Fig. 2). Before depositing, the adversary acquires a flash loan of b ASSET. At time t_2 she deposits *those* borrowed funds instead of her own. For now, we assume that the borrowing of money is free and there is no cost for the flash loan (we

---

[4] To do so, she uses a fresh identity to suppress potential suspicions. Most validators have a real-world presence and can be held legally accountable [24, p. 29], but this validator is pseudonymous.

revisit this assumption in the full version of this paper [31]). During equivocation, the adversary does not want to be holding any stASSET of her own, as the price of stASSET is about to drop. She also needs to repay the acquired flash loan. Therefore, after the adversary obtains $s = \frac{s_0}{b_0}b$ stASSET from the deposit, she immediately sells[5] them for $b = \frac{b_0}{s_0}s$ ASSET in the open market, at time t_3. She uses the obtained b ASSET to repay the flash loan. The acts of taking the flash loan, depositing, swapping, and returning the flash loan, can all be performed in a single transaction.

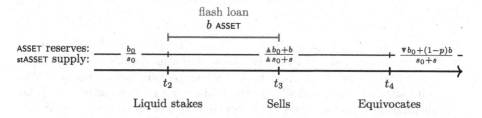

Fig. 2. Timeline of the attack with no initial capital.

The adversary has now managed to add b ASSET delegated to validator $\mathcal{V}$ in the protocol's delegation pool while not currently holding any stASSET. The loss has been averted. At this time, even though the stASSETs have changed hands, the liquid staking protocol cannot redelegate its ASSETs instantly due to $\delta > 0$. The adversary can now equivocate at time t_4 and, as before, cause the price of stASSET to drop.

Making the Attack Profitable. The profitable version of the attack (Fig. 3) works similarly to the above attack, but with some extra steps. As before, the adversary begins by spawning the colluding validator $\mathcal{V}$, deposits b ASSET, obtained by a flash loan, at time t_2, sells the acquired s stASSET to repay the flash loan at time t_3, and equivocates at time t_4.

A small extra trick will allow her to profit. Before forcing the price of stASSET to drop, at time $t_0 < t_4$ the adversary *shorts* stASSET: She takes a loan of z stASSETs and sells them for $b^* = z\frac{b_0}{s_0}$ ASSET in the market. Lastly, at time $t_5 > t_4$ after the price drop, the adversary closes her short position by repaying z stASSET. To recover this amount of stASSET, at time t_5, the adversary *deposits* $b' = \frac{b_0}{s_0}(1 - p\frac{b}{b_0+b})z$ ASSET into the protocol, which allows her to issue the exact required stASSET to be paid back. This concludes the attack.

Her total profits from the attack are $\alpha = b^* - b' = z\frac{b_0}{s_0}p\frac{b}{b_0+b}$ ASSET. A larger short position $z\frac{b_0}{s_0}$ and a larger stASSET price drop percentage $p\frac{b}{b_0+b}$, yields higher profits for the adversary.

---

[5] Instead of *selling*, the adversary can *redeem*, but this may incur an unbonding delay, which can be rectified by taking a loan. See the full version of this paper [31] for more details.

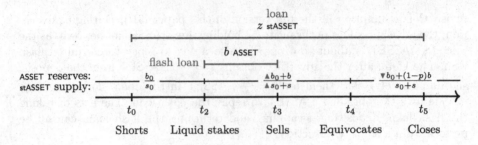

Fig. 3. Timeline of the profitable attack.

So far, we have allowed the adversary to take a loan indiscriminately without any concern for collateral. In practice, loan platforms require a collateral, so the attack impact will be limited by the adversary's initial capital available for collateralization. Let u ASSET be the initial capital of the adversary. If no overcollateralization is required she can obtain a loan of up to $z = u\frac{s_0}{b_0}$ stASSET and then sell them back for $b^* = u$ ASSET. Her profit relative to her initial capital is then $\alpha = up\frac{b}{b_0+b}$ ASSET.

6   Exempt Delegations

Exempt delegations (proposed in LSM [2]) are a mechanism to alleviate the Principal–Agent problem in liquid staking. In this mechanism, an exempt delegation amount c ASSET is associated with each validator. It is a measure of the validator's trustworthiness. The liquid staking protocol is now redesigned to impose restrictions on how much of the protocol's pooled moneys can be delegated to a particular validator based on the validator's exempt delegation. The restriction is parameterized by a factor ϕ (in practice, $\phi > 1$) and is given by the inequality $b \leq \phi c$: Only up to ϕc ASSETs are allowed to be delegated in aggregate by the liquid staking protocol to a validator with a reserve of c ASSET in exempt delegations.

A new validator begins its lifecycle with $c = 0$. They can then raise their own exempt delegation amount by locking aside a chosen amount of ASSET, and marking it as *exempt*. Those assets are delegated to the validator as usual. However, the *exempt* marking means that those delegated assets cannot be part of the liquid staking protocol pool, but must remain locked aside. Additionally, these specially marked delegations are slashed[6] at a potentially higher rate $q \geq p$. Exempt delegated assets cannot be undelegated in a way that causes a violation of $b \leq \phi c$.

Principals, whether wise or unwise, are not expected to participate in exempt delegations; instead, it is the validator who exempt delegates to themselves (or someone who trusts the validator for extrinsic reasons). This means that, in case

---

[6] We abstract some of the irrelevant implementation details here. See the full version of this paper [31] for how the real protocol works in the context of Cosmos.

of validator misbehavior, the exempt delegation slashing qc is a penalty that only affects the validator.

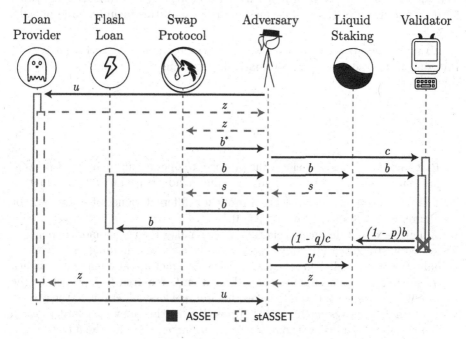

Fig. 4. Sequence diagram of the attack with exempt delegations.

This raises the cost of the attack described in the previous section. The adversary must first, at time t_1 (where $t_0 < t_1 < t_2$), exempt delegate a sufficient amount $c \geq \frac{b}{\phi}$ ASSET to $\mathcal{V}$ before she can liquid stake b ASSET. Whereas the stASSETs corresponding to those b ASSETs can be, as before, sold at t_3 to separate the agent from the principal, the c amount remains with the agent, holding her financially liable to misbehavior. After equivocation at t_4, in addition to any other costs, the adversary loses qc ASSET. At the conclusion of the attack, the adversary undelegates the unslashed $(1-q)c$ ASSET exempt delegation. The sequence diagram of the refined attack is illustrated in Fig. 4.

The attack may remain profitable despite exempt delegations. To maximize her shorting leverage, the adversary wants to use all of her initial capital u ASSET to obtain the z stASSET loan. Upon swapping z for b^* ASSET, the adversary can then use part of it as c. The rational adversary should not waste any unnecessary resources on c; therefore, after choosing b she can set $c = \frac{b}{\phi}$. Since the maximum amount the adversary exempt delegates cannot be more than her initial capital u ASSET, it must always hold that $b \leq u\phi$.

The profit of the attack now becomes $\alpha = b^* - b' - qc$. Solving for $\frac{d\alpha}{db} = 0$ yields the optimal $b = \sqrt{upb_0\frac{\phi}{q}} - b_0$, which maximizes the adversary's profit, subject to the constraint $0 \leq b \leq u\phi$.

The intuition for why exempt delegations protect the system is that, for the adversary to profit from the short, she must cause a significant shift in the price. The shift in the price is determined by the factor $p\frac{b}{b_0+b}$, so the adversary aims for a large b. But because $b \leq \phi c$ must be respected, this incurs a large penalty $qc = \frac{q}{\phi}b$.

To make the attack irrational, we select the parameter $\frac{\phi}{q}$ such that $\alpha \leq 0$. Plugging in the adversarially optimal value for b in the inequality $\alpha \leq 0$ and solving for $\frac{\phi}{q}$ yields

$$\frac{\phi}{q} \leq \frac{b_0}{pu}. \tag{$*$}$$

Plugging the values we believe the protocol to operate under into p, b_0 and u, we calculate a secure $\frac{\phi}{q}$ for an assumed maximum adversarial market domination $\frac{u}{b_0}$. In Fig. 5, we show the adversarial profit for different values of $\frac{\phi}{q}$ and $\frac{u}{b_0}$. For the figure, we used a slashing rate $p = 0.5$.

A higher exempt delegation slashing rate q makes the attack more expensive. This is because a larger portion of the exempt delegation c, holding the adversary accountable, is slashed. A lower exempt delegation factor ϕ also makes the attack more expensive since a larger exempt delegation is required to liquid stake the same b ASSET. Hence, a lower $\frac{\phi}{q}$ makes the protocol less vulnerable to the attack. We recommend always setting $q = 1$ if possible, as this allows for larger values of ϕ, increasing liquidity, without any harm to anyone besides the adversary.

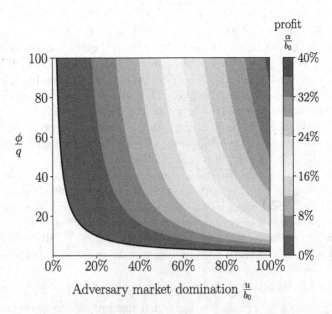

Fig. 5. Adversarial profitability based on market domination $\frac{u}{b_0}$ and parameter $\frac{\phi}{q}$. The white area indicates secure parametrizations.

Repeating the Attack. If the adversary finds herself in a situation where the attack is profitable, the attack can be repeated in quick succession to siphon off almost all of the money in the liquid staking protocol. This corresponds to moving across the x axis in Fig. 5. As the attack repeats, b_0 decreases and u increases as money moves from the reserves of the staking protocol to the hands of the adversary. We conclude that the protocol must be configured with enough margin such that the conditions for the attack never emerge.

Proportional Representation vs Fair Punishment. Proportional representation and fair punishment, as indicated in Sect. 5, are conflicting properties in liquid staking. Without exempt delegations ($\phi = \infty$), the protocol has full proportional representation, as the principal can signal delegation to any agent of their choice without restriction. There, an adversary can always cause unfair punishment of principals. However, with the introduction of exempt delegations, if we make $\frac{\phi}{q}$ smaller, the pool of available agents to choose from is reduced to only the wealthy amongst them, so proportional representation becomes limited. For a sufficiently small $\frac{\phi}{q}$, the protocol has fair punishment in the rational model.

Acknowledgements. The authors wish to thank Joachim Neu for the suggestion of the repeated attack; Zaki Manian, Aidan Salzmann and Vish Modali for the insights on the history and implementation details of liquid staking; Viraj Nadkarni for the fruitful discussions during the development of our model; Ertem Nusret Tas, Vasiliy Shapovalov, Nikolaos Kamarinakis, Dimitris Karakostas and Aleksis Brezas for reading early versions of the paper and providing valuable feedback; and Harry Karavassilis and Zeta Avarikioti for the creative contributions. We are grateful to the Algorand Centres of Excellence MEGA-ACE programme managed by Algorand Foundation for partially funding this paper. Any opinions, findings, and conclusions or recommendations expressed in this material are those of the authors and do not necessarily reflect the views of Algorand Foundation.

References

1. Lido: Ethereum Liquid Staking (2020)
2. Liquidity staking module (2022). https://github.com/iqlusioninc/liquidity-staking-module
3. Agrawal, S.: Mesh security. In: Presentation at Cosmoverse 2022 (2022)
4. Angeris, G., Kao, H.-T., Chiang, R., Noyes, C., Chitra, T.: An analysis of uniswap markets (2021)
5. Badertscher, C., Gaži, P., Kiayias, A., Russell, A., Zikas, V.: Ouroboros genesis: composable proof-of-stake blockchains with dynamic availability. In: Proceedings of the 2018 ACM SIGSAC Conference on Computer and Communications Security, pp. 913–930 (2018)
6. Bentov, I., Pass, R., Shi, E.: Snow white: provably secure proofs of stake. IACR Cryptol. ePrint Arch. **2016**, 919 (2016)
7. Bowman, J., Modali, V., Mortaki, R.: Quicksilver protocol, the cosmos liquid staking zone (2022)

8. Buchman, E.: Tendermint: Byzantine fault tolerance in the age of blockchains. PhD thesis, University of Guelph (2016)
9. Buchman, E., Kwon, J.: Cosmos whitepaper: a network of distributed ledgers (2016)
10. Buchman, E., Kwon, J., Milosevic, Z.: The latest gossip on BFT consensus. arXiv preprint arXiv:1807.04938 (2018)
11. Buterin, V.: Slasher: a punitive proof-of-stake algorithm (2014). https://blog.ethereum.org/2014/01/15/slasher-a-punitive-proof-of-stake-algorithm
12. Buterin, V.: Minimal slashing conditions (2017). https://medium.com/@VitalikButerin/minimal-slashing-conditions-20f0b500fc6c
13. Buterin , V., Griffith, V.: Casper the friendly finality gadget. arXiv preprint arXiv:1710.09437 (2017)
14. Buterin, V., et al.: Combining GHOST and Casper. arXiv preprint arXiv:2003.03052 (2020)
15. Cosmos SDK Team. Cosmos SDK Staking module. https://docs.cosmos.network/v0.47/modules/staking
16. David, B., Gaži, P., Kiayias, A., Russell, A.: Ouroboros praos: an adaptively-secure, semi-synchronous proof-of-stake blockchain. In: Nielsen, J.B., Rijmen, V. (eds.) EUROCRYPT 2018. LNCS, vol. 10821, pp. 66–98. Springer, Cham (2018). https://doi.org/10.1007/978-3-319-78375-8_3
17. EigenLayer Team. EigenLayer: The Restaking Collective (2023). https://2039955362-files.gitbook.io//files/v0/b/gitbook-x-prod.appspot.com/o/spaces%2FPy2Kmkwju3mPSo9jrKKt%2Fuploads%2F2dCfPgItRfQbX25KriQv%2Fwhitepaper.pdf?alt=media&token=d4d94480-3f01-4e63-bc92-a0658ea37aab
18. Gilad, Y., Hemo, R., Micali, S., Vlachos, G., Zeldovich, N.: Algorand: scaling byzantine agreements for cryptocurrencies. In: Proceedings of the 26th Symposium on Operating Systems Principles, pp. 51–68 (2017)
19. Gudgeon, L., Werner, S., Perez, D., Knottenbelt, W.J.: DeFi protocols for loanable funds: interest rates, liquidity and market efficiency. In: Proceedings of the 2nd ACM Conference on Advances in Financial Technologies, pp. 92–112 (2020)
20. Jensen, M.C., Meckling, W.H.: Theory of the firm: managerial behavior, agency costs and ownership structure. J. Finan. Econ. **3**(4), 305–360 (1976)
21. Kiayias, A., Russell, A., David, B., Oliynykov, R.: Ouroboros: a provably secure proof-of-stake blockchain protocol. In: Katz, J., Shacham, H. (eds.) Annual International Cryptology Conference. LNCS, vol. 10401, pp. 357–388. Springer, Springer (2017)
22. King, S., Nadal, S.: Ppcoin: peer-to-peer crypto-currency with proof-of-stake. Self-published Paper **19**(1) (2012)
23. Lutsch, F.: Delegation vouchers: a design concept for liquid staking positions (2019). https://medium.com/chorus-one/delegation-vouchers-cfb511a29aac
24. Lutsch, F.: Liquid staking research report (2020). https://mirror.chorus.one/liquid-staking-report.pdf
25. Manian, Z.: ADR ADR-061: liquid staking (2022). https://docs.cosmos.network/v0.47/architecture/adr-061-liquid-staking
26. Mill, J.S.: Of true and false democracy; representation of all, and representation of the majority only (1862)
27. pStake Team. pStake: Unlocking Liquidity for Staked Assets. https://pstake.finance
28. Rocket Pool Team. Rocket Pool. https://rocketpool.net
29. Smith, A.: The Wealth of Nations (1776)

30. Stride. Stride: Multichain liquid staking. https://www.stride.zone
31. Tzinas, A., Zindros, D.: The principal-agent problem in liquid staking. Cryptology ePrint Archive (2023)
32. Werner, S.M., Perez, D., Gudgeon, L., Klages-Mundt, A., Harz, D., Knottenbelt, W.J.: SoK: Decentralized Finance (DeFi). arXiv preprint arXiv:2101.08778 (2021)
33. Yun, T., Lee, J., King, S.: ICS-027: interchain accounts (2019). https://github.com/cosmos/ibc/blob/main/spec/app/ics-027-interchain-accounts/README.md

Detecting Privileged Parties on Ethereum

Michael Fröwis$^{(\boxtimes)}$ and Rainer Böhme

Department of Computer Science, Universität Innsbruck, Innsbruck, Austria
michael.froewis@gmail.com

Abstract. The promise of smart contracts (computer programs running on a decentralized virtual computer) lies in the ability to execute agreements without the risk of interference by powerful intermediaries. However, in practice, many smart contracts reintroduce privileged parties on the application layer. They are programmed to enforce that certain functions can only be executed by the owners of defined accounts. We propose and validate a method to detect such privileged parties from binary smart contract code on the Ethereum platform. Our open-source implementation, Ethpector, can be used to verify claims about "zero-trust," reveal ownership structures, forensically analyze networks of virtual shell organizations, and may support auditors when testifying ownership of intangible assets on Ethereum held by conventional legal entities.

Keywords: Smart Contracts · Governance · Audits · Forensics · Ownership Pattern · Ethereum Virtual Machine · Symbolic Execution

1 Introduction

Privileged parties are entities that can unilaterally exercise control over a system on which ordinary users interact. Decentralized systems are often designed to minimize the influence of privileged parties in order to reduce the number of entities users have to trust. This design principle can make systems more robust to failures of individual components and arguably more trustworthy as a whole.

While, "zero-trust" transactions will probably remain a utopian vision [3,17], Ethereum today provides the technical means to avoid certain trust relationships. Yet, at the current state of Ethereum and its ecosystem, it is often unclear if services offered on the platform indeed require less trust that centralized alternatives. In many cases, trust relationships are merely less apparent to users, disguised in opaque program code, and renounced in marketing language.

It is instructive to illustrate this on a simplified technology stack as shown in Fig. 1. A decentralized network of miners participates in a protocol which establishes consensus on the state of a replicated machine. This machine offers a programming interface for applications (i. e., smart contracts) to run on. While a decentralized platform is a *necessary* precondition for decentralized applications, it is *not sufficient*. Developers can re-introduce privileged parties on a higher layer by specifying that certain functions check the identity (i. e., Ethereum address) of the caller against constants or state variables before execution.

© International Financial Cryptography Association 2024
A. Essex et al. (Eds.): FC 2023 Workshops, LNCS 13953, pp. 470–488, 2024.
https://doi.org/10.1007/978-3-031-48806-1_30

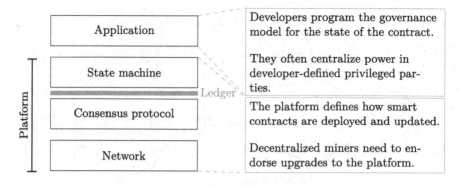

Fig. 1. Governance on different layers of the Ethereum technology stack.

To understand why privileged parties matter, consider the issues involved in updating smart contracts. Whenever code on Ethereum is prepared to be updatable (e. g., to be able to patch security vulnerabilities), there is some party in control of the update [14]. This party has exceptional control over whatever this application does. In fact, for the scope of the application, this party's power is comparable to that of an operator of a centralized system. For example, the party authorized to update the smart contract of a token system is at least as powerful as a conventional bank, the very type of intermediary cryptocurrency systems set out to remove. The party can freeze accounts, adjust balances, or shut down the entire token system. Even if there is no 'wild-card' option to replace the code, the deployed code may allow privileged parties to update parameters of the system, such as creating or destroying tokens, adjusting fees, or reassigning the privilege to other parties. From a users' perspective, this situation could be worse than when dealing with a regulated bank because there is little hope for legal redress. Besides legal and regulatory uncertainty, operators of token systems are barely accountable. They are often identified by nothing more than pseudonyms on social media or code sharing platforms. These examples highlight the need for a technical method to detect the privileged parties of any given smart contract before interacting with it.

Existing solutions to this problem are unsatisfactory. The canonical approach to identify all privileged parties (or verify the absence of them) is to review the source code of the smart contract. In a second step, one has to replicate the compile process to ensure that the deployed code indeed implements the functionality specified in the source code. Third, one has to inspect the transaction that deployed the smart contract to ensure that it cannot change in the future [10]. This laborious manual process requires deep technical understanding of the platform as well as of the application in question. Clearly, this approach does not scale. It also does not work for smart contracts whose source code is not publicly available.

Contribution: This paper presents Ethpector, a tool that facilitates the automatic extraction of privileged parties from smart contract binaries. We start

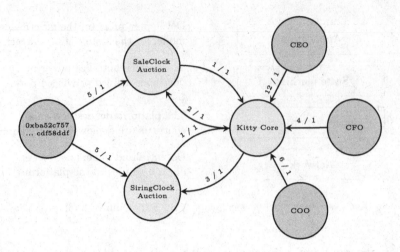

Fig. 2. The governance structure of the CryptoKitties contract. Orange nodes represent code accounts, gray nodes are externally owned accounts. The edge annotations mean: number of functions controlled/by n parties (one slot). (Color figure online)

with a motivating example in Sect. 2. Section 3 proposes our method to extract privileged parties, which we evaluate against a curated set of ground-truth data in Sect. 4. We discuss applications and limitations in Sect. 5. Section 6 discusses related work before Sect. 7 concludes. **Ethpector** is an open-source implementation of the proposed method. It can be used to replicate all results in this paper.

2 Motivating Example

Established in late 2017, CryptoKitties belong to the first digital collectibles on the Ethereum platform. They became precursors of the NFT hype. Figure 2 visualizes the governance structure of the CryptoKitties contract.[1] The addresses labeled CEO, COO, and CFO can execute the privileged function **pause** to halt all contract activity, which in effect freezes all kitties. Furthermore, the CEO is authorized to invoke **setGeneScienceAddress**, which sets a new reference to the account responsible for creating kitties. This address controls how unique new kittens are and thus may influence their valuation [18]. The power of these privileged parties stands in contrast to the claims made on the CryptoKitty website:[2]

---

[1] The UNESCO defines governance as: "...structures and processes that are designed to ensure accountability, transparency, responsiveness, rule of law, stability, equity and inclusiveness, empowerment, and broad-based participation."; See http://www.ibe.unesco.org/en/geqaf/technical-notes/concept-governance, Accessed: 14 June 2022.

[2] https://www.cryptokitties.co/about, Accessed 18 Jan 2022.

"... each CryptoKitty is one-of-a-kind and 100% owned by you. It cannot be replicated, taken away, or destroyed."

Meanwhile, users seem to happily trust the privileged parties of this contract, or might simply be unaware of this governance structure.

Our Ethpector tool, which generated the governance structure in Fig. 2, is designed to extract such privileged parties automatically from a smart contract binary. This enables users to scrutinize claims and understand power relations before sending funds to a contract. Applied iteratively, our method allows to reveal ownership structures and track them through networks of "shell contracts", Ethereum's equivalent to shell companies that are commonly used to conceal wealth and decision power in the real world.

Yet another use case of Ethpector is when auditors certify virtual assets on a real-world entity's balance sheet. While holdings of ether and standard tokens can be verified with common techniques, there is no canonical way to testify ownership of – or other kinds of privileged access to – smart contracts. To the best of our knowledge, the method presented here is the first to tackle this problem in generality for arbitrary smart contracts.

3   Proposed Method

Smart contracts can implement privileged parties in many different ways. Our aim is to identify functions in EVM binaries where parts can only be executed by a privileged party. Moreover, we want to be able to identify the privileged party by its Ethereum address.

3.1   Dead End: Heuristic Pattern Matching

We first considered to heuristically extract information from the most common standardized interfaces. This approach as been used widely in the literature, for instance to analyze token flows from log entries of popular token standards [4–8,15,16]. We identified the *ownership pattern* as a common form to manage a single privileged party. This pattern keeps an owner address in the smart contract's state.

This variable is typically initiated with the sender of the transaction that deploys the code. The pattern's interface supports an getOwner function, which can be called on the local node to identify the privileged party. Changes of ownership (i. e., of the privileged party) can be tracked by watching for calls to changeOwner or by observing OwnerSet logs emitted by the contract.

To evaluate the coverage of an approach solely relying on the ownership pattern, we classify all newly deployed smart contracts in a time window of two months in summer 2022 (891 170 contracts in total). We consider all smart contracts that export functions using Ethereum's Application Binary Interface (ABI). Among the contracts which do not export any function, we consider all

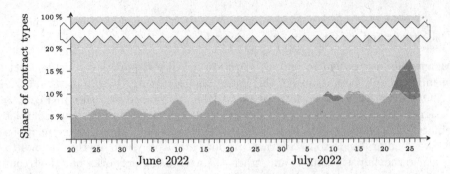

Fig. 3. Prevalence of the common ownership pattern in newly created smart contracts (orange) using a signature-based detector. Our baseline (red) are all contracts with known interfaces, such as ERC20. Gray contracts are likely multi-sig wallets, but cannot be analyzed with the proposed method. (Color figure online)

deployments with known bytecode.[3] Those mainly include forwarder contracts used to create fresh deposit addresses and upgradable proxy contracts. Figure 3 shows the results over time using a 3-day rolling window. Observe that only 5–10% of the relevant contracts implement the vanilla ownership pattern. The simple approach sketched in the previous paragraph would thus fail for at least 85% of the cases where Ethpector can in principle extract some information. Also the CryptoKitties contract used as motivating example in Sect. 2 could not be analyzed with the ownership pattern heuristic. These numbers highlight the need for a more sophisticated approach using symbolic execution.

3.2 Symbolic Execution

Symbolic execution [12] is a common technique in program analysis, often used to find bugs or to generate test cases automatically. Symbolic execution tries to explore all possible execution paths through a program in a systematic manner. For that purpose, the input to the program is intentionally left unspecified (or *symbolic*). On each control flow decision, the symbolic execution engine tries to explore both branches. To avoid the exploration of unreachable paths, the engine uses a satisfiability modulo theories (SMT) solver to find program inputs that satisfy the path constraints leading to the branch. Paths for which no suitable input is found are skipped.

For our purpose we are interested in control flow decisions within a function that depend on the caller, i.e., the sender of the message or transaction which

---

[3] For 36% of the deployed contracts we cannot infer a contract type. They neither export functions nor belong to the our set of known bytecodes. The database of known interfaces and bytecodes is curated from public sources, e.g., https://eips.ethereum.org/, GitHub etc. A complete list of items can be found at https://github.com/uibk-ethpector/ethpector/blob/main/src/ethpector/classify/classification.py; function and event signatures are obtained from the 4-bytes directory and etherface.io.

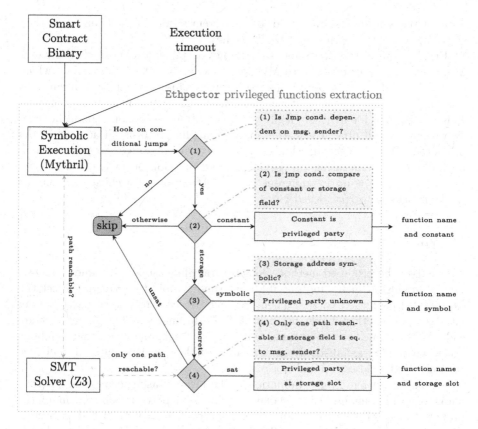

Fig. 4. Flow chart of `Ethpector`'s privileged function detection.

invokes the function.[4] Moreover, we want to find control flow decisions where one of the branches can only be reached if the caller is a privileged party either (a) stored as constant in the binary or (b) read from a storage field. If we have found such a control flow decision, we want to extract the address of the privileged party. In case (a), we can read the encoded party directly from the binary. This means we go back to the `PUSH` instruction that placed the constant on the stack. In case (b), we need to extract the slot in permanent storage that holds the address. This storage slot is encoded in the path constraint and can be obtained by analyzing the structure of the path constraint. We use the path constraint as well as information we gain from tainting all values introduced by loads from permanent storage. We compare both values to avoid wrong extractions. Finally, to ensure that the extracted data is correct, we use the SMT solver to verify that

---

[4] In principle, one could also look for the origin, i. e., the party who signed the transaction. To the best of our knowledge, almost all authorization decisions on Ethereum are based on the message sender.

if we set the identified storage field to the current sender of the transaction then we in fact can only reach one of the branches.

Figure 4 shows the proposed binary analysis pipeline as a flow chart. Our `Ethpector` implementation uses Mythril[5] as symbolic execution engine, which in turn depends on Microsoft's Z3 SMT solver. Observe that we can run into cases where we detect the existence of a privileged party, but fail to identify it. This can happen for multi-sig logic which conditions access on general boolean expressions. In all other cases, the analysis pipeline returns an address of the privileged party, or a storage slot. Given the extracted storage slot, we can look up the current value using the `getStorageAt` function of an Ethereum node. Repeating this look-up for different points in time on an archive node lets us track changes of the privileged party.

4   Validation

We validate the proposed method along several dimensions. First and foremost, we are interested in finding out if the method is able to correctly detect the existence of privileged parties. Then, for each detected privileged party, we are interested in whether it can be identified. Additional variables of interest are code coverage and execution time, which is not negligible given that symbolic execution tries to exhaustively explore all possible execution paths. Finally, we compare to the closest related work.

A main challenge in the validation is the lack of task-specific ground-truth data. The only reliable way to identify privileged parties independent of the proposed method is to carry out the manual code review described in Sect. 1. However, this depends on the availability of the source code. Since manual code review does not scale, we have to keep the size of the ground-truth data limited. This, in turn, means that the results become more sensitive to the sample selection. The naive approach to sample $x\%$ of all smart contracts deployed on Ethereum in the past year is prone to biases given that the overwhelming majority of deployments are proxy or forwarder contracts. Those are very short and generally easy to analyze. Therefore, such a sample would over-estimate the accuracy of the method while almost never testing its limits.

To overcome these issues, we compose a validation dataset of 41 non-trivial smart contracts by combining two sources. We identify 28 relevant smart contracts from the list of top gas consumers provided by EthGasStation.[6] Starting from the top, we take each smart contract for which Etherscan has source code. If the smart contract is invoked via a proxy pattern, we do not only analyze the proxy but try to include the contract on the address it resolves to. This applies to seven cases. Since the so-obtained dataset was still biased towards proxy contracts, we balance it by adding selected popular contracts of several diverse cat-

---

[5] https://github.com/ConsenSys/mythril, Accessed: 07 June 2022.
[6] https://ethgasstation.info/json/gasguzz.json, Accessed: 13 May 2022. The ranking aggregates gas use over 1500 blocks (roughly six hours).

Table 1. Extraction results compared to our ground-truth data.

	Name	F in Abi	TP F	FP F	FN F	TP O	FP O	FN O	Owners/Slots
0	0x: Coinbase Wallet Proxy	14	6	0	0	1	0	0	1 / 1
1	1inch v4: Router	23	4	0	0	1	0	0	1 / 1
2	BendDao: Bend Token	16	0	0	0	0	0	0	0 / 0
3	BendDao: Bend Token Proxy	6	6	0	0	1	0	0	1 / 1
4	BosonRouter	33	8	0	0	1	0	0	1 / 1
5	Center: USD Coin	52	12	0	0	2	0	0	2 / 5
6	Center: USD Coin Proxy	6	6	0	0	1	0	0	1 / 1
7	CryptoKitties	59	17	0	0	5	0	0	5 / 6
8	EMOBUDDIES	43	13	0	1	1	0	0	1 / 1
9	ENS: ETH Registrar Controller	22	5	0	0	1	0	0	1 / 1
10	FloatingCats	43	11	1	1	1	0	0	1 / 1
11	Gem: GemSwap 2	41	19	0	0	1	0	0	1 / 2
12	GnosisSafe Mastercopy 1.1.1	31	0	0	0	0	0	0	0 / 0
13	KaijuFrenz: KAIJUFRENZ Token	54	14	0	0	1	0	0	1 / 1
14	LooksRare: Exchange	23	7	0	0	0	1	1	1 / 1
15	Merkle distributor	19	7	0	0	1	0	0	1 / 1
16	Merkle distributor Proxy	6	6	0	0	1	0	0	1 / 1
17	MetaPunk: Minter	45	13	0	4	1	0	0	1 / 1
18	OpenSea: Registry	21	6	0	0	1	0	0	1 / 1
19	OpenSea: Wyvern Exchange v2	36	5	0	0	1	0	0	1 / 1
20	Polygon Matic: Bridge Proxy	7	3	0	0	1	0	0	1 / 1
21	Polygon Matic: Bridge RootChainManager	41	0	0	0	0	0	1	0 / 0
22	Proxy to 34cfac64 ... 83fe3f5f	1	0	0	0	0	0	0	0 / 0
23	ProxyAdmin ?	9	5	0	0	1	0	0	1 / 1
24	RaidParty: Game Party	28	0	0	0	0	0	0	0 / 0
25	RaidParty: Game Party Proxy	6	6	0	0	1	0	0	1 / 1
26	Saitama Inu: SAITAMA Token	24	5	0	1	1	0	0	1 / 1
27	Shiba Inu: SHIB Token	13	0	0	0	0	0	0	0 / 0
28	StrongBlock: Service Proxy	6	6	0	0	1	0	0	1 / 1
29	Strongblock: Service V19	102	32	0	0	1	0	0	1 / 7
30	Strongblock: Service V20	107	29	1	0	1	0	0	1 / 7
31	SushiSwap: Router	25	1	0	0	1	0	0	1 / 0
32	TRIBE X: TRIBEX Token	61	21	0	1	1	0	0	1 / 1
33	Tether: USDT Stablecoin	33	10	0	0	1	0	0	1 / 1
34	Tornado.Cash: Router	12	2	0	0	2	0	0	2 / 0
35	Uniswap V2: Router 2	25	1	0	0	1	0	0	1 / 0
36	Uniswap V3: Positions NFT	39	1	0	3	1	0	0	1 / 0
37	Uniswap V3: Router	18	1	0	0	1	0	0	1 / 0
38	Uniswap V3: Router 2	40	1	0	0	1	0	0	1 / 0
39	Wandernauts: WANDERNAUT Token	39	11	0	3	1	0	0	1 / 2
40	Wrapped Ether	12	0	0	0	0	0	0	0 / 0
	TOTAL:	1241	300	3	14	39	1	2	
	ACC, REC, F1:		0.99	0.96	0.97	0.98	0.95	0.96	

egories, such as multi-sig wallets, AdminProxy, and not to forget CryptoKitties. Table 2 in the appendix lists details for all elements of the validation dataset.

We generate ground-truth by downloading the source code for all contracts and manually extracting all functions that require authorization. This caused an effort of several working days by the Solidity expert on the research team. Additionally, we use Etherscan's read contract feature to collect the addresses set in permanent storage that are used for the authorization decisions. We use this manually curated data to evaluate the performance of our automated approach.

Table 1 reports the extraction performance of our method for each contract. We evaluate the capability to detect the existence of a privileged party on the level of functions. Column "F in Abi" lists the number of exported functions per contract. The following three columns count true positives, false positives, and false negatives, respectively. Overall, our method achieves 99% accuracy and 96% recall on a total of 1241 exported functions. Turning to the identification of privileged parties, the numbers are naturally smaller as few contracts handle more than one privileged party. We measure 98% accuracy and 95% recall across our validation dataset.

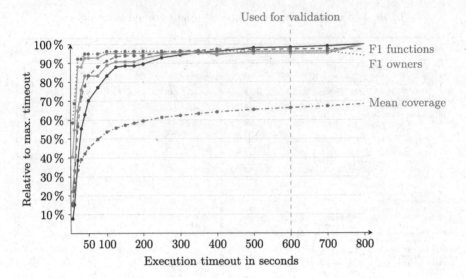

Fig. 5. Number of privileged functions (blue), owners (orange) and slots (red) found depending on the execution timeout of the symbolic execution. (Color figure online)

These results are obtained with a timeout of 600 s on a commodity AMD Ryzen 7 Pro[7] machine with 32 GB RAM. This runtime is not long enough to achieve complete code coverage except for very short contracts. To evaluate the sensitivity of the performance evaluation to the choice of the timeout, we repeat the extraction with varying timeout and report key indicators in Fig. 5. Observe that the number of detected items plateaus after 300 s (and would allow a rough approximation after just 60 s). Likewise, the performance metrics (here: F1-scores) are largely insensitive to the timeout once it exceeds one minute. While this is still too slow to be attractive for realtime analysis of all deployed smart contracts, it is sufficiently fast for the exploration of governance structures in selected parts of the ecosystem. Note that the mean code coverage is far below 100%. The nonetheless good performance takes advantage of the fact that authorization decisions typically appear early in the execution path and a breadth-first search strategy. This means the symbolic execution engine needs less time to reach the crucial instructions. Moreover, it is less likely that we miss the relevant branches since the path constraints remain lean and are unlikely to overwhelm the SMT solver. The mean code coverage of 65% for the 600 s timeout hides tremendous heterogeneity, with individual coverages ranging between 20 and 100%. As plotted in Fig. 6 for each element in our validation set, the coverage is negatively correlated with the bytecode size, but can still vary by a factor of two between smart contracts of the same size.

To complete the validation, we compare Ethpector to a concurrent effort. Ma et al. [13] propose a static analysis pipeline starting from source code to find backdoors in token systems. (Recall that Ethpector is much more general.)

---

[7] 5850U at 1.90–4.40 GHz, 8 cores, 16 threads, and 16 MB cache.

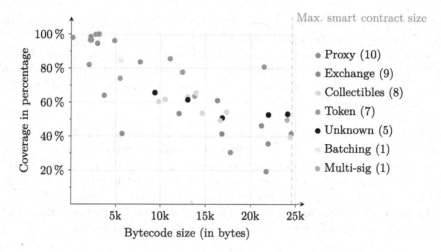

Fig. 6. Scatter plot of bytecode size and code coverage. Timeout 600 s.

They discover 190 backdoors in deployed ERC20 contracts.[8] We feed the 157 unique addresses on their list into our method. `Ethpector` correctly identifies and extract (at least one) privileged party in 156 cases, suggesting a true positive rate of 99%. The only contract where `Ethpector` failed[9] to extract the privileged party stores the administrator account in a mapping structure. While we cannot calculate false positives from the biased data, we note that the presence of a privileged party is generally suspicious in an ERC20 contract. For completeness, in the appendix we show `Ethpector`'s console output for the SoarCoin smart contract, the motivating example in [13]. The backdoor therein has caused a loss of $6.6 million to an Australian firm in 2018. `Ethpector` exposes its privileged functions `zero_fee_transaction` and `drain`.

5   Discussion

Next we discuss applications before we move on to limitations in Subsect. 5.2.

5.1   Applications

Verifying Zero-Trust. Many smart contract projects start off with a central controlling party and the promise to switch to "zero-trust" in the future. The transition from central control to "zero-trust" is typically conducted by setting the owner to an address known not to be controlled by any party e.g., zero. `Ethpector` can identify where in the storage of the smart contract the owners is stored. With this information, changes in ownership can be tracked with the

---

[8] https://github.com/EthereumContractBackdoor/PiedPiperBackdoor/blob/main/ Backdoor_List.md, Accessed 18 Oct 2022.

[9] Ethereum address `0xa821f14fb6394e82839f5161f214cacc90372453`.

information from an Ethereum node. Our method does not require any knowledge about the smart contract, such as known interfaces or self-reporting.

Figure 7 demonstrates this by plotting all changes of privileged parties for all contracts in our validation dataset. Only one smart contract of our validation dataset (the SAITAMA Token) changed its owner to "zero-trust" on 7 July 2021, 7 days after creation.[10]

Audits. Auditors are often tasked to verify the opposite of "zero-trust." Companies that offer services in the Ethereum ecosystem might want to declare their smart contract operations as intangible assets on their conventional balance sheet. To attest that an entity actually "owns" a deployed smart contract, auditors could verify if this is reflected in privileged access to managing functions of the smart contract. Our method allows third parties to do exactly this in an automated manner, i.e., without costly review of the source code.

Detecting Privileged Parameters. For all privileged functions detected with our method, `Ethpector` can extract the storage slots to which the function writes. Slots that are written by one privileged function and read by other (not privileged) functions indicate the existence of a privileged parameter. The analysis results for the SoarCoin contract in Fig. 8 (appendix) demonstrates this. The function `set_centralAccount` is privileged and the only one to write into storage slot 3, suggesting that it holds a privileged parameter. Access to the critical function `zero_fee_transaction`, which reportedly enabled the scam, is controlled by this slot.

Detecting Update Privileges. `Ethpector` also extracts calls and their call targets from the binaries. This information in combination with the check for parameter changes can be used to detect updatable proxies, the common way to keep smart contract code maintainable (and break the immutability feature). More specifically, a smart contract with a privileged function to change an address field that is in turn used to redirect calls is likely used to make the contract updatable. Watching this address field over time allows us to track code updates. Note that our method does not rely on knowledge about the exact update pattern used.

Address Clustering and Network Analysis. For many types of cryptoasset analytics, including forensic investigations, it is useful to lift the unit of analysis from the individual address level to the level of real-world entities. Address clustering is concerned with inferring which addresses belong to the same entity. Detecting privileged parties enables to automatically consider smart contracts as well as their controlling accounts as one entity. Similarly, if the same party is detected to have privileges in multiple smart contracts, they can be treated as one

---

[10] The code for generating the figure can be found at https://github.com/uibk-eth pector/ethpector/blob/main/experiments/privileged-parties/paper/storage_evoluti on.py.

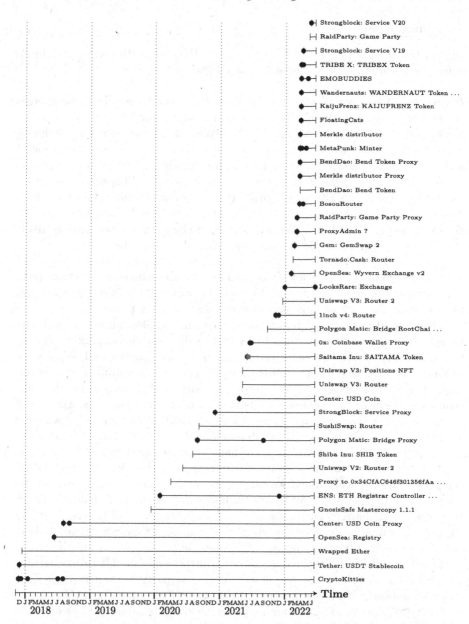

Fig. 7. Changes of privileged parties over time in the validation dataset. Bars are contract lifetimes; black dots indicate changes of privileged parties; red dots (only one in the chart) indicate change to zero, a convention for "zero-trust." (Color figure online)

conglomerate. `Ethpector` enables a range of applications to study dependencies between smart contracts on the level of their governance structures, potentially uncovering networks of virtual shell organizations.

5.2 Limitations

Obviously our approach has some limitations. We start with conceptual limits before we discuss the most salient technicalities.

Conceptual. A common pattern to distribute the control over global parameters of the system are governance tokens (e. g., Uniswap, MakerDAO). Voting protocols enable the token-holders to jointly make system-wide decisions. While a concentration of tokens in a single party could effectively fulfill our definition of a privileged party, we do not consider this problem here.

We also caution against premature conclusions when `Ethpector` detects a privileged party. The existence of a privileged party does not always imply central control. Exceptions may occur when the identified party is the address of a multi-signature wallet. If such a wallet is realized off-chain, we cannot distinguish it from any other externally owned account using blockchain data only.

Technical. Symbolic execution faces well-known limitations in practice: path explosion, unbounded loops, and the NP-hardness of the SMT problem all require tradeoffs, such as imposing timeouts and skipping paths [2].

The method as proposed fails to detect certain complex administration patterns involving more than one owner (e. g., multi-sig). The challenging smart contracts use advanced data structures in order to manage parties and assign roles to them. While some of the structures could in principle be unrolled, `Ethpector` skips them in the interest of avoiding false positives. This is because the data structures resemble those commonly used to manage token balances. Traversing them would incur the risk that many token functions could be falsely identified as granting privileged access. After all, token holders *are* privileged parties compared to non-holders; but this is not what `Ethpector` is designed to look for. A particular challenging data structure are mappings (i. e., hash tables). Often the address is used as key; and we cannot extract any value before knowing the address we are looking for. As Ethereum nodes do not support enumerating all keys, one would have to customize a node to keep track of all keys so that the correct key–value pair can be known in the analysis. `Ethpector` handles these cases by detecting the existence of a privileged party but fails to identify it.

Finally, our method inspects one smart contract at a time. It cannot resolve authorization patterns that request the privileged party (or other access control information) from other smart contracts using function calls. If this type of authorization becomes more common, the method can be adapted to be aware of common interfaces. This is easier to realize than executing inter-contract communication symbolically.

6 Related Work

This work connects to a number of research strands. We focus on the most relevant ones.

Governance of Cryptocurrency Platforms. Azouvi et al. [1] explore the governance structure of Bitcoin and Ethereum by reviewing the community of contributors to the respective public source-code repositories and discussion boards. They find that only a small number of contributors make up for most of the discussions and code contributions. This suggests a rather centralized governance structure at the level of the development workflow. The authors acknowledged that the centralization seen in the source-code contributions does not directly imply strong centralization of decision making in general. In particular cryptocurrencies diversify control by having miners or validators as gatekeepers.

In contrast to [1], our work is not concerned with the governance structures of the cryptocurrency platforms themselves, but the governance of user-defined applications running on these platforms. Unlike platforms, smart contracts do not have a built-in gatekeeper. The developers alone decide how to distribute control. For example, a significant share of updatable smart contracts are controlled by a single party [14]. This suggests that the governance structures on the Ethereum application layer could be a lot more centralized than the one of the underlying cryptocurrency platform.

Immutability and Code Updates. Fröwis and Böhme [9] study the immutability of the control flow of smart contracts using static program analysis. Using heuristics, they estimate that, in 2017, 40% of the code accounts on Ethereum host program code that could change its some parts of its code by updating dynamic references. Medhi et al. [14] review approaches to update smart contract implementations. They distinguish between retail and wholesale changes. The former affect parameters; the latter replace the complete implementation. Their measurements focuses on wholesale changes, in particular updates made possible through dynamic references between smart contracts. Between September 2020 and July 2021 they find that in almost 50% of the identified contracts, a single externally owned account is authorized to update. More recently, Fröwis and Böhme [10] explore a novel way to update code that became available on Ethereum after the Constantinople platform upgrade in early 2019. Using a heuristic indicator, they find more than 100k "potentially updatable" accounts. However, only 41 accounts actually got updated using this method.

Our work is concerned with the more general task of identifying functions of a smart contract that can only be executed by a privileged party. The most popular form of code updates via dynamic references relies on privileged functions only an authorized administrator account can call. Therefore, our method can be applied to detect updatable code. While `Ethpector` cannot extract the indicators used in [10], it is arguably more reliable in detecting the preconditions for such updates than the heuristic approach. The most relevant precondition is whether a `SELFDESTRUCT` instruction is reachable in the execution path.

Backdoors in Token Systems. In concurrent work, Ma et al. [13] propose a static analysis pipeline starting from source code and tailored to identify backdoors in smart contracts implementing token systems. The authors develop detectors for five common backdoors observed in the wild and evaluate their accuracy using active fuzzing. All of the backdoors studied by them require the existence of a privileged party. Although `Ethpector` cannot identify the exact conditions that invoke a backdoor, it is capable of identifying privileged functions. Our method requires bytecode only and is not limited to a specific type of smart contract.

Concurrent Work. After completing this research, we became aware of a master's thesis by Gorgoris [11]. The tool described therein, `ithildin`, resembles `Ethpector`. It reaches comparable performance for the detection of privileged parties, although using different benchmark data.

7   Conclusion

We have proposed, implemented, and validated a method to automatically extract privileged parties from EVM binaries using symbolic execution. Our artifact, `Ethpector`, is available on GitHub[11] under an open-source license. It enables a range of applications in research and practice, including the verification of claims about "zero-trust," revelation of ownership structures, and support for forensic analyses of networks of virtual shell organizations. While it cannot replace a thorough code review, it can substantially speed up independent sanity checks; or make them available to audiences who cannot perform a code review.

Future work could refine the detection of more complex authorization patterns, notably boolean expressions involving multiple conditions and privileged parties stored in mapping structures. Both should help to complete the picture by eliminating the (still quite small) gray areas in Fig. 3, where `Ethpector` is not yet applicable.

Acknowledgements. This work has received funding from the Austrian Research Promotion Agency (FFG), the Austrian Security Research Programme (KIRAS), and the Austrian Blockchain Center (ABC).

---

[11] https://github.com/uibk-ethpector/ethpector.

A Validation Data

Table 2. Composition of our validation dataset.

	Name	Address	Proxy Implementation	Code Coverage	Type
0	0x: Coinbase Wallet Pro...	0xe66b31678d6c16e9ebf358268a790b763c133750	-	0.82	proxy
1	1inch v4: Router	0x1111111254fb6c44bac0bed2854e76f90643097d	-	0.46	exchange
2	BendDao: Bend Token	0x02863c14603c3b157379999f567ddece151e9153	-	0.73	token
3	BendDao: Bend Token Pro...	0x0d02755a5700414b26ff040e1de35d337df56218	0x02863c ... 151e9153	0.96	proxy
4	BosonRouter	0x0a393aef6dbcd7e7088acf323f9d28b093b9ab5a	-	0.60	exchange
5	Center: USD Coin	0xa2327a938febf5fec13bacfb16ae10ecbc4cbdcf	-	0.81	token
6	Center: USD Coin Proxy	0xa0b86991c6218b36c1d19d4a2e9eb0ce3606eb48	0xa2327a ... bc4cbdcf	0.98	proxy
7	CryptoKitties	0x06012c8cf97bead5deae237070f9587f8e7a266d	-	0.75	token
8	EMOBUDDIES	0xc995756e8e6a319f209623d0c8f7629dc5636129	-	0.62	collectibles
9	ENS: ETH Registrar Cont...	0x283af0b28c62c092c9727f1ee09c02ca627eb7f5	-	0.66	ens
10	FloatingCats	0xa514ede519870c62d35130ca18e4134e86244255	-	0.60	collectibles
11	Gem: GemSwap 2	0x83c8f28c26bf6aaca652df1dbbe0e1b56f8baba2	-	0.54	collectibles
12	GnosisSafe Mastercopy 1...	0x34cfac646f301356faa8b21e94227a3583fe3f5f	-	0.49	multisig
13	KaijuFrenz: KAIJUFRENZ ...	0xc92090f070bf50eec26d849c88a68112f4f3d98e	-	0.52	collectibles
14	LooksRare: Exchange	0x59728544b08ab483533076417fbbb2fd0b17ce3a	-	0.41	exchange
15	Merkle distributor	0x7529834a5974e2d5fff3d0f0591e9a5ca2ca1619	-	0.84	batching
16	Merkle distributor Prox...	0x1b5d2904be3e4711a848be09b17dee89e6a5bc27	0x752983 ... a2ca1619	0.96	proxy
17	MetaPunk: Minter	0x67401149e3e88b10dd92821eb6302f4dee8191bc	-	0.60	other services
18	OpenSea: Registry	0xa5409ec958c83c3f309868babaca7c86dcb077c1	-	0.64	proxy
19	OpenSea: Wyvern Exchang...	0x7f268357a8c2552623316e2562d90e642bb538e5	-	0.19	exchange
20	Polygon Matic: Bridge P...	0xa0c68c638235ee32657e8f720a23cec1bfc77c77	0x6abb75 ... 105fd5f5	0.95	proxy
21	Polygon Matic: Bridge R...	0x6abb753c1893194de4a83c6e8b4eadfc105fd5f5	-	0.51	other services
22	Proxy to 34cfac64 ... 8...	0xe24f4870ab85de8e356c5fc56138587206c70d99	0x34cfac ... 83fe3f5f	0.98	proxy
23	ProxyAdmin ?	0x1f0e8a86e398f0f2fd285a36d2f1ee85d6bbc9c5	-	1.00	proxy
24	RaidParty: Game Party	0x62e4760a69ce31865a09cfc7cdc27432eb4433db	-	0.49	collectibles
25	RaidParty: Game Party P...	0xd311bdacb151b72bddfee9cbdc414af22a5e38dc	0x83d0c1 ... 1ac57fcc	0.82	proxy
26	Saitama Inu: SAITAMA To...	0x8b3192f5eebd8579568a2ed41e6feb402f93f73f	-	0.64	token
27	Shiba Inu: SHIB Token	0x95ad61b0a150d79219dcf64e1e6cc01f0b64c4ce	-	0.96	token
28	StrongBlock: Service Pr...	0xfbddadd80fe7bda00b901fbaf73803f2238aa655	0xdcbf1e ... 9d5a41cf	0.96	proxy
29	Strongblock: Service V1...	0xc2899dfcb0a81b73e89e4a99cd24ab26d8a78295	-	0.53	other services
30	Strongblock: Service V2...	0x88f6ed8fb519612a03730e4b5a5c1581a7d0c305	-	0.54	other services
31	SushiSwap: Router	0xd9e1ce17f2641f24ae83637ab66a2cca9c378b9f	-	0.34	exchange
32	TRIBE X: TRIBEX Token	0xff9981d2c6c6d612e03e4a32f5488e552eeae285	-	0.63	collectibles
33	Tether: USDT Stablecoin	0xdac17f958d2ee523a2206206994597c13d831ec7	-	0.86	token
34	Tornado.Cash: Router	0xd90e2f925da726b50c4ed8d0fb90ad053324f31b	-	0.41	privacy
35	Uniswap V2: Router 2	0x7a250d5630b4cf539739df2c5dacb4c659f2488d	-	0.36	exchange
36	Uniswap V3: Positions N...	0xc36442b4a4522e871399cd717abdd847ab11fe88	-	0.40	collectibles
37	Uniswap V3: Router	0xe592427a0aece92de3edee1f18e0157c05861564	-	0.54	exchange
38	Uniswap V3: Router 2	0x68b3465833fb72a70ecdf485e0e4c7bd8665fc45	-	0.41	exchange
39	Wandernauts: WANDERNAUT...	0x793daf78b74aadf1eda5cc07a558fed932360a60	-	0.67	collectibles
40	Wrapped Ether	0xc02aaa39b223fe8d0a0e5c4f27ead9083c756cc2	-	1.00	token
	TOTAL:			0.66	

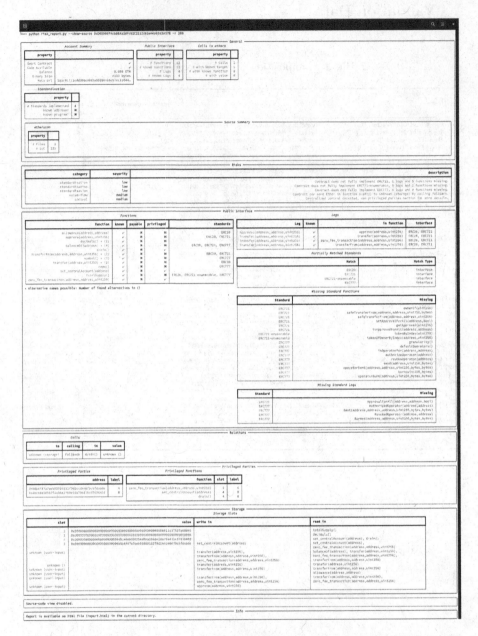

Fig. 8. Example output of the `Ethpector` console UI. The address under analysis is the SoarCoin smart contract. Its privileged function `zero_fee_transaction` is a backdoor that caused a loss of $6.6 million to an Australian firm [13].

References

1. Azouvi, S., Maller, M., Meiklejohn, S.: Egalitarian society or benevolent dictatorship: the state of cryptocurrency governance. In: Zohar, A., et al. (eds.) FC 2018. LNCS, vol. 10958, pp. 127–143. Springer, Heidelberg (2019). https://doi.org/10.1007/978-3-662-58820-8_10
2. Baldoni, R., Coppa, E., D'elia, D.C., Demetrescu, C., Finocchi, I.: A survey of symbolic execution techniques. ACM Comput. Surv. **51**(3), 1–39 (2018)
3. Bratspies, R.M.: Cryptocurrency and the myth of the trustless transaction. Mich. Telecommun. Technol. Law Rev. **25**, 1 (2018)
4. Chen, T., et al.: Tokenscope: automatically detecting inconsistent behaviors of cryptocurrency tokens in Ethereum. In: Proceedings of the 2019 ACM SIGSAC Conference on Computer and Communications Security, pp. 1503–1520 (2019)
5. Chen, W., Zhang, T., Chen, Z., Zheng, Z., Lu, Y.: Traveling the token world: a graph analysis of ethereum ERC20 token ecosystem, pp. 1411–1421. Association for Computing Machinery, New York, NY, USA (2020)
6. Di Angelo, M., Salzer, G.: Tokens, types, and standards: identification and utilization in ethereum. In: 2020 IEEE International Conference on Decentralized Applications and Infrastructures (DAPPS), pp. 1–10. IEEE (2020)
7. Di Angelo, M., Salzer, G.: Identification of token contracts on ethereum: standard compliance and beyond. Int. J. Data Sci. Anal. **16**, 333–352 (2021)
8. Di Angelo, M., Salzer, G.: Towards the identification of security tokens on ethereum. In: 2021 11th IFIP International Conference on New Technologies, Mobility and Security (NTMS), pp. 1–5. IEEE (2021)
9. Fröwis, M., Böhme, R.: In code we trust? measuring the control flow immutability of all smart contracts deployed on ethereum. In: Garcia-Alfaro, J., Navarro-Arribas, G., Hartenstein, H., Herrera-Joancomartí, J. (eds.) Data Privacy Management, Cryptocurrencies and Blockchain Technology, ESORICS 2017 International Workshops. Lecture Notes in Computer Science, vol. 10436, pp. 357–372. Springer, Cham (2017). https://doi.org/10.1007/s41060-021-00281-1
10. Fröwis, M., Böhme, R.: Not all code are create2 equal. In: Matsuo, S., et al. (eds.) FC 2022. LNCS, vol. 13412, pp. 516–538. Springer, Cham (2022). https://doi.org/10.1007/978-3-031-32415-4_3
11. Gorgoris, P.: Identifying administrators of smart contracts from transaction data. Master's Thesis, TU Wien (2021)
12. King, J.C.: Symbolic execution and program testing. Commun. ACM **19**(7), 385–394 (1976)
13. Ma, F., et al.: Pied-piper: revealing the backdoor threats in ethereum ERC token contracts. Trans. Softw. Eng. Methodol. **32**(3), 1–24 (2022)
14. Mehdi Salehi, J.C., Mannan, M.: Not so immutable: upgradeability of smart contracts on ethereum. In: Matsuo, S., et al. (eds.) FC 2022. LNCS, vol. 13412, pp. 539–554. Springer, Cham (2022). https://doi.org/10.1007/978-3-031-32415-4_33
15. Somin, S., Gordon, G., Altshuler, Y.: Network analysis of ERC20 tokens trading on ethereum blockchain. In: Morales, A.J., Gershenson, C., Braha, D., Minai, A.A., Bar-Yam, Y. (eds.) ICCS 2018. SPC, pp. 439–450. Springer, Cham (2018). https://doi.org/10.1007/978-3-319-96661-8_45
16. Victor, F., Lüders, B.K.: Measuring ethereum-based ERC20 token networks. In: Goldberg, I., Moore, T. (eds.) FC 2019. LNCS, vol. 11598, pp. 113–129. Springer, Cham (2019). https://doi.org/10.1007/978-3-030-32101-7_8

17. Vidan, G., Lehdonvirta, V.: Mine the gap: bitcoin and the maintenance of trust-lessness. New Media Soc. **21**(1), 42–59 (2019)
18. Zhang, L.: Your CryptoKitty isn't forever - why DApps aren't as decentralized as you think (2017). https://medium.com/loom-network/your-crypto-kitty-isnt-forever-why-dapps-aren-t-as-decentralized-as-you-think-871d6acfea. Accessed 31 Dec 2021

Breaking Blockchain Rationality
with Out-of-Band Collusion

Haoqian Zhang[(⊠)], Mahsa Bastankhah, Louis-Henri Merino,
Vero Estrada-Galiñanes, and Bryan Ford

École Polytechnique Fédérale de Lausanne (EPFL), Lausanne, Switzerland
{haoqian.zhang,mahsa.bastankhah,louis-henri.merino,
vero.estrada,bryan.ford}@epfl.ch

Abstract. Blockchain systems often rely on rationality assumptions for
their security, expecting that nodes are motivated to maximize their
profits. These systems thus design their protocols to incentivize nodes
to execute the honest protocol but fail to consider out-of-band collusion. Existing works analyzing rationality assumptions are limited in
their scope, either by focusing on a specific protocol or relying on non-
existing financial instruments. We propose a general rational attack on
rationality by leveraging an external channel that incentivizes nodes to
collude against the honest protocol. Our approach involves an attacker
creating an out-of-band bribery smart contract to motivate nodes to
double-spend their transactions in exchange for shares in the attacker's
profits. We provide a game theory model to prove that any rational node
is incentivized to follow the malicious protocol. We discuss our approach
to attacking the Bitcoin and Ethereum blockchains, demonstrating that
irrational behavior can be rational in real-world blockchain systems when
analyzing rationality in a larger ecosystem. We conclude that rational
assumptions only appear to make the system more secure and offer a
false sense of security under the flawed analysis.

1 Introduction

Blockchain systems often rely on rationality assumptions to ensure their security by providing financial incentives for adhering to the honest protocol. For
example, in Proof-of-Work, miners are incentivized to work on the longest chain
as it increases their expected chances of having their blocks accepted in the
blockchain. Similarly, in Proof-of-Stake, such as the one recently adopted by
Ethereum [4], validators are disincentivized from malicious behavior, such as
signing two blocks with the same height, due to the loss of part of their deposits.
These incentive mechanisms seem to secure these systems as any entity deviating
from the honest protocol would have a lower or negative expected return.

However, as many previous works demonstrated [1,5,6,8,10,12], those mechanisms might not be incentive-compatible, *i.e.*, there exists a more profitable
alternative strategy that deviates from the honest protocol. For instance, selfish
mining is a strategy to increase miners' expected return by deviating from the

© International Financial Cryptography Association 2024
A. Essex et al. (Eds.): FC 2023 Workshops, LNCS 13953, pp. 489–501, 2024.
https://doi.org/10.1007/978-3-031-48806-1_31

longest-chain rule expected by the Bitcoin mining protocol [6]. Whale attacks incentivize miners to fork the chain to include an off-the-blockchain transaction with a substantial transaction fee [12].

Whereas those previous works focus on specific protocols within individual blockchain systems, we question the incentive mechanism at a meta-level: Are those blockchain systems rely on rationality assumptions secure in general? We try to answer this research question by considering attacks beyond their ecosystem taking into account the broader influences of the outside world on the system. What is considered irrational behavior within their ecosystem might be rational when analyzing rationality in the context of a larger ecosystem.

We demonstrate that rationality assumptions can be defeated by attacks driven by rationality. Specifically, an attacker creates an out-of-band bribery smart contract that incentivizes nodes to double-spend the attacker's transactions. In return, the attacker can then share the profits from the double-spending with colluded consensus nodes, offering a financial incentive for them to commit the attack in the first place. Such an attack can happen in permissionless or permissioned blockchains, as long as they adopt some fashion of rationality assumptions.

A closely related work by Ford and Böhme [7] also offer a general rational attack on rationality. However, their attack method relies on financial instruments that are either non-existent or not well-established in the cryptocurrency markets. We, on the other hand, eliminate the need for non-existent financial instruments and significantly relaxes the requirements to launch the attack.

To prove that out-of-band collusion breaks blockchain systems' rationality assumptions, we propose a game theory model and use it to analyze a blockchain system before and after launching our attack. We find that in the absence of the attack, following the honest protocol is a strict Nash equilibrium that discourages nodes from deviating; however, in the presence of our attack, the honest protocol becomes a weakly dominated strategy. In particular, we identify a finite sequence of deviations from the honest protocol where each deviating node obtains at least the same reward as before the deviation. This sequence ultimately leads to a state where all the nodes follow our attack. Furthermore, we prove that following our attack is a strict Nash equilibrium, thus disincentivizing further deviation.

We provide an outline of the steps required to break the longest-chain rule in Bitcoin and the deposit-slashing protocol in Ethereum. Our work implies that rationality assumptions only appear to make the system more secure and provide a false sense of security.

2 Assumptions Underlying the Attack

This section introduces the following assumptions for our attack model:

Assumption 1: We consider the target system S to be an open financial payment network operating on blockchain rails, where any client can initiate a transaction. S is maintained by a set of rational nodes $\mathcal{N} = \{1, 2, \ldots, n\}$ who seek to maximize their profits. We assume that each node, $i \in \mathcal{N}$, has the power of v_i, *i.e.*, the voting power to decide the next block in the blockchain system. For example, the voting power in a Proof-of-Work blockchain is the nodes' computational power and the voting power in a Proof-of-Stake blockchain is nodes' stake amount, whereas the voting power in a practical Byzantine Fault Tolerance (PBFT) blockchain is the existence of an approved node. We normalize the power distribution such that the sum of all the nodes' power is equal to 1: $\sum_{i=1}^{n} v_i = 1$. For simplicity, we assume that the number of nodes and their power distribution remains constant; however, our model also applies to the dynamic number of nodes with smooth power changes.

Assumption 2: We assume the existence of an open system S' that supports smart contracts and has access to a perfect oracle mechanism $\mathcal{O}$ that can access real-time state information on S without manipulation. To avoid S' and $\mathcal{O}$ being attacked by the same rational attack, we assume that S' and $\mathcal{O}$ do not rely on any rationality assumption, and their security assumptions hold. For example, S' could be a PBFT-styled blockchain, where at most f of $3f + 1$ nodes can fail or misbehave, and $\mathcal{O}$ can solely rely on trusted hardware [3] to provide truthful information from S.

Assumption 3: The system S leverages, in some fashion, rationality assumptions to incentivize nodes to follow the S-defined honest protocol $\mathcal{P}_h$. Mathematically, we assume there is a well-known power threshold t such that, within a time period, if $\mathcal{N}_h \subset \mathcal{N}$ with $\sum_{i \in \mathcal{N}_h} v_i > t$ follows the honest protocol $\mathcal{P}_h$, for $i \in \mathcal{N}_h$ expects to receive a reward of $\mathcal{R}_{h,i} > 0$, and for $i \notin \mathcal{N}_h$ expects to obtain a reward $\mathcal{R}_{d,i}$. We assume that $\forall i \in \mathcal{N}, \mathcal{R}_{d,i} < \mathcal{R}_{h,i}$. $\mathcal{R}_{d,i}$ can be negative, *i.e.*, a node receives punishment for deviating from $\mathcal{P}_h$.

Assumption 4: We assume the existence of a malicious protocol $\mathcal{P}_m$ that differs from the expected behavior such that, within the same time period, if $\mathcal{N}_m \subset \mathcal{N}$ with $\sum_{i \in \mathcal{N}_m} v_i > t$ follows the malicious protocol $\mathcal{P}_m$, for $i \in \mathcal{N}_m$ can expect to receive a reward of $\mathcal{R}_{m,i}$, and for $i \notin \mathcal{N}_m$ can expect to obtain a reward of $\mathcal{R}_{d',i}$. We assume that $\forall i \in \mathcal{N}, \mathcal{R}_{d',i} < \mathcal{R}_{m,i}$ and $\mathcal{R}_{m,i} > \mathcal{R}_{h,i}$ as the malicious protocol is only worthwhile for attackers if it provides them with greater rewards. In Sect. 5.1, we show that there always exists a malicious protocol capable of double-spending attacks to satisfy this assumption in real-world blockchain systems.

Assumption 5: We assume that the underlying consensus requires $t \geq \frac{1}{2}$ to avoid nodes split into two independent functional subsets. We also assume that no single node can abuse the system, meaning that $\forall i \in \mathcal{N}, v_i < t$. For simplicity, we assume that if neither $\mathcal{P}_h$ nor $\mathcal{P}_m$ has enough nodes to execute, S loses liveness, and nobody gets any reward.

Algorithm 1: Bribery smart contract to incentivize collusion

Init *Upon creating the bribery smart contract:*
  Set T_e as the expiration time
  Set $\mathcal{P}_m$ as the malicious protocol
  Deposit $\mathcal{D}_m$ by the magnate
  $\mathcal{N}_m \leftarrow \varnothing$
  $order \leftarrow \mathcal{P}_h$

Commit *Upon receiving node i's commitment request:*
  $\mathcal{N}_m \leftarrow \mathcal{N}_m \cup i$
  Deposit $\mathcal{D}_i$ by i

Attack *Upon $\sum_{i \in \mathcal{N}_m} v_i > t$:*
  $order \leftarrow \mathcal{P}_m$

Distribute *Upon receiving the request from $i \in \mathcal{N}_m$ for the first time:*
  if *Attack is successful and i has executed $\mathcal{P}_m$* **then**
    Distribute $v_i \mathcal{D}_m + \mathcal{D}_i$ to i
  end
  if *Attack is not successful and $T_{now} > T_e$* **then**
    Distribute $\mathcal{D}_i$ to i
  end

---

3 Rational Attack on Rationality

This section presents our attack on rationality at a high-level. We begin by demonstrating that no rational node would execute $\mathcal{P}_m$ without collusion. We then introduce an attacker who creates a *Bribery Smart Contract* on S' that incentivizes the nodes on S to launch the attack.

Without Collusion: In the absence of collusion between nodes, each node is incentivized to follow the honest protocol $\mathcal{P}_h$; no single rational node will deviate from $\mathcal{P}_h$ as the expected reward is lower than that of following $\mathcal{P}_h$ ($\mathcal{R}_{d,i} < \mathcal{R}_{m,i}$ in Assumption 3). Therefore, when there is no collusion, S is secure under the rational assumption (we present a game theory analysis in Sect. 4.1). However, one cannot optimistically assume that such collusion will not exist.

Magnate-Coordinated Collusion: When an S' exists, an attacker (referred to as a *magnate*) can use it to coordinate collusion between nodes (Assumption 2). To defeat S, the magnate can create a bribery smart contract to attract nodes (referred to as *minions* and denoted by $\mathcal{N}_m$).

We use the double spending attack induced by the magnate as an example to illustrate a possible malicious protocol $\mathcal{P}_m$. The magnate needs to use a bribery smart contract to specify the transaction to be reverted, and order minions to work on a fork that allows the magnate to double-spend the transaction. To ensure the attack's success, the magnate must guarantee that each node can expect a higher reward, $i.e.$, $\mathcal{R}_m > \mathcal{R}_h$. In the case of this double-spending attack, each node can still expect to receive the rewards that a node executing $\mathcal{P}_h$ would typically get, such as block rewards and transaction fees. However, nodes can now expect to receive a share of the profits obtained by the magnate through double-spending by having the nodes execute $\mathcal{P}_m$. Therefore, the magnate has successfully produced a reward $\mathcal{R}_m$ strictly greater than $\mathcal{R}_h$. Note that the double spending attack is just one example of a malicious protocol. As long as the malicious protocol $\mathcal{P}_m$ produces a higher reward, $i.e.$, $\mathcal{R}_m > \mathcal{R}_h$, it works in our model to defeat rationality.

We outline the design of the bribery smart contract (Algorithm 1) on S' that would enable the magnate to execute the attack successfully. All parties must be held accountable if any party defects to ensure a successful attack in practice. During the creation of the smart contract, the magnate thus deposits $\mathcal{D}_m$ to be shared among the nodes if the attack is successful. In addition, when joining the bribery smart contract, each minion is required to deposit $\mathcal{D}_i$ to be slashed in case of a defect. When the minions' total voting power exceeds t, the bribery smart contract orders them to execute $\mathcal{P}_m$. The smart contract then can monitor the attack through the oracle $\mathcal{O}$ (Assumption 2) and upon success, returns the deposits with a share of $\mathcal{D}_m$ to each minion. If the magnate fails to attract enough minions to commit the attack, the deposits are still returned to each minion after an expiration time, making the commitment of the attack by a node risk-free. The magnate can also require a large $\mathcal{D}_i$ as each colluded node expects to get back $\mathcal{D}_i$ eventually (we discuss how to choose $\mathcal{D}_i$ in Sect. 4.2). However, if a minion does not follow the order from the bribery smart contract, their deposit is burned, thus incentivizing each minion to follow the order.

Given the bribery smart contract, a rational node is incentivized to commit and execute $\mathcal{P}_m$, as, intuitively, every node can benefit. If a node does not participate in the attack, it can, at most, obtain $\mathcal{R}_h$. However, if a node joins the attack, it will receive at least $\mathcal{R}_h$ with the opportunity of increasing its reward to $\mathcal{R}_m$. We offer a game theory analysis on node collusion in Sect. 4.2. We emphasize that, in this attack, the magnate does not even need to control any part of S or S', making such an attack doable with a low barrier to launch.

4 Game Theoretic Analysis

In this section, we formalize the behavior of S nodes and examine the possibility of deviation first without any collusion and then with collusion through the bribery smart contract on S'.

In the absence of collusion, following the honest protocol $\mathcal{P}_h$ is a strict Nash equilibrium, meaning that no player will deviate as deviation leads to a lower payoff. However, in the presence of the bribery smart contract, following the protocol $\mathcal{P}_h$ is a weakly dominated strategy and thus is no longer a strict Nash equilibrium. In particular, we identify a sequence of deviations from $\mathcal{P}_h$ where each deviant node obtains at least the same payoff as before. We show that this sequence of deviations ends with following the bribery smart contract orders. Furthermore, we prove that following the bribery smart contract orders is a strict Nash equilibrium, yielding the maximum payoff of the game. As a result, no rational player would deviate from it.

Additionally, we provide a bound on the amount of money that minions should deposit in the bribery smart contract to ensure that they do not deviate from the bribery smart contract's commands.

4.1   Game 0: Without Collusion

We model the behavior of the nodes in the absence of any external factors as a strategic-form game $\Gamma_0 = (\mathcal{N}, \{S_h, S_m\}^n, \text{Utility}_i^0(.)_{i \in \mathcal{N}})$. $\mathcal{N} = \{1, 2, \ldots, n\}$ is the set of nodes (players) of the game. Each node i has power v_i such that $\sum_{i \in \mathcal{N}} v_i = 1$. Each player can choose the honest strategy S_h (corresponding with the protocol $\mathcal{P}_h$) or the malicious strategy S_m (corresponding with the protocol $\mathcal{P}_m$). We denote the chosen strategy of node i by s_i.

We define V_h as the total power of the nodes that choose strategy S_h and V_m as the total power of the nodes which follow S_m, i.e.,

$$V_h := \sum_{i \in \mathcal{N}} v_i 1_{\{s_i = S_h\}}$$

$$V_m := \sum_{i \in \mathcal{N}} v_i 1_{\{s_i = S_m\}} = 1 - V_h.$$

Finally, we define the utility function of node i, $\text{Utility}_i^0(.)$, which is a function of i's and other players' strategies as follows:

$$\text{Utility}_i^0(s_1, \ldots, s_n) = \begin{cases} \mathcal{R}_{h,i} & \text{If } s_i = S_h \quad \& \quad V_h > t \\ \mathcal{R}_{d',i} & \text{If } s_i = S_h \quad \& \quad V_m > t \\ \mathcal{R}_{d,i} & \text{If } s_i = S_m \quad \& \quad V_h > t \\ \mathcal{R}_{m,i} & \text{If } s_i = S_m \quad \& \quad V_m > t \\ 0 & \text{If } V_h, V_m \leq t \end{cases}$$

with $\mathcal{R}_{h,i} > \mathcal{R}_{d,i}, \mathcal{R}_{m,i} > \mathcal{R}_{h,i} > 0, \mathcal{R}_{m,i} > \mathcal{R}_{d',i}$.

Suppose $V_h > t$, i.e., majority power is dedicated to the strategy S_h, player i obtains reward $\mathcal{R}_{h,i}$ by following S_h and obtains $\mathcal{R}_{d,i}$ otherwise. Similarly, when the majority adopts S_m, player i obtains reward $\mathcal{R}_{m,i}$ by following S_m and gets $\mathcal{R}_{d',i}$ otherwise. We assume that $\mathcal{R}_{m,i} > \mathcal{R}_{h,i}$ (Assumption 4). If both V_h and V_m are smaller than t, all the nodes receive a payoff of 0 (Assumption 5).

Theorem 1: In the strategic-form game Γ_0 if $\forall i \in \mathcal{N}$, $\mathcal{R}_{d,i} < \mathcal{R}_{h,i}$ and $\max_{i \in \mathcal{N}} v_i \leq t$, the strategy S_h is a strict Nash Equilibrium.

Proof: We should prove that when all nodes play strategy, S_h, and an arbitrary node i deviates to S_m, i obtains less payoff. We use overline to denote a variable if i deviates.

When everybody plays S_h, $V_h = 1$, and if i deviates then $\overline{V_h} = 1 - v_i$. One of the following two cases will occur:

- If $v_i < 1 - t$, $\overline{V_h} > t$; therefore, even if i deviates, $\mathcal{P}_h$ executes, and i gets $\mathcal{R}_{d,i}$ which is strictly less than $\mathcal{R}_{h,i}$.
- If $v_i \geq 1 - t$, $\overline{V_h} \leq t$ and $\mathcal{P}_h$ does not execute with enough power in S if i deviates. As we assumed that $v_i \leq t$ and i is the only player that plays $\mathcal{P}_m$, we will have $\overline{V_m} = v_i < t$; therefore, $\mathcal{P}_m$ executes with enough nodes neither and every node, including i, receives utility 0. As $\mathcal{R}_{h,i} > 0$, i gets less payoff if deviates.

Theorem 1 implies that in the absence of any external factors, given an initial honest behavior in S, deviating from $\mathcal{P}_h$ has strictly less utility. Therefore, nodes do not deviate from the honest protocol.

4.2 Game 1: Magnate-Coordinated Collusion

We define Game $\Gamma_1 = (\mathcal{N}, \{S_h, S'_m\}^n, \text{Utility}_i^1(.)_{i \in \mathcal{N}})$ to describe S in the presence of an external factor: the bribery smart contract (Algorithm 1). Each node has two strategies S_h, S'_m. S_h is the honest strategy as described before. S'_m denotes the strategy of committing to the bribery smart contract and following its commands. We can interpret S'_m as a colluding version of S_m which nodes only run $\mathcal{P}_m$ if they are sure that enough voting power is dedicated to $\mathcal{P}_m$.

Similarly, we denote the overall power of players who choose S_h by V_h; furthermore, we denote the overall power of minions (players who choose strategy S'_m) by V'_m with relation $V_h + V'_m = 1$. Note that V'_m does not necessarily represent the real power dedicated to $\mathcal{P}_m$ because if $V'_m \leq t$ then the bribery smart contract orders minions to follow $\mathcal{P}_h$ and no one follows $\mathcal{P}_m$; only when $V'_m > t$, the bribery smart contract orders minions to follow the protocol $\mathcal{P}_m$.

To incentivize minions to follow the bribery smart contract's orders unconditionally, the bribery smart contract requires the minions to deposit some money at the time of commitment. Magnate should choose a large enough deposit such that it rules out any order violation. In Theorem 2, we find a deposit function that satisfies this necessity.

Theorem 2: *If the bribery smart contract sets the deposit for all the minions as described in the Eq. 1, under no circumstances any minion has the incentive to deviate from the bribery smart contract commands.*

$$D > \max_{i \in \mathcal{N}}(\mathcal{R}_{m,i} + \max\{|\mathcal{R}_{d,i}|, |\mathcal{R}_{d',i}|\}) \qquad (1)$$

Proof: Consider node i that has committed to the bribery smart contract and has deposited value $\mathcal{D}_i$. i receives a payoff x if it follows the bribery smart contract commands and gets a payoff $y - \mathcal{D}_i$ if it deviates from the commands where x, y are valid utility values, i.e., $x, y \in \{\mathcal{R}_{m,i}, \mathcal{R}_{h,i}, \mathcal{R}_{d,i}, \mathcal{R}_{d',i}\}$ and their value depend on the strategy of other players. Our objective is to select $\mathcal{D}_i$ in such a way that deviates from the commands of the bribery smart contract are always more detrimental than any other strategy, regardless of what strategies other players are pursuing. Hence, the following should hold for any valid x, y:

$$y - \mathcal{D}_i < x \rightarrow \mathcal{D}_i > y - x$$

We know that as $\mathcal{R}_{h,i}, \mathcal{R}_{m,i} > 0$, $(\max\{\mathcal{R}_{h,i}, \mathcal{R}_{m,i}\} + \max\{|\mathcal{R}_{d,i}|, |\mathcal{R}_{d',i}|\}) = \mathcal{R}_{m,i} + \max\{|\mathcal{R}_{d,i}|, |\mathcal{R}_{d',i}|\}$ is an upper bound on $y - x$; therefore, it suffices to choose $D > \max_{i \in \mathcal{N}}(\mathcal{R}_{m,i} + \max\{|\mathcal{R}_{d,i}|, |\mathcal{R}_{d',i}|\})$

The implication of Theorem 2 is that if a rational node commits to the bribery smart contract, it always follows the bribery smart contract commands. Therefore there are only two possible strategies for the nodes, either playing the honest strategy or committing all of their power to the bribery smart contract and following its orders. If we use a deposit function that does not satisfy Eq. 1, in some cases, some minions might benefit by deviating from the bribery smart contract orders and dedicating less power to the specified protocol by the bribery smart contract even if they have committed to the bribery smart contract. Thus Theorem 2 is essential for defining Γ_1. Now we can define the utility function of the game Γ_1 as follows:

$$\text{Utility}_i^1(s_1, \ldots, s_n) = \begin{cases} \mathcal{R}_{h,i} & \text{If } s_i = \mathsf{S}_h & \& & V_h > t \\ \mathcal{R}_{d',i} & \text{If } s_i = \mathsf{S}_h & \& & V_m' > t \\ \mathcal{R}_{h,i} & \text{If } s_i = \mathsf{S}_m' & \& & V_h > t \\ \mathcal{R}_{m,i} & \text{If } s_i = \mathsf{S}_m' & \& & V_m' > t \\ \mathcal{R}_{h,i} & \text{If } V_h, V_m' \leq t \end{cases}$$

with $\mathcal{R}_{m,i} > \mathcal{R}_{h,i} > 0, \mathcal{R}_{m,i} > \mathcal{R}_{d',i}$.

The key difference between game Γ_1 and Γ_0 is that the minions are now colluding and as a result, they will not execute protocol $\mathcal{P}_m$ when $V_h > t$ to avoid the penalty $\mathcal{R}_{d,i}$.

Theorem 3: *In the strategic-form game Γ_1, the strategy S_h is not a strict Nash equilibrium, and even further, if any subset of nodes deviates from S_h to S_m', the deviating nodes always get at least the same payoff as if they were playing strategy S_h.*

Proof: Without the deviation $V_h = 1$, $V_m' = 0$ and every node i obtains reward $\mathcal{R}_{h,i}$. We denote the set of nodes that deviate from S_h to S_m' as $\mathcal{N}_m$, while the rest of the nodes $\mathcal{N} - \mathcal{N}_m$ play strategy S_h. We use the overlined variable to show the value of that variable if deviation takes place.

- If the overall power of $\mathcal{N}_m$ is equal or less than t, i.e., $\overline{V_m'} \leq t$, the bribery smart contract will order running protocol $\mathcal{P}_h$; therefore, the members of $\mathcal{N}_m$ will run $\mathcal{P}_h$. As other nodes also run $\mathcal{P}_h$, all the nodes no matter if they are a member of $\mathcal{N}_m$ or not will get the same reward as before, i.e., $\mathcal{R}_{h,i}$.

– If the overall power of $\mathcal{N}_m$ is greater than t, i.e., $\overline{V_m'} > t$, the bribery smart contract will order running protocol $\mathcal{P}_m$; therefore, the members of $\mathcal{N}_m$ will run $\mathcal{P}_m$ and will obtain reward $\mathcal{R}_{m,i}$, and the rest of the nodes will get the utility $\mathcal{R}_{d',i}$. As $\mathcal{R}_{d',i} < \mathcal{R}_{m,i}$, the nodes that deviate will get a better payoff, and the nodes that do not deviate are better off by deviating.

Theorem 4: *In the strategic-form game Γ_1, if $\mathcal{R}_{d',i} < \mathcal{R}_{m,i}$ and $\mathcal{R}_{h,i} < \mathcal{R}_{m,i}$, the strategy S_m' is a strict Nash Equilibrium.*

Proof: When all the nodes play S_m' we have $V_m' = 1$, and every node i obtains reward $\mathcal{R}_{m,i}$. If player i deviates to S_h, one of the following two cases will occur:

– If $v_i < 1 - t$, $\overline{V_m'} = 1 - v_i > t$; thus, the bribery smart contract orders to run $\mathcal{P}_m$ and i will receive $\mathcal{R}_{d',i} < \mathcal{R}_{m,i}$.
– If $v_i \geq 1 - t$, $\overline{V_m'} = 1 - v_i \leq t$; thus, the bribery smart contract orders to follow $\mathcal{P}_h$ and every node, as well as i, gets the honest reward $\mathcal{R}_{h,i} < \mathcal{R}_{m,i}$.

Implication: In a functional system where nodes execute the honest protocol without any collusion, no node has the incentive to deviate. However, with collusion, strategy S_h becomes a weakly dominated Nash equilibrium. Specifically, any colluding subset of nodes would receive at least the same payoff as before. Hence, it is rational for them to deviate in order to seek a higher payoff. Once the subset with power larger than t deviates, the nodes strictly benefit from deviation (as $\mathcal{R}_{m,i} > \mathcal{R}_{h,i}$); thus, we expect S to transition to a state where everybody plays S_m'. From this point, as S_m' is a strict Nash equilibrium, no party will deviate from it. In summary, we have identified a sequence of deviations where each node receives at least the same payoff as before, and eventually, the system settles into a strict Nash equilibrium and remains there.

Coming back to the example of a double-spending attack organized by a magnate, Theorem 3 states that starting from a healthy system S, if any subset of nodes commit their power to the bribery smart contract and run the double-spending attack if the bribery smart contract orders so, the minions will never get a less payoff than playing the honest strategy. Moreover, Theorem 4 suggests that starting from a situation where all the nodes commit to the bribery smart contract and execute the double spending attack, if a node deviates and plays the honest strategy, the deviant node gets strictly less payoff after deviation.

5   Sketch to Break Real-World Blockchain Systems

We illustrate a malicious protocol that generally exists in real-world blockchain systems, and then we discuss how we can use it to attack Bitcoin and Ethereum.

5.1   Double-Spending as Malicious Protocol

We present there always exists a malicious protocol $\mathcal{P}_m$ enabling double-spend attacks in S, illustrated in Fig. 1. A colluded node executes the $\mathcal{P}_m$ when the

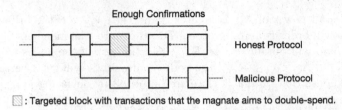

: Targeted block with transactions that the magnate aims to double-spend.

Fig. 1. In a real-world blockchain system, given an honest protocol $\mathcal{P}_h$, the magnate can always construct a malicious protocol $\mathcal{P}_m$ with a higher total reward by double-spending transactions through reverting a confirmed block.

block that contains the target transactions receives enough block confirmations. The protocol aims to revert the block by working a fork, which allows the magnate to double-spend the transactions confirmed previously. When the fork becomes the valid chain, $\mathcal{P}_m$ finishes.

5.2   Breaking the Longest-Chain Rule in Bitcoin

Bitcoin's protocol incentivizes the nodes to adopt the longest-chain rule when mining a new block. This behavior assumption applies to the rationality principle: As long as more than 50% of the nodes follow the longest-chain rule, any rule-deviating node would reduce its expected chance to mine new accepted blocks and thus its expected reward. Therefore, the longest-chain rule is consistent with our Assumption 3.

We now sketch the attacking method based on double-spending. Once a magnate selects a transaction to double spend, they create a bribery smart contract with the malicious protocol $\mathcal{P}_m$ in an attempt to reverse the transaction by creating a fork. The magnate is required to put up a deposit $\mathcal{D}_m$ proportional to the expected reward for double spending this transaction. Similar to an auction contract, the magnate also specifies a time T_e when the contract expires.

Once the bribery smart contract is published, any rational node is incentivized to join the bribery smart contract and, when enough nodes have joined, follow $\mathcal{P}_m$ due to the expected reward increase over following $\mathcal{P}_h$. The bribery smart contract requires nodes to deposit $\mathcal{D}_i$ in case they defect. $\mathcal{D}_i$ needs to be more than the block rewards and transactions fees that can be reverted by the fork. If the bribery smart contract successfully attracts more than 50% of the nodes, then the nodes launches the attack. While launching the attack, each node submits proofs to the bribery smart contract that it is following $\mathcal{P}_m$. Since Bitcoin uses Proof-of-Work as the underlying consensus algorithm, proofs can be hash results that satisfy a difficulty requirement, similar to how miners prove their work to a mining pool [11].

5.3   Breaking the Deposit-Slashing Protocol in Ethereum

In the recent upgrade of the Merge [4], Ethereum changed its consensus algorithm to Proof-of-Stake. To incentivize honest nodes and punish malicious ones, Ethereum adopts a deposit-slashing protocol, where each node must deposit some cryptocurrency. A node can withdraw its deposit entirety when exiting the consensus group if no other node can prove that it violated the protocol. Ethereum utilizes the deposit-slashing protocol to punish the double-sign behavior, *i.e.*, a node signs two blocks with the same height, thus mitigating the double-spending issues.

The magnate can adopt a similar strategy to break the deposit-slashing protocol. The magnate still tries to double spend transactions to create additional rewards for the colluded nodes. The colluded nodes need to work on the fork indicated by the magnate after the targeted transaction is confirmed. By doing so, each colluded node needs to sign two blocks with the same height, a behavior violating the deposit-slashing protocol. Thus, the colluded node is subject to be slashed if anyone submits the proof to the blockchain. However, as long as all the colluded nodes do not allow the proof to be included on the blockchain in the first place, the slashing will never happen.

To prove that a node has executed the $\mathcal{P}_m$, the bribery smart contract has to verify that it has voted to the fork indicated by the magnate and has not voted for any block with proof potentially slashing other colluded nodes before exiting the consensus group. The second condition effetely delays the verification time; However, as long as the magnate attracts enough nodes, the magnate is in total control of the blockchain before the colluded nodes exit the consensus group.

6   Discussion

Our work reveals the weakness of blockchain systems that depend on rationality for security. Despite this weakness, to the best of our knowledge, no major cryptocurrency has suffered from rational attacks [2,16], even with the usual concentration of voting power in the hands of a few [13].

The absence of such an attack may result from other factors. First, it may be because the attack is hard to communicate and coordinate, *i.e.*, every node must be aware of such a bribery smart contract, rendering such attacks hard to be realized in real-world blockchain systems. Second, cryptocurrency stakeholders may be unwilling to conduct such an attack due to the potential loss of faith in the cryptocurrency market, leading to significant price drops; thus, it is irrational to launch such an attack if we consider the monetary value of the cryptocurrency [2]. Finally, some actors may choose not to participate in such an attack out of altruism, even though the strategy does not maximize their profits.

Nevertheless, our theoretical conclusion is that rationality is insufficient for security; thus, its use results in a false sense of security, and such an attack could happen at any moment. Our work implies that to build a secure blockchain system, we have to rely on non-rational assumptions, such as threshold assumptions

500 H. Zhang et al.

(*i.e.*, a certain percentage of the nodes are truly honest, even though this would lead to profit loss) and police enforcement (*e.g.*, nodes would face legal prosecution if not following the honest protocol).

7 Related Work

The earliest work attacking blockchain rationality is selfish mining, demonstrating that the Bitcoin mining protocol is not incentive-compatible [6]. They prove that, in the current Bitcoin architecture, even if the adversary controls less than 50% of the hashing power, it can launch the attack successfully and earn more benefits than honest behavior.

Following the selfish mining attacks, several works attack blockchain incentive mechanisms, such as whale attacks [12], block withholding [5], stubborn mining [15], transaction withholding [1], empty block mining [8], and fork after withholding [10]. However, these previous works only discuss the attacks in a specific protocol.

Ford et al. first outline a general method to attack rationality, arguing that rationality is self-defeating when analyzing rationality in the context of a large ecosystem [7]. Although the attack generally applies to any blockchain system, it builds upon some derivatives on financial markets, which are either non-existing or non-mature, indicating the attack is not practical any time soon. To our knowledge, our work is the first practical and general attack on rationality assumptions for various blockchain systems.

Finally, utilizing smart control to incentivize malicious behaviors is a well-known strategy in the blockchain space. McCorry et al. present various smart contracts that enable bribing of miners to achieve a strategy that benefits the briber [14]. Juels et al. propose criminal smart contracts that encourage the leakage of confidential information [9].

8 Conclusion

This paper proposes an attacking method that breaks the rationality assumptions in various blockchain systems. The attack utilizes an out-of-band smart contract to establish the collusion between nodes coordinated by a magnate. Unlike previous works which attack rationality for a specific protocol or rely on non-existent financial instruments, our method is more general and practical. Our result indicates that the rationality assumptions do not increase the system's security and might provide a false sense of security under the flawed analysis.

Acknowledgments. This research was supported in part by U.S. Office of Naval Research grant N00014-19-1-2361, the AXA Research Fund, the PAIDIT project funded by ICRC, the IC3-Ethereum Fund, Algorand Centres of Excellence programme managed by Algorand Foundation, and armasuisse Science and Technology. Any opinions, findings, and conclusions or recommendations expressed in this material are those of the author(s) and do not necessarily reflect the views of the funding sources.

References

1. Babaioff, M., Dobzinski, S., Oren, S., Zohar, A.: On bitcoin and red balloons. In: ACM Conference on Electronic Commerce, pp. 56–73. ACM (2012)
2. Badertscher, C., Garay, J., Maurer, U., Tschudi, D., Zikas, V.: But why does it work? a rational protocol design treatment of bitcoin. In: Nielsen, J.B., Rijmen, V. (eds.) EUROCRYPT 2018. LNCS, vol. 10821, pp. 34–65. Springer, Cham (2018). https://doi.org/10.1007/978-3-319-78375-8_2
3. Costan, V., Devadas, S.: Intel sgx explained. Cryptology ePrint Archive (2016)
4. The merge (2022). https://ethereum.org/en/upgrades/merge/. Accessed 03 Oct 2022
5. Eyal, I.: The miner's dilemma. In: IEEE Symposium on Security and Privacy (Oakland), pp. 89–103. IEEE (2015)
6. Eyal, I., Sirer, E.G.: Majority is not enough: bitcoin mining is vulnerable. Commun. ACM **61**(7), 95–102 (2018)
7. Ford, B., Böhme, R.: Rationality is self-defeating in permissionless systems. arXiv preprint arXiv:1910.08820 (2019)
8. Houy, N.: The bitcoin mining game. https://ssrn.com/abstract=2407834 (2014)
9. Juels, A., Kosba, A., Shi, E.: The ring of Gyges: using smart contracts for crime. aries **40**, 54 (2015)
10. Kwon, Y., Kim, D., Son, Y., Vasserman, E., Kim, Y.: Be selfish and avoid dilemmas: fork after withholding (FAW) attacks on Bitcoin. In: ACM Conference on Computer and Communications Security (CCS), pp. 195–209. ACM (2017)
11. Lewenberg, Y., Bachrach, Y., Sompolinsky, Y., Zohar, A., Rosenschein, J.S.: Bitcoin mining pools: a cooperative game theoretic analysis. In: Proceedings of the 2015 International Conference on Autonomous Agents and Multiagent Systems, pp. 919–927 (2015)
12. Liao, K., Katz, J.: Incentivizing blockchain forks via whale transactions. In: Brenner, M., et al. (eds.) FC 2017. LNCS, vol. 10323, pp. 264–279. Springer, Cham (2017). https://doi.org/10.1007/978-3-319-70278-0_17
13. Mariem, S.B., Casas, P., Romiti, M., Donnet, B., Stütz, R., Haslhofer, B.: All that glitters is not bitcoin-unveiling the centralized nature of the BTC (IP) network. In: NOMS 2020–2020 IEEE/IFIP Network Operations and Management Symposium, pp. 1–9. IEEE (2020)
14. McCorry, P., Hicks, A., Meiklejohn, S.: Smart contracts for bribing miners. In: Zohar, A., et al. (eds.) FC 2018. LNCS, vol. 10958, pp. 3–18. Springer, Heidelberg (2019). https://doi.org/10.1007/978-3-662-58820-8_1
15. Nayak, K., Kumar, S., Miller, A., Shi, E.: Stubborn mining: generalizing selfish mining and combining with an eclipse attack. In: 2016 IEEE European Symposium on Security and Privacy (EuroS&P), pp. 305–320. IEEE (2016)
16. Wang, Z., Lv, Q., Lu, Z., Wang, Y., Yue, S.: ForkDec: accurate detection for selfish mining attacks. Secur. Commun. Netw. **2021**, 1–8 (2021)

Author Index

A

Angeris, Guillermo 266

B

Bar-On, Yogev 247
Bastankhah, Mahsa 489
Becker, Ingolf 113
Blom, Michelle 79
Böhme, Rainer 470
Brigner, Paul 141

C

Chatzigiannis, Panagiotis 367
Chen, Shiping 133, 208
Cohen, Samuel N. 303
Cortier, Véronique 3

D

de Valence, Henry 266
Debant, Alexandre 3
di Angelo, Monika 439
Diamandis, Theo 266

E

Estrada-Galiñanes, Vero 489
Evans, Alex 266

F

Feichtinger, Rainer 165
Felten, Edward W. 355
Feng, Ding 320
Finogina, Tamara 34
Ford, Bryan 489
Fritsch, Robin 165
Fröwis, Michael 470
Fu, Shange 133, 208

G

Gaudry, Pierrick 3
Germouty, Paul 420
Gervais, Arthur 320
Glondu, Stéphane 3

H

Haenni, Rolf 47
Haines, Thomas 19
Heimbach, Lioba 337
Herranz, Javier 34
Higuchi, Taishi 286
Hitsch, Rupert 320

J

Jin, Shan 367
Johnson, Nicholas A. G. 266

K

Kakebayashi, Michi 216
Katayama, Ken 141
Koenig, Reto E. 47
Kumaresan, Ranjit 367

L

Larraia, Enrique 420
Locher, Philipp 47

M

Mamageishvili, Akaki 355
Mansour, Yishay 247
Merino, Louis-Henri 489
Milionis, Jason 262
Minaei, Mohsen 367
Moallemi, Ciamac C. 262
Mohanty, Susil Kumar 405
Molchanovsky, Leon 197
Moreno-Sanchez, Pedro 367

N

Nejadmalayeri, Ali 197

O

Ordekian, Marilyne 113
Otsuka, Akira 286

© International Financial Cryptography Association 2024
A. Essex et al. (Eds.): FC 2023 Workshops, LNCS 13953, pp. 503–504, 2024.
https://doi.org/10.1007/978-3-031-48806-1

P
Paleo, Bruno Woltzenlogel   197
Prescott, Rodney W.   197
Presto, Gerard P.   216

Q
Qin, Kaihua   320

R
Raghuraman, Srinivasan   367
Roenne, Peter   19
Roughgarden, Tim   262

S
Sabaté-Vidales, Marc   303
Saereesitthipitak, Schwinn   385
Salzer, Gernot   439
Schertenleib, Eric   337
Šiška, David   303
Spertus, Jacob V.   95
Stark, Philip B.   63
Stuckey, Peter J.   79
Sutopo, Anggrio   19
Szpruch, Łukasz   303

T
Teague, Vanessa   79
Tripathy, Somanath   405
Tzinas, Apostolos   456

V
Vasek, Marie   113
Vonlanthen, Yann   165
Vukcevic, Damjan   79

W
Wang, Qin   133, 208
Wang, Ye   320
Wattenhofer, Roger   165, 320, 337

Y
Yamamoto, Go   186
Yao, Yaxing   320
Yu, Jiangshan   133, 208
Yuyama, Tomonori   141, 216

Z
Zamani, Mahdi   367
Zhang, Haoqian   489
Zhang, Wei   420
Zindros, Dionysis   385, 456

Printed in the United States
by Baker & Taylor Publisher Services